Internetw
with NetWare
TCP/IP

Karanjit S. Siyan, Ph.D.

Peter Rybaczyk

Peter Kuo, Ph.D.

New Riders Publishing, Indianapolis, Indiana

Internetworking with NetWare TCP/IP

By Karanjit S. Siyan, Peter Rybaczyk, and Peter Kuo

Published by:
New Riders Publishing
201 West 103rd Street
Indianapolis, IN 46290 USA

Printed in the United States of America 1 2 3 4 5 6 7 8 9 0

Warning and Disclaimer

This book is designed to provide information about the NetWare network operating system. Every effort has been made to make this book as complete and as accurate as possible, but no warranty or fitness is implied.

The information is provided on an "as is" basis. The author(s) and New Riders Publishing shall have neither liability nor responsibility to any person or entity with respect to any loss or damages arising from the information contained in this book or from the use of the disks or programs that may accompany it.

Publisher *Don Fowley*
Publishing Manager *Emmett Dulaney*
Marketing Manager *Mary Foote*
Managing Editor *Carla Hall*

Acquisitions Editor
Mary Foote

Project Editor
John Sleeva

Copy Editors
Laura Frey
Cliff Shubs

Technical Editor
Tim Petru

Associate Marketing Manager
Tamara Apple

Acquisitions Coordinator
Stacia Mellinger

Publisher's Assistant
Karen Opal

Cover Designer
Alam Hashimoto

Cover Production
Aren Howell

Book Designer
Sandra Schroeder

Production Manager
Kelly Dobbs

Production Team Supervisor
Laurie Casey

Graphics Image Specialists
Brad Dixon
Clint Lahnen
Laura Robbins

Production Analysts
Jason Hand
Bobbi Satterfield

Production Team
Heather Butler
Angela Calvert
Kim Cofer
Dan Caparo
Tricia Flodder
Aleata Howard
Erika Millen
Beth Rago
Erich J. Richter
Christine Tyner

Indexer
Tom Dinse

About the Authors

Karanjit S. Siyan, Ph.D. is president of Kinetics Corporation. He has authored international seminars on Solaris & SunOS, TCP/IP networks, PC Network Integration, Windows NT, Novell networks, and Expert Systems using Fuzzy Logic. He teaches advanced technology seminars in the United States, Canada, Europe, and the Far East. Dr. Siyan has published articles in *Dr. Dobbs Journal, The C Users Journal, Databased Advisor,* and research journals, and is actively involved in Internet research. Karanjit has been involved with NetWare since 1985. He holds a Ph.D in Computer Science. Before working as an independent consultant, Karanjit worked as a senior member of technical staff at ROLM Corporation, and as a software developer and technical manager on numerous projects. As part of his consulting work, Karanjit has written a number of custom compiler and operating system development tools. His interests include Unix-based, NetWare-based, Windows NT-based, and OS/2 networks. He is actively involved in the application of many computer science disciplines, such as networks, operating systems, programming languages, databases, expert systems and computer security. Dr. Siyan is a Microsoft Certified Professional for Windows NT, and holds a Master CNE and ECNE certification for Novell-based networks, and has written numerous books. Karanjit Siyan is based in Montana where he lives with his wife. He can be reached at his e-mail address of *karanjit@siyan.com.*

Peter Rybaczyk is a practicing Certified NetWare Engineer for the consulting firm PME Enterprises. He specializes in consulting and complete support of PC-based installations with emphasis on Novell NetWare. Peter's services include sales, installation, support of custom-configured stand-alone PCs, LANs, peer-to-peer networks, WANs, satellite based database access, and Internet access setup. He also specializes in the installation and troubleshooting of applications software, data recovery, and hardware maintenance. Peter has also been an instructor for Learning Tree International, teaching advanced technologies courses on managing PC networks, installing Novell NetWare, advanced NetWare administration, networking technologies, and internetworking. Peter is coauthor of *PC Network Administration,* published by McGraw Hill.

Peter Kuo, Ph.D., is the president of DreamLAN Network Consulting, a Toronto-based firm specializing in connectivity and network management. Peter is the first Canadian Enterprise Certified Netware Engineer (ECNE) and Master CNE, and is a Certified NetWare Instructor. His areas of expertise include advanced NetWare topics such as network management, IBM, and Unix connectivity issues. Peter is a SysOp on NetWire (CompuServe), supporting many advanced sections for Novell, such as connectivity, network management, NetWare 4.x (NDS), and client software. He is also a member of Novell's Professional Developer's Program.

Trademark Acknowledgments

Acknowledgments

From Karanjit Siyan

One of the more pleasurable tasks of being an author is to thank the people responsible for the success of a book. My heartfelt thanks to my wife Dei for her love and support. I wish to thank my father, Ahal Singh, and my mother, Tejinder; my brothers, Harjit, Jagjit; my sisters, Kookie and Dolly. Thanks also to Margaret Cooper Scott, Cathryn and Bob Foley, Craig and Lydia Cooper, Robert and Janie Cooper, Heidi and Steve Bynum, Barbara and Edward L. Scott (Scotty), and Jacquelyn McGregor for their love and support. Special thanks to Mother, Saint Germain, Bhagwan Krishna, and Babaji. Without their spiritual support, this book would not have been possible.

I want to thank Peter Rybaczyk, and Peter Kuo for the development of some of the chapters in this book. Peter Rybaczyk wrote the chapters on managing TCP/IP protocols using INETCFG and building Internet servers using NetWare, and Peter Kuo wrote the chapter on LAN WorkPlace and WorkGroup. Other good friends who provided excellent company during the development of this book include Edward and Mary Kramer, Maria Elizabeth Rybaczyk, and Dr. Caspari. I want to thank Drew and Blythe Heywood for their friendship and good will.

I want to thank Bob Sanregret and Anders Amundson, who initially got me interested in writing teaching materials on computer networks. I also wish to thank the many people at Learning Tree for their help and support on various projects. In particular, I would like to thank John Moriarty, Rick Adamson, Dr. David Collins, Eric Garen, Fancesco Zambowni, Richard Beaumont, Mark Drew, David O'Neal, Mike Lopez, Julane Marx, and many others.

Finally, I also want to extend my thanks to the many people at New Riders: Emmett Dulaney for his cheerful attitude and faith in my abilities, and John Sleeva, project editor, for his editorial skills.

From Peter Rybaczyk

I wish to extend my deepest thanks to my beloved wife, Maria Elizabeth, for her patience and support during the writing of this book. A big thanks also to the staff at New Riders, including Mary Foote, John Sleeva, and Laura Frey. I also want to thank the marketing and technical staffs at Micro Computer Systems, Puzzle Systems, and Firefox for supplying evaluation copies of their products.

Contents at a Glance

Table of Contents

Introduction

The staff of New Riders Publishing is committed to bringing you the very best in computer reference material. Each New Riders book is the result of months of work by authors and staff who research and refine the information contained within its covers.

As part of this commitment to you, the NRP reader, New Riders invites your input. Please let us know if you enjoy this book, if you have trouble with the information and examples presented, or if you have a suggestion for the next edition.

Please note, though: New Riders staff cannot serve as a technical resource for NetWare or for questions about software- or hardware-related problems.

If you have a question or comment about any New Riders book, there are several ways to contact New Riders Publishing. We will respond to as many readers as we can. Your name, address, or phone number will never become part of a mailing list or be used for any purpose other than to help us continue to bring you the best books possible. You can write us at the following address:

New Riders Publishing
Attn: Publisher
201 W. 103rd Street
Indianapolis, IN 46290

If you prefer, you can fax New Riders Publishing at (317) 581-4670.

You can also send e-mail to New Riders at the following Internet address:

`edulaney@newriders.mcp.com`

NRP is an imprint of Macmillan Computer Publishing. To obtain a catalog or information, or to purchase any Macmillan Computer Publishing book, call (800)428-5331.

Thank you for selecting *Internetworking with NetWare TCP/IP!*

Part I

TCP/IP Transport

Understanding TCP/IP Networks

TCP/IP-based networks play an increasingly important role in computer networks. Perhaps one reason for their appeal is that they are based on an open specification that is not controlled by any vendor. This chapter will examine the origins of TCP/IP networks and the commercial uses of this protocol.

Overview of TCP/IP Networks

Before examining the details of TCP/IP networks, you must understand what TCP/IP is. To help you understand TCP/IP networks, this section examines the events that led to the commercial uses of TCP/IP.

What Is TCP/IP?

People use the acronym TCP/IP to refer to a number of different concepts and ideas. The most popular use of the term TCP/IP describes two related communications protocols utilized for data transport. TCP stands for *Transmission Control Protocol,* and IP stands for *Internet Protocol.* The term TCP/IP is not limited just to these two protocols, however. Frequently, the term TCP/IP is used to refer to a group of protocols related to the TCP and IP protocols such as the User Datagram Protocol (UDP), File Transfer Protocol (FTP), Terminal Emulation Protocol (TELNET), and so on.

Figure 1.1 shows a sample TCP/IP network that uses TCP/IP. In this figure, TCP/IP refers to the data transport protocol and the applications that use TCP/IP, such as FTP and TELNET.

Networks that use TCP/IP are called TCP/IP *internets.* Figure 1.1 is an example of a TCP/IP internet. A distinction must be made between TCP/IP *internet* and the *Internet.* The Internet is currently the largest network in the world, with thousands of computers. It spans several continents and is predominantly based on TCP/IP.

The Origins of TCP/IP

In the late 1960s, *DARPA* (the Defense Advanced Research Project Agency), in the United States, noticed that there was a rapid proliferation of computers in military communications. Computers, because they can be easily programmed, provide flexibility in achieving network functions that is not available with other types of communications equipment. The computers then used in military communications were manufactured by different vendors and were designed to interoperate with computers from that vendor only. Vendors used proprietary protocols in their communications equipment. The military had a multivendor network but no common protocol to support the heterogeneous equipment from different vendors.

The Role of DARPA

To solve these problems, the U.S. Department of Defense (DoD) mandated a common set of protocols. The reasons for having a common set of protocols were the following:

- **To simplify procurement.** By mandating a common set of protocols, it is possible for the military to prepare a request or proposal that specified that communications products use the common protocol.

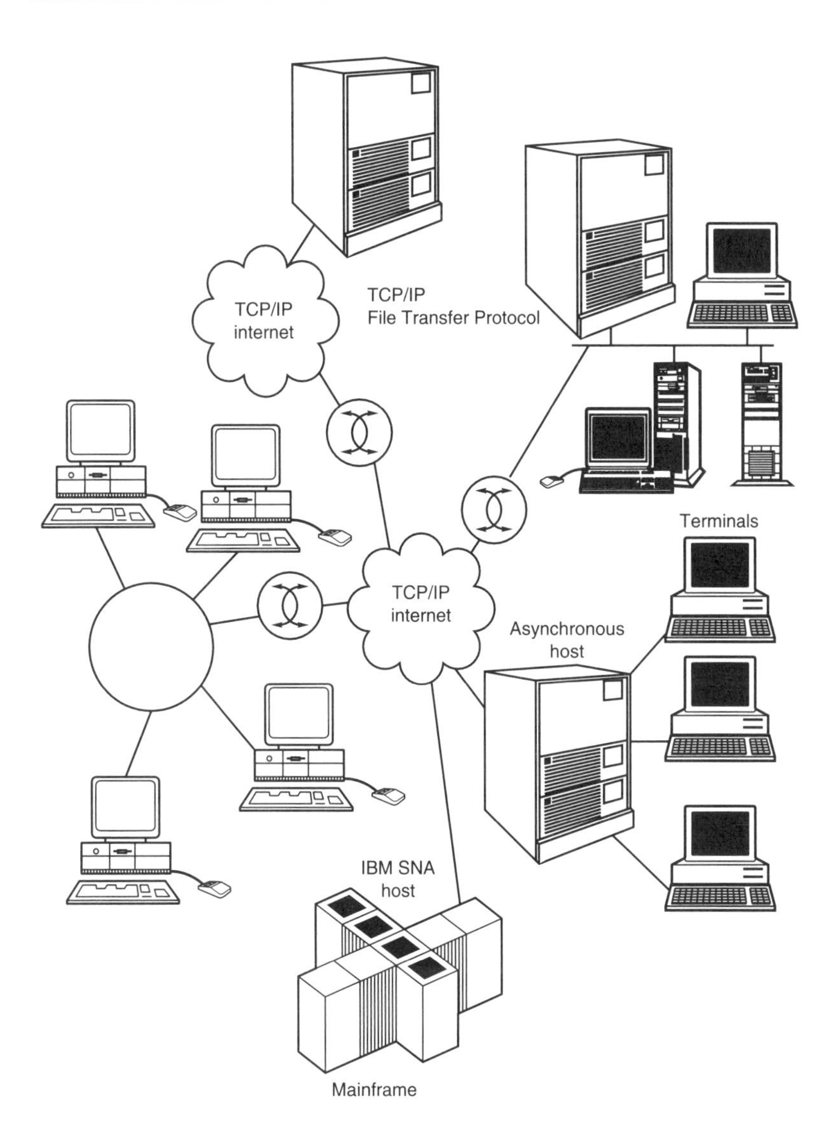

Figure 1.1

An example of a TCP/IP internet.

- **To foster competition among vendors.** Vendors compete with each other based on the merits of their implementation of a standard protocol. If a common set of protocols were not required, vendors could implement their proprietary protocols, against which other vendors could not compete.
- **To enable interoperability.** By requiring vendors to use a common set of protocols, interoperability between equipment from different vendors becomes a reality. If equipment from different vendors, implementing a common protocol, cannot interoperate, the problem is probably one of difference in implementation. Vendors can then refer to the standard specification of the protocol to isolate the problem.

- **To encourage vendor productivity and efficiency.** Vendors can focus their attention on a single protocol rather than spread their efforts trying to implement several protocols. This makes vendors' efforts more productive.

The Early DARPA Experiments

In 1969, an interesting experiment was conducted to use a computer network to connect the following sites:

- University of California, Los Angeles (UCLA)
- University of California, Santa Barbara (UCSB)
- University of Utah
- SRI International

Figure 1.2 shows the sites involved. This was the beginning of the famous ARPAnet (Advanced Research Project Agency Network). The experiment was a success. Additional sites were added to the network.

Figure 1.2

The four-node ARPAnet experiment.

• Sites include

– University of California, Los Angeles (UCLA)
– University of California, Santa Barbara (UCSB)
– University of Utah
– SRI International

ARPAnet = Advanced Research Projects Agency Network

In 1972, ARPAnet was demonstrated with 50 packet switched nodes (PSNs) and 20 hosts. Like the previous four-node experiment, this too was a success, and it set the stage for large-scale deployment of PSNs and hosts on the ARPAnet.

Novell's documents say that TCP/IP was an experiment conducted by the DoD in the 1970s. The actual experiments began in 1969.

The ARPAnet Evolution

The ARPAnet continued to grow and went through a series of transformations. Prior to 1986, the ARPAnet consisted of specialized military networks connected with the ARPAnet (see fig. 1.3). After 1986, the specialized military networks formed their own network that was not connected to any other network. The Defense Data Network (DDN) was created with links to the ARPAnet (see fig. 1.4).

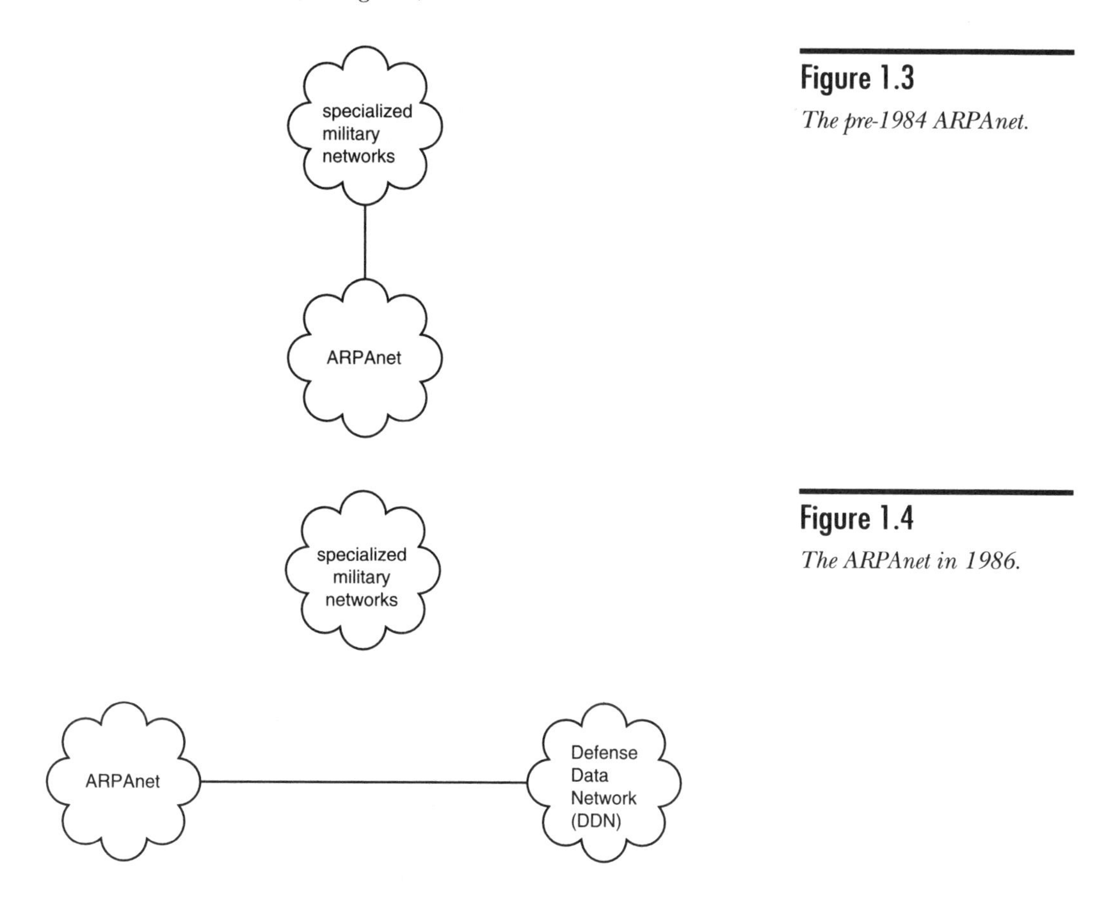

Figure 1.3

The pre-1984 ARPAnet.

Figure 1.4

The ARPAnet in 1986.

By 1986, the ARPAnet had expanded to encompass all major universities, the military network called *MILNET*, Research Laboratories such as Cadre and Tartan at Carnegie-Mellon University (CMU), and satellite links to several international sites (see fig. 1.5).

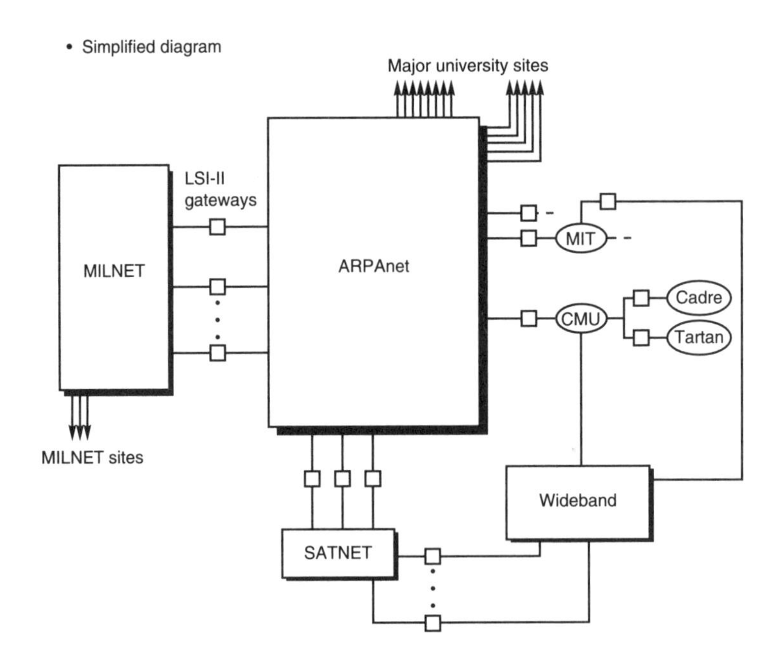

Figure 1.5
The ARPAnet in 1986.

Gradually, the ARPAnet itself was replaced by the Internet. The Internet is experiencing rapid commercialization and is no longer the exclusive domain of universities and research organizations. There is currently more network traffic from commercial organizations than any other source on the Internet.

The original backbone of the Internet in the United States was National Science Foundation Network (NSFNET). Management of the NSFNET was contracted to Advanced Network Services (ANS). When commercialization of the Internet began, an ANSNET backbone was formed for carrying the commercial traffic. The ANSNET backbone was also managed by ANS. Actually, both NSFNET and ANSNET traffic were carried over the same physical links, but two virtual backbones were run over it.

The Internet Community

The earlier Internet community consisted of universities such as Stanford, UCLA, MIT, the University of California at Santa Barbara, the University of Utah, the University of Hawaii, and the University of California at Berkeley, as well as research organizations such as SRI International, Rand Corporation, the Institute of Advanced Computation, and the company Bolt, Beranek, and Newman (BBN).

Currently, the Internet community has expanded to include commercial organizations and individual users. The Internet community includes all major universities, research organizations, corporations, individual users, and Internet providers.

Internet providers are commercial organizations that sell access to the Internet. Table 1.1 shows a list of some of the Internet providers.

Table 1.1 Internet Providers

Internet Access Provider	Contact
AlterNet	UUNET Technologies, Inc. 800-488-6383 703-204-8000 alternet-info@uunet.uu.net
Internet Express	719-520-1700 ID: new, password: newuser Local access area codes: 303, 719 klaus@usa.net
DELPHI	800-365-4636 Local access areas: Boston, Kansas City walthowe@delphi.com
Dial-in-cerf	Provided by CERFNET 800-876-2373 619-455-3900 Local access area codes: 213, 310, 415, 510, 619, 714, 818 help@cerf.net
NEARnet	617-873-8730 Local access codes: 508, 603, 617 nearnet-join@nic.near.net
NETCOM	408-554-Unix info@netcom.com
NorthWestNet	206-562-3000 nic@nwnet.net
NYSERnet	315-453-2912 info@nysernet.org
PSInet	703-620-6651 all-info@psi.com
WELL	The Whole Earth 'Lectronic Link 415-332-6106 ID: newuser info@well.sf.ca.us
World	Software Tool & Die 617-739-9753 ID: new 617-739-0202 office@world.std.com

The Transition from Proprietary Networks to Open TCP/IP Networks

Earlier commercial computers were based around proprietary vendor products. Two classic examples of these are IBM's System Network Architecture (SNA) network and Digital's DECnet (see fig. 1.6).

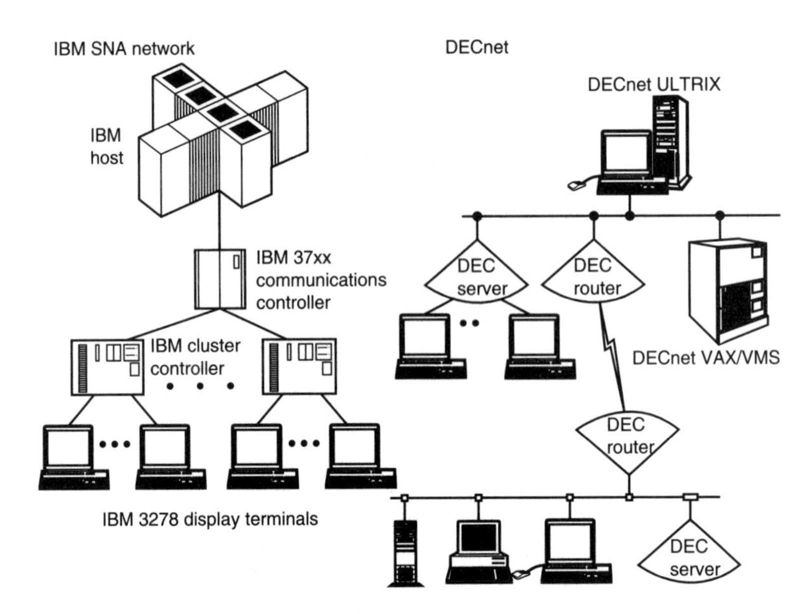

Figure 1.6
Two proprietary networks.

IBM's SNA network has traditionally been hierarchical. The IBM host communicates with communications controllers that off-load the communications processing from the IBM host. The communications controller in turn communicates with the IBM cluster controller that acts like a terminal server to IBM 3278/3279 page-mode display terminals.

Digital's DECnet Phase IV is built around the DECnet suite of protocols, and DECnet Phase V uses both DECnet and OSI protocols. DECnet has a more peer-to-peer orientation at both the physical network and protocol levels when compared with IBM's SNA network.

IBM's SNA networks have evolved to become more peer-to-peer at the API and upper protocol level, as can be seen with the introduction of Advanced Peer-to-Peer Communications (APPC) and Advanced Peer-to-Peer Networks (APPN).

Both of these proprietary solutions, IBM's SNA and Digital's DECnet, have become more open with the availability of TCP/IP (and OSI) support. IBM, VAX or Alpha-based hosts can be accessed using TCP/IP protocols and services.

Both IBM and DEC have intensified their efforts in the TCP/IP market. For example, IBM now off-loads TCP/IP processing from the IBM mainframes to the IBM 3172 Interconnect Controller or to a RISC System 6000 running TCP/IP. The IBM 3172 Interconnect Controller acts as a front-end processor and removes the host out of processing TCP/IP communications. The 3172 is an Intel 80486 micro channel platform running TCP/IP on OS/2. This off-load technology is primarily aimed at MVS, VM mainframes that are currently at peak capacity.

A Multivendor Network

One reason vendors have begun providing more open solutions based around TCP/IP is that users have demanded freedom from proprietary solutions. Proprietary solutions "lock" users to a particular vendor's platform. While this may be advantageous to vendors, it can lead to more expensive networking solutions for the user.

Using a common protocol such as TCP/IP promotes a more competitive market where users can pick the best TCP/IP protocol stack from a wide range of choices.

Figure 1.7 shows an example of a multivendor network based around TCP/IP. This figure shows an HP-9000 class machine running HP-UX that comes with TCP/IP software. It also shows SUN workstations running SunOS or Solaris, VAX/VMS running TCP/IP for VMS or Wollongong's TCP/IP for VMS, Novell NetWare 3.x/4.x running TCP/IP, UnixWare TCP/IP, IBM VM host running TCP/IP for VM or Fibronics TCP/IP, IBM PC with NCSA TCP/IP software, and MacTCP. This is only a partial list. TCP/IP implementations are available on every major computing platform ranging from mainframes and minicomputers to workstations and microcomputers.

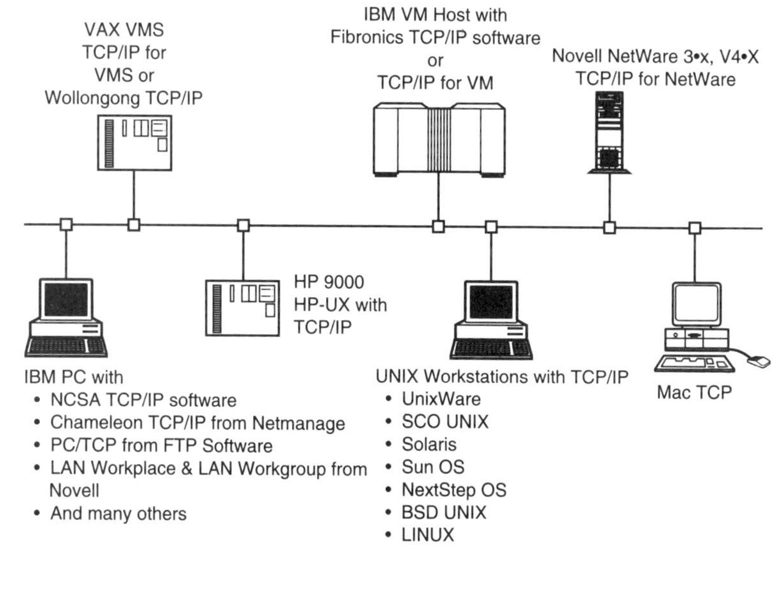

Figure 1.7

A multivendor TCP/IP implementation.

HP-UX, SunOS/Solaris, and UnixWare are examples of TCP/IP implementations on a Unix platform. TCP/IP is implemented as a standard part of BSD Unix and Unix System V.

Originally, TCP/IP was implemented in the kernel of the 4.2 BSD Unix operating system. 4.2 BSD Unix was a very influential version of Unix, and is one of the reasons for TCP/IP's widespread popularity. Most universities and many research organizations use BSD Unix.

Today, most host machines on the Internet run a direct descendant of BSD Unix. In addition, many commercial versions of Unix, such as SUN's SunOS and Digital's Ultrix, were derived from 4.2 BSD Unix. Unix System V TCP/IP implementation has also been heavily influenced by BSD Unix, as has been Novell's TCP/IP implementation on DOS (LANWorkplace products) and NetWare 3.x/4.x.

TCP/IP Vendor Revenues

There are many job opportunities in the area of computer networks that require knowledge of TCP/IP. Figures 1.8 and 1.9 show the shift in TCP/IP vendor revenues and number of TCP/IP vendors. Both of these graphs indicate a rising interest in TCP/IP. Figure 1.8 shows that the market size, in terms of revenues, has increased for U.S.-based companies. It also shows that most of the growth has been in the commercial sector.

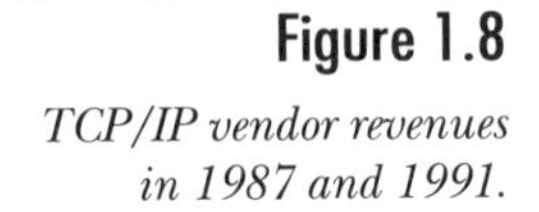

Figure 1.8

TCP/IP vendor revenues in 1987 and 1991.

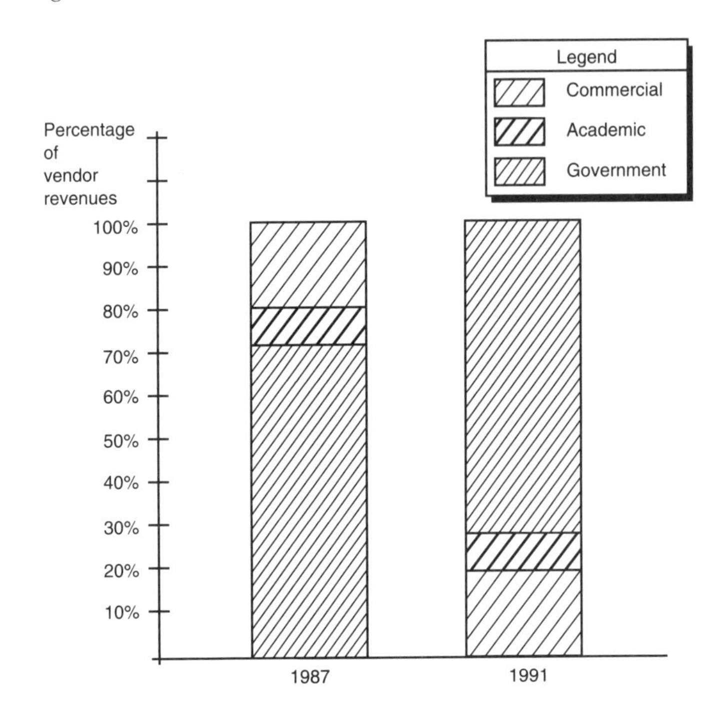

Source: Infonetics, *Network World*, Newton-Evans Research Co.

Figure 1.9 shows that a rapid increase in the number of vendors providing TCP/IP-based products around 1985. There are several reasons for this growth. One of the major reasons is that the microcomputer market grew dramatically around this time, and several vendors began developing TCP/IP protocols and applications for microcomputers. Another reason is that vendors grew tired of waiting for OSI protocols to mature while there was already a mature TCP/IP protocol suite and services that had a proven track record for a number of years.

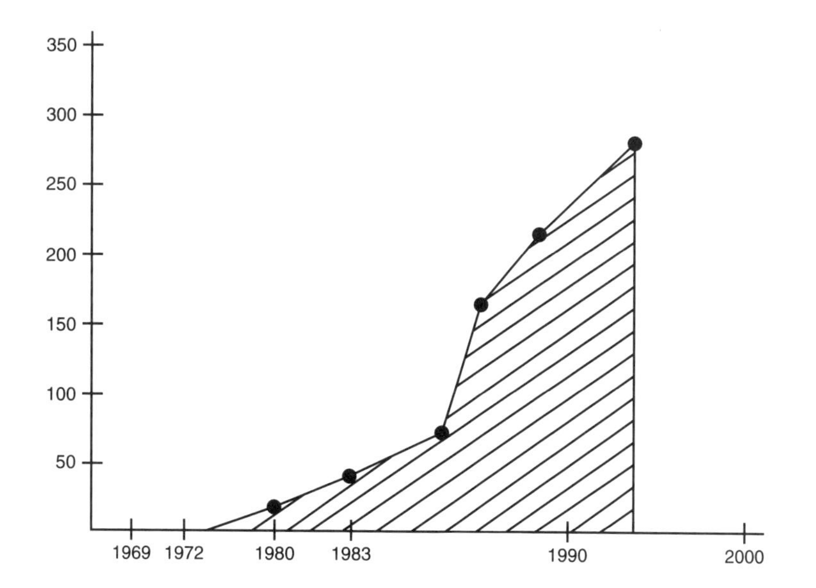

Source: Infonetics

Figure 1.9

The number of TCP/IP vendors from 1969 to the present.

The Driving Forces behind TCP/IP

TCP/IP delivers today what OSI protocols have promised for a number of years. The areas where TCP/IP was originally weak compared to OSI protocols was in the area of application services. OSI had a far richer variety of standard application services than TCP/IP. In recent years, as a result of strenuous efforts by those in the Internet community, TCP/IP proponents have narrowed the gap between OSI application offerings and TCP/IP applications. Some of the more promising OSI applications such as X.500 are being implemented on TCP/IP based networks.

The three factors driving growth in TCP/IP today are the following:

- **Growth in network management tools.** The most widely implemented network management protocol today is Simple Network Management Protocol (SNMP). This protocol makes use of TCP/IP protocols. Many network vendors of products such as hubs, bridges, and routers provide SNMP agents. These SNMP agents use the TCP/IP stack. The graph in figure 1.9, therefore, also includes hardware vendors.
- **Promise of interoperability.** Having a set of common protocols allows the interoperability of products from different vendors. For true interoperability using TCP/IP, vendors should use not only TCP/IP but also TCP/IP application services.
- **Interest in the commercialization of the Internet.** The Internet today is predominantly based on TCP/IP protocols and application services. As the general public interest in using the Internet continues to grow, and the ensuing "information superhighway" continues to increase, you can expect a corresponding increase in interest in TCP/IP protocols and services.

The Evolution of TCP/IP

Figure 1.10 shows the evolution of TCP/IP. This figure shows events of note that occurred with respect to TCP/IP growth. The time-line begins with the four-node ARPAnet experiment in 1969 and the ARPAnet demo in 1972. From 1978 to 1980 there was a great deal of interaction between the TCP/IP researchers and implementers and the researchers at Xerox's Palo Alto Research facility who were working on Xerox Network System (XNS). As a result of this interaction, XNS's RIP (Routing Information Protocol) was adopted for use in BSD Unix. Because BSD Unix was popular, RIP became widely used on TCP/IP networks. The influence of BSD Unix was felt around 1980 when this operating system was deployed at many sites.

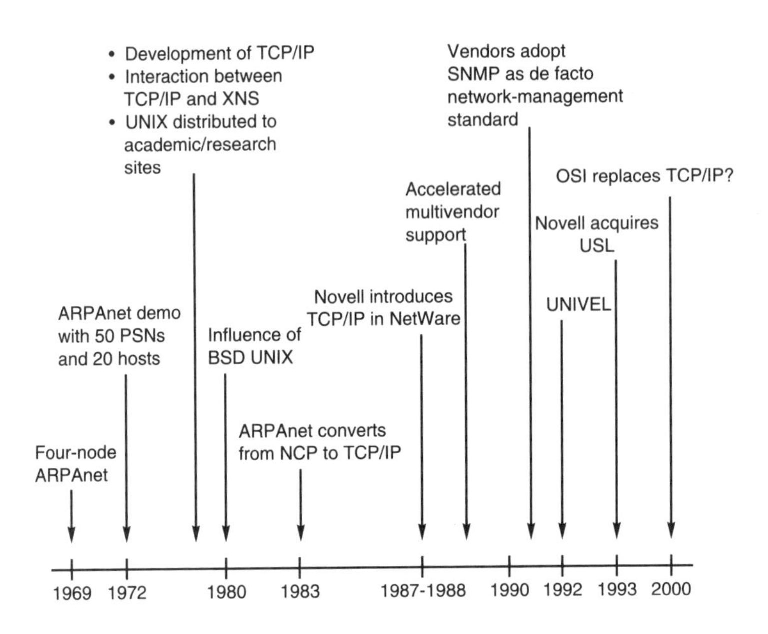

Figure 1.10
The evolution of TCP/IP.

Figure 1.10 shows why TCP/IP's RIP and Novell's IPX RIP have more in common besides the name. They both have a common ancestor—XNS RIP. Another protocol derived from XNS RIP is AppleTalk's Routing Table Maintenance Protocol (RTMP).

In 1983, the ARPAnet, which had been using Network Control Protocol (NCP)—not to be confused with NetWare Core Protocol, began converting to TCP/IP.

In 1987, Novell introduced TCP/IP in NetWare 3.x. Novell had acquired Excelan of San Jose and used the technology gained as a result of this acquisition to introduce TCP/IP protocols and applications in several of its products.

In the late 1980s, multivendor support for TCP/IP accelerated. In the early 1990s, SNMP became a de facto standard for management of TCP/IP networks. SNMP is not restricted to using TCP/IP protocols. For example, SNMP can also run on Novell's Internetwork Packet Exchange protocol (IPX) and OSI's Connectionless Network Protocol (CLNP).

In 1992, a joint USL (Unix Systems Laboratories) and Novell venture called *UNIVEL* was formed to integrate Unix and NetWare in a product called *UnixWare*. This was followed by the acquisition of USL by Novell and its renaming to the *Unix Systems Group* (USG).

Overview of TCP/IP Applications

Several TCP/IP applications such as FTP and TELNET were mentioned earlier in this chapter. The section provides an overview of these applications.

TCP/IP Applications

Figure 1.11 shows some of the more popular TCP/IP applications. This figure shows a TCP/IP internet with users that are accessing TCP/IP applications on hosts that are remote from the users.

In this figure, user A is at a workstation, using a TELNET session to log on remotely to a VMS host. The TELNET application enables the user to access another host remotely. For this to take place, there are two components of software that must be running. You need a TELNET client application running at the user's workstation. The TELNET client application takes the user's keystrokes and sends them (either a character at a time or a line at a time) to the remote host. At the remote host, you need a TELNET server component. This TELNET server component takes the user's typed-in characters and submits it to the operating system as if they were typed in by a locally attached terminal. The TELNET server is responsible for taking the host's response and sending it to the TELNET client running at the user's workstation.

User B, in figure 1.11, is using an FTP session to transfer files between his or her workstation and an IBM host. The FTP application enables a user to access another host's file system interactively. Once an FTP session is established, the user can type special FTP commands that will enable the user to browse directories and files on the remote system. The user can issue commands for uploading or downloading files between the workstation and the FTP host. For an FTP session to work, you need two software components. You need an FTP client application running at the user's workstation, which enables you to send interactive commands to the FTP host. At the remote host you need an FTP server component, which processes the user's FTP commands and interacts with the file system of the host that it runs on.

Figure 1.11

An overview of TCP/IP applications.

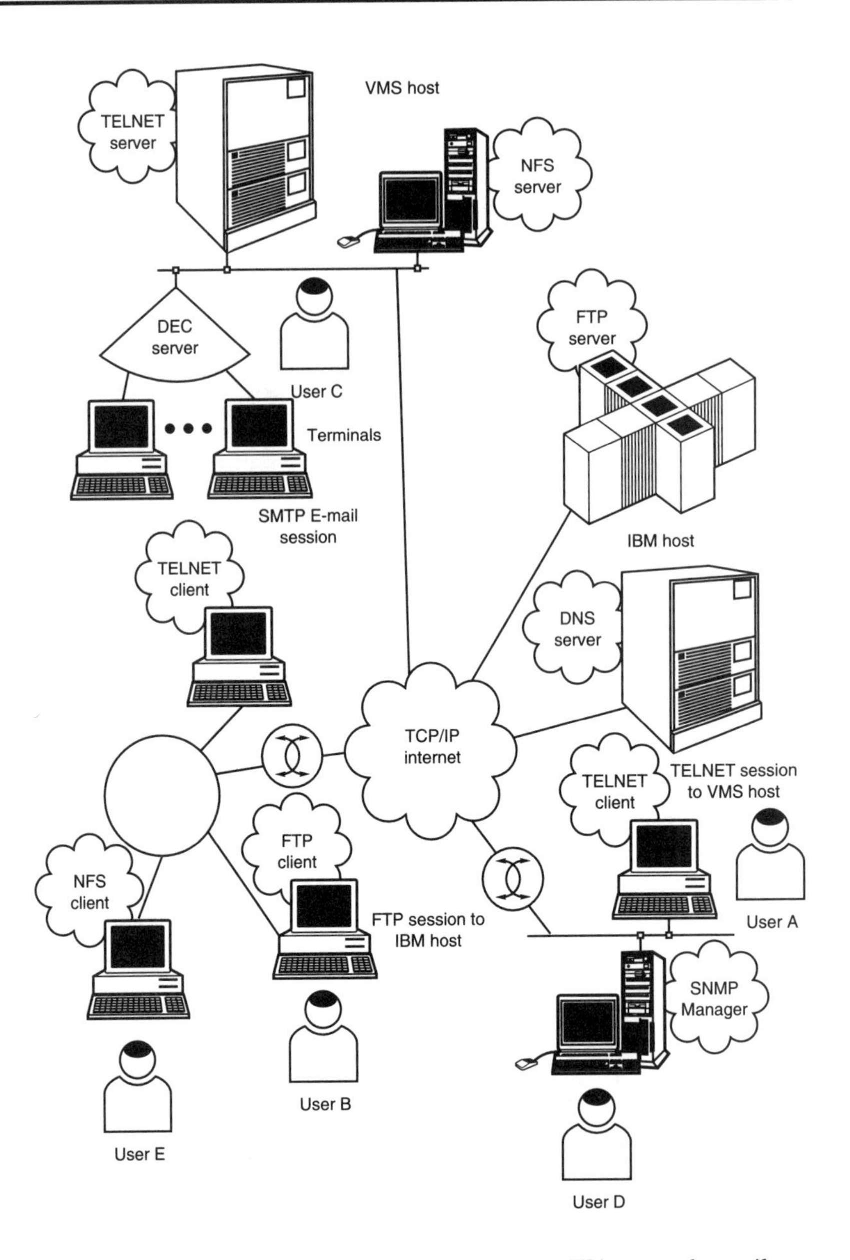

User C, in figure 1.11, is using the Simple Mail Transfer Protocol (SMTP) to send e-mail to other users on the network. The mail software running at the user's workstation takes the e-mail message composed by the user and deposits it into an outgoing mail area. A program that runs in the background takes the e-mail and sends it to the destination host. The mail is then deposited in the mailbox on the host. This mailbox is that of the user who is the recipient of the e-mail.

User D, in figure 1.11, is using SNMP to access information on devices on the network. The user is running SNMP manager software that sends requests in a special SNMP message format to a device, querying the device for management information. Management information is information that the SNMP manager finds useful for monitoring and controlling the device. An SNMP agent running on the device responds to the SNMP requests. The replies sent by the SNMP agent are used by the SNMP Manager to manage the device.

User E, in figure 1.11, is using Network File System (NFS) to access file services on a remote host directly. This means that the file system at the remote host appears to the workstation as an extension of the file system on that workstation. This enables the user to access the remote file system using the commands of the local workstation operating system. For NFS to work, you need two software components. The NFS client application running at the user's workstation connects with the file system on the NFS host. An NFS server component running on the remote host interacts with the file system of the host that it runs on and allows its file system to be treated as a local file system at the user's workstation.

The *Domain Name System* (DNS) server shown in figure 1.11 is used for TCP/IP applications to refer to host names by their symbolic names rather than by their network address. When a TCP/IP application such as TELNET wishes to log onto the VMS host, it can use a symbolic name for the VMS host. The DNS server will resolve this symbolic name to the network address that will be used by the TELNET application to contact the VMS host.

Table 1.2 summarizes the TCP/IP applications discussed in this section.

Table 1.2 TCP/IP Applications Summary

Application Service	Description
TELNET	Enables users to log in remotely across a TCP/IP network to any host supporting this protocol.
FTP	Enables users to transfer files between computers on a TCP/IP network.
SMTP	Enables users to send electronic mail to other users on the TCP/IP network.
SNMP	Allows remote management of devices such as bridges, routers, and gateways on the network.
DNS	Acts as an electronic directory and clearinghouse for names of network resources.

The Internet

The former ARPAnet has gradually been replaced by the Internet. The Internet is not a single network. It is a conglomeration of several networks. The predominant protocols used are TCP/IP, and the applications are TCP/IP-based. But not all networks on the Internet use TCP/IP. An example of this is the BITNET and the CREN. These use IBM's SNA protocols. In order for these networks to interact with other networks that use TCP/IP, protocol translations by gateways must be performed.

Even though the Internet continues to undergo commercialization, it provides an incomparable test network for developing new protocols and application services. For example, a great deal of experimentation and research on OSI application services is conducted on the Internet.

Sample Networks on the Internet

Table 1.3 contains some of the networks that make up the Internet. This list is by no means exhaustive. It is meant to give you an idea of the range of participation on the Internet by international communities.

TABLE 1.3 NETWORKS ON THE INTERNET

Network	Description
NSFNET	National Science Foundation Network. The backbone network in the U.S.
CSNET	Computer Science Network. Affordable internet services using X.25 for small schools and organizations.
Cypress Net	Provides low-cost and low-volume Internet access centered around Purdue University.
MILNET	U.S. Department of Defense (DoD) network. Originally part of ARPAnet.
BITNET	Because It's Time Network. Uses IBM mainframes and low-cost 9600 bps links.
CREN	Consortium for Research and Education Network. Successor to CSNET and BITNET.
EARN	European Academic Research Network. Uses BITNET technology. A network for Europe, the Middle East, and Africa.
JANET	Joint Academic Network. A network for universities and Research Institutions in the U.K.

Network	Description
CDNet	Network services to Canadian research, education and advanced development community.
NRCnet	Canadian National Research Council network. Modeled after NSFNET.
ACSnet	Australian Computer Science Network. Used by universities, research institutions, and industry.
Kogaku-bu	Established at the University of Tokyo. Uses a proprietary 100 Mbps fiber backbone network.

NFSNET is a general-purpose internet providing access to scientific computing resources, data and information initially organized and partly funded by NSF. It consists of a three-level internetwork comprised of the following:

- The backbone: a transcontinental network that connects separately administered networks, NSF supercomputer centers.
- Mid-level networks: regional, discipline-based, and supercomputer consortium networks.
- Campus-wide networks connected to mid-level networks.

Since the demise of ARPANET, NFSNET has replaced it as general-purpose backbone. Management and operation of it are the responsibility of Merit, Inc. End-user support to the research community is provided by a NIC at BBN.

On the NFSNET, packet switch nodes called *Nodal switching subsystems* (NSS) are used. Each NSS consists of nine IBM RT/PCs running AIX connected to token ring networks for redundancy. Within each NSS, a Routing Control Processor (RCP) mediates access between more than 1 NSS. Backbone routing software within each NSS uses IS-IS. Mid-level networks are connected using EGP.

CSNET, established in January 1981, consisted of the Computer Science departments of schools and universities. Membership is now more general and includes industrial, academic, government, and non-profit institutions engaged in computer-related research or advanced development in science and engineering. This network is mostly confined to the U.S. and Canada but has links to Australia, Finland, France, Germany, Israel, Japan, Korea, New Zealand, Sweden, Switzerland, China, and the U.K.

CSNET *CIC* (Computer and Information Center) is administered by BBN.

BITNET is a cooperative network serving more than 2,300 hosts (IBM) at several hundred sites in 32 countries. The underlying protocol is NJE, with some sites running NJE on top of TCP/IP. In Europe, there are plans to migrate to ISO protocols. Major constituents of BITNET are in the U.S., Mexico, Japan, Singapore, Taiwan, and Korea (Asian parts are known as Asianet). BITNET is known as NetNorth in Canada and EARN in Europe.

In October 1988, the boards of CSNET and BITNET voted to merge the two into a single net called the CREN. The merger was completed in 1989.

EARN was formed in 1983. EARN's charter states that it is a network for Europe, the Middle East, and Africa. Recent voting has ratified Morocco, Tunisia, Egypt, and India as members. EARN is registered in France and its board of directors consist of members from each member country. EARN uses the technology used in BITNET and is part of BITNET. Many EARN hosts are IBM VM and DEC VAX VMS machines. Gateways exist to other networks, such as JANET in the U.K. and HEANET in Ireland.

JANET was established to provide consolidated links among universities and research institutions in the U.K. JANET is funded by the Computer Board for Universities and Research Councils (CB) and is limited to the following:

- Universities
- Laboratories or institutes funded by research councils
- Individual members of polytechnics or other institutes of further education that hold research council grants
- Polytechnics that may join the network but are charged

Services in JANET include mail, file transfer, remote login, and remote job entry. LANs connected to JANET tend to be X.25 campus switches, Cambridge Rings (CR82 standard), Ethernet, and IEEE 802.3. Wide-area links are X.25 at the network layer. JANET Packet Switching Exchanges (JPSE) are based on GEC 4000 processors. JANET uses a domain name system similar to the Internet DNS, but the order of the domain name parts is opposite, with the root on the left. For instance, to send mail from JANET to the Internet, the gateway is at uk.ac.ucl.cs.nss at the University of London Computer Center (ULCC).

CDNET is administered by the CDNet Headquarters at the University of British Columbia (UBC) and is independent of Canadian Department of Defense. Most machines are DEC VAX or Sun file servers (about 60 percent Unix and 40 percent VMS). Most wide-area links are X.25 at 2400 bps (ranging from 1200 bps to 9600 bps) provided through DATAPAC. There are leased-line connections to the NFSNET backbone. Gateways exist to CSNET and BITNET.

NRCNET is modeled after NFSNET to provide faster services than currently offered by NetNorth and CDNET. It uses the three-level model of backbone, mid-level, and campus LANs.

ACSNET is based on the Sydney Unix Network (SUN) software developed at the University of Sydney. The network was started in 1979. It provides mail and file transfer traffic among researchers, academia, and industry. Wide-area links include leased lines, dial-up lines, and X.25.

Kogaku-bu, established in 1987, uses TCP/IP over a Toshiba 100 Mbps fiber backbone network that connects Ethernet LANs. Protocols are not FDDI because the technology predates FDDI. The data link protocol on the ring is called TOTOLAN/RING. Applications include TELNET and FTP. Mainframe remote login access using Japanese character sets have been managed by putting TELNET in the transparent mode and using the character conversion capabilities of the IBM TSS TIOP2 program on the mainframe.

The IAB and the Internet Society

Figure 1.12 shows the interrelationships between the various bodies that have an impact on the Internet.

The *Internet Activities Board* (IAB) provides focus, direction, and coordination of TCP/IP-related protocols. This body guides the evolution of the Internet. It is comprised of the Internet Research Task Force (IRTF) and the Internet Engineering Task Force (IETF). The *Federal Networking Council* (FNC) is the U.S government regulatory body that serves as an advisory body. As the Internet gets even more commercialized, the influence of the FNC will be even further reduced.

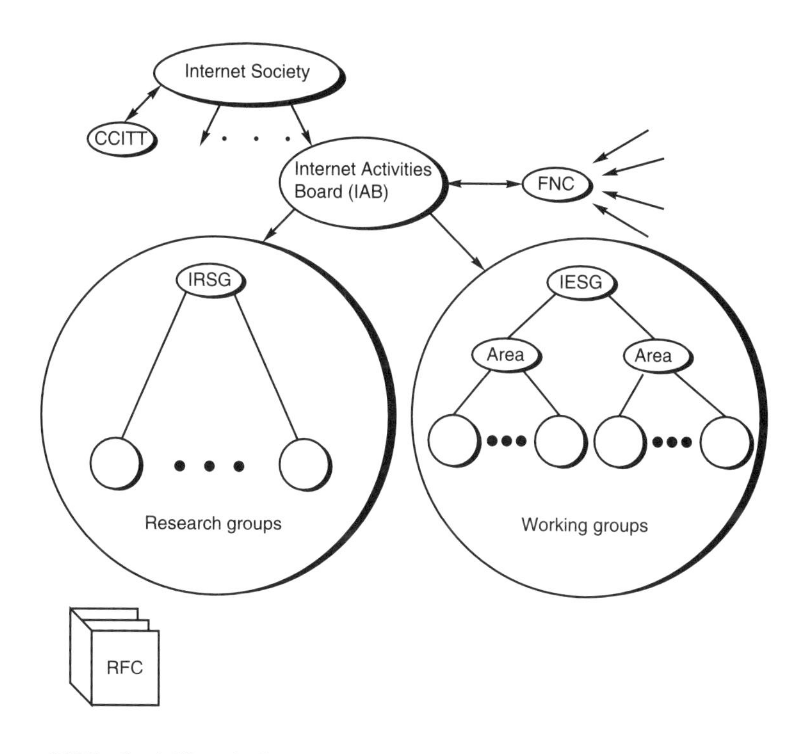

Figure 1.12

The structure of the IAB.

The Internet Engineering Task Force is managed by the Internet Engineering Steering Group (IESG). It is divided into areas, with areas divided into working groups. The IETF focuses on short- to medium-term engineering problems.

The Internet Research Task Force is managed by the Internet Research Steering Group (IRSG). It focuses on long-term research problems.

The IETF has the following broad technical areas. The actual areas may change over time depending on the needs of the Internet.

- Applications
- Host protocols
- Internet protocols
- Routing
- Network management
- OSI interoperability
- Operations
- Security

The IETF has many working groups. Some of these are authentication, domain names, dynamic host configuration, host requirements, interconnectivity, Internet MIB, joint management, Telnet, user documents, and so on.

A more recent development is the formation of the Internet Society. The *Internet Society* promotes the use of the Internet for collaboration on research topics on the Internet. It provides a forum for industry, educators, government, and users. It is involved with the recommendation of procedures and technical standards for the global Internet and private internets.

Membership in the Internet Society is open to everyone for an annual membership fee. As this book goes to press, the regular membership is $70 per year. It is $25 per year for students. You can contact the Internet Society at the following address:

Internet Society
Suite 100
1895 Preston White Drive
Reston, VA 22091-5434
U.S.A.

E-mail: isoc@isoc.org
Telephone: 703-648-9888
Fax: 703-620-0913

RFCs and IENs

The primary method for communicating new ideas on protocols, research, and standards is through *Requests For Comments* (RFCs). When a researcher comes up with a new protocol, research, or tutorial on a topic, the researcher can submit this as an RFC document. Thus, RFCs consist of Internet standards, proposals for new or revised protocols, implementation strategies, tutorials, collective wisdom, and so on.

Not all RFCs are Internet Protocol Standards, even though all Internet Protocol Standards have an RFC number. The list of official Internet Protocol Standards is published regularly. This list is also an RFC. When a new RFC is published on the same topic, it contains a statement about which RFC it replaces. Thus, RFC 1600 is published as

> 1600 Postel, J., ed. INTERNET OFFICIAL PROTOCOL STANDARDS. 1994 March; 36 p. (Format: TXT=80958 bytes) (Obsoletes RFC 1540)

Notice that this RFC listing states that RFC 1600 is the Internet Official Protocol Standards, and that it obsoletes RFC 1540 on the same topic.

Anyone can submit an RFC, as long as it follows guidelines established by RFC 1543.

> 1543 Postel, J. Instructions to RFC Authors. 1993 October; 16 p. (Format: TXT=31384 bytes) (Obsoletes RFC 1111)

When you write an RFC, you must submit it to the editor-in-chief, whose e-mail address is

> RFC-Editor@ISI.EDU

Earlier documents and standards on the ARPAnet were written as *Internet Engineering Notes* (IENs). These have been replaced by RFCs.

Some of the RFCs are actually poems. Some examples are RFCs 968 and RFC 1121. Here are some interesting poems by two of the founders of the Internet: Vincent Cerf, the father of the Internet, and Leonard Kleinrock, who did major analytical work on the Internet.

Twas the Night Before Start-up
Vint Cerf, 1985 (RFC 968)

Twas the night before start-up and all through the net,
not a packet was moving; no bit nor octet.
The engineers rattled their cards in despair,
hoping a bad chip would blow with a flare.
The salesmen were nestled all snug in their beds,
while visions of data nets danced in their heads.
And I with my datascope tracings and dumps
prepared for some pretty bad bruises and lumps.
When out in the hall there arose such a clatter,
I sprang from my desk to see what was the matter.

There stood at the threshold with PC in tow,
An ARPANET hacker, all ready to go.
I could see from the creases that covered his brow,
he'd conquer the crisis confronting him now.
More rapid than eagles, he checked each alarm
and scrutinized each for its potential harm.

On LAPB, on OSI, X.25!
TCP, SNA, V.35!

His eyes were afire with the strength of his gaze;
no bug could hide long; not for hours or days.
A wink of his eye and a twitch of his head,
soon gave me to know I had little to dread.
He spoke not a word, but went straight to his work,
fixing a net that had gone plumb berserk;
And laying a finger on one suspect line,
he entered a patch and the net came up fine!

The packets flowed neatly and protocols matched;
the hosts interfaced and shift-registers latched.
He tested the system from Gateway to PAD;
not one bit was dropped; no checksum was bad.
At last he was finished and wearily sighed
and turned to explain why the system had died.
I twisted my fingers and counted to ten;
an off-by-one index had done it again...

THE BIG BANG!
(or the birth of the ARPANET)
Leonard Kleinrock (RFC 1121)

It was back in '67 that the clan agreed to meet.
The gangsters and the planners were a breed damned hard to beat.
The goal we set was honest and the need was clear to all:
Connect those big old mainframes and the minis, lest they fall.

The spec was set quite rigid: it must work without a hitch.
It should stand a single failure with an unattended switch.
Files at hefty throughput 'cross the ARPANET must zip.
Send the interactive traffic on a quarter second trip.

The spec went out to bidders and 'twas BBN that won.
They worked on soft and hardware and they all got paid for fun.
We decided that the first node would be we who are your hosts
And so today you're gathered here while UCLA boasts.

I suspect you might be asking "What means FIRST node on the net?"
Well frankly, it meant trouble, 'specially since no specs were set.
For you see the interface between the nascent IMP and HOST.
Was a confidential secret from us folks on the West coast.

BBN had promised that the IMP was running late.
We welcomed any slippage in the deadly scheduled date.
But one day after Labor Day, it was plopped down at our gate!
Those dirty rotten scoundrels sent the damned thing out air freight!

As I recall that Tuesday, it makes me want to cry.
Everybody's brother came to blame the other guy!
Folks were there from ARPA, GTE, and Honeywell.
UCLA and ATT and all were scared as hell.

We cautiously connected and the bits began to flow.
The pieces really functioned—just why I still don't know.
Messages were moving pretty well by Wednesday morn.
All the rest is history—packet switching had been born!

ROSENCRANTZ AND ETHERNET
Vint Cerf, 1989 (RFC 1121)

All the world's a net! And all the data in it merely packets
come to store-and-forward in the queues a while and then are
heard no more. 'Tis a network waiting to be switched!

To switch or not to switch? That is the question. Whether
'tis wiser in the net to suffer the store and forward of
stochastic networks or to raise up circuits against a sea
of packets and, by dedication, serve them.

To net, to switch. To switch, perchance to slip!
Aye, there's the rub. For in that choice of switch,
what loops may lurk, when we have shuffled through
this Banyan net? Puzzles the will, initiates symposia,
stirs endless debate and gives rise to uncontrolled
flights of poetry beyond recompense!

RFCs

You can obtain Request For Comments from several sources. If you do not have access to the Internet, you can contact:

SRI International, Room EJ291
333 Ravenswood Avenue
Menlo Park, CA 94025
415-859-3695
NIC@SRI-NIC.ARP

Table 1.4 shows some of the RFC sites that are available. The primary repositories will have the RFC available when it is first announced, as will many secondary repositories. Some secondary repositories may take a few days to make available the most recent RFCs.

Table 1.4 RFC Sites

Host Name	Primary/Secondary
DS.INTERNIC.NET	Primary
NIS.NSF.NET	Primary
NISC.JVNC.NET	Primary
VENERA.ISI.EDU	Primary
WUARCHIVE.WUSTL.EDU	Primary
SRC.DOC.IC.AC.UK	Primary
FTP.CONCERT.NET	Primary
FTP.SESQUI.NET	Primary
SUNIC.SUNET.SE	Secondary
CHALMERS.SE	Secondary
WALHALLA.INFORMATIK.UNI-DORTMUND.DE	Secondary
MCSUN.EU.NET	Secondary
FUNET.FI	Secondary
UGLE.UNIT.NO	Secondary
FTP.DENET.DK	Secondary
MUNNARI.OZ.AU	Secondary
NIC.CERF.NET	Secondary
FTP.UU.NET	Secondary

Summary

TCP/IP-based networks play an increasingly important role in computer networks. TCP/IP networks are based on an open protocol specification that is not controlled by any vendor. This chapter examined the origins of TCP/IP networks and the commercial uses of this protocol. The chapter briefly explained some common uses of TCP/IP protocols.

This chapter also discussed the relationship between the Internet and the older ARPAnet, and the professional bodies that influence research and development of the Internet protocols.

TCP/IP Network Protocol Architecture

This chapter explores the TCP/IP layering concepts. A familiarity with TCP/IP layering concepts is important because these concepts provide insight into the different protocol elements needed for TCP/IP applications. The TCP/IP protocol elements will be shown in relationship to the OSI and the DoD models. These models are important for a conceptual understanding of the TCP/IP protocol stack. You will learn how IP addresses can be specified for a TCP/IP network interface, and you will learn about the importance of using subnets on a TCP/IP network.

TCP/IP can operate on a wide variety of physical networks. This chapter examines some of the more common transports on which TCP/IP can run.

TCP/IP Protocol Layering

A TCP/IP network such as that shown in figure 2.1 can be organized into the following major network elements:

- Physical connections
- Protocols
- Applications

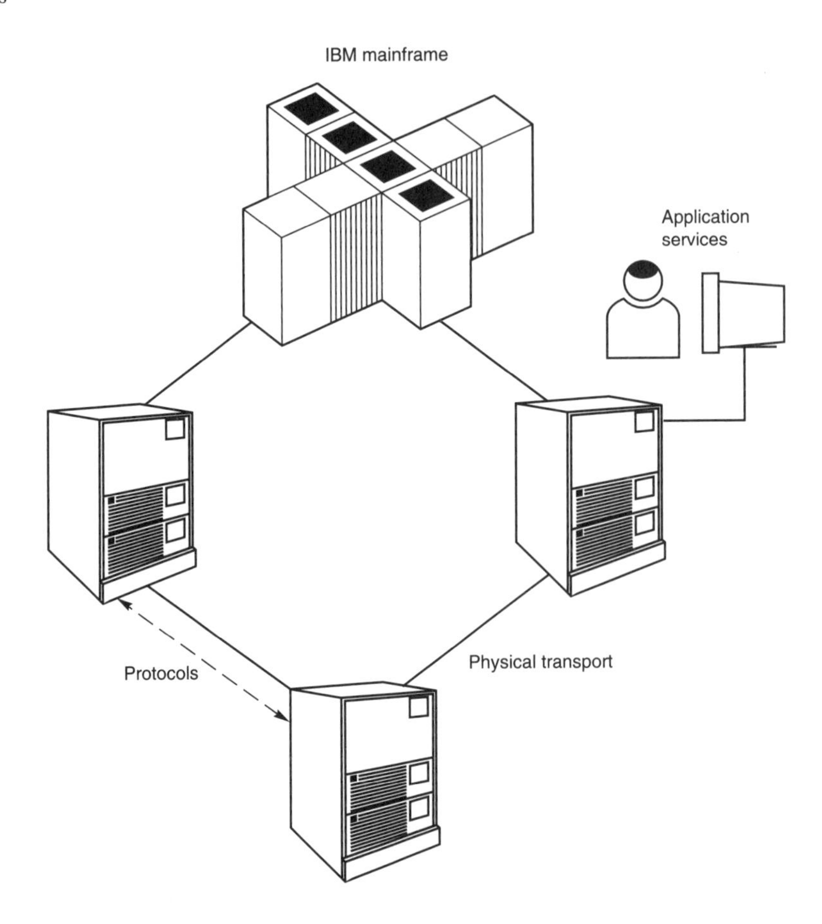

Figure 2.1
Elements of a TCP/IP network.

The physical connections provide the medium over which the bits comprising the messages can be transmitted. The physical connections could be coaxial cable, twisted-pair wiring (shielded or unshielded), fiber optic, telephone lines, leased lines, microwave links, infrared links, radio links, or satellite links. There are many choices for the physical connections of a network. You must make your choice based on factors such as bandwidth of medium, ease of installation, maintenance, media cost, and end-equipment cost.

The physical connections represent the lowest level of logical functionality needed by the network. To operate the network, you need to have a standard set of rules and regulations that all devices must obey to be able to communicate and interoperate with each other. The rules and regulations by which devices on the network communicate are called *protocols*. A variety of such rules and regulations (protocols) exist, and these rules provide different types of functions for a network.

Network applications use the underlying network protocols to communicate with network applications running on other network devices. The network protocols in turn use the network physical connections to transmit the data.

When you consider that network operation consists of physical connections, protocols, and applications, you can see that these network elements form a hierarchy: the applications at the very top and the physical connections at the bottom. The protocols provide the bridge between the applications and the physical connections.

To understand the hierarchy between the network elements and the functions that they perform, you need a "yard stick" or model for defining these functions. One commonly accepted model is the OSI reference model.

The OSI Reference Model

Before you can understand networking protocols, you need to learn the terminology used to define them. The preeminent model for comparing protocols is the *Open Systems Interconnection* (OSI) reference model. Today, all vendors compare their proprietary, industry-standard, or international standard protocol implementations against the OSI reference model.

The OSI reference model was developed in 1978 by the International Organization of Standards (ISO) to specify a standard that could be used for the development of open systems and as a yardstick to compare different communication systems. Network systems designed according to OSI framework and specifications speak the same language; that is, they use similar or compatible methods of communication. This type of network system allows products from different vendors to interoperate.

In the early days of computer networks (prior to the OSI model), the proprietary computer network architecture reigned supreme. An organization interested in installing a computer network examined the choices available from vendors such as IBM, DEC, HP, and Honeywell. Each of those choices had its own proprietary architecture; the capability to interconnect networks from different vendors was almost nonexistent.

Once committed to buying equipment from a specific vendor, the organization was virtually locked in. Updates or modifications to the system were provided by the vendor, and because the vendor had a closed proprietary architecture, no one could compete with that vendor in supplying equivalent services. Prices were determined based on what the customer could bear without complaining too much.

Today's users probably realize that in many areas of the computer industry, this picture has not changed much. Proprietary architecture history is still around, but the OSI model can, at the very least, provide you with a clearer picture of how different network components relate to each other.

Layers of the OSI Model

The OSI model has seven layers, as shown in figure 2.2. The layers, working from the bottom up, include the following:

1. Physical
2. Data Link
3. Network
4. Transport
5. Session
6. Presentation
7. Application

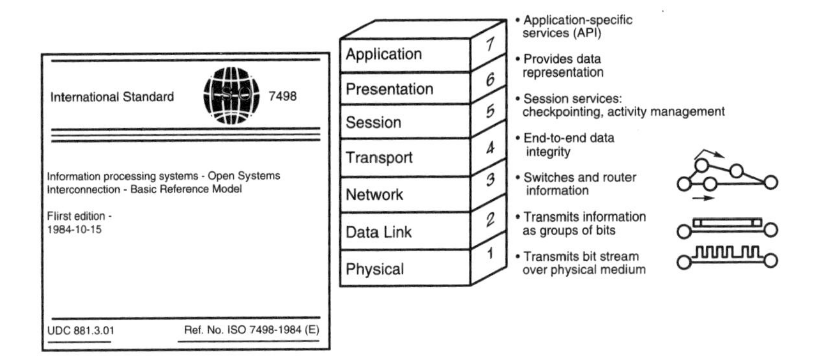

Figure 2.2
The OSI reference model.

The following five principles were applied to determine the layers in figure 2.2:

- A layer should be created only when a different level of abstraction is needed.
- Each layer should provide a well-defined function.
- The function of each layer should be chosen so that it defines internationally standardized protocols.

- The layer boundaries should be chosen to minimize the information flow across layer interfaces.
- Distinct functions should be defined in separate layers, but the number of layers should be small enough that the architecture does not become unwieldy.

The functions of each of these seven layers are described in the following sections.

Physical Layer

The *physical layer* transmits bits over a communication channel. The bits may represent database records or file transfers; the physical layer is oblivious to what those bits represent. The bits can be encoded as digital 1s and 0s or in analog form. The physical layer involves the mechanical, electrical, and procedural interfaces over the physical medium.

Data Link Layer

The *data link layer* builds on the transmission capability of the physical layer. The bits that are transmitted/received are grouped in logical units called a *frame.* In the context of LANs, a frame can be a token ring or Ethernet frame.

The bits in a frame serve specific purposes. The beginning and end of a frame may be marked by special bit patterns. In addition, the bits in a frame are divided into an address field, control field, data field, and error control field. Figure 2.3 shows a typical data link frame. You see more specific examples of the data link frame in the discussion of Ethernet and token ring LANs.

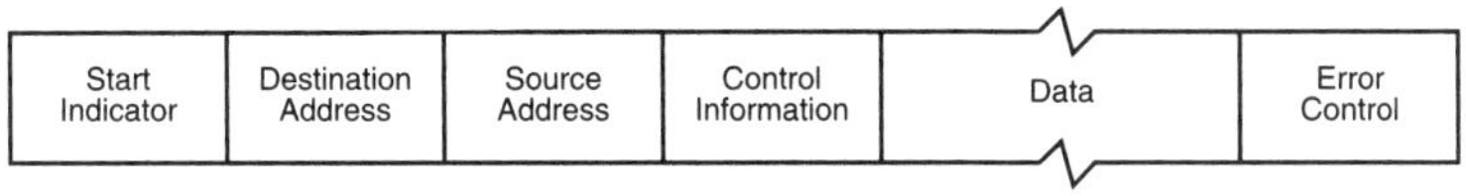

Start Indicator	Destination Address	Source Address	Control Information	Data	Error Control

Figure 2.3

A typical data link layer frame.

The *address* field(s) contains the sender and receiving node address. The *control* field is used to indicate the different types of data link frames, which include data frames and frames used for managing the data link channel. The *data* field contains the actual data being transmitted by the frame. The error control field usually detects errors in the data link frame. The data link layer also is the first layer in which you see error control concerns. The error control field is usually a hardware-generated *checksum* that is used to detect errors in the data link frame.

Network Layer

The *network layer* builds on the node-to-node connection provided by the data link layer. The node-to-node data link services are extended across a network by this layer. An additional service provided by the data link layer is how to route *packets* (units of information at the network layer) between nodes connected through an arbitrarily complex network.

Besides routing, the network layer may help eliminate congestion as well as regulate flow of data. The network layer also makes it possible for two networks to be interconnected by implementing a uniform addressing mechanism. Ethernet or token ring LANs, for instance, have different types of data link addresses. To interconnect these two networks, you need a uniform addressing mechanism that can be understood by both token ring and Ethernet. For NetWare-based networks, this capability is provided by the *Internet Packet Exchange* (IPX), a network layer protocol. For TCP/IP based networks, this capability is provided by the *Internet Protocol* (IP).

Transport Layer

The *transport layer* provides enhancements to the services of the network layer. This layer helps ensure reliable data delivery and end-to-end data integrity. To ensure reliable delivery, the transport layer builds on the error control mechanisms provided by the lower layers. If the lower layers do not do a good enough job, the transport layer has to work harder. This layer is the last chance for error recovery. In fact, when it comes to providing error free delivery, you could say, "The buck stops here" at the transport layer.

The transport layer also may be responsible for creating several logical connections over the same network connection, a process called *multiplexing*. Multiplexing (or time sharing) occurs when a number of transport connections share the same network connection.

The transport layer is the middle layer of the OSI model. The three lower layers constitute the *subnet* portion of the network model, and the three upper layers are usually implemented by networking software on the node. The transport layer also is usually implemented on the node; its job is to convert an unreliable subnet into a more reliable network.

Because of multiplexing, several software elements (OSI terminology uses the term *protocol entity)* share the same network layer address. To identify each software element within the transport layer, a more general form of addressing is necessary. These addresses, called *transport addresses*, usually are a combination of the network layer address and a transport Service Access Point (SAP) number. Sometimes the names *sockets* or *port numbers* are used to identify transport addresses.

Examples of transport protocols used by NetWare are Sequenced Exchange Protocol (SPX), Packet Exchange Protocol (PXP), and the Transmission Control Protocol (TCP) that is used in TCP/IP networks.

Session Layer

The *session layer* makes use of the transport layer to provide enhanced session services. Examples of a session include a user being logged in to a host across a network or a session being established for the purpose of transferring files.

- Dialog control
- Token management
- Activity management

A session, in general, allows two-way communications (full duplex) across a connection. Some applications may require alternate one-way communications (half duplex). The session layer has *dialog control*, which can provide two-way or one-way communications.

For some protocols, it is essential that only one side attempt a critical operation at a time. To prevent both sides from attempting the same operation, a control mechanism, such as the use of *tokens*, can be implemented. When using the token method, only the side holding a token is permitted to perform the operation. Determining which side has the token and how it is transferred between the two sides is known as *token management.*

The use of the word *token* here should not be confused with token ring operation. Token management is a much higher level concept at layer five of the OSI model. IBM's Token-Ring operation belongs to layers two and one of the OSI model.

If you are performing a one-hour file transfer between two machines, and network crashes occur approximately every 30 minutes, you may never be able to complete the file transfer. After each transfer aborts, you have to start over again. To avoid this problem, you can treat the entire file transfer as a single activity with checkpoints inserted in the data stream. That way, if a crash occurs, the session layer can synchronize to a previous checkpoint. This operation of managing an entire activity is called *activity management.*

Presentation Layer

The *presentation layer* manages the way data is represented. Many ways of representing data exist, such as ASCII and EBCDIC for text files, and 1s or 2s complement representation for numbers. If the two sides involved in communication use different data representations, they will not be able to understand each other. The presentation layer represents data with a common syntax and semantics. If all the nodes used and understood this common language, misunderstanding in data representation could be eliminated. An example of this common language is Abstract Syntax Representation, Rev 1 (ASN.1), an OSI recommendation. Another example of a protocol that corresponds to this layer is the External Data Representation (XDR) protocol that is used in the Network File System (NFS). NFS is discussed in Chapter 11, "Internetworking with NetWare NFS."

Application Layer

The *application layer* contains the protocols and functions needed by user applications to perform communication tasks. Examples of common functions include the following:

- Protocols for providing remote file services, such as open, close, read, write, and shared access to files
- File transfer services and remote database access
- Message handling services for e-mail applications
- Global directory services to locate resources on a network
- A uniform way of handling a variety of system monitors and devices
- Remote job execution

Many of these services are called *Application Programming Interfaces* (APIs). APIs are programming libraries that an application writer can use to write network applications.

In NetWare, NetWare Control Protocol (NCP) is an example of an application layer protocol. For TCP/IP, examples of application layer protocols are FTP, SMTP, and TELNET.

Layered Protocol Envelopes

The OSI reference model can be helpful in understanding the data exchange between two computer systems, called *End Systems* (ES) in OSI terminology. Consider two such end systems shown in figure 2.4.

Figure 2.4

OSI protocol layering and communications.

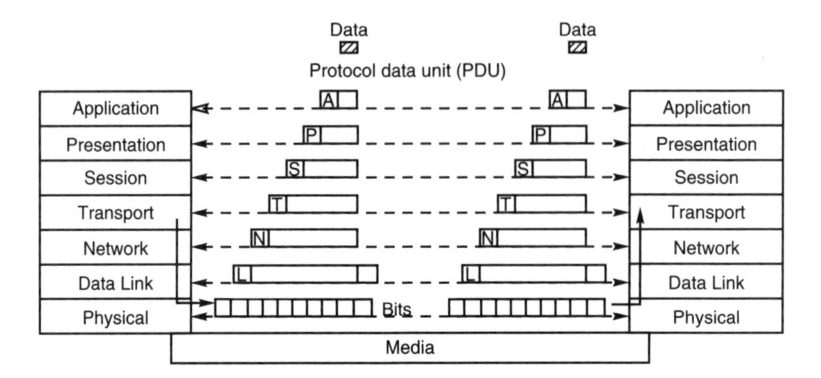

- Data travels *down* through layers at *local* end
- Protocol-control information (headers/trailers) used as *envelope* at each layer
- Data travels *up* through layers at *remote* end
- Protocol-control information (headers/trailers) *removed* as information passes up

In this figure, messages are to be sent from one end system to the other end system. The application layer processes the message and adds some application bits as header information to the message. These application bits are called *Protocol Control Information* (PCI) in OSI terminology and consist of information about the processing done on the message. Additionally, the PCI may contain information identifying the application entities (source and destination application layer address). The PCI, plus the original message, is called the *Application Protocol Data Unit* (APDU).

The APDU is sent to the layer below the presentation layer. The presentation layer adds its PCI to the data (APDU) received from the application layer, and the resulting message is the *Presentation Protocol Data Unit* (PPDU). At this point the original message is encapsulated in the APDU, and the APDU is in turn encapsulated as the PPDU.

As each layer adds its own header information to the message received from its upper layer, it is like taking the data and placing it inside an *envelope*. The envelope with its contents forms the PDU (or packet) for that layer.

This process continues all the way down to the physical layer. At the data link layer, usually a *trailer* field is added to the data. This trailer field is a checksum field covering the data link layer frame and is generated by the data link layer hardware mechanism (network boards). It is added at the end because the hardware mechanism computes the checksum as the data is pumped out serially over the line. The checksum is usually a CRC (Cyclic Redundancy Checksum) for most LAN/WAN devices.

At the physical layer the "header" information may take the form of an indication informing the receiver of a packet arrival. On Ethernet networks, this is a 56-bit preamble that is used by the receiver to synchronize itself.

At the remote end, the physical layer receives the bits and strips off any physical layer synchronization bits and sends the resulting data to the data link layer. The remote-data link layer groups the bits it receives into a frame and checks to see if the CRC is valid. After the data link layer processes the received frame, it strips off the data-link PCI (data-link header and CRC) and sends the resulting NPDU (Network PDU) to the network layer for processing.

At each remote end-system layer, the PDU is processed based on the PCI (header) information for that layer. The PCI is removed and the data portion of the PDU is sent to the upper layer. This process continues until the remote application layer completes its processing and the original data is recovered.

If you examine layers at the local end-system and the remote end-system, the layers in the OSI model seem to communicate with the corresponding *peer* layer. For this reason, the OSI model describes peer-to-peer protocols between the layers. For example, the transport layers at the two end-systems appears to be communicating with each other. To accomplish this communication, the transport layer has to make use of the infrastructure provided by the layers (network, data link, physical layers) below it.

The OSI model provides an easy-to-understand conceptual view of communication. In actual practice, the layers are not as well defined as shown in the OSI model. For example, an implementation may not have a distinct separation between the presentation and application layer. Many of the functions of the presentation layer, such as a universal data encoding/decoding, may be performed in the application layer by calling appropriate data encoding/decoding programming language functions.

The DoD Model

The OSI model was created in 1979, although protocol layering concepts existed long before they were formalized by the OSI model. An example of an earlier successful protocol that used protocol layering concepts was the TCP/IP protocol suite. Because of TCP/IP's historic ties with the Department of Defense, the TCP/IP protocol layering is called the *DoD Model.*

Figure 2.5 describes the DoD model, which consists of four layers.

Figure 2.5

The DoD model.

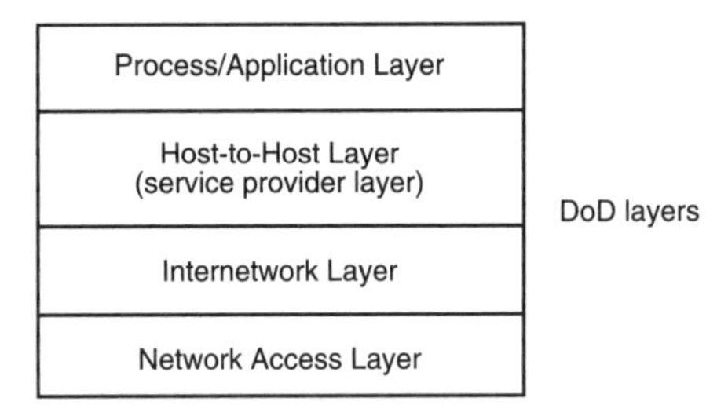

The bottommost layer is the *Network Access* layer. The Network Access layer represents the physical connection components such as the cables, transceivers, network boards, link protocols, LAN access protocols (such as CSMA/CD for Ethernet and token access for token ring), token bus, and FDDI. The Network Access layer is used by the *Internetwork* layer.

The Internetwork layer is responsible for providing a logical address for the physical network interface. The DoD model's implementation of the Internetwork layer is the *Internet Protocol* (IP). This layer provides a mapping between the logical address and the physical address provided by the Network Access layer, by using *Address Resolution Protocol* (ARP) and *Reverse Address Resolution Protocol* (RARP). Problems, diagnostic information, and unusual conditions associated with the IP protocol are reported by a separate protocol called the *Internet Control Message Protocol* (ICMP) that also operates at the Internetwork layer. The Internetwork layer is also concerned with routing of packets between hosts and networks. The Internetwork layer is common to the DoD upper layers. The upper layer that directly uses the Internetwork layer is the *Host-to-Host* layer.

The Host-to-Host protocol implements connections between two hosts across a network. The DoD model implements two Host-to-Host protocols: *Transmission Control Protocol* (TCP) and *User Datagram Protocol* (UDP). The TCP protocol is responsible for reliable, simultaneous, full-duplex connections. The term *reliable* means TCP takes care of transmission errors by resending the portion of data that was in error. The Process/Application layers that use TCP do not have to be concerned with reliability of data transmission because this is handled by TCP.

TCP also provides for simultaneous connections. Several TCP connections can be established at a host and data can be sent simultaneously, independent of data on other connections. TCP provides full-duplex connections, which means that data can be sent and received on a single connection. The UDP protocol is not as robust as TCP and can be used by applications that do not require the reliability of TCP at the Host-to-Host layer.

The Process/Application layer provides applications that use the Host-to-Host layer protocols (TCP and UDP). Examples of these applications are File Transfer Protocol (FTP), Terminal Emulation (TELNET), Electronic Mail (SMTP), and Simple Network Management Protocol (SNMP). The Process/Application layer represents the user's interface to the TCP/IP protocol stack.

If you compare the functionality of the DoD model with the OSI model, you can see that they are similar. Figure 2.6 shows these similarities.

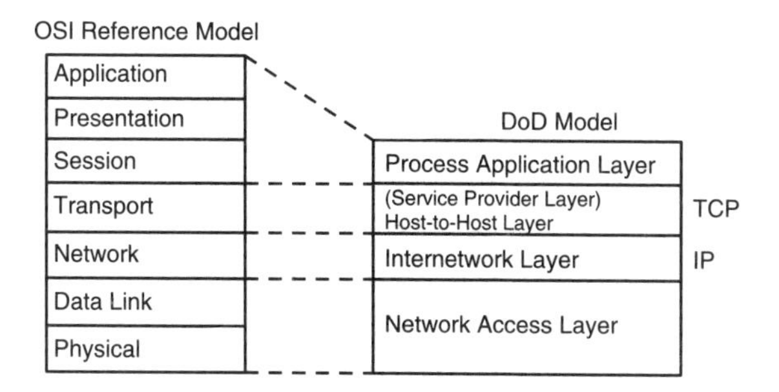

Figure 2.6

OSI versus DoD model.

The Network Access layer of the DoD model corresponds to two layers of the OSI model: the physical layer and the data link layer.

The Internetwork layer of the DoD model corresponds to the network layer of the OSI model.

The Host-to-Host layer of the DoD model corresponds to the transport layer of the OSI model.

The Process/Application layer of the DoD model corresponds to three layers of the OSI model: session layer, presentation layer, and application layer.

Table 2.1 summarizes the correspondence between layers of the OSI and DoD models by name and by the number of the OSI layer.

TABLE 2.1 DOD AND OSI COMPARISON SUMMARY

DoD Layer	OSI Layer Number	OSI Layer
Network Access	1	Physical
	2	Data link
Internetwork	3	Network
Host-to-Host	4	Transport
Process/Application	5	Session
	6	Presentation
	7	Application

Data-Flow across TCP/IP Networks

Figure 2.7 shows communication between two hosts using the DoD model. If you contrast this with figure 2.4, you can see the similarity of communications between the OSI and the DoD models.

Figure 2.7

DoD Protocol layering and communications.

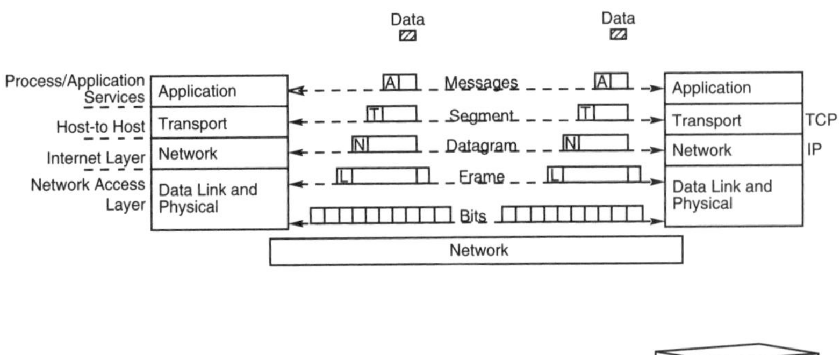

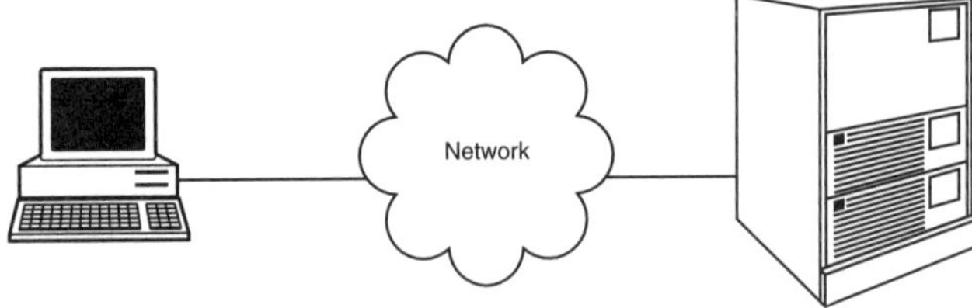

The data transmitted by a host is encapsulated by the header protocol of the Process/Application layer. The Application/Process layer data is in turn encapsulated by the Host-to-Host (TCP or UDP) layer. The Host-to-Host layer protocol is in turn encapsulated by the Internetwork layer (IP). Finally, the Internetwork layer protocol is encapsulated by the Network Access layer protocol.

When the encapsulated data is received by the remote host, it decapsulates the headers at each of the DoD model layers and sends the resulting data to the layer above it until the original data is recovered.

An important difference between the OSI and DoD models is the difference in terminology used to describe data at each layer. In the OSI model, the term *Protocol Data Unit* (PDU) was used to describe data at a layer. In the DoD model, the term *message* is used to describe data at the Process/Application layer. The term *segment* is used to describe data at the Host-to-Host layer. The term *datagram* is used to describe data at the Internetwork layer, and the term *frame* is used to describe data at the Network Access layer.

TCP/IP Protocol Suite

The TCP/IP protocols and applications, often called the *TCP/IP protocol suite*, are defined by Request for Comments (RFCs) and Standard numbers. Table 2.2 shows the RFCs and the Standard numbers for the protocols used by the DoD model. Although all Internet standards have an RFC number, not all RFCs are part of the Internet Official Standards. Many RFCs are concerned with experimental and proposed standards; some are just tutorials. Vendors are required to comply with the list of official Internet standards. The RFC describing the list of Internet Official Protocol standards, at the time of writing this book, is RFC 1600. It is important to realize that table 2.2 contains only the more well-known standards. Appendix A contains a more detailed list of RFCs and Standards.

TABLE 2.2 STANDARDS USED IN THE DOD MODEL

Standard Name	Standard Number	RFC	DoD Model Layer
File Transfer Protocol (FTP)	9	959	Process/ Application
Telnet Protocol (TELNET)	8	854, 855	Process/ Application
Trivial File Transfer Protocol (TFTP)	33	1350	Process/ Application
Simple Mail Transfer Protocol (SMTP)	10	821	Process/ Application
Simple Network Management Protocol (SNMP)	15	1157	Process/ Application
Domain Name System (DNS)	13	1034, 1035	Process/ Application
Mail Routing and the Domain System (DNS-MX)	14	974	Process/ Application
Transmission Control Protocol (TCP)	7	793	Host-to-Host
User Datagram Protocol (UDP)	6	768	Host-to-Host
Internet Protocol (IP)	5	791	Internet
IP subnet extension	5	950	Internet
IP Broadcast Datagrams	5	919	Internet
IP Broadcast Datagrams with Subnets	5	922	Internet
Internet Control Message Protocol	5	792	Internet

TCP/IP Implementation Hierarchy

The TCP/IP protocol suite has evolved to include a rich set of application services that can utilize a variety of physical networking technologies, such as WANs, LANs, radio, satellite links, and Integrated Services Digital Network (ISDN) lines.

Figure 2.8 shows a partial list of TCP/IP application services and a large variety of Network Access protocols that support TCP/IP. The application services are shown in relationship to the DoD model. An implementation may support only a few of the application services or other protocols, such as ARP, RARP, proxy ARP, and routing protocols. For example, the TCP/IP host in figure 2.8 supports only the TCP/IP application services FTP, TELNET, and SMTP.

Figure 2.8

TCP/IP implementation hierarchy.

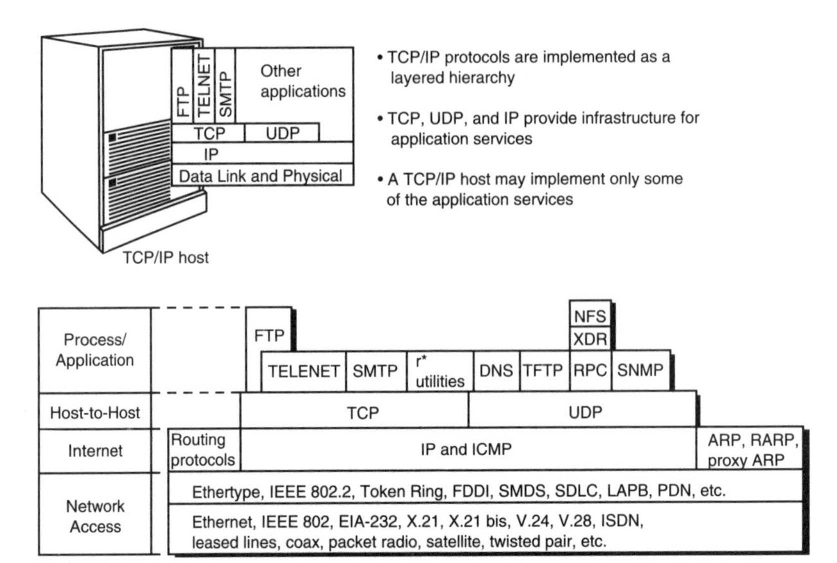

The application services in figure 2.8 are called "TCP/IP application services" because of their historical association with the TCP/IP protocol. There is nothing to prevent the application services described by the Process/Application layer from being built around a different transport or network layer protocol. SNMP, for example, is historically associated with TCP/IP but can also run on an IPX protocol stack (RFC 1420), AppleTalk protocol stack (RFC 1419), and the OSI protocol stack (RFC 1418). Similarly, services that are traditionally non–TCP/IP-based, such as NetWare Core Protocol (NCP), which normally runs on an IPX network protocol, and X.500, which uses the OSI protocols, can also run on TCP/IP. The NetWare/IP product from Novell provides NCP services over TCP/IP, and the ISO Development Environment (ISODE) provides X.500 services over TCP/IP.

Protocol Multiplexing and Demultiplexing

Figure 2.9 shows TCP/IP communications between two hosts. Each host is running TCP/IP application services such as FTP, TELNET, Trivial File Transfer Protocol (TFTP), and SMTP.

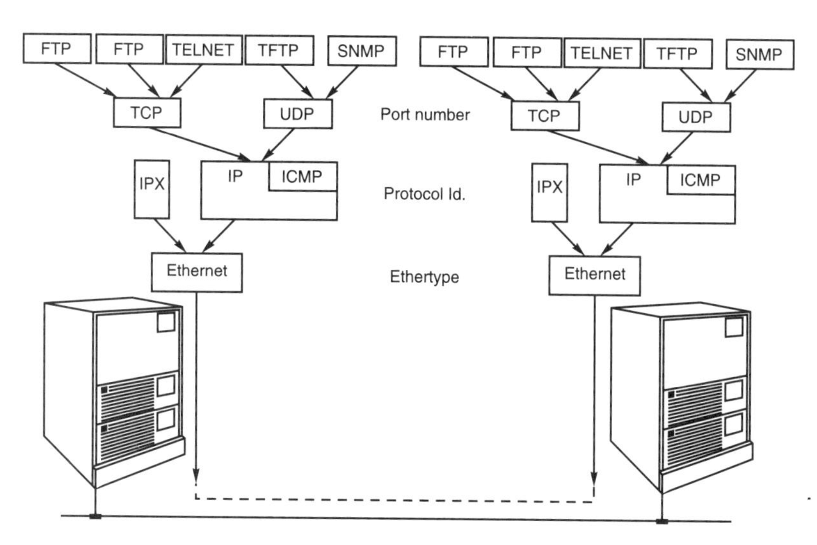

Figure 2.9

Protocol multiplexing and demultiplexing.

Several sessions exist between the hosts that use FTP. You might ask the question: How does networking software on each host distinguish between multiple applications or protocols at a given layer?

For instance, the Ethernet in figure 2.9 supports IP and ICMP protocols and potentially other protocols such as IPX and AppleTalk's IDP. How does Ethernet determine that a packet arriving from a network interface is destined for IP or ICMP? To make this distinction, Ethernet uses a 2-byte Ethertype field that is part of the Ethernet frame (see fig. 2.10). Table 2.3 shows some of the values of Ethertype fields used for network layer protocols. Using table 2.3, you can see that Novell has been assigned an Ethertype of 8137 and 8138. The Ethertype value of 8137 is used for Novell's IPX protocol.

The Ethertype field at the data link layer makes it possible to multiplex several network protocols at the sender and demultiplex them at the receiver (see fig. 2.11).

6 bytes	6 bytes	2 bytes	max of 1500 bytes	4 bytes
Destination Address	Source Address	Ethertype		CRC

Figure 2.10

2-byte Ethertype field used for protocol multiplexing/demultiplexing.

Figure 2.11

Multiplexing/demultiplexing using the Ethertype field.

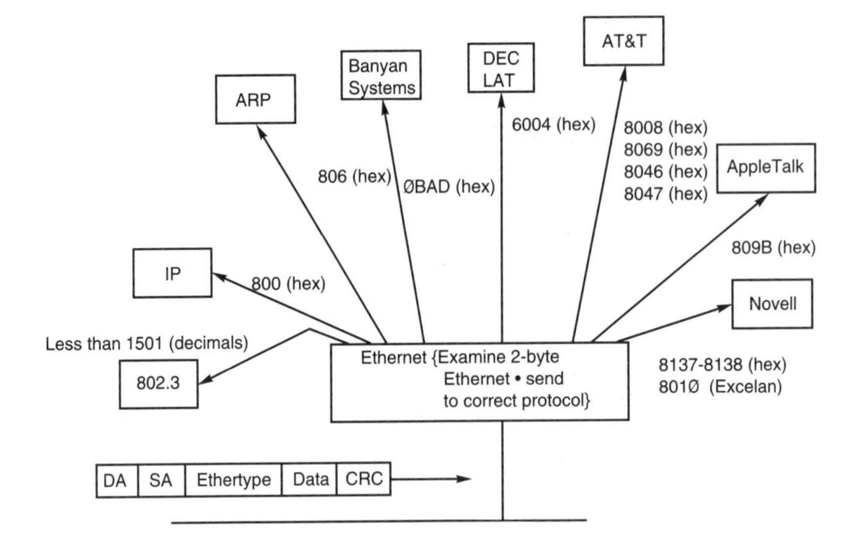

Table 2.3 Example Ethertype Value Used for Data Link Layer Multiplexing/Demultiplexing

Ethertype Value (Decimal)	Ethertype Value (Hexadecimal)	Protocols or Organizations to which Ethertype Field Is Assigned
0 - 1500	0 - 05DC	IEEE 802.3 length field
1536	0600	XEROX NS IDP
2048	0800	DoD IP
2049	0801	X.75 Internet
2050	0802	NBS Internet
2051	0803	ECMA Internet
2052	0804	Chaosnet
2053	0805	X.25 Level 3
2054	0806	ARP (Address Resolution Protocol)
2055	0807	XNS Compatibility
2076	081C	Symbolics Private
2184 - 2186	0888 - 088A	Xyplex
2304	0900	Ungermann-Bass Net Debugger
2560	0A00	Xerox IEEE 802.3 PUP
2561	0A01	PUP Address Translation
2989	0BAD	Banyan Systems
4096	1000	Berkeley Trailer Negotiation

Ethertype Value (Decimal)	Ethertype Value (Hexadecimal)	Protocols or Organizations to which Ethertype Field Is Assigned
4097 - 4101	1001 - 100F	Berkeley Trailer encapsulation/IP
5632	1600	Valid Systems
16962	4242	PCS Basic Block Protocol
21000	5208	BBN Simnet
24576	6000	DEC Unassigned (Experimental)
24577	6001	DEC MOP Dump/Load
24578	6002	DEC MOP Remote Console
24579	6003	DEC DECNET Phase IV Route
24580	6004	DEC LAT
24581	6005	DEC Diagnostic Protocol
24582	6006	DEC Customer Protocol
24583	6007	DEC LAVC, SCA
24584 - 24585	6008 - 6009	DEC Unassigned
24586 - 24590	6010 - 6014	3COM Corporation
28672	7000	Ungermann-Bass download
28674	7002	Ungermann-Bass dia/loop
28704 - 28713	7020 - 7029	LRT
28720	7030	Proteon
28724	7034	Cabletron
32771	8003	Cronus VLN
32772	8004	Cronus Direct
32773	8005	HP Probe
32774	8006	Nestar
32776	8008	AT&T
32784	8010	Excelan (Novell)
32787	8013	SGI diagnostics
32788	8014	SGI network games
32789	8015	SGI reserved
32790	8016	SGI bounce server
32793	8019	Apollo Computers
32815	802E	Tymshare
32816	802F	Tigan, Inc.

continues

Table 2.3, Continued

Ethertype Value (Decimal)	Ethertype Value (Hexadecimal)	Protocols or Organizations to which Ethertype Field Is Assigned
32821	8035	Reverse ARP
32822	8036	Aeonic Systems
32824	8038	DEC LANBridge
32825 - 32828	8039 - 803C	DEC Unassigned
32829	803D	DEC Ethernet Encryption
32831	803F	DEC LAN Traffic Monitor
32832 - 32834	8040 - 8042	DEC Unassigned
32836	8044	Planning Research Corp.
32838 - 32389	8046 - 8047	AT&T
32841	8049	ExperData
32859	805B	Stanford V Kernel exp.
32860	805C	Stanford V Kernel prod.
32864	805D	Evans & Sutherland
32866	8062	Counterpoint Computers
32869 - 32870	8065 - 8066	Univ. of Mass. @ Amherst
32871	8067	Veeco Integrated Auto
32872	8068	General Dynamics
32873	8069	AT & T
32874	806A	Autophon
32876	806C	ComDesign
32877	806D	Computgraphic Corp.
32878 - 32887	806E - 8077	Landmark Graphics Corp.
32890	807A	Matra
32891	807B	Dansk Data Elektronik
32892	807C	Merit Internodal
32893 - 32895	807D - 807F	Vitalink Communications
32896	8080	Vitalink TransLAN III
32897 - 32899	8081 - 8083	Counterpoint Computers
32923	809B	AppleTalk
32924 - 32926	809C - 809E	Datability
32927	809F	Spider Systems Limited

Ethertype Value (Decimal)	Ethertype Value (Hexadecimal)	Protocols or Organizations to which Ethertype Field Is Assigned
32931	80A3	Nixdorf Computers
32932 - 32947	80A4 - 80B3	Siemens Gammasonics, Inc.
32960 - 32963	80C0 - 80C3	DCA Data Exchange Cluster
32966	80C6	Pacer Software
32967	80C7	Applitek Corporation
32968 - 32972	80C8 - 80CC	Intergraph Corporation
32973 - 32975	80CD - 80CE	Harris Corporation
32975 - 32978	80CF - 80D2	Taylor Instruments
32979 - 32980	8CD3 - 80D4	Rosemount Corporation
32981	80D5	IBM SNA Service on Ethernet
32989	80DD	Varian Associates
32990 - 32991	80DE - 80DF	Integrated Solution TRFS
32992 - 32995	80E0 - 80E3	Allen-Bradley
32996 - 33008	80E4 - 80F0	Datability
33010	80F2	Retix
33011	80F3	AppleTalk AARP (Kinetics)
33012 - 33013	80F4 - 80F5	Kinetics
33015	80F7	Apollo Computer
33023	80FF - 8103	Wellfleet Communications
33031 - 33033	8107 - 8109	Symbolics Private
33072	8130	Waterloo Microsystems
33073	8131	VG Laboratory Systems
33079 - 33080	8137 - 8138	Novell, Inc.
33081	8139 - 813D	KTI
33100	814C	SNMP Research
36864	9000	Loopback
36865	9001	3COM(Bridge) XNS Sys. Mgmt.
36866	9002	3COM(Bridge) TCP Sys
36867	9003	3COM(Bridge) loopdetect
65280	FF00	BBN VITAL-LanBridge cache

When the IP layer receives a packet from Ethernet it has to distinguish between packets that need to be processed by the TCP or UDP protocol module. It does this by examining an 8-bit Protocol Id field of the IP packet. Table 2.4. shows some common values for the Protocol Id field. These values can also be found in the SYS:ETC/PROTOCOL file on NetWare servers and /etc/protocols file on Unix hosts.

TABLE 2.4 EXAMPLE PROTOCOL ID VALUES USED FOR NETWORK LAYER MULTIPLEXING/DEMULTIPLEXING

Protocol Id	Next Layer Protocol in IP Packet
0	Reserved
1	Internet Control Message Protocol (ICMP)
2	Internet Group Management Protocol (IGMP)
4	IP in IP encapsulation
5	Stream IP
6	Transmission Control Protocol (TCP)
8	Exterior Gateway Protocol (EGP)
9	Any private interior gateway protocol (example: CISCO's IGP)
11	Network Voice Protocol (NVP-II)
12	Parc Universal Protocol (PUP)
16	Chaos protocol
17	User Datagram Protocol (UDP)
21	Packet Radio Measurement (PRM)
22	XEROX NS IDP (XNS-IDP)
29	ISO Transport Protocol Class 4 (ISO-TP4)
30	Bulk Transfer Protocol (NETBLT)
36	Express Transport Protocol (XTP)
37	Datagram Delivery Protocol (DDP)
75	Packet Video Protocol (PVP)
80	ISO Internet Protocol (ISO-IP)
83	VINES

When the TCP or UDP protocol modules receive a packet from the IP layer, they have to distinguish between packets that need to be processed by an application service such as FTP, TELNET, SMTP, and SNMP. The TCP and UDP protocol modules do this by examining the 16-bit port number field of their respective packets. Tables 2.5 and 2.6 show a few common values for port numbers for TCP and UDP. Because TCP and UDP protocol modules are distinct from each other, their port number address spaces are distinct. Also notice that some TCP/IP applications are listed in both tables 2.5 and 2.6 with the same port number. This is because these application services are available over both TCP and UDP. The port number values supported on a system can be found in the SYS:ETC/SERVICES file on NetWare servers and /etc/services file on Unix hosts.

TABLE 2.5 EXAMPLE PORT NUMBER VALUES USED FOR TCP MULTIPLEXING/DEMULTIPLEXING

TCP Port Number	Application Layer Service
0	Reserved
1	TCP Port Service Multiplexor
2	Management Utility
3	Compression Process
5	Remote Job Entry
7	Echo
9	Discard
11	Active Users (systat)
13	Daytime
17	Quote of the Day (QUOTD)
20	FTP data port
21	FTP control port
23	Telnet
25	SMTP
35	Any private printer server
37	Time
39	Resource Location Protocol
42	Host name server (nameserver)
43	Who Is (nicname)
49	Login Host Protocol (login)
52	XNS Time Protocol
53	Domain Name Server (domain)
54	XNS clearing house
66	Oracle SQL*NET (sql*net)
67	Bootstrap Protocol Server (bootps)
68	Bootstrap Protocol Client (bootpc)
70	Gopher protocol
79	Finger protocol
80	World Wide Web HTTP

continues

Table 2.5, Continued

TCP Port Number	Application Layer Service
88	Kerberos
94	Trivoli Object Dispatcher (objcall)
95	SUPDUP
102	ISO-TSAP
107	Remote Telnet Service (rtelnet)
108	SNA Gateway Access Server (snagas)
110	Post Office Protocol—Version 3 (POP3)
111	Sun Remote Procedure Call (sunrpc)
119	Network News Transfer Protocol (NNTP)
123	Network Time Protocol (NTP)
134	INGRES-NET Service
137	NETBIOS Naming Service (netbios-ns)
138	NETBIOS Datagram Service (netbios-dgm)
139	NETBIOS Session Service (netbios-ssn)
142	Britton-Lee IDM
191	Prospero
194	Internet Relay Chat Protocol (irc)
201	AppleTalk Routing Maintenance (at-rtmp)
202	AppleTalk Name Binding (at-nbp)
213	IPX
215	Insigniax (Soft PC)
217	dBASE Unix
372	Unix Listserv
519	unixtime
525	Time Server (timed)
533	For emergency broadcasts (netwall)
556	RFS server (remoterfs)
565	Who Am I (whoami)
749	Kerberos Administration (kerberos-adm)
767	Phone (phonebook)
1025	Network Blackjack (blackjack)
1352	Lotus Notes (lotusnote)
7000 to 7009	Used by Andrew File System (AFS)
17007	ISODE Directory User Agent (isode-dua)

TABLE 2.6 EXAMPLE PORT NUMBER VALUES USED FOR UDP MULTIPLEXING/DEMULTIPLEXING

UDP Port Number	Application Layer Service
0	Reserved
2	Management Utility
3	Compression Process
5	Remote Job Entry
7	Echo
9	Discard
11	Active Users (systat)
13	Daytime
17	Quote of the Day (QUOTD)
35	Any private printer server
37	Time
39	Resource Location Protocol
42	Host name server (nameserver)
43	Who Is (nicname)
49	Login Host Protocol (login)
52	XNS Time Protocol
53	Domain Name Server (domain)
54	XNS clearing house
66	Oracle SQL*NET (sql*net)
67	Bootstrap Protocol Server (bootps)
68	Bootstrap Protocol Client (bootpc)
69	Trivial Transfer Protocol (tftp)
70	Gopher protocol
79	Finger protocol
80	World Wide Web HTTP
88	Kerberos
94	Trivoli Object Dispatcher (objcall)
95	SUPDUP
102	ISO-TSAP
107	Remote Telnet Service (rtelnet)
108	SNA Gateway Access Server (snagas)
110	Post Office Protocol—Version 3 (POP3)

continues

Table 2.6, Continued

UDP Port Number	Application Layer Service
111	Sun Remote Procedure Call (sunrpc)
119	Network News Transfer Protocol (NNTP)
123	Network Time Protocol (NTP)
134	INGRES-NET Service
137	NETBIOS Naming Service (netbios-ns)
138	NETBIOS Datagram Service (netbios-dgm)
139	NETBIOS Session Service (netbios-ssn)
142	Britton-Lee IDM
161	SNMP
162	SNMP Traps
191	Prospero
194	Internet Relay Chat Protocol (irc)
201	AppleTalk Routing Maintenance (at-rtmp)
202	AppleTalk Name Binding (at-nbp)
213	IPX (Used for IP Tunneling)
215	Insignia (Soft PC)
217	dBASE Unix
372	Unix Listserv
513	Maintains database on who is logged in to machines on a local net and the load average of the machine (who)
519	unixtime
525	Time Server (timed)
533	For emergency broadcasts (netwall)
556	RFS server (remoterfs)
565	Who Am I (whoami)
749	Kerberos Administration (kerberos-adm)
767	Phone (phonebook)
1025	Network Blackjack (blackjack)
1352	Lotus Notes (lotusnote)
7000 to 7009	Used by Andrew File System (AFS)
17007	ISODE Directory User Agent (isode-dua)

TCP/IP Implementation and the Host Operating System

The performance of a TCP/IP implementation, its configuration, and its ease of maintenance depend on the operating system platform on which it runs. To show the interaction between the TCP/IP protocol and the application, vendors try to show the operating system as part of the OSI model. Unfortunately, the operating system does not fit neatly into the OSI model because the OSI model is designed for communication functions. The operating system has its own multiple-layer model. One such model is shown in figure 2.12.

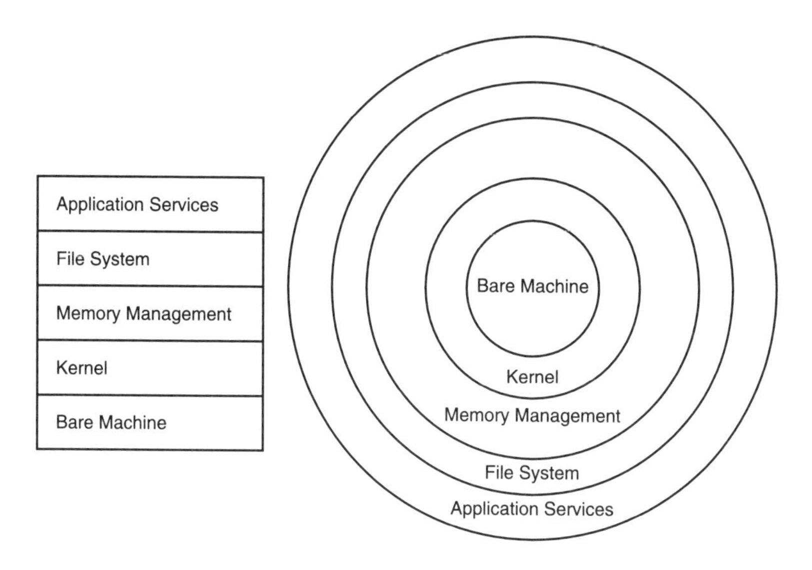

Figure 2.12

Operating system layering.

Compare this figure with figure 2.2; you can see that these models are distinct. An operating system is a program that is a resource manager. The network communication system (modeled by the OSI model) is just one resource the operating system has to manage. In many operating systems, the network communication system is treated as part of the I/O Manager of the operating system.

Although the operating system is theoretically not necessary for running TCP/IP—the TCP/IP protocol could be embedded in ROM in an embedded application—most commercial implementations of TCP/IP interact with the operating system.

TCP/IP's interaction with the operating system can be classified in any of the following ways:

- As part of the operating system kernel
- As a device driver
- As an application process

In operating systems such as Unix and NetWare, TCP/IP is implemented as part of the operating system kernel. This type of TCP/IP implementation tends to be fast because there is little overhead in accessing the OS kernel for communication functions.

Operating systems that have device driver implementations of TCP/IP include VMS, OS/2, MS Windows, Windows NT, and MS-DOS. In MS Windows, the VxD virtual device driver implements the TCP/IP stack as a 32-bit driver that uses extended memory and avoids the use of base memory of the Intel processor. (Base memory is memory below 640 KB.)

Operating systems that have application process implementations of TCP/IP are IBM's mainframe operating systems MVS and VM, MS Windows, and MS-DOS. Some MS-Windows and MS-DOS TCP/IP implementations use terminate-and-stay-resident (TSR) programs and Dynamic Link Libraries (DLLs).

Unless the TSR can be loaded in upper memory by using DOS's LOAD HIGH command, the TSR resides in base memory where it must compete for memory with other applications.

If the TCP/IP stack is to be used only from within MS Windows, it can be implemented as a Dynamic Link Library. A standard interface, called the *WinSock* (Windows Socket) interface to this DLL, has been defined by vendors such as Microsoft, Novell, and FTP Software. Vendors that provide the WinSock DLL include Novell, Microsoft, Beam & Whiteside, FTP Software, and NetManage. Public domain versions of WinSock are also available (example: Trumpet WinSock).

TCP/IP Network Services

The TCP/IP network services consist of the following:

- Application services
- Host-to-Host services
- Internet services
- Network Access services

These services correspond to the layers of the DoD model.

This section examines some of the more important TCP/IP application services, including the following:

- FTP
- TFTP
- TELNET
- SMTP
- DNS

File Transfer Using FTP

The *File Transfer Protocol* (FTP) uses the TCP transport protocol to transfer files between two computers reliably. TCP is used as the transport protocol because of its guaranteed delivery of services.

FTP enables the user to access files and directories interactively on remote hosts, and to perform directory operations, such as the following:

- List files in a remote or local directory
- Rename and delete files (if you have permission)
- Transfer files from remote host to local host (download)
- Transfer files from local host to remote host (upload)

Figure 2.13 shows a transfer of a file from the local host to the remote host. The FTP session to perform this transfer is outlined in this figure. The FTP session is initiated by the FTP client across a TCP/IP network. The computer the remote client logs into is called the *FTP host.* The FTP host must have a software component called the *FTP server* that interacts with the file system of the host.

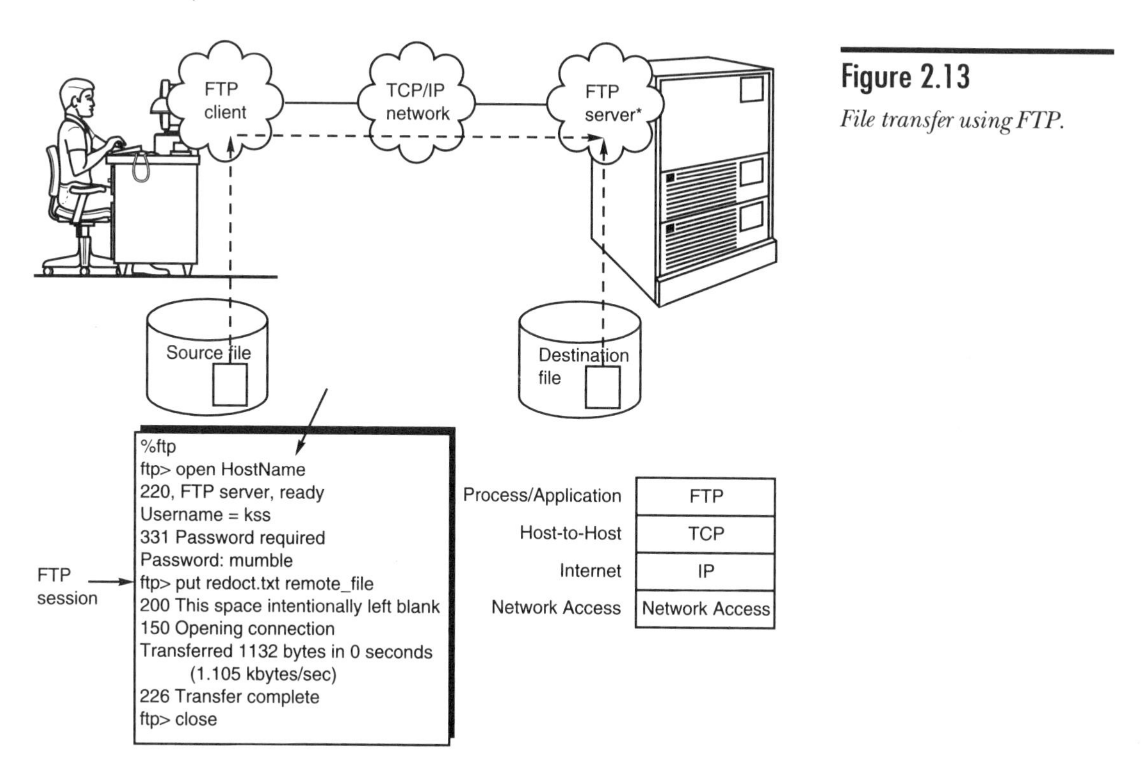
FTP client
TCP/IP network
FTP server*
Source file
Destination file
%ftp
ftp> open HostName
220, FTP server, ready
Username = kss
331 Password required
Password: mumble
ftp> put redoct.txt remote_file
200 This space intentionally left blank
150 Opening connection
Transferred 1132 bytes in 0 seconds
(1.105 kbytes/sec)
226 Transfer complete
ftp> close
FTP session
Process/Application
Host-to-Host
Internet
Network Access
FTP
TCP
IP
Network Access
* FTP server is also called FTP daemon.

Figure 2.13

File transfer using FTP.

In general, to use FTP or any other TCP/IP application service, you must have a client version of these applications. These client TCP/IP applications are available on Unix hosts. For DOS clients, you will have to purchase separate products such as those from Novell (LAN WorkPlace), FTP Software, Inc. (PC/TCP or OnLAN), Wollongong (Pathways), or from a variety of other vendors.

To start an FTP session, you can use the following command:

```
ftp  [hostname]
```

The *hostname* is the symbolic name or IP address of the host that you are logging into. If the *hostname* is left out, you can issue a number of FTP commands. If you type the help command or ?, you can obtain help on the FTP commands. The list that follows outlines some of the FTP commands available while logged into the INTERNIC.NET host:.

```
ftp> ?
Commands may be abbreviated.  Commands are:
!        cr          macdef   proxy      send
$        delete      mdelete  sendport   status
account  debug       mdir     put        struct
append   dir         mget     pwd        sunique
ascii    disconnect  mkdir    quit       tenex
bell     form        mls      quote      trace
binary   get         mode     recv       type
bye      glob        mput     remotehelp user
case     hash        nmap     rename     verbose
cd       help        ntrans   reset      ?
cdup     lcd         open     rmdir
close    ls          prompt   runique
```

If you want to perform an FTP session to the host INTERNIC.NET, use this command:

```
ftp INTERNIC.NET
```

If you know the IP address of the host, such as the FTP server for Novell, you can use the following command:

```
ftp 137.65.4.1
```

Please be aware that to connect to hosts outside your network environment, you will need access to these hosts through a TCP/IP internetwork. One way to access another host is through the Internet.

You must specify a username and a password to log into an FTP host. The FTP server uses the FTP host's underlying authentication mechanism to verify the privileges an FTP user should have. This means that if you have a user account, for instance Bob, on the computer acting as the FTP host, you can log in as user Bob, and use the same password that you would normally use to log into that computer's native operating system. Many FTP hosts provide *anonymous* logins. This means that if you were to specify the username *anonymous* and a password of *guest* (some computers expect an e-mail address containing the @ character), you can log into the FTP host with a limited set of privileges determined by the system administrator of the FTP host.

The following is a short guided tour of an FTP session to the INTERNIC.NET host:

1. Type the **ftp** command and supply the name of the host:

```
% ftp internic.net
```

   The % symbol in the preceding command is the default Unix prompt. *internic.net* is the hostname and uses the Domain Name Syntax discussed later in this chapter.

2. If the host is reachable, a message similar to the following appears. Details of the sign-on messages may differ. The following is an example of the sign-on message for the INTERNIC.NET host. This is the host on the Internet that is responsible for Internet Registration services.

```
Connected to internic.net.
220-*****Welcome to the InterNIC Registration Host  *****
    *****Login with username "anonymous" and password "guest"
    *****You may change directories to the following:
      policy            - Registration Policies
      templates         - Registration Templates
      netinfo           - NIC Information Files
      domain            - Root Domain Zone Files
220 And more!
Name (internic.net:karanjit):
```

   As the message indicates, you can log in as the user *anonymous* with password *guest.*

3. Supply the username and password:

```
Name (internic.net:karanjit): anonymous
331 Guest login ok, send "guest" as password.
Password:guest
230 Guest login ok, access restrictions apply.
ftp>
```

4. After you are logged in, you can use the ? or help command, as follows:

```
ftp>?
Commands may be abbreviated.  Commands are:
!         cr          macdef   proxy       send
$         delete      mdelete  sendport    status
account   debug       mdir     put         struct
append    dir         mget     pwd         sunique
ascii     disconnect  mkdir    quit        tenex
bell      form        mls      quote       trace
binary    get         mode     recv        type
bye       glob        mput     remotehelp  user
```

```
case      hash      nmap      rename      verbose
cd        help      ntrans    reset       ?
cdup      lcd       open      rmdir
close     ls        prompt    runique
```

5. The command to see your current directory on the FTP host is *pwd.*

```
ftp> pwd
257 "/" is current directory.
```

The status of each FTP command is returned as a numeric code such as 257, and a text message accompanying it.

6. To see a list of files in the current directory, use the ls or dir command.

```
ftp> ls
200 PORT command successful.
150 Opening ASCII mode data connection for file list.
bin
usr
dev
etc
pub
policy
templates
home
netinfo
domain
ls-ltR
netprog
archives
rfc
226 Transfer complete.
99 bytes received in 0.04 seconds (2.4 Kbytes/s)
```

This just lists the files and does not give information about the size of a file or whether it is a directory. To see this information, it is preferable to use the dir command.

```
ftp> dir
200 PORT command successful.
150 Opening ASCII mode data connection for /bin/ls.
total 22
drwxr-xr-x  2 root     1             512 Mar 22 21:40 archives
dr-xr-xr-x  2 root     1             512 Feb 25  1993 bin
drwxr-xr-x  2 root     1             512 Mar  9  1993 dev
drwxr-xr-x  2 root     1             512 Apr  1  1993 domain
dr-xr-xr-x  2 root     1             512 Feb 25  1993 etc
drwxr-xr-x  2 root     1             512 Mar  9  1993 home
```

```
-rw-r--r--  1 root     1              9035 May  4 19:12 ls-ltR
drwxr-xr-x  2 root     1              1024 Apr 14 14:57 netinfo
drwxr-xr-x  2 root     1               512 Apr  1  1993 netprog
drwxr-xr-x  2 root     1              1024 May  4 19:11 policy
drwxr-xr-x  4 root     1               512 Apr 20 15:01 pub
lrwxrwxrwx  1 root     1                 6 Aug  9  1993 rfc -> _policy
drwxr-xr-x  2 root     1               512 May  3 19:54 _templates
drwxr-xr-x  3 root     1               512 Feb 25  1993 usr
226 Transfer complete.
875 bytes received in 0.25 seconds (3.4 Kbytes/s)
```

The information is reported in the Unix style list format because you are logged into a Unix system.

7. If you know that you are logged into a Unix system acting as an FTP server, you can use the following useful trick:

   If you use the ls command, the Unix ls command is executed. You can supply to the ls command any of the Unix options, such as the *-lR* option that gives a recursive long form list of files in subdirectories. You should realize that the *-lR* option is not a part of the standard FTP commands, and only works for Unix FTP servers or those FTP servers that emulate this behavior. The following example shows the output of the ls *-lR* command. You can use this to get a quick overview of the files available on the FTP host.

```
ftp> ls -lR
200 PORT command successful.
150 Opening ASCII mode data connection for /bin/ls.
total 22
drwxr-xr-x  2 root         512 Mar 22 21:40 archives
dr-xr-xr-x  2 root         512 Feb 25  1993 bin
drwxr-xr-x  2 root         512 Mar  9  1993 dev
drwxr-xr-x  2 root         512 Apr  1  1993 domain
dr-xr-xr-x  2 root         512 Feb 25  1993 etc
drwxr-xr-x  2 root         512 Mar  9  1993 home
-rw-r--r--  1 root        9035 May  4 19:12 ls-ltR
drwxr-xr-x  2 root        1024 Apr 14 14:57 netinfo
drwxr-xr-x  2 root         512 Apr  1  1993 netprog
drwxr-xr-x  2 root        1024 May  4 19:11 policy
drwxr-xr-x  4 root         512 Apr 20 15:01 pub
lrwxrwxrwx  1 root           6 Aug  9  1993 rfc -> policy
drwxr-xr-x  2 root         512 May  3 19:54 templates
drwxr-xr-x  3 root         512 Feb 25  1993 usr
:
  (and more output)
:
usr/lib:
```

```
total 576
-r-xr-xr-x  1 root        40960 Feb 25  1993 ld.so
-rwxr-xr-x  1 root       516096 Feb 25  1993 libc.so.1.8
-rwxr-xr-x  1 root        24576 Feb 25  1993 libdl.so.1.0
226 Transfer complete.
remote: -lR
9228 bytes received in 1.2 seconds (7.5 Kbytes/s)
```

8. To change your directory to a particular directory, such as rfc, use the cd command, as follows:

```
ftp> cd rfc
250 CWD command successful.
```

9. To see a list of the files in the /rfc directory, use ls or dir.

```
ftp> ls
200 PORT command successful.
150 Opening ASCII mode data connection for file list.
asn.index
domain.index
index
master.index
network.index
rfc1009.txt
rfc1011.txt
rfc1031.txt
:
  (and more output)
:
226 Transfer complete.
496 bytes received in 0.045 seconds (11 Kbytes/s)
```

10. If you try to get a file that does not exist, such as the file rfc1365.txt, FTP displays the following message:

```
ftp> get rfc1365.txt
200 PORT command successful.
550 rfc1365.txt: No such file or directory.
```

Remember that filenames under Unix are case-sensitive.

11. To copy a file from the FTP server to the local host, the FTP command is as follows:

```
get remotefile [localfile]
```

remotefile is the name of the file on the remote host, and *localfile* is the name of the file on the local machine. If *localfile* is not specified, the local file is given the same name as the remote file.

For text files, FTP performs the proper carriage return to carriage-return/linefeed conversions between different operating systems if the transfer mode is ASCII. To use the ASCII transfer mode, use the FTP command ascii. To transfer binary files, use the command image or binary to disable carriage-return/linefeed conversions.

The following shows the FTP get command:

```
ftp> get rfc1400.txt
200 PORT command successful.
150 Opening ASCII mode data connection for rfc1400.txt (13009 _bytes).
226 Transfer complete.
local: rfc1400.txt remote: rfc1400.txt
13404 bytes received in 0.78 seconds (17 Kbytes/s)
```

12. To close the current FTP connection, use the close command.

```
ftp> close
221 Goodbye.
ftp>
```

13. To exit FTP completely, use the bye command. This command also closes existing FTP connections before exiting FTP:

```
ftp> bye
%
```

Trivial File Transfer Protocol

The File Transfer Protocol uses TCP to achieve reliable communications across a network. If the network is inherently reliable (as is true on most LANs), or a simpler file transfer protocol is needed, you can use the User Datagram Protocol (UDP) as the underlying transport (Host-to-Host) protocol. An example of a file transfer protocol that uses UDP is the Trivial File Transfer Protocol (TFTP).

Figure 2.14 shows a TFTP session used to transfer files between two hosts. TFTP can be used to transfer files between hosts without requiring user authentication. Files can be transferred by just specifying the filename. Because a user account and a password are not required for transferring files in TFTP, many system administrators disable TFTP on their systems, or restrict the types of files that can be transferred. Implementations can also deny access to a file unless every user on the host can access the file.

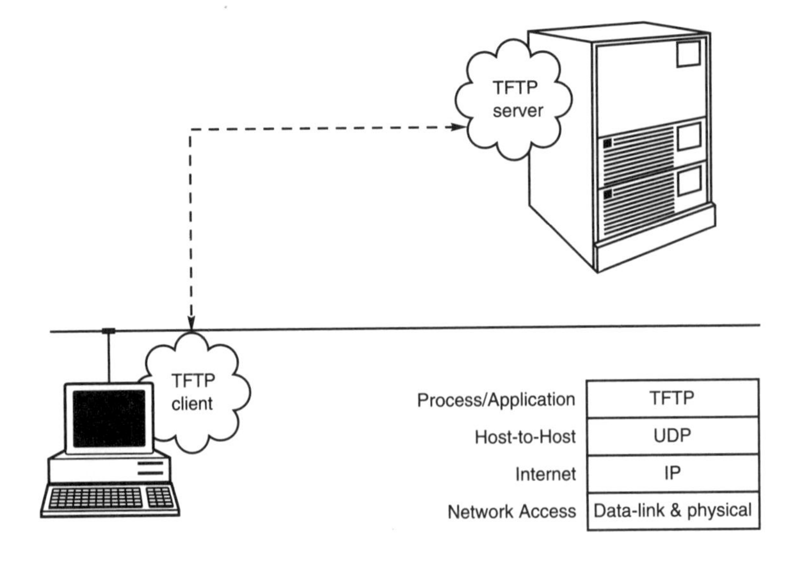

Figure 2.14
A TFTP session.

TFTP is used in conjunction with diskless workstations that need to download a boot image of the operating system from a server. The TFTP protocol is small enough to be efficiently implemented on a Boot ROM on the workstation's network board. Sun Unix workstations use TFTP in conjunction with RARP or BOOTP. RARP and BOOTP can be used to obtain the IP address of the workstation. TFTP is used for downloading the operating system image.

Terminal Emulation Using TELNET

The TELNET protocol is used for emulating a terminal connection to a remote host. It makes use of TCP as a transport protocol to transmit information from a user's keyboard to the remote host, and displays information from the remote host to the user workstation's display.

Figure 2.15 shows a TELNET session. To support a TELNET session, you must have a TELNET client component running at the user's workstation and a TELNET server running at the remote host. A TCP/IP session is set up between the TELNET client and the TELNET server. As the user types the keyboard commands, the characters are received by the TELNET server component and sent to the operating system on which the TELNET server runs. The characters appear as if they were typed in by a locally attached terminal.

The results of the commands are sent by the TELNET server to the TELNET client. The TELNET client displays the results received from the TELNET server on the user workstation's display unit. To the person using the TELNET client, the response seems to be from a machine attached locally to the workstation.

After you are logged in, you can type any command that you are permitted on the remote operating system. To log into a remote host, you must have an account on that machine.

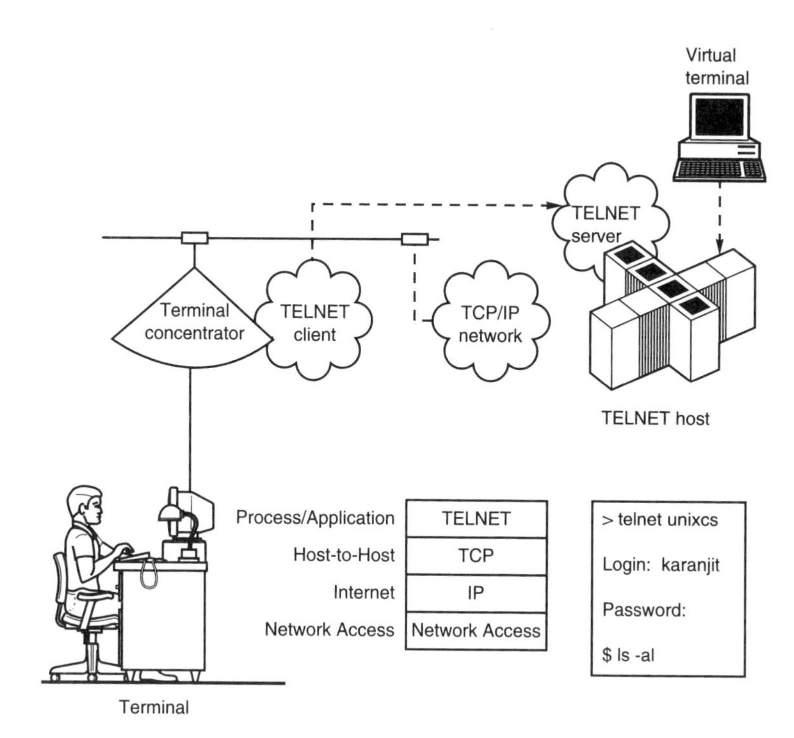

Figure 2.15
TELNET session.

The following is an example of a TELNET session to a Unix host:

```
% telnet world.std.com
Trying 192.74.137.5 ...
Connected to world.std.com.
Escape character is '^]'.
* To create an account on The World login as new, no password.
SunOS Unix (world)
login: karanjit
Password:password
Last login: Tue May 10 17:52:29 from karanjit-slip.cs
OS/MP 4.1C Export(STD/arlie)#15: Fri Mar 18 17:25:40 1994
           Welcome to the World!  A 6 CPU Solbourne 6E/900.
       Public Access Unix -- Home of the Online Book Initiative
         Type 'help' for help!  -- Stuck?  Try 'help HINTS'.
       When you see MORE, hit the space bar for the next page.
             Use 'exit' or 'logout' to leave the system.
                 Still Stuck?  Send mail to 'staff'.
You have mail.
Over disk quota on /home/ie, time limit has expired, remove 120K
TERM = (vt100)
Erase is Backspace
No new messages.
```

```
An authority is a person who can tell you more about something than you really care
to know.
from: postel@isi.edu [no subject]
% ls -alr
total 1011
 -rw------  1 karanjit   21852  Apr 13   21:56   veronica
drwx------  2 karanjit     512  Dec 28    1992   temp
 -rw------  1 karanjit    4780  Jun  4    1993   snapip.dmp
 -rw------  1 karanjit    1319  Jul  9    1993   Index
 -rw------  1 karanjit       8  Apr 13   20:43   .sh_history
 -rw------  1 karanjit    7035  May 10   17:53   .pinerc
drwx------  2 karanjit     512  Apr 13   20:01   .nn
 -rw------  1 karanjit  138402  Apr 13   20:01   .newsrc.bak
-rw-r--r--  1 karanjit  138102  Apr 13   20:01   .newsrc
-rw-r--r--  1 karanjit       4  Apr  7   12:55   .msgsrc
 -rw------  1 karanjit      11  Dec 28    1992   .mh_profile
-rw-r--r--  1 karanjit     386  Dec 19    1992   .login
 -rw------  1 karanjit       0  Apr  7   17:35   .gopherrc
-rw-r--r--  1 karanjit     538  Dec 19    1992   .emacs
drwx------  2 karanjit     512  Jan 22    1993   .elm
-rw-rw-r--  1 karanjit     799  Feb  1    1993   .cshrc
 -rw------  1 karanjit       0  Dec 19    1992   .addressbook
drwxrwxr-x  1911 root    61952  May 24   12:55   ..
drwx------  7 karanjit    1024  May 10   17:56   .
% ping novell.com
novell.com is alive
% logout
```

Mail Services Using SMTP

Mail services is perhaps the most widely used application on the Internet. Several protocols for mail services are available, but the most widely used is Simple Mail Transfer Protocol (SMTP).

SMTP allows ASCII text messages to be sent to mail boxes on TCP/IP hosts configured with mail services. Figure 2.16 shows a mail session that uses SMTP. A user who wants to send mail interacts with the local mail system through the User Agent (UA) component of the mail system. The mail is deposited in a local mail outgoing mail box. A sender-SMTP process periodically polls the outgoing box and, when it finds a mail message in the box, establishes a TCP connection with the destination host to which mail is to be sent. The Receiver-SMTP process at the destination host accepts the connection, and the mail message is sent on that connection. The Receiver-SMTP process deposits the mail message in the destination mail box on the destination host. If no mailbox with the specified name exists on the destination host, a mail message is sent to the originator indicating that the mailbox does not exist.

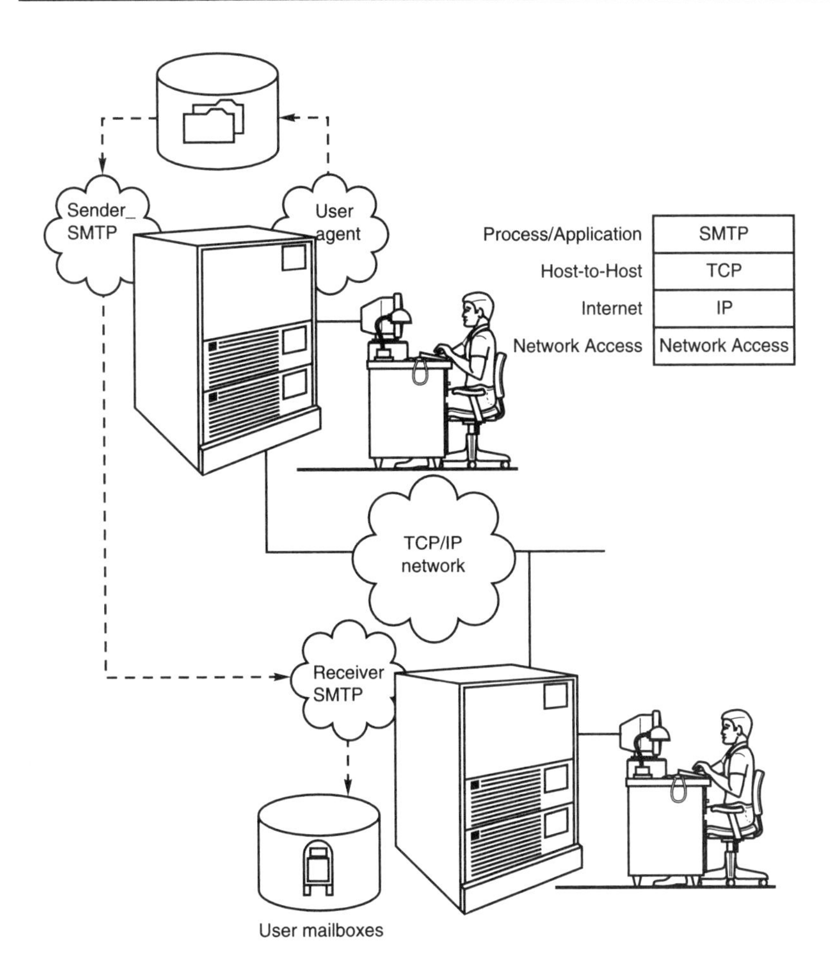

Figure 2.16

An SMTP session.

Mail addresses used in SMTP follow the RFC 882 standard. The mail headers are often referred to as "882 headers." An example of an 882 address is as follows:

```
KSS@SHIVA.COM
```

The text string before the @ symbol specifies the mailbox name, and the text string after it specifies the hostname. If the mailbox name contains special characters, such as the percent symbol (%), the mailbox name will be given a special encoding so that it can be used by mail gateways. In the mail address of KSS@SHIVA.COM, the text string KSS is the name of the mailbox on host SHIVA.COM.

SMTP expects the destination host receiving the mail to be online. Otherwise, a TCP connection cannot be established with the destination host. For this reason, it is not practical to establish an SMTP session with a desktop machine because they are often turned off at the end of the day. In many network environments, SMTP mail is received by an SMTP host that is always active on the network. This SMTP host provides a mail drop service. Workstations interact with the SMTP host and retrieve messages using a client/server mail protocol such as POP3 (Post Office Protocol, Version 3) described in RFC 1460.

If you want to send non-text messages using SMTP, you can encode the message as a text message by using the UUENCODE utility available on many systems. The receiver has to decode the encoded message using a utility called UUDECODE. Another way of sending non-text messages is to use the Multipurpose Internet Mail Extensions (MIME) protocol. MIME is described in RFCs 1521, 1522, 1563.

A sample mail session using the Unix mail program illustrates how the user can interact with the User Agent (UA).

```
% mail
Mail version SMI 4.0 Thu Jul 23 13:52:20 PDT 1992  Type ? for help.
"/usr/spool/mail/karanjit": 1 message
>   1 kss@RAMA.COM    Mon Apr 25 19:32 5148/153370
& ?
cd [directory]                  chdir to directory or home if none given
d [message list]                delete messages
e [message list]                edit messages
f [message list]                show from lines of messages
h                               print out active message headers
m [user list]                   mail to specific users
n                               goto and type next message
p [message list]                print messages
pre [message list]              make messages go back to system mailbox
q                               quit, saving unresolved messages in mbox
r [message list]                reply to sender (only) of messages
R [message list]                reply to sender and all recipients of messages
s [message list] file           append messages to file
t [message list]                type messages (same as print)
top [message list]              show top lines of messages
u [message list]                undelete messages
v [message list]                edit messages with display editor
w [message list] file           append messages to file, without from line
x                               quit, do not change system mailbox
z [-]                           display next [previous] page of headers
!                               shell escape
A [message list] consists of integers, ranges of same, or usernames separated by
spaces.  If omitted, Mail uses the current message.
& m karanjit@kscs.com
Subject: Mail demonstration message
This is a demonstration on using the
simple mail program interface.
When done you must type period (.)
:-)
.
```

```
EOT
& h
(Print out active message headers)
>   1 kss@RAMA.COM    Mon Apr 25 19:32 5148/153370
& p
(Print message. Message now follows)
Message  1:
From kss@RAMA.COM Mon Apr 25 19:32:35 1994
Return-Path: <kss@RAMA.COM>
Received: by world.std.com (5.65c/Spike-2.0)
        id AA01519; Mon, 25 Apr 1994 19:31:33 -0400
Received: from sita.RAMA.COM by relay1.UU.NET with SMTP
        (5.61/UUNET-internet-primary) id AAwnfh17101; Mon, 25 Apr 94 19:21:26 -0
400
Received: by sita.RAMA.COM (5.67/PERFORMIX-0.9/08-16-92)
        id AA03921; Mon, 25 Apr 94 16:21:21 -0700
Date: Mon, 25 Apr 94 16:21:21 -0700
From: kss@RAMA.COM (K S)
Message-Id: <9404252321.AA03921@learn1.Lrntree.COM>
To: karanjit@world.std.com
Status: RO
X-Status: D
#! /bin/sh
# This is a shell archive.  Remove anything before this line, then unpack
# it by saving it into a file and typing "sh file".  To overwrite existing
# files, type "sh file -c".  You can also feed this as standard input via
# unshar, or by typing "sh <file", e.g..  If this archive is complete, you
# will see the following message at the end:
#               "End of shell archive."
# Contents:  INSTALL Makefile Prospero RCS README acalloc.c archie.c
#   archie.man atalloc.c dirsend.c get_pauth.c get_vdir.c p_err_text.c
#   pauthent.h pcompat.h perrno.h pfs.h pmachine.h pprot.h ptalloc.c
#   regex.c stcopy.c support.c uw-copyright.h vl_comp.c vlalloc.c
# Wrapped by darwin@king.csri on Wed Jan  5 20:28:52 1994
PATH=/bin:/usr/bin:/usr/ucb ; export PATH
if test -f 'INSTALL' -a "${1}" != "-c" ; then
  echo shar: Will not clobber existing file \"'INSTALL'\"
else
echo shar: Extracting \"'INSTALL'\" \(1725 characters\)
sed "s/^X//" >'INSTALL' <<'END_OF_FILE'
X[Last changed: 07/31/91]
(Rest of message....)
& x
(Quit and do not change system mailbox)
%
```

Domain Name System (DNS)

The examples of sending e-mail messages discussed in the preceding section used a symbolic name for the hostname on which the mailbox resided. In general, users can more easily remember symbolic names for names of hosts. The alternative is to remember the IP address of the host. The IP address of a hostname is a 32-bit number, which most people find difficult to use and remember. The TCP/IP protocol software, on the other hand, uses the IP address. Any symbolic name used by the TCP/IP application service is translated to the equivalent 32-bit IP address. This translation is performed by the *Domain Name System* (DNS).

The DNS system essentially acts as a names database (also called a *name server*). When given a hostname, DNS translates it to an IP address. DNS can also do reverse translations (also called *pointer queries*), which means that given an IP address, DNS can return the hostname registered for that IP address.

DNS is implemented as a distributed database for looking up name-to-IP address associations. Another way of performing the name lookup is to keep the name-to-IP address information in a static file. On Unix systems, this static file is the /etc/hosts file. On NetWare servers, this static file is kept in the SYS:ETC/HOSTS file. The following sample host file format shows this organization:

```
# Local network host addresses
#
#ident "@(#)hosts    1.1 - 88/05/17"
#
127.0.0.1       local lb localhost loopback
144.19.74.1     sparc1 sp1
144.19.74.2     sparc2 sp2
144.19.74.3     sparc3 sp3
144.19.74.4     sparc4 sp4
144.19.74.5     sparc5 sp5
144.19.74.6     sparc6 sp6
144.19.74.7     sparc7 sp7
144.19.75.1     sparc8 sp8
144.19.75.2     sparc9 sp9
144.19.75.3     sparc10 sp10
144.19.75.4     sparc11 sp11
144.19.75.5     sparc12 sp12
144.19.75.6     sparc13 sp13
144.19.75.7     sparc14 sp14
144.19.74.101   cdos
144.19.74.102   server1 s386 nw
144.19.74.103   spws sparcsrv sps ss
144.19.74.201   sparcc1 spc1
144.19.74.202   sparcc2 spc2
```

The IP address 127.0.0.1 is a special address called the *loopback address*. Packets sent to this address never reach the network cable. The loopback address can be used for diagnostic purposes to verify that the internal code path through the TCP/IP protocols is working. The loopback address can also be used by client applications to communicate with software programs running on the same machine. In other words, the loopback address can be used for the local host.

Each <IP Address, Host name> pair is expressed on a single line using the style shown in the hosts file. The multiple hostnames for the host are alias names. The protocol software, if configured to perform name resolution using this static host file, looks up the information for resolving a name. Consider the following command:

```
telnet sp14
```

The protocol software uses the following entry in the hosts file to resolve the name sp14:

```
144.19.75.7     sparc14 sp14
```

The name sp14 is an alias for the hostname sparc14. The corresponding IP address is 144.19.75.7. The protocol software resolves the name sp14 to 144.19.75.7. The preceding command then becomes:

```
telnet 144.19.75.7
```

The static host file approach has a number of problems. As the number of hosts on a network becomes large, it is increasingly difficult to keep this file up to date. In addition, many organizations have more than one network administrator. It is difficult for these administrators to coordinate with each other every time host files need to be changed. Even keeping this information in a large central static file quickly becomes unmanageable as the number of entries in this file becomes large.

The DNS system was developed to overcome the problems of name resolution on a large IP network. It provides a distributed database of names and IP addresses. The names could be hostnames or names of mail exchanger hosts. It also has provisions for keeping text descriptions of hostnames and for providing name resolution for other protocol families besides TCP/IP (such as Chaosnet and XNS). It is, however, used predominantly for resolving hostnames for the TCP/IP protocols.

Figure 2.17 shows DNS operation; a TELNET session is being initiated using the command telnet archie.ans.net.

A portion of this TELNET session is shown:

```
% telnet archie.ans.net
Trying 147.225.1.2...
Connected to nis.ans.net.
Escape character is '^]'.
AIX telnet (nis.ans.net)
IBM AIX Version 3 for RISC System/6000
Copyrights by IBM and by others 1982, 1990.
login:
```

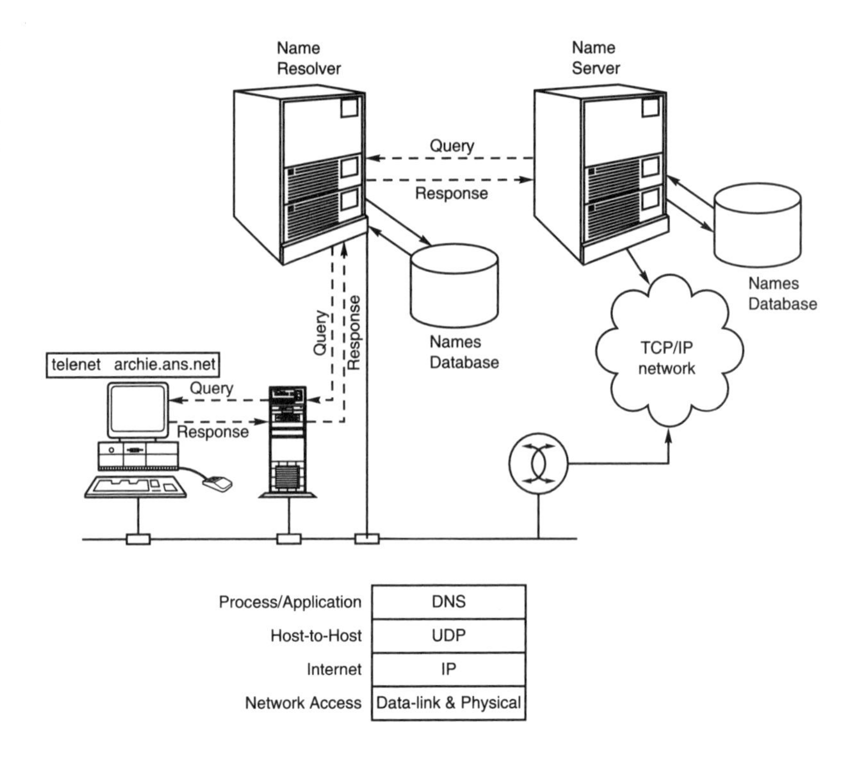

Figure 2.17

A DNS name resolution example.

The immediate response from the telnet session is the following message:

```
Trying 147.225.1.2...
```

The TCP/IP software translated the hostname archie.ans.net to the 32-bit IP address 147.225.1.2. DNS performed this translation.

TCP/IP application software can be configured to use DNS to resolve names. When a TCP/IP application encounters a hostname, it sends a query to a *name resolver* to translate the name to an IP address. On many Unix systems, the name resolver can be on the same workstation where the query was issued. If the name resolver cannot find the answer, it sends the query to a known *name server.* Typically, the name server exists on the workstation's network. If the name server cannot find the answer, the query can be sent to another name on the TCP/IP network.

The DNS system relies on a query/response type behavior and uses the UDP protocol as a transport protocol. The UDP protocol is more suited for applications that are query/response based because there is no overhead of maintaining a connection for transmitting data. The TCP protocol also can be used for query/response-based applications, but it requires an initial opening of a connection and a breakdown of the connection when the query/response is done. If only a single query/response or an occasional query/response transaction is expected, the overhead of establishing and breaking a connection can be excessive.

The most widely used implementation of DNS is the *Berkeley Internet Name Domain* (BIND) server, originally made available on BSD Unix, but now available on most Unix platforms. On Unix systems, it is often called the *named* (name daemon) program. The NetWare/IP product contains an implementation of BIND, in the form of the NAMED.NLM.

Windows NT has an implementation of DNS server called the *WINS* program.

BIND implementations for DOS and OS/2 are available from FTP Software. A simple Windows front-end for BIND is available from Chameleon's NETMANAGE product.

Domain Names

The examples of the hostnames in the preceding section have periods in them. These types of names use a hierarchical naming convention.

In the hierarchical name scheme used in DNS, names are organized into a hierarchical tree. At the top of the tree is the root domain named by the period symbol (.). Because all names have this common root, the period is omitted when specifying the hierarchical name in most TCP/IP applications. Below the root domain are top-level domains (see fig. 2.18). These reflect how names are organized. Table 2.7 shows examples of top-level domains.

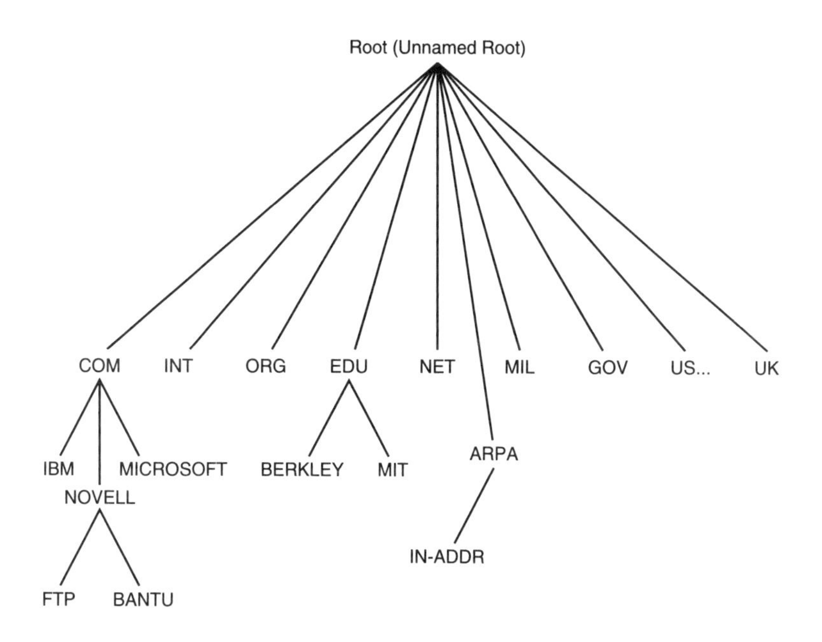

Figure 2.18

Hierarchical names in DNS.

The two-letter designations are assigned to countries as per the CCITT standards (now called ITU standards) and the ISO-3166 standard (except for Great Britain, which uses UK rather than the designated GB). These are the same country designations used for specifying country objects in NetWare Directory Services. Below the top-level domains are middle-level domains. There can be a number of middle-level names. Each name is separated from another by use of the period (which can never occur as part of the name of a domain). The length of a complete domain name is shown here:

```
archie.ans.net
```

A name cannot exceed 255 characters. In the name archie.ans.net, the name of the host is as follows:

```
archie
```

This domain is named:

```
ans.net
```

If another host were in the same domain whose name was sparky, its fully qualified name (FQN) would be the following:

```
sparky.ans.net
```

Many of the middle-level names refer to names of organizations. An organization is free to define subdomains within the organization. If it does this it should provide appropriate name services to resolve names in these subdomains. For instance, consider the organization SCS that has been given the following domain name:

```
SCS.COM
```

If this organization has separate networks for its Corporate, Marketing, and Research arms, it could define three separate subdomains named CORP, MKTG, RESCH, and provide a DNS server or a number of DNS servers to resolve names on its networks. The domains in this case would be the following:

- CORP.SCS.COM
- MKTG.SCS.COM
- RESCH.SCS.COM

Table 2.7 Examples of Some Top-Level Domains

Top Level Domain	Description
COM	Commercial organization
EDU	Education institution. Universities, schools, and so on
MIL	Military
GOV	Government, U.S.A.
NET	Network provider
ORG	Organization
ARPA	ARPAnet. Now historical. Still used for inverse address mapping

Top Level Domain	Description
INT	International organization
US	U.S.A.
CA	Canada
UK	United Kingdom
DE	Germany
SE	Sweden
FR	France
IN	India
CN	China
JA	Japan

As local government agencies, schools, and community colleges join the Internet, the Domain Name organization under the U.S. domain has become more complex. The Internet Network Information Center (INTERNIC) has guidelines on the U.S. domain organization.

Membership in the U.S. domain is open to any computer in the United States. In the past, the computers registered in the U.S. domain were primarily owned by small companies or individuals with computers at home. The U.S. Domain has grown and currently registers hosts in federal and state government agencies, technical/vocational schools, K12 schools, community colleges, private schools, libraries, city and county government agencies, as well as in businesses and homes.

The U.S. Domain hierarchy is subdivided into states, and then locality (that is, city or county), and then organization or computer name and so on. The state codes are those assigned by the U.S. Postal Service. Within the state name, locality names such as cities, counties, or some other local names are used, but not incorporated entities.

Registered names under locality can be of the following types:

- *hostname*.CI.*locality*.*state*.US (for city government agency)
- *hostname*.CO.*locality*.*state*.US (for county government agency)
- *hostname*.*locality*.*state*.US (for businesses)

The code of CI is used for a city government, and CO is used for a county government. Businesses are registered directly under the *locality* name.

If a county and a city have the same locality name, uniqueness is still maintained because of the use of the CO or CI keyword.

Cities can be designated by their full names (spelled out with hyphens replacing spaces, as in San-Francisco or New-York), or by a city code. The preference should be to use the full city name. If it is appropriate, you can also use the well-known city abbreviation known throughout a locality. However, it is very desirable if all users in the same city use the same designator for the city. That is, any particular locality should have just one DNS name.

For example, the Fire Department of Park County in Montana (MT) could have the following DNS name:

```
Fire-Dept.CO.Park-County.MT.US.
```

The state code is the postal code—MT for Montana. The *locality* is the Park County. The keyword *CO* designates that this a reference to the county government. The *Fire-Dept* is the name of the department in the Park County government.

Besides CO and CI, other codes such as the ones listed here are used:

- **K12.** Used for public school districts
- **PVT.** Used in the place of a school district name to designate private schools
- **CC.** Used for state-wide or Community colleges
- **TEC.** Used for Technical and Vocational schools and colleges
- **LIB.** Used with libraries for state, region, city, and county
- **STATE.** Used for state government agencies
- **GEN.** General independent entity that does not fit easily into any other structure listed. These could be state-wide associations, clubs, or domain parks
- **FED.** Used for agencies of the federal government
- **DNI.** Distributed National Institutes. This branch is to be used for organizations that span state, regional, and other organizational boundaries and that are national in scope

The general syntax of the domain names that use these codes are as follows:

- *school.district.*K12.state.US
- *school-name.*PVT.K12.state.US
- *school-name.*CC.state.US
- *school-name.*TEC.state.US
- *org-name.*STATE.state.US
- *org-name.*GEN.CA.US
- *org-name.*FED.US
- *org-name.*DNI.US

Figure 2.19 shows the second-level domains under US. Figure 2.20 shows third-level domains under the example state of California. Figure 2.21 shows a view of state, regional, and general agencies. Figure 2.22 shows the locality domains for Los Angeles and Santa Monica.

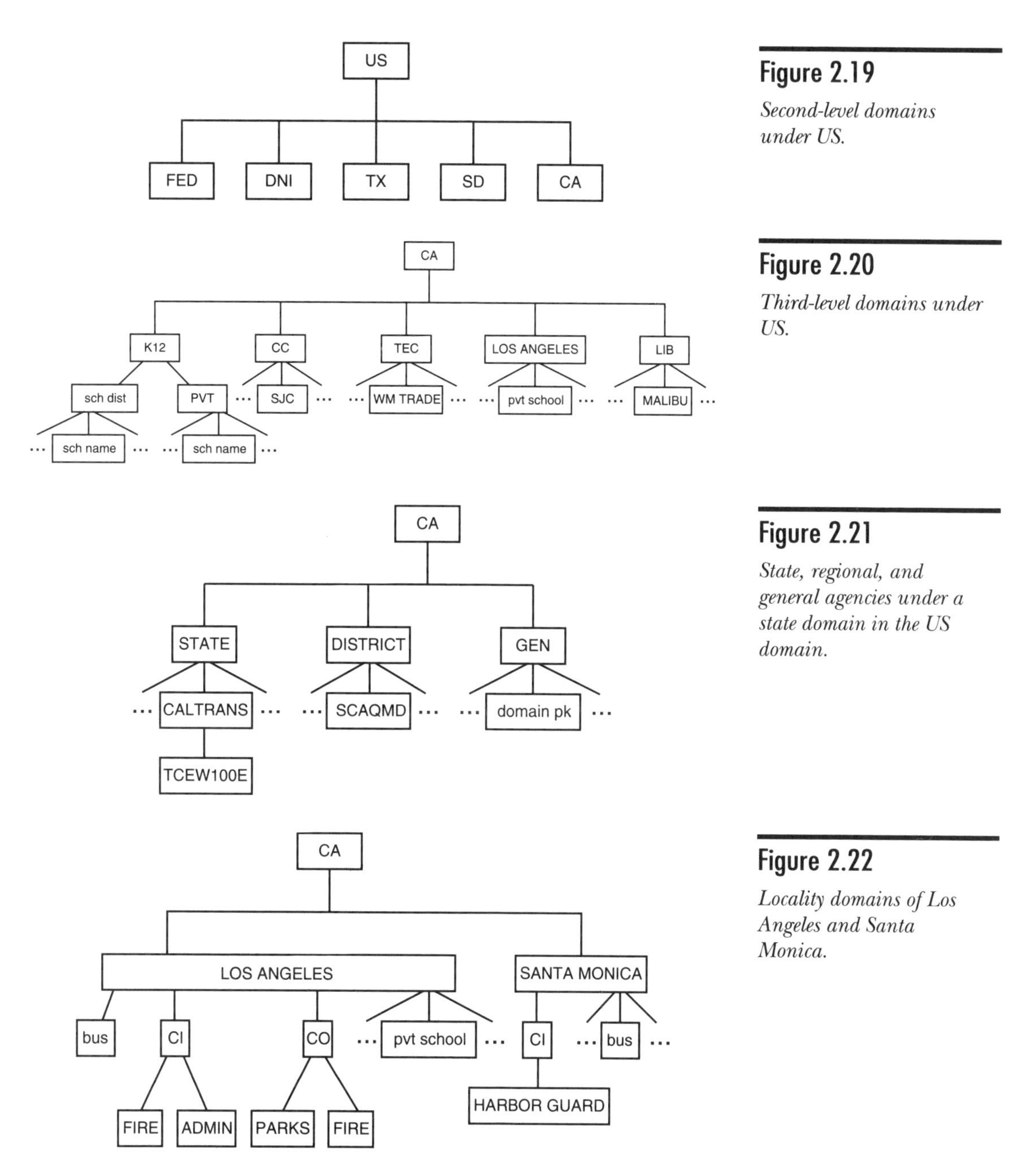

Figure 2.19

Second-level domains under US.

Figure 2.20

Third-level domains under US.

Figure 2.21

State, regional, and general agencies under a state domain in the US domain.

Figure 2.22

Locality domains of Los Angeles and Santa Monica.

Anyone requesting to register a host in the U.S. must fill a special US Domain Template obtainable by sending a message to the US Domain registrar (us-domain@isi.edu). Questions can be sent by e-mail to us-domain@isi.edu, or you can call Ann Cooper, USC/ Information Sciences Institute, (310) 822-1511.

If you want to register a name in a delegated zone, you should register with the contact for that zone. You can obtain this file through anonymous FTP. The file is in-notes/delegated-domains.txt from venera.isi.edu. Alternatively, you can send an e-mail message to RFC-INFO@ISI.EDU and include the following as the only text in the message:

```
Help: us_domain_delegated_domains
```

The U.S. domain is currently supported by the following seven name servers:

- VENERA.ISI.EDU
- NS.ISI.EDU
- RS.INTERNIC.NET
- NS.CSL.SRI.COM
- NS.UU.NET
- ADM.BRL.MIL
- EXCALIBUR.USC.EDU

Although a DNS server is not required for each domain, it is common to have one or more for each domain being served. Figure 2.18 would have several DNS servers for the root domain. These would know about names of the top-level domains such as COM, EDU, MIL, ORG, NET, and others.

A number of name servers manage the domain names at the root domain. These root domain servers, at the time of this writing, are shown in the following table:

Hostname	Net Addresses	Server Program
NS.INTERNIC.NET	198.41.0.4	BIND (Unix)
NS.NIC.DDN.MIL	192.112.36.4	BIND (Unix)
NS1.ISI.EDU	128.9.0.107	BIND (Unix)
AOS.ARL.ARMY.MIL	128.63.4.82 192.5.25.82	BIND (Unix)
C.NYSER.NET	192.33.4.12	BIND (Unix)
TERP.UMD.EDU	128.8.10.90	BIND (Unix)
NS.NASA.GOV	192.52.195.10 128.102.16.10	BIND (Unix)
NIC.NORDU.NET	192.36.148.17	BIND (Unix)

Several DNS servers can be used for a domain to perform load balancing, avoid unnecessary network traffic, and for reliability in case the primary DNS server is not available. In this setup, the COM domain would have one or more DNS servers that know the names of all commercial organizations in the COM domain. Within the COM domain, a subdomain such as IBM.COM will have its own DNS servers for that domain. Hosts within a domain will query the local DNS server for the domain to resolve names. For example, the host WORLD.STD.COM would query the DNS server for the domain STD.COM to find out the IP address of the host FTP.NOVELL.COM or the IP address of ATHENA.SCS.ORG. When this query is resolved, the results are usually cached locally for a configurable period of time.

The DNS servers for a domain need to resolve names of hosts in their domains. Secondary DNS servers in a domain must know the IP address of the primary server in the domain so that it can contact it and resolve a name query. A DNS server must also know the IP address of the parent DNS server.

DNS uses UDP as a transport protocol to send DNS queries and receive responses from DNS servers.

If you have an Internet connection and access to the whois client program, you can use this client utility to obtain information on a domain and the person(s) responsible for administering the domain.

The following are results of running the whois utility on some interesting domain names:

```
% whois novell.com
Novell, Inc. (NOVELL-DOM)
   122 East 1700 South
   Provo, UT 84606
   Domain Name: NOVELL.COM
   Administrative Contact, Technical Contact, Zone Contact:
      Richardson, Mark  (MR46)  mark_richardson@NOVELL.COM
      (801) 429-7974
   Record last updated on 24-Sep-92.
   Domain servers in listed order:
   NS.NOVELL.COM         137.65.1.1, 137.65.4.1
   NS.UTAH.EDU         128.110.124.120
   CCNUCB.COLORADO.EDU      128.138.238.34

% whois microsoft.com
Microsoft Corporation (MICROSOFT-DOM)
   3635 157th Avenue
   Building 11
   Redmond, WA 98052
   Domain Name: MICROSOFT.COM
   Administrative Contact:
      Kearns, Paul  (PK47)  postmaster@MICROSOFT.COM
      (206) 882-8080
```

```
   Technical Contact, Zone Contact:
      NorthWestNet Network Operations Center  (NWNET-NOC)  noc@nwnet.net
      (206) 685-4444
   Record last updated on 11-Apr-94.
   Domain servers in listed order:
   DNS1.NWNET.NET       192.220.250.1
   DNS2.NWNET.NET       192.220.251.1
   NS1.BARRNET.NET    131.119.245.5

% whois nic.ddn.mil
Government Systems, Inc. (DIIS)
   14200 Park Meadow Dr., Suite 200
   Chantilly, VA 22021
   Hostname: NIC.DDN.MIL
   Nicknames: DIIS.DDN.MIL
   Address: 192.112.36.5
   System: SUN running Unix
   Host Administrator:
      McCollum, Robert  (RM584)  bobm@NIC.DDN.MIL
      (703) 802-8476
   Domain Server DDN user assistance     (800) 365-3642 NIC@NIC.DDN.MIL
                                      (703) 802-4535
      Computer Operations      (703) 802-4535   ACTION@NIC.DDN.MIL
      WHOIS updates, user registration          REGISTRAR@NIC.DDN.MIL
      Host changes and updates                  HOSTMASTER@NIC.DDN.MIL
      Suggestions                               SUGGESTIONS@NIC.DDN.MIL
   Record last updated on 17-Sep-92.
To see this host record with registered users, repeat the command with a star ('*')
before the name; or, use '%' to show JUST the registered users.
The InterNIC Registration Services Host ONLY contains Internet Information (Networks,
ASN's, Domains, and POC's).
Please use the whois server at nic.ddn.mil for MILNET Information.

% whois 130.57
```

(The preceding line is querying whois service for a domain name for IP net address of 130.57.0.0—class B address. You learn about class addresses later in this chapter.)

```
Novell, Inc. (NET-NOVELL-WEST)
   122 East 1700 South
   Provo, UT  84606
   Netname: NOVELL-WEST
   Netnumber: 130.57.0.0
   Coordinator:
      Richardson, Mark  (MR46)  mark_richardson@NOVELL.COM
      (801) 429-7974
```

```
   Domain System inverse mapping provided by:
   NS.NOVELL.COM                137.65.1.1, 137.65.4.1
   NEWSUN.NOVELL.COM            130.57.4.1
   Record last updated on 28-Sep-92.

% whois 1
```

(The preceding line is querying whois service for a domain name for IP net address of 1.0.0.0—class A address—actually the first class A address ever assigned! You learn about class addresses later in this chapter.)

```
BBN Communications Corporation (ASN-BBN)
   33 Moulton Street
   Cambridge, MA 02238
   Autonomous System Name: BBN-CORE-GATEWAYS
   Autonomous System Number: 1
   Coordinator:
      Brescia, Michael  (MB)  BRESCIA@BBN.COM
      (617) 873-3662
   Record last updated on 27-Jun-91.
The InterNIC Registration Services Host ONLY contains Internet Information (Networks,
ASNs, Domains, and POCs). Please use the whois server at nic.ddn.mil for MILNET
Information.
```

Network File System (NFS)

Network File System (NFS) is a file service protocol originally developed by Sun Microsystems and licensed to a large number of vendors, including Novell. It allows a computer on which the NFS server software is running to export its file systems to other clients. *Exporting* a file system means that it is made available to clients on a variety of different operating system platforms as long as they are running the NFS client software.

Figure 2.23 shows that the NFS server is exporting the /usr/public directory. This exported directory can be accessed simultaneously by Unix NFS clients, Macintosh NFS clients, IBM PC DOS clients, and VAX/VMS NFS clients.

Figure 2.23
Using NFS.

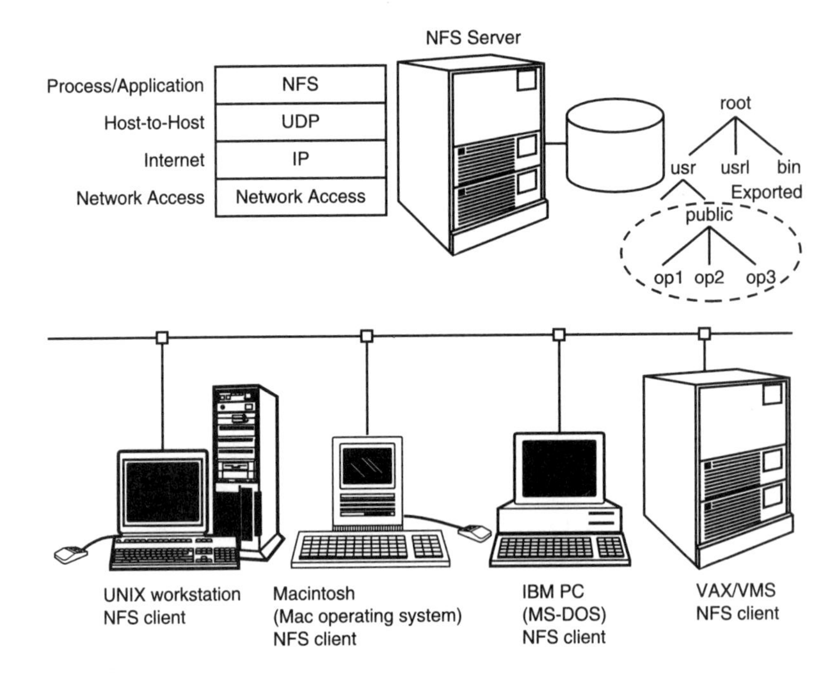

Each NFS client views the file system exported by the NFS server in the environment of the client's native file system. For example, a DOS NFS client accesses the exported file system through a network drive letter assignment; a Unix NFS client sees the exported file system linked to its local file system.

The NFS file system messages are sent using the UDP transport protocol.

Simple Network Management Protocol (SNMP)

SNMP can be used to manage a TCP/IP network. The *SNMP Manager* is a special station on the network that can send management queries to other nodes being managed on the network. Figure 2.24 shows an example SNMP management scenario. The managed nodes on the networks can be bridges, routers, and hosts. Each node that is managed must run a special program called the *SNMP agent.* The SNMP agent accepts the queries sent by the SNMP Manager and sends back the requested information.

SNMP uses the UDP as a transport protocol to send and receive requests. Chapter 5 discusses SNMP in more detail.

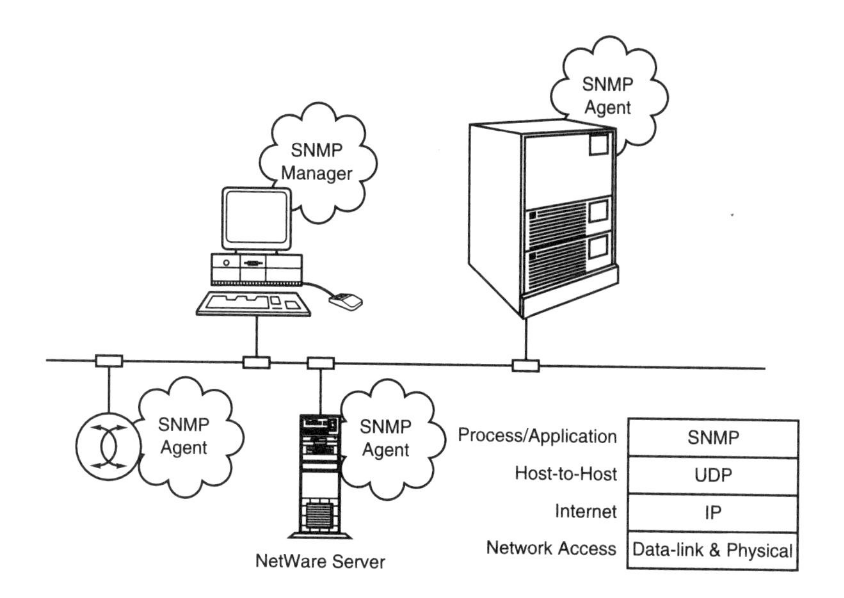

Figure 2.24

Use of SNMP.

Protocol Summary for Applications

Table 2.8 shows a summary of the transport protocol usage of the TCP applications discussed in this section. All the applications in table 2.8 use the IP protocol.

TABLE 2.8 TRANSPORT PROTOCOL USAGE SUMMARY

Process/Application Layer	Transport Protocol
FTP	TCP
TELNET	TCP
SMTP	TCP
DNS	UDP
NFS	UDP
SNMP	UDP
TFTP	UDP

Host-to-Host and Internet Layer Protocols

The DoD model uses two protocols at the Host-to-Host layer: TCP and UDP. The DoD model uses the IP and ICMP protocols at the DoD Internetwork layer. For broadcast networks (Ethernet, token ring, FDDI, and others), additional protocols such as the ARP and RARP can be used to support the Internet layer. Highlights of the TCP, UDP, and IP protocols are examined in the following sections.

Transmission Control Protocol (TCP)

The *Transmission Control Protocol* (TCP) provides reliable, full-duplex connections between two hosts. The connections that TCP provides are analogous to telephone circuits and are called *virtual circuits.* Figure 2.25 shows a TCP connection between two hosts.

Figure 2.25

TCP connection used to transmit data.

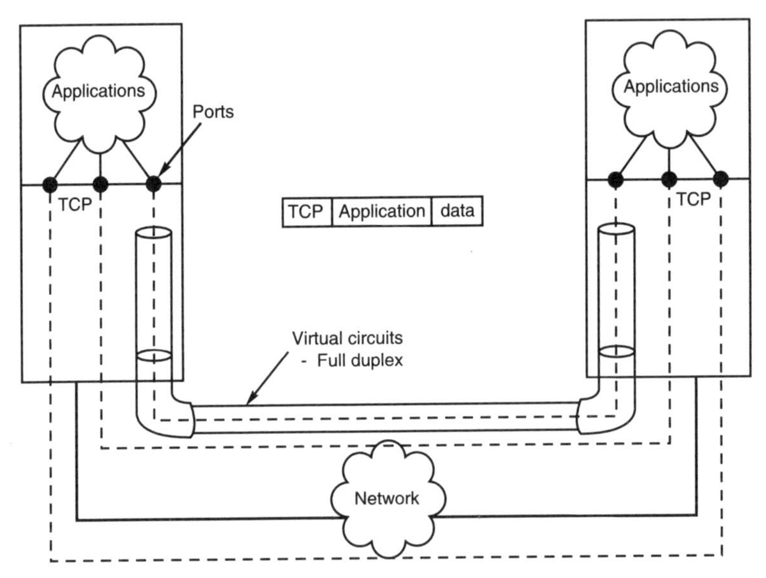
• Uses virtual circuits
- Similar to telephone circuits
- Open connection
- Reliable data transfer
Applications
Ports
TCP
TCP | Application | data
Applications
TCP
Virtual circuits
- Full duplex
Network
Virtual circuits are not suitable for packet broadcasts.

For TCP to be used for the transmission of data, a connection must be established between the two hosts. This is similar to the process of establishing a connection between two telephones. After the connection is established, port numbers that act as logical identifiers are used to identify the virtual circuit. On a TCP virtual circuit, data can be transmitted in either direction simultaneously. This is called *full duplex operation.* The TCP connection is maintained for the duration of data transmission. If no more data transmission is expected on the TCP circuit, the connection can be closed. Closing a connection releases any operating system resources such as memory and state tables needed to keep the connection alive.

TCP has its own built-in mechanism for reliable data transmission. Message segments not received at the destination are automatically present at the expiration of a time-out interval. The time-out interval is dynamic and takes into account factors such as changing delays caused by network congestion and alternate routes being used by underlying network services.

Although TCP is suited for applications that require reliable data transmission, it is not suited for applications that require broadcast traffic. To send a broadcast datagram to multiple destinations, TCP would have to establish a virtual circuit to each destination host, and then send the datagram on each one of the virtual circuits. This is a time-consuming and resource-intensive process. For applications that depend on broadcasts, UDP is a more suitable transport layer protocol.

Applications discussed in this book that use TCP are FTP, TELNET, and SMTP.

User Datagram Protocol (UDP)

The *User Datagram Protocol* (UDP) can send data without requiring that a data-circuit be established. Each data unit is sent with complete source and destination IP addresses and port numbers that identify the application level processes involved in the data exchange. UDP is similar to ordinary postal services because complete addressing information is sent with each UDP message.

UDP is called a connectionless transport protocol because it does not use a pre-established connection to transmit data. Figure 2.26 shows the use of UDP to exchange data between two hosts.

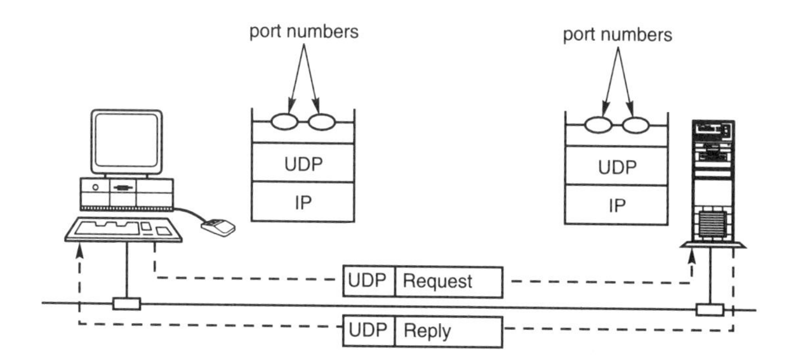

Figure 2.26

UDP connection used to transmit data.

UDP has less overhead than TCP. On the other hand, UDP does not guarantee that data arrives in the order in which it is sent; TCP guarantees that messages are assembled in the order in which they are sent. UDP includes an optional checksum that can be used to ensure data integrity of the message being sent. If additional reliability, such as data being received in the order in which it was sent (called *sequenced delivery*), is required, the application level process/protocol has to provide for it.

A big advantage UDP has over TCP is that it is more suited for applications that require broadcast data. A single datagram can be broadcast on the network by specifying a broadcast address on the destination address.

UDP is popular in many LAN-based applications that are broadcast based and do not require the complexity of TCP. Applications that use UDP are NFS, DNS, SNMP, and TFTP. UDP is also used for IP Tunneling (see Chapter 4, "TCP/IP Routing Support in NetWare") and by NetWare/IP to send NetWare Core Protocol (NCP) over IP.

Internet Protocol (IP)

The *Internet Protocol* (IP) is used to encapsulate TCP and UDP message segments (see fig. 2.27). The IP provides a logical network address for the hardware network interlace. This logical network address is a 32-bit address (called the IP address) and can be used to identify separate physical networks joined by interconnecting devices called *routers.* The logical IP address provided by the Internet Protocol identifies the destination network and the host address on that network to which the data is to be sent. It can therefore be used for routing a data unit, called a *datagram,* to its correct destination.

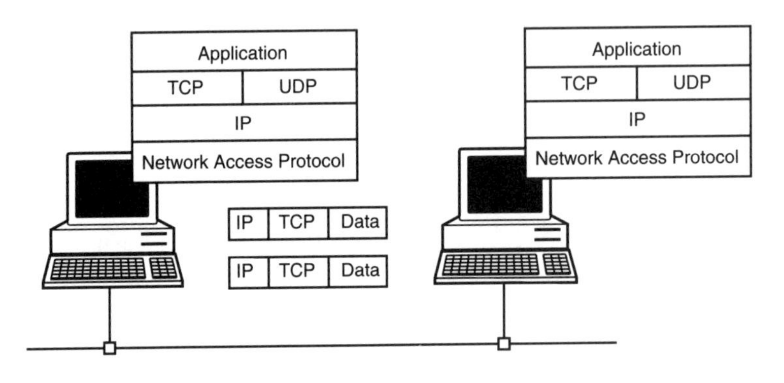

Figure 2.27
The IP protocol.

The IP protocol is a connectionless protocol: it does not require the establishment of a virtual circuit for sending a datagram.

Internet Control Message Protocol (ICMP)

The *Internet Control Message Protocol* (ICMP) is used to report problems encountered with the delivery of a datagram, such as an unreachable host or unavailable port. ICMP can also be used to send an echo request packet to a host to see if it is "alive." The host that receives an ICMP echo request sends back an ICMP reply packet if it is "alive" and still functioning. This is called the "PING" test.

ICMP can also be used by router devices to send an ICMP redirect message to other devices indicating that a better path has been found.

Network Access Layer

Because of TCP/IP's popularity, it has been implemented on every major physical network architecture available for LANs and WANs. TCP/IP protocol software can be used on LANs such as IEEE LANs, Ethernet, Local Talk, and Fiber Distributed Data Interface (FDDI). WANs that support TCP/IP include X.35, Frame Relay, ISDN, Point-to-Point circuits, and Asynchronous Transfer Mode (ATM).

This section examines some of the common LAN transports.

IEEE LANs

The Institute of Electrical and Electronics Engineers (IEEE) undertook Project 802 in February of 1980 to identify and formalize LAN standards for data rates not exceeding 20 megabits per second (Mbps). Standardization efforts resulted in the IEEE 802 LAN standards. The number 802 was chosen to mark the calendar date when IEEE undertook the LAN standardization efforts (80 for 1980, 2 for February).

Figure 2.28 shows the IEEE LAN standards in relationship to the OSI model. You can see that the primary emphasis of the IEEE committee was to standardize the hardware technologies used at the physical and data link layers. This is not surprising considering that networking hardware such as network interface cards and LAN wiring can be modeled completely by the two lower OSI layers.

The IEEE standards divide the OSI data link layer into two sub-layers: the Media Access Control (MAC) and the Logical Link Control (LLC). The MAC layerworks with media access techniques utilized to control access to a shared physical medium. Token ring and Ethernet have different implementations of the MAC layer because they use different methods to share the physical media.

All IEEE LANs have the same LLC layer, as defined by standard 802.2. The advantage of a common sublayer such as the LLC is that upper-layer mechanisms can be the same regardless of what kind of networking hardware you use.

Figure 2.28 shows the interface between upper layer protocols and the LLC layer defined by Link Service Access Points (LSAPs). LSAPs are logical data link addresses. A single MAC address, such as an Ethernet address, can have multiple LSAP addresses. These multiple addresses enable multiple end-point connections to exist between two nodes on a LAN.

The LLC layer also provides the options of virtual circuit (connections-oriented) or datagram (connectionless) services, or a combination of these two.

Unacknowledged datagram services are modeled after postal services. In the datagram approach, every packet contains complete addressing information, including destination and source addresses. No special effort is made to ensure that packets arrive intact or in the correct order. Unacknowledged datagram services are called *Type 1 services.*

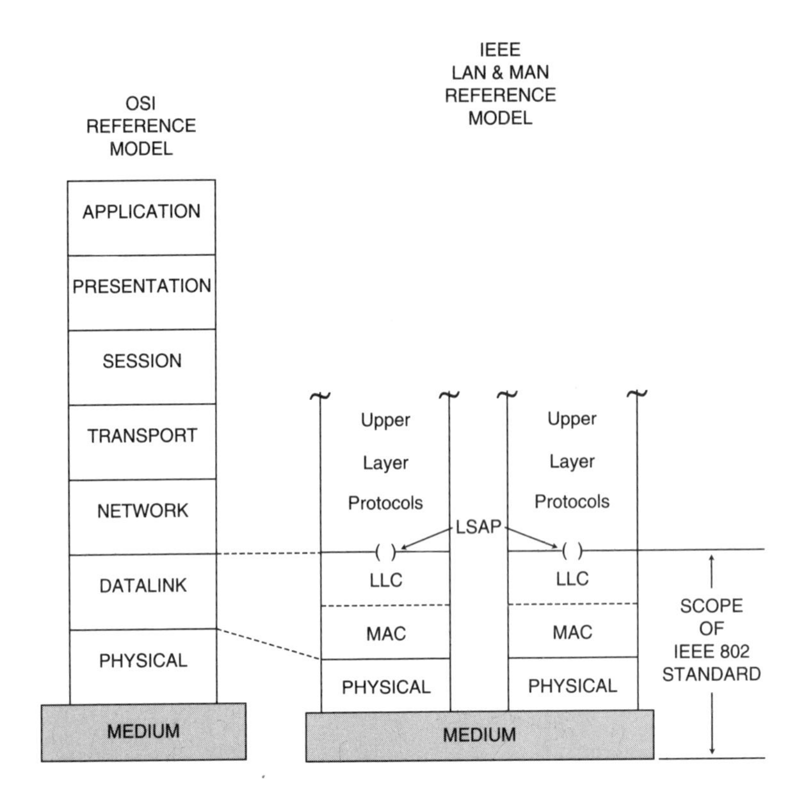

Figure 2.28

Relationship of the IEEE 802 standard to the OSI model.

In a virtual-circuit, a special effort is made to ensure that packets arrive error-free in the order they were sent. Virtual circuits are modeled after the telephone system and require that a connection be established between two nodes before data can be exchanged between them. When data transfer is complete, this virtual circuit needs to be closed or terminated. Virtual-circuit services are called *Type 2 services.*

Acknowledged datagram services, a combination of datagram and virtual circuits, are called *Type 3 services.* With these services, an effort is made to correct data errors by retransmitting packets that have data errors.

Figure 2.29 shows how the IEEE committee has identified the choices at the different layers. Each of the choices represents a standard protocol or specification. Table 2.9 describes their IEEE numbers and meanings.

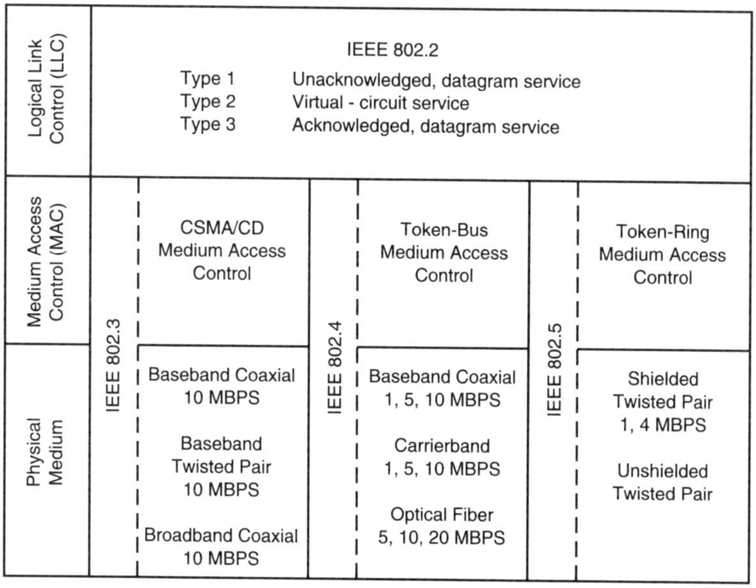

Logical Link Control (LLC)

IEEE 802.2

Type 1 Unacknowledged, datagram service
Type 2 Virtual - circuit service
Type 3 Acknowledged, datagram service

Medium Access Control (MAC)

Physical Medium

IEEE 802.3

CSMA/CD Medium Access Control

Baseband Coaxial 10 MBPS

Baseband Twisted Pair 10 MBPS

Broadband Coaxial 10 MBPS

IEEE 802.4

Token-Bus Medium Access Control

Baseband Coaxial 1, 5, 10 MBPS

Carrierband 1, 5, 10 MBPS

Optical Fiber 5, 10, 20 MBPS

IEEE 802.5

Token-Ring Medium Access Control

Shielded Twisted Pair 1, 4 MBPS

Unshielded Twisted Pair

Figure 2.29

Services defined by various IEEE 802 standards.

Table 2.9 IEEE Standards

IEEE Standard	Meaning
IEEE 802.1	LAN bridging
IEEE 802.2	Logical Link Control (LLC)
IEEE 802.3	Standardization of Ethernet technology; includes 100BASE-TX, 100 BASE-TF, 100 BASE-T4 (Fast Ethernet)
IEEE 802.4	Token bus standard
IEEE 802.5	Token ring standard
IEEE 802.6	Metropolitan Area Network (MAN)
IEEE 802.7	Broadband technical advisory
IEEE 802.8	Fiber optic technical advisory
IEEE 802.9	Integrated Voice/Data (IVD)
IEEE 802.10	LAN security
IEEE 802.11	Wireless LANs
IEEE 802.12	100BASE-VG (100VG-AnyLAN)

Detailed discussion of the IEEE standards is beyond the scope of this book. If you are interested in more details, refer to *NetWare Professional Reference, Fourth Edition* (New Riders Publishing) from the same author.

Ethernet II

Ethernet was proposed as a standard by Digital Equipment Corporation, Intel, and Xerox. The first Ethernet standard was published in September 1981 and was called the DIX 1.0. DIX stands for **D**igital (DEC), **I**ntel, and **X**erox. DIX 1.0 was followed by DIX 2.0, published in November 1982. Today, this standard is also referred to as the Ethernet II standard.

Meanwhile, Project 802 from the IEEE had undertaken LAN standardization efforts. Not surprisingly, Digital, Intel, and Xerox proposed the adoption of Ethernet as a standard. IBM, based on prototypes built at IBM's Zurich Lab, proposed the token ring as a standard. The Ethernet proposal became known as the IEEE 802.3, and the token ring proposal became the IEEE 802.5. The IEEE 802.3 standard is not quite the same as the Ethernet standard; important differences exist. Although 802.3 and Ethernet are incompatible standards, the term *Ethernet* is used in LANs to designate 802.3-compliant networks. This book bows to common usage and uses the term Ethernet for both standards, making distinctions as required when a specific standard is discussed.

Figure 2.30 shows two classic examples of Ethernet topologies: Thick Wire Ethernet and Thin Wire Ethernet. Figure 2.31 shows the Ethernet 10BASE-T technologies. Some of the network parameters concerned with distance rules for these types of networks are summarized in these figures. Today, the most common Ethernet type is the Thin Wire Ethernet (also called 10BASE2). The 10BASE-T and 100BASE-TX standards use Unshielded Twisted Pair (UTP).

Ethernet Frame Structure

Both Ethernet-II and IEEE 802.3 have a minimum frame size of 64 bytes and a maximum frame size of 1,518 bytes.

Ethernet II Frame

The Ethernet II frame (see fig. 2.32) begins with a preamble of eight octets (one octet = eight bits) consisting of an alternating pattern 1010 that ends in 101011. At 10 Mbps, this preamble is of 6.4 microsecond duration and is sufficient time for the receiving station to synchronize and get ready to receive the frame.

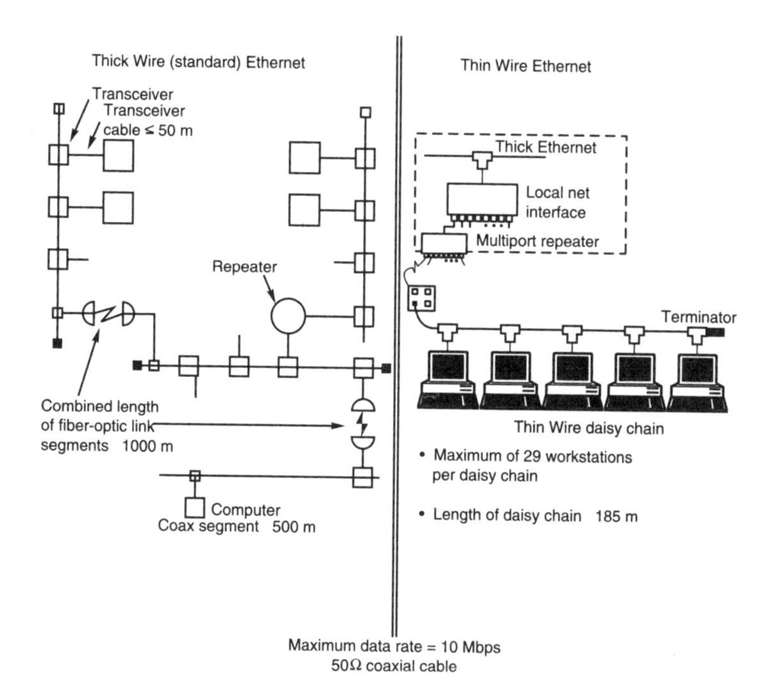

Figure 2.30

Thick Wire and Thin Wire Ethernet.

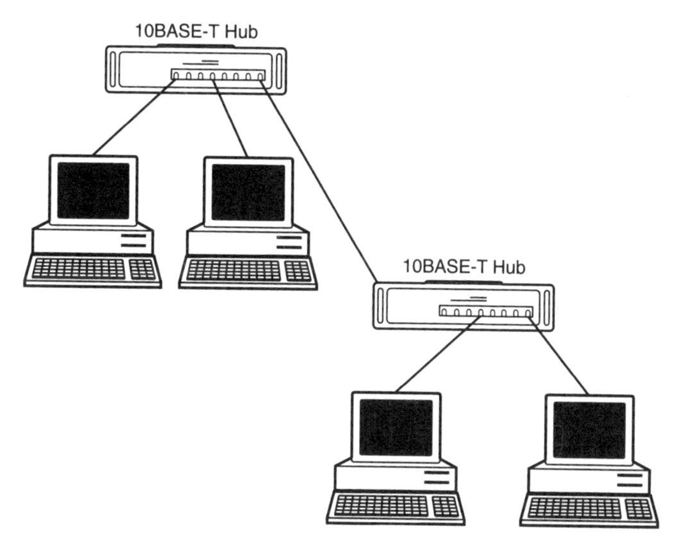

Figure 2.31

10BASE-T.

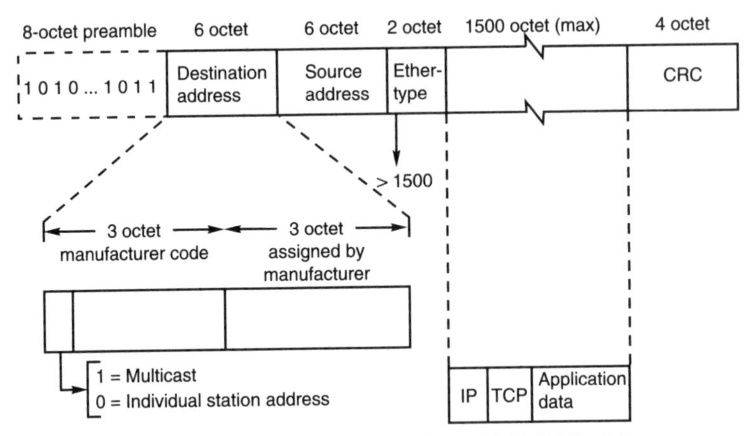

Figure 2.32
Ethernet II frame.

The Destination Address (DA) and the Source Address (SA) fields follow this preamble. Each address field is six octets long. The first three octets represent a manufacturer's code; the remaining three octets are assigned by the manufacturer. This assignment is made so that an Ethernet card will have a unique six-octet address. This address is usually burned into a ROM chip on the Ethernet card. The least significant bit (LSB) of the first octet is the Physical/Multicast bit. It is 0 for an Ethernet address. A value of 1 for this LSB indicates a multi-cast address. For instance, a hex value of FFFFFFFFFFFF—all 1s—for the DA field represents a broadcast. The manufacturer's code was formerly assigned by Xerox; it is now assigned by IEEE.

Table 2.10 lists a few of the more common manufacturer IDs used in IEEE LANs.

TABLE 2.10 MANUFACTURER IDs FOR IEEE ADDRESSES

Manufacturer	Manufacturer ID for IEEE Addresses
Novell	00 00 1B 08 00 14
3COM	02 60 8C
DEC	AA 00 04
IBM	08 00 5A
SUN	08 00 20

For additional details on manufacturer IDs, refer to the RFC 1340 on Assigned Numbers.

The *Type field,* also referred to as *Ethertype,* is a two-octet field used to indicate the type of data in the data field. Thus, if the Ethernet frame is used to carry NetWare data, the Ethertype value will be 8137 hex. If it is used to carry DoD Internet Packet (IP) data, it will have the value 0800 hex. XNS packets used in 3COM networks will have the value 0600 hex. This field is used by network drivers or the network layer to demultiplex data packets to the appropriate protocol stack. It allows multiple protocol stacks to run on a single Ethernet card.

The *Data Unit field* is a variable length field that can range from 46 to 1,500 octets. The remaining fixed length fields add up to 18 bytes.

The *FCS* field is generated by the Ethernet hardware at the end of the Data field and is a 32-bit Cyclic Redundancy Checksum (CRC) over the Address, Type, and Data fields. It is used to detect errors in transmission. Bad frames are retransmitted.

IEEE 802.3 Frame

The IEEE frame shown in figure 2.33 begins with a preamble of seven octets (one octet = eight bits) consisting of an alternating pattern 1010. At 10 Mbps, this preamble is of 5.6 microseconds' duration, which is a sufficient amount of time for the receiving station to synchronize and get ready to receive the frame.

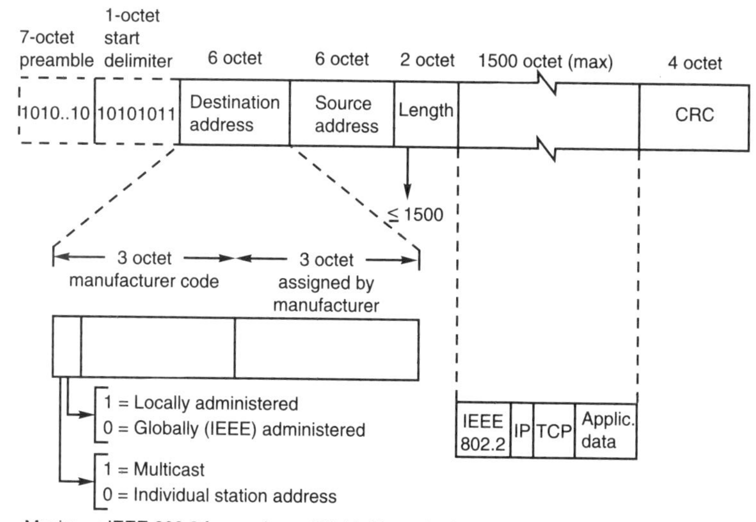

Figure 2.33

IEEE 802.3 frame.

The Start Frame Delimiter (SFD) follows after the preamble and is defined by the pattern 10101011. Note in the following formula that the IEEE 802.3 preamble and the SFD field combined are identical to the eight-octet Ethernet preamble:

IEEE 802.3 preamble + SFD = Ethernet preamble

The *DA* and the *SA fields* follow the SFD. Each address field can be six octets or two octets long. The six-octet addressing is the most common. The first three octets represent a manufacturer's code, and the remaining octets are assigned by the manufacturer. This assignment is made so that any two Ethernet and IEEE cards will have a unique six-octet address. This address is usually burned into a ROM chip on the IEEE 802.3 card. The LSB of the first octet represents the *Individual/Group field* and is similar to the Physical/Multicast field in Ethernet. The next bit is the *Universe/Local* (U/L) *field* and indicates if the addressing is global or local.

The *Length field* follows the address fields and is two octets long. It indicates the data size of the 802.3 frame. A minimum of 46 octets of LLC is required to make up the minimum size of 64 octets. The maximum value of this field is 1,500 to make a maximum frame size of 1,518 octets.

The Data Unit field is a variable length field containing 46 to 1,500 octets of LLC data.

The *FCS field* is generated by the IEEE 802.3 hardware at the end of the Data field and is a 32-bit Cyclic Redundancy Checksum (CRC) over the Address, Type, and Data fields. It is used to detect errors in transmission. Bad frames are retransmitted.

Differences between Ethernet II and IEEE 802.3

Ethernet II and IEEE 802.3 differ in several ways. You can see that Ethernet II uses a two-byte Type field to indicate the type of data. The Type field values were at one time assigned by Xerox; they are now assigned by IEEE. Instead of the Type field, IEEE 802.3 has a two-byte Length field. The length information for Ethernet Packets is supplied by a higher layer. In some cases, the NIC can determine the length of the frame based on hardware mechanisms, find out the bits received, and pass this information to upper layers. For IEEE 802.3 frames, the "type" information is supplied by the IEEE 802.2 (Logical Control Layer) frame that is part of the Data Unit field. Figure 2.34 illustrates the LLC frame format.

For example, a hex code of E0 indicates a NetWare packet. A hex code of AA is reserved to transmit upper layer packets generated by non-IEEE LANs. This is referred to as the *Sub Net Access Protocol* (SNAP) mechanism. A complete description of SNAP can be found in RFC-1042.

Ethernet has no provision to pad the data to make a minimum Ethernet frame of 64 bytes. IEEE 802.3 frames have a Length field to encode the pad information. In Ethernet, the padding has to be performed by upper layers.

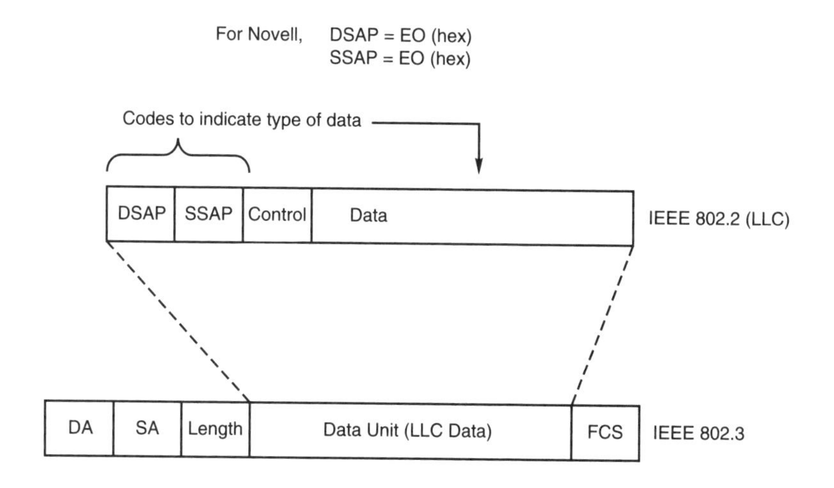

Figure 2.34

"Type" information in IEEE 802.3.

Although IEEE 802.3 uses the IEEE 802.2 (LLC) to provide the "type" format, Novell's use of the frame type called ETHERNET_802.3 did not use the IEEE 802.2 (LLC) type frame. The term "Ethernet *raw* frame type" is sometimes used to indicate Novell's ETHERNET_802.3 frame type. Novell has defined a frame type of ETHERNET_802.2 to describe the frame type shown in figure 2.33. This frame type uses the IEEE 802.2 (LLC) to represent "type" information.

IEEE 802.5

IEEE 802.5 specifies token ring options (see fig. 2.35) at data rates of 1 Mbps, 4 Mbps, and 16 Mbps. The 1 Mbps rate uses UTP wiring. Initially, the 16 Mbps rate used STP wiring. Demand within the industry to have a 16 Mbps data rate on UTP wiring resulted in several products that are now available to support UTP wiring for 4 Mbps and 16 Mbps token rings. For a long time, a 16 Mbps UTP version was not available from IBM. IBM has teamed with Synoptics Communications to propose a 16 Mbps UTP standard to the IEEE 802.5 committee.

The 16 Mbps stations have an option called the *early token release mechanism.* In this option, the 16 Mbps stations do not wait for the return of the data frame to place the token on the network. This mechanism allows up to two data frames to be transmitted on a token ring LAN at a time.

IP Protocol Elements

When two TCP/IP hosts are connected through a network, each protocol layer of the TCP/IP host communicates with the corresponding protocol layer of the other TCP/IP host.

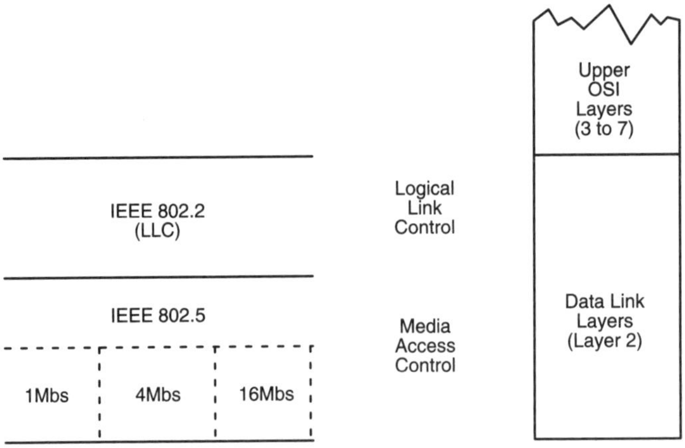

Figure 2.35
IEEE 802.5 options for token ring.

The DoD model discussed earlier in this chapter comprises four layers: the Process/Application layer, Host-to-Host layer, Internetwork Layer, and Network Access layer. As each of these protocol layers communicate with the peer layer of the remote TCP/IP host, they use their own addressing.

The Process/Application layer uses hostnames. Because the Process/Application layer is seen directly by users, it makes sense for this layer to use hostnames, which are much easier to identify and remember. The Host-to-Host layer uses port numbers to describe the interface points to this layer. The port numbers can be seen as the addresses of the software processes that reside on the same TCP/IP host. The Internet layer uses IP addresses. An IP address is needed for each network interface in a TCP/IP host. TCP/IP hosts that have multiple network interfaces (such as hosts acting as routers) are called *multi-homed hosts.*

Table 2.11 summarizes the addressing method used in each of the DoD layers.

TABLE 2.11 ADDRESSING METHOD IN THE DOD MODEL

DoD Layer	Addressing Method
Process/Application	Hostname
Host-to-Host	Port number
Internet	IP address
Network Access	Hardware address (MAC address)

Process/Application Layer Addressing

Hostnames are used as addresses in the Process/Application layer. The hostnames are translated (mapped) to IP addresses by using either DNS or a hostname file.

DNS was discussed earlier in this chapter in the section "Domain Name System (DNS)." For small networks, a static host table can be used to perform the mapping between hostnames and IP addresses. This avoids the expense of configuring and maintaining a DNS server. Figure 2.36 shows the translation between hostnames and IP addresses using a hostname file. The hostname file is the /etc/hosts file on Unix servers. On NetWare servers, the hostname file is implemented by SYS:ETC/HOSTS file.

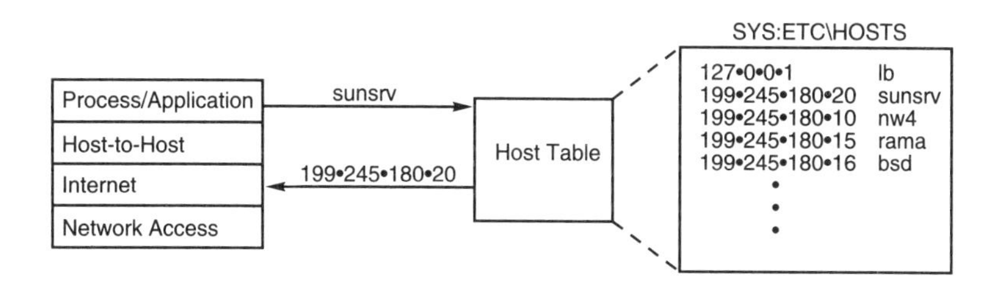

Figure 2.36

Host name translation using a hostname file.

Internet Layer Addressing

The Internet Layer addresses are represented by 32-bit numbers called *IP addresses.* Each network interface in a node that supports an IP stack must have an IP address assigned to it. The IP address is a logical address independent of the underlying network hardware or network type.

IP Address Classes (Class A, B, C, D, E)

The IP address consists of two parts: a network ID (*netid*) and a host ID (*hostid*), as shown in figure 2.37. The most significant bits are used to determine how many bits are used for netid and the hostid. Five address classes are currently defined: Class A, B, C, D, and E. Of these, class A, B, and C addresses are assignable. Class D is reserved for multicasting and is used by special protocols to transmit messages to a select group of nodes. Class E is reserved for future use.

0 8
0 | netid | hostid — Class A

0 1 16
1 | 0 | netid | hostid — Class B

0 1 2 24
1 | 1 | 0 | netid | — Class C

0 1 2 3
1 | 1 | 1 | 0 | multicast — Class D

1 | 1 | 1 | 1 | 0 | reserved for future use — Class E

Figure 2.37

IP address classes.

Although IP address classes A, B, C, D, and E exist, the Novell documentation speaks of only the address classes A, B, and C.

The netid portion of the IP address is similar to the network number used in IPX protocols. It identifies the network uniquely. Interconnected networks must have unique netids. If your network is going to be connected to other networks such as the Internet, you must apply to a central authority to obtain a netid (network number) not in use by anyone else. The central Internet Address Network Authority (IANA) is listed here.

To connect to the MILNET:

DDN Network Information Center

14200 Park Meadow Drive, Suite 200

Chantilly, VA 22021, USA

E-mail address: HOSTMASTER@NIC.DDN.MIL

To connect to the Internet:

Network Solutions

InterNIC Registration Services

505 Huntmar Park Drive

Herndon, VA 22070

E-mail address: HOSTMASTER@INTERNIC.NET

Older reference works on TCP/IP may list the Stanford Research Institute (SRI) as the IANA. This no longer is true; but you can still obtain RFCs from SRI.

Reasons for Using Specific Address Classes

The different types of IP address classes are defined to address the needs of networks of different sizes. On request, the network registration authority assigns a network number (the netid field) to an organization. It is the sole responsibility of an organization that has been allocated a network number to assign the host numbers (the values for the hostid field).

The number of hosts that can be assigned for a given network number depends on the number of bits in the hostid field. The number of bits in the hostid field depends on the address class to which the network number belongs. A class A network number has the largest number of bits in the hostid field and therefore has the largest number of hosts. Similarly, a class C address has the smallest number of bits in the hostid field and therefore has the smallest number of hosts. Table 2.12 shows the number of networks and nodes possible with each address class.

TABLE 2.12 REASONS FOR USING SPECIFIC ADDRESS CLASS

Address Class	Number of Networks	Number of Nodes
A	127	16,777,214
B	16,383	65,534
C	2,097,151	254

A class A network is suitable for very large networks, but because its netid field (refer to fig. 2.37) is only 7 bits, there can be only 127 such networks. The original ARPAnet is an example of a class A network. Class B networks are medium-size networks and are suited for medium to large organizations. Class C networks are suited for small organizations, in which each network can have no more than 254 nodes.

Dotted Decimal Notation

The 32-bit number is represented for convenience as four decimal numbers corresponding to the decimal value of the four bytes that make up the 32-bit IP address. The decimal numbers are separated by periods (.). This shorthand notation for IP addresses is called *dotted decimal notation.* The following shows an IP address in its binary form and in dotted decimal notation:

IP Address = 10010000 0001011 01001010 1001001

IP Address = 144.19.74.201

Figure 2.38 shows the relationship between the binary representation of the IP address and the dotted decimal notation. From this figure, you can see that the first group of 8 bits (10010000) that has a decimal value of 144 becomes the first decimal number of the dotted decimal IP address. Similarly, the second, third, and fourth groups of 8 bits are each represented by their decimal values in the dotted decimal notation.

• To make a 32-bit binary number more human-readable, dotted decimal notation is used
32 bits
IP address
8-bits 8-bits 8-bits 8-bits
10010000 00010011 01001010 11001001
IP address is divided into four 8-bit fields.
144 19 74 201
8-bit binary number is converted to decimal value.
d1 • d2 • d3 • d4
d1, d2, d3, and d4 must be between 0 and 255.
Example: Dotted decimal 144 • 19 • 74 • 201

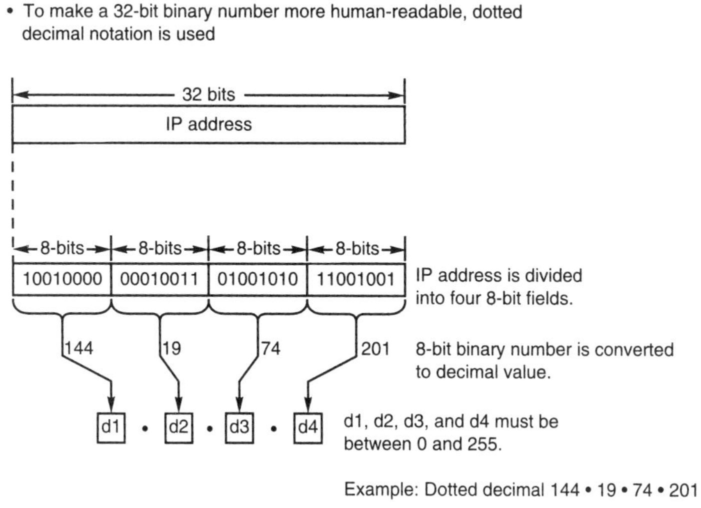

Figure 2.38

Dotted decimal notation.

Calculating an Address Class

Given an IP address in the dotted decimal notation form, it is important to know which address class it belongs to. The IP address class determines the number of bits assigned to the hostid field. The size of the hostid field limits the number of hosts that can be on the network. Another reason for knowing the address class is because it can be used to determine how to divide a network into smaller networks called *subnets.*

One method of determining the IP address class is to convert the IP address into its binary form and to examine the first few most significant bits (bits on the left of the binary pattern for the IP address). The most significant bits of an IP address determine the IP address class. From figure 2.37, you can see that if the most significant bit of the IP address is a 0, the IP address is a class A address. If the first two most significant bits of the IP address are 10, the IP address is a class B address; and if the first three most significant bits of the IP address are 110, the IP address is a class C address. Table 2.13 summarizes these rules.

Table 2.13 Determining IP Address Class from the Most Significant Bits of the IP Address

Most Significant Bits	IP Address Class
1	Class A
10	Class B
110	Class C
1110	Class D

Consider an IP address of 137.65.4.1. If you convert this IP address to its binary representation, you obtain the following 32-bit pattern:

1001001 01000001 00000100 00000001

The most significant two bits of this bit pattern are 10. Therefore, the IP address 137.65.4.1 is a class B address.

Consider another example in which the IP address is 199.245.180.10. If you convert this IP address to its binary representation, you obtain the following 32-bit pattern:

1100111 11110101 10110100 00001010

The most significant three bits of this bit pattern are 110. Therefore, the IP address 199.245.180.10 is a class C address.

Although this technique works, it is a laborious way of determining the IP address class because it involves converting the IP address to a bit pattern. Fortunately, a simpler way is available. Consider the class B address shown in figure 2.39. For a class B address, the two most significant bits are 10. The minimum value of the first 8 bits occurs when the remaining 6 bits are 0; the maximum value occurs when the remaining 6 bits are 1.

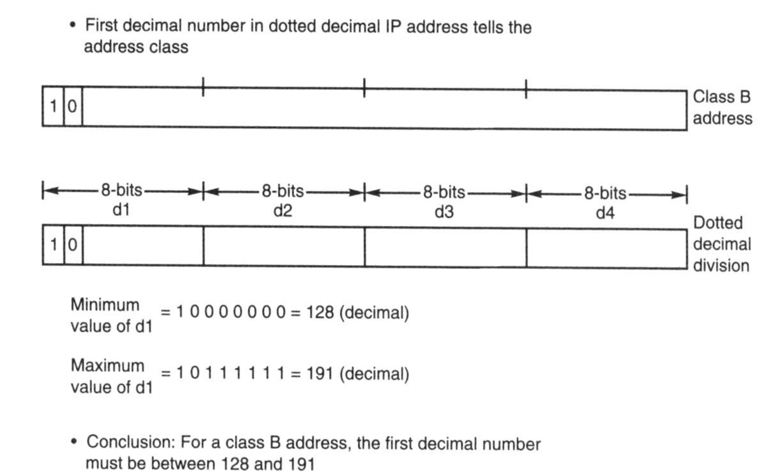

Figure 2.39

Determining IP address class.

Therefore, the minimum value of the first 8 bits of a class B address is 10000000 and the maximum value is 10111111. These minimum and maximum values correspond to a decimal value of 128 and 191. This means that if the first decimal number of an IP address in the dotted decimal notation is a number between 128 and 191 (inclusive), the IP address is a class B address. In the preceding example of an IP address of 137.65.4.1, the number 137 is between 128 and 191, and therefore 137.65.4.1 is a class B address.

Using the same reasoning, the minimum and maximum for the first decimal number of a class A and class C address in its dotted decimal notation form can be worked out as shown:

- Minimum value of first decimal for class A = 00000000 = 0
- Maximum value of first decimal for class A = 01111111 = 127
- Minimum value of first decimal for class C = 11000000 = 192
- Maximum value of first decimal for class C = 11011111 = 223

Table 2.14 shows the range of values for the first decimal number of an IP address in the dotted decimal notation. This table can be used to determine the IP address class by merely examining the first decimal number of an IP address.

TABLE 2.14 DETERMINING IP ADDRESS CLASS FROM THE FIRST DECIMAL NUMBER OF AN IP ADDRESS EXPRESSED IN DOTTED DECIMAL NOTATION

IP Address Class	Minimum	Maximum
A	0	126
B	128	191
C	192	223
D	224	239
E	240	247

Consider the following questions:

1. What is the IP address class for 40.12.33.1?
2. What is the IP address class for 191.122.65.234?
3. What is the IP address class for 204.17.206.10?

By examining table 2.14, the first decimal number of 40 in the IP address 40.12.33.1 indicates that it is a class A address. The first decimal number of 191 in the IP address 191.122.65.234 indicates that it is a class B address; and the first decimal number of 204 in the IP address 204.17.206.10 indicates that it is a class C address.

Software Loopback

If you examine table 2.14, you will see that the number 127, which should be in the class A range of values, is missing. This number is reserved for the software loopback address. Any packet sent by a TCP/IP application to an IP address of 127.*X.X.X*, with *X* being any number from 0 to 255, results in the packet coming back to the application without reaching the network media. The packet is copied from transmit to receive buffer on the same computer. This is why the IP address 127.*X.X.X* is called a *loopback* address. The software loopback address can be used as a quick check to see that the TCP/IP software is properly configured.

Although any address of the type 127.*X.X.X* indicates a loopback address, NetWare servers use the IP address 127.0.0.1; many Unix systems use a software loopback address of 127.1.

Special IP Addresses

A hostid value of 0 or all 1s is never assigned to an individual TCP/IP host. An IP address with a hostid value of 0 indicates the network itself. Therefore, the IP address of 137.53.0.0 indicates the class B network 137.53.

If the hostid value contains all 1s in the bit pattern, it indicates a directed broadcast address. A directed broadcast address is seen by all nodes on that network. Therefore, for the network number 137.53, the broadcast address is 137.153.255.255. The network number 137.53 is a class B address and has 16 bits in the hostid field. If 1s are used for the 16 bits of the hostid, they correspond to a decimal value of 255.255.

Another type of broadcast, called the *local broadcast*, is represented by the value of 255.255.255.255. This type of broadcast can be used in local area networks, where a broadcast never crosses a router boundary.

An important exception to all 1s in the hostid field used for broadcasts is TCP/IP software derived from 4.2 BSD Unix. 4.2 BSD Unix used the convention of all 0s in the hostid field to indicate a broadcast address. At the time 4.2 BSD Unix was written, the RFCs were unclear about the convention used for broadcast addresses. This was clarified in later RFCs, which stated that all 1s in the hostid field should be used for broadcast addresses. 4.3 BSD Unix was modified to conform to the RFCs.

Software derived from 4.2 BSD Unix, unless modified, can still use the all 0s broadcast convention. If hosts that use all 0s to broadcast are placed on the same physical network as hosts that use all 1s for broadcasts, the broadcast mechanism will not work as expected. A symptom of this is failure of TCP/IP applications on the specific network to work correctly.

An IP address of 0.0.0.0 is used to refer to the network itself. The 0.0.0.0 address is also used in routing tables to indicate the network entry for the default router's (often called *default gateway*) IP address.

Subnet Masks

After an IP network number has been assigned for a network, it is up to the network administrator to assign values for the host number field.

Consider an IP network number of 149.108.0.0. Sixteen bits are assignable for this network number, and this gives a total of 2^{16} possible host number combinations. Two to the power of 16 is equal to 65536. Out of 65536 combinations, the pattern consisting of all 1s (broadcast) cannot be used. In addition, the pattern consisting of all 0s (the network itself) should not be used for host number assignments. Thus, from a total of 65536 host numbers, two host numbers cannot be used, resulting in a total number of 65534 hosts (refer to table 2.12).

Figure 2.40 shows the network number 149.108.0.0 (called Network 1) connected to the Internet using a router. All traffic for network number 149.108.0.0 is sent to the router for that network. It is possible to have 65534 hosts on the network. If the network is inside a building, probably fewer than 65534 hosts will be on the same physical network in the building. However, the network does have the capacity to grow up to 65534 hosts, even though this may not be practical.

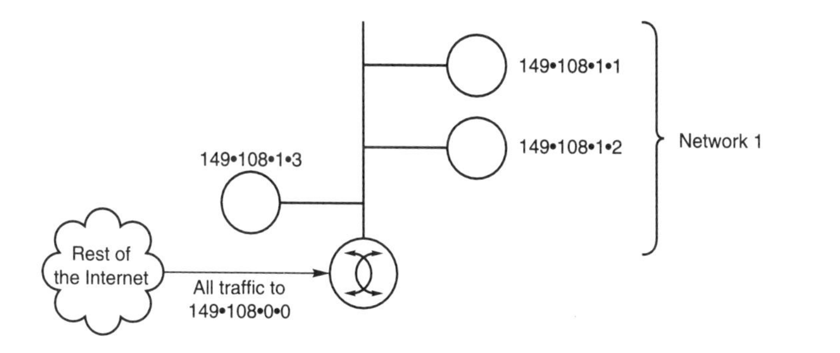

Figure 2.40
A class B network connected to the Internet.

If the organization decides to build a second network, perhaps in a separate building, and have this also connected to the Internet, what network number should the organization use? If the network number of 149.108.0.0 was also used for the new second network, then the first and the second networks will be the same because the IP router cannot distinguish between these by examining the netid field of the IP address for a host on these networks.

A different network number assignment that belongs to class A, B, or C could be used, but this involves applying for a new network number assignment even though many hostid bit patterns on network 1 are not in use and may never be used. A better way would be to use some of the bits in the hostid field for distinguishing between the two networks and leave the rest for the host number assignments. This scheme is called *subnetting*, and the resulting networks are called *subnets*. The scheme for subnetting is documented in RFC 950.

Figure 2.41 shows that a second network (Network 2) can be connected to the first network and the rest of the Internet using the same router used in figure 2.40, provided it had an extra unused port. In figure 2.41, the first byte of the hostid field is used to distinguish between the two networks; the bits used to distinguish between the two networks are called *subnet numbers*. Therefore, network 1 has been given a subnet number value of 1 and network 2 a subnet number value of 2.

Figure 2.41

A class B network connected to the Internet using subnets.

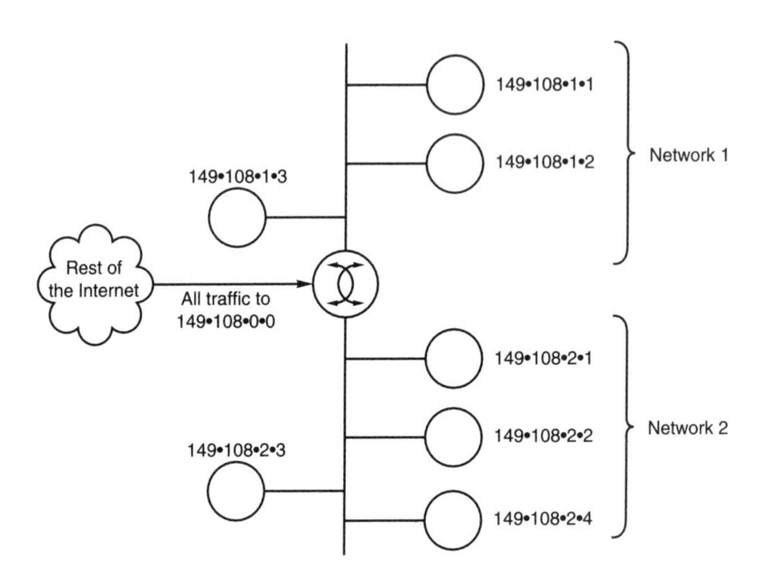

Subnetting is a scheme that enables you to break a network into smaller networks using the same network number assignment. The advantages of subnetting include the following:

- ◆ Simplified administration
- ◆ Restructuring of internal networks without affecting external networks
- ◆ Improved security

Simplified administration results from the capability to use routers to partition networks using logical boundaries. This often allows smaller networks to be administered independently and more efficiently. The smaller networks may even be managed by their own independent network administration staff. This type of setup even avoids or eliminates certain types of political problems between department staffs that may want to have greater control over their network.

The use of subnets allows the network to be structured internally without the rest of the connected network being aware of changes in the internal network. In figure 2.41, the internal network has been divided into two subnets, but external traffic coming from the internal network is still sent to the network address 149.108.0.0. It is up to the router (see fig. 2.41) that belongs to the organization to make a further distinction between IP addresses belonging to its subnets. An important benefit of the internal network being "invisible" to external networks is that an organization can achieve this internal restructuring without having to obtain an additional network number. With the internetwork running out of network numbers, this is a great advantage.

Because the structure of the internal subnetworks are not visible to external networks, use of subnets results in an indirect improvement in network security.

Figure 2.42 shows the relationship between the different fields of an IP address and subnetworks that have been discussed so far. If the subnets in figure 2.42 are to be connected, routers must be used between them. Moreover, the routers must understand that subnetting is being used and how many bits of the hostid field are being used for subnets.

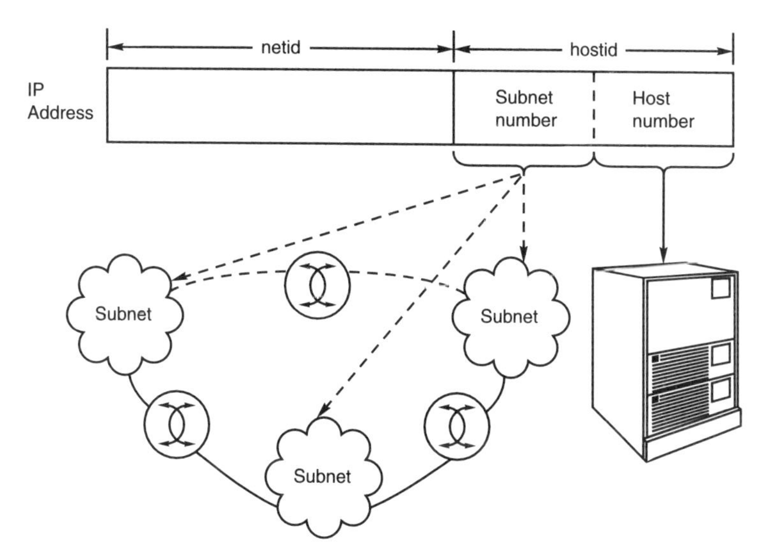

Figure 2.42

Subnets and subnet numbers.

The router in the example of figure 2.41 must be made to understand that the hostid field of the IP address is to be treated specially—a part of it used for the subnet number and the remaining part for the host number. This information is typically represented to the router as the subnet mask.

The subnet mask is used by routers and hosts on a subnet to interpret the hostid field in such a way that they can determine how many bits are being used for subnetting. The subnet mask divides the hostid field into the subnet number and the host number. The subnet mask is a 32-bit number whose value is formed by using the following rules:

- Ones (1s) in the subnet mask correspond to the position of the netid and subnet number in the IP address.
- Zeros (0s) in the subnet mask correspond to the position of the host number in the IP address.

Figure 2.43 shows an application of the previously stated rules. This figure shows a class B network number used for subnetting. Eight bits of the hostid field are being used for the subnet number. The resulting subnet mask is also shown in figure 2.43. The subnet mask is a 32-bit pattern and is conventionally written in a dotted decimal notation form. Because a group of eight 1s corresponds to a decimal value of 255, the subnet mask of figure 2.43 can be written in the following manner:

255.255.255.0

Figure 2.43

Subnet mask representation.

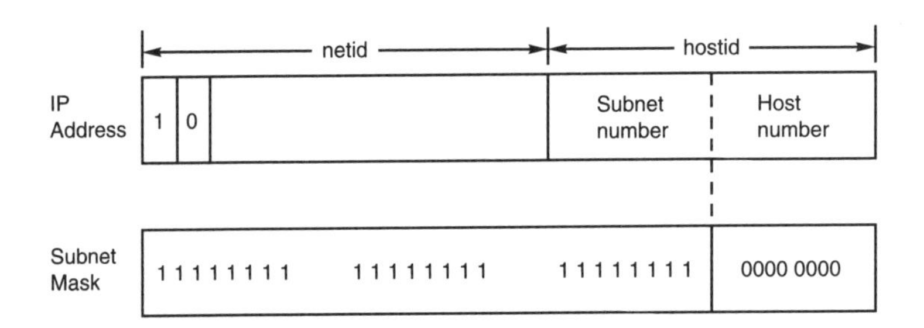

If a subnet mask value of 255.255.0.0 is used for a class B address, this would indicate that no subnetting is being used. A class B address has 16 bits of netid field. This netid field is accounted for by the first two 255s (255.255) in the 255.255.0.0 subnet mask value. The remaining value of 0.0 must correspond to the host number. No 1s are in the subnet mask for the subnet number or field, and therefore no subnetting is being used.

If the same subnet mask value of 255.255.0.0 was used for a class A address, it would indicate that subnetting is being used. A class A address has 8 bits of netid field. This netid field is accounted for by the first 255 in the 255.255.0.0 subnet mask value. The remaining 255 must correspond to the subnet number, which is 8 bits long.

If a subnet mask value of 255.255.255.0 is used for a class C address, this would indicate that no subnetting is being used. A class C address has 24 bits of netid field. This netid field is accounted for by the first three 255s (255.255.255) in the 255.255.255.0 subnet mask value. The remaining value of 0 must correspond to the host number. No 1s are in the subnet mask for the subnet number field, and therefore no subnetting is being used.

If a subnet mask value of 255.255.0.0 was used for a class C address, this would be an illegal value. A class C address has 24 bits of netid field, but the first two 255s in the 255.255.0.0 account for only 16 bits of the netid. There should be at least another 255 to cover the remaining 8 bits of netid.

The subnet mask value is usually required at the time you specify the IP address for a host or router. It can be expressed as the dotted decimal notation value seen in earlier examples. An alternate form used by some TCP/IP software is a hexadecimal pattern or a dotted hexadecimal notation. Therefore, a subnet mask of 255.255.255.0 can also be expressed in the following ways:

FFFFFF00(hex pattern)

0xFF.0xFF.0xFF.0xFF.0x00 (a dotted hexadecimal notation)

The dotted hexadecimal notation is an alternative form that can be used with NetWare's TCPIP.NLM. A subnet number (portion of the hostid field designated for subnetting) value of all 0 bits or all 1 bits is not permitted.

The subnet mask is usually stored in an internal database. For Unix systems, it can be stored in /etc/rc.local or /etc/netd.cf files. For NetWare, the subnet mask is stored in the SYS:ETC/AUTOEXEC.NCF file. On DOS/Windows implementations, it depends on the TCP/IP software. For example, LAN Workplace stores it in the NET.CFG file; NCSA's Telnet package uses the CONFIG.TEL file.

In retrospect, it might have been better if the designers of the subnet scheme had used an alternative representation different from the subnet mask to specify the number of bits to be used for subnetting. For instance, they could have designed the subnet mask so that the subnet is represented by a single number called the "subnet bits" that is the size of the subnet number field starting from the most significant part of the hostid field. Some software, such as FTP Software, Inc.'s PC/TCP, enables you to specify subnetting in precisely this manner. With this software, the TCP/IP software could figure out the subnet mask values based on this information, which would have prevented several generations of network administrators from becoming confused about subnet masks!

The problem with subnet masks is that administrators often must work with unfamiliar bit (or hex) patterns. For a systems programmer working in assembly or C/C++ languages, working with bit patterns is natural and easy, but for ordinary mortals such as network administrators it can be a daunting task.

If you are having difficulties grasping subnet masks, do not despair. The basic idea is simple; it is just working with bits that may be unfamiliar. Practice using the examples in this chapter to help you understand their layout.

RFC 950 contains a detailed description of the subnetting procedure.

Conversion between Decimal and Binary Numbers

As you work through the following examples of subnet masks and IP addresses, you will come across situations in which you need to convert between decimal numbers and their binary values. This section is a short tutorial in performing these conversions.

First, examine the problem of converting a binary number to a decimal value. You later learn how to convert a decimal number to its binary form.

Consider an 8-bit binary pattern of 10101000 whose decimal value you need to find to solve an IP address problem. Please note that, because IP addresses are typically represented in a dotted decimal notation in which 8 bits of the IP address are converted to a decimal value, only 8-bit patterns are discussed in this section.

The binary number of 10101000 uses a base 2 system, just as a decimal number such as 143 uses a base 10 system.

The term *bit* is commonly used to describe a 1 or 0 and is a contraction of the words *b*inary digi*t*. Binary means a value of 2, and therefore bit patterns use a base 2 system just as decimal numbers use a base 10 system.

In a decimal number such as 143, the 1 represents the 100's position; the 4 represents the 10's position; and the 3 represent the 1's position. The digit 1 represents the 100's position because two digits are to the right of it. The two digits to the right of 1 correspond to a magnitude of 10 to the power of 2 (10^2), or 100. Similarly, the digit 4 in the number 143 represents the 10's position because one digit is to the right of it. The 1 digit to the right of 4 corresponds to magnitude of 10 to the power of 1, or 10. Finally, the digit 3 in the number 143 represents the 1's position because zero digits are to the right of it. The 0 digits to the right of 4 correspond to magnitude of 10 to the power of 0, or 1.

Now consider again the bit pattern of 10101000. The 1 in the left-most position of this bit pattern has seven bits to the right of it. This 1 must correspond to a magnitude of 2 to the power of 7, or 2^7. The value of 2^7 is 128. You can use table 2.15 to find the decimal value for the powers of 2 up to 7, or you can use a simple mathematics trick to find out the decimal value. 2^7 can be expressed as a product of 2^3, 2^3, and 2, as shown in the following:

$$2^7 = 2^3 \times 2^3 \times 2^1 = 8 \times 8 \times 2 = 128$$

In the preceding equation, the index 7 has been expressed as the sum of 3 + 3 + 1.

The next 1 in the bit pattern of 10101000 has five bits to the right of it. It's magnitude is 2^5 or 32 (see table 2.15). The remaining 1 in the bit pattern of 10101000, has three bits to the right of it. Its magnitude is 2^3 or 8. You could write the bit pattern of 10101000 in the following form:

$$10101000 = 1 \times 2^7 + 0 \times 2^6 + 1 \times 2^5 + 0 \times 2^4 + 1 \times 2^3 + 0 \times 2^2 + 0 \times 2 + 0 \times 1$$

$$= 128 + 32 + 8 = 168$$

Table 2.15 Powers of 2

Power of 2	Decimal value
2^0	1
2^1	2
2^2	4
2^3	8
2^4	16
2^5	32
2^6	64
2^7	128

Now consider the problem of converting the number 145 to a binary 8-bit pattern. One way of performing this conversion is to use entries in table 2.15 and express 145 as the sum of powers of 2. This can be done as follows:

$144 = 128 + 16 + 1 = 2^7 + 2^4 + 2^0$

From the preceding discussion, 2^7 consists of a binary pattern of 1 with 7 0s after it. 2^4 consists of a binary pattern of 1 with 4 0s after it. 2^0 consists of a binary pattern of 1 with no 0s after it.

$2^7 = 10000000$

$2^4 = 00010000$

$2^0 = 00000001$

Adding up these bit patterns yields the following answer:

$144 = 128 + 16 = 10000000 + 00010000 + 00000001 = 10010001$ (binary pattern)

You can use the table in 2.15 to convert base 10 numbers to binary patterns or use an alternate technique, which uses the following rules:

1. Divide the number by 2. Call the quotient (whole number) of the division Q, and the remainder R.
2. Place the remainder R in the binary pattern. The placement of the remainder (0 or a 1 because you are dividing by 2) starts with the right-most position and gradually works its way to the left.
3. Use the quotient Q as the number to divide in step 1. Repeat this process until the quotient becomes a zero.

Apply these rules to convert 145 to a binary pattern:

Round 1:

Divide 145 by 2.

Quotient is 72.

Remainder is 1.

Bit pattern is 1.

Round 2:

Divide 72 by 2.

Quotient is 36.

Remainder is 0.

Bit pattern is 01.

Round 3:

Divide 36 by 2.

Quotient is 18.

Remainder is 0.

Bit pattern is 001.

Round 4:

Divide 18 by 2.

Quotient is 9.

Remainder is 0.

Bit pattern is 0001.

Round 5:

Divide 9 by 2.

Quotient is 4.

Remainder is 1.

Bit pattern is 10001.

Round 6:

Divide 4 by 2.

Quotient is 2.

Remainder is 0.

Bit pattern is 010001.

Round 7:

Divide 2 by 2.

Quotient is 1.

Remainder is 0.

Bit pattern is 0010001.

Round 8:

Divide 1 by 2.

Quotient is 0 (stop the algorithm).

Remainder is 1.

Bit pattern is 10010001.

Because the quotient is a 0, you stop the conversion. The resulting bit pattern of 10010001 is the answer.

Subnet Example Problem: Using Class B Address with Subnet Mask on a Byte Boundary

Given the following IP address and subnet mask values:

IP address = 128.12.34.71

Subnet Mask = 255.255.255.0

What is the value of the following:

Subnet number = ?

Host number = ?

Directed broadcast address = ?

Examine the subnet mask of 255.255.255.0. You can see that the division of 1s and 0s in the subnet mask fall on a byte boundary. The byte boundary simplifies the calculation.

The IP address 128.12.34.71 is a class B address because 128 is between 128 and 191 (see table 2.14). The first two 255s of the subnet mask of 255.255.255.0 correspond to the 16 bits of a class B *netid.* The remaining 255 must therefore correspond to the subnet number on the IP address. Therefore, the subnet number is 34. To express this in the dotted decimal notation, you would type the following:

Subnet number = 0.0.34.0

The 0 in the subnet mask of 255.255.255.0 corresponds to the host number. The host number in the IP address must be 71. To express this in the dotted decimal notation, you would type the following:

Host number = 0.0.0.71

The directed broadcast for the network must have all 1s in the host number field. Therefore, the last byte of the subnet must have all 1s. To express this in the dotted decimal notation, you would type the following:

Directed broadcast address = 128.12.34.255

Subnet Example Problem: Using Class C Address with Subnet Mask on a Non-Byte Boundary

Given the following IP address and subnet mask values:

IP address = 192.55.12.120

Subnet Mask = 255.255.255.240

What is the value of the following:

Subnet number = ?

Host number = ?

Directed broadcast address = ?

When you examine the subnet mask of 255.255.255.240, you can see that the division of 1s and 0s in the subnet mask is in the last byte on a bit boundary. The bit boundary complicates the calculation.

As an aid to computing the desired values, the bit patterns for the various values to be computed are shown in figure 2.44.

The IP address 192.55.12.120 is a class C address because 192 is between 192 and 223 (see table 2.14). The first three 255s of the subnet mask of 255.255.255.240 correspond to the 24 bits of a class C *netid.* The remaining 240 must therefore correspond to the subnet number on the IP address. The decimal value 240 has a bit pattern of 1110000. The following is the subnet mask represented as a bit pattern:

11111111 11111111 11111111 11110000

The last four 1s correspond to the subnet number field in the IP address. The following is the bit pattern representation of the IP address with the subnet field highlighted in bold:

11000000 00110111 00001100 **0111**1000

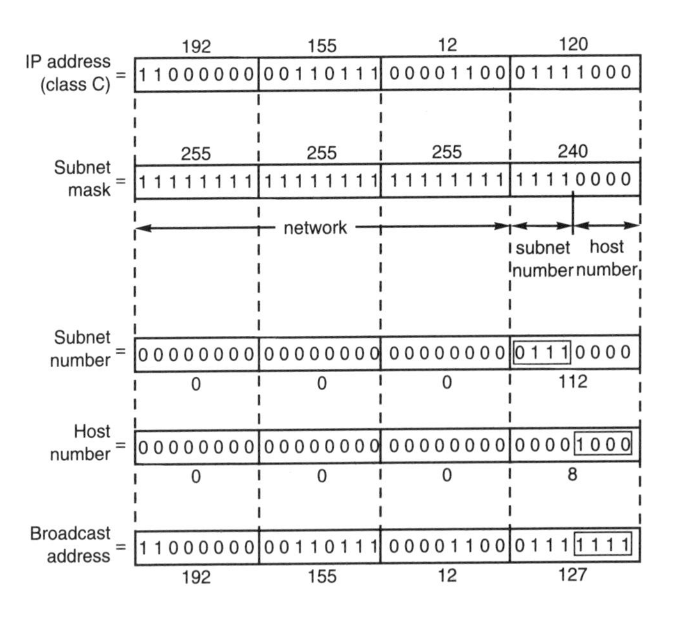

Figure 2.44

Subnet example solution.

The subnet number field bit pattern of 0111 has a decimal value of 7, but this value is part of the last 8-bit value of the IP address. The subnet number expressed as a bit pattern is shown here:

00000000 00000000 00000000 01110000

The subnet number expressed in the dotted decimal notation is shown here:

Subnet number =0.0.0.112

The 0s in the subnet mask of 255.255.255.240 correspond to the host number. The host number in the IP address is shown in bold in the IP address pattern:

11000000 00110111 00001100 0111**1000**

The host number expressed as a bit pattern is shown here:

00000000 00000000 00000000 00001000

The host number expressed in the dotted decimal notation is shown here:

Subnet number = 0.0.0.8

The directed broadcast for the network must have all 1s in the host number field. Therefore, the last four bits of the subnet must have all 1s.

The directed broadcast address expressed as a bit pattern is shown here:

11000000 00110111 00001100 0111**1111**

The directed broadcast address expressed in the dotted decimal notation is shown here:

Directed broadcast address = 192.55.12.127

Non-Byte Boundary Subnet Masks

In the preceding example, a subnet mask of 255.255.255.240 is used. The last decimal number 240 translated into a bit pattern of 11110000. In general, it is useful to know the bit pattern representations when a subnet number field of 1 to 7 bits is used. Table 2.16 shows the decimal subnet size, and the decimal values in the subnet mask. The table assumes that the subnet number bits are all contiguous. This is normally true for most real-world networks.

TABLE 2.16 SUBNET SIZE AND DECIMAL VALUES

Subnet Size(bits)	Bit Pattern	Decimal Value
1	10000000	128
2	11000000	192
3	11100000	224
4	11110000	240
5	11111000	248
6	11111100	252
7	11111110	254

The RFCs do not prohibit the subnet numbers from being non-contiguous. That is, it is possible to have a subnet mask where the subnet number bits and host number bits may alternate! For example, it is possible to have the following subnet mask for a class B address:

11111111 11111111 **10110101 00001111**

or

255.255.171.15

In this subnet mask, nine subnet number bits (bold in the bit pattern) exist, but they are interspersed with the host number bits.

Even though the RFCs allow such monstrosities, most TCP/IP software will not function with non-contiguous subnet number bits. No useful purpose is served in using such subnet masks, except to confound future network administrators.

Answering IP Address and Subnet Mask Questions

This section provides the solutions to some typical IP address and subnet mask questions.

1. What is the network address of a TCP/IP host that has an IP address of 203.23.32.34?

Answer: 203.23.32

Reason: The address 203.23.32.34 is a class C address (see table 2.14). For a class C address, the first three bytes are the network address. Therefore, the first three bytes of 203.23.32.34 are the network address.

2. What is the node (or host) address of a TCP/IP host that has an IP address of 182.23.32.34?

Answer: 32.34

Reason: The address 182.23.32.34 is a class B address (see table 2.14). For a class B address, the first two bytes are the network address, and the last two bytes are the host address. Therefore, the last two bytes of 182.23.32.34 are the node address.

3. What is the subnet mask for 184.231.138.239, if first ten bits of node address is used for subnetting?

   A. 255.255.192.0

   B. 255.255.224.0

   C. 255.255.255.224

   D. 255.255.255.192

Answer: Choice D (255.255.255.192)

Reason: The IP address 184.231.138.239 is a class B address. This means that the first two bytes of 184.231.138.192 are the network address. Its subnet mask must have two bytes of all 1s for the first two bytes of the network address. In addition, because the first ten bits of the host address (also called node address) are used for subnetting, ten bits of all 1s must follow the 1s corresponding to the network address field. The subnet mask will therefore be the following:

11111111 11111111 **11111111 11**000000

The bits in bold in the subnet mask correspond to the subnet number. The dotted decimal value of this subnet mask is as follows:

255.255.255.192

4. Which of the following hosts must use a router to communicate with the host 129.23.144.10 if the subnet mask is 255.255.192.0?

   A. 129.23.191.21

   B. 129.23.127.222

   C. 129.23.130.33

   D. 129.23.148.127

Answer: Choice B (129.23.127.222)

Reason: The subnet mask of 255.255.192.0 translates to a bit pattern of

11111111 11111111 **11**000000 00000000

The address 129.23.144.10 is a class B address (see table 2.14). The first two bytes of the class B address are the network address. In the subnet mask of 255.255.192.0, the first two bytes cover the network address of the class B address. The last two bytes, 192.0, describe the subnet mask. In the previously stated bit representation of the subnet mask, the subnet bits are shown in bold. The subnet mask 255.255.192.0 has two subnet bits.

The IP address of 123.23.144.10 has a host address (*hostid*) of 144.10. Because the subnet mask of 255.255.192.0 is used, the first two bits of this host address are the subnet number. If you convert 144.10 to a binary pattern, you receive

10010000 00001010

The subnet bits are the first two bits of 10. Hosts that have the bit pattern of 10 in these first two bits of the host address (subnet number) will be on the same network and will not require a router to communicate with each other. A host that has a different subnet number (different value from 10 in the first two bits of host address) will require a router to communicate with host 123.23.144.10. The previously stated question becomes one of finding the first two bits of the host address for the following:

129.23.191.21

129.23.127.222

129.23.130.33

129.23.148.127

The host address of 129.23.191.21 is 191.21, which converts into the following:

- The bit pattern of 191.21 is 10111111 00010101.
- Subnet bits are 10, which is the same as subnet bits for 123.23.144.10.

The host address of 129.23.127.222 is 127.222, which converts into the following:

- The bit pattern of 127.222 is 01111111 11011110.
- Subnet bits are 01, *different* from subnet bits for 123.23.144.10.

The host address of 129.23.130.33 is 130.33, which converts into the following:

- The bit pattern of 130.33 is 10000010 00100001.
- Subnet bits are 10, which is the same as subnet bits for 123.23.144.10.

The host address of 129.23.148.127 is 148.127, which converts into the following:

- The bit pattern of 148.127 is 10010100 01111111.
- Subnet bits are 10, which is the same as subnet bits for 123.23.144.10.

The only host with a subnet number different from 123.23.144.10 is 129.23.127.222. Therefore, the answer to the question is the host 129.23.127.222.

You may have observed that only the bit pattern of the third byte was needed because the subnet number was in this byte. You could have just converted the third byte to a binary number and examined the first two bits of the IP addresses.

5. Which IP address is located on the same subnet as 130.12.127.231 if the subnet mask is 255.255.192.0?

   A. 130.45.130.1

   B. 130.22.130.1

   C. 130.12.64.23

   D. 130.12.167.127

Answer: Choice C (130.12.64.23)

Reason: All choices have a class B address, but choices A and B can be eliminated because they have network addresses of 130.45 and 130.22, which are different from the network address of host 130.12.120.231. Because choices A and B have different network addresses than 130.12, they cannot be on the same subnetwork.

Choices C and D are on the same class B network because they have the same network address of 130.12, but you are informed that subnetting is in use. Therefore, these addresses could be on different subnets. The subnet mask is 255.255.192.0. This subnet mask has a bit representation of

11111111 11111111 **11**000000 00000000

The first two bytes of all 1s in the subnet mask correspond to the network address of the class B address. The 1s in the third byte correspond to the subnet number. Only the first two bits of the first byte host address (*hostid*) are used as a subnet number. Because of this, you need only examine the third byte of the IP address to answer the question.

The subnet number of IP address 130.12.127.231 is in the third byte. The third byte, which has a value of 127, has a bit pattern of

01111111

The subnet number is the first two bits and has a value of 01.

The third byte of IP address 130.12.64.23 is 64. This has a bit pattern of

01000000

The subnet number is the first two bits and has a value of 01.

The third byte of IP address 130.12.167.63 is 167. This has a bit pattern of

10100111

The subnet number is the first two bits and has a value of 10.

Only the IP address 130.12.64.23 has the same subnet number as the IP address 130.12.127.231, and therefore the answer is 130.12.64.23.

Using Different Subnet Masks for a Network

In the examples covered so far, the same subnet mask was used for a given network. For a network address of 134.65.0.0, a class B address, the subnet mask could be 255.255.255.0, which means that eight bits of the host address field are used for subnetting. TCP/IP enables you to use different subnet masks for the same network address of 134.65.0.0. For example, a subdivided network of the network 134.65.0.0 could use a subnet mask of 255.255.255.192 whereas another uses a subnet mask of 255.255.255.0. When different subnet masks are used, there are restrictions on what combinations of host IP addresses and subnet masks can be used. Setting up such subnet masks requires advanced knowledge and skill in bit manipulation and is beyond the scope of this book.

Novell documentation explicitly warns about using different subnet masks for a network address, and recommends against its use. The current RIP algorithm used on NetWare servers does not handle a mix of different subnet masks for the same network address. As a result of this RIP limitation, the network topology reported by RIP would not accurately reflect the network topology that you have set up.

Need for Address Resolution

The DNS is used to provide an association between symbolic names for host and the IP address. Knowing the symbolic name, a host can discover the corresponding IP address. To transmit a message to a host on a network with a broadcast capability, such as in Ethernet and token ring, the sender must know the hardware address of the destination host. The hardware address, also called the MAC (Media Access Control) address, is needed in the MAC header of the packet used to send a message. The host software knows the IP address of the destination by using DNS or a table lookup. Figure 2.45 shows the problem of determining the hardware address of the destination host.

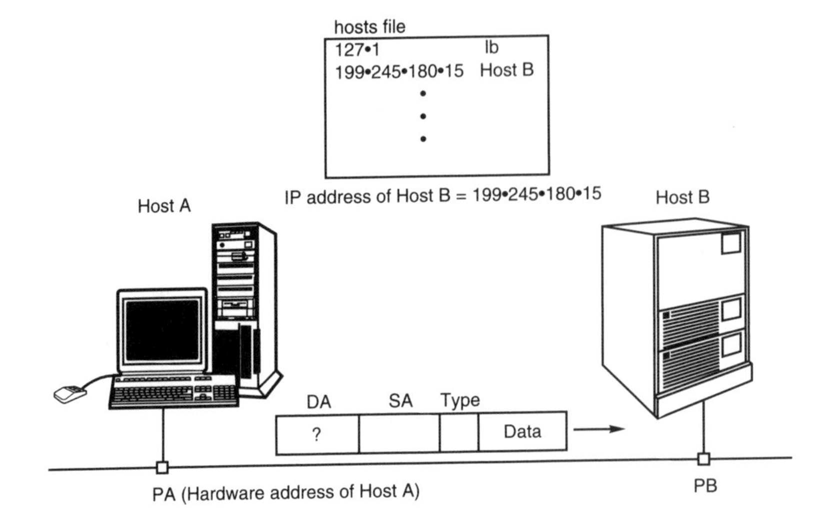

Figure 2.45

Need for address resolution.

Determining MAC Address

One method of solving the problem was to use a table of IP address and MAC address associations similar to the hosts file table discussed earlier. The problem with this approach is that if a network board is replaced on a host, the MAC address will probably change, and this table will have to be updated. If the network board was changed by a technician, it is unlikely that he or she will inform the administrator of this change immediately.

A more flexible scheme is needed to dynamically determine the MAC address knowing a host's IP address. This dynamic mechanism is implemented as a separate protocol called the *Address Resolution Protocol.*

Address Resolution Protocol (ARP)

Figure 2.46 shows how ARP works. In this figure, Host A wants to determine the hardware address of destination B before it sends a message.

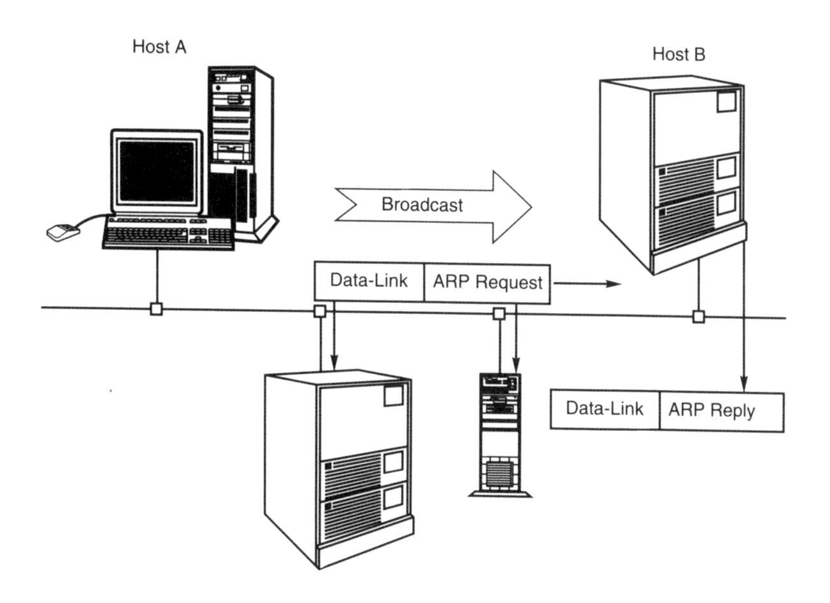

Figure 2.46
ARP operation.

Host A sends a MAC broadcast frame called the *ARP request frame* on the network. The ARP request frame contains the sender Host A's IP and MAC address and the destination B's IP address. The ARP request frame contains a place-holder field for destination B's hardware address. All nodes on the physical network receive the broadcast ARP request frame. All other nodes that receive the broadcast frame will compare its IP address to the IP address in the ARP request. Only the host that has the same IP address as the one requested in the ARP request frame will respond.

If Host B exists on the network, it will respond with its IP address encoded in an ARP reply frame. The Host A initializes its ARP cache table (kept in RAM) with the answer contained in the ARP reply. The ARP cache entries are timed out after a certain period, which can be configured in some TCP/IP implementations. Typically, the ARP cache time-out is 10 minutes. After an ARP cache entry has timed-out for a specific host, the ARP request frame is sent again to discover the host's hardware address.

Many TCP/IP implementations enable you to make manual entries in the ARP cache table. Normally, no need exists to make manual entries in the ARP table; the dynamic ARP operation determines the IP address and hardware associations. ARP entries made manually are not timed out and can be used to fix problems with incorrect entries in the ARP table because of duplicate IP address problems or malfunctioning software.

The assumption in the operation of the ARP protocol is that the underlying physical network supports a broadcast capability. This is true in LANs such as Ethernet, token ring, FDDI, and ARCnet.

Note Other related address resolution protocols, besides the ARP protocol, are RARP (Reverse Address Resolution Protocol) and Proxy ARP.

RARP is used to discover the IP address, when the hardware address is known, and can be used in diskless workstations. RARP is described in RFC 903.

Proxy ARP can be used in networks that use old TCP/IP software that does not understand subnetting. Proxy ARP is described in RFC 1027.

Summary

This chapter explored the TCP/IP layering concepts in terms of the OSI reference and DoD models. These models were explained as an aid to understanding how TCP/IP components interact with each other. The different classes of IP address were explained, and you learned how IP networks can be divided into smaller networks called subnets. Most large networks use subnets, and it is important for administrators of these networks to understand when subnets are needed and how to use subnet masks to describe subnetting.

Toward the end of this chapter, you also learned about the more common network technologies, such as Ethernet and token ring, that can be used with TCP/IP.

Managing Basic TCP/IP Protocol Elements in NetWare

This chapter discusses the features of NetWare TCP/IP implementation on NetWare 3.x and 4.x servers. The NetWare TCP/IP support implemented by the TCPIP.NLM is outlined. As you read through this chapter, you will learn the names and contents of the configuration files that work with TCP/IP software and the procedure and parameters used to configure the TCP/IP stack on NetWare servers.

Overview of NetWare TCP/IP

NetWare TCP/IP support exists at the workstation and the server (see fig. 3.1). At the workstation, the following products from Novell implement TCP/IP support:

- ◆ LAN WorkPlace
- ◆ LAN WorkGroup

At the server, TCP/IP support is implemented by the TCPIP.NLM and a number of support NLMs. The focus of this chapter is primarily on TCP/IP support at the NetWare server. TCP/IP support at the workstation is beyond the scope of this book.

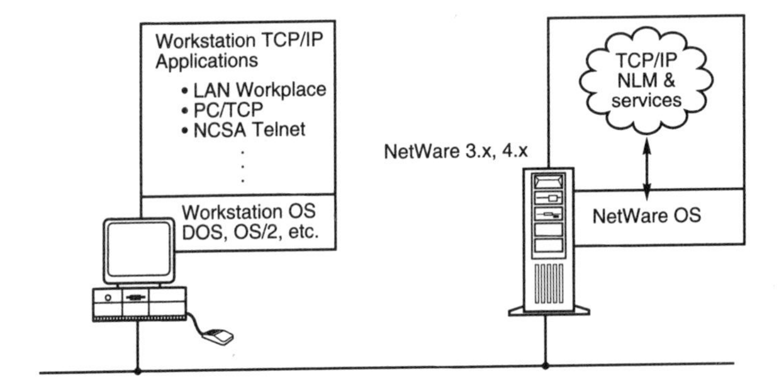

Figure 3.1

Server versus workstation.

NetWare TCP/IP Features

NetWare TCP/IP NLMs implement the following functionality:

- ◆ Network management using SNMP
- ◆ IP routing
- ◆ IP tunneling

The TCP/IP NLMs that come with NetWare do not implement application services such as NetWare NFS, Mail gateways, or FTP. These services are purchased as separate products.

Network Management Using SNMP

The NetWare TCP/IP NLMs come with an SNMP agent implemented by SNMP.NLM. This SNMP agent runs on NetWare servers and allow an SNMP manager to obtain information about TCP/IP network statistics and parameters on the NetWare server. The SNMP manager could be a third-party product such as Hewlett-Packard's OpenView or Sun Microsystems's SUN NetManager. Novell provides a simple SNMP manager that is implemented by TCPCON.NLM.

Figure 3.2 shows how SNMP can be used on a network. The SNMP manager in this figure is implemented by the TCPCON.NLM. The TCPCON.NLM can be used to query devices on the network that have an SNMP agent. Such a device could include a NetWare server that is running the SNMP.NLM.

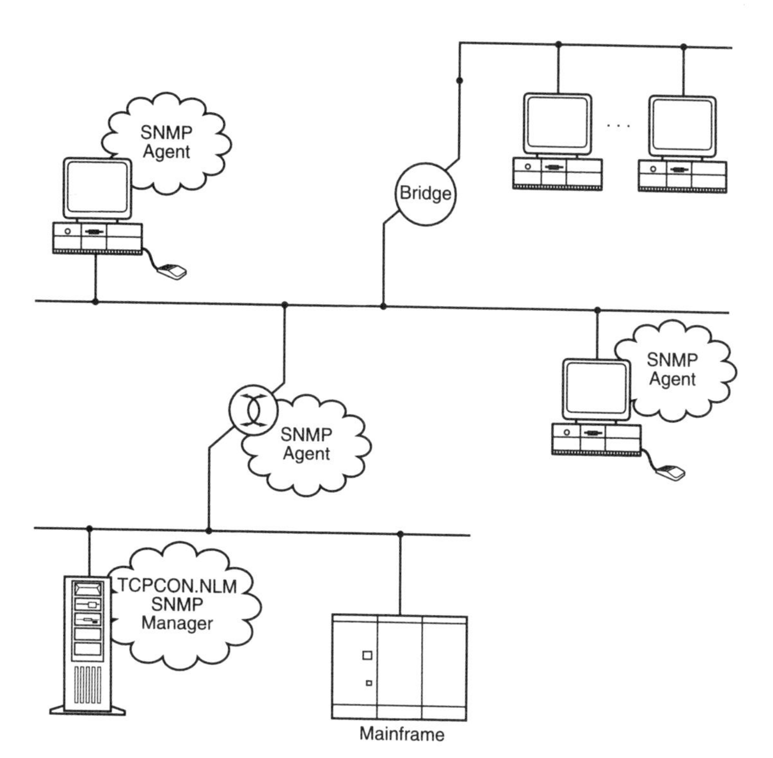

Figure 3.2

Example of network using SNMP.

IP Routing

NetWare TCP/IP NLMs on a NetWare server can be configured to forward IP packets between networks. A NetWare server with this configuration acts as an IP router. Figure 3.3 shows an example of a NetWare server acting as an IP router. The NetWare server must have an NIC for each network it connects to. At a minimum, it must have two NIC boards. The NetWare server can also act as a file server and provide IP routing functions, or it can be configured as an IP router only. The NetWare server can also act as a router for other protocols such as IPX and AppleTalk.

Figure 3.3

IP routing on a NetWare server.

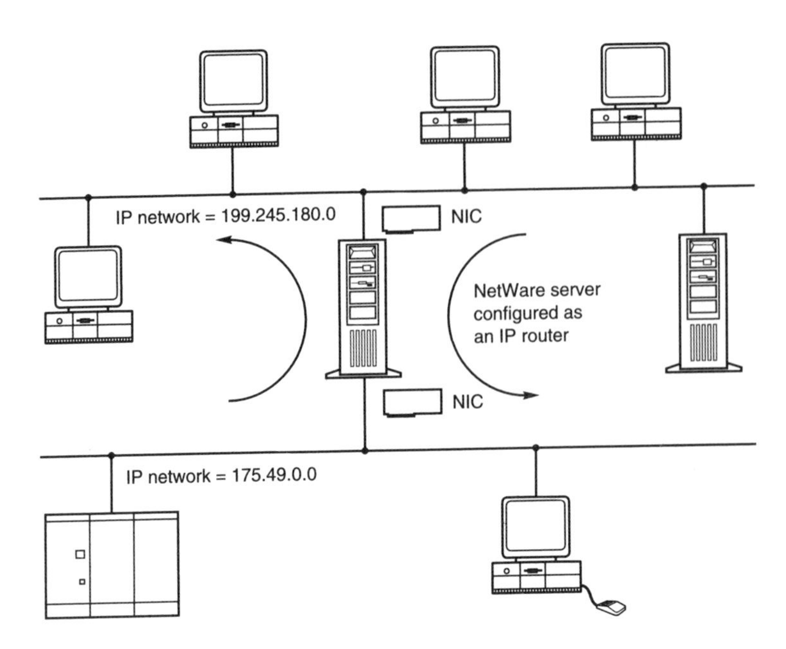

IPX Tunneling

Consider two IPX networks, network A and network B, that are far apart and not directly connected to each other (see fig. 3.4). If the networks are a considerable distance apart, they can be connected by a leased line, frame relay, X.25, or other wide area network technologies. If a connection is available through a TCP/IP network such as the Internet, however, it may be cost effective for the two IPX networks to use the TCP/IP network to connect with each other. The problem here is that a TCP/IP network does not understand IPX packets. An IP router will reject an IPX packet and prevents its transmission because it does not understand IPX packets. One way of solving this problem is to disguise the IPX packet as an IP packet for transmission across an IP network. This is done by a technique known as *IPX tunneling*.

In IPX tunneling, the IPX packets are encapsulated by IP packets for delivery across IP networks (see fig. 3.5). *Encapsulation* means that the IPX packet is treated as data inside a UDP/IP packet. The IP header contains the information needed by the IP routers to transmit the encapsulated IPX packet to the destination network. The UDP header is used to identify the port number used for the encapsulation and decapsulation process at source and destination. The UDP port number 213 has been assigned for this purpose.

When the NetWare server on the destination network receives an IP packet on UDP port number 213, the server knows that this packet contains an IPX packet. A decapsulation process waiting on this port decapsulates the IP packet to obtain the original IPX packet.

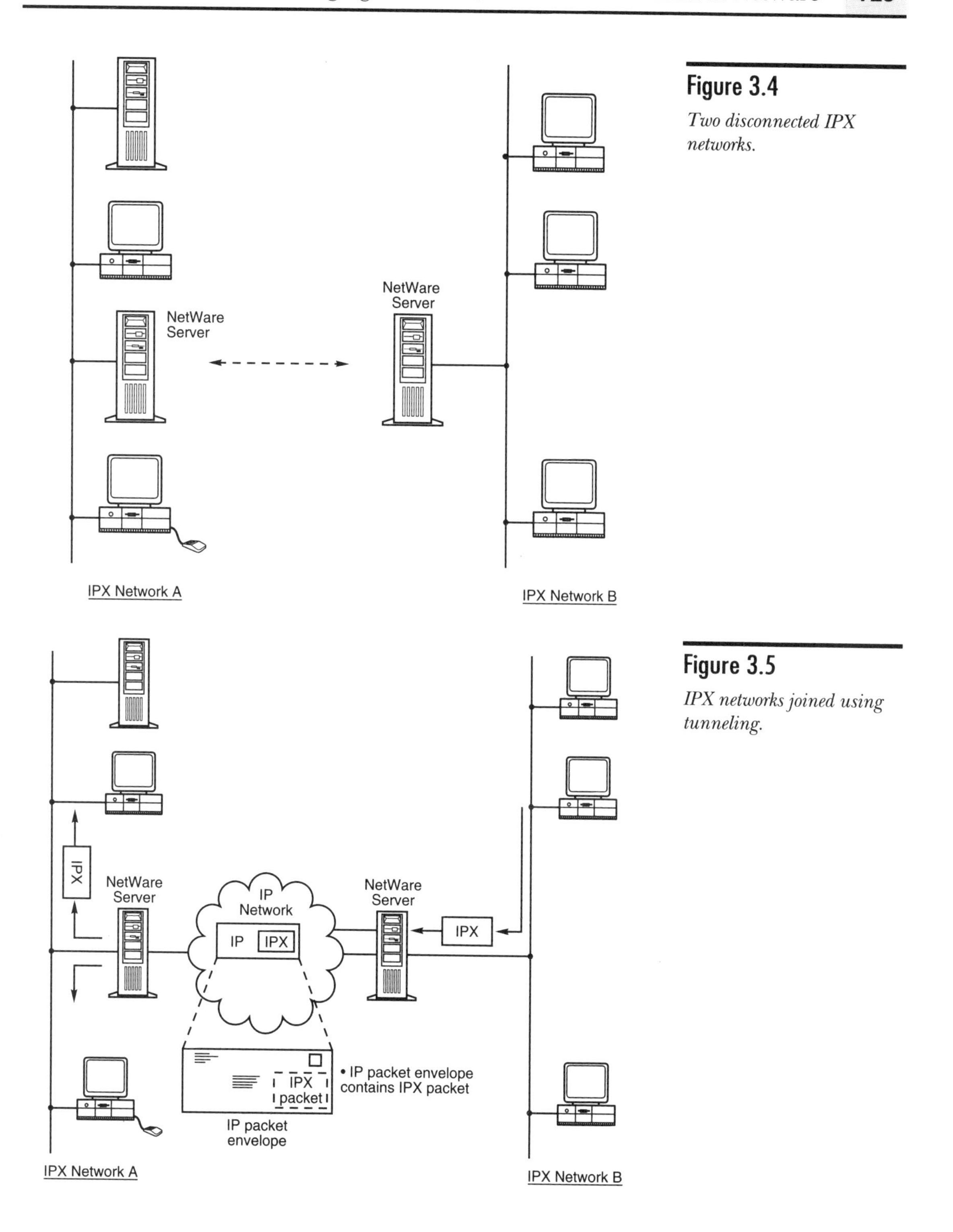

Figure 3.4

Two disconnected IPX networks.

Figure 3.5

IPX networks joined using tunneling.

Other NetWare TCP/IP Application Support

The TCP/IP support that comes with NetWare 3.x and 4.x products provides the TCP/IP transport and network protocol stack support. TCP/IP applications such as NFS services, mail gateway services, and TCP/IP development must be purchased separately. The following are the services and products that use the TCPIP.NLM:

- NFS and Line printer daemon
- Mail gateway
- TCP/IP developer's toolkit

Figure 3.6 shows these services using the TCP/IP protocol stack (TCPIP.NLM) that is included with the NetWare operating system.

Figure 3.6

Other TCP/IP products.

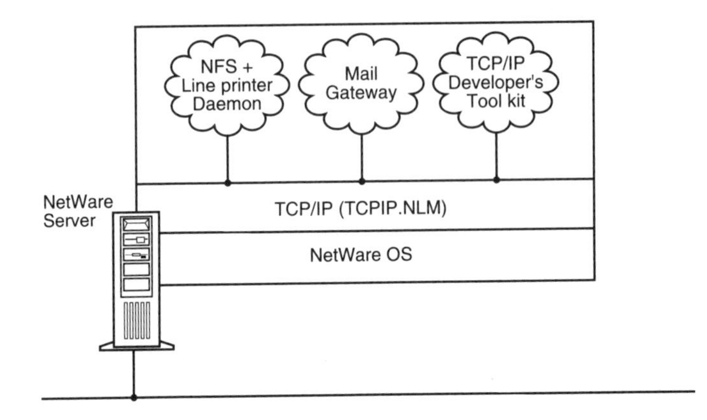

NFS and Line Printer Daemon Support

The NFS services and line printer daemon (LPD) support are available through the separate NetWare NFS product. NetWare NFS enables a NetWare server to act as an NFS server. NFS (Network File System) is the de facto method used on Unix systems to provide a distributed and remote file system on the network. When NFS is run on a NetWare server, Unix clients can access the file services on a NetWare server as if it were on the local Unix machine. Unix clients can also send print jobs to the NetWare NFS server through a line printer daemon that runs on the NetWare server. The line printer daemon is included with the NetWare NFS product. NetWare NFS also includes print gateway services that allow NetWare clients to send print jobs to a Unix printer.

The NetWare NFS product is discussed in detail in Chapter 11, "Internetworking with NetWare NFS."

Mail Gateway

The *mail gateway* is a separate product and provides conversion between Simple Mail Transfer Protocol (SMTP) and Novell's Message Handling System (MHS) messaging standard. With the SMTP mail gateway product, users of MHS mail can exchange e-mail with SMTP mail users. SMTP is used on the Internet; if an Internet connection is available, MHS users can exchange e-mail with users on the Internet.

TCP/IP Developer's Kit

The *TCP/IP developer's kit* is a separate product available for developers to write custom TCP/IP applications. Two popular programming interfaces are used with TCP/IP—the sockets interface and the Transport Layer Interface (TLI). The sockets interface has been popularized by BSD Unix. Many applications have been written that use the sockets interface. Programs written to these programming interfaces can be easily ported to the NetWare operating system.

The TLI interface was developed by AT&T and is a standard part of System V Release 4 Unix. Figure 3.7 shows the 4.3 BSD sockets and TLI interfaces to the NetWare TCP/IP. The Streams interface is used to provide a uniform interface to different transport protocols.

The BSD sockets interface is built into the CLIB.NLM. Use of the TLI interface requires the STREAMS.NLM and the TLI.NLM, which are part of the standard NetWare software. The STREAMS.NLM is autoloaded by the CLIB.NLM if it has not been loaded on the NetWare server.

NetWare TCP/IP Configuration

Figure 3.7 shows that Streams provides a common programming interface to different types of transport protocols. In a similar manner, the *Open Data-link Interface* (ODI) is used to provide a common interface for transport protocols so that these protocols can share an NIC or communicate with a different NIC.

To configure the TCP/IP interface, you must configure the following interfaces:

- The ODI interface
- The TCP/IP protocol stack

The ODI Interface

Figure 3.8 shows the ODI interface supporting multiple transport protocols, such as TCP/IP, SPX/IPX, and AppleTalk.

Figure 3.7

Programming interfaces for NetWare TCP/IP.

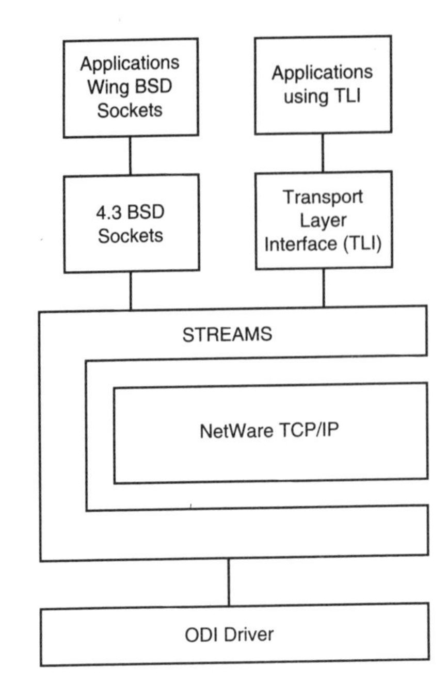

Figure 3.8

The ODI interface.

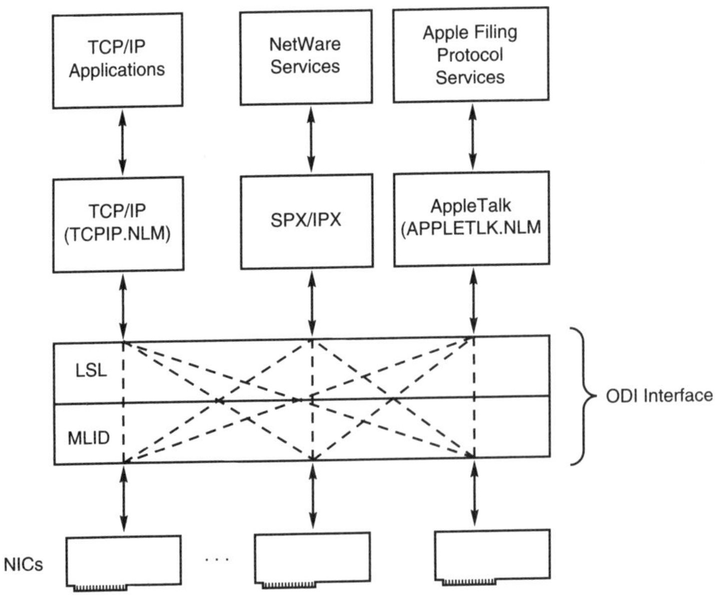

The ODI interface provides network adapters with the capability to support different network protocols. Prior to ODI and similar mechanisms (NDIS, Packet Driver—now called Crynwr drivers), a separate driver had to be written for each protocol stack. It was difficult to get these separate drivers to coexist on a workstation, making it difficult to support more than one protocol stack.

The key components of ODI layers are the Link Support Layer (LSL) and the Multiple Link Interface Driver (MLID). The *Link Support Layer* provides a logical view of the network adapter. The transport protocols are written to interface with this logical view.

On NetWare workstations, the Link Support Layer has to be loaded as a separate module. On NetWare servers there is no separate Link Support Layer NLM. The Link Support function is integrated into the operating system kernel.

The Ethernet, Token Ring, and ARCnet networking technologies correspond to the first and second layers of the OSI model. NE2000.LAN, TOKEN.LAN, and RXNET.LAN are examples of MLID drivers used at the NetWare server. Other types of network boards can have different names. These drivers correspond to a portion of the data link layer.

The drivers are written to interface with the Link Support Layer. The LSL, which does not map well onto the OSI model, represents the boundary between the data link and the network layers. Because the LSL provides the interface between MLID drivers and the upper layer protocols, the LSL can be thought of as covering a portion of the data link layer and the lower portion of the network layer of the OSI model.

The LSL is a key element in the ODI specification. It *virtualizes* the network adapter by providing a logical view of the network adapter. The network layer software does not have to be rewritten to understand the low-level mechanics and operational details of a new network adapter. The network layer software "sees" a well-defined virtual interface to any network adapter. The well-defined virtual interface means that protocol stacks can be written to interface with the network adapter in a standard way.

The practical significance of the virtual interface is that the network layer protocol needs to be written just once to this virtual interface. When a new type of network adapter is built, the manufacturer writes an MLID driver for it that can hook into the LSL layer. The LSL provides the same virtual interface to this board, and the protocol software does not need to be rewritten for the new network adapter.

The same MLID driver can support new types of protocol software, as long as the protocols are written to the virtual interface provided by LSL. The MLID driver is capable of handling packets from different protocol stacks delivered to it by the LSL.

On receiving the different protocol packets from the network, the MLID forwards the packet to the LSL without interpreting the packet contents. The LSL is responsible for sending the packets to the correct protocol stack.

The LSL acts as a software switch through which multiple protocol packet types travel and are delivered to the correct MLID or the correct protocol stack. To provide this routing, the LSL contains information about the MLIDs and the protocol stacks it supports. When MLID drivers or protocol stacks are loaded, they register information about themselves with the LSL. The registered information includes items such as network adapter information, protocol stack information, and binding information.

When an MLID such as the NE2000.LAN loads, the LSL assigns a logical number to the network adapter. When a protocol stack loads and registers with the LSL, it also is assigned a logical protocol stack number. Up to 16 such protocol stacks can be supported.

The LSL also keeps information on the send-and-receive event control blocks (ECBs)—data structures used for transmitting and receiving packets, and that contain packet ID information. The LSL uses the packet ID information in ECBs, and information about network adapters and protocol stacks registered with it, to route packets.

The LSL has a set of routines for the LAN adapters below it and the protocol stacks above it. The LSL calls these routines to move data packets. Each network adapter registers a send routine and a control routine, for example. Also associated with each network adapter is a packet buffer area. The *packet buffer area* makes it possible for multiple adapters of the same type to have only one MLID that is loaded reentrantly. In this case, even though the adapters have the same send and control routines, those adapters have a different data area. The protocol stacks above the LSL also register a similar set of support routines with the LSL.

Every packet on a network has a Media Access Control (MAC) frame that encapsulates the communications protocol packet (IPX, AppleTalk, TCP/IP). The MAC is the lower sublayer of the data link layer. For LANs, it represents the mechanisms by which a node on the LAN acquires access to the physical LAN. Within the ODI-based node, a protocol ID (PID) consisting of one to six bytes is added to the beginning of the frame. This PID identifies the MAC frame and the communications protocol contained in the MAC frame. A code of 8137 (hexadecimal), for instance, is used to indicate an Ethernet II MAC frame that has IPX data inside it; a code of 800 (hexadecimal) indicates an IP packet inside the MAC frame. The LSL uses the PID value to route the packet to the appropriate protocol stack.

On NetWare servers, the ODI-specific parameters are stored in the AUTOEXEC.NCF file. This enables the server to initialize the ODI interface when the server is booted. The configuration parameters for the ODI interface are specified using the server LOAD and BIND commands.

Configuring the TCP/IP Protocol Stack

The TCP/IP protocol uses configuration information stored in a number of database files (actually text files) that are kept in the SYS:ETC directory. The TCP/IP protocol software that runs on the NetWare server and uses these database files is stored as NetWare Loadable Modules (NLMs) in the SYS:SYSTEM directory.

Figure 3.9 shows an overview of the configuration files and TCP/IP software for NetWare servers.

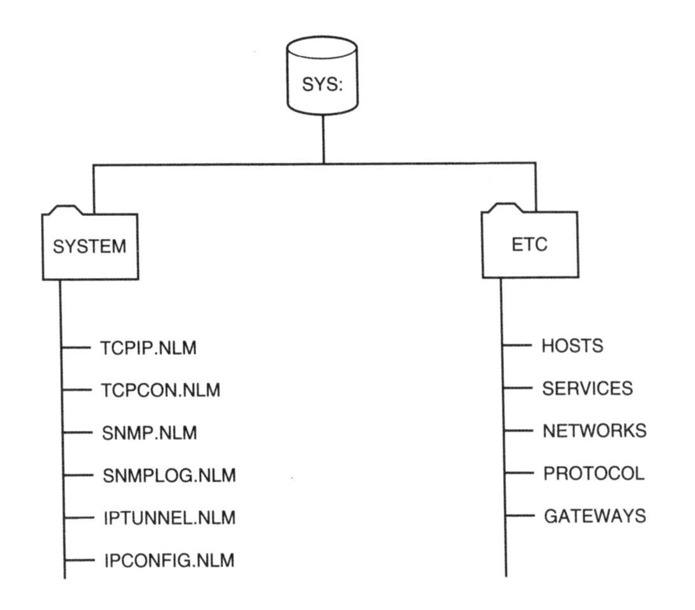

Figure 3.9

TCP/IP configuration files and NLMs.

The major TCP/IP database configuration files used for NetWare servers are the following:

- SYS:ETC\HOSTS
- SYS:ETC\SERVICES
- SYS:ETC\PROTOCOL
- SYS:ETC\NETWORKS
- SYS:ETC\GATEWAYS

These files are also used on many Unix systems, where they are kept in the /sys/etc directory. NetWare uses the same syntax and format used in the corresponding Unix files except for the file SYS:ETC\PROTOCOL. In Unix, this file has the name /etc/protocols. Because of DOS's filename limitation of eight characters for file names, the PROTOCOLS file is truncated to PROTOCOL. All the database files are text files and can be modified using a text editor.

A brief summary of the function of these database files is shown in table 3.1.

Table 3.1 Summary of TCP/IP Database Configuration Files

Configuration File	Description
HOSTS	Contains mappings between IP addresses and host names.
SERVICES	Lists all application services and the transport and port numbers they use.

continues

Table 3.1, Continued

Configuration File	Description
PROTOCOL	Lists protocols and their protocol number (used in IP headers).
NETWORKS	Lists network names and their corresponding IP network number.
GATEWAYS	Contains static routes used by IPCONFIG.NLM to enter in the server routing table.

The TCP/IP NLMs in the SYS:SYSTEM directory work together to provide services to TCP/IP applications. Some of the TCP/IP NLMs, such as TCPCON and IPCONFIG, use configuration parameters stored in the database files in the SYS:ETC directory. Table 3.2 lists the NLMs bundled with the NetWare 3.x and NetWare 4.x operating system products.

Additional services, such as NFS, FTP, and print gateways, are purchased as separate add-on products.

Table 3.2 Summary of TCP/IP NLMs

NLM	Description
TCPIP.NLM	Implements the TCP/IP protocol stack.
TCPCON.NLM	Provides a TCP/IP console interface. Acts as an SNMP manager.
IPTUNNEL.LAN	Driver for the IP Tunnel. Used to provide IPX communications via an IP Tunnel.
SNMP.NLM	SNMP Agent. Provides SNMP support so that management information can be read by an SNMP manager.
SNMPLOG.NLM	SNMP Logger. Used to log SNMP-related events.
PING.NLM	Implements the PING utility for diagnostics and troubleshooting. Available only in NetWare 3.12 (and higher) and NetWare 4.x. Not available in NetWare 3.11.

The HOSTS File

The HOSTS file on a NetWare server is used by the TCP/IP NLMs to look up the IP address of host names. Each line in the HOSTS text file contains information in the following format:

```
IP Address    hostname   [alias [...] ]    #comment
```

The *IP Address* is the IP address in dotted decimal notation. Hexadecimal numbers can be used but must be preceded by *0x*. For example, the IP address 129.13.45.67 can be expressed in the dotted hexadecimal notation form as

```
0x81.0xD.0x2D.0x43
```

The *hostname* is the name of the system with a given IP address. It must be separated from the IP address by one or more white spaces (blanks, tab characters). The host name cannot contain a tab, space, or number sign (#) and must be unique in the hosts file.

The *alias* is an alternate name for the host name. You can use domain names; that is, names containing a period (.). Here is an example of a line that uses domain names:

```
199.245.180.222   rama.kinetics.com  ra
```

The domain name *rama.kinetics.com* has an IP address of 199.245.180.222. The name *ra* is an alias for *rama.kinetics.com.*

Typically, the alias is a shorter name for the host. A host can have from one to 10 aliases.

The *#comment* is used to place comments. All characters between the # and the end-of-line are ignored and treated as comments. The #comment can be placed on a line by itself.

The following is a sample SYS:ETC/HOSTS file:

```
# SYS:ETC/HOSTS file for NW4CS
# "IP Address", "Hostname"
127.0.0.1        localhost loopback lb
199.245.180.91        boston rport180
199.245.180.211       london rport211
199.245.180.101       cdoserv.kinetics.com cdoserv
199.245.180.1         shiva.kinetics.com shiva mahadeva
199.245.180.2         vishnu.kinetics.com vishnu rama
199.245.180.3         brahma.kinetics.com brahma
199.245.180.4         wks1.kinetics.com wks1 wk1
199.245.180.5         wks2.kinetics.com wks2 wk2
199.245.180.5         wks3.kinetics.com wks3 wk3
199.245.180.6         wks4.kinetics.com wks4 wk4
199.245.180.7         wks5.kinetics.com wks5 wk5
199.245.180.8         wks6.kinetics.com wks6 wk6
199.245.180.9         wks7.kinetics.com wks7 wk7
199.245.180.10        wks8.kinetics.com wks8 wk8
199.245.180.11        wks9.kinetics.com wks9 wk9
144.19.74.102         386 nwcs
144.19.74.201         cs
```

The SERVICES File

The SERVICES file is used to identify the following:

- Names of services
- Transport protocol
- Port number used by the service

The names of services are programs that run in the Process/Application layer of the DoD model. Examples of these services are TELNET, FTP, SMTP, SNMP, and so on. These services could use a transport protocol such as TCP or UDP. The SERVICES configuration file identifies the transport protocol that is used. Some services are available through both the TCP and UDP transport protocols. In this case, the service is listed twice: once for the TCP protocol and once for the UDP protocol. The port number identifies the application service that uses the transport protocol.

This SERVICES file accompanies the TCP/IP product and contains common TCP/IP services; you should not have to modify it.

Each line in the SERVICES text file contains information in the following format:

```
service       port/transport      [alias]    #comment
```

The *service* is an identifier representing the name of the service. Example values of services are telnet, ftp, ftp-data, smtp, snmp. The service name cannot contain a tab, space, or number sign (#) and must be unique in the services file.

The optional *alias* identifies other names by which this service is known.

The *#comment* is used to place comments. All characters between the # and the end-of-line are ignored and treated as comments. The *#comment* can also be placed on a line by itself.

On NetWare servers, a sample SERVICES file is kept in the SYS:ETC/SAMPLES directory. A sample SERVICES for a NetWare 4.x server is shown here:

```
#
# SYS:ETC\SERVICES
#
#   Network service mappings.  Maps service names to transport
#   protocol and transport protocol ports.
#
echo          7/udp
echo          7/tcp
discard       9/udp      sink null
discard       9/tcp      sink null
systat       11/tcp
daytime      13/udp
daytime      13/tcp
netstat      15/tcp
```

```
ftp-data     20/tcp
ftp          21/tcp
telnet       23/tcp
smtp         25/tcp      mail
time         37/tcp      timserver
time         37/udp      timserver
name         42/udp      nameserver
whois        43/tcp      nicname       # usually to sri-nic
domain       53/udp
domain       53/tcp
hostnames   101/tcp      hostname      # usually to sri-nic
sunrpc      111/udp
sunrpc      111/tcp
#
#
# Host specific functions
#
tftp         69/udp
rje          77/tcp
finger       79/tcp
link         87/tcp      ttylink
supdup       95/tcp
iso-tsap    102/tcp
x400        103/tcp                    # ISO Mail
x400-snd    104/tcp
csnet-ns    105/tcp
pop-2       109/tcp                    # Post Office
uucp-path   117/tcp
nntp        119/tcp      usenet        # Network News Transfer
ntp         123/tcp                    # Network Time Protocol
NeWS        144/tcp      news          # Window System
#
# Unix specific services
#
# these are NOT officially assigned
#
exec        512/tcp
login       513/tcp
shell       514/tcp      cmd           # no passwords used
printer     515/tcp      spooler       # experimental
courier     530/tcp      rpc           # experimental
biff        512/udp      comsat
who         513/udp      whod
syslog      514/udp
talk        517/udp
route       520/udp      router routed
```

```
new-rwho    550/udp      new-who      # experimental
rmonitor    560/udp      rmonitord    # experimental
monitor     561/udp                   # experimental
ingreslock 1524/tcp
snmp        161/udp                   # Simple Network Mgmt _Protocol
snmp-trap   162/udp      snmptrap     # SNMP trap (event) _messages
```

A sample Unix /etc/services file taken from UnixWare is also shown as follows. In this file, you can see that there are many similarities between these two files. The UnixWare /etc/services file is a little more comprehensive because the Unix platform supports a wider range of services than NetWare.

```
#ident   "@(#)cmd-inet:common/cmd/cmd-inet/etc/services   _1.8.7.3"
#ident "$Header: /sms/sinixV5.4es/rcs/s19-full/usr/src/cmd/_cmd-#inet/etc/services,
➥v 1.1 91/02/28 16:30:47 ccs Exp $"
#
#   assigned numbers from rfc1060
#
tcpmux            1/tcp
echo              7/tcp
echo              7/udp
discard           9/tcp      sink null
discard           9/udp      sink null
systat           11/tcp      users
systat           11/udp      users
daytime          13/tcp
daytime          13/udp
netstat          15/tcp
netstat          15/udp
qotd             17/tcp      quote
qotd             17/udp      quote
chargen          19/tcp      ttytst source
chargen          19/udp      ttytst source
ftp-data         20/tcp
ftp              21/tcp
telnet           23/tcp
smtp             25/tcp      mail
time             37/tcp      timserver
time             37/udp      timserver
name             42/tcp      nameserver
name             42/udp      nameserver
whois            43/tcp      nicname      # usually to sri-nic
whois            43/udp      nicname      # usually to sri-nic
nameserver       53/udp      domain
nameserver       53/tcp      domain
apts             57/tcp                   # any private _terminal service
apfs             59/tcp                   # any private file _service
```

```
bootps          67/udp      bootp
bootpc          68/udp
tftp            69/udp
rje             77/tcp      netrjs       # any private rje
finger          79/tcp
link            87/tcp      ttylink
supdup          95/tcp
hostnames      101/tcp      hostname     # usually to sri-nic
iso-tsap       102/tcp
x400           103/tcp                   # ISO Mail
x400-snd       104/tcp
csnet-ns       105/tcp                   # CSNET Name Service
pop-2          109/tcp                   # Post Office
sunrpc         111/udp      rpcbind
sunrpc         111/tcp      rpcbind
auth           113/tcp      authentication
sftp           115/tcp
uucp-path      117/tcp
nntp           119/tcp      usenet readnews untp # Network _News Transfer
eprc           121/udp
ntp            123/tcp                   # Network Time _Protocol
ntp            123/udp                   # Network Time _Protocol
NeWS           144/tcp      news         # Window System
iso-tp0        146/tcp
iso-ip         147/tcp
bftp           152/tcp
snmp           161/udp
snmp-trap      162/udp
cmip-manage    163/tcp
cmip-agent     164/tcp
print-srv      170/tcp
#
# Unix specific services
#
# these are NOT officially assigned
#
exec           512/tcp
login          513/tcp
shell          514/tcp      cmd          # no passwords used
printer        515/tcp      spooler      # line printer _spooler
timed          525/udp      timeserver
courier        530/tcp      rpc          # experimental
# uucpd is not supported by System V Unix.
uucp           540/tcp      uucpd        # uucp daemon.
biff           512/udp      comsat
who            513/udp      whod
```

```
syslog          514/udp
talk            517/udp
ntalk           518/udp
route           520/udp      router routed
new-rwho        550/udp      new-who       # experimental
rmonitor        560/udp      rmonitord     # experimental
monitor         561/udp                    # experimental
pcserver        600/tcp                    # ECD Integrated PC _board srvr
ingreslock     1524/tcp
nfsd           2049/udp                    # NFS server daemon
listen         2766/tcp                    # sysv listener _service
ttymon         2767/tcp                    # sysv tty service
xserver0       6000/tcp                    # X-Window Server _Display 0
pppmsg          911/tcp                    # PPP daemon

#   Univel specific service registration
apfs          36938/spx                    # any private file _service
apts          38939/spx                    # any private _terminal service
auth          36940/spx      authentication
bftp          36941/spx
biff          36914/ipx      comsat
bootpc        36915/ipx
bootps        36916/ipx      bootp
chargen       36942/spx      ttytst source
chargen       36917/ipx      ttytst source
cmip-agent    36943/spx
cmip-manage   36944/spx
courier       36945/spx      rpc           # experimental
csnet-ns      36946/spx                    # CSNET Name Service
daytime       36947/spx
daytime       36918/ipx
discard       36919/ipx      sink null
discard       36948/spx      sink null
echo          36820/ipx
echo          36949/spx
eprc          36821/ipx
exec          36950/spx
finger        36951/spx
ftp           36952/spx
ftp-data      36953/spx
hostnames     36954/spx      hostname      # usually to sri-nic
ingreslock    36955/spx
iso-ip        36956/spx
iso-tp0       36957/spx
iso-tsap      36958/spx
link          36959/spx      ttylink
```

```
listen       36960/spx                    # sysv listener _service
login        32867/spx
monitor      36822/ipx                    # experimental
name         36923/ipx    nameserver
name         36962/spx    nameserver
nameserver   36924/ipx    domain
nameserver   36963/spx    domain
netstat      36925/ipx
netstat      36964/spx
new-rwho     36926/ipx    new-who         # experimental
# nfsd       36927/ipx                    # NFS server daemon
nntp         36965/spx  usenet readnews untp # Network News _Transfer
ntp          36928/ipx                    # Network Time _Protocol
ntp          36966/spx                    # Network Time _Protocol
pcserver     36967/spx                    # ECD Integrated PC _board srvr
pop-2        36968/spx                    # Post Office
print-srv    36969/spx
printer      36970/spx    spooler         # line printer _spooler
qotd         36929/ipx    quote
qotd         36971/spx    quote
rje          36972/spx    netrjs          # any private rje
rmonitor     36930/ipx    rmonitord       # experimental
route        36931/ipx    router routed
sftp         36973/spx
shell        36974/spx    cmd             # no passwords used
smtp         36975/spx    mail
snmp         36879/ipx
snmp-trap    36880/ipx
sunrpc       36889/ipx    rpcbind
sunrpc       36890/spx    rpcbind
supdup       36976/spx
syslog       36932/ipx
systat       36933/ipx    users
systat       36977/spx    users
talk         36934/ipx
telnet       36978/spx
tftp         33683/ipx
time         36935/ipx    timserver
time         36979/spx    timserver
ttymon       36980/spx                    # sysv tty service
uucp         36981/spx    uucpd           # uucp daemon
uucp-path    36982/spx
who          36936/ipx    whod
whois        36937/ipx    nicname         # usually to sri-nic
whois        36983/spx    nicname         # usually to sri-nic
x400         36984/spx                    # ISO Mail
```

```
x400-snd      36985/spx
install       36986/spx              # Univel network _installation server
xserver0      32998/spx              # X-Window Server _Display 0
```

Notice that the Univel specific entries in the /etc/services file on UnixWare contain services described for protocols other than TCP/IP, such as SPX and IPX.

In addition to the SERVICES file, tables 2.5 and 2.6 in Chapter 2 also contain information on port numbers used for TCP and UDP services.

The PROTOCOL File

The PROTOCOL file is used to identify the names of protocols and the corresponding protocol number. The protocol number for the Internet suite of protocols is the value protocol identifier (protocol id) field of the IP header. The *protocol id* field is used to identify the upper layer protocol that uses the Internet Protocol.

The PROTOCOL file accompanies the TCP/IP product and contains common protocols; you should not have to modify it.

Each line in the PROTOCOL text file contains information in the following format:

```
protocol_name   protocol_number   [alias]   #comment
```

The *protocol_name* is an identifier representing the name of the protocol; the *protocol_number* is the number used in the IP header to identify the protocol. The protocol name cannot contain a tab, space, or number sign (#) and must be unique in the protocol file.

The optional *alias* identifies other names by which this protocol is known. Usually the *protocol_name* is in lowercase characters and an alias is included that lists the service in uppercase characters.

The *#comment* is used to place comments. All characters between the # and the end-of-line are ignored and treated as comments. The *#comment* can also be placed on a line by itself.

The PROTOCOL file for NetWare servers is listed here:

```
#
# SYS:ETC\PROTOCOL
#
#   Internet (IP) protocols
#
ip     0   IP   # internet protocol, pseudo protocol number
icmp   1   ICMP # internet control message protocol
igmp   2   IGMP # internet group multicast protocol
ggp    3   GGP  # gateway-gateway protocol
tcp    6   TCP  # transmission control protocol
pup   12   PUP  # PARC universal packet protocol
udp   17   UDP  # user datagram protocol
```

A sample Unix /etc/protocols file taken from UnixWare is also shown as follows. You can see the many similarities between the files on the NetWare and Unix systems. The UnixWare /etc/protocols file is a little more comprehensive because the Unix platform supports a wider range of protocols than NetWare.

```
#ident   "@(#)cmd-inet:common/cmd/cmd-inet/etc/protocols   _1.1.2.1"
#ident "$Header: /sms/sinixV5.4es/rcs/s19-full/usr/src/cmd/cmd-#inet/etc/protocols,
➥v 1.1 91/02/28 16:30:45 ccs Exp $"
#
# Internet (IP) protocols
#
ip        0   IP        # internet protocol, pseudo protocol _number
icmp      1   ICMP      # internet control message protocol
ggp       3   GGP       # gateway-gateway protocol
tcp       6   TCP       # transmission control protocol
egp       8   EGP       # exterior gateway protocol
pup      12   PUP       # PARC universal packet protocol
udp      17   UDP       # user datagram protocol
hmp      20   HMP       # host monitoring protocol
xns-idp  22   XNS-IDP   # Xerox NS IDP
rdp      27   RDP       # "reliable datagram" protocol
```

The NETWORKS File

The NETWORKS file is used to identify the networks that exist on the internetwork. The NETWORKS file is similar in concept to the HOSTS file. Although the HOSTS file contains the association between host addresses and host names, the NETWORKS file contains the association between network addresses of network names.

Each line in the NETWORK text file contains information in the following format:

```
network_name   network_number[/subnet_mask]    alias #comment
```

The *network_name* is an identifier representing the name of the network; the *network_number* is the netid part of the IP Address for the network (see Chapter 2, "TCP/IP Network Protocol Architecture"). The network name cannot contain a tab, space, or number sign (#) and must be unique in the networks file.

The *subnet_mask* for the network can be expressed in dotted decimal or dotted hexadecimal notation. The square brackets ([ ]) in the previously stated syntax for the NETWORKS file entry indicate that the subnet mask is optional. If the subnet mask is left out, a default mask indicating that no subnet mask is being used is specified.

The optional *alias* identifies other names by which this protocol is known. Usually the *protocol_name* is in lowercase characters and an alias is included that lists the service in uppercase characters.

The *#comment* is used to place comments. All characters between the # and the end-of-line are ignored and treated as comments. The *#comment* can also be placed on a line by itself.

The network names specified in the NETWORKS file can be used in configuration utilities and commands that reference the network address. For example, the network name can be used in the GATEWAYS file as an alternative to using the network addresses. This file can be modified by network administrators so that network names can be used in configuration commands and utilities instead of the more difficult to remember network addresses.

The following is a sample of a NETWORKS file on NetWare servers:

```
#
# SYS:ETC\NETWORKS
#
#   Network numbers
#
loopback    127           # fictitious internal loopback network
novellnet   130.57        # Novell's network number
#
# Internet networks
#
arpanet       10   arpa   # historical network
milnet        26          # not so historical military net
ucb-ether     46          # Go bears!
```

It is interesting that the network UCB-ETHER has a comment of "Go bears!" The NETWORKS file on NetWare servers is taken from a sample configuration on a host at the University of California, Berkeley. The football team at the University of California, Berkeley is called "Bears," which explains this comment, and also the origin of the TCP/IP code used in NetWare.

The following is a sample NETWORKS file that comes with UnixWare. This has fewer entries than the sample NETWORKS file on NetWare servers, but more entries can be added at the discretion of the network Administrator.

```
#ident   "@(#)cmd-inet:common/cmd/cmd-inet/etc/networks   _1.1.2.1"
#ident "$Header: /sms/sinixV5.4es/rcs/s19-full/usr/src/cmd/cmd-inet/etc/networks,
➥v 1.1 91/02/28 16:30:43 ccs Exp $"
#
# Internet networks
#
loopback   127
#
# Internet networks
#
arpanet      10      arpa
```

The GATEWAYS File

The GATEWAYS file contains information on routes used by the NetWare server when it acts as an IP router. The utility IPCONFIG.NLM uses the information in the GATEWAYS file to initialize the routing table at the server.

The format of the GATEWAYS file is discussed in greater detail in Chapter 4, "TCP/IP Routing Support in NetWare," which discusses internetworking and routing issues.

Configuring TCP/IP

To configure TCP/IP NLMs on NetWare servers, several parameters need to be specified. Some parameters are optional; others, such as specifying the IP address of an interface, are mandatory. This section describes the configuration procedure for TCP/IP on NetWare servers.

Configuring STARTUP.NCF and AUTOEXEC.NCF

When packets arrive at the NetWare server, they are temporarily stored in an area of the server memory called the *packet receive buffers*. The number of such packet receive buffers and their size can affect the performance of TCP/IP software.

Configuring the Size of Packet Receive Buffers

The size of a packet that can be transmitted is determined by the network's physical access mechanism and driver limitations. On the server side, NetWare enables you to define the maximum size of a packet that can be processed by the file server. When a workstation makes a connection to the server, the packet size is negotiated, based on the settings of the network driver being used at the workstation. This parameter value needs to be large enough to accommodate the maximum packet size used by a workstation. Generally, a large packet size can speed communications but consumes more RAM.

The maximum size of the packet receive buffers should accommodate the largest data-link layer packet size the server can receive on any of the server's network boards. For Ethernet, the maximum packet size is 1,514 bytes (excluding CRC). For Token Ring, the maximum packet size is determined by *Token Holding Time* (THT). For a 4 Mbps Token Ring, the maximum packet size is 4,096 bytes. If the NetWare server contains an Ethernet and a 4 Mbps Token Ring network board, the maximum packet size should be set to 4,096 bytes.

The maximum packet size is set by the MAXIMUM PHYSICAL RECEIVE PACKET SIZE set parameter. The default value of this parameter is 1,514 bytes. To set this parameter to a value such as 4,096 bytes, you can use the following command:

```
SET MAXIMUM PHYSICAL RECEIVE PACKET SIZE = 4096
```

To set the MAXIMUM PHYSICAL RECEIVE PACKET SIZE to a non-default value every time the NetWare server starts, you can place the SET MAXIMUM PHYSICAL RECEIVE PACKET SIZE command in the STARTUP.NCF file on the NetWare server's boot directory.

All nodes on the network must be configured to use a packet size that the server can handle. There is a certain amount of inefficiency involved when packets on a network do not utilize the entire space reserved for handling the largest packet on the network. On the other hand, this enables disparate networks that have different packet sizes to use the same NetWare server.

Configuring the Number of Packet Receive Buffers

The number of packet receive buffers should be sufficient to allow normal network traffic loads. Packets are placed in the packet receive buffers while waiting for their turn to be processed. If the amount of packet receive buffers is insufficient to handle network traffic, the server may drop packets. Even though upper-layer protocol mechanisms may cause the dropped packets to be re-sent, the loss of packets results in an inefficiency on the network, which should be avoided.

The maximum number of packet receive buffers is set by the MAXIMUM PACKET RECEIVE BUFFERS set parameter. This parameter has a default value of 100. To increase the parameter to, say 200, you can use the following console command:

```
SET MAXIMUM PACKET RECEIVE BUFFERS=200
```

To set the MAXIMUM PACKET RECEIVE BUFFERS to a non-default value every time the NetWare server starts, you can place the SET MAXIMUM PACKET RECEIVE BUFFERS command in the AUTOEXEC.NCF file in the NetWare server's SYS:SYSTEM directory.

The server needs to keep a certain number of packet buffers in RAM to avoid being overrun by data. Normally, the server allocates receive buffers dynamically, based on its needs. NetWare enables you to set an upper limit on the number of packet receive buffers the operating system can allocate.

You can monitor the number of packet receive buffers by running the MONITOR.NLM utility from the server console. The main screen of the MONITOR utility shows the number of packet receive buffers that have been allocated. If this number begins to approach the current value of the MAXIMUM PACKET RECEIVE BUFFERS, you may want to increase this parameter until you have at least one packet receive buffer per workstation. For OS/2 and MS Windows, increase this value based on the number of simultaneously running network applications at the workstations. Allow for at least one buffer per application. The MONITOR.NLM can be used also to monitor the No ECB available count errors. If these errors are being reported, increase this parameter in increments of 10. For EISA and MCA server machines, increase this parameter to allow for five to 10 packet receive buffers per EISA/MCA network board. If the number of file service processes reported by MONITOR.NLM is close to its maximum, you can increase the maximum number of service processes to reduce the need for more packet receive buffers. The parameter value ranges from 50 to 2,000, with a default of 100.

If you configure the number of packet receive buffers to a large value, the packet receive buffers may not be fully utilized. In addition, there will be less server memory available for caching, which could result in a drop in performance.

Besides using the SET command to modify the MAXIMUM PHYSICAL RECEIVE PACKET SIZE and MAXIMUM PACKET RECEIVE BUFFERS parameters, you can use the SERVMAN.NLM on NetWare 4.x servers to modify these values.

Loading and Configuring Steps for TCP/IP NLMs

Figure 3.10 summarizes the loading and configuration steps for TCP/IP NLMs.

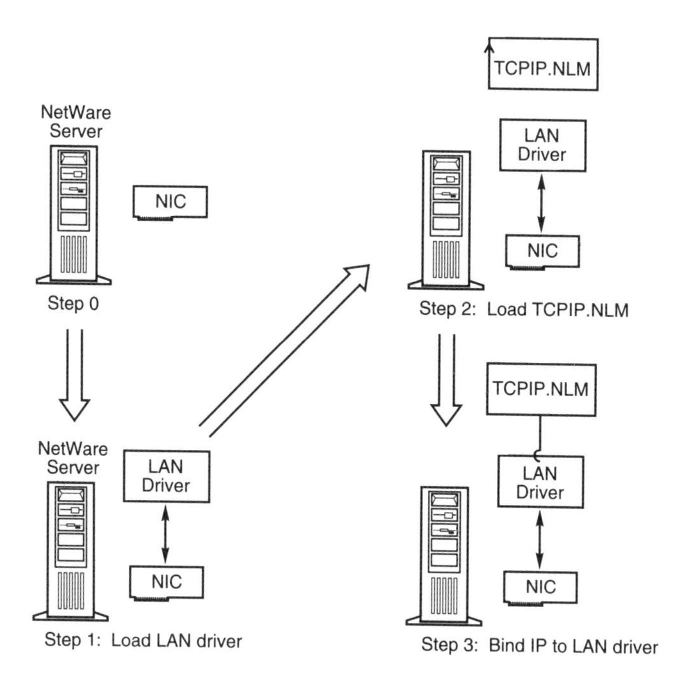

Figure 3.10

Load and configuration steps for TCP/IP NLMs.

The NetWare server must be properly installed with NetWare software. This is described as step 0 in figure 3.10. The same network board that is used for IPX communications can also be used by the TCP/IP NLMs because the network board drivers are based on ODI, which allows multiple protocol stacks to use the same board. If the NetWare server is to connect to non-IPX networks, such as a TCP/IP network, you may want to have an additional network board at the NetWare server that connects the NetWare server to the TCP/IP network.

Loading the LAN Driver

In step 1 of figure 3.10, the network board driver must be loaded by using the LOAD command and the following general syntax:

```
LOAD NETWORK_DRIVER  [parameters]
```

The LOAD command is issued at the server console to load and run the network board driver NetWare Loadable Module. The network board drivers for the NetWare servers are written as NLMs.

The *NETWORK_DRIVER* is replaced by the name of the ODI driver. By convention, ODI drivers on a NetWare server have a LAN extension. Examples of these drivers are NE2000.LAN, TOKEN.LAN, and SMC8000.LAN.

The *parameters* that follow the name of the driver specify the interrupt request number, I/O port address, memory base address, and DMA channel used by the network board. Network board drivers are written with a range of allowable parameter values. You must select a parameter value that matches the network board settings. When the network board driver loads, it initializes the network board. If the parameters specified on the LOAD command for the network board driver do not match the network board settings, an error message appears on the console. Most network board drivers are written so that they will not load in server memory unless they can communicate with the network adapter.

Table 3.3 shows typical parameters used for a large number of network board drivers. Token Ring boards require special parameters, which are listed in table 3.4.

Table 3.3 Card Parameters in LOAD NETWORK_DRIVER Command

Parameter	Meaning
DMA	Specifies the DMA channel number of the NIC.
INT	Specifies the IRQ level the NIC is set to.
MEM	Refers to the base memory address of RAM on the NIC.
PORT	Specifies the I/O port address setting of the NIC.
NODE	Overrides node address on NICs that permit it, such as NICs that use IEEE MAC-addressing schemes.
RETRIES	Denotes the number of times the NIC driver retries failed packet transmissions. Default for most adapters is 5. This parameter can be set as high as 255.
SLOT	Used for MCA and EISA bus computers. Tells NOS the NIC to link the driver to. Hardware parameters, such as I/O port and IRQ, are set by using the reference disk.
NAME	Specifies a unique name (up to 17 characters) for an NIC. Useful for many NICs of the same type. NAME can be used in the BIND command.
FRAME	Specifies the type of MAC layer encapsulation to be used. Used for Ethernet and Token Ring.

TABLE 3.4 TOKEN RING SPECIFIC PARAMETERS FOR LOAD TOKEN COMMAND

Parameter	Meaning
LS	Specifies the number of IEEE 802.5 link stations.
SAPS	Denotes the number of Service Access Points for Token Ring driver.
TBC	Refers to the Transmit Buffer Count for Token Ring driver. The default is set to 2.
TBZ	Refers to the Transmit Buffer Size for Token Ring driver. Values range from 96 to 65,535, although not all values are supported. The default value is 0, and it implies the maximum that works for the NOS or the NIC.

Frame Format Parameters

Most of the network board parameters in tables 3.3 and 3.4 are fairly straightforward. The one that might require a little explanation is the FRAME parameter. The FRAME parameter can be used for Ethernet and Token Ring NICs and tells the NIC driver the type of header to be used for packets. In other words, FRAME controls the MAC layer encapsulation.

In Chapter 2, you learned that many modern Ethernet NICs can generate either IEEE 802.3 encapsulation or Ethernet II (version 2.0) encapsulation. NetWare's default Ethernet encapsulation is IEEE 802.3 for NetWare 3.11 and IEEE 802.2 for NetWare 3.12 (and higher) and NetWare 4.x.

This IEEE 802.3 frame encapsulation (see fig. 3.11) corresponds to a FRAME value of ETHERNET_802.3. If a NetWare server's Ethernet interface is configured for ETHERNET_802.3 only, it means that the NetWare server, by default, can speak only to stations or other computers that can understand the IEEE 802.3 headers in the packets.

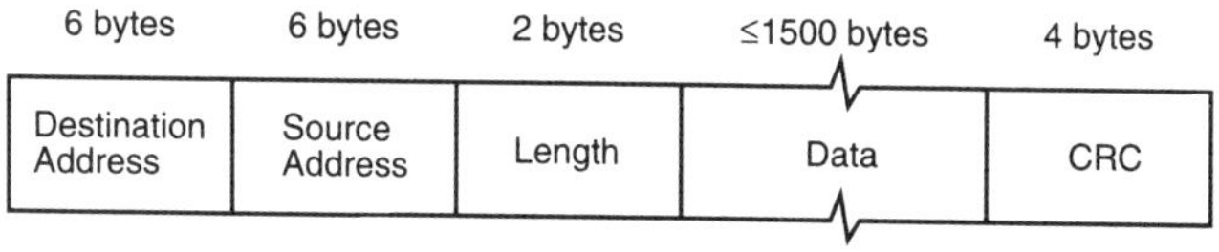

6 bytes	6 bytes	2 bytes	≤1500 bytes	4 bytes
Destination Address	Source Address	Length	Data	CRC

Figure 3.11

IEEE 802.3 (ETHERNET_802.3) encapsulation.

Similarly, the IEEE 802.2 frame encapsulation corresponds to a FRAME value of ETHERNET_802.2. If a NetWare server's Ethernet interface is configured for ETHERNET_802.2 only, it means that the NetWare server, by default, can speak only to stations or other computers that can understand the IEEE 802.2 headers in the packets.

If ETHERNET_802.2 is used for the FRAME parameter, it implies an IEEE 802.2 MAC layer encapsulation. In addition, the data portion of the IEEE 802.3 frame contains an IEEE 802.2 frame (see fig. 3.12). IEEE 802.2 or *Logical Link Control* (LLC) enables the specification of the type of upper-layer data that is encapsulated. For example, when the Destination Service Access Point (DSAP) and Source Service Access Point (SSAP) values are E0 (hexadecimal), the IEEE 802.2 frame is carrying an IPX packet. By using LLC, multiple sessions are possible between Link Service Access Points (LSAPs). If NetWare servers are being used on a network that uses IEEE 802.2, you should configure the NIC driver to use IEEE 802.2 encapsulation.

Figure 3.12

IEEE 802.2 (ETHERNET_802.2) encapsulation.

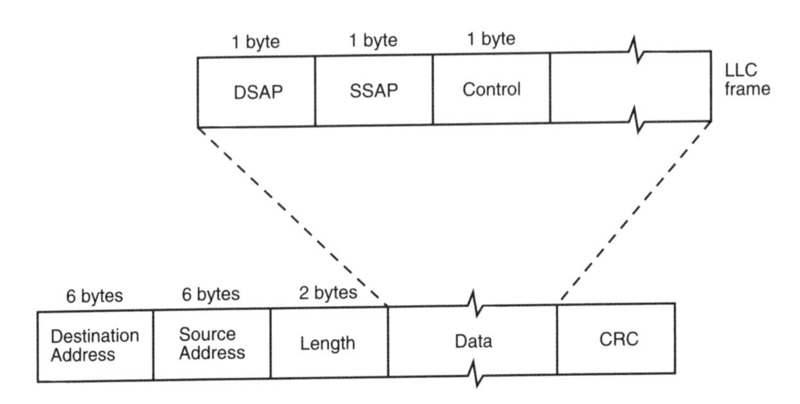

Correctly speaking, the IEEE 802.3 frame should always be used in conjunction with the IEEE 802.2 (LLC) frame. Historically, this was not done with Novell's ETHERNET_802.3. For this reason, Novell's ETHERNET_802.3 frame is called the *raw* Ethernet frame. With the release of NetWare 3.12 and NetWare 4.x, Novell began using the IEEE 802.2 frame in conjunction with IEEE 802.3 frame encapsulation. Novell calls this type of frame encapsulation ETHERNET_802.2.

Configuring Ethernet for TCP/IP

The TCP/IP protocol stack on NetWare servers, when configured for the Ethernet network board, requires an Ethernet II encapsulation. The Ethernet II has a 2-byte *type*, which is a field immediately following the 6-byte destination and source address fields. The IEEE 802.3 frame also uses the 6-byte destination and source address fields, but these are followed by a 2-byte *length* field that specifies the length of the packet. The Ethernet *type* field of the Ethernet II frame has a value of more than 1,500 (decimal). This enables the Ethernet II frame to be easily distinguished from the IEEE 802.3 frame that uses the *length* field whose value is less than or equal to 1,500. Remember that 1,500 is the maximum legal size of the data portion of an Ethernet or IEEE 802.3 packet.

To communicate with TCP/IP-based networks that typically use an Ethernet II frame encapsulation, NetWare provides the flexibility of changing the MAC layer encapsulation to Ethernet II (see fig. 3.13). This is done by setting the FRAME parameter in the LOAD *NETWORK_DRIVER* command to ETHERNET_II.

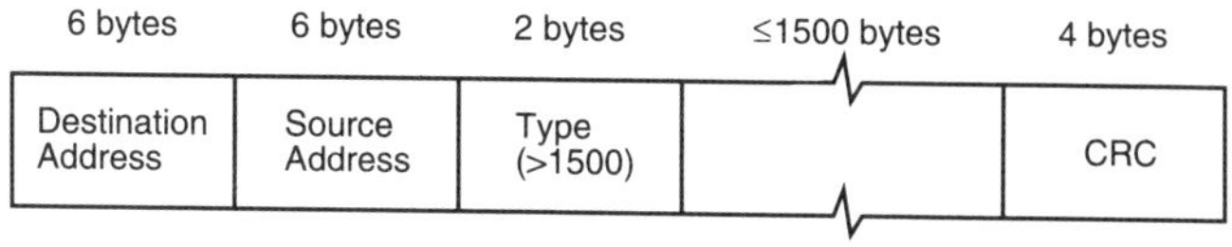

6 bytes	6 bytes	2 bytes	≤1500 bytes	4 bytes
Destination Address	Source Address	Type (>1500)		CRC

Figure 3.13
ETHERNET II encapsulation.

If the network driver has already been loaded with a frame type of ETHERNET_802.3 or ETHERNET_802.2, you must reload this driver with the ETHERNET_II frame type if you are configuring the network board for TCP/IP. When you load a network board driver that has already been loaded, only one copy of the network board driver is kept in memory. The additional load of the network driver is called a *reentrant* load because it uses a single copy of the program code for the driver.

Consider the following LOAD command in an AUTOEXEC.NCF file that is set up for IPX communications on an Ethernet NE2000 board:

```
LOAD NE2000 port=300 INT=5
```

Because no frame parameter was specified in the LOAD command, a default frame type will be assumed. If the LOAD command was issued on a NetWare 3.11 server, the ETHERNET_802.3 frame type will be used. On a NetWare 3.12 or NetWare 4.x server, the ETHERNET_802.2 frame type is used. If the same NE2000 board is to be used for TCP/IP communications, you must use a frame type of ETHERNET_II. This can be done by another LOAD command that loads the driver a second time. The following statements illustrate this concept:

```
LOAD NE2000 port=300 INT=5
LOAD NE2000 port=300 INT=5 frame=ETHERNET_II
```

The second LOAD command uses the same copy of the network driver loaded by the first LOAD command, but it has a different frame type—ETHERNET_II—that can be used by the TCP/IP protocols.

Another value for the FRAME parameter is ETHERNET_SNAP. The ETHERNET_SNAP frame encapsulation is used on Macintosh-based networks. If you are using a Macintosh client to communicate with a NetWare TCP/IP server, you should configure the Ethernet interface on the NetWare server with ETHERNET_SNAP.

The SNAP in ETHERNET_SNAP stands for Sub-Network Access Protocol. SNAP, described in RFC 1042, was developed as a means to send IP datagrams and Address Resolution Protocols (ARPs) used in the Internet over IEEE 802.3, IEEE 802.4 (Token Bus), IEEE 802.5 (Token Ring), and FDDI networks. IP datagrams historically have been tied to

Ethernet II frames; SNAP offers a way of transporting them across non-Ethernet II networks. The SNAP mechanism, however, is general enough to be used by other protocols, such as AppleTalk Phase 2 used for Macintosh networks. NetWare 3.x supports AppleTalk and TCP/IP-based networks and defines a FRAME value of ETHERNET_SNAP for Ethernet and TOKEN-RING_SNAP for Token Ring networks.

The use of SNAP is illustrated in figure 3.14. The first three bytes of IEEE 802.2 and the SNAP protocol are the same; that is, the LLC headers are the same. This is not surprising because SNAP was designed to use IEEE 802.2. In SNAP, a special value of AA (hex) for the Destination Service Access Point (DSAP) and Source Service Access Point (SSAP) in the LLC header means that the next five bytes (40 bits) contain a special PROTOCOL IDENTIFIER. The first three bytes of the PROTOCOL IDENTIFIER represent the Organizational Unit Identifier (OUI) and, as the name suggests, is unique to an organization. Apple's OUI, for example, is 00 00 F8 (hex). The remaining two bytes contain information similar to the Ether Type field used for Ethernet.

Figure 3.14

SNAP frame encapsulation for Ethernet.

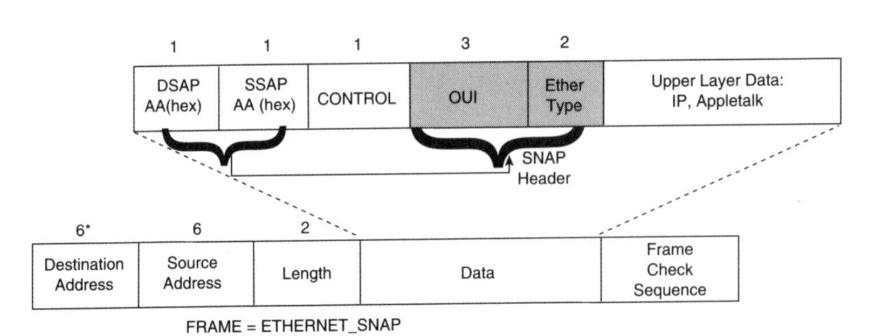

The translation of an Ethernet II frame to SNAP format is shown in figure 3.15. The OUI is assumed to be 00 00 F8. In this translation, notice that the size of the frame grows by eight bytes, which represents the SNAP header length. If the original Ethernet II had a maximum size of 1,500 bytes for the data size, this translates to a data frame size of 1508. This exceeds the maximum data frame size of 1,500 bytes for IEEE 802.3 and can potentially cause problems for IEEE 802.3 networks.

Configuring Token Ring for TCP/IP

For Token Ring, the possible FRAME values are TOKEN-RING and TOKEN-RING_SNAP. The TOKEN-RING frame value is used for sending IPX data, and the TOKEN-RING_SNAP is a requirement for TCP/IP packets. TOKEN-RING uses the IEEE 802.2 header in its data portion, and TOKEN-RING_SNAP uses the SNAP header in the data portion of the Token Ring frame (see fig. 3.16).

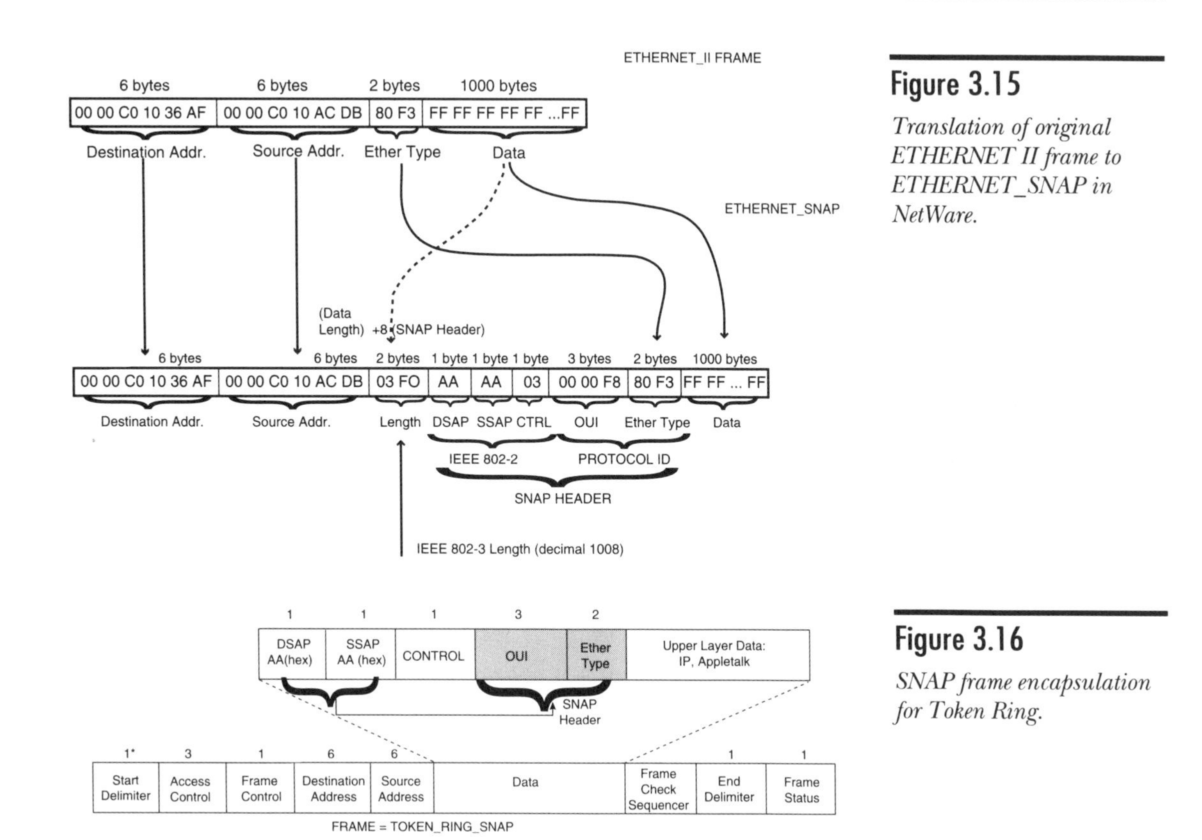

Figure 3.15

Translation of original ETHERNET II frame to ETHERNET_SNAP in NetWare.

Figure 3.16

SNAP frame encapsulation for Token Ring.

Consider the following LOAD command in an AUTOEXEC.NCF file set up for IPX communications on an IBM Token Ring board.

```
LOAD TOKEN
```

Because no frame parameter was specified in the LOAD command, a default frame type is assumed. On NetWare 3.x and NetWare 4.x servers, the default frame type of TOKEN-RING is used. If the same Token Ring board is to be used for TCP/IP communications, you must use a frame type of TOKEN-RING_SNAP. This can be done by another LOAD command that loads the driver a second time, as in the following example:

```
LOAD TOKEN
LOAD TOKEN frame=TOKEN-RING_SNAP
```

The second LOAD command uses the same copy of the network driver loaded by the first LOAD command, but it has a different frame type (TOKEN-RING_SNAP) that can be used by the TCP/IP protocols.

Summary of Frame Types

Table 3.5 summarizes the different frame types discussed in this section.

TABLE 3.5 FRAME PARAMETER VALUES

FRAME	Meaning
ETHERNET_802.3	Default Ethernet encapsulation.
ETHERNET_II	Ethernet II encapsulation. Uses Ether Type value of 8137 (hex) for IPX packets.
ETHERNET_802.2	LLC encapsulation in Ethernet data.
ETHERNET_SNAP	SNAP encapsulation in Ethernet data.
TOKEN-RING	Default Token Ring encapsulation. IEEE 802.2 (LLC) encapsulation in Token Ring data.
TOKEN-RING_SNAP	SNAP encapsulation in Token Ring data.

Frame Type for ARCnet

ARCnet uses the default framing parameter for both IPX and TCP/IP; no special framing parameter is needed. The default frame parameter for ARCnet is RX-NET.

Using a Single Frame Type on an Ethernet Network

It is possible to use a single frame type for all servers, routers, and workstations on an Ethernet network. IPX is flexible enough to use either of the ETHERNET_802.3, ETHERNET_802.2, and ETHERNET_II frame types. Novell's TCP/IP implementation, on the other hand, requires the use of an ETHERNET_II frame type on an Ethernet network. If a single frame type is to be used for both IPX and TCP/IP, it must be ETHERNET_II.

An organization may be interested in simplifying the configuration by using the ETHERNET_II frame type on NetWare servers, routers, and workstations.

On NetWare 3.x and 4.x servers, the use of ETHERNET_II for both IPX and TCP/IP means using a single LOAD command to load the driver with a frame type of ETHERNET_II. For an NE2000, the command may look similar to the following:

```
LOAD NE2000 port=300 int=5 frame=ETHERNET_II
```

On NetWare 2.x servers, you must run ECONFIG on the NET$OS.EXE program that contains the boot image of the operating system. The following is an example of configuring the NetWare 2.x server boot image:

```
ECONFIG NET$OS.EXE lantype:E
```

lantype is A, B, C, or D. The designation A refers to the first network board that is configured for the NetWare server, B the second board, C the third board, and D the fourth board. NetWare 2.x servers and external routers can have a maximum of four network boards.

The utility ECONFIG can be used to change the frame encapsulation for NetWare shells, routers, and NetWare 2.x operating system images. This utility can be found on the WSGEN or SHGEN disks of the NetWare 2.x distribution.

When you type **ECONFIG** at the DOS prompt, you receive the following information about its usage:

```
Usage: econfig [volume:]file [parameter list]
[parameter list] is one of the following:
SHELL:[configuration type]
AD:[configuration type]
[configuration type] = N, E [type constant]
[type constant] = 0 FFFF (8137 is Novell's assigned type constant)
Example: econfig os.exe a:n; b:e 8137; c:e 15af
         econfig shell.com shell:e 8137
```

To configure a NetWare workstation that uses non-ODI drivers, use the following command to configure IPX.COM:

```
ECONFIG IPX.COM SHELL:E 8137
```

The constant 8137 is the Ethernet Type field value assigned to Novell. To verify the configuration change, type the following:

```
ECONFIG IPX.COM
```

You will see the following message if the change is successful:

```
SHELL: Ethernet Typefield: 8137(Assigned Novell type constant)
```

If you want to change the shell back to the Novell IEEE 802.3 encapsulation, use the following command:

```
ECONFIG IPX.COM SHELL:N
```

To configure an external router that runs the program ROUTER.EXE so that it uses the Ethernet frame type of ETHERNET_II, use the following command:

```
ECONFIG    ROUTER.EXE    lantype:E
```

lantype is A, B, C, or D for the LAN Board order.

You cannot use ECONFIG to change the frame types for workstations that use ODI drivers. For NetWare workstations with ODI drivers, add the following lines to NET.CFG in the Link Driver Section:

```
FRAME     ETHERNET_II
PROTOCOL  IPX  8137  ETHERNET_II
```

Here is an example of NET.CFG with these lines:

```
Link Driver  SMCPLUS
INT    #1    3
PORT    #1    280
FRAME     ETHERNET_II
PROTOCOL  IPX  8137  ETHERNET_II
```

Loading the TCP/IP NLM

After the LAN drivers have been loaded, step 2 of the TCP/IP configuration requires that the TCPIP.NLM be loaded (refer to fig. 3.10).

The following LOAD command is used for loading the TCPIP.NLM:

```
LOAD TCPIP
```

The TCPIP.NLM depends on a number of other NLMs. If these are not in memory at the time of loading TCPIP.NLM, they are automatically loaded (*autoloaded*). Figure 3.17 shows the TCIP.NLM load dependency order.

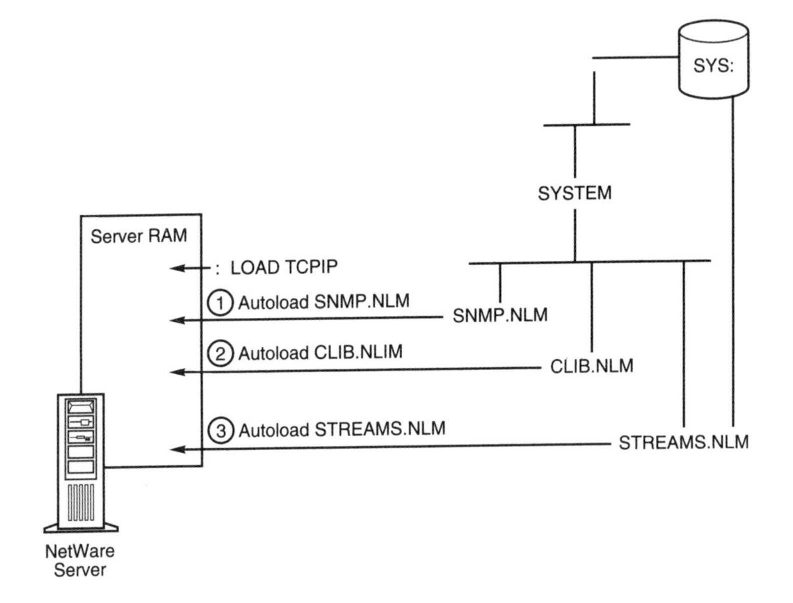

Figure 3.17

The TCPIP.NLM load dependency order.

The TCPIP.NLM depends on the SNMP.NLM. The SNMP.NLM is the SNMP agent that runs on NetWare servers, and can be used by SNMP management workstations to query parameters about the NetWare server. If the SNMP.NLM is not loaded in the server memory at the time of loading TCPIP.NLM, the SNMP.NLM is autoloaded.

The SNMP.NLM in turn depends on the CLIB.NLM. If the CLIB.NLM is not loaded in the server memory at the time of loading TCPIP.NLM, the CLIB.NLM is autoloaded.

The CLIB.NLM in turn depends on the STREAMS.NLM. If the STREAMS.NLM is not loaded in the server memory at the time of loading TCPIP.NLM, the STREAMS.NLM is autoloaded.

The CLIB.NLM and STREAMS.NLM are used by other application NLMs, and may already be loaded at the server. If these NLMs are not already loaded, you will see console messages on-screen indicating they are being autoloaded.

The following is the full syntax for loading the TCPIP.NLM:

```
LOAD TCPIP  [FORWARD={Yes¦No}]  [RIP={Yes¦No}]   [TRAP=IP _Address]
```

The parameters used to configure TCPIP are for IP routing and SNMP traps. Table 3.6 shows a brief description of the TCPIP.NLM parameters.

TABLE 3.6 TCPIP.NLM PARAMETERS

Parameter	Description
FORWARD	Enables or disables IP forwarding. If set to Yes (enabled), server acts as an IP router. If set to No (disabled), disables forwarding of IP packets. Default is No.
RIP	Enables or disables RIP. If set to Yes (enabled) and forwarding is enabled (FORWARD=Yes), the NetWare server will actively participate in the RIP algorithm. It will use RIP to broadcast information on routes it knows. If set to No (disabled), server will not use RIP messages or send RIP messages. Default is Yes, which means that RIP operation is enabled at the server.
TRAP	Specifies the destination IP address to which the SNMP agent (SNMP.NLM) running at the server sends trap messages. Default is the software loop-back IP address of 127.0.0.1. If the TRAP messages are sent to another NetWare server, it must be configured for TCP/IP and have the SNMP logger running at the server if messages are to be logged in a file.

The following are a few examples of loading TCPIP:

Loading TCPIP: Example 1

To enable RIP and IP forwarding but not send SNMP messages, you can use the following commands:

```
LOAD  TCPIP  FORWARD=Yes  RIP=Yes
```

or

```
LOAD  TCPIP  FORWARD=Yes
```

The RIP parameter was left out in the second LOAD statement because its default value is *Yes*.

Loading TCPIP: Example 2

To disable RIP and disable IP forwarding, you can use the following commands:

```
LOAD  TCPIP  FORWARD=No  RIP=No
```

or

```
LOAD  TCPIP   RIP=No
```

The FORWARD parameter was left out in the second LOAD statement because its default value is *No*.

Loading TCPIP: Example 3

To forward trap messages to SNMP manager at 199.245.180.10 and enable IP forwarding and RIP, you can use the following commands:

```
LOAD  TCPIP  TRAP=199.245.180.10 RIP=Yes  FORWARD=YES
```

or

```
LOAD  TCPIP FORWARD=YES   TRAP=199.245.180.10
```

The RIP parameter was left out in the second LOAD statement because its default value is *Yes*. The previous example also illustrates that the parameters can be placed after the LOAD TCPIP in any order.

TCPIP may fail to load if the protocol numbers assigned to IP and ARP have been assigned to other protocols. Normally, this should not happen because ARP and IP have been assigned the protocol numbers of 806 (hex) and 800 (hex), respectively, by the Internet standards. If you are running experimental protocol modules on the server, and these modules are using the protocol numbers assigned to ARP and IP, TCPIP.NLM will not load and will produce one of the following messages:

```
Could not register ARP

Could not register IP (LSL error code=xx)
```

The solution to the previous problem is to remove the protocol software that is claiming the protocol numbers assigned to IP and ARP.

Binding IP Protocol to the Network Board Driver

After the TCPIP.NLM has been loaded, step 3 (refer to fig. 3.10) of the TCP/IP configuration requires the binding of the IP protocol to the network driver. *Binding* of IP to the network board driver sets the communications between the TCP/IP stack and the LAN Driver.

When the TCPIP.NLM is loaded, it is only resident in server memory, and it does not know about the network board that it will be using. The TCPIP.NLM needs to be informed about the network interface in a separate step called "binding the protocol to the network board driver." This binding process is similar to that used for IPX, but because the protocol is IP, it requires a different set of parameters.

The general syntax for binding IP to the network board driver is the following:

```
BIND IP NETWORK_DRIVER   [parameters]
```

The *parameters* specify IP Address, subnet mask, and routing information. Table 3.7 summarizes the BIND parameters that are used for IP, and table 3.8 shows the default values of these parameters and which parameters are required and optional. The BIND parameters GATE, DEFROUTE, COST, and POISON are covered in greater detail in Chapter 4.

If the server has insufficient memory, the BIND IP command can fail and display any of the following error messages:

```
Could not add interface to routing database

Interface allocation failed

IP could not get enough memory to remember interface
```

If the server is short on memory, you get the message ARP could not allocate resource tag. You must unload other NLMs or add more server memory.

Table 3.7 BIND Parameters for IP

Parameter	Description
ADDR	This is the IP Address of the network interface that IP will be using. This must be specified and there is no default value. If ADDR is not specified TCPIP prompts you for a value. IP requires a different IP address for each interface it is bound to. If you assign a duplicate IP address to an interface, you will see an error message that says `The interface, IP Address1, is connected to the same network as the interface using IP Address2.` If you are using the server router with two network boards, each network board must be assigned a different and unique IP address that is compatible

continues

Table 3.7, Continued

Parameter	Description
	with the IP address of the network they connect to. The TCP/IP software checks for illegal addresses, such as addresses that are not class A, B, or C; or an attempt to use a loop-back address for a network interface. On detecting illegal parameter values, an appropriate message is sent to the server console. In addition, the host field cannot be all zeros or all ones. An attempt to make the host field in the IP address all zeros or ones will produce the error message `IP Address is illegal`. Host field zeros or all ones.
MASK	This is the subnet mask and it is used to implement subnetting. All nodes on the same physical network must have the same subnet mask. A *physical* network is defined as one that does not cross a router boundary. Subnet masks are discussed in detail in Chapter 2. If a subnet mask is not specified, IP assumes that the network is not subdivided into subnetworks, and a default is used. For class A, B, and C addresses, the default masks are respectively 255.0.0.0, 255.255.0.0, and 255.255.255.0. The subnet number field cannot be all zeros or all ones as per RFC 950. An attempt to make the subnet number field in the IP address all zeros or ones will produce the error message `IP Address is illegal`. Subnet field is zeros or all ones. If you use different subnet masks within the same network and create duplicate IP addresses, the TCP/IP software can detect these error conditions and will generate error messages of the form `Cannot support IP Address1` with subnet mask Mask1 because it conflicts with IP Address2 with subnet mask Mask2, or an address IP is already supporting on another interface.
BCAST	This is the broadcast address used for the network interface. The default value is all ones (255.255.255.255), which means a local broadcast. This is normally not changed. TCP/IP software derived from 4.2 BSD may not understand the local broadcast. In this case, you can change the BCAST parameter to use a broadcast address that is compatible with other nodes on the network. Software derived from 4.2 BSD Unix, typically use an all zeros broadcast. This means for a class B network address of 135.23, the all zero broadcast address would be 135.23.0.0. If you are using a mix of 4.2 BSD Unix nodes and NetWare servers, it is best to use an all ones broadcast address. In the example of network address 135.23, an all ones broadcast address would be 135.23.255.255. BSD Unix nodes can be configured to use an all ones broadcast address by using the ifconfig Unix utility.
ARP	Specifies if you are using ARP. Must be set to Yes for broadcast networks such as LANs. When set to No, the host portion of the address is mapped directly to the local hardware address. Mapping the host portion of the address to the local hardware address is possible with Ethernet, and is used in DECnet.

Parameter	Description
GATE	Specifies IP address of default router for this network. IP uses this gateway value to reach other networks that are not directly connected to the NetWare server. If this parameter is not used, NetWare TCP/IP gathers default route information from RIP. If RIP is set to Yes, Novell does not recommend using the GATE parameter. There is no default value for this parameter. When the GATE parameter is specified, a status message of Using IP Address as a default gateway is returned.
DEFROUTE	If set to Yes, the server advertises itself as a default router for other nodes on the network. The default value is No. When DEFROUTE=YES is specified, a status message of `Configured as default router for this network` should be displayed.
COST	Specifies metric cost to be used with RIP in a decimal value that can range from 1 to 16. The value of 16 means that the interface is unreachable and corresponds to a cost of 16. For this reason, only use values from 1 to 15. The default value for the COST parameter is 1. The lower cost value interfaces are selected over higher cost interfaces for routing of packets. When the COST parameter is specified, a status message informing you that the `Interface cost is set to xx` is returned.
POISON	Controls use of "poison reverse" in RIP. *Poison reverse* is a mechanism that determines how routing updates on failed links are sent on the network. When POISION=YES is specified, you will see a status message `Using 'poison reverse'` in RIP's split horizon.

TABLE 3.8 SUMMARY OF DEFAULT AND REQUIRED/ OPTIONAL STATUS OF BIND PARAMETERS

Parameter	Argument Value	Default Value	Required/ Optional
ADDR	IP address	none	required
MASK	network mask	standard	optional
BCAST	IP address	255.255.255.255	optional
ARP	yes/no	yes	optional
GATE	IP address	none	optional
DEFROUTE	yes/no	no	optional
COST	integer	1	optional
POISON	yes/no	no	optional

The following are examples of the use of the BIND IP parameters:

Using BIND IP Parameters: Example 1

To specify an IP address of 132.13.46.1 for the interface and a subnet mask of 255.255.0.0, use the following:

```
BIND  IP   TO   IPNET  ADDR=132.13.46.1  MASK=255.255.0.0
```

or

```
BIND  IP   TO   IPNET  ADDR=132.13.46.1
```

Note that the IPNET used in this and the following examples refers to the name of the network board driver that is loaded with the appropriate frame type. For example, if an NE2000 Ethernet board is being used for TCP/IP, and you want to identify it by the name IPNET, you would use the following:

```
LOAD NE2000 port=300 int=5 frame=ETHERNET_II name=IPNET
BIND IP TO IPNET ADDR=132.13.46.1
```

Using BIND IP Parameters: Example 2

To specify an IP address of 132.13.47.7 for the interface and a subnet mask of 255.255.255.0, will the following statement work?

```
BIND  IP   TO   IPNET  ADDR=132.13.47.7
```

Answer: No. The previous statement assumes a default mask of 255.255.0.0, because 132.13.47.7 is a class B address and no MASK parameter is specified. The default mask of 255.255.0.0 is different from the mask of 255.255.255.0 that was required in the example.

The following is the correct BIND statement for example 2:

```
BIND  IP   TO   IPNET  ADDR=132.13.47.7  MASK=255.255.255.0
```

Using BIND IP Parameters: Example 3

To specify an IP address of 199.245.180.2 for the interface, a subnet mask of 255.255.255.192, and a broadcast mask of 199.245.180.63, you can use the following:

```
BIND  IP   TO   IPNET  ADDR=199.245.180.2    MASK=255.255.255.192
BCAST=199.245.180.63
```

Using BIND IP Parameters: Example 4

To specify that poison reverse be used for the IP address of 199.245.180.131 for the interface and a subnet mask of 255.255.255.240, and that the interface be used as a default router on the network, you can use the following:

```
BIND IP TO IPNET ADDR=199.245.180.131 MASK=255.255.255.240 POISON=YES DEFROUTE=YES
```

TCP/IP Configuration Case Studies

Case Study 1: The NetWare server is on an Ethernet network and has the following statements in its AUTOEXEC.NCF file:

```
LOAD   NE2000  INT=3 PORT=300   NAME=NOVNET
BIND   IPX  TO NOVNET   NET=6F5A
```

Write down the configuration statements to configure a TCP/IP interface on the same network so that the interface has an IP address of 129.222.15.2, a subnet mask of 255.255.255.0 with no forwarding of IP packets, and with RIP enabled.

Answer: The configuration statements that should be placed in the AUTOEXEC.NCF file can be the following:

```
LOAD   NE2000  INT=3 PORT=300   NAME=NOVNET
BIND   IPX  TO NOVNET   NET=6F5A
LOAD NE2000 INT=3 PORT=300 FRAME=ETHERNET_II NAME=IP_A
LOAD TCPIP FORWARD=NO RIP=YES
BIND IP TO IP_A ADDR=129.222.15.2 MASK=255.255.255.0
```

Case Study 2: The NetWare server is on a Token Ring network and has the following statements in its AUTOEXEC.NCF file:

```
LOAD   TOKEN   NAME=TRNET
BIND   IPX  TO TRNET   NET=6E6F
```

Write down the configuration statements to configure a TCP/IP interface on the same network so that the interface has an IP address of 199.245.180.193, a subnet mask of 255.255.255.224 with no forwarding of IP packets, with RIP enabled, and a broadcast address of 199.245.180.255.

Answer: The configuration statements that should be placed in the AUTOEXEC.NCF file can be the following:

```
LOAD   TOKEN   NAME=TRNET
BIND   IPX  TO TRNET   NET=6E6F
LOAD TOKEN NAME=TR_IPNET FRAME=TOKEN-RING_SNAP
LOAD TCPIP FORWARD=NO RIP=YES
BIND IP TO TR_IPNET ADDR=199.245.180.193 MASK=255.255.255.224
BCAST=199.245.180.255
```

Unloading TCP/IP

If you want to reconfigure the TCP/IP parameters on the NetWare server, such as IP address, subnet mask, and broadcast address, you can do so without bringing the server down. To change TCP/IP parameters that are specified in the BIND or LOAD TCPIP statements, you have to execute these commands after you unbind or unload the TCPIP.NLM. The procedure for unloading the TCPIP.NLM is described in figure 3.18.

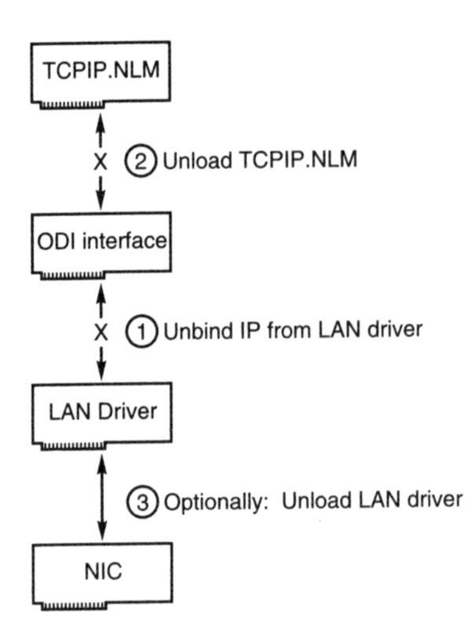

Figure 3.18
Unloading TCP/IP NLMs.

To unload the TCPIP.NLM, these steps must be performed in the reverse order of the load sequence:

1. Unbind IP from LAN driver. To do so, use the UNBIND IP FROM *LAN_DRIVER* command.
2. Unload the TCPIP NLM. This is done using the UNLOAD TCPIP command.
3. Optionally unload LAN_DRIVER if not in use.

NetWare 4.x Options for Configuring TCP/IP

In addition to the methods described in this chapter, NetWare 4.x offers the use of the INETCFG.NLM for configuring TCP/IP and other protocol services.

The INETCGF.NLM presents a graphical user interface with parameter choices for configuring the TCP/IP NLMs. The INETCFG menu controls the setting of the following:

- ◆ Network Boards
- ◆ Protocols
- ◆ Bindings

If you use the INETCFG.NLM, the LOAD and BIND statements in the AUTOEXEC.NCF are commented by placing the # character before each such statement. Additionally, the following statements are added to the AUTOEXEC.NCF file:

```
LOAD CONLOG
LOAD SNMP
INITIALIZE SYSTEM
    .
    .

UNLOAD CONLOG
```

The CONLOG.NLM captures console messages generated during server startup and logs them to the SYS:ETC\CONSOLE.LOG file. This is a text file and can be examined for troubleshooting server startup problems.

The INITIALIZE SYSTEM causes the processing of the information entered through the INETCFG.NLM.

The UNLOAD CONLOG is placed at the end of the AUTOEXEC.NCF file and stops the logging of console messages to conserve disk space. If obtaining a log of console messages is more important than conserving disk space, you can remove the UNLOAD CONLOG statement from the AUTOEXEC.NCF file.

The INETCFG NLM is covered in greater detail in Chapter 6, "Managing TCP/IP Protocols Using INETCFG."

Summary

In this chapter you learned the features of NetWare TCP/IP for NetWare 3.x and 4.x servers. The basic TCP/IP NLMs and configuration files for implementing a TCP/IP stack on a NetWare server are bundled with NetWare server distribution. Additional services, such as NFS, Line Printer Daemon, SMTP mail gateway, and developer's toolkit, are available as separate products.

You learned about the different configuration files that come with the TCP/IP software for NetWare and how to configure the TCPIP.NLM on a NetWare server. The discussion on parameters used with LOAD TCPIP and BIND IP statements were presented with several examples and case studies to facilitate your understanding of this topic.

TCP/IP Routing Support in NetWare

This chapter examines how you can use NetWare TCP/IP to connect several TCP/IP networks. In the previous chapter, you learned that a NetWare TCP/IP server can be configured as an IP router. This chapter will show you how to do this. For IP routers to respond dynamically to changes in network topologies, they must exchange routing messages. This chapter examines the different ways to configure NetWare IP routers.

Introduction to Routing

In the previous chapter, you learned about the GATE (short for *gateway*) parameter that you can use in the BIND IP command to specify the IP address of the default router. The use of a gateway parameter to specify the IP address of an IP router may at first appear to be puzzling. Historically, the devices now called *routers* by the data communications industry were once called gateways. The term *gateways* now means something entirely different. Moreover, at one time, Novell called its IPX routers bridges.

Before you can understand routing, you must understand the differences between repeaters, bridges, routers, and gateways.

An Internetworking Device Model

An effective way to understand the differences between repeaters, bridges, routers, and gateways is to use the OSI model for describing these differences.

Figure 4.1 shows the connectivity between two LANs described in terms of the OSI model. The type of processing needed to provide the connection between two networks at any layer of the OSI model defines whether the device is a repeater, bridge, router, or gateway.

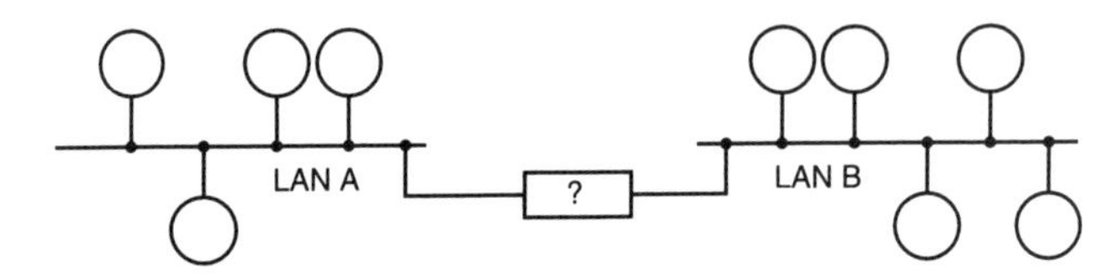

Figure 4.1

Internetworking devices and the OSI model.

Repeaters, Bridges, Routers, and Gateways

If the connectivity between two networks is provided by a device operating at the physical layer of the OSI model, the device is called a *repeater*. The physical layer of the OSI model deals with signal representation on the transport media, not the "meaning" of the bits. On receiving a signal on one of its ports, the repeater device, because it operates at the physical layer, amplifies and retimes the signal and sends the regenerated signal to all of the remaining ports. In 10BASE-T and 100BASE-T Ethernet networks, the repeater device is called a *concentrator* or *hub*. On Token Ring networks, the repeater function is performed by each Token Ring card.

If the connectivity between two networks is provided by a device operating at the data link layer of the OSI model, the device is called a *bridge*. The data link layer of the OSI model deals with *frames* of information. Each frame usually has a sender and destination identification field. For LANs, these fields are called *MAC addresses*. The bridge operates at the data link layer. On receiving a signal on one of its ports, the bridge uses the MAC address fields in the data link header to determine on which port to send the packet. Because bridges operate at the data link layer, the networks connected by the bridges have the same network layer, and they form part of the same logical network.

If the connectivity between two networks is provided by a device operating at the network layer of the OSI model, the device is called a *router*. The network layer of the OSI model deals with routing issues and with the logical addresses of nodes on the network. Each packet in the network layer has a sender and destination network address. For TCP/IP networks, the network addresses are the IP addresses. On receiving a packet, the router uses the network address fields in the data link header to determine on which port to send the packet. Because routers operate at the network layer, the networks connected by the routers must have a unïque network identification. For IP networks, this unique network identification is the network number or *netid* (see Chapter 2, "TCP/IP Network Protocol Architecture") of the IP address of the nodes on the network.

The term *gateway* was formerly used to describe routers. The meaning of the term gateway has changed over the years. If the two networks use different protocols at the upper layers (layer 4 and above) or use completely different protocols, a protocol translation involving several OSI layers is needed. The internetworking device that performs this protocol translation is called a *gateway*. One example of a gateway is application gateways. Application gateways perform protocol translation at the application layer of the OSI model. An application gateway could perform e-mail conversions between Novell's MHS standard and SMTP. Other examples would be a file-transfer gateway between FTP and the equivalent OSI file-transfer protocol (called FTAM, File Transfer and Access Management), or a terminal emulation gateway between TELNET and OSI's VT (Virtual Terminal) protocol.

Because this chapter deals with internetworking issues, the remainder of the discussion will be focused on routers.

The Role of the Router

Figure 4.2 shows a model of a router. A router has two or more ports that can be used for sending or receiving packets. In figure 4.2, the router's ports are designated as an input or output port. This is a simplified view of the router designed to give a conceptual understanding of how routers operate. In actual routers, the ports are bi-directional and are capable of receiving and transmitting data on any port.

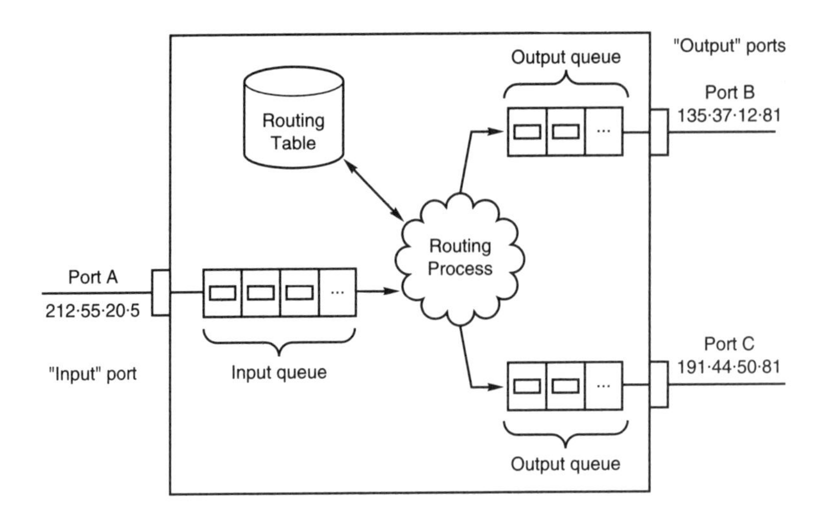

Figure 4.2

Operation of a router.

When a packet arrives at an input port, the router process examines the network layer header of the packet. If the router process is busy processing another packet, the incoming packet is placed in an input queue associated with the port, awaiting its turn to be processed. If the packets arrive more quickly than they can be processed, the number of packets in the queue (called the *length* of the queue), can exceed the size of the queue. When this happens, incoming packets can be lost. A higher-layer protocol mechanism such as TCP on both the sender and receiver recovers the lost packets by retransmitting them.

The router process implements the router operation. In software-based routers such as Novell's Multi Protocol Router (MPR), the router process is a software program activated on the router hardware. On high-performance routers, such as those from Cisco, Wellfleet, 3COM, and DEC, the router process is implemented in firmware or special hardware. The IP routing function that comes with NetWare TCP/IP is built into TCPIP.NLM.

The router process examines the destination address of the incoming packet and consults a database of routing information called the *routing table.* The router process sends the packet to one of its output ports based on information in the routing table and the destination address in the packet.

The entries in the routing table can be made manually, initialized from a file containing routes, or updated dynamically. In modern routers, the routing table is updated dynamically. For router updates to occur dynamically, the routers communicate routing information to each other. The mechanism used to communicate routing information between routers is called a *routing protocol.* Examples of routing protocols for TCP/IP are Routing Information Protocol (RIP) and Open Shortest Path First (OSPF).

Some protocols, such as OSI's Intermediate System to Intermediate System (IS-IS) and Novell's NetWare Link Service Protocol (NLSP), can send routing information independently of the network layer protocol.

If a packet is sent to an output port that is busy transmitting a previous packet, the new packet is placed in the output queue associated with the port.

The network directly connected to one of the router's ports is called a *directly connected network.* A router's ports must have an IP address assigned to them that is compatible with the network address of their directly connected network. This is because a router's port is seen by other nodes as a TCP/IP interface on the directly connected network. For example, if port B of the router (refer to fig. 4.2) connects to a class B network with the IP address 135.37.0.0, port B's IP address must have the same network address, 135.37. For example, port B's IP address could be 135.37.12.81. The host address of the IP address, 12.81, is assigned by the network Administrator, and must be different from all other IP addresses on the network directly connected to port B.

IP Routing Example

All hosts that need to send an IP packet to a network, other than the directly connected network, must have a locally maintained routing table. Hosts learn about networks through routers and through routing tables with which they can be initialized. The routing information about networks kept at a host is called the *host routing table.* A common misconception is that only routers keep a routing table. In the next example, you learn that hosts keep a minimal routing table used to send packets to remote hosts and networks.

The host routing table should not be confused with the routing table maintained at routers. The host routing table contains only information about other networks or hosts that the sender host is interested in reaching. The host may acquire this information from other routers. Routers maintain a more general-purpose routing table, which knows many networks, as well as the next router to which a packet should be forwarded. Routers actively participate in the routing algorithms of the network and know the costs for reaching a specific network.

When a host sends an IP packet, it performs the following operations:

- If the network address (netid) of the packet is the same as the network address of the directly connected network, the packet is sent directly to the destination. In this case, routing is not required.

- If the network address (netid) of the packet is different from the network address of the directly connected network, the packet is sent to a router. The IP address of the router port is obtained by consulting the host's routing table.

- If there is no entry in the host routing table for the destination network or host, the default router entry is used. The default router entry is initialized with the IP address of the router port to which a packet will be sent, if there is no explicit entry in the router's table for the destination network or host. If there is no default router entry, the packet cannot be routed, and an error is reported to the host that the destination is not reachable.

To understand how a TCP/IP host uses its routing table, and how routing works, consider the example shown in figure 4.3.

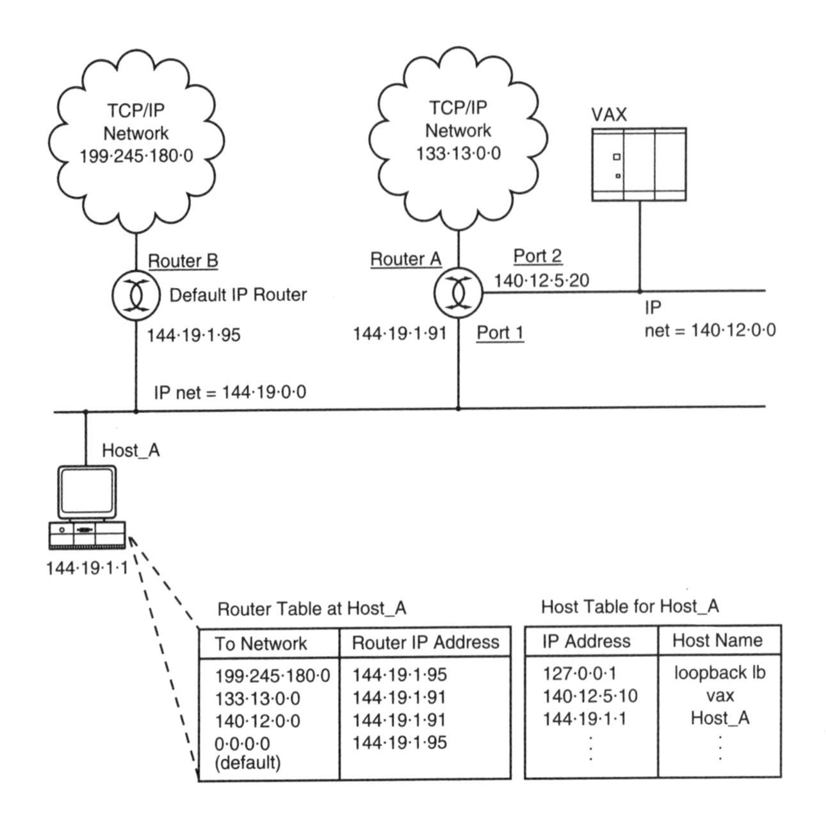

Figure 4.3

Routing at the host.

This example shows Host_A with the IP address 144.19.1.1 on an Ethernet network 144.19.0.0 that needs to initiate a TELNET session to the host vax on the IP network with the address 140.12.0.0. The two networks are joined together with a router. The router port's IP address is 144.19.1.91 on network 144.19.0.0, and 140.12.5.20 on network 140.12.0.0. There is another router on network 144.19.0.0 with the IP address 144.19.1.95. This router acts as a default router for the network 144.19.0.0. This means that all IP packets whose destination networks are not explicitly entered in a host's routing table will be forwarded to the default router at 144.19.1.95. In this example, the Host_A's host routing table has been initialized with the following entries:

To Network	Router IP Address (Next Hop)
199.245.180.0	144.19.1.95
133.13.0.0	144.19.1.91
140.12.0.0	144.19.1.91
0.0.0.0 (default)	144.19.1.9

All IP packets to be sent to the class C network address 199.245.180.0 must be forwarded to the router 144.19.1.95; all IP packets to be sent to the class B network address 140.12.0.0 must be forwarded to the router 144.19.1.91. Additionally, packets sent to class B network 133.13.0.0 must be forwarded to the router 144.19.1.91. Packets sent to any other network must be forwarded to the default router 144.19.1.95. The default router is indicated by the entry 0.0.0.0. The router at IP address 144.19.1.95 is explicitly listed for network 199.245.180.0 and also acts as a default router.

Host_A has a host's file containing host names and their IP addresses. (See Chapter 2 for an understanding of the purpose and structure of the hosts file.) The contents of this host file are as follows:

# IP Address	Host Name
127.0.0.1	loopback lb
140.12.5.10	vax
144.19.1.1	Host_A

It is possible for a host to use DNS to resolve host names, but in this example, it is assumed that the local host file is used for resolving host names.

The following steps describe the sequence of events that takes place when Host_A executes the command:

```
telnet vax
```

1. Host_A consults its host's file and finds that the IP address of host vax is 140.12.5.10.
2. Host_A compares the network address of the destination IP address with the network address of the directly connected network. Host_A discovers that the network address of the destination is 140.12.0.0 and the network address of the directly attached network is 144.19.0.0.

   Because these network addresses are different, Host_A consults its host routing table for an entry for network 140.12.0.0. The entry for 140.12.0.0 is found in the host routing table. This entry indicates that the packet to the host vax must be forwarded to the router port with the IP address 144.19.1.91
3. Host_A needs to determine the hardware address of the router's port to send a packet to that port. Remember that IP packets are encapsulated by the data link layer for transmission by the underlying network (Ethernet, in this case). Host_A uses the ARP protocol to discover the router's hardware address. This address goes into the MAC header as the destination address of the MAC frame (see fig. 4.4). The source address in the MAC header is the hardware address of Host_A.

Figure 4.4

A packet sent to the local router from a sender.

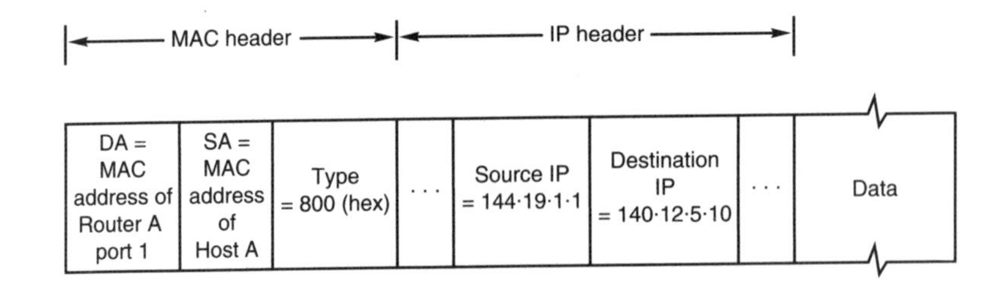

DA = Destination Address
SA = Source Address
• MAC header assumed to be for Ethernet
• Only IP address fields in IP header are shown

4. The router examines the IP header of the packet received and realizes that the destination IP address is on a network connected directly to one of its ports. The router uses ARP to discover the destination host's MAC address (host vax's MAC address) and places it in the destination address of the MAC frame. The router places its port hardware address in the source address of the MAC Frame (see fig. 4.5).

Figure 4.5

A packet sent to a destination from a router.

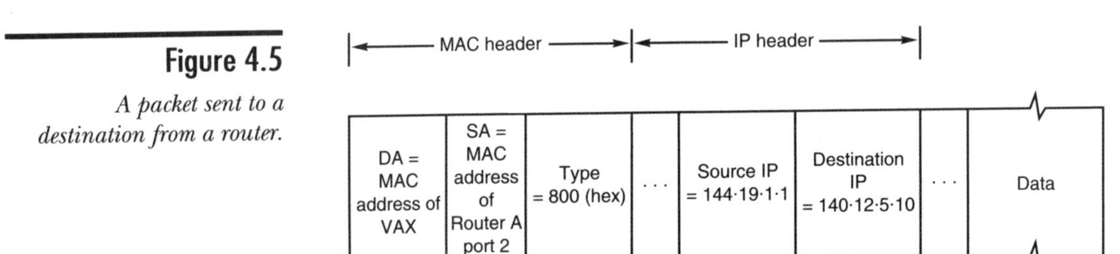

NetWare Routing Configuration

The TCPIP.NLM enables a NetWare server to act as an IP router. The IP router can learn about other networks using a routing protocol such as RIP. Besides using RIP, there are other ways that the NetWare TCP/IP router can learn about routes.

The NetWare TCP/IP router can learn about other networks and hosts (see fig. 4.6) using the following:

- The TCP/IP console program, TCPCON.NLM
- The IP configuration utility, IPCONFIG.NLM
- The Routing Information Protocol, RIP
- The Internet Control Message Protocol, ICMP

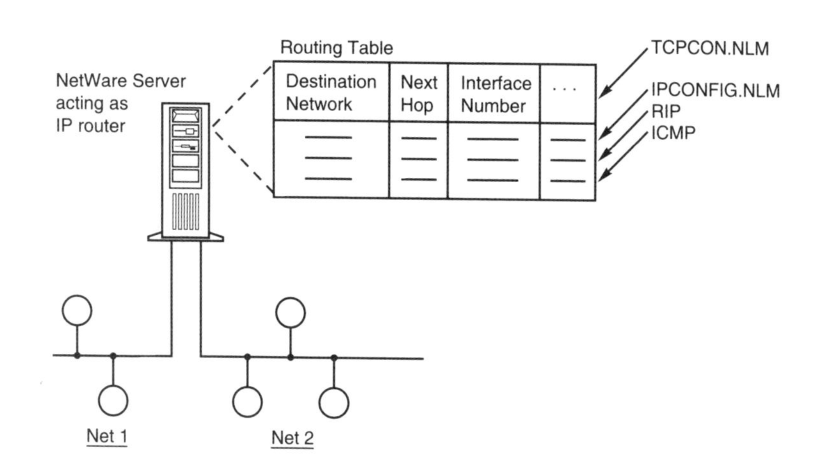

Figure 4.6

Methods for updating the IP routing table.

Routing Table and TCPCON

To modify the routing table using TCPCON, follow these steps:

1. From the NetWare server console, enter the following command:

   ```
   LOAD TCPCON
   ```

   For TCPCON to load, your NetWare server must be configured with TCP/IP. See Chapter 3, "Managing Basic TCP/IP Protocol Elements in NetWare," for details about TCP/IP configuration.

   When TCPCON loads, the main screen appears, as shown in figure 4.7.

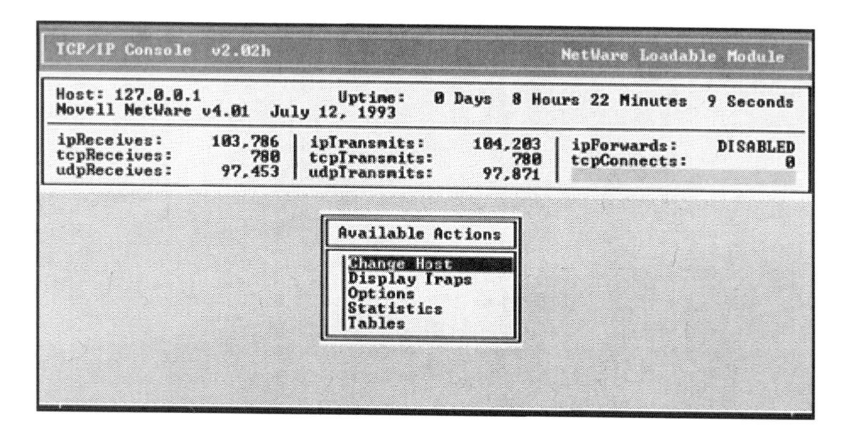

Figure 4.7

TCPCON's main menu.

2. From the TCPCON main screen, select Tables.

   A list of tables appears, as shown in figure 4.8.

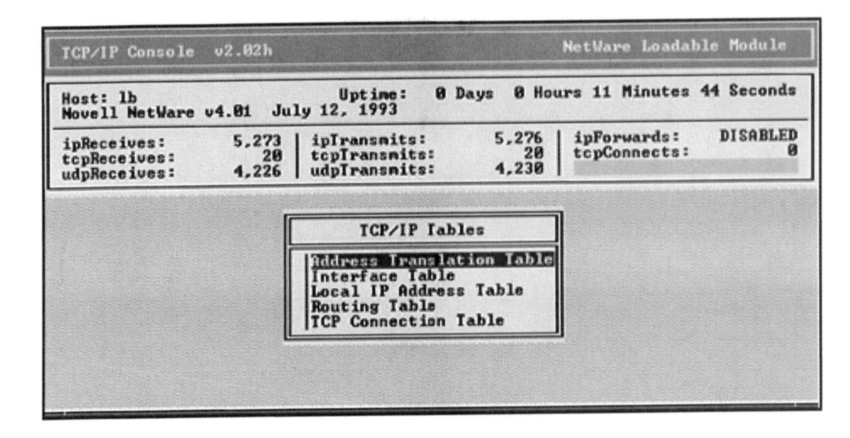

Figure 4.8

The TCP/IP Tables options in TCPCON.

3. From the tables menu, select Routing Table.

   The Routing Table screen appears, as shown in figure 4.9.

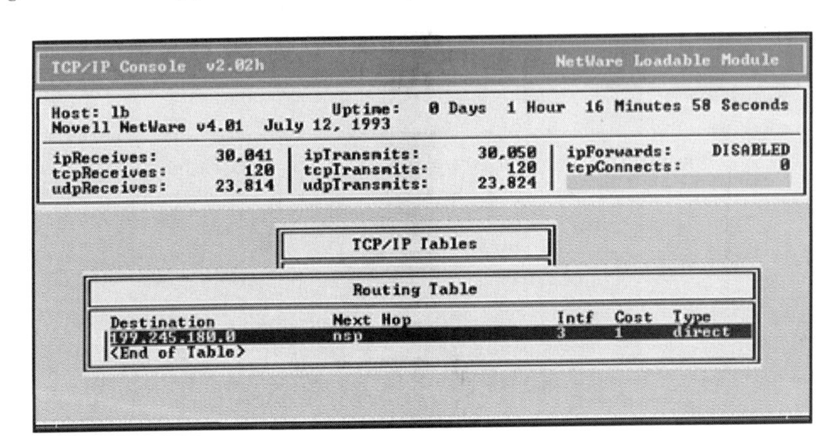

Figure 4.9

The Routing Table screen.

4. Press Insert or Enter to create an IP routing table entry. The router entry screen appears (see fig. 4.10).

If you examine the routing table entries in figure 4.10, you notice that some of the routing table entry names have either a colon (:) or a colon-dot (:.) next to them. The colon signifies that the value is read-only, and the colon-dot signifies that the value can be modified.

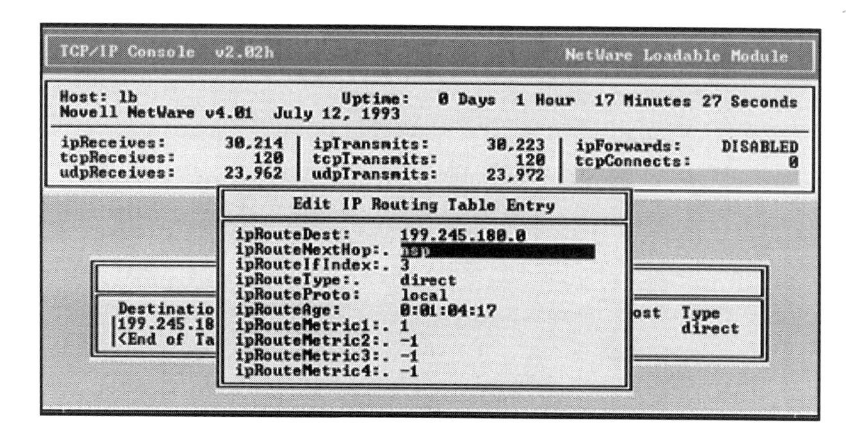

Figure 4.10

The Edit IP Routing Table Entry screen.

Table 4.1 gives a description of the routing table entry names.

TABLE 4.1 ROUTING TABLE ENTRY NAMES

Routing Table	Description
ipRouteDest	The IP address of the destination network or host. A value of 0.0.0.0 indicates a default route. The IP address can be in dotted decimal notation, or it can be a symbolic name from the HOSTS or NETWORKS file. This field is modifiable.
ipRouteNextHop	The IP address of router-to-forward packets destined for the address in ipRouteDest. This field is modifiable.
ipRouteIfIndex	This identifies the number of network interfaces used to reach the router. By default, the network interface for which a driver is loaded first is called *interface number 1.* All other network interfaces are numbered in the same order in which their device drivers are loaded. This field is modifiable.
ipRouteType	This parameter has the value of either *direct* or *remote.* It indicates if a destination is connected to a directly attached network. Remote destinations require one or more routers. This field is modifiable.
ipRouteProto	This indicates the source used to make the entry. The values for this parameter can be netmgmt, local, icmp, or rip. Local indicates that the utility IPCONFIG was used to make the router entry. This field is read-only.
ipRouteAge	This parameter indicates the time in the format *days:hours:minutes:secs* since the routing entry was made. This field is read-only.
ipRouteMetric	This parameter indicates the routing cost metric associated with the route. Usually, this is referred to as the *hop count.* It indicates the number of routers a packet must pass through to get to the destination. This field is modifiable.

OSPF (Open Shortest Path First) is a link-state protocol used with TCP/IP and has many characteristics that make it superior to RIP. It will be included in later releases of NetWare 4.x. For a discussion on how link state-routing protocols operate, see the author's *NetWare Professional Reference, Fourth Edition,* published by New Riders Publishing.

When IPCONFIG.NLM is loaded, it reads the contents of the file SYS:ETC\GATEWAYS (see fig. 4.11). This file contains network and host-specific routes, their metric cost, and whether or not the entry is "permanent" for the duration of the router activation. A permanent router entry is one that cannot be modified unless the router is stopped and a different value for the router entry is made.

Figure 4.11

Using IPCONFIG.

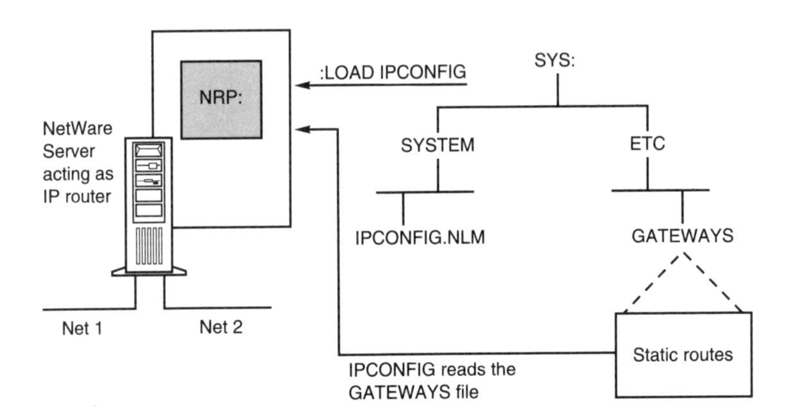

After IPCONFIG.NLM finishes processing SYS:ETC\GATEWAYS, it automatically unloads. The IPCONFIG exists in the server RAM only for the duration that the SYS:ETC\GATEWAYS file is being read and processed.

On Unix systems there is an /etc/gateway file that is read by the utility routed (pronounced "route-dee"). The format of the SYS:ETC\GATEWAYS file is the same as the format of the /etc/gateways file used in Unix.

The IPCONFIG utility should be loaded only after the TCP/IP stack is configured properly. Proper configuration of TCP/IP implies that the TCPIP.NLM has been loaded and that IP is bound to the network interface.

Each line in the SYS:ETC\GATEWAYS file has the following syntax:

```
NET net_name[/net_mask] GATEWAY router_addr [METRIC cost] [ACTIVE ¦ PASSIVE]
```

or

```
HOST host_name GATEWAY router_addr [METRIC cost] [ACTIVE ¦ PASSIVE]
```

The entries for networks begin with the reserved word NET, and entries for specific hosts begin with the reserved word HOST.

The *net_name* is the name of the network that is defined in the SYS:ETC\NETWORKS file. The *net_mask* is the subnet mask for the network. The *net_mask* is optional. If you do not specify it, a default subnet mask is assumed. The default *net_mask* value indicates that no subnetworking is being used.

The *host_name* is the name of the network that is defined in the SYS:ETC\HOSTS file.

The *router_addr* is the IP address of the router port on the directly connected network to which packets for the specified network or host should be forwarded.

The *cost* is an estimate of the expense of routing through a specific router port. The *cost* is an optional parameter. If you do not specify a value, a *cost* of 1 is assumed for routing through the specified router. The *cost* parameter can have a value from 1 to 15. A value of 16 implies that the network or host is unreachable through the specified router address.

The reserved words ACTIVE and PASSIVE identify the router as an active or passive router. If the router is specified as PASSIVE, the router on which IPCONFIG is being run assumes that the specified router cannot participate in routing message exchanges (RIP), and the route is flagged as permanent in the routing table. If the router is specified as ACTIVE, the router on which IPCONFIG is being run assumes that the specified router can communicate its routing table. If no message is received from the active router for a period of time, the routing entry for that route is expired. If neither the reserved word ACTIVE or PASSIVE is specified, a default of PASSIVE is assumed—that is, router entries are marked as permanent.

Table 4.2 summarizes the parameters used in the GATEWAYS file.

TABLE 4.2 THE GATEWAYS FILE PARAMETERS

Parameter	Description
NET *net_name*	*net_name* refers to the IP address of the network or name of network in the NETWORKS file. It is the final destination to which to route the packet.
HOST *host_name*	*host_name* refers to the IP address of the host or name of host in the HOSTS file. It is the final destination to which to route the packet.
GATEWAY *router_addr*	*router_addr* refers to the IP address of the router to which to forward packets.
METRIC *cost*	*cost* refers to the cost of the route. The value ranges from 1 to 16 (unreachable). For RIP, this metric refers to the hop count. If not specified, a value of 1 is assumed.
ACTIVE | PASSIVE	Routes can be ACTIVE or PASSIVE. ACTIVE routes are automatically expired after a certain period of time, if new information on that route is not received. PASSIVE routes remain permanently in memory and are not expired. If not specified, routes default to PASSIVE routes.

The following are examples of the use of the GATEWAYS file.

Example 1

```
NET 133.65.0.0 GATEWAY 144.79.4.3 PASSIVE
```

In this example, a packet to the network 133.65.0.0 can be sent to the router at 144.79.4.3. This entry is marked as permanent in the routing table because it is assumed that router entry 144.79.4.3 cannot participate in routing message exchanges. The cost of this route defaults to a value of 1.

The NetWare TCP/IP router on which IPCONFIG is loaded to process the entry in the SYS:ETC\GATEWAYS file must be on the network 144.79.0.0, because the specified router 144.79.4.3 must be on the directly connected network.

Example 2

```
NET 17.0.0.0 GATEWAY 199.245.180.91
```

In this example, a packet to the network 17.0.0.0 can be sent to the router at 199.245.180.91. This route entry defaults to a PASSIVE route. This means that the route is marked as permanent in the routing table because it is assumed that router 199.245.180.91 cannot participate in routing message exchanges. The cost of this route defaults to a value of 1.

The NetWare TCP/IP router on which IPCONFIG is loaded to process the entry in the SYS:ETC\GATEWAYS file must be on the network 199.245.180.0, because the specified router 199.245.180.91 must be on the directly connected network.

Example 3

```
NET 233.230.225.0 GATEWAY 129.24.10.11 ACTIVE
```

In this example, a packet to the network 233.230.225.0 can be sent to the router at 129.24.10.11. This route entry is marked ACTIVE. It is assumed that router 129.24.10.11 can participate in routing message exchanges. If no router updates are heard from the router 129.24.10.11 about the route to 233.230.225.0, the specified router entry will be timed-out and removed from the router table. The cost of this route defaults to a value of 1.

The NetWare TCP/IP router on which IPCONFIG is loaded to process the entry in the SYS:ETC\GATEWAYS file must be on the network 129.24.0.0, because the specified router 129.24.10.11 must be on the directly connected network.

Example 4

```
NET 23.0.0.0 GATEWAY 12.24.10.11 ACTIVE METRIC 4
```

In this example, a packet to the network 23.0.0.0 can be sent to the router at 12.24.10.11. This route is marked as being ACTIVE. Router 12.24.10.11 can participate in routing message exchanges. If no router updates are heard from the router 12.24.10.11 about the route to 233.230.225.0, the specified router entry will be timed-out and removed from the router table. The cost of this route is set to a value of 4. If another route with a lower cost than 4 to network 23.0.0.0 is received by the router, it will be selected over the specified route.

The NetWare TCP/IP router on which IPCONFIG is loaded to process the entry in the SYS:ETC\GATEWAYS file must be on the network 12.0.0.0, because the specified router 12.24.10.11 must be on the directly connected network.

Example 5

```
HOST 134.33.43.2 GATEWAY 12.24.10.11 ACTIVE METRIC 3
```

In this example, a packet to the host 134.33.43.2 can be sent to the router at 12.24.10.11. This is an example of a host-specific route. Most router table entries are for networks, but it is possible to specify entries for important hosts. This route entry is marked as ACTIVE. It is assumed that router 12.24.10.11 can participate in routing message exchanges. If no router updates are heard from the router 12.24.10.11 about the route to host 134.33.43.2, the specified router entry will be timed-out and removed from the router table. The cost of this route is set to a value of 3. If another route with a lower cost than 3 to the host 134.33.43.2 is received by the router, it will be selected over the specified route.

The NetWare TCP/IP router on which IPCONFIG is loaded to process the entry in the SYS:ETC\GATEWAYS file must be on the network 12.0.0.0, because the specified router 12.24.10.11 must be on the directly connected network.

Using the Routing Information Protocol (RIP)

The Routing Information Protocol (RIP) specified in RFC 1058 is an example of a distance-vector routing protocol. In a distance-vector routing protocol such as RIP, the entire routing table is broadcast at periodic intervals to all other routers. Each entry of the routing table that is broadcast contains the following information:

```
<destination, hop count>
```

The *destination* is the network address of the network or the host address of the host that is reachable through the router at a cost of *hop count*. The routing table is broadcast at a default interval of 30 seconds. The neighbor routers update their routing table based on this route table broadcast. Routers that are neighbors are assumed to be one hop away.

In the example in figure 4.12, routers R2, R4, and R5 are neighbors of router R1.

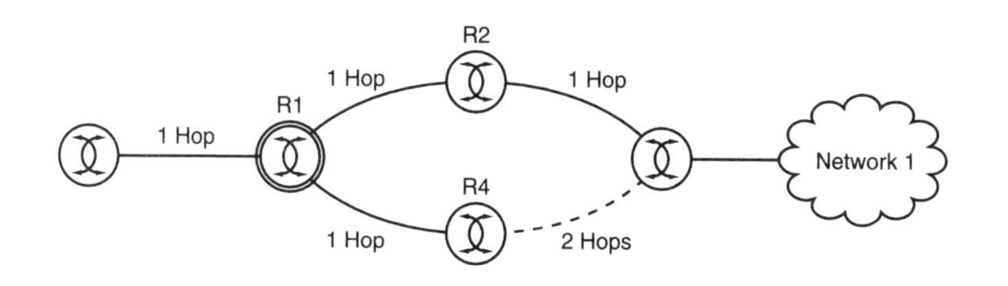

Figure 4.12

A best route cost example using RIP.

If R1 receives a router update from R2, R4, or R5 about the routes reachable through them, it performs the following actions:

The router R1 adds 1 to the route path cost (metric) received from the neighbors, and takes the minimum of these routes. A value of 1 is added to the route path cost reported by the neighbor, because the router, R1, is one hop away from the neighbor's, by definition. If a neighbor's route path cost to destination is *x* hops, R1's route path cost must be $x + 1$ hops away.

In general, the minimum hop count is calculated from the following formula:

Min {hop count information from neighbor router + 1}

Applying this to figure 4.12, assume that R2 reports that the cost to reach a network N1 is two hops and R4 reports that the cost to reach network N1 is three hops:

Hop count information from neighbor R2 = 2

Hop count information from neighbor R3 = 3

The best path to reach N1 from R1 is computed as follows:

Minimum {(Hop count information from neighbor R2 + 1),
Hop count information from neighbor R3 + 1)}

= Minimum {(2+1), (3+1)}
= Minimum {3, 4}

= 3 (through router R2)

The cost metric for a route usually represents the hop count, but a route can be configured to advertise a cost metric that is different from the hop count. This can be used to make some routes attractive and other routes unattractive. For example, if there is a relatively slow link between two LANs, the link can be given a higher cost metric to make it less attractive than other links that are faster. A fast link yields a better performance and can be made more attractive by reducing its cost metric.

The Internet Control Message Protocol (ICMP)

The Internet Control Message Protocol (ICMP) is part of the Internet Layer of the DoD model and is described in RFC 792. No special configuration is needed to configure ICMP—it is part of the Internet layer implemented by TCPIP.NLM. ICMP is used to report errors on the IP datagrams. It does not make the IP protocol layer more reliable. Though ICMP reports errors on the Internet layer, it does not make the data transmission more reliable—it is up to an upper layer protocol such as TCP to make the Internet layer more reliable. ICMP reports information on network parameters, errors on the network, and it can also be used to diagnose the network. Figure 4.13 shows the different ICMP services that are available. The ICMP services include the following:

- Using echo to test availability of a TCP/IP host
- Measuring the timestamp

- Indicating whether the Time to Live has expired
- Indicating whether the destination network or host is unreachable
- Detecting errors in IP parameters in the IP header
- Redirecting messages for better routes
- Determining the subnet address mask of the network to which the host is attached
- Providing the source quench to inform source to slow down sending of packets

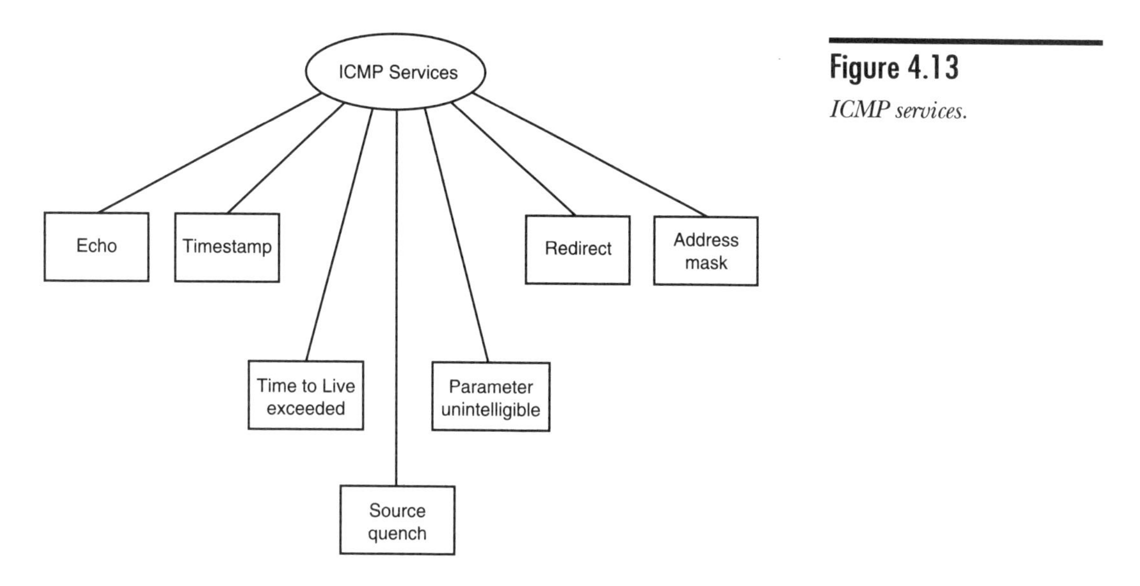

Figure 4.13

ICMP services.

A detailed discussion of the different types of ICMP services is beyond the scope of this book. This book's discussion focuses on the ICMP Redirect messages that can be used to update router tables for a NetWare TCP/IP router.

Figure 4.14 shows a network that has two IP routers attached to a LAN. The routers are used to provide connection to an IP network that connects to remote hosts. Assume that initially only one, Router 1, is connected to the LAN. The workstation on the LAN will have its host routing table set to use Router 1. If a new router, Router 2, is attached to the LAN, the workstation on the LAN will not know about this new router unless its host table has been explicitly initialized with the new router, Router 2. ICMP can be used to initialize the workstation with information about Router 2. Because Router 1 and Router 2 exchange routing messages, Router 1 may know that a packet sent to Router 1 from the workstation can be sent through a better route if it was sent to Router 2. In this case, Router 1 will send an ICMP redirect message to the workstation that informs the workstation that there is a better route to the destination through Router 2. The workstation can then initialize its routing table with the new route through Router 2.

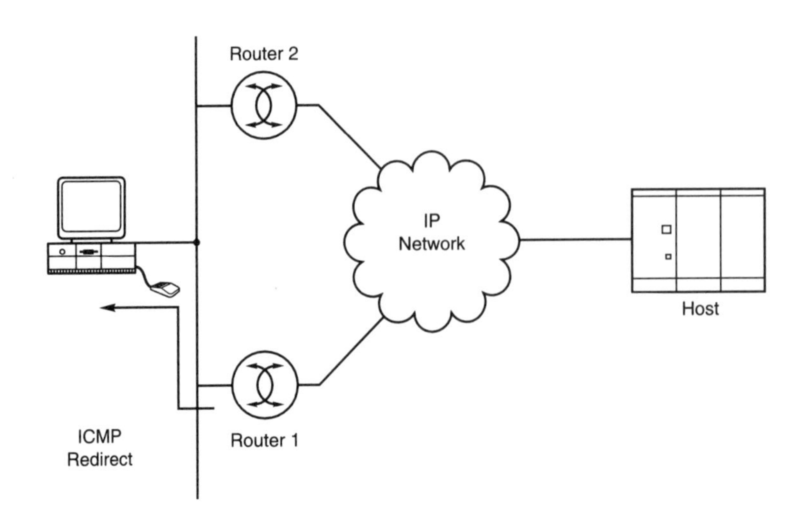

Figure 4.14
Using ICMP redirect messages.

This discussion assumes that the node attached to the LAN is a workstation. If the node is a NetWare TCP/IP server, its routing table can also be initialized using ICMP redirect messages.

BSD 4.2-derived TCP/IP software ignores ICMP redirect messages. This causes routers that discover a better path to send an ICMP redirect message for every packet sent on an inefficient path. The additional traffic generated because of the ICMP redirect messages cause additional stress on the network. BSD 4.3 fixed the problem, but the new redirect route times-out after a period of time, and then reverts to the old route. The whole process repeats, but this is still better than an ICMP redirect for every packet that is sent.

Router Configuration Steps

To configure a NetWare server as an IP router, you must have at least two or more NICs in the NetWare TCP/IP server connected to distinct network segments (see fig. 4.15).

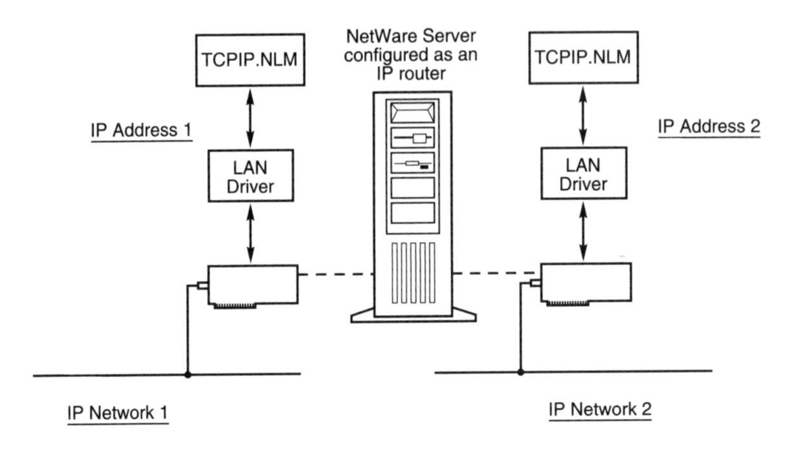

Figure 4.15
NetWare TCP/IP router configuration.

The following is a summary of the steps needed to configure a NetWare TCP/IP router from the server console. These commands can also be placed in the AUTOEXEC.NCF file.

1. Load LAN drivers.

   If two NICs are of the same type, the same driver must be loaded reentrantly a second time with the correct frame type needed for TCP/IP. Remember that NetWare TCP/IP requires that Ethernet use a frame type of ETHERNET_II and Token Ring use a frame type of TOKEN-RING_SNAP.

2. Load TCPIP.NLM.

3. Bind IP to the LAN driver.

TCPIP NLM Configuration Parameters for Routing

The TCPIP.NLM must be loaded with a FORWARD=Yes parameter. You should also set RIP=Yes to have the NetWare TCP/IP server participate in routing exchanges (see fig. 4.16).

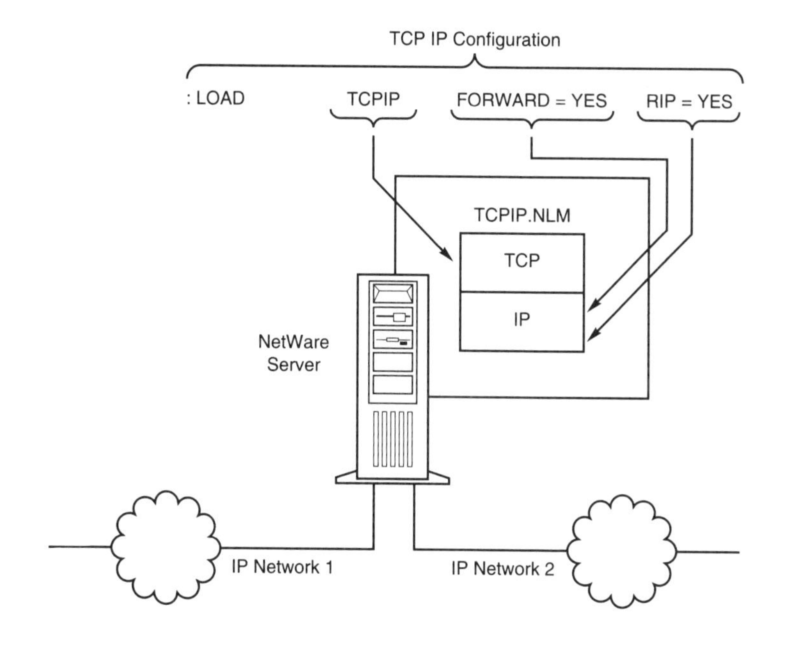

Figure 4.16
Configuring TCPIP.NLM for routing.

When RIP is set to Yes, the NetWare TCP/IP server updates its routing table based on information received through RIP messages. If the NetWare TCP/IP server also acts as an IP router, it sends RIP update messages to other routers. The default value for the RIP parameter is Yes.

In situations where you suspect routing updates to be erroneous because of incorrect routing messages, you may want to set RIP=No. Setting RIP=No ignores RIP update messages. If you are disabling RIP updates, you may want to use static routes specified through the SYS:ETC\GATEWAYS file and IPCONFIG.NLM.

BIND IP Routing Parameters

When IP is bound to the network driver that has been loaded with the correct frame type, you must at a minimum specify the IP address of the network interface. The IP address is specified through the ADDR parameter. Optionally, you can specify the subnet mask (MASK parameter) or the broadcast address (BCAST parameter). Chapter 3 discusses many of the BIND IP parameters in detail. The following BIND IP parameters have a special meaning for routers:

- COST
- DEFROUTE
- POISON

These BIND parameters are specified in the BIND IP statement as follows:

```
BIND IP TO IPNET ADDR=ipaddr COST=metric POISON={Yes¦No} DEFROUTE={Yes¦No}
otherparams
```

Although the COST parameter can have a value from 1 to 16, the POISON and DEFROUTE parameters only can have a value of Yes or No.

The COST Parameter

If the NetWare TCP/IP server is acting as a router, the COST parameter on the BIND IP statement represents the cost of routing packets through the server's interface.

The COST parameter normally represents the hop count. Usually each router on the path adds a hop count of 1 to the total cost of reaching the destination. However, the route path cost can be changed to discourage the NetWare TCP/IP server from being used as a router. You may want to do this to reduce the impact of IP routing on the NetWare TCP/IP server. This is true especially if the server is used for executing workstation requests and other file-server related functions as well.

The COST parameter can be set to a value from 1 to 16. A value of 16 implies that the router is unreachable and for all practical purposes is synonymous to a value of infinity.

Consider the network in figure 4.17, where the NetWare TCP/IP server and another router are used to link network segments 201.15.81.0 and 201.12.23.0. The server network interface 201.12.23.102 is configured with the following BIND IP statement:

```
BIND IP TO IPNET ADDR=201.12.23.102 COST=5
```

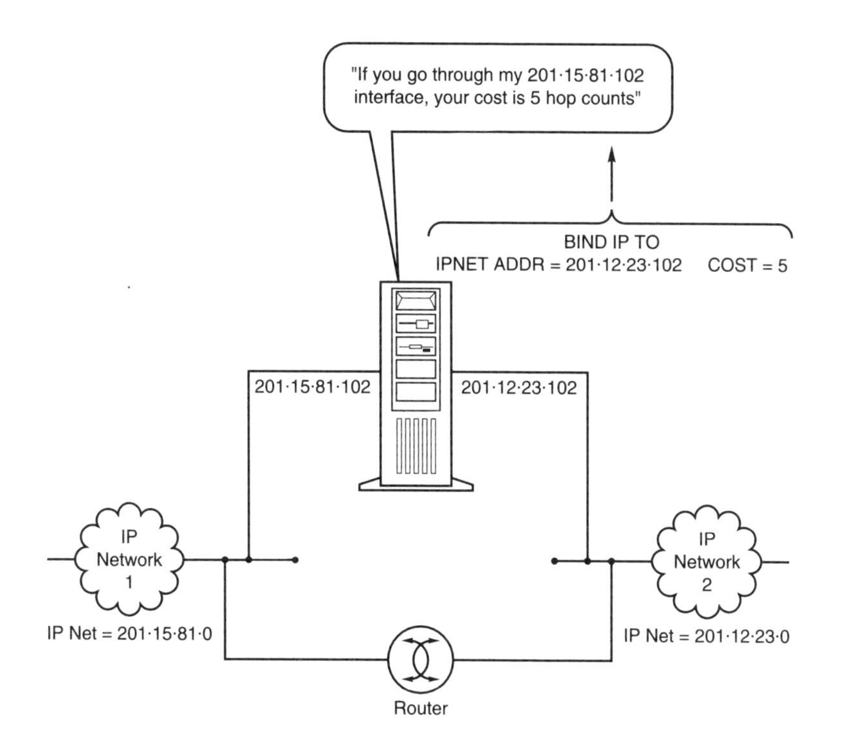

Figure 4.17

Using the COST parameter.

The NetWare TCP/IP server will advertise that the cost of reaching it through its 201.12.23.102 interface is 5. This will discourage the use of the server as a router through the 201.12.23.102 network interface. If the alternate router shown in figure 4.17 has a lower cost than the 201.12.23.102 interface, it will be selected as a preferred router over the NetWare TCP/IP server.

The DEFROUTE Parameter

If the NetWare TCP/IP server is acting as a router, the DEFROUTE parameter on the BIND IP statement can be used to advertise the server as a default router on the network.

The DEFROUTE parameter can have only the value Yes or No. If the DEFROUTE parameter is set to Yes, the router advertises that destination network 0.0.0.0 can be reached through itself with a cost of 1. The network entry 0.0.0.0 in the router table indicates that the specified router address is used as a default router. The default value of the DEFROUTE parameter is No.

The DEFROUTE parameter is used to override default router entries in hosts on network, and enables a server to hide routing information on this network.

Consider the network shown in figure 4.18, which has two routers. Initially, the workstations on the network are configured to use the router, R1, as a default router. The NetWare TCP/IP server is then configured with the following BIND IP statement:

```
BIND IP TO IPNET ADDR=135.105.7.97 DEFROUTE=YES
```

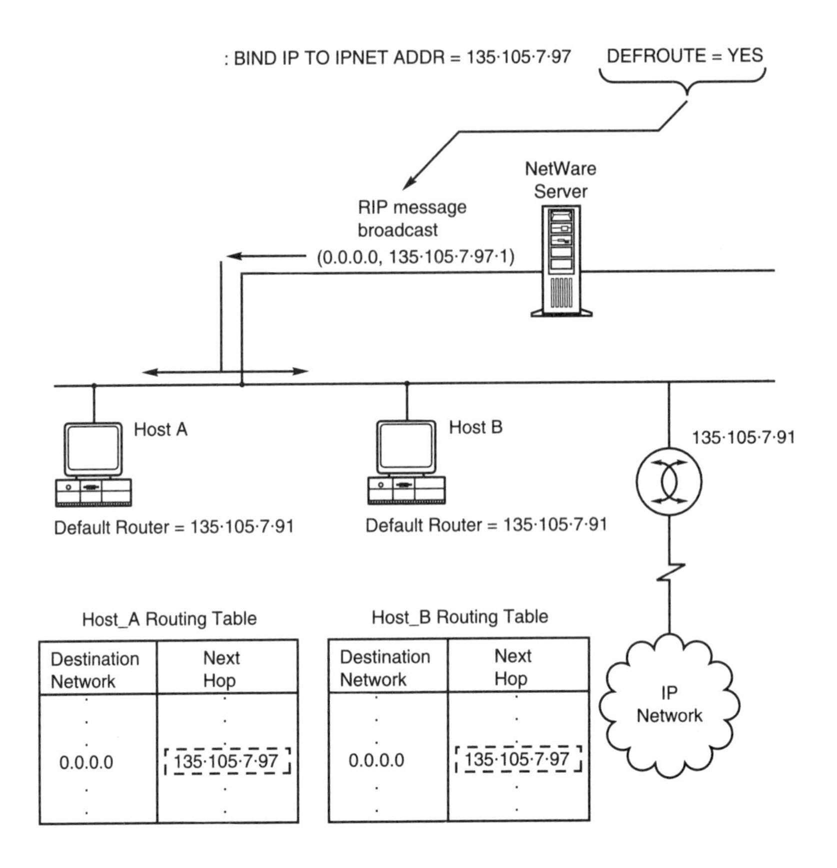

Figure 4.18

Using the DEFROUTE parameter.

As a result of the previous binding, if RIP=Yes is enabled when TCPIP.NLM was loaded, RIP messages will be broadcast on the network 135.105.0.0 announcing that the network 0.0.0.0 can be reached through the network interface 135.105.7.97 at a cost of one hop. The workstations on receiving this RIP broadcast will change their default router to 135.105.7.97, the network interface on the NetWare TCP/IP router. If a network is not reachable through the new default router interface, and there is no explicit entry for the network in the host routing table for the workstation, the network will be unreachable and effectively hidden from the workstations. Be careful to select the default route values correctly. An incorrectly specified value (by setting DEFROUTE=Yes) could result in making routing loops or the destination networks unreachable.

The POISON Parameter

If the POISON parameter is set to Yes in the BIND IP command for a NetWare TCP/IP server acting as a router, it broadcasts RIP packets indicating that all routes learned through the interface specified in the BIND IP command are unreachable. It does this by broadcasting a value of 16 as a metric.

The POISON parameter is used as one of the solutions to a problem with RIP called the count-to-infinity problem.

RIP routers, by default, exchange routing at periodic intervals (for example, every 30 seconds). The RIP message contains a list of all routes known to that router. In other words, each RIP message contains the entire routing table of the router. For large networks the routing table tends to be large and the RIP messages are proportionately large. A router, on receiving a RIP message from its neighbor, recomputes the routes in its table based on the new information, and sends the recomputed routing table on its next broadcast interval. As links go up and down, it may take several broadcast intervals before the routers have a consistent view of the network. This problem is known as *slow convergence.*

In addition to slow convergence, RIP has no authentication mechanism to prevent an intruder from broadcasting an incorrect RIP message. Other known problems that plague distance-vector-based methods are the count-to-infinity problem and the absence of routing domains so that routing in a designated area or domain can be accomplished without impacting other areas of the network.

The count-to-infinity problem is a classic problem associated with distance vector schemes of which RIP is an example. This problem arises when a router (Router B) sends recomputed information about a route to a router (Router A) from which it originally received the information (see fig. 4.19). If a link connected to Router A is broken, Router A waits for its next broadcast interval to send information about unreachable destinations to its neighbor.

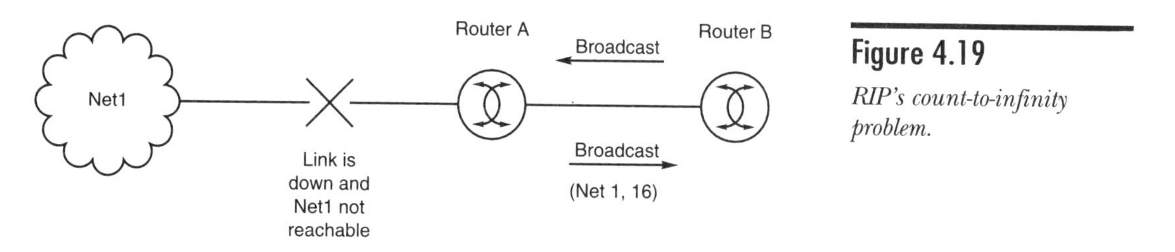

Figure 4.19

RIP's count-to-infinity problem.

Meanwhile, Router B doesn't know about destinations that are unreachable, and sends its routing table to Router A before Router A can send its broadcast. This routing table contains old information about the status of the links, including the link which is down. Router A thinks that the unreachable destinations are reachable through Router B and updates its table with incorrect information. Because Router B is a neighbor, Router A adds its distance from Router B to the route path information received from Router B. When Router A broadcasts its incorrect routing table to Router B, Router B adds its distance from Router A to reach destinations through Router A. At each broadcast interval the distance-metric to reach the unreachable destinations grows until they reach a value that is assumed to be infinity. In RIP, this value is 16 hops.

One solution to the count-to-infinity problem of RIP is *split-horizon,* and another is *poison reverse.* In split-horizon, you do not report information about destinations from routers from which you originally received the information.

In poison reverse, changed information is sent immediately without waiting for the next broadcast interval. The link that is down is announced as a "poison" route to the rest of the network. This poison route is announced for several broadcast intervals. The poison reverse feature is enabled by setting POISON=Yes in the BIND IP statement. Setting POISON=Yes generates some extra traffic when links go down, but the benefit is that the network stabilizes more quickly.

The problems of RIP can be avoided by using link state protocols such as Open Shortest Path First (OSPF). OSPF is intended as a feature of NetWare TCP/IP in later releases. For more information on link state and distance vector routing protocols, refer to the author's *NetWare Professional Reference, Fourth Edition,* from New Riders Publishing.

Case Study 1: Connecting Separate IPX and TCP/IP Networks

Figure 4.20 shows two separate networks that need to share the NetWare server NWTCP. Network 1 consists of IPX clients on a Token Ring network and needs to access the NWTCP server. Network 2 consists of TCP/IP hosts connected to the NWTCP server using a NE2000 board. Write down the configuration commands for the AUTOEXEC.NCF file for the server NWTCP. Don't worry about the parameter settings for the NICs in the LOAD LAN_DRIVER command for this case study. The Ethernet interface for NWTCP server has the IP address 199.245.180.10.

Figure 4.20

Separate IPX and TCP/IP networks.

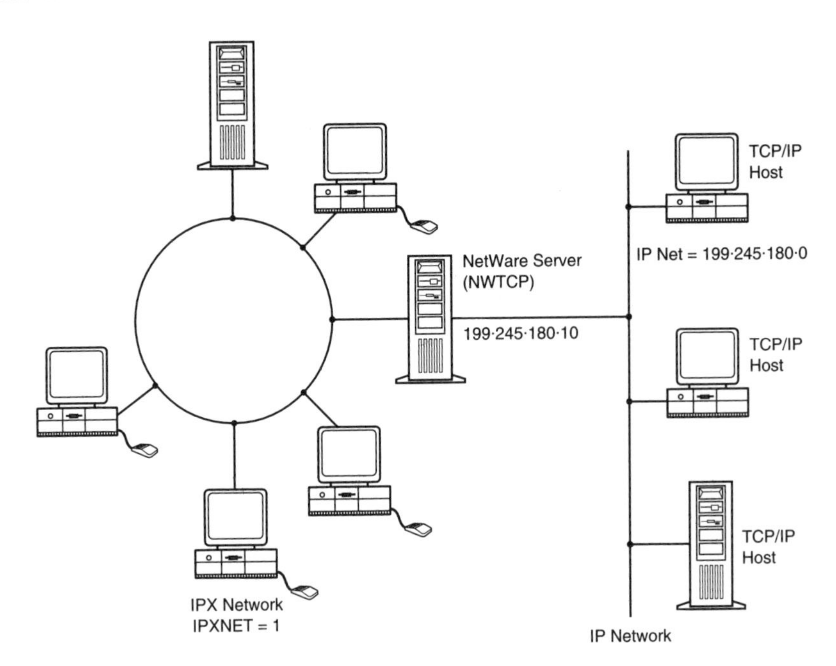

In this case study, the NetWare TCP/IP acts as a shared file server between Networks 1 and 2, but does not provide routing functions. Network 1 has only IPX clients and Network 2 has only TCP/IP clients.

The AUTOEXEC.NCF file can contain the following statements:

```
# Configure Token Ring interface for IPX on network 1
LOAD TOKEN NAME=IPXNET1
BIND IPX TO IPXNET1 NET=1

# Configure Ethernet interface for IP on network 2
LOAD NE2000 NAME=IPNET2 FRAME=ETHERNET_II
LOAD TCPIP FORWARD=NO
BIND IP TO IPNET2 ADDR=199.245.180.10
```

Case Study 2: Connecting a Mixed IPX and TCP/IP Network through a NetWare TCP/IP Router

Figure 4.21 shows two separate networks that need to share the NetWare server NWTCP. The server NWTCP also acts as an IP router connecting the two networks. Network 1 consists of IPX and TCP/IP clients on a Token Ring network and connected to the NWTCP server. Network 2 also consists of IPX and TCP/IP clients connected to the NWTCP server via an NE2000 board. Write down the configuration commands for the AUTOEXEC.NCF file for the server NWTCP. Don't worry about the parameter settings for the NICs in the LOAD LAN_DRIVER command for this case study. The Ethernet interface for NWTCP server has the IP address of 199.245.180.10 and the Token Ring interface has an IP address of 134.45.23.44.

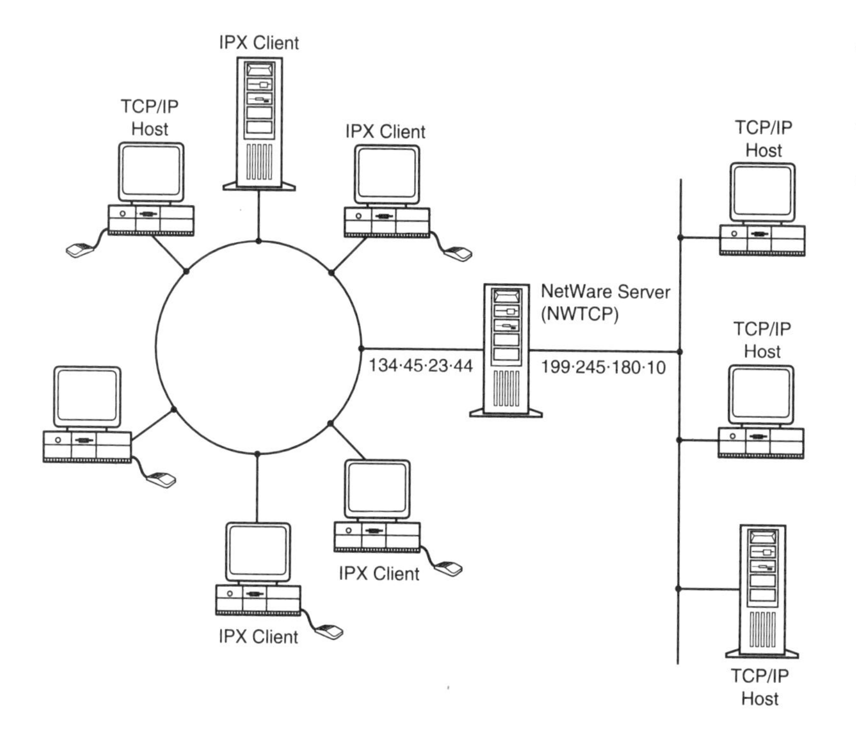

Figure 4.21

A mixed IPX and TCP/IP network connected through a NetWare TCP/IP router.

In this case study, the NetWare TCP/IP acts as a shared file server between Networks 1 and 2, and also provides routing functions.

The AUTOEXEC.NCF file can contain the following statements:

```
# Configure Token Ring interface for IPX on Network 1
LOAD TOKEN NAME=IPXNET1
BIND IPX TO IPXNET1 NET=1

# Load TCPIP with forwarding and RIP enabled
LOAD TCPIP FORWARD=YES RIP=YES

# Configure Token Ring interface for IP on Network 1
LOAD TOKEN NAME=IPNET1 FRAME=TOKEN-RING_SNAP
BIND IP TO IPNET1 ADDR=134.45.23.44

# Configure Ethernet interface for IPX on Network 2
LOAD NE2000 NAME=IPXNET2
BIND IPX TO IPXNET2 NET=2

# Configure Ethernet interface for IP on Network 2
LOAD NE2000 NAME=IPNET2 FRAME=ETHERNET_II
BIND IP TO IPNET2 ADDR=199.245.180.10
```

Case Study 3: Connecting a Mixed IPX and TCP/IP Network through a NetWare TCP/IP Router Using Subnetting

Figure 4.22 shows two separate networks that need to share the NetWare server NWTCP. The server NWTCP also acts as an IP router connecting the two networks. There is only one class B address, 182.52.0.0, assigned for both networks. It has been decided to have no more than 1000 nodes on each physical network that connects to an IP router. Network 1 consists of IPX and TCP/IP clients on a Token Ring network and needs to connect to the NWTCP server. Network 2 also consists of IPX and TCP/IP clients connected to the NWTCP server via an NE2000 board. Write down the configuration commands for the AUTOEXEC.NCF file for the server NWTCP. Don't worry about the parameter settings for the NICs in the LOAD LAN_DRIVER command for this case study.

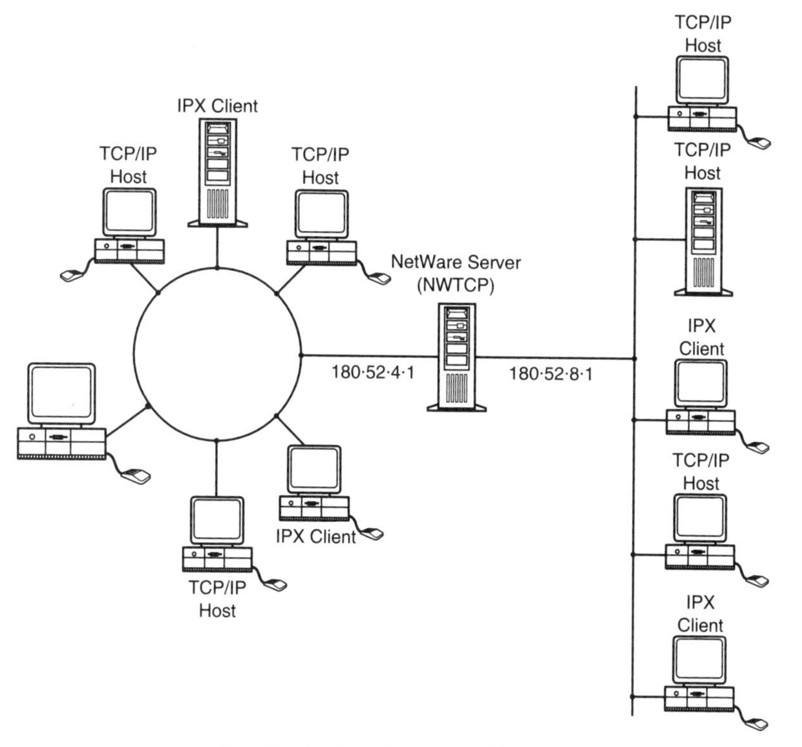

Figure 4.22

Subnetting through a NetWare TCP/IP router.

In this case study, the NetWare TCP/IP acts as a shared file server between networks 1 and 2, and also provides routing functions.

Because only one class B address has been assigned for the network, the network must be subnetted. The host number must contain enough bits to accommodate up to 1000 hosts. If the number of bits in the host number field is 10, it will accommodate the requirement of 1000 nodes. With 10 bits for a host number, a class B address, the subnet number is 6 bits long (16–10), and the subnet mask is 255.255.252.0 (see Chapter 2 for more information about subnet masks).

In general, if there are a maximum of N hosts that need to be on a subnetted network, the number of bits used for the host number H and the number of subnet number bits S can be computed from the following equations:

$2^{H-1} < N$
$2^{H} >= N$
$S = I - n$
$1 <= H < I$

in which

I = 24 for class A address
I = 16 for class B address
I = 8 for class C address

The Ethernet and Token Ring interface on the NWTCP server must be assigned a unique IP address. Assume that the subnet number for Network 1 is 1 and the subnet number for Network 2 is 2 (other values could also be selected). Select the NWTCP server's IP address for the Token Ring interface to be 180.52.4.1 so that it belongs to subnet number 1. Select the NWTCP server's IP address for the Ethernet interface to be 180.52.8.1 so that it belongs to subnet number 2. There are many other selections for IP addresses for the NWTCP server; the choice can be arbitrary as long as the IP addresses selected are on their respective subnetworks. To review subnet masks, see Chapter 2.

The AUTOEXEC.NCF file can contain the following statements:

```
# Configure Token Ring interface for IPX on Network 1
LOAD TOKEN NAME=IPXNET1
BIND IPX TO IPXNET1 NET=1

# Load TCPIP with forwarding and RIP enabled
LOAD TCPIP FORWARD=YES RIP=YES

# Subnet of 6 bits used for the class B address
LOAD TOKEN NAME=IPNET1 FRAME=TOKEN-RING SNAP
BIND IP TO IPNET1 ADDR=180.52.4.1 MASK=255.255.252.0

# Configure Ethernet interface for IPX on Network 2
LOAD NE2000 NAME=IPXNET2
BIND IPX TO IPXNET2 NET=2

# Configure Ethernet interface for IP on Network 2
LOAD NE2000 NAME=IPNET2 FRAME=ETHERNET_II

# Subnet of 6 bits used for the class B address
BIND IP TO IPNET2 ADDR=180.52.8.1 MASK=255.255.252.0
```

IP Tunneling

Consider two IPX networks that are separated by an IP network (see fig. 4.23). In order for these two IPX networks to communicate, you could establish separate IPX links between the two networks, or you could use an existing IP network. Very often, using an existing IP network is more cost-effective than establishing a separate network. This technique is called *tunneling*. Tunneling can be used whenever you need to connect two or more networks by means of an existing network that uses a different network protocol. The network using a different network layer protocol is called the *foreign network*.

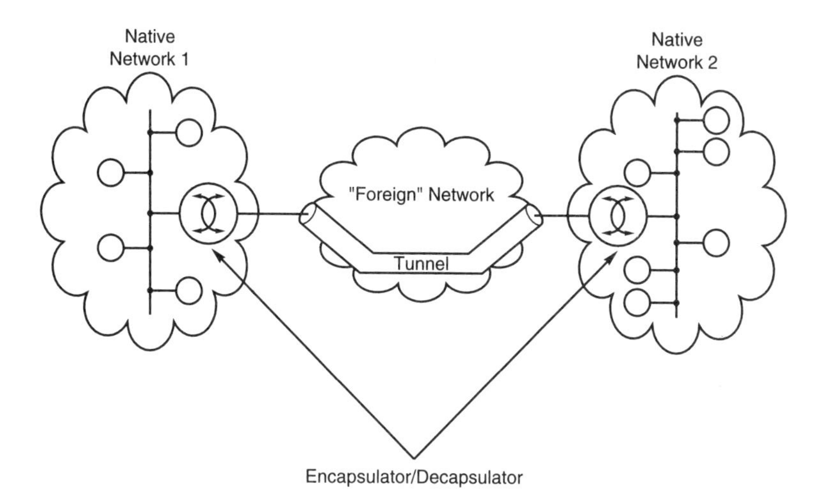

Figure 4.23
Tunneling concepts.

A NetWare TCP/IP server can be configured to act as an encapsulator/decapsulator. The encapsulator takes the IPX packet and encapsulates it with the network layer header of the foreign network. In the case of IP tunneling, the foreign network is an IP network. The encapsulation in this case consists of placing the IPX packet as data inside an IP packet.

The encapsulated IPX packet appears as an IP packet to the IP network. The routers in the IP network are able to route this IP packet to the decapsulator on the destination IPX network. The decapsulator on the destination network is configured on a NetWare TCP/IP server, and it strips the IP header, thereby recovering the original IPX packet. This IPX packet can then be sent to its destination on the IPX network.

RFC 1241 contains additional details on the mechanics of tunneling and encapsulation on an IP network.

Protocols Used for Tunneling IPX across IP Networks

The encapsulator/decapsulator functions described in the previous section are accomplished by the IPTUNNEL.LAN driver. The IPTUNNEL.LAN driver is included with the NetWare 3.x and NetWare 4.x TCP/IP software.

The IPTUNNEL.LAN driver encapsulates IPX packets within an IP packet and a UDP Header (see fig. 4.24). The User Datagram Protocol (UDP) is used for specifying the port numbers of the encapsulator/decapsulator processes. As discussed in Chapter 2, the UDP transport protocol can be used to specify port numbers on the source and destination nodes. The port numbers are used for identifying software processes on the source and destination nodes that are involved in the message exchange.

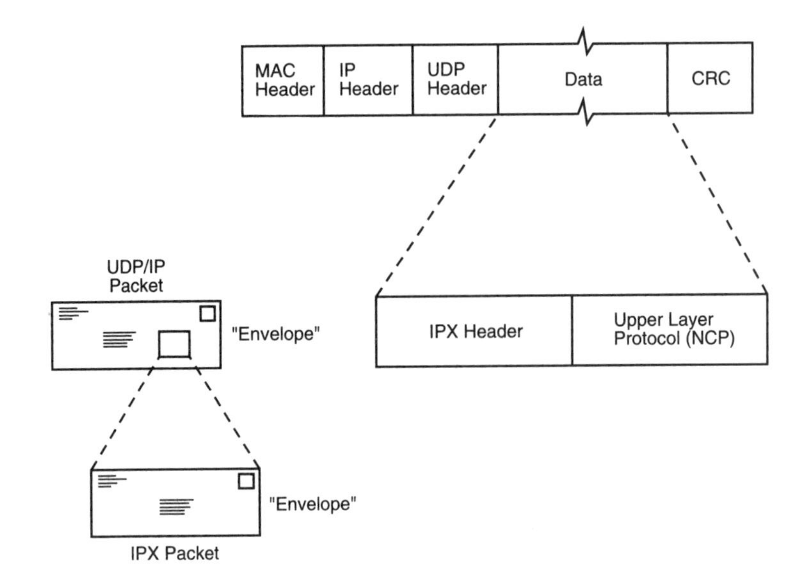

Figure 4.24

IP tunneling protocols.

The source port number in the UDP header for an IPX packet encapsulated by UDP/IP headers identifies the encapsulation process on the sending NetWare TCP/IP server; the destination port number in this UDP header identifies the decapsulation process on the receiving NetWare TCP/IP server on the destination IPX network. For NetWare's IPTUNNEL.LAN, a UDP port of 213 is used. This is a port reserved for Novell's use of IP tunneling.

The IPTUNNEL driver at destination removes the IP and UDP headers and recovers the original IPX packet. UDP cannot guarantee sequenced delivery of packets, but it can be used to provide an optional checksum for additional data integrity. When IPTUNNEL is configured, the UDP checksums can be enabled to protect the packets from errors.

Because UDP cannot guarantee sequenced delivery of packets, this must be provided by an upper layer protocol. In NetWare environments, sequencing and error recovery is performed by the NetWare Core Protocol (NCP).

The IP Tunnel Driver

IP tunneling requires a host on each of the source and destination IPX networks to act as an encapsulator/decapsulator.

One host serves as an encapsulator and the other serves as a decapsulator. The encapsulation/decapsulation function on the hosts can be performed by any of the following:

- The IPTUNNEL.LAN driver and NetWare TCP/IP NLMs
- An IP Tunnel Client Driver from LAN Workplace for DOS 4.0 and above
- Schneider & Koch's SK-IPX/IP Gateway
- Schneider & Koch's SK-IPX/IP Gateway Client

The IP Tunnel Client driver for LAN Workplace can be used to connect a single workstation to an IPX network using IP tunneling. The Schneider & Koch products are third-party products. Their discussion is beyond the scope of this book.

Configuring IP Tunneling

The steps required to configure IP tunneling when IPTUNNEL.LAN is used are shown in figure 4.25. The IPTUNNEL.LAN driver is treated as a network board driver. The steps for configuring it are as follows:

1. Load the IPTUNNEL.LAN driver.
2. Bind IPX to the IPTUNNEL driver.

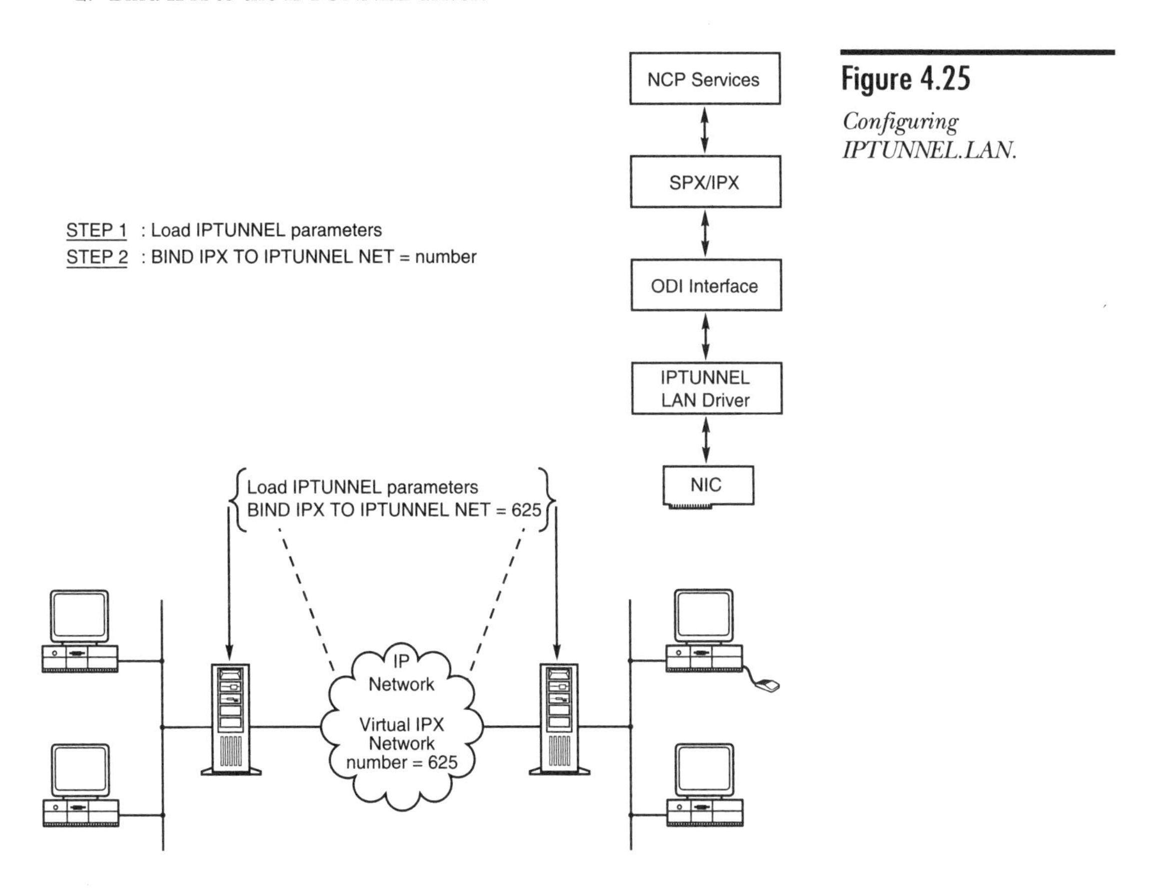

Figure 4.25
Configuring IPTUNNEL.LAN.

When IPTUNNEL is loaded, you must specify the peer NetWare TCP/IP servers on other IPX networks connected by the IP tunnel that must receive broadcast packets, such as SAP packets from the NetWare TCP/IP server. The broadcasts are sent through the IP tunnel to only the designated networks. In IPX networks, broadcasts are used as a standard method of communicating information about availability of services (SAP broadcasts). Broadcasts are not practical on an IP network that can consist of a large number of hosts and slow WAN links. In fact, if the Internet is used, the network can consist of millions of hosts.

When IPX is bound to the IPTUNNEL, you must specify the IPX network number of the IP network. The connecting IP network is treated by IPX as a virtual IPX network. The IP Tunnel configuration on all the NetWare TCP/IP servers must use the same IPX network number assigned to the connecting IP network.

Loading IPTUNNEL

When the IPTUNNEL is loaded, you must specify a peer list of other NetWare TCP/IP servers that must receive the SAP broadcasts. This is done using the PEER parameter, which lists the IP addresses of remote NetWare TCP/IP servers. The PEER parameter can accept only one IP address value, so if more than one peer exists, the IPTUNNEL must be loaded again with the different PEER address value. If IPTUNNEL is loaded more than once, only one copy of IPTUNNEL.LAN is loaded in server memory (reentrant loading). The second LOAD of the IPTUNNEL is used to register a new PEER IP address value.

In the following example, the NetWare TCP/IP server's peers are at IP address 123.23.34.3, 133.65.65.87, and 203.12.77.97. The loading of IPTUNNEL should use the PEER parameters as shown by the following:

```
LOAD IPTUNNEL PEER=123.23.34.3
LOAD IPTUNNEL PEER=133.65.65.87
LOAD IPTUNNEL PEER=203.12.77.97
```

Each use of LOAD IPTUNNEL that uses the PEER parameter adds the specified IP address to the peer list. There is no limit to the number of IP addresses added to the peer list, but you must keep in mind that for every broadcast, IPTUNNEL duplicates and transmits information in the broadcast packet to each IP address in the peer list. As the peer list becomes large, so does the amount of time spent sending individual packets to the peer NetWare TCP/IP servers.

The following is the general syntax of the LOAD IPTUNNEL statement:

```
LOAD IPTUNNEL PEER=peer_addr CHKSUM=[ Yes ¦ No ] LOCAL=ip_addr PORT=port# SHOW=[ Yes
➥¦ No ]
```

The IPTUNNEL parameters are described in table 4.3.

TABLE 4.3 IPTUNNEL PARAMETERS

Parameters	Description
PEER=*peer_addr*	*peer_addr* is the address of the host that must receive NetWare broadcasts. To add additional peers, repeat the command with the PEER parameter. The server duplicates and transmits each broadcast packet to each entry in the peer list. Other NetWare servers at the end of the IP tunnel should be in the peer list. DOS workstations should not be added to the peer list.
CHKSUM=[Yes I No]	If set to Yes (the default), checksums are enabled to guard against transmission errors. Setting CHKSUM to No may increase performance slightly at risk of data errors.
LOCAL=*ip_addr*	Used to disambiguate between boards when TCP/IP NLM is bound to more than one board. Default is the first interface the TCP/IP NLM was bound to.
PORT=*port#*	Specifies port number to be used by UDP. This uniquely identifies the IP Tunnel processes that must handle the IP Tunnel packet. Default value is 213 and is the official value assigned for this purpose. This value is not usually changed unless Schneider & Koch products are used, in which case a value of 59139 must be used.
SHOW=[Yes I No]	When set to Yes, the IPTUNNEL.NLM displays the current settings for the other parameters. Used for diagnostic purposes.

Case Study 5: Configuring an IP Tunnel between Two IPX Networks

Figure 4.26 shows two separate IPX networks connected using an IP Tunnel. Servers A and B are used to connect their networks to the IP Tunnel. The IP Tunnel has an IPX network number assignment of 225. Assume that Server A attaches to the IP internet using NE2000 boards and Server B attaches to the local network using IBM Token-Ring. Write down the configuration commands for the AUTOEXEC.NCF file for Servers A and B.

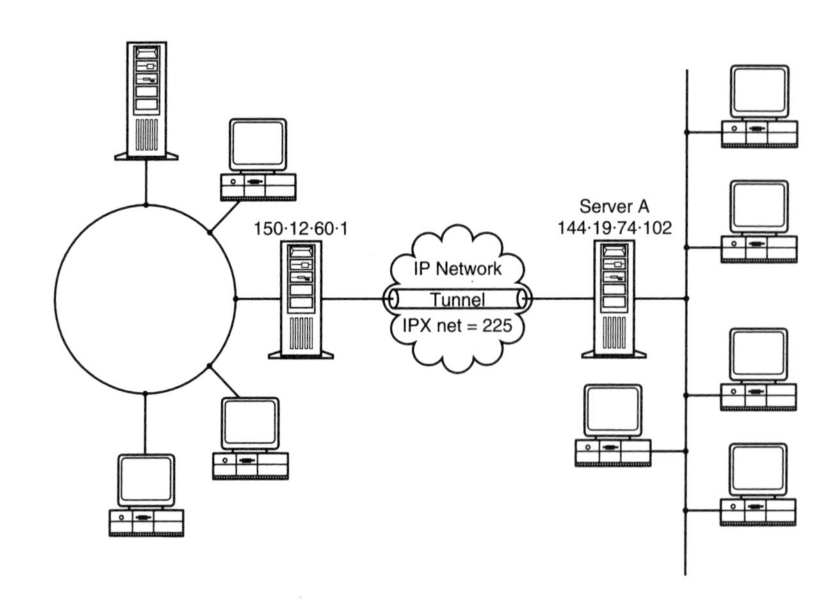

Figure 4.26

IP tunneling between two IPX networks.

Server A

```
# Load NE2000 driver
LOAD NE2000 NAME=IPNET FRAME=ETHERNET_II
# Load TCP/IP stack
LOAD TCPIP
# Bind IP to IPNET
BIND   IP TO  IPNET ADDR=144.19.74.102
# Load IPTUNNEL twice for each peer
LOAD IPTUNNEL   PEER=150.12.60.1
# Bind IPX to virtual IPX network
BIND IPX TO IPTUNNEL NET=225
```

Server B

```
# Load Token Ring driver
LOAD TOKEN NAME=IPNET FRAME=TOKEN-RING_SNAP
# Load TCP/IP stack
LOAD TCPIP
# Bind IP to IPNET
BIND   IP TO  IPNET ADDR=150.12.60.1
# Load IPTUNNEL twice for each peer
LOAD IPTUNNEL   PEER=144.19.74.102
# Bind IPX to virtual IPX network
BIND IPX TO IPTUNNEL NET=225
```

Case Study 6: Configuring an IP Tunnel between Three IPX Networks

Figure 4.27 shows three separate IPX networks connected using an IP Tunnel. Servers A, B, and C are used to connect their networks to the IP Tunnel. The IP Tunnel has an IPX network number assignment of 625. Assume that each server attaches to the IP internet and the local networks using NE2000 boards. Write down the configuration commands for the AUTOEXEC.NCF file for servers A, B, and C.

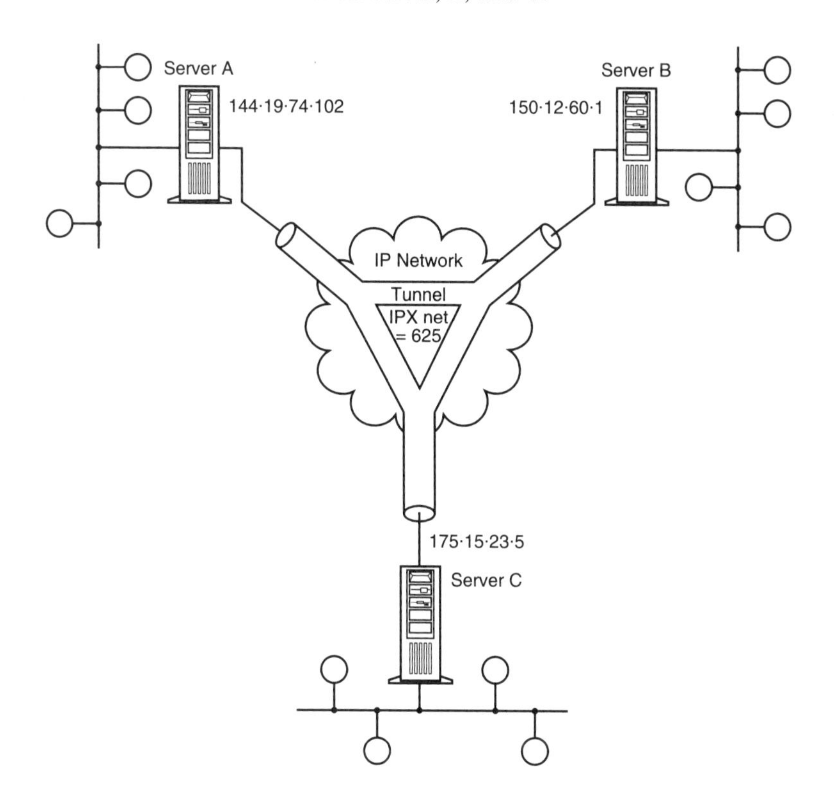

Figure 4.27

IP Tunneling between three IPX networks.

Server A

```
# Load NE2000 driver
LOAD NE2000 NAME=IPNET FRAME=ETHERNET_II
# Load TCP/IP stack
LOAD TCPIP
# Bind IP to IPNET
BIND   IP TO  IPNET ADDR=144.19.74.102
# Load IPTUNNEL twice for each peer
LOAD IPTUNNEL   PEER=150.12.60.1
LOAD IPTUNNEL   PEER=175.15.23.5
# Bind IPX to virtual IPX network
BIND IPX TO IPTUNNEL NET=625
```

Server B

```
# Load NE2000 driver
LOAD NE2000 NAME=IPNET FRAME=ETHERNET_II
# Load TCP/IP stack
LOAD TCPIP
# Bind IP to IPNET
BIND   IP TO  IPNET ADDR=150.12.60.1
# Load IPTUNNEL twice for each peer
LOAD IPTUNNEL   PEER=144.19.74.102
LOAD IPTUNNEL   PEER=175.15.23.5
# Bind IPX to virtual IPX network
BIND IPX TO IPTUNNEL NET=625
```

Server C

```
# Load NE2000 driver
LOAD NE2000 NAME=IPNET FRAME=ETHERNET_II
# Load TCP/IP stack
LOAD TCPIP
# Bind IP to IPNET
BIND   IP TO  IPNET ADDR=175.15.23.5
# Load IPTUNNEL twice for each peer
LOAD IPTUNNEL   PEER=144.19.74.102
LOAD IPTUNNEL   PEER=150.12.60.1
# Bind IPX to virtual IPX network
BIND IPX TO IPTUNNEL NET=625
```

Configuring IPTUNNEL for a DOS Workstation

In some cases there may be a need for a DOS workstation to connect to an IPX network through an IP network. In this case an IP tunnel can be used to connect the DOS workstation to a NetWare TCP/IP server on the IPX network (see fig. 4.28). Both the DOS workstation and the NetWare TCP/IP server must be configured to use IP tunneling. NetWare TCP/IP servers can be configured with IPTUNNEL.LAN. DOS workstations can be configured with the IPTUNNEL.EXE driver that comes with LAN Workplace for DOS.

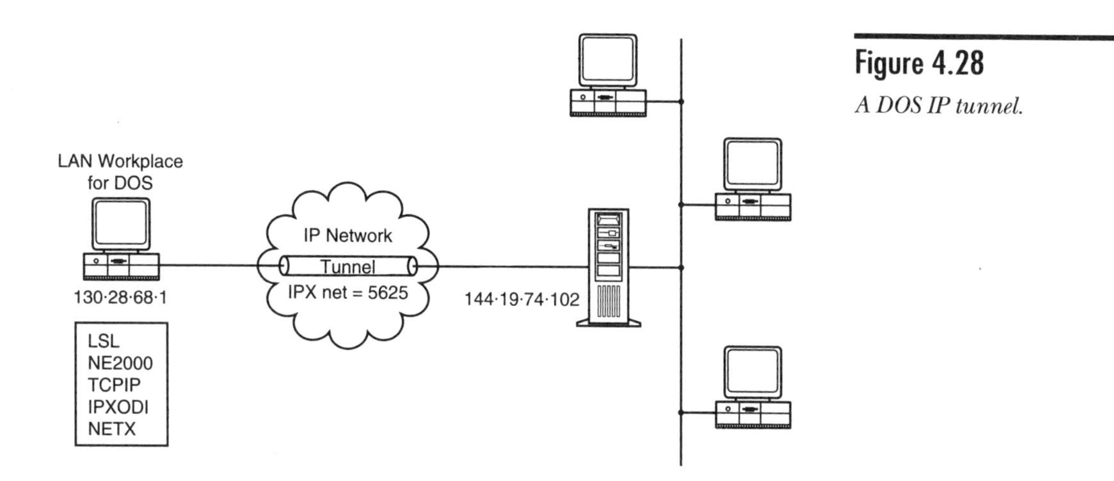

Figure 4.28

A DOS IP tunnel.

Load the DOS tunnel driver as a TSR by entering the following command at the DOS workstation:

```
IPTUNNEL
```

To remove the DOS tunnel from memory, use the following command:

```
IPTUNNEL U
```

At the DOS workstation, the following modules can be loaded:

```
LSL                  ; Load Link Support Layer interface
NE2000               ; Load the ODI NIC driver at workstation
TCPIP                ; Load LAN Workplace TCP/IP stack
IPTUNNEL             ; Load DOS IP Tunnel interface
IPXODI               ; Load SPX/IPX stack
NETX or VLM          ; Load shell or VLM
```

The NET.CFG file at the DOS workstation should look similar to the following. The IPTUNNEL specific parameters are shown in bold. Table 4.4 contains a description of the DOS IP tunnel parameters used in the NET.CFG.

```
LINK SUPPORT
     buffers      8  1568
     mempool      4096

PROTOCOL  TCPIP
     bind               ne2000
     ip_address         130.20.68.1
     ip_router          130.20.68.91
     ip_netmask         255.255.0.0
```

```
PROTOCOL  IPX
     bind          IPTUNNEL       ;  Bind IPX to IPTUNNEL

LINK  DRIVER      IPTUNNEL
     gateway      144.19.74.102   ; Gateway address is IP _address
                                  ; of NetWare server

     port         213             ;  Port # is 213 (default).
     checksum     yes             ;  UDP checksums are enabled

LINK DRIVER NE2000
     int        #1     3
     port           #1     300
     frame      ethernet_ii
```

Table 4.4 DOS IP Tunnel Parameters in NET.CFG

Parameter	Description
gateway	This parameter enables you to specify the IP addresses of the IP tunnel gateways. You can specify up to 10 gateway addresses. If this parameter is not specified, a default value of 255.255.255.255 is used. This value specifies a local broadcast, and enables the DOS client to find IP tunnel gateways attached to the local network. If a remote gateway is used, you must specify a specific entry for each remote gateway.
port	This specifies the UDP port number to be used for IP tunneling. If not specified, the port number defaults to 213, the port number assigned for IPX by the Assigned Numbers RFC. Earlier versions (prior to 1.3) of the Schneider & Koch SK-IPX/IP client and server products used a port number value of 59139. If you are using this third-party product, you should set the port number to the specified value.
checksum	The IP tunnel can use UDP checksums to ensure data integrity of the tunneled IPX packet. UDP checksums are enabled by default. To disable UDP checksums, you can specify a value of No for this parameter.

Summary

This chapter introduced you to routing concepts and how IP routing can be used to interconnect a number of TCP/IP networks. The differences between interconnecting devices such as repeaters, bridges, routers, and gateways were explored. You learned that IP routers can respond dynamically to changes in network topologies. You learned the different ways NetWare IP routers can be configured, with knowledge of the network topology. Several case studies involving a mix of IPX and IP routers were examined, and you learned how a NetWare TCP/IP could be configured to solve real world problems. If you need to connect several IPX networks using an IP network, you can use IP tunneling. IP tunneling can be configured at a NetWare TCP/IP server and at an IPX client.

SNMP Support for TCP/IP Networks in NetWare

TCP/IP networks use a standard management protocol called Simple Network Management Protocol (SNMP). The SNMP protocol is widely used in the industry. Although SNMP was developed as a solution for network management on TCP/IP networks, it is not limited to those networks. The SNMP protocol can be run on other transport protocols such as Internet Packet Exchange (IPX), Open Systems Interconnections (OSI), and ConnectionLess Network Protocol (CLNP). This chapter focuses on the SNMP support that is available on NetWare servers. NetWare server software is distributed with an SNMP agent and a simple SNMP manager.

Learning the Basics of TCP/IP Network Management

In this section the fundamental concepts of SNMP are presented. These concepts apply to SNMP implementations on any platform, including NetWare.

A Model for Network Management

Figure 5.1 shows a model for network management. In this model, the network consists of several devices in which a management agent is running. The management agent has knowledge of the device parameters on which it runs. Some of the device parameters are specific to the device that is managed. Router devices, for example, have parameters that describe the routing table. All devices can be expected to have some common parameters, such as the name of the device, how long the device has been active *(up time)*, and so on.

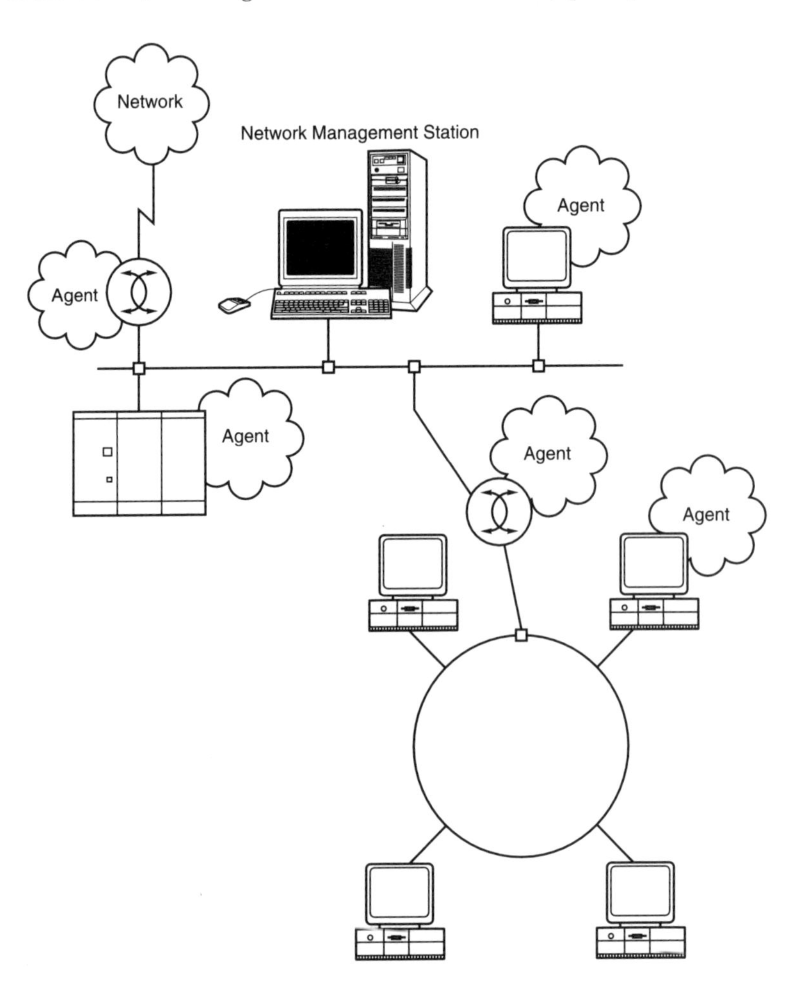

Figure 5.1

A model for network management.

Figure 5.1 shows that the agents can be managed by a special device called the *Network Management Station* (NMS). The Network Management Station can issue specific requests to a device for information on its network parameters. The agent for the device receives these requests and sends back the requested information. The Network Management Station, on receiving the reply, knows the values of the requested parameters and can use this information to deduce the state of the device and whether the device requires attention.

It would also be important to prevent an unauthorized Network Management Station from obtaining information on the devices on the network. This capability requires that some authentication scheme be implemented to prevent unauthorized access.

Figure 5.2 shows the goal of network management. The network is shown as a "cloud" that has both input and output. The network *input* is the shared data and the activity generated by users of the network. The network *output* is the increased efficiency that results from information sharing. The network is subject to disturbances in the form of computers, devices, and network links becoming inoperable. The goal of network management is to monitor the status of the network and use control mechanisms to achieve the desired output (increased efficiency) despite network disturbances.

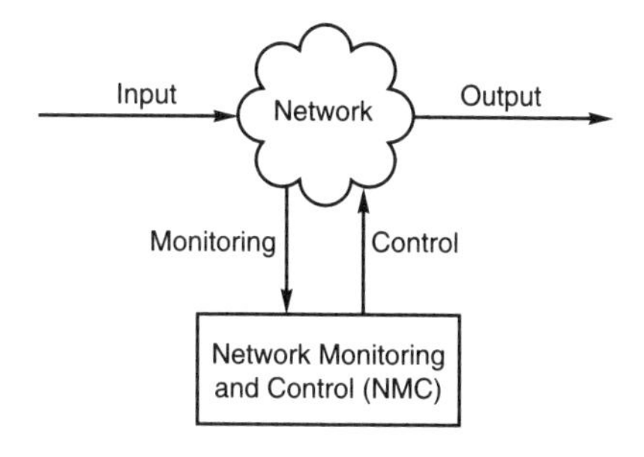

Figure 5.2

The goal of network management.

The mechanisms used for monitoring and controlling the network should have a minimal impact on the network. In other words, the protocols used to collect information should not impact the performance of the network or the devices that are managed. If the network management mechanism uses most of the network bandwidth, little is available for the network users. In this case the network traffic is disrupted. Similarly, the network agents running on the devices should not consume a great deal of processing power on their devices; otherwise, the device might not be able to perform its normal functions in the desired time.

The Managed Node

The device that is being managed by the Network Management Station is called the *managed node.* The managed node has parameters that the Network Management Station can query and obtain values for (see fig. 5.3). A *management protocol* is used to establish communications between the Network Management Station and the managed node and to send queries and receive responses. An example of this management protocol is SNMP.

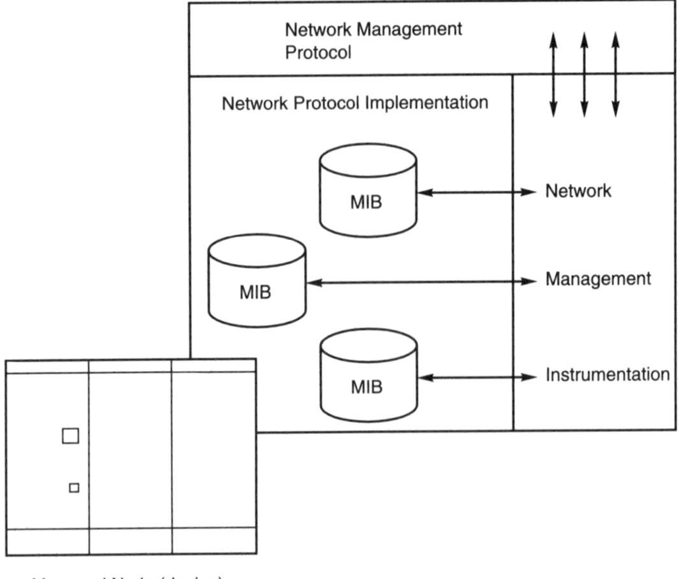

Figure 5.3
The managed node.

The management protocol interfaces with the network management instrumentation within the managed node. The management instrumentation has internal knowledge of the parameters and memory locations within the managed node. When a query is received through the management protocol, such as SNMP, the network management instrumentation receives the request and accesses the managed node's parameters. The results are reported back to the NMS by the management instrumentation, using the network management protocol.

In the discussion of SNMP, the managed node is often called the *managed device.* These terms are used interchangeably in this chapter.

Relevant RFCs for SNMP

SNMP is described by a number of RFCs (Requests for Comments). The following is a list of some of the more important RFCs:

RFC 1450 by Case, J.; McCloghrie, K.; Rose, M.; Waldbusser, S. "Management Information Base for Version 2 of the Simple Network Management Protocol (SNMPv2)." 1993 April; 27 pp.

RFC 1449 by Case, J.; McCloghrie, K.; Rose, M.; Waldbusser, S. "Transport Mappings for Version 2 of the Simple Network Management Protocol (SNMPv2)." 1993 April; 24 pp.

RFC 1448 by Case, J.; McCloghrie, K.; Rose, M.; Waldbusser, S. "Protocol Operations for Version 2 of the Simple Network Management Protocol (SNMPv2)." 1993 April; 35 pp.

RFC 1447 by Galvin, J.; McCloghrie, K. "Party MIB for Version 2 of the Simple Network Management Protocol (SNMPv2)." 1993 April; 50 pp.

RFC 1446 by Galvin, J.; McCloghrie, K. "Security Protocols for Version 2 of the Simple Network Management Protocol (SNMPv2)." 1993 April; 51 pp.

RFC 1445 by Galvin, J.; McCloghrie, K. "Administrative Model for Version 2 of the Simple Network Management Protocol (SNMPv2)." 1993 April; 47 pp.

RFC 1444 by Case, J.; McCloghrie, K.; Rose, M.; Waldbusser, S. "Conformance Statements for Version 2 of the Simple Network Management Protocol (SNMPv2)." 1993 April; 32 pp.

RFC 1443 by Case, J.; McCloghrie, K.; Rose, M.; Waldbusser, S. "Textual Conventions for Version 2 of the Simple Network Management Protocol (SNMPv2)." 1993 April; 31 pp.

RFC 1442 by Case, J.; McCloghrie, K.; Rose, M.; Waldbusser, S. "Structure of Management Information for Version 2 of the Simple Network Management Protocol (SNMPv2)." 1993 April; 54 pp.

RFC 1441 by Case, J.; McCloghrie, K.; Rose, M.; Waldbusser, S. "Introduction to Version 2 of the Internet Standard Network Management Framework." 1993 April; 13 pp.

RFC 1420 by Bostock, S. "SNMP over IPX." 1993 March; 4 pp. (Obsoletes RFC 1298).

RFC 1419 by Minshall, G.; Ritter, M. "SNMP over AppleTalk." 1993 March; 7 pp.

RFC 1418 by Rose, M. "SNMP over OSI." 1993 March; 4 pp. (Obsoletes RFCs 1161, 1283).

Management Information Base (MIB)

The parameters in the managed node are called *management objects*. The set of parameters in a managed node is called the *Management Information Base* (MIB). You can conceptually regard the MIB as a database. Each of the objects in the MIB, also called *variables*, has a number associated with it that is used to uniquely identify the object. This number is called the object id. The *object id* is based on a hierarchical numbering scheme and enables the variable in the MIB to be ordered. The ordering of the variables, given an object id for a variable, enables you to determine the "next" variable that follows. The ordering of the MIB variables is conceptually similar to the indexing that orders records in a database.

An MIB variable also includes a status flag indicating whether the variable is read-only or has read-write access.

A certain set of standard MIB variables exists for the different protocol elements of TCP/IP. These MIB variables describe parameter values for IP, ICMP, TCP, SNMP, Exterior Gateway Protocol (EGP), and Address Translation tables.

Data-link interfaces such as Ethernet, Token Ring, SMDS, and ATM have their own sets of MIB variables. A vendor of a special device might even have MIB variables specific to that device. MIB variables that are specific to a vendor's device are called *proprietary MIBs*.

Certain interface mechanisms enable an SNMP manager to take a description of a proprietary MIB and compile it so that it becomes part of the MIB variables known to the SNMP Manager.

The Management Paradigm in SNMP

The Network Management Station for SNMP is called the *SNMP Manager.* The SNMP Manager uses a management paradigm called the *remote debugging* paradigm (see fig. 5.4). In this paradigm, the SNMP Manager is like a programmer at a workstation debugging programs from a remote location. Such a hypothetical programmer would be interested in reading the values of variables in the program and changing the values of certain critical variables. Likewise, the SNMP Manager should be able to read and update values of MIB variables on the managed devices. The SNMP Manager should be able to perform the following actions:

- Read or Read-Write of MIB variables
- Trap-directed polls
- Simple traversal of variables in the managed node

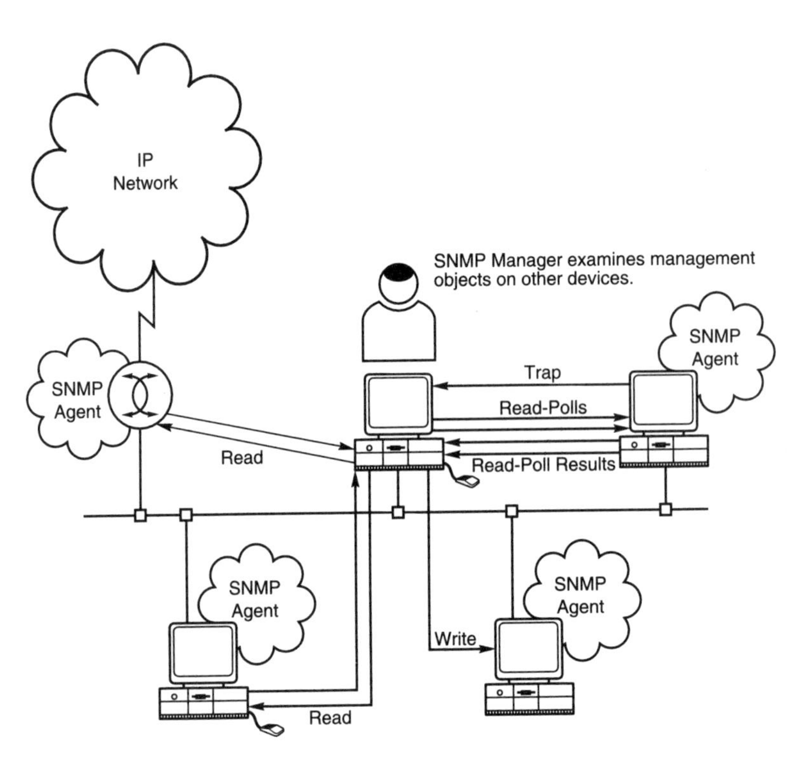

Figure 5.4
The SNMP management paradigm.

When an exceptional condition occurs at a managed device, such as the failure of a link or a critical change in the status of the device, the managed device sends a trap SNMP message to the SNMP Manager. The *trap message* indicates the event that caused the generation of the message. The SNMP Manager then must respond to the trap message. The SNMP Manager can simply log the message in a trap log file or take more extensive action. The SNMP Manager can, for instance, request additional information from the device that generated the trap message. The additional information can be obtained through read requests for specific MIB variables. If the SNMP Manager is programmed for control of the device, it can issue a write request to modify the value of an MIB variable.

All control actions within SNMP occur as "side effects" of the modification of an MIB variable. If a device is to be powered-off remotely from an SNMP Manager, for example, the SNMP Manager can send a write request to modify a defined MIB variable called the *ifPowerOff* variable. The managed device can be programmed so that the *ifPowerOn* variable acts in the following way: the value of the variable is normally 1; if the value is 0, the device is powered off. The managed device, on sensing a value of 0 in its *ifPowerOn* variable, initiates a device shutdown.

Because the MIB variables are ordered according to their object identifiers, the SNMP Manager can traverse all the variables in the device using an SNMP command called *GetNext*. This process is called a *simple traversal* of the MIB.

Because SNMP uses side effects to initiate control actions, the SNMP commands consist of only the following:

- Get—read a MIB variable
- Set—write a MIB variable
- GetNext—return the next MIB variable
- Trap—send to SNMP Manager to report exceptional conditions

SNMP Commands and Protocols

Figure 5.5 shows the SNMP commands and the transport and protocols on which SNMP depends. The SNMP Manager can issue any of the following commands:

- Get
- GetNext
- Set

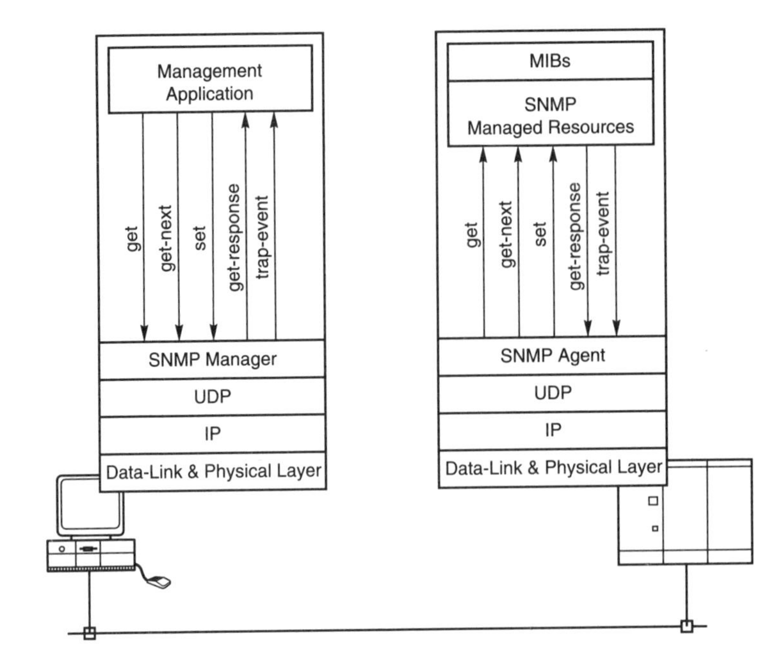

Figure 5.5

SNMP commands and protocols.

The SNMP Manager sends these commands to the SNMP agent using the UDP/IP protocols. The SNMP agent can send a Get_Response SNMP command in reply to the SNMP Get request or GetNext request from the SNMP Manager. The SNMP Set command from the SNMP Manager is not explicitly acknowledged. In other words, a Set_Response command sent from the SNMP agent to the SNMP Manager does not exist. The Trap events are sent from the SNMP agent to the SNMP Manager when exceptional conditions occur in the managed device.

SNMP Traps

When an unusual condition occurs in the SNMP device, the SNMP agent alerts the SNMP Manager through SNMP *traps*. Figure 5.6 shows a sample network with some of the trap messages that can be generated by SNMP agents.

The SNMP agent must be configured to send trap messages to an SNMP Manager station. Table 5.1 summarizes the different SNMP trap messages that can be generated.

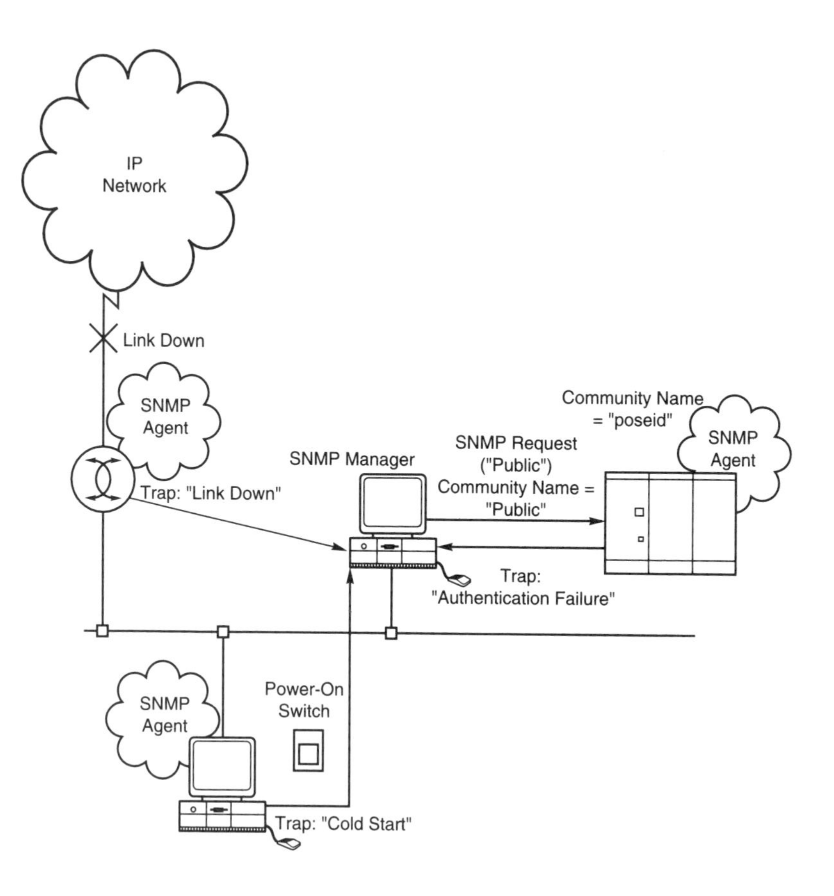

Figure 5.6
SNMP traps.

TABLE 5.1 SNMP TRAP MESSAGES

Parameter	Description
`Link up or Link down`	When a network interface on the managed device fails, a Link down trap message is generated; if the network interface comes back to life, a Link up trap message is generated.
`Cold start or Warm start`	When an SNMP agent starts, a Cold start trap message is generated. If the SNMP initializes its table, a Warm start trap message is generated.
`Authentication failure`	When an SNMP agent receives an SNMP request with a community name that does not match the community name with which the device is configured, an Authentication failure trap message is generated.
`Loss of EGP neighbor`	When an SNMP agent cannot communicate with its EGP neighbor, a Loss of EGP neighbor trap message is generated.

On a NetWare network, except for the loss of EGP neighbor trap, any of the preceding trap messages can occur.

Note The EGP protocol at one time was widely used on the Internet. Its inclusion as an SNMP trap message is to support those sites that might still be using it.

Examining NetWare SNMP Components

On NetWare servers, the SNMP agent is implemented by SNMP.NLM, and the SNMP Manager is implemented by TCPCON.NLM. Configuring and using SNMP on NetWare servers involves setting SNMP parameters for these NLMs. The SNMPLOG.NLM acts as a SNMP logger process that logs traps to a file for later examination.

Using the NetWare SNMP Agent

The SNMP.NLM works with the NetWare TCP/IP protocol stack TCPIP.NLM to provide SNMP services to SNMP Managers such as TCPCON.NLM or a third-party SNMP Manager, such as Castle Rock Computing's SNMPc, Sun Microsystems's Sun Net Manager, Hewlett-Packard's OpenView, and so on.

The SNMP.NLM provides access to the MIB variables for the TCP/IP parameters. Initially, only support for MIB-I definition of the MIB variables was available. MIB-II support is expected at the time this book goes to press. MIB-II contains more extensive MIB variables than is contained in the MIB-I definition.

Figure 5.7 shows the use of an SNMP.NLM on a NetWare server. The SNMP.NLM agent responds to polls (queries) about NetWare TCP/IP parameters from an SNMP Manager.

You can configure the SNMP.NLM with separate community names for monitoring, controlling, and receiving trap messages. These community names accompany SNMP requests and are used by the SNMP agent to authenticate the request. The SNMP agent accepts only requests that contain a community name that matches the community name for the function being performed. If the SNMP request does not contain a matching community name, it is discarded and an Authentication failure trap message is generated.

Loading the SNMP Agent on NetWare Servers

The SNMP.NLM is automatically loaded when TCP is loaded, if the SNMP.NLM is not already loaded in memory. If SNMP is automatically loaded through TCPCON, it establishes the default community names. If the SNMP agent is to be configured with nondefault community names, you must load the SNMP.NLM explicitly, using the LOAD command. When you load SNMP.NLM explicitly, you can specify community name parameters for monitoring, control, and traps.

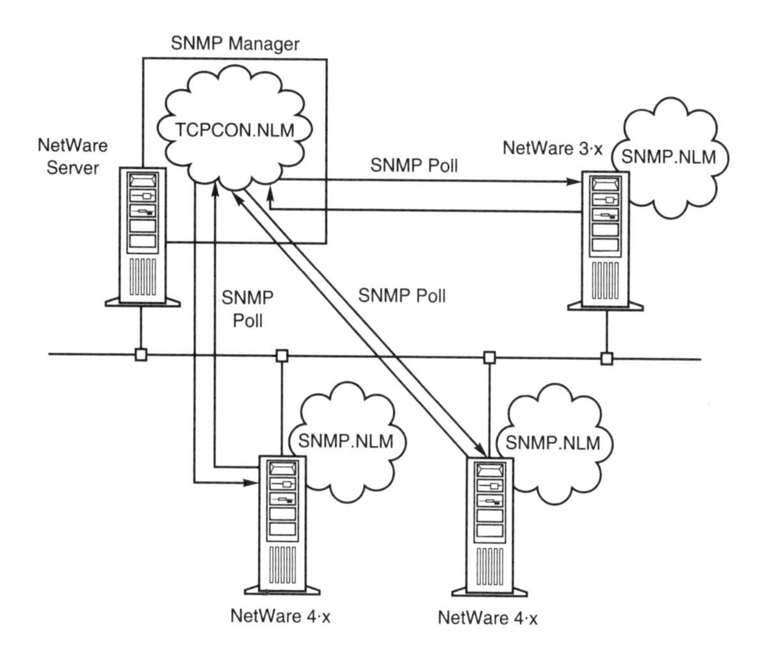

Figure 5.7

The SNMP.NLM agent.

The following is the syntax of the SNMP parameters:

```
LOAD SNMP MONITORCOMMUNITY=name CONTROLCOMMUNITY=name
TRAPCOMMUNITY=name
```

If you use the NetWare 4.x INETCFG utility to configure the server, the LOAD SNMP command parameters are configured in the INETCFG configuration file.

The parameter options MONITORCOMMUNITY, CONTROLCOMMUNITY, and TRAPCOMMUNITY set the parameters for the monitor, control, and trap communities, respectively (see fig. 5.8).

The *monitor community* refers to the SNMP Managers that provide the specified monitor community name to read the MIB variables of the managed device. Thus, if an SNMP Manager is to read MIB variables, the SNMP request that it issues must contain a community name that matches the community name specified by the MONITORCOMMUNITY parameter. The MONITORCOMMUNITY parameter can be abbreviated by the letter M.

The *control community* refers to the SNMP Managers that provide the specified control community name to read or write the MIB variables of the managed device. Thus, if an SNMP Manager is to read or write MIB variables, the SNMP request that it issues must contain a community name that matches the community name specified by the CONTROLCOMMUNITY parameter. The CONTROLCOMMUNITY parameter can be abbreviated by the letter C.

Figure 5.8

SNMP community names.

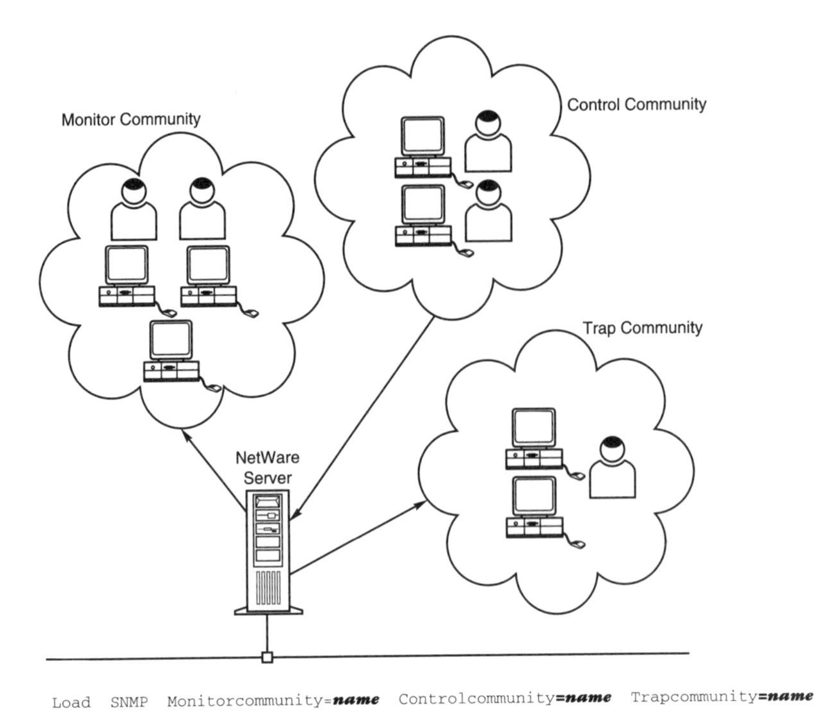

The *trap community* name refers to the SNMP Managers that can receive the trap messages generated by the SNMP agent. The trap messages generated by the SNMP agent contain the community name specified by the TRAPCOMMUNITY name. The SNMP Manager must be configured with the community name specified by the TRAPCOMMUNITY parameter; otherwise, the SNMP manager discards the trap message. The SNMP Manager to receive the trap message is specified by the TRAP parameter when TCPIP.NLM is loaded. To specify that SNMP Manager at 199.245.180.9 should receive the trap messages for the SNMP.NLM agent, for example, you can use the following command line:

```
LOAD TCPIP TRAP=199.245.180.9
```

Table 5.2 summarizes the meanings of the different community parameters.

Table 5.2 SNMP Community Names

Community Name	Description
MONITORCOMMUNITY	Used by SNMP Managers in the SNMP request to read MIB variables.
CONTROLCOMMUNITY	Used by SNMP Managers in the SNMP request to read or write MIB variables.
TRAPCOMMUNITY	The SNMP.NLM agent sends the name specified by this parameter in trap messages to the SNMP Manager specified by the TRAP parameter of TCPIP.NLM.

The community names specified by the MONITORCOMMUNITY, CONTROLCOMMUNITY, and TRAPCOMMUNITY parameters are case sensitive and can be up to 32 characters long. Community names can include any characters except space, tab, colon (:), semicolon(;), equal sign (=), number sign (#), and left bracket ([).

If you enter any of the MONITORCOMMUNITY, CONTROLCOMMUNITY, and TRAPCOMMUNITY parameters with an equal sign (=) only, any community name in the SNMP request from the SNMP Manager is accepted. In other words, using only the equal sign (=) after the community name parameter disables authentication, and therefore any community name can be used. The following examples disable authentication for the community names that precede the equal sign:

```
LOAD SNMP MONITORCOMMUNITY=
LOAD SNMP CONTROLCOMMUNITY=
LOAD SNMP TRAPCOMMUNITY=
LOAD SNMP MONITORCOMMUNITY= CONTROLCOMMUNITY= TRAPCOMMUNITY=
LOAD SNMP M= C=
LOAD SNMP C= T=
LOAD SNMP M= C= T=
```

In the last three examples, the community name parameters are abbreviated to their first letters only.

If you enter the community name parameter *without* the equal sign (=), the access function specified by that community name is disabled. In the following examples, the access functions specified by the community names are disabled:

```
LOAD SNMP MONITORCOMMUNITY
LOAD SNMP CONTROLCOMMUNITY
LOAD SNMP TRAPCOMMUNITY
LOAD SNMP MONITORCOMMUNITY CONTROLCOMMUNITY TRAPCOMMUNITY
LOAD SNMP M
LOAD SNMP C
LOAD SNMP M C T
```

In the last three examples, the community name parameters are abbreviated to their first letters only.

If monitor access is disabled, as shown by the following statements, the SNMP Managers are unable to read the MIB variables for the managed device.

```
LOAD SNMP MONITORCOMMUNITY
LOAD SNMP M
```

If control access is disabled, as shown by the following statements, the SNMP Managers are unable to read and write to (change) the MIB variables for the managed device. A community name specified for read/write access also is valid for read access.

```
LOAD SNMP CONTROLCOMMUNITY
LOAD SNMP C
```

If trap access is disabled, as shown by the following statements, trap messages are not generated by the managed device.

```
LOAD SNMP TRAPCOMMUNITY
LOAD SNMP T
```

If SNMP is autoloaded or you do not specify the SNMP community options in the LOAD SNMP command, the MONITOR-COMMUNITY and TRAPCOMMUNITY parameter values default to "public," and the CONTROLCOMMUNITY is disabled.

The following examples set the community name parameters to non-default values:

Example 1

```
LOAD SNMP M=Jacobi
```

In this example, SNMP Managers that are configured with a community name "Jacobi" can monitor the SNMP agent. The trap community has a default name of "public," and the control community is disabled.

Example 2

```
LOAD SNMP C
```

In this example, read/write of MIB variables is disabled. The trap community has a default name of "public."

Example 3

```
LOAD SNMP C=
```

In this example, any SNMP Manager can read and write the MIB variables. The trap community has a default name of "public."

Example 4

```
LOAD SNMP M=SCS  C=RAI-ERNON  T=RAI-GWAUXLN
```

In this example, SNMP Managers that are configured with a community name RAI-GWAUXLN can monitor and receive trap messages from the SNMP agent. Also, SNMP Managers with a community name of RAI-ERNON can read and write the MIB variables.

Example 5

```
LOAD SNMP M= C=secret
```

In this example, any SNMP Manager can read the MIB variables, but only the SNMP Managers with a community name of "secret" can read and write the MIB variables. The trap community has a default name of "public."

Example 6

```
LOAD SNMP TRAPCOMMUNITY=SECRET
LOAD TCPIP ADDR=144.19.74.1 TRAP=144.19.74.102
```

Use this command line to specify that trap messages on interface 144.19.74.1 be sent to 144.19.74.102 with a community name of SECRET.

Understanding Security Issues with SNMP-I

The community names included in SNMP messages are sent in the "clear," without any encryption. You thus can discover the community names by using a protocol analyzer. A protocol analyzer can display the contents of the SNMP packets. Also, because the community name is not encrypted, you easily can find the string of characters used for the community name.

SNMP-II uses an improved scheme based on public key encryption and the message digest algorithm.

Using the SNMP Logger

An SNMP trap logger that can log trap messages in a file for later review is available for NetWare servers. The SNMP trap logger is implemented by SNMPLOG.NLM and is loaded after TCPIP.NLM. SNMPLOG.NLM is included in the NetWare server distribution software. SNMPLOG.NLM does not require any parameters, and you can load it by using the following console command:

```
LOAD SNMPLOG
```

While SNMPLOG is running, it processes trap messages sent to the NetWare TCP/IP server and writes them to the binary file SYS:ETC\SNMP$LOG.BIN (see fig. 5.9). If SNMPLOG is not loaded, SNMP trap messages can still be received, but they are not logged in to a file.

To disable the logging of trap messages, you can unload SNMPLOG by using the following command:

```
UNLOAD SNMPLOG
```

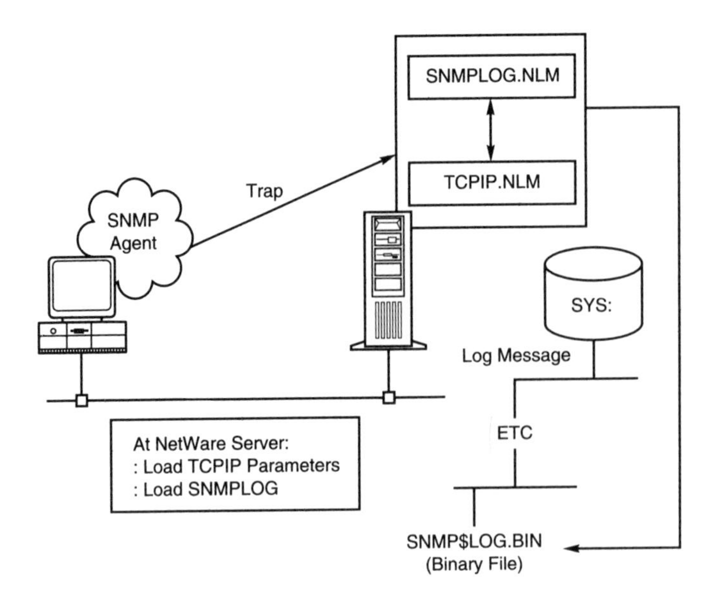

Figure 5.9
The SNMP logger.

Loading TCPCON

The TCPCON.NLM acts as a simple SNMP Manager. You can load it by using the following syntax:

```
LOAD TCPCON [target][community=name][help={Yes¦No}]
     [poll=rate] [retry=count][sort={Yes¦No}]
     timeout=secs]
```

Internal initialization errors occur if the server is short on memory or system resources, causing TCPCON to fail to load. The following messages are generated by possible TCPCON initialization errors:

```
TCPCON user interface initialization failed.
TCPCON help screen initialization failed.
TCPCON help screen access failed.
UDP socket initialization failed.
UDP socket connect failed.
UDP socket bind failed.
UDP socket ioctl failed.
```

Table 5.3 contains a summary of the TCPCON parameters.

TABLE 5.3 TCPCON PARAMETERS

Parameter	Description
target	Provides the name in the HOSTS file or IP address of the target host to be monitored. If not specified, a default value of the software loop back (127.0.0.1) is assumed, which means that information is presented for the local host only.
community=*name*	Used by SNMP agents to determine the type of MIB access that TCPCON should be given. A text string of up to 32 characters is included with an SNMP request. Remember that by default SNMP.NLM gives read-only access with community name "public" to the MIB and denies write access to the MIB. If the SNMP agent is configured with a different community name, you must specify this name using the community parameter.
help={Yes|No}	If set to Yes (the default), enables the loading of the TCPCON help text file. A value of No prevents the loading of the help file and disables help.
poll=*rate*	Specifies the SNMP request message poll rate in seconds. The TCPCON sends SNMP requests at the frequency specified to update its statistics display. The default poll rate is 1 second; the value can range from 0 to 900 seconds. A value of 0 specifies continuous polling.
retry=*count*	Number of consecutive unanswered requests that should be sent before declaring that the selected host is unreachable. The message Host Unavailable is displayed if the host cannot be polled successfully. The value must be between 1 and 100 and has a default value of 3.
sort={Yes|No}	Controls whether symbolic names in the HOSTS and NETWORKS files are presented in a sorted order or the order of listing in the file. Default value is Yes; that is, names are presented in a sorted order.
timeout=*secs*	Specifies the time in seconds that TCPCON should wait for a response before retrying. The default is 1 second, which should be adequate for most networks. You might want to increase this value for a very large network or if you are experiencing unusual delays.

Looking at the Special Keys Used with TCPCON

When using TCPCON, keep in mind that some notations and keys have special meanings.

A colon (:) following a field in TCPCON implies a *read-only* field.

A colon and period (:.) following a field in TCPCON identifies a *read-write* field.

Table 5.4 summarizes the special keys and their uses for navigating TCPCON.NLM.

TABLE 5.4 SPECIAL TCPCON KEYS

Key	Purpose
Enter	Selects the currently highlighted value.
Ins	Adds a new entry to a writeable table.
Del	Removes an entry from a writeable table or selects and clears the hostname field.
Tab	Toggles between the hostname and the IP address display.

Using TCPCON

The following sections give you a guided tour in the use of TCPCON.NLM. When TCPCON.NLM is used to examine variables on remote nodes, it issues SNMP get requests to obtain this information.

To Load TCPCON

If an SNMP device is available, specify its IP address or hostname, as in the following example:

```
LOAD TCPCON  nameOrIPaddress
```

Figure 5.10 shows the main TCPCON screen in which TCPCON.NLM was loaded with the following command:

```
LOAD TCPCON 199.245.180.55
```

The top part of the TCPCON screen shows the hostname or IP address of the device being monitored. The hostname is displayed if it exists in the local SYS:ETC\HOSTS file; otherwise, the IP address is displayed. In figure 5.10, the IP address of 199.245.180.55 is displayed. If the name of the SNMP device was not specified when TCPCON was loaded, the loopback address (127.0.0.1, the local server) is displayed (see fig. 5.11).

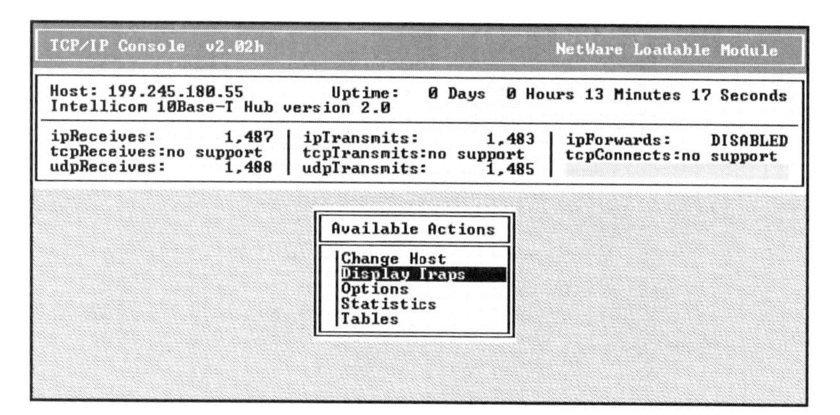

Figure 5.10

The TCPCON main screen for an SNMP device.

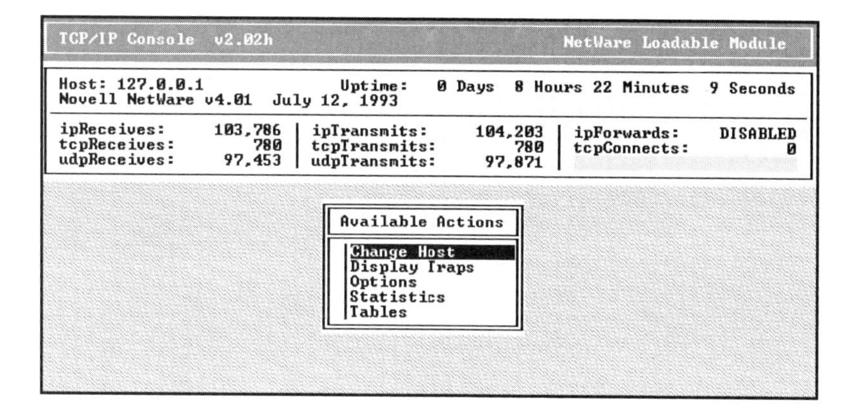

Figure 5.11

The TCPCON main screen for a local server.

All the statistics displayed refer to the device being monitored. Below the hostname is a brief description of the system being monitored. Figure 5.10 shows that the name of the SNMP device is Intellicom 10Base-T Hub version 2.0. Figure 5.11 has the generic name of Novell NetWare v4.01 July 12, 1993.

The Uptime value shows the length of time that the TCP/IP protocol stack has been running on the server in days, hours, minutes, and seconds. Figure 5.10 shows that the SNMP device at 199.245.180.55 has been running for 13 minutes and 17 seconds; and figure 5.11 shows that the TCP/IP stack on the local NetWare server at 127.0.0.1 has been running for 8 hours, 22 minutes, and 9 seconds.

The space below the Uptime field is blank under normal conditions. This field is used to display warning messages such as those listed in table 5.5.

TABLE 5.5 TCPCON WARNING MESSAGES

Message	Description
`Host Unavailable`	The specified host does not respond to SNMP messages. The SNMP agent might be inactive or configured with a different community name.
`Read Only Access`	An attempt to modify a read-only MIB variable was denied. Another reason for this message is that the community name in the SNMP request does not match the read/write community name established at the target system.
`Memory Shortage`	The NetWare server on which TCPCON is running is short on memory. As a result, an attempt to allocate memory failed.
`Msg Build Failure`	A diagnostic message indicating that an attempt to build an SNMP message failed. This message indicates an unusual problem with TCPCON.
`Msg Send Truncated`	A diagnostic message indicating that the UDP transport truncated the SNMP request message. This message indicates an unusual problem with TCPCON.
`Msg ID Mismatch`	The SNMP ID field in the response message did not match the request message. (Each SNMP message has an SNMP ID field that is used to associate an SNMP response with the SNMP request.) This message indicates a problem in the SNMP device being monitored.
`Msg Name Mismatch`	The SNMP community name in the response message does not match the community name in the SNMP request message.
`Msg Parse Failure`	The SNMP response message is invalid, perhaps because it was corrupted.
`Reply Msg Too Big`	The size of the SNMP response message is excessively large.
`Unknown Object`	The SNMP device does not support the requested MIB object.
`Bad Object Value`	The SNMP response contains an object value that is invalid for the specified object type.

The other statistics on the TCPCON main screen indicate the number of TCP and UDP transmit and receive packets, the number of forwarded IP packets, and the number of TCP connections. Figure 5.11 shows that the ipForwards is disabled because the NetWare server is not configured as a router. The ipForwards for the Intellicom Hub is also disabled because the Intellicom hub cannot act as a router (refer to fig. 5.10). The tcpConnects for the Intellicom Hub shows a value of no support because the TCP protocol is not supported on the hub (refer to fig. 5.10). This setting is typical of most network hubs that support only the UDP/IP protocol needed for the SNMP agent.

To monitor a different SNMP device, select Change Host from the Available Actions menu.

You then see a prompt for a new hostname or IP address (see fig. 5.12). You also can enter a hostname that is already defined in the local SYS:ETC\HOSTS file. Press the Ins key to see a list of possible hostnames (see fig. 5.13).

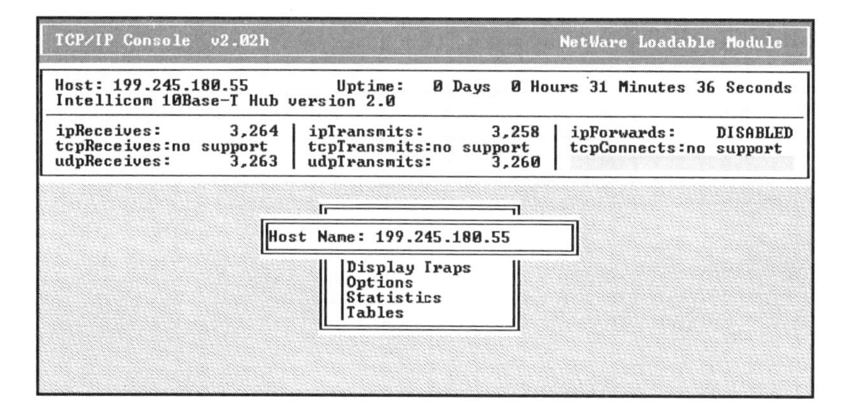

Figure 5.12

Using the Change Host option.

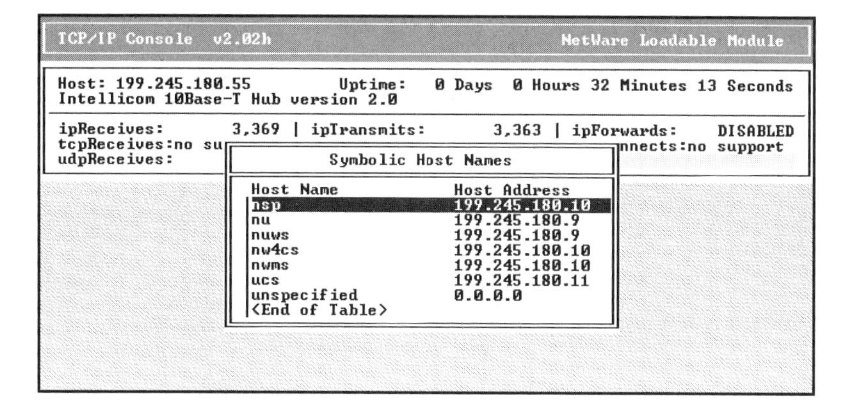

Figure 5.13

The list of hostnames for the TCPCON Change Host option.

To View Logged Trap Messages

Select Display Traps from the Available Actions menu to see a list of trap messages sent to the local NetWare TCP/IP server. The most recent traps are placed at the top of the list.

Figure 5.14 shows the trap log at a NetWare server. The trap log contains a number of Authentication Failure and Cold Start trap messages from the SNMP device at 199.245.180.55.

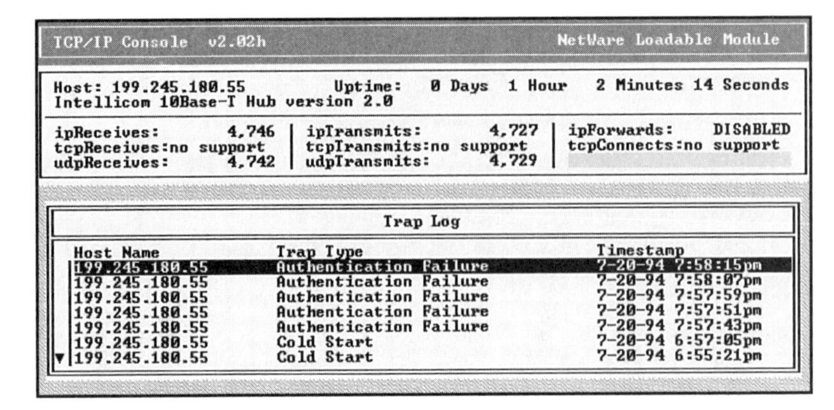

Figure 5.14
TCPCON trap messages.

When you exit the Display Trap option, you are asked whether you want to delete the trap log. The default is Yes, so if you do not want to delete the trap log, be careful and select No. Each entry in the trap log contains the hostname, type of trap, and times at which the trap took place. The hostnames are displayed in their symbolic form if an entry for the hostname is in the SYS:ETC\HOSTS file. If the hostnames have not been defined in the SYS:ETC\HOSTS file, their IP addresses are displayed. To toggle between the display hostnames and their IP addresses, you can use the Tab key.

The trap type can be any of the following:

- Cold start
- Warm start
- Link down
- Link up
- Authentication failure
- Routing neighbor loss
- Enterprise-specific *NN*

The enterprise-specific trap type is used to indicate vendor-specific events defined for the managed device. The decimal code *NN* indicates a vendor-specific code. You need to consult the vendor's documentation to determine the meaning of this code.

To Configure TCPCON Options

TCPCON gives you the flexibility of changing many of its default options such as community name, request retry count, request poll interval, and reply timeout interval. The following outlines the meanings of the TCPCON configurable parameters and how you can change them. Select Options from the Available Actions menu. The screen shown in figure 5.15 appears. The Community Name option has a default value of public. The default value for the Reply Timeout Interval option is 1 second. If no response is received within this time, the request is repeated a number of times as set in the Request Retry Count option (the default is 3). The SNMP requests are sent out by the parameter indicated in Request Poll Interval option. The "Options" parameters are the same as the ones that you set from the LOAD TCPCON command. Using the "Options" choice enables you to change these parameters without unloading and reloading TCPCON.

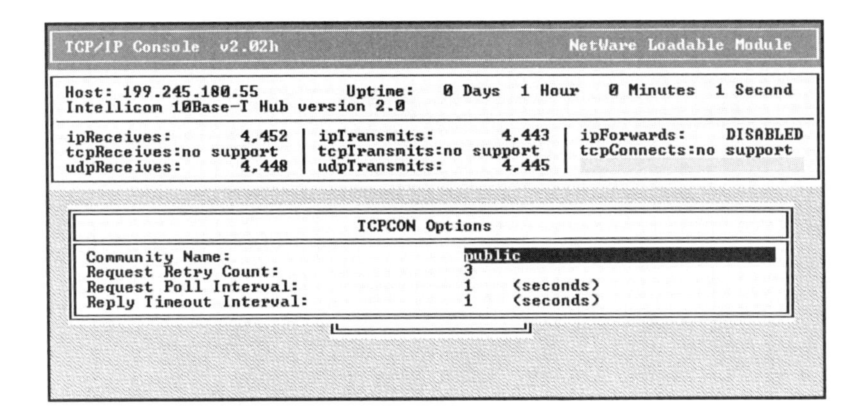

Figure 5.15

The TCPCON Options settings.

The name specified in the Community Name field must match the community name configuration for the SNMP device being monitored; otherwise, SNMP authentication failure trap messages are generated by the SNMP device. Additionally, the summary display of the TCPCON screen shows unknown for the statistic fields, and the HOST UNAVAILABLE message appears in the lower right corner of the TCPCON screen.

To Observe ICMP, IP, TCP, and UDP Statistics

Observing statistics on the operation of a protocol gives you valuable insight into the operation of the protocol software. The following is an outline of how to display these statistics. Select Statistics from the Available Actions menu.

The screen shown in figure 5.16 appears. Selecting each of the options in the TCP/IP Statistics menu enables you to view the individual statistics for the selected protocol.

Figures 5.17 to 5.20 show the statistics for the ICMP, IP, TCP, and UDP protocol types. The values of the fields shown in these figures are the names of the SNMP MIB variables defined in the SNMP standard for MIB-I. The SNMP MIB variables (also called objects) that you can change are identified by the colon/dot (:.) combination. MIB variables that are read-only are identified by a single colon (:).

Figure 5.17—ICMP statistics—shows that all the ICMP MIB variables are read-only. The ICMP parameters on this screen were generated by using the PING utility, which uses the ICMP protocol.

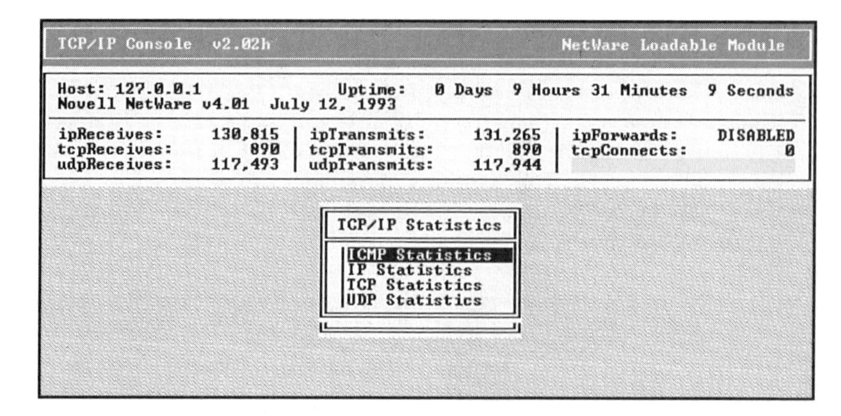

Figure 5.16

The TCP/IP Statistics options.

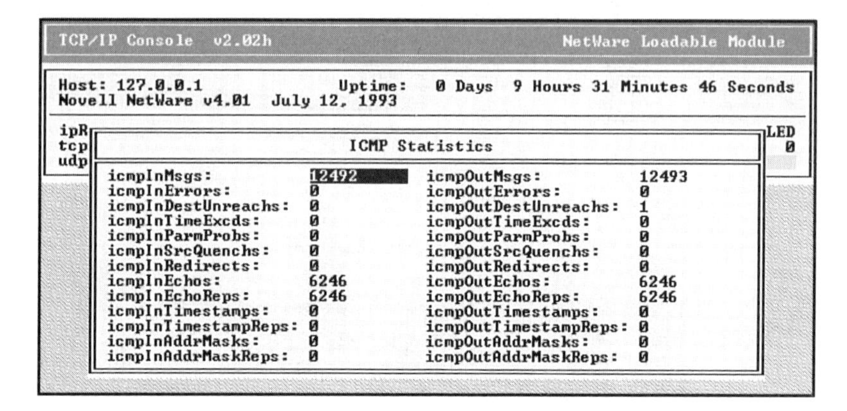

Figure 5.17

ICMP statistics.

Figure 5.18—IP statistics—shows that with the exception of ipForwarding and ipDefaultTTL, which are read-write, all the IP MIB variables are read-only. The ipDefaultTTL has a default value of 128 seconds and is the maximum time the IP packet can exist on the network. Routers that forward an IP packet are expected to decrease the *Time To Live* (TTL) value of the IP packet by the amount of time spent processing it. At a minimum, they are required to decrease the TTL field by 1. The TTL field in IP packets is meant to prevent routing loops. A *routing loop* occurs when an IP packet gets into an endless loop because links on the network are down.

Figure 5.19—TCP statistics—shows that all the IP MIB variables are read-only. The tcpRtoAlgorithm has a value of vanj. This parameter refers to the TCP round-trip timeout algorithm. NetWare's TCP implementation uses the Van Jacobson timeout algorithm.

Figure 5.20—UDP statistics—shows that all the UDP MIB variables are read-only.

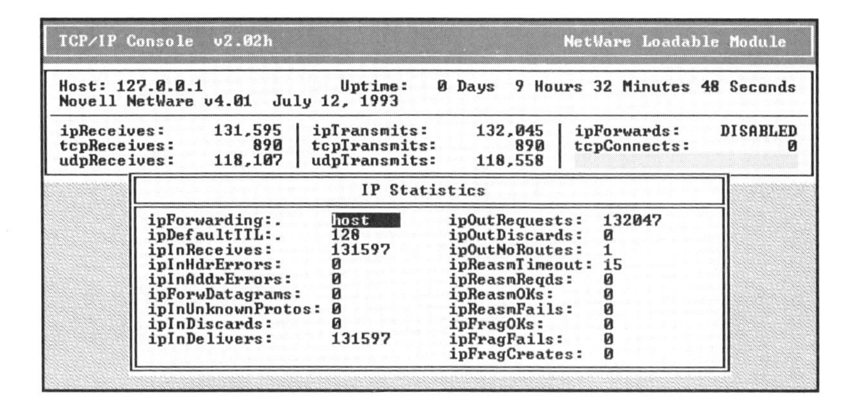

Figure 5.18

IP statistics.

```
TCP/IP Console  v2.02h                              NetWare Loadable Module

Host: lb                    Uptime:   0 Days  0 Hours 10 Minutes 15 Seconds
Novell NetWare v4.01  July 12, 1993

ipReceives:         4,525 | ipTransmits:        4,527 | ipForwards:    DISABLED
tcpReceives:           20 | tcpTransmits:          20 | tcpConnects:          0
udpReceives:        3,624 | udpTransmits:       3,627 |

                             TCP Statistics
     tcpRtoAlgorithm:  vanj          tcpAttemptFails:  0
     tcpRtoMin:        111           tcpEstabResets:   0
     tcpRtoMax:        118800        tcpCurrEstab:     0
     tcpMaxConn:       -1            tcpInSegs:        20
     tcpActiveOpens:   2             tcpOutSegs:       20
     tcpPassiveOpens:  2             tcpRetransSegs:   0
```

Figure 5.19

TCP statistics.

```
TCP/IP Console  v2.02h                              NetWare Loadable Module

Host: lb                    Uptime:   0 Days  0 Hours 10 Minutes 50 Seconds
Novell NetWare v4.01  July 12, 1993

ipReceives:         4,827 | ipTransmits:        4,830 | ipForwards:    DISABLED
tcpReceives:           20 | tcpTransmits:          20 | tcpConnects:          0
udpReceives:        3,868 | udpTransmits:       3,872 |

                       UDP Statistics
                udpInDatagrams:     3870
                udpNoPorts:         1
                udpInErrors:        0
                udpOutDatagrams:    3874
```

Figure 5.20

UDP statistics.

Monitoring TCP/IP Tables

The TCP/IP tables in TCPCON are used to display the *Address Resolution Protocol* (ARP) table, routing table, interface table, hosts table, and the TCP connection table. The information in these tables is used to troubleshoot TCP/IP-related problems. The following is an outline on how to perform these tasks. Select Tables from the Available Actions menu. The screen shown in figure 5.21 appears. Selecting each of the options in the TCP/IP Tables menu enables you to view ARP, interface, hosts, routing, and TCP connection tables.

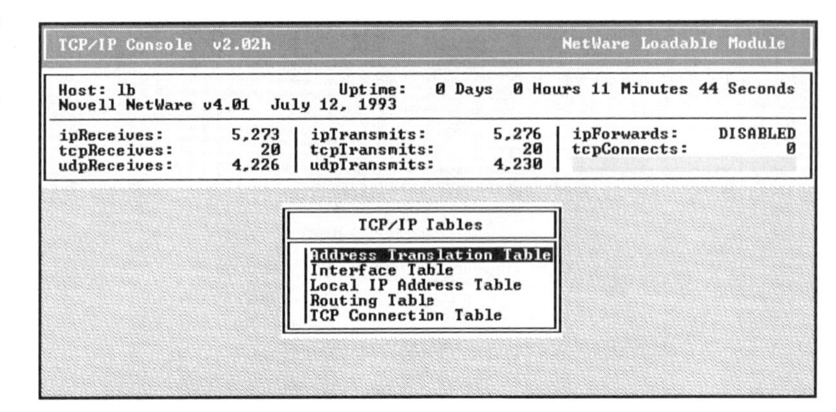

Figure 5.21
The TCP/IP Tables menu.

The Address Translation Table

Select Address Translation Table from the TCP/IP Tables menu to view the ARP table for the node being monitored (see fig. 5.22). The NetWare server's ARP table has two entries. These entries show names of IP nodes with which the server has communicated recently. As you learned in Chapter 3, ARP table entries are removed when they exceed a certain timeout value. You can use the Tab key to toggle between IP addresses and symbolic hostnames. Figure 5.23 shows the same ARP table in figure 5.22 after the Tab key was used to display IP addresses.

To temporarily solve IP address duplication and IP address to MAC address mapping problems, you can add and modify entries in the ARP table by pressing the Ins key. Unless you are comfortable with these issues, you should not make manual entries. Manual entries, unlike entries made dynamically with the ARP protocol, are not timed out.

The Interface Table

Select Interface Table from the TCP/IP Tables menu to view the logical network interfaces defined for the node being monitored. Figure 5.24 shows that three NE2000 interfaces, numbered from 1 to 3, are defined. The MAC addresses of the three interfaces in figure 5.24 are the same; they have a value of 00-40-05-28-B7-2A. The three interfaces correspond to the NE2000 driver being loaded three times with different frame types. You can obtain additional information on the interface by highlighting the interface and pressing Enter.

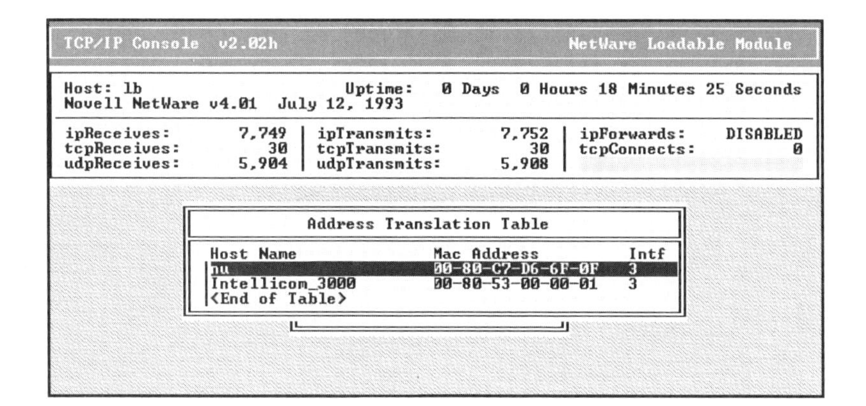

Figure 5.22

The Address Translation Table with symbolic hostnames.

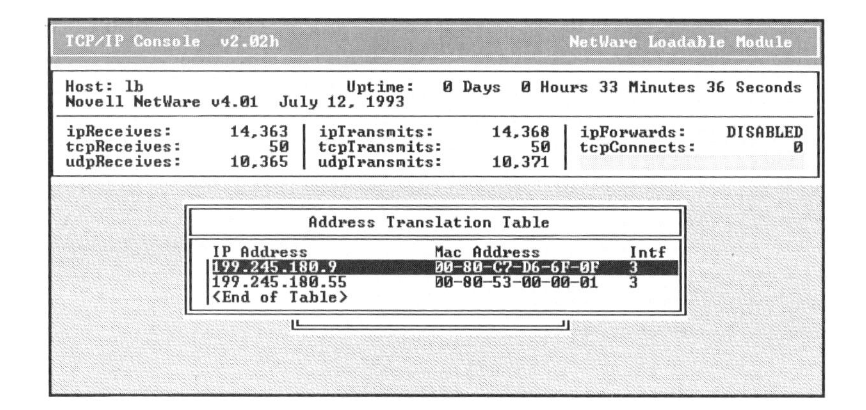

Figure 5.23

The Address Translation Table with IP addresses.

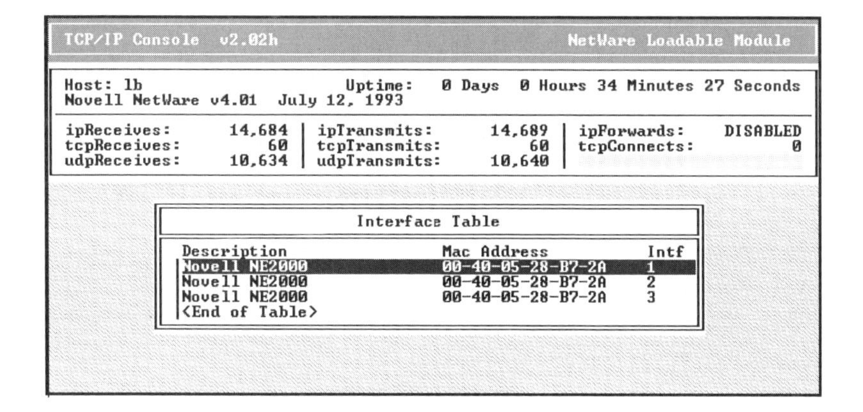

Figure 5.24

The Interface Table screen.

In figures 5.25 through 5.27, the interfaces correspond to the frame types of ETHERNET_802.3, ETHERNET_802.2, and ETHERNET_II. The value of ifType in figures 5.25 and 5.26 is iso88023-csmacd; and the value in figure 5.27 is ethernet-csmacd. The is88023 refers to ISO 8802/3, and csmacd refers to the Media Access Control method of Carrier Sense Multiple Access with Collision Detect (CSMA/CD) used in Ethernet. The ISO 8802/3 is the International Organization of Standard's (ISO's) designation for IEEE 802.3.

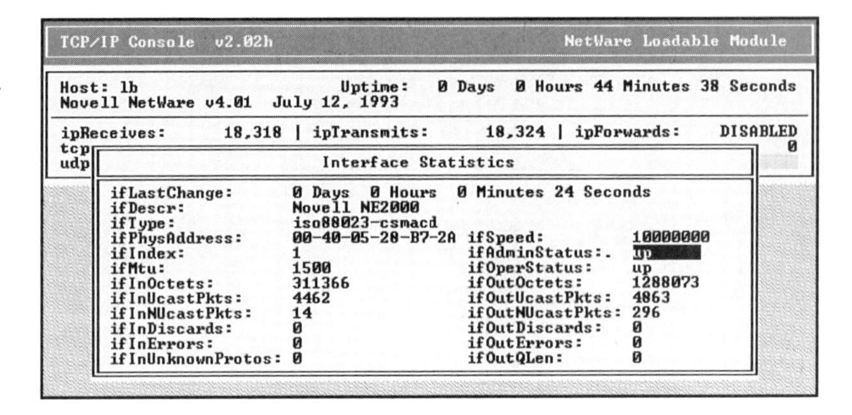

Figure 5.25

Interface statistics for NE2000 Interface 1 (frame ETHERNET_802.3).

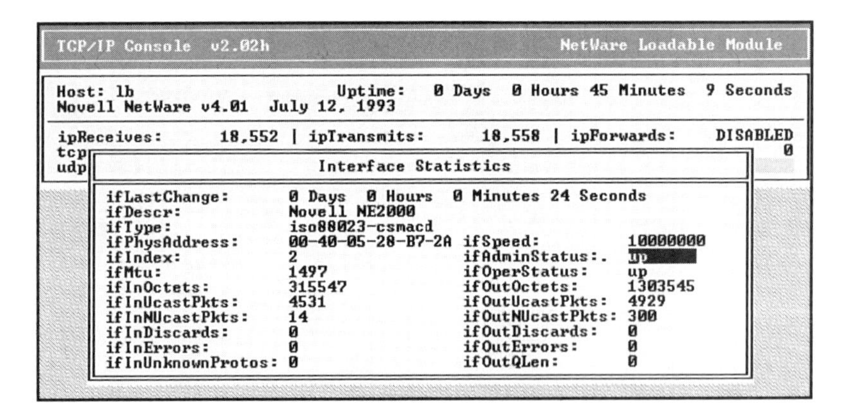

Figure 5.26

Interface statistics for NE2000 Interface 1 (frame ETHERNET_802.2).

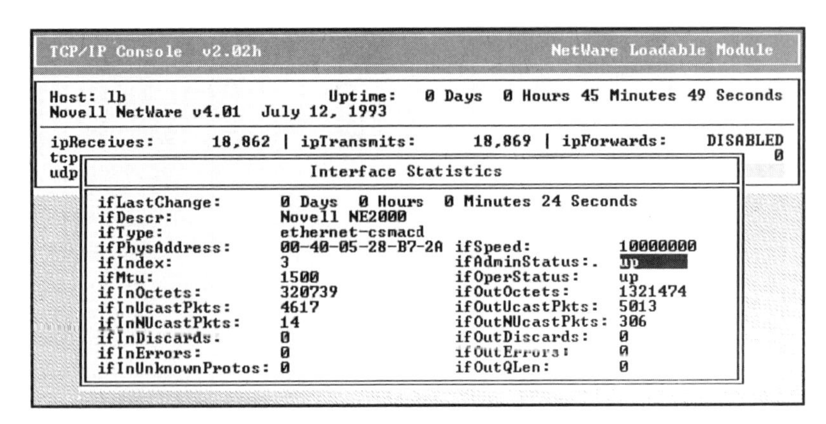

Figure 5.27

Interface statistics for NE2000 Interface 1 (frame ETHERNET_II).

The Local IP Address Table

Select Local IP Address Table from the TCP/IP Tables menu to view the local IP addresses of the TCP/IP node's network interfaces (see fig. 5.28). Each entry contains the hostname (or IP address), address mask (subnet mask), network interface number, and an indication of the type of broadcast that is supported at that interface. The entries in this table are for display purposes and cannot be modified.

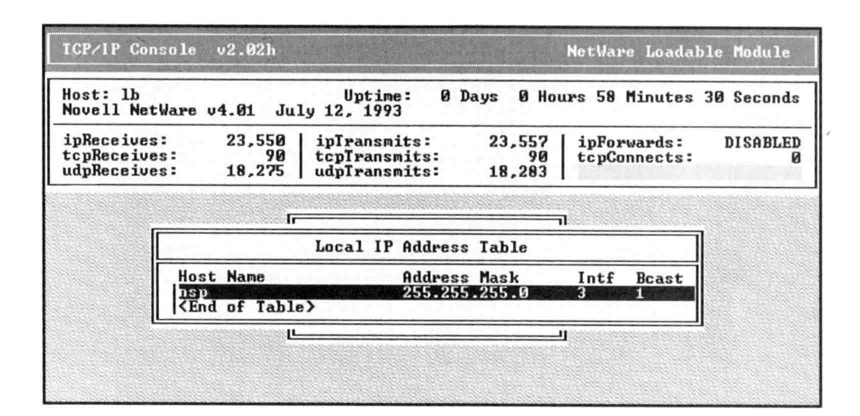

Figure 5.28

The Local IP Address Table.

The Routing Table

Select Routing Table from the TCP/IP Tables menu to view the routing table for the selected TCP/IP node (see fig. 5.29). Because the node is not configured as a TCP/IP router, only the network entry for the directly connected network of 199.245.180.0 is shown. Each entry contains the destination network, next hop (router address), network interface number for the next hop router, cost of route, and type of route (direct or remote). If destination networks are entered in the SYS:ETC\NETWORKS file, they are displayed in symbolic form. You can use the Tab key to toggle between symbolic names and the dotted decimal notation for the networks.

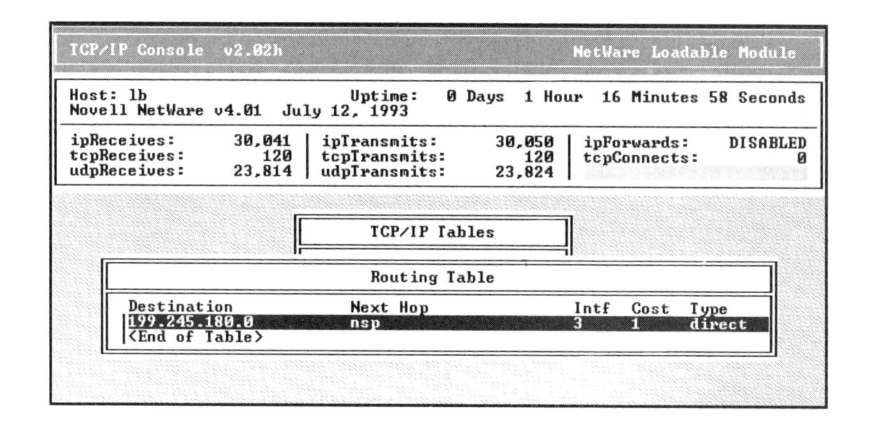

Figure 5.29

The Routing Table.

The direct routes are permanent entries made at the time of IP initialization. The remote routes are for networks that are reachable only through a router. Press Enter on any of the routes to see more information on the router table entry (see fig. 5.30). For a more detailed discussion about the fields in figure 5.30, see Chapter 4, "TCP/IP Routing Support in NetWare."

Figure 5.30

A routing table entry.

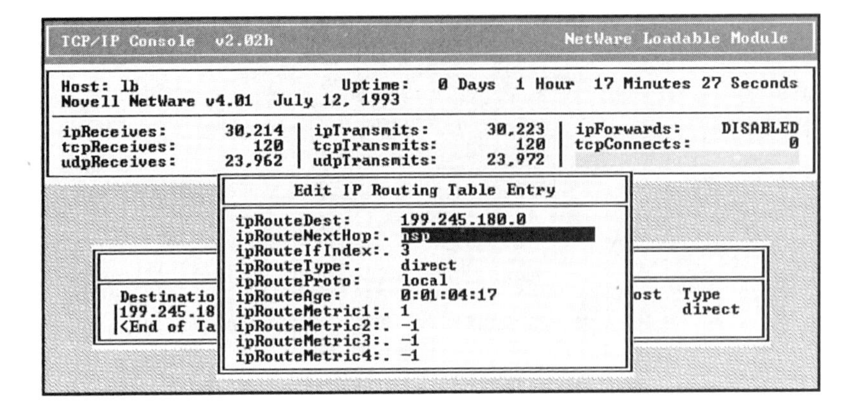

The TCP Connection Table

Select TCP Connection Table from the TCP/IP Tables menu to show the TCP Connection Table for the selected TCP/IP node (see fig. 5.31). The TCP Connection Table contains an entry for each connection between the local host and a remote host. Each entry contains the source hostname and port number, destination host and port number, and the status of the connection. In figure 5.31, because no TCP connections exist, the connection state for all the services is listen, and the local and remote host columns read unspecified.

Figure 5.31

The TCP Connection Table.

TCP/IP Console v2.02h NetWare Loadable Module

Host: lb Uptime: 0 Days 1 Hour 20 Minutes 24 Seconds
Novell NetWare v4.01 July 12, 1993

ipReceives: 31,265 | ipTransmits: 31,275 | ipForwards: DISABLED
tcpReceives: 130 | tcpTransmits: 130 | tcpConnects: 0
udpReceives: 24,856 | udpTransmits: 24,867

TCP Connection Table

Local Host	Port	Remote Host	Port	State
unspecified	echo	unspecified	none	listen
unspecified	discard	unspecified	none	listen
unspecified	chargen	unspecified	none	listen
unspecified	domain	unspecified	none	listen
unspecified	111	unspecified	none	listen
unspecified	396	unspecified	none	listen
unspecified	1025	unspecified	none	listen

Summary

SNMP has gained widespread acceptance as a standard protocol for managing TCP/IP networks. NetWare 3.x and 4.x servers support SNMP by providing an agent (SNMP.NLM) that can be queried by any SNMP Manager. A simple SNMP Manager (TCPCON.NLM) also is included with the NetWare software distribution.

In this chapter, you learned to load and configure the SNMP agent for NetWare servers and the SNMP logger used to record trap messages. You also learned how to use TCPCON.NLM to perform simple management tasks.

Managing TCP/IP Protocols Using INETCFG

INETCFG is an NLM that facilitates menu-driven configuration and the ongoing management of network communication protocols running on a NetWare server. The protocols include IPX, TCP/IP, and AppleTalk. Routing protocols such as RIP (Routing Information Protocol) and OSPF (Open Shortest Path First) are also configured using INETCFG. This chapter discusses the features of INETCFG, concentrating on the configuration of TCP/IP.

Overview of INETCFG

A menu-driven approach to protocol configuration as implemented by INETCFG minimizes the chances of introducing syntax and spelling errors into configuration files where protocol configuration statements are stored. When a NetWare server is configured without the use of INETCFG, the configuration statements for network protocols are contained in AUTOEXEC.NCF. Without INETCFG, these protocols are configured in a text-editing mode using the text editor provided within the NetWare INSTALL utility. AUTOEXEC.NCF statements beginning with LOAD and BIND commands are examples of typical protocol configuration statements. The LOAD command loads drivers, while the BIND command associates these drivers with the appropriate protocols. The LOAD command is also used for loading other protocol-related NLMs into the server memory.

When INETCFG is loaded for the first time from a server console, a "Yes/No" menu comes up on the server console (see fig. 6.1). It gives you the option to extract the existing LAN driver, protocol, and remote configuration commands from AUTOEXEC.NCF, and to place them in two configuration files located in the SYS:ETC directory. The two configuration files in the SYS:ETC directory are INITSYS.NCF and NETINFO.CFG, which are created when the Yes option is chosen, as shown in figure 6.1.

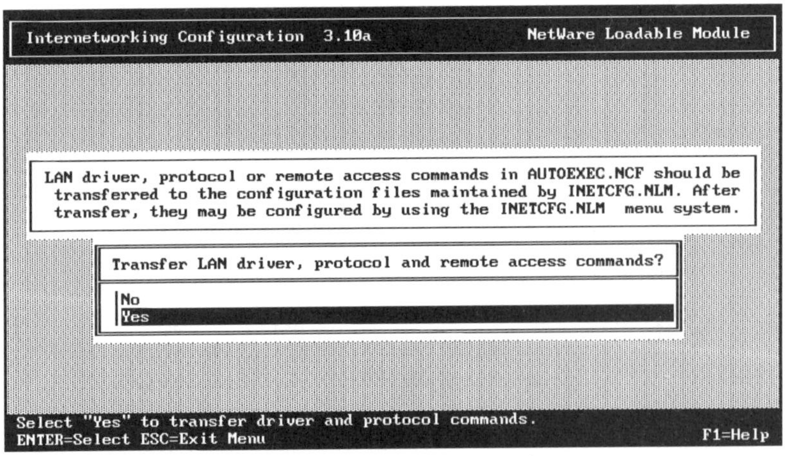

```
Internetworking Configuration  3.10a                NetWare Loadable Module

LAN driver, protocol or remote access commands in AUTOEXEC.NCF should be
 transferred to the configuration files maintained by INETCFG.NLM. After
 transfer, they may be configured by using the INETCFG.NLM  menu system.

      Transfer LAN driver, protocol and remote access commands?
      No
      Yes

Select "Yes" to transfer driver and protocol commands.
ENTER=Select ESC=Exit Menu                                          F1=Help
```

Figure 6.1

Menu options when INETCFG is loaded for the very first time from a NetWare server console.

The statements transferred out of the AUTOEXEC.NCF are commented in the file and left there for reference (see fig. 6.2). After INITSYS.NCF and NETINFO.CFG are created, they are maintained by the INETCFG NLM. It is not recommended that these two files be modified through any other means except through the use of INETCFG.

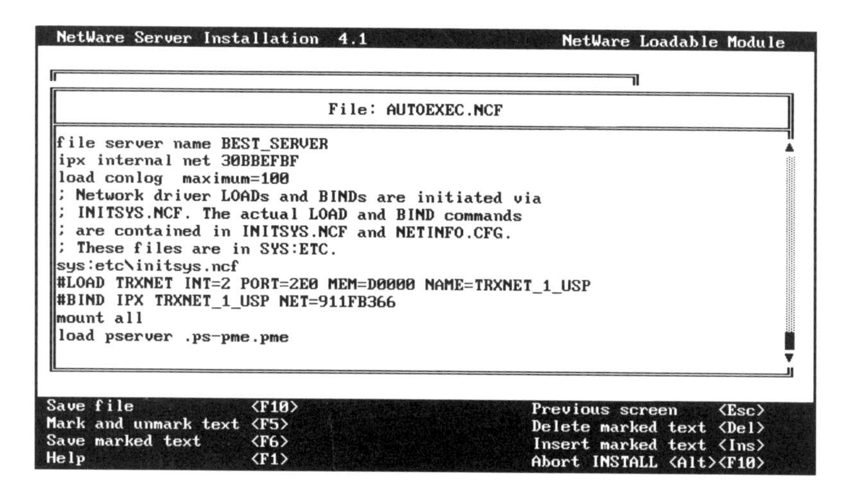

Figure 6.2

AUTOEXEC.NCF modified by INETCFG.

Configuring NetWare Servers with INETCFG.NLM

When INETCFG is invoked subsequent to the initial transfer of configuration statements from AUTOEXEC.NCF, the Internetworking Configuration menu appears, as shown in figure 6.3. The menu choices explained in the following steps are used to configure and manage a NetWare server.

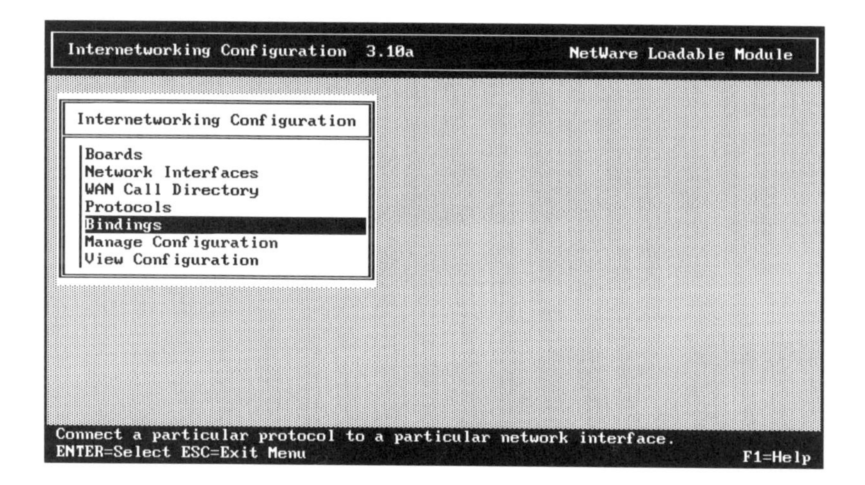

Figure 6.3

The INETCFG Internetworking Configuration menu.

Using the Boards Menu Option

The Boards option allows the configuration of network cards that are installed in the file server. A sample display resulting from invoking this option is shown in figure 6.4. This display, however, is a result of manually configuring only one network card in AUTOEXEC.NCF and having that configuration statement transferred out of AUTOEXEC.NCF when INETCFG is first invoked.

Figure 6.4

Display of a configured network card in the Boards configuration menu. Transferred from AUTOEXEC.NCF.

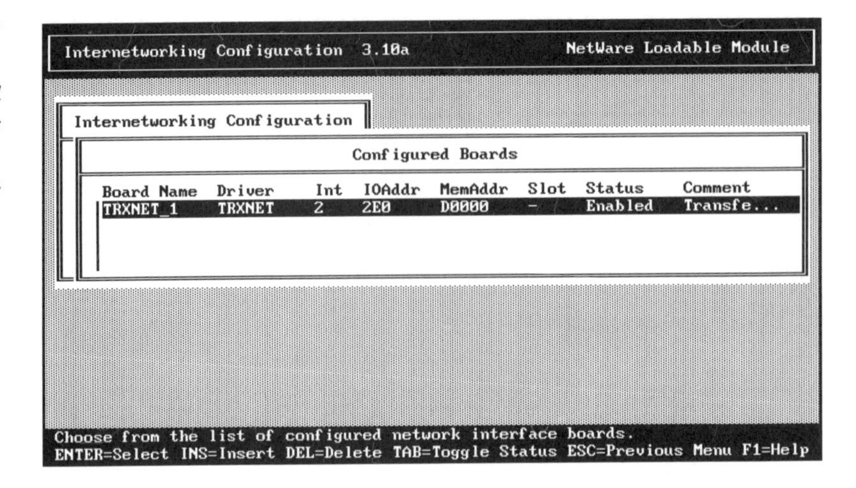

Because multiple network cards can be and typically are installed in NetWare servers, they are configured from this menu option by pressing the Ins key. Next, you must select a driver (see fig. 6.5) and specify the board parameters such as the interrupt (IRQ), I/O port, and shared memory address (see fig. 6.6). In the example shown in figure 6.5, the selected driver is NE2000.

If a desired driver does not appear on the screen as shown in figure 6.5, the appropriate driver files must be obtained from the network card vendor and copied into the SYS:SYSTEM directory. Note that you are not asked to specify the frame type because INETCFG automatically supplies the frame type as a function of the assigned driver. You must also determine that the board parameters do not conflict with each other when installing them in the server.

Figure 6.5

Choice of network card drivers in the Boards configuration menu.

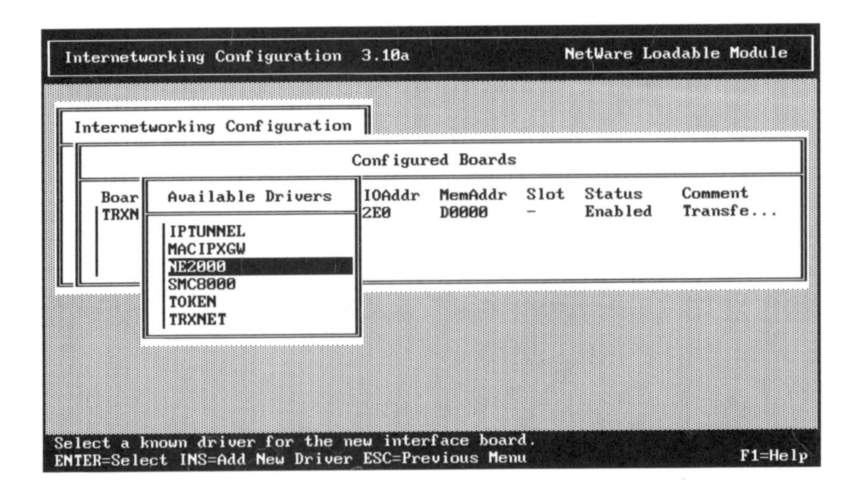

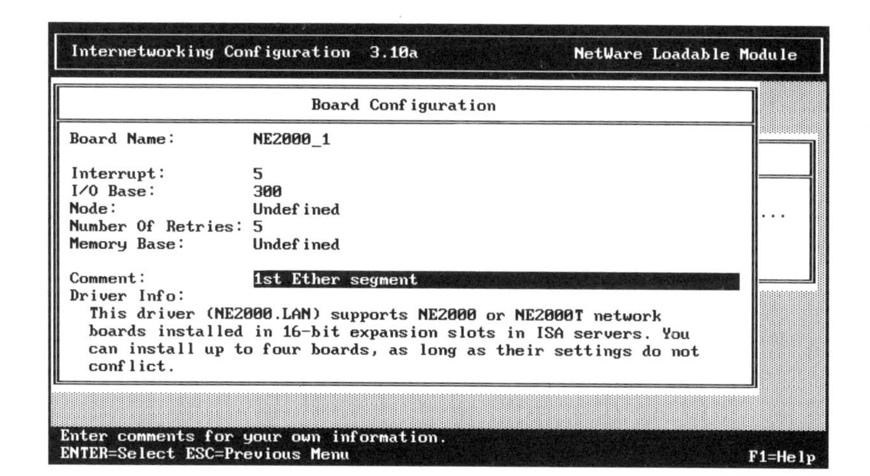

Figure 6.6

Network card parameters in the Boards configuration menu.

Note the display of the Boards menu option after two additional NE2000 compatible boards were installed in the server and configured through this option (see fig. 6.7).

Internetworking Configuration 3.10a NetWare Loadable Module

Internetworking Configuration

Configured Boards

Board Name	Driver	Int	IOAddr	MemAddr	Slot	Status	Comment
TRXNET_1	TRXNET	2	2E0	D0000	–	Enabled	Transfe...
NE2000_1	NE2000	5	300	–	–	Enabled	1st Eth...
NE2000_2	NE2000	A	320	–	–	Enabled	2nd Eth...

Choose from the list of configured network interface boards.
ENTER=Select INS=Insert DEL=Delete TAB=Toggle Status ESC=Previous Menu F1=Help

Figure 6.7

Boards configuration display after two boards were configured through INETCFG. The first board was transferred from AUTOEXEC.NCF.

When there is a need to change any of the board parameters, it can be done by highlighting a configured board and pressing Enter. Doing this displays the screen shown in figure 6.8. The board chosen in this example is the second NE2000 board.

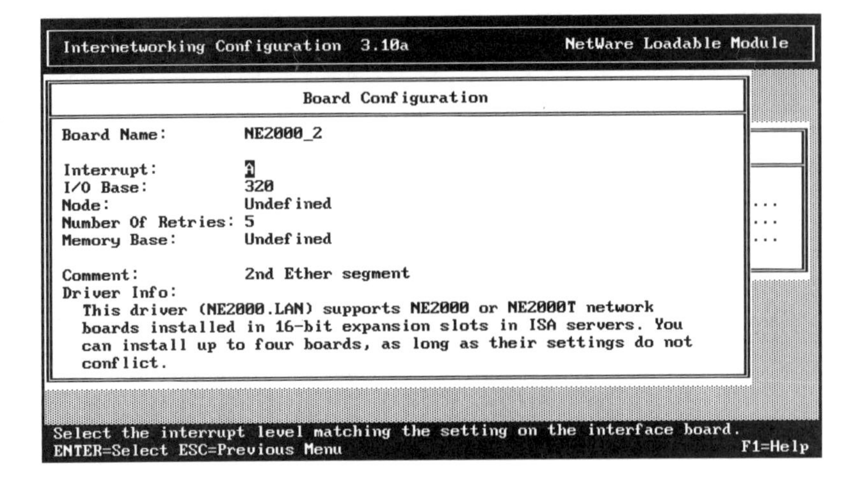

Figure 6.8

Editing network card parameters in the Boards configuration menu.

Keep in mind when you are reconfiguring a board through INETCFG, that the IRQ, I/O address, and shared memory address parameters must also be changed on the board itself. These parameters can be changed through the jumper settings or with the appropriate utilities supplied by the manufacturer of the board.

Tip Board parameters set through INETCFG do not affect the settings on the boards themselves.

If an attempt is made to configure an additional board that conflicts with the IRQ, I/O, or shared memory address parameters of an existing board, INETCFG will display the warning message shown in figure 6.10. In the example shown in figure 6.9, an attempt was made to configure a third NE2000 board (NE2000_3) with the same IRQ as the second NE2000 compatible board named NE2000_2.

```
Internetworking Configuration  3.10a              NetWare Loadable Module

                          Board Configuration
Board Name:          NE2000_3

Interrupt:           A
I/O Base:            300
Node:                Undefined
Number Of Retries:   5
Memory Base:         Undefined

Comment:             Unspecified
Driver Info:
  This driver (NE2000.LAN) supports NE2000 or NE2000T network
  boards installed in 16-bit expansion slots in ISA servers. You
  can install up to four boards, as long as their settings do not
  conflict.

Select the base I/O address matching the setting on the interface board.
ENTER=Select ESC=Previous Menu                                    F1=Help
```

Figure 6.9

A NE2000_3 board modified to have the same IRQ as NE2000_2 board.

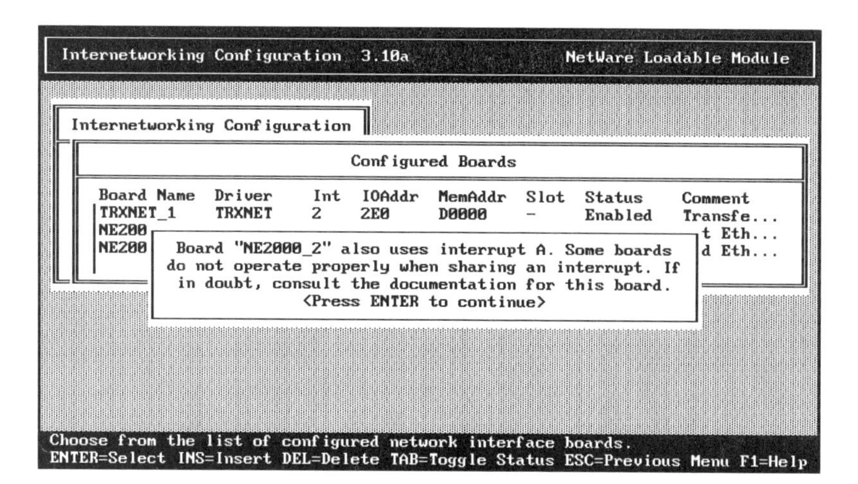

Figure 6.10

The warning message displayed by INETCFG when there is a conflict between parameters of the configured boards.

Configuring boards with conflicting parameters can only result in a malfunctioning server and is depicted here for instructional purposes only. INETCFG does not deter you from installing configurations with board parameters that conflict (see fig. 6.11). This figure shows that an NE2000_3 board was configured with an IRQ and I/O port address conflicting with the NE2000_2 board, even though the NE2000_3 was not physically installed in the server.

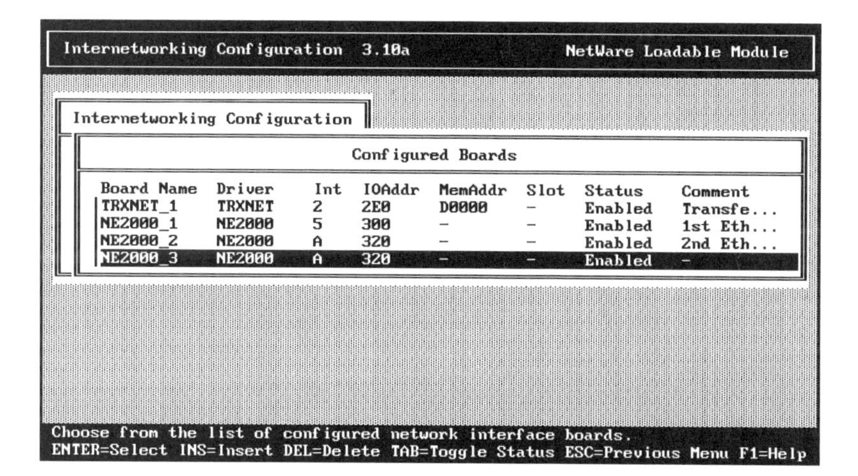

Figure 6.11

Boards configured with conflicting parameters.

You can delete a misconfigured board by highlighting the problem board and pressing the Delete key. A screen requesting deletion confirmation of a misconfigured board is shown in figure 6.12.

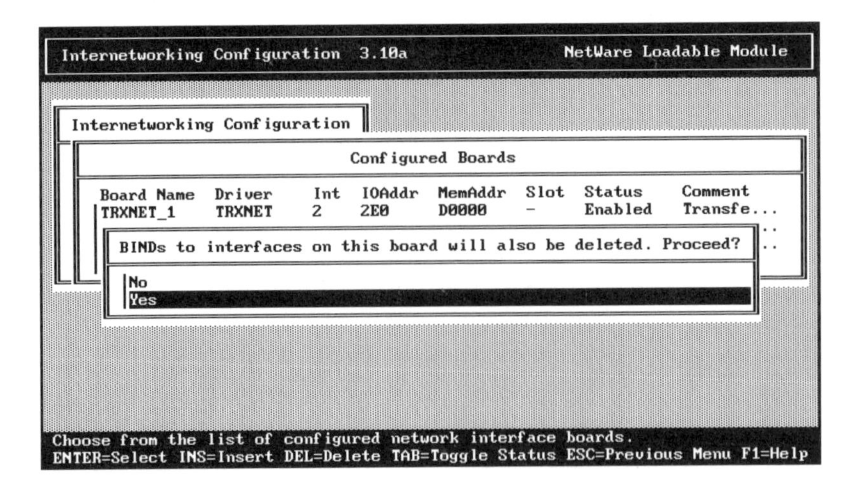

Figure 6.12

The Delete option in the Boards menu.

Using the Network Interface Option

The Network Interfaces option is a "display only" option that acts as an extension of the Boards menu option. For every defined board or network card in the server there is an entry in the Network Interface menu. The Network Interfaces screen appears as it is shown in figure 6.13 for all the boards defined in the Boards option menu. Highlighting one of the interfaces and pressing Enter results in the message shown in figure 6.14, that no further configuration is required.

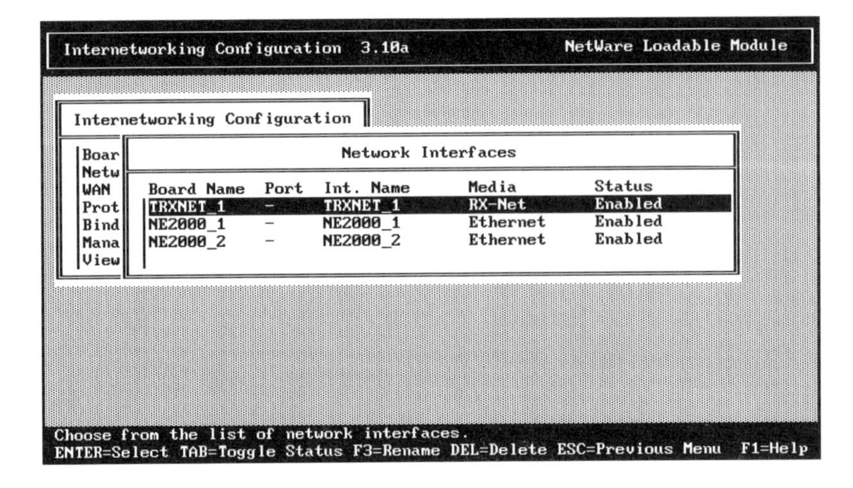

Figure 6.13

A display of network interfaces in the Network Interfaces menu.

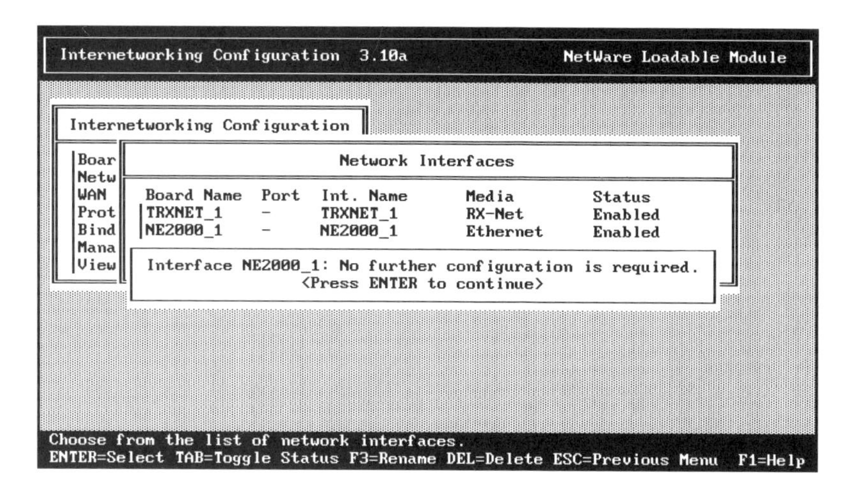

Figure 6.14

The warning message in the Network Interfaces menu that no further configuration is required.

The contents of the Network Interfaces menu option are used in subsequent actions when the IPX and TCP/IP protocols are bound to the network boards.

If you had WAN boards, you would configure them at this point by using the WAN Call Directory options. Configuring the WAN Call Directory requires the NetWare Multiprotocol Router, and is not discussed in this chapter. Please refer to the MPR documentation for installation and configuration instructions.

Using the Protocols Option

The Protocol Configuration menu screen is shown in figure 6.15. AppleTalk, IPX, TCP/IP, as well as user-specified protocols can be configured through this menu option. Sample AppleTalk configuration screens are displayed for reference in figures 6.16 and 6.17. Figure 6.16 shows the initial AppleTalk configuration screen, and figure 6.17 displays the AppleTalk Update-based Router Protocol (AURP) configuration.

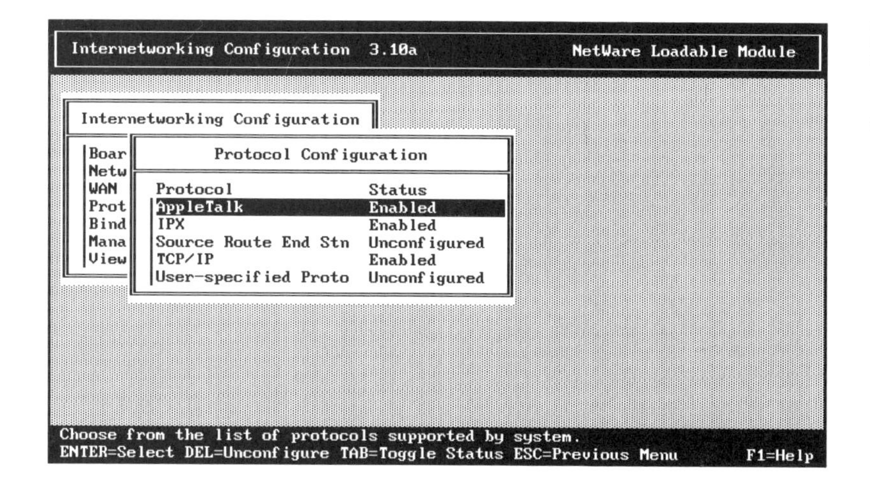

Figure 6.15

The Protocol Configuration menu.

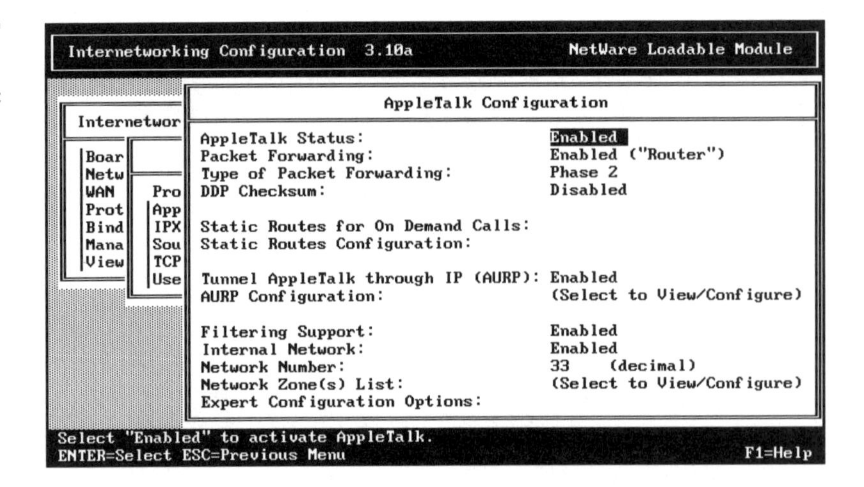

Figure 6.16

The AppleTalk Configuration menu.

```
Internetworking Configuration  3.10a                NetWare Loadable Module

                          AppleTalk Configuration
Internetwor
                     Appl            AURP Configuration
Boar                 Pack
Netw                 Type  UDP Port:          387
WAN       Pro        DDP   UDP Checksum:      Enabled
Prot      App
Bind      IPX        Stat  Local IP Address:  199.245.180.10
Mana      Sou        Stat  Remote Peers List: (Select to View/Configure)
View      TCP              Expert Options:    (Select to View/Configure)
          Use        Tunn
                     AURP Configuration:                 (Select to View/Configure)

                     Filtering Support:                  Enabled
                     Internal Network:                   Enabled
                     Network Number:                     33    (decimal)
                     Network Zone(s) List:               (Select to View/Configure)
                     Expert Configuration Options:

AURP must use one of IP addresses configured to identify itself to its peers.
ENTER=Select ESC=Previous Menu                                          F1=Help
```

Figure 6.17

The AppleTalk Configuration options continued.

Figures 6.18, 6.19 and 6.20 show some of the options that are available to you when configuring IPX.

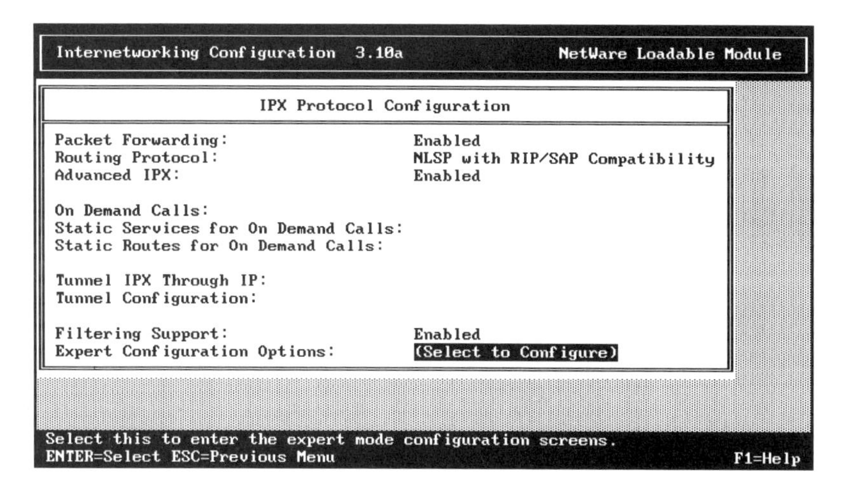

Figure 6.18

The IPX Configuration menu.

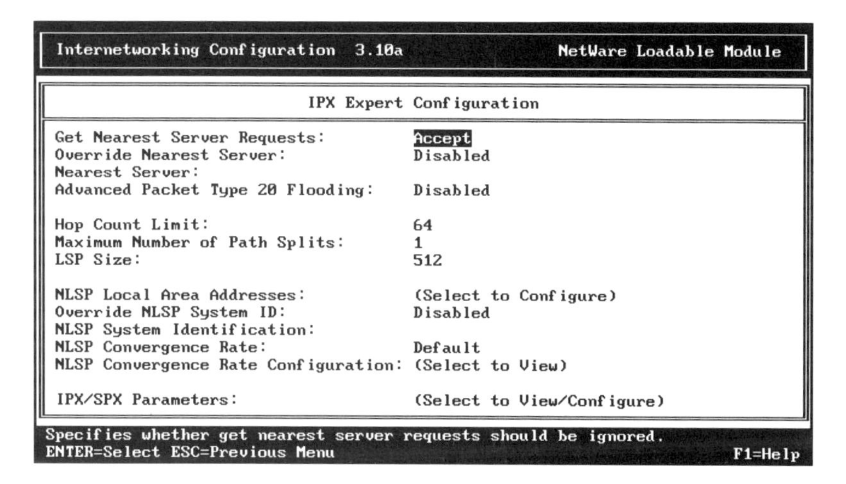

Figure 6.19

The IPX Expert Configuration menu.

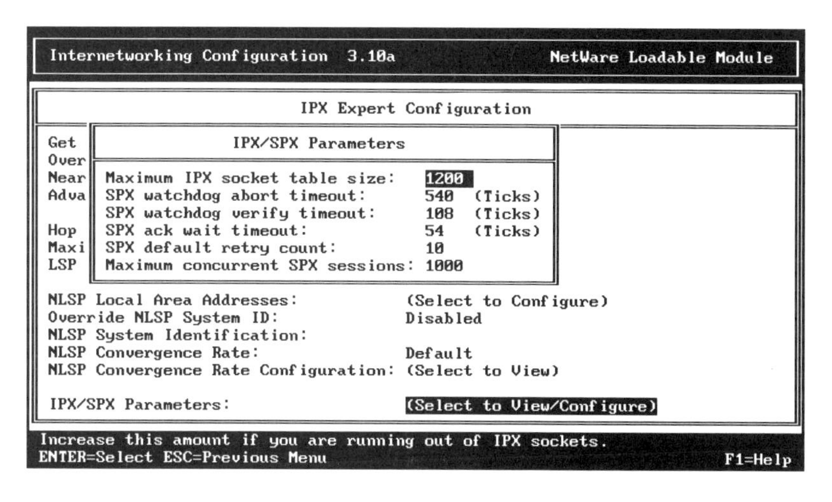

Figure 6.20

The IPX/SPX Configuration parameters.

The details of the configuration of these protocols are outside the scope of this chapter. For additional details on IPX see *NetWare: The Professional Reference, Fourth Edition* from New Riders.

TCP/IP configuration options are described in detail in the section entitled "Configuring TCP/IP Parameters with INETCFG NLM."

Using the Bindings Option

The Bindings option allows the protocols to be bound to the network cards. A sample binding of IPX to an ARCnet card named TRXNET_1 is shown in figure 6.21. The display is the result of the original transfer of configuration statements from AUTOEXEC.NCF.

Figure 6.21

The display of an IPX binding to a network card named TRXNET_1 in the Bindings menu.

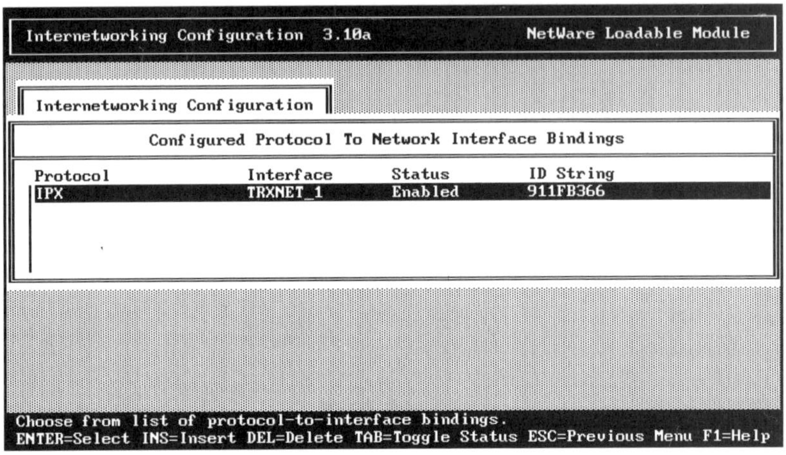

```
Internetworking Configuration  3.10a               NetWare Loadable Module

 Internetworking Configuration

            Configured Protocol To Network Interface Bindings

 Protocol                  Interface       Status         ID String
 IPX                       TRXNET_1        Enabled        911FB366

Choose from list of protocol-to-interface bindings.
ENTER=Select INS=Insert DEL=Delete TAB=Toggle Status ESC=Previous Menu F1=Help
```

You will now step through the process of binding TCP/IP to one of the NE2000 cards, defined as NE2000_1. First, press the Ins key and select the TCP/IP protocol, as shown in figure 6.22.

Figure 6.22

The Protocol selection option in the Bindings menu.

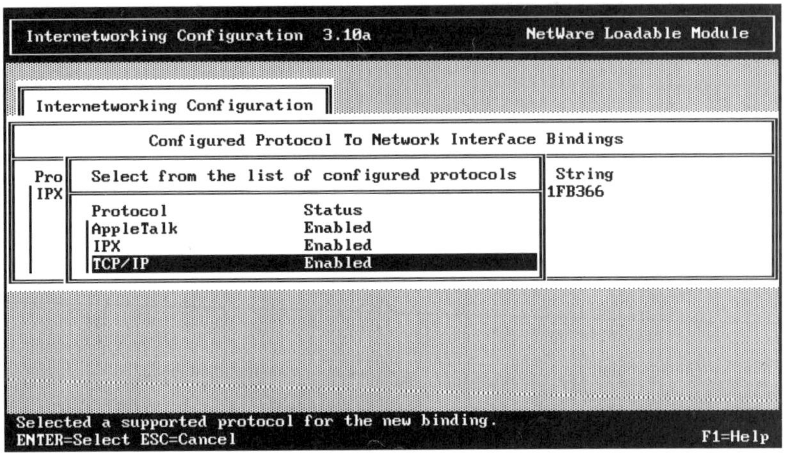

```
Internetworking Configuration  3.10a               NetWare Loadable Module

 Internetworking Configuration

            Configured Protocol To Network Interface Bindings

 Pro   Select from the list of configured protocols    String
 IPX                                                   1FB366
       Protocol                    Status
       AppleTalk                   Enabled
       IPX                         Enabled
       TCP/IP                      Enabled

Selected a supported protocol for the new binding.
ENTER=Select ESC=Cancel                                              F1=Help
```

Next, press the Enter key to display a screen like the one shown in figure 6.23, listing all the available network interfaces to which the selected protocol can be bound. In this example, the interfaces are for one ARCnet card and two Ethernet cards named TRXNET, NE2000_1, and NE2000_2, respectively. Note the similarity of this screen to what is shown in figure 6.6, which displays all the available network interfaces.

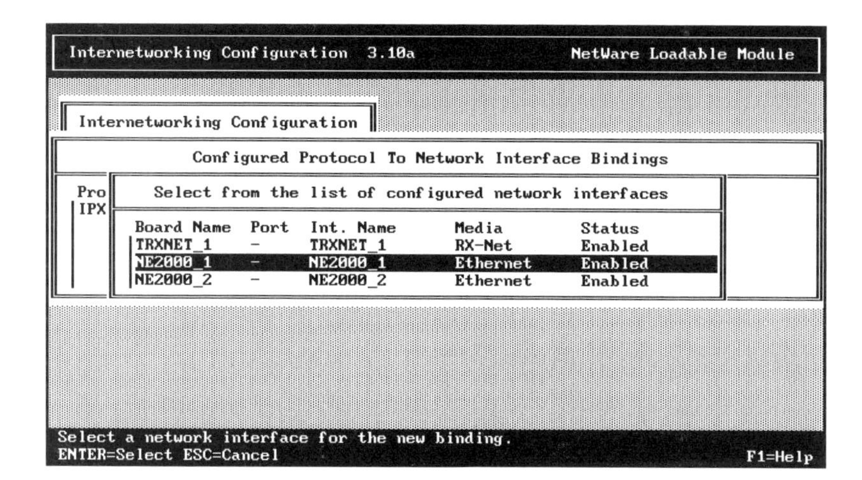

Figure 6.23

Network interface card selection option in the Bindings menu.

Selecting NE2000_1 and pressing Enter opens the subsequent screen, which requires the specification of the IP address, subnet mask, RIP, and OSPF options, as shown in figure 6.24. When an IP address is specified, a default subnet mask is supplied automatically.

```
Internetworking Configuration 3.10a              NetWare Loadable Module

Internetworking Configuration
              Configured Protocol To Network Interface Bindings
Pro                    Binding TCP/IP to a LAN Interface
IPX   Network Interface:                       NE2000_1

      Local IP Address:                        199.245.180.10
      Subnetwork Mask of Connected Network:    FF.FF.FF.0

      RIP Bind Options:                        (Select to View or Modify)
      OSPF Bind Options:                       (Select to View or Modify)
      Expert TCP/IP Bind Options:              (Select to View or Modify)

Subnet mask for interface's IP network.
ENTER=Select ESC=Previous Menu                                    F1=Help
```

Figure 6.24

TCP/IP protocol parameters in the Bindings menu.

When the preceding steps of binding TCP/IP to NE2000_1 are completed, the Bindings menu includes an additional entry, as shown in figure 6.25 (compared to the initial Bindings display shown in figure 6.21).

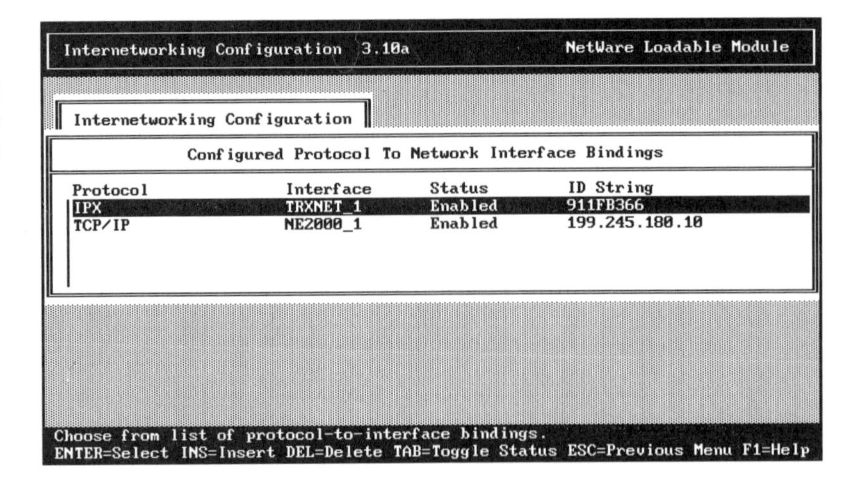

Figure 6.25

The "Configured Protocol To Network Interface Bindings" list in the Bindings menu.

Using the Manage Configuration Option

The Manage Configuration option allows the setup of SNMP to manage the internetwork configuration. SNMP (Simple Network Management Protocol) was first developed for the purpose of managing routers. In INETCFG, SNMP is configured through two options in the Manage Configuration submenu (see fig. 6.26).

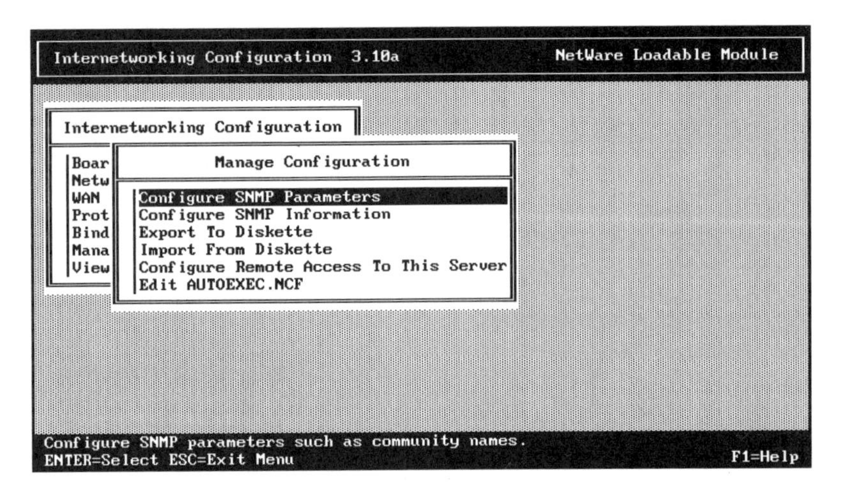

Figure 6.26

The Manage Configuration menu.

The option to configure SNMP information enables you to enter very basic information about the node to be managed—that is, the server. Server name, type of hardware, physical location, and human contact can be entered as shown in figure 6.27.

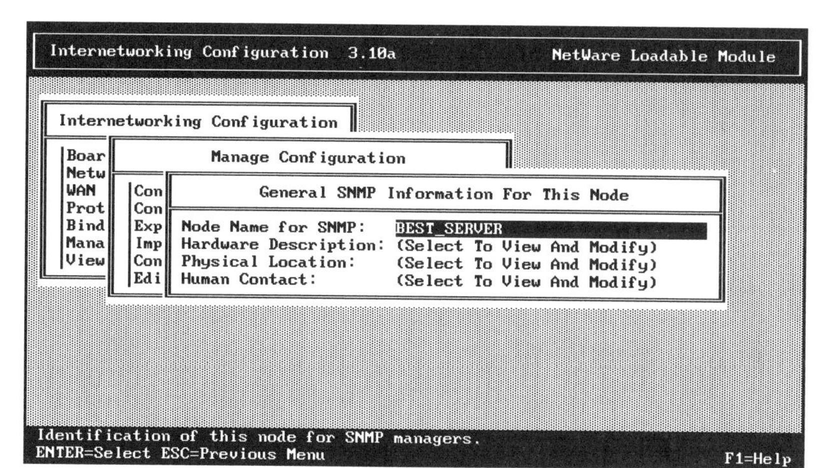

Figure 6.27

General SNMP options.

The option to configure SNMP parameters allows you to define SNMP community names as a means of implementing a simple authentication scheme. Three types of SNMP communities have been defined: monitor, control, and trap (see fig. 6.28).

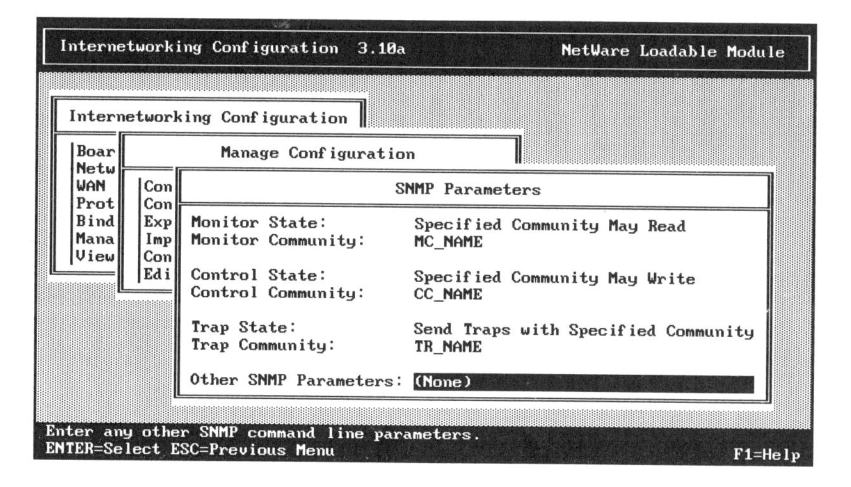

Figure 6.28

SNMP community options in the SNMP Parameters dialog box.

SNMP managers in a monitor community can make requests to read local Management Information Base (MIB) variables from the managed devices or SNMP agents. MIB is a repository of data collected by SNMP agents throughout the network. Routers managed by SNMP are examples of SNMP agents collecting data in their local MIBs.

The community names in the managers must match the community names in the managed devices before a successful exchange between a manager and a managed device can take place.

SNMP managers in a control community can make requests to read and write to the MIBs of the managed devices. Writing to the MIBs of managed devices is for the purpose of setting alarm thresholds. An alarm threshold may be a certain number of packets per second, as an example.

When an SNMP agent has reached a threshold set by a manager, it issues a trap message. Only the managers authenticated by the Trap Community name can receive trap messages.

The same community name may be specified for all three communities if there is only one SNMP manager on the network.

Using the View Configuration Option

The View Configuration option of the Internetworking Configuration menu expands into a submenu, as shown in figure 6.29.

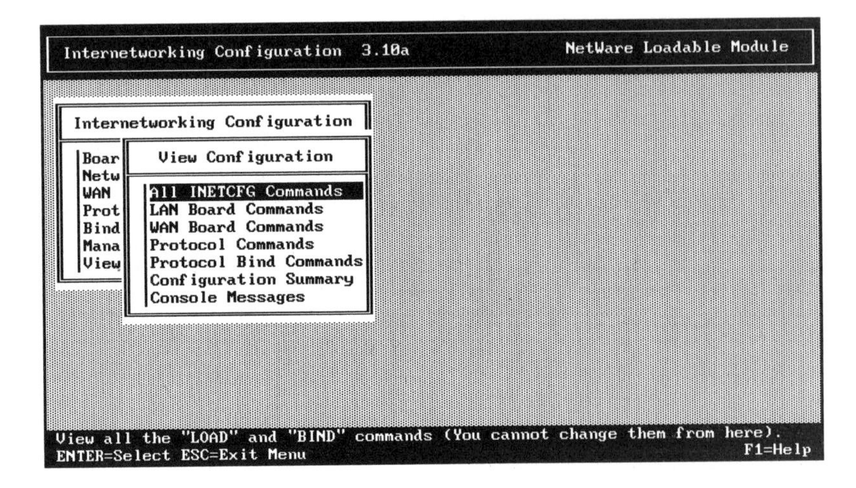

Figure 6.29
The View Configuration menu.

The options in this submenu allow the viewing in a "read-only" mode of the commands created via INETCFG. All the commands can be viewed using the first option (All INETCFG Commands), or groups of commands can be displayed using the subsequent options. The display format of groups of commands relating to LAN boards, WAN boards, protocols, and protocol bindings is very useful for troubleshooting and isolating problems. The last option in this submenu, "Console Messages," allows the viewing of all the console messages generated from the time the file server began to boot. Your ability to view console messages is useful in troubleshooting as file server messages go off the screen. The console messages displayed through this option are stored in a CONSOLE.LOG file in the SYS:ETC directory.

Tip

The TRXNET driver for ARCnet cards that is distributed with NetWare fails to load when loaded reentrantly, meaning that TRXNET cannot be bound to IPX and IP protocols for the same card. It also means that when you have multiple ARCnet cards in a server, IPX and IP cannot be configured simultaneously. The View Console messages option was helpful in the discovery and troubleshooting of this problem. An updated version of TRXNET needs to be obtained by you if you are planning to use ARCnet with IP and IPX.

Configuring TCP/IP Parameters with INETCFG NLM

The TCP/IP Protocol Configuration screen from INETCFG is depicted in figure 6.30. You get to this screen by selecting the Protocols options from the Internetworking Configuration menu, then selecting the TCP/IP protocol.

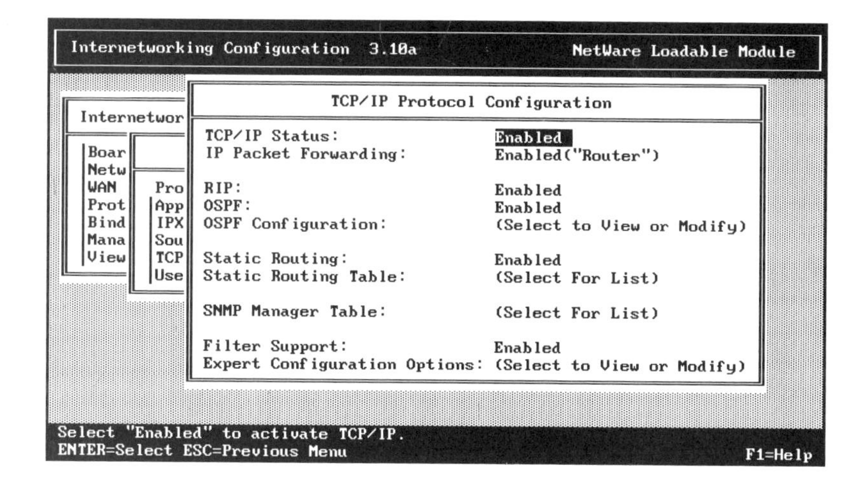

Figure 6.30
The TCP/IP Protocol Configuration menu.

All of the configuration choices shown in figure 6.30 are explained in the following sections.

Understanding the TCP/IP Status Field

The TCP/IP Status can either be Enabled (the default) or Disabled. The Enabled option determines whether the TCP/IP protocol will be activated when the system is initialized. If enabled, TCP/IP will be activated during system initialization according to the configuration specified in the subsequent choices. If disabled, TCP/IP will not be activated at system initialization, but the configuration will be retained. If the server is used for occasional Internet access, the administrator might enable or disable the TCP/IP status as needed while maintaining the configuration.

Understanding the IP Packet Forwarding Option

Setting this parameter will determine whether or not the server is going to be used as an IP router or an end node. An IP router is able to receive IP packets and forward them to other destinations. An end node can receive IP packets but it does not forward any further. When this parameter is enabled, the server can act as an IP router. Using the OSI vernacular, a router is appropriately considered as an intermediate system. A router acts as a relay between the transmitter and the receiver or between two end nodes. When the IP forwarding parameter is disabled, the server will act as an end node. It will be able to initiate IP packet transmissions to other nodes, as well as receive packets from other nodes, but it will not act as a relay or a router between the end nodes or end systems. The default setting for this parameter is Enabled (see fig. 6.31).

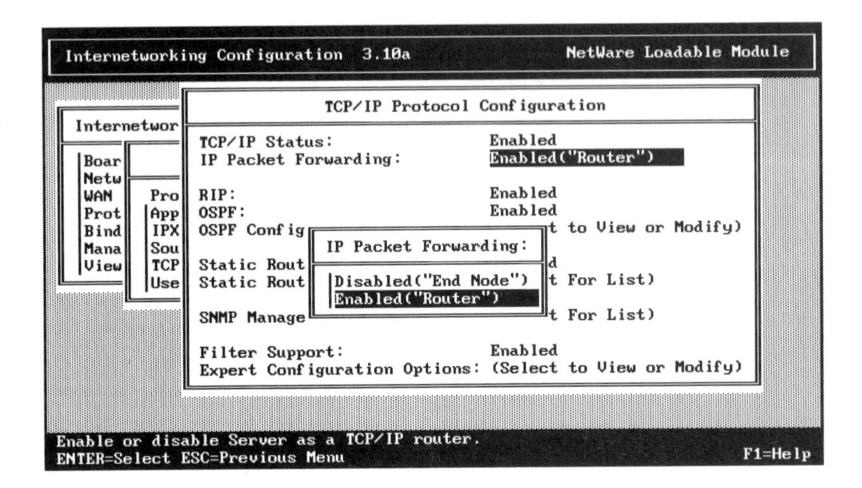

Figure 6.31

IP forwarding options in the TCP/IP Protocol Configuration menu.

Understanding the RIP Field

RIP is a very simple distance-vector protocol used to create and maintain routing tables. RIP table entries can be either dynamic or static. Dynamic RIP table entries are created through periodic broadcast exchanges between routers. Static RIP table entries are configured manually by you when static routing is enabled. See the sections that follow on Static Routing and Static Routing Table for more information.

RIP table entries consist of the following three major elements:

- ◆ The distance required to reach the final destination.
- ◆ The IP addresses of the destination networks.
- ◆ The direction or vector required to reach the destination. The direction is represented by the IP address of the next router or the next hop along the way to the final destination.

RIP distance is typically defined as the number of routers an IP packet must traverse before reaching its destination and is referred to as the number of hops. IP RIP is typically implemented with a maximum of 15 hops. A network destination with a hop count of 16 is considered to be unreachable. An IP packet destined for a network that has a hop count of 16 in a RIP table will be discarded.

The basic requirement of a distance-vector routing protocol like RIP is that routers participating in it through dynamic routing must maintain a table entry for every possible destination in an internetwork. As an internetwork grows, so does the size of the router tables. IP RIP routers exchange their entire table contents with their neighbors through broadcasts that occur every 30 seconds. This creates a considerable amount of broadcast traffic consuming a greater and greater portion of the available bandwidth as the internetwork grows larger.

RIP was never designed with the idea of running on very large internetworks and is not considered to be a very scalable routing protocol. It is, however, a popular solution for smaller networks. The maximum hop count of 15 is considered to be a serious limitation of RIP for large networks.

The other limitation of RIP is that its simple hop count metric does not take into account other criteria such as the speed of router interfaces, line costs, and load when dynamically creating routing tables. This means that a route with a very slow interface but only one router between the transmitter and a receiver would be considered a better route than a high speed route with several routers between the end stations.

RIP can be configured to partially overcome the problem of the simple hop count metric and take into account the speed of router interfaces. RIP permits network managers to assign a "cost" metric to the router ports. The cost metric effectively becomes the distance. The total distance between the sending and the receiving stations is the sum of the "costs" of the network interfaces a packet must traverse. There is an inverse relationship between an interface cost and the line speed of that interface. The higher the line speed, the lower the cost; the lower the line speed, the higher the cost.

Because RIP packets do not carry subnet information, RIP supports only a single IP subnet mask; that is, RIP does not support variable subnet masks on the internetwork.

A RIP-based internetwork consists of active/passive devices or machines. Active devices are routers. Passive devices are hosts or end nodes. Active devices advertise their tables through regular broadcasts. Passive devices listen to the broadcasts but do not do any advertising on their own.

The RIP option can be Enabled or Disabled. The default for RIP is to be Enabled (see fig. 6.32). If RIP is Disabled the server will not participate in dynamic RIP exchanges. Instead, it will use OSPF, EGP, static routing, or a default gateway to exchange information with the rest of the internetwork.

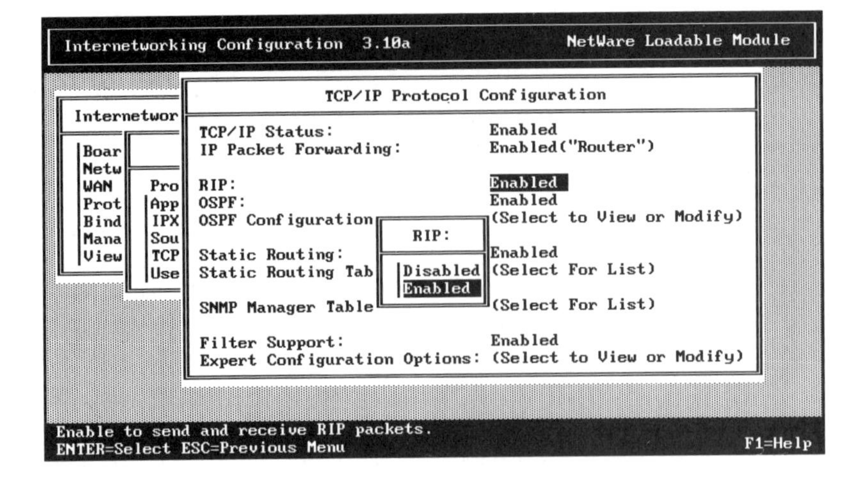

Figure 6.32
Enable/Disable RIP options in the TCP/IP configuration menu.

RIP typically refers to the original RIP, version I. A new version of RIP, RIP II, has been developed to deal with some of the limitations of the original RIP. RIP II provides better security through authentication and support for variable subnet masks. For additional information on RIP II see RFC 1732.

Understanding the OSPF Field

OSPF was developed to overcome the limitations of RIP. OSPF is considered to be a link-state protocol and its philosophy is entirely different from that of RIP. Instead of maintaining distances to all possible destinations in an internetwork, OSPF routers maintain a "topological map" of the network. This map consists of the descriptions or the state of the links in an internetwork. A link is considered to be a segment connecting any two routers. It is identified by the interface identifiers of the connected routers, a link number, and a metric.

OSPF was designed to be a scalable routing protocol that would facilitate routing in large internetworks. OSPF supports "hierarchical routing" through the concept of "areas." Each area acts as an independent network and is uniquely identified by an area ID. Routers belonging to a given area must be assigned the same area ID. An area ID is a 32-bit number that is expressed in a dotted decimal notation like an IP address. Area ID addresses, however, should not be confused with IP addresses. Multiple areas in an internetwork are joined together through a backbone area, which by default has an ID of 0.0.0.0. Routers that connect OSPF areas to the backbone area are known as area border routers or ABRs. The backbone area must be physically contiguous to act as a backbone. In the event that a backbone area becomes partitioned for geographical reasons, different OSPF areas can still be reconnected through the use of "virtual links." For more informtion, see the section "Virtual Link Configuration" later in this chapter.

The advantage of OSPF areas is that most of the routers in a given area need only be aware of the topology in that area. This translates into a smaller database of the "topology map" from which the routes are calculated, and improves the router performance. Only the area border routers that connect OSPF areas to the backbone have to maintain multiple sets of the link-state or topology map databases. ABRs maintain one link-state database for the area to which they belong and a summary of link-state databases for other areas connected to the backbone.

Like RIP, OSPF can either be Enabled or Disabled. The default setting for OSPF is to be Disabled (see fig. 6.33).

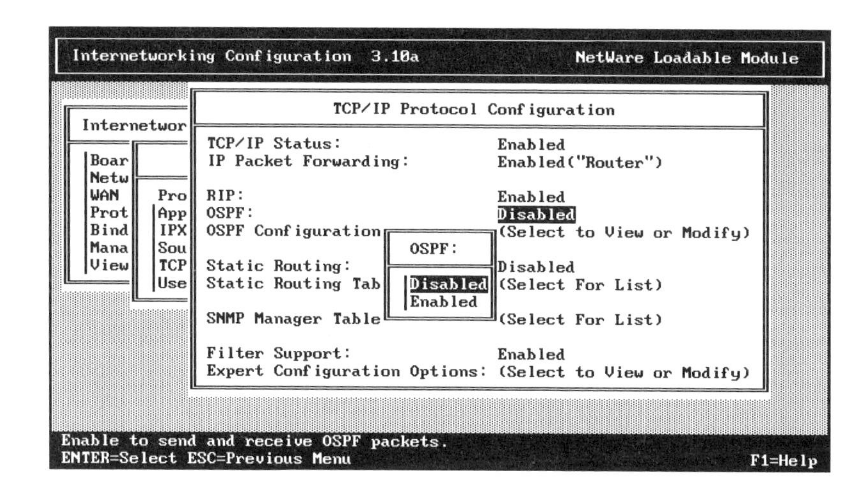

Figure 6.33

Enable/Disable OSPF option in the TCP/IP configuration menu.

If OSPF is Disabled, the server will have to use RIP, EGP, static routing, or a default gateway to exchange information with the rest of the internetwork. If OSPF is Enabled, it needs to be configured through the OSPF Configuration option explained in the next section.

Using the OSPF Configuration Option

The OSPF configuration options are shown in figure 6.34.

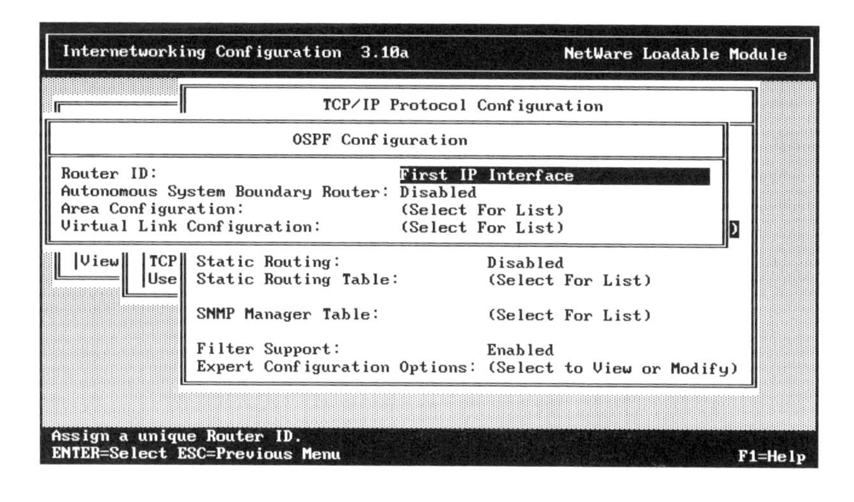

Figure 6.34

OSPF configuration submenu when OSPF is enabled in the TCP/IP configuration menu.

The parameters in figure 6.34 are explained in the following sections.

Router ID

Every router within an OSPF domain must be identified by a unique 32-bit number expressed in a dotted decimal notation similar to the way the IP addresses and OSPF area IDs are expressed. The router ID number can be assigned by the network administrator or defaults can be used. The default is the IP address of the first router interface. When the screen shown in figure 6.34 first comes up, the "First IP Interface" appears in place of the ID. By pressing Enter you can supply an ID in a dotted decimal notation (see fig. 6.35).

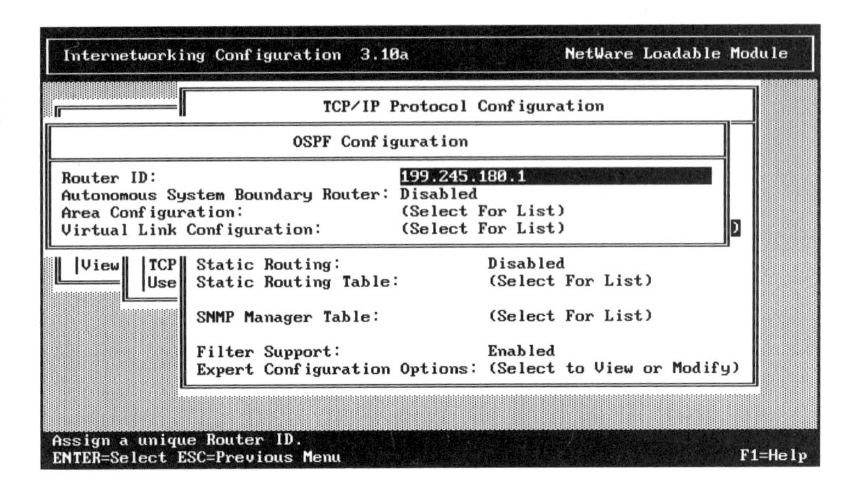

Figure 6.35
Entry of the OSPF Router ID parameter in the OSPF Configuration submenu.

Autonomous System Boundary Router

Large internetworks can be broken into routing domains known as autonomous systems. Different autonomous systems can run different routing protocols. Communication between autonomous systems takes place through the autonomous system boundary routers or ASBRs. ASBRs typically run a protocol like EGP (Exterior Gateway Protocol) in addition to OSPF. EGP is explained in the section "EGP Configuration." ASBRs further facilitate hierarchical routing. When an OSPF router is configured as an ASBR, OSPF allows this router to learn about routes supplied by EGP coming from other autonomous systems. ASBRs should not be confused with ABRs, which are Area Border Routers connecting different OSPF areas to the backbone.

Autonomous system boundary routers can also be configured to exclude specific routes. This requires the enabling of the filter support parameter and configuring of the exclusion routes through the FILTCFG menu-driven NLM. The default configuration for autonomous system boundary router is DISABLED (see fig. 6.36).

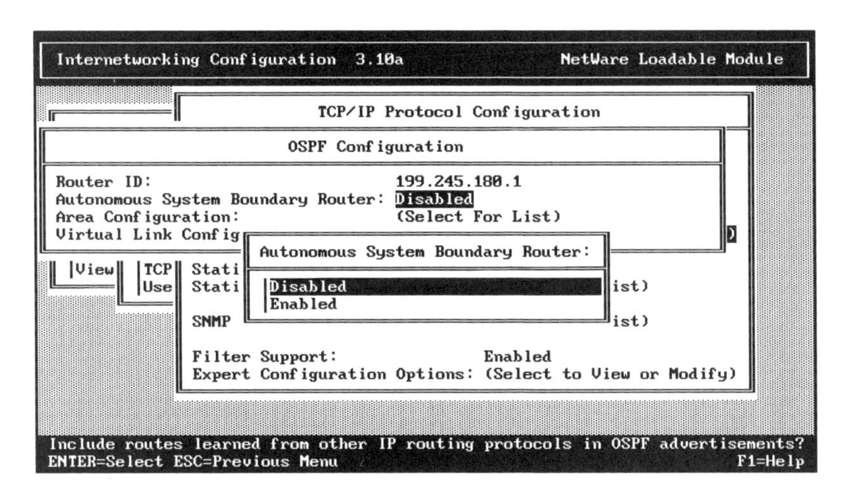

Figure 6.36

Enable/Disable option for an Autonomous System Boundary Router in the OSPF submenu.

Area Configuration

Whenever OSPF is enabled, the backbone area with an ID of 0.0.0.0 is configured by default. Additional areas can be defined by pressing the INS key and supplying the requested parameters (see figs. 6.37 and 6.38).

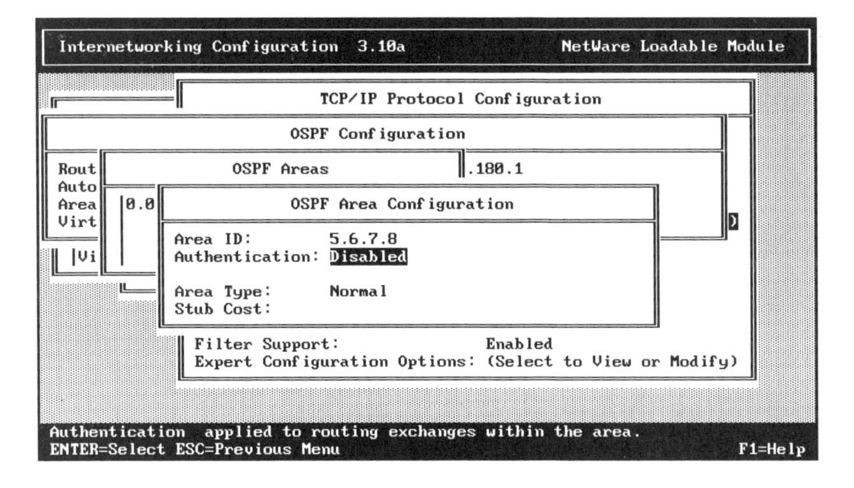

Figure 6.37

The OSPF Area Configuration submenu.

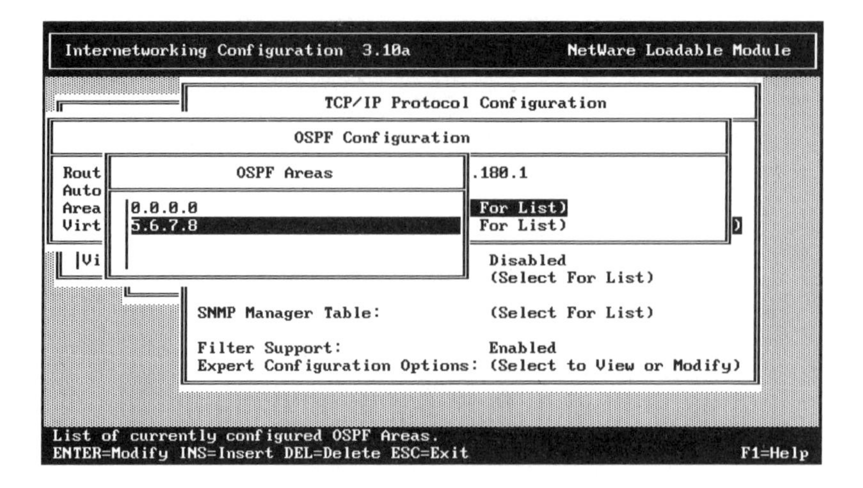

Figure 6.38

The OSPF area definitions.

In the example shown in figures 6.37 and 6.38, an area 5.6.7.8 was defined as a normal area. An area can be defined either as normal or stub. In a stub area, routers do not maintain link-state databases of routes external to the OSPF domain. External route advertisements are not propagated through a stub area. In a stub area, all external routes are summarized by a default route that has a cost associated with it known as the stub cost. The stub cost is the cost of the default route advertised to the stub area. Area 7.7.7.7 was configured as a stub area with a stub cost of 1, which is the default (see fig. 6.39).

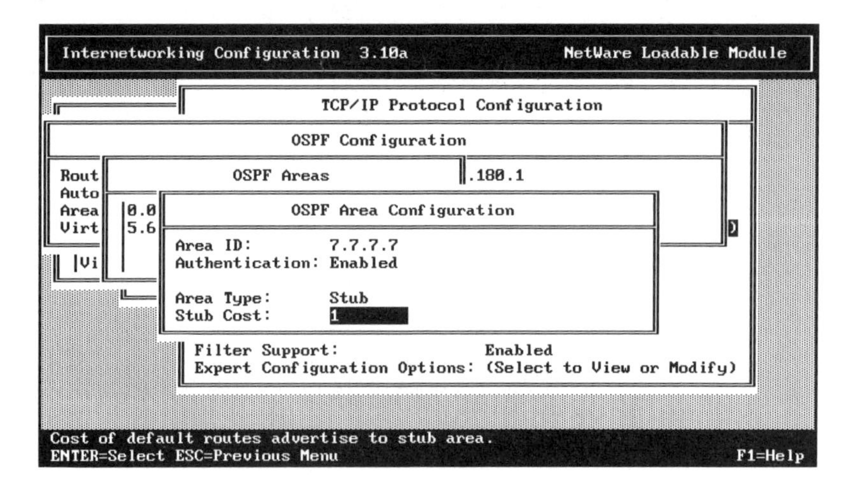

Figure 6.39

The OSPF area parameters.

In a normal area, routers support external routes and propagate external route advertisements.

Virtual Link Configuration

In the event that an OSPF backbone area had to be partitioned, a "virtual link" can be configured to connect two areas that no longer share a connection through the backbone. Figure 6.40 shows the parameters that must be supplied to configure a virtual link.

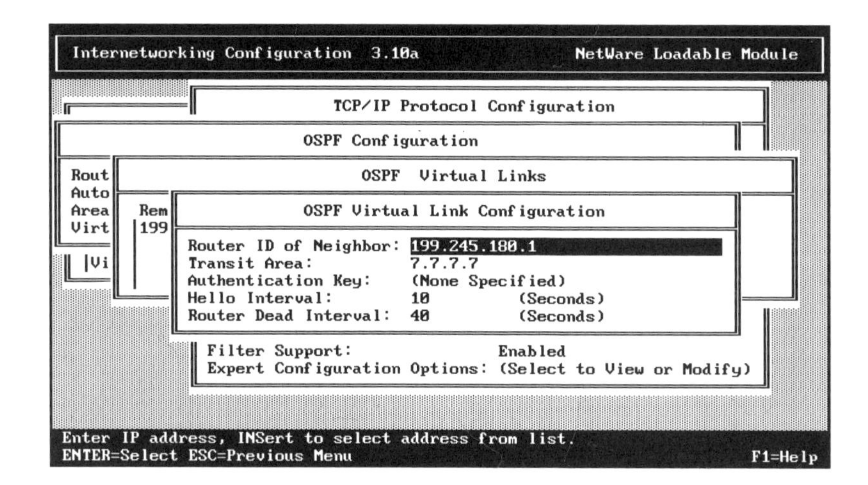

Figure 6.40

OSPF virtual link parameters.

The two key parameters in a virtual link configuration are the following:

- **Remote router ID.** A router ID is typically the IP address of its first interface. In this case, it is the ID of the destination router to which the virtual link is being established.
- **Transit area.** The transit area represents an OSPF area through which the virtual link must pass. Assume that an OSPF backbone area had to be split for political, economic, or other reasons and another OSPF area is inserted between the two parts of the backbone. This new area that now separates the two parts of the backbone becomes the transit area.

After a virtual link has been configured, the screen that displays the configuration information resembles figure 6.41.

Figure 6.41

A configured OSPF virtual link.

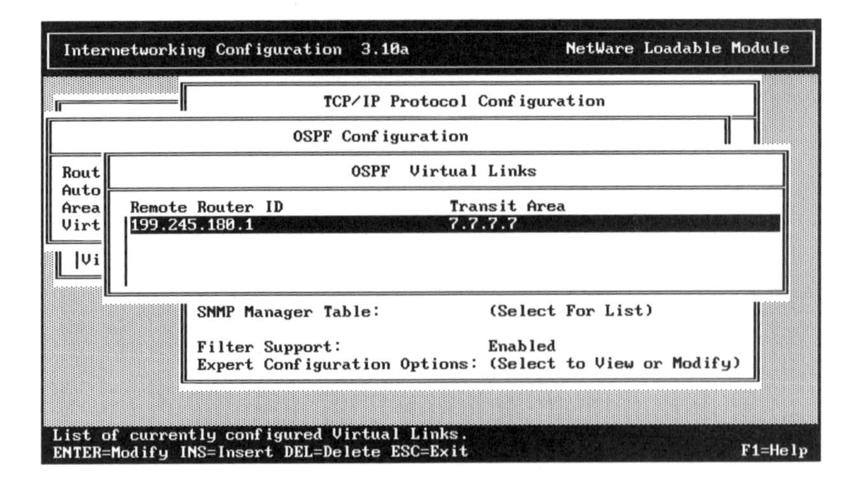

Configuring Static Routing

Static versus dynamic routing determines how a router's routing tables are constructed and maintained. Static route entries for a host or a router are manually configured by you. With dynamic routing, the routing tables are created and maintained by protocols like RIP or OSPF through periodic broadcast exchanges between routers. One reason for static routing is to reduce the amount of broadcast traffic on the network. Other reasons include security and backups for dynamic routes. Static routes can also be used in a case where a dynamic RIP route would exceed the maximum of 15 hops. The default for this option should be Disabled.

The static routing table displays the list of configured static routes (see fig. 6.42). Press the INS key to configure new static routes. Highlighting an existing table entry expands it into a screen, like the example shown in figure 6.43, where the static route parameters can be changed.

Figure 6.42

Definitions of TCP/IP static routes.

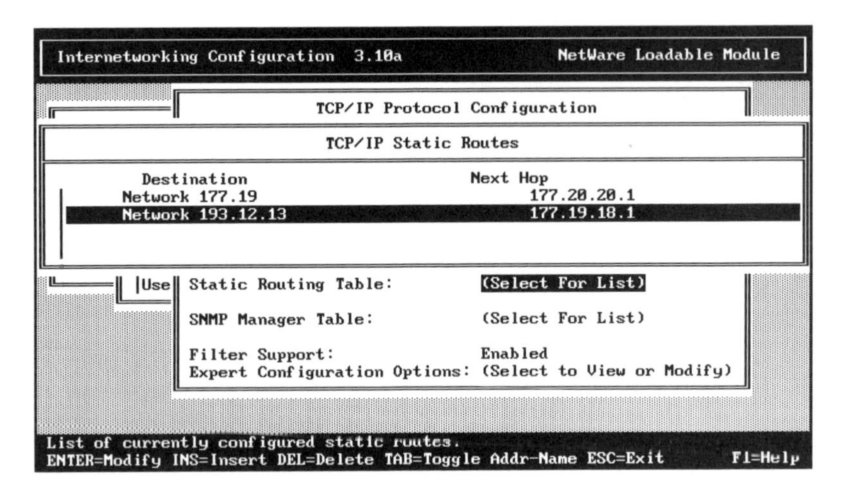

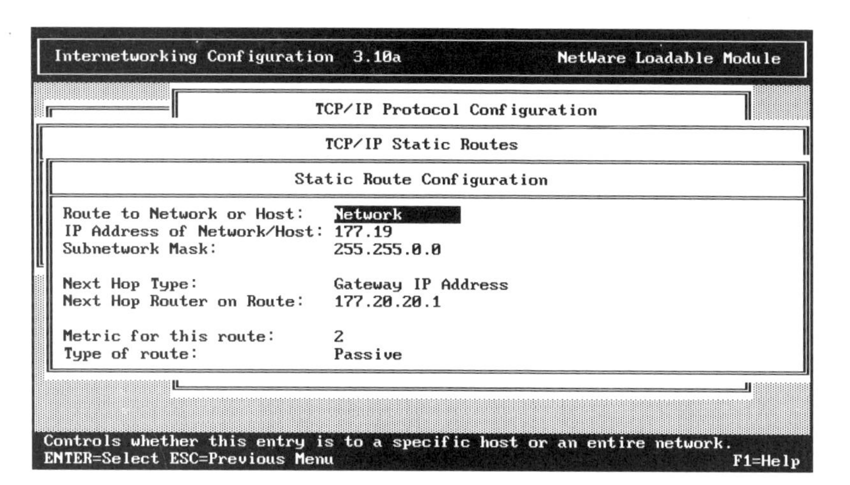

Figure 6.43

Static route configuration.

The static route parameters include the following:

- **Route to Network or Host.** This parameter defines the route type: network, host, or default route. The default choice is a network route.
- **IP Address of Network/Host.** If a network route type was specified in the preceding parameter, then only the network portion of the IP address needs to be entered here. See the explanation of IP address classes. If a host route is selected in the preceding parameter, then the IP address of the host including the network and the host portion must be entered here. If a default route is selected, then this parameter is not entered.
- **Subnetwork Mask.** The subnetwork mask is specified by having all of the bits representing the global and the local network portion set to one. A subnet mask for a class B address using subnetting on the first octet of the local portion (host id) would be 255.255.255.0. A subnet mask for a class C address subnetting on the four high order bits of the host octet is 255.255.255.240. Refer to Chapter 2, "TCP/IP Network Protocol Architecture," for a more detailed explanation of IP subnetting.
- **Next Hop Type.** This parameter indicates whether the next hop along the way is an IP router or a WAN destination.
- **Next Hop Router on Route.** This parameter represents the IP address of closest router along the route to the final destination. It has to be a router that is attached to the same network as the server. The network portions of the server address and this address need to be same.
- **Metric for this route.** This number represents the number of hops to the destination. It is equivalent to the "cost" of the route.
- **Type of route.** A static route can be either active or passive. If a route is active it means that if a router discovers a lower cost dynamic route to the destination it will use that route instead, until such time that the lower cost route becomes unavailable. When the static route type is defined as passive, the router will always use it regardless of whether it discovers a lower cost route to the same destination.

Configuring the SNMP Manager Table

The SNMP manager table defaults to the loopback address for "this" network, which is 127.0.0.1. This address can be deleted and a new IP address of a station that will act as an SNMP manager can be supplied by you. See figures 6.44 and 6.45 showing the default manager address and a new address supplied after the default was deleted. The SNMP manager is a network management station that intercepts trap messages from a router and presents them in a graphical format for analysis by a network manager.

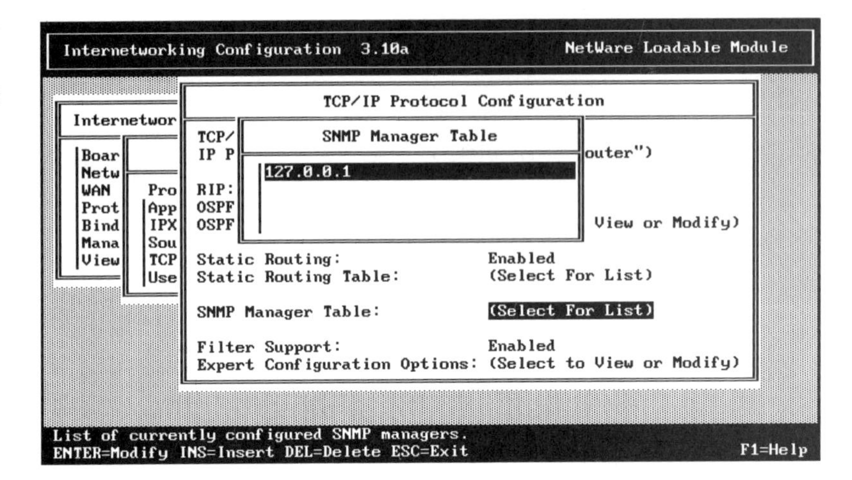

Figure 6.44

The SNMP default manager table.

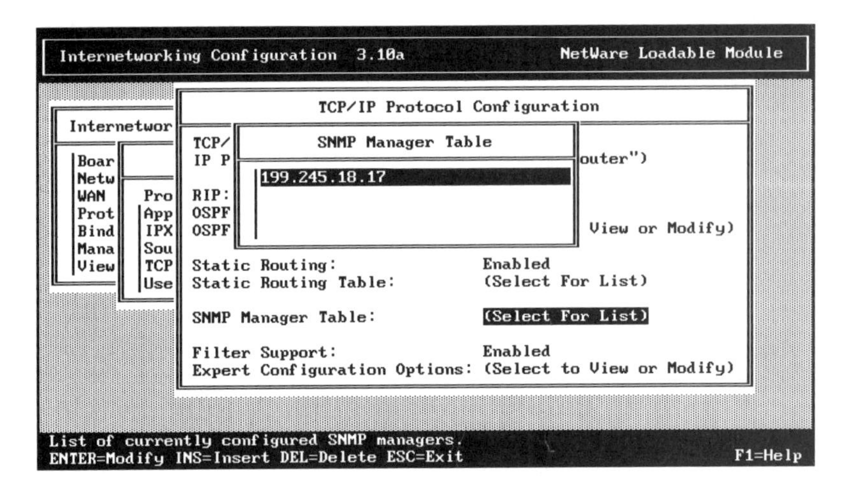

Figure 6.45

The SNMP configured manager table.

SNMP is configured on a NetWare server through the use of a TCPCON utility. TCPCON is a menu-driven NLM that also enables viewing of statistics for protocols configured through INETCFG.

Configuring the Filter Support

When the filter support option is Enabled (refer to fig. 6.30) it will activate packet filters configured through the FILTCFG NLM. FILTCFG can be used to configure filters for TCP/IP, IPX, and AppleTalk (see fig. 6.46).

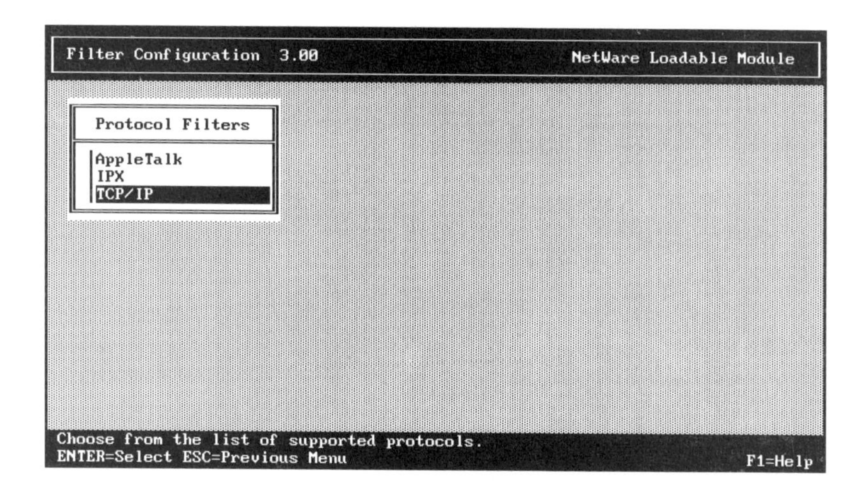

Figure 6.46

The FILTCFG main menu.

When filter support is enabled, incoming and outgoing packets are analyzed against the filter values. Filtering is set up so that some packets are not allowed to leave a network and other packets are prevented from coming in. Filtering is one of the means of implementing network security. For the TCP/IP protocol, filtering can also be used to limit undesirable routes from being added to routing tables. The TCP/IP filtering options are shown in figure 6.47.

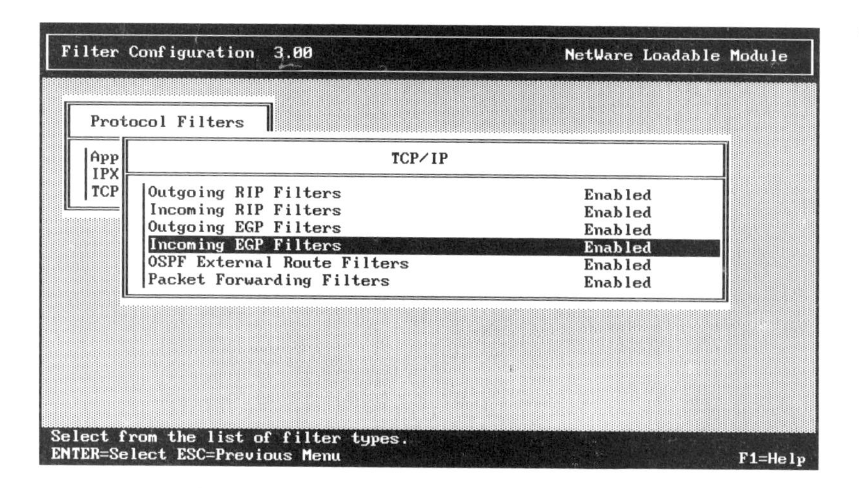

Figure 6.47

The TCP/IP filter options in FILTCFG.

Each one of the options shown in figure 6.47 expands into a screen that allows the entry of specific values. A sample screen for outgoing RIP filters is shown in figure 6.48.

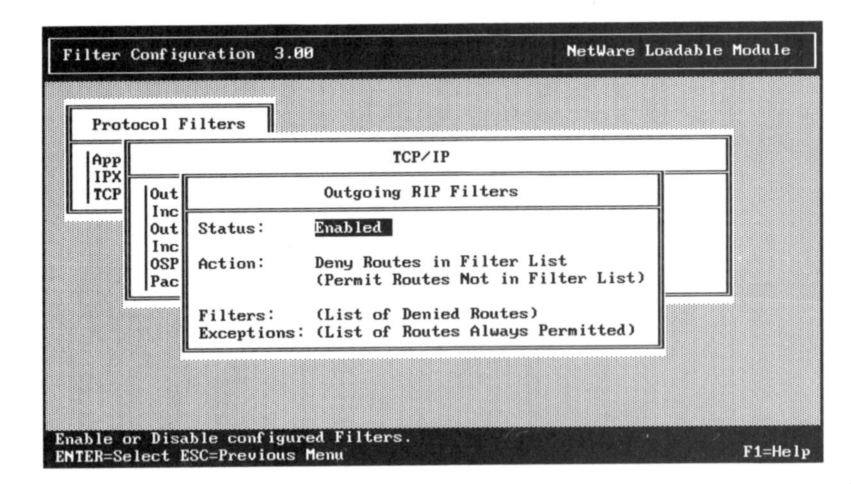

Figure 6.48
The RIP filter options in FILTCFG.

Understanding the Expert Configuration Options

This option (refer to fig. 6.30) expands into a screen as shown in figure 6.49. The options are explained in the sections that follow.

```
Internetworking Configuration 3.10a                NetWare Loadable Module

                  TCP/IP Protocol Configuration
 Internetwor  TC            TCP/IP Expert Configuration
              IP
 Boar             Directed Broadcast Forwarding:  Enabled
 Netw     Pro RI
 WAN      App OS  BootP Forwarding Configuration: (Select to View or Modify)
 Prot     IPX OS
 Bind     Sou     EGP:                            Enabled
 Mana     TCP St  EGP Configuration:              (Select to View or Modify)
 View     Use St

              SNMP Manager Table:            (Select For List)

              Filter Support:                Enabled
              Expert Configuration Options:  (Select to View or Modify)

Forward broadcasts to specific network or subnetwork.
ENTER=Select ESC=Previous Menu                                      F1=Help
```

Figure 6.49
TCP/IP Expert Configuration options.

Directed Broadcast Forwarding

Directed broadcasting is a means of sending a packet across an internetwork to all of the hosts on a network specified in the directed broadcast address. Directed broadcasts are forwarded by routers unless the directed broadcast forwarding option is Disabled. Only the hosts with the network IP address corresponding to the directed broadcast network address will receive the broadcast packet. All other hosts on all of the other nets in the internetwork will be bypassed. For example, a directed broadcast address of 193.32.17.255 is meant only for all the hosts on the network 193.32.17.0. It is not meant for any other nodes in the internetwork of which 193.32.17.0 is only one net.

If the directed broadcast parameter is enabled in a router that is not directly attached to the network specified in the directed broadcast address, then that router will forward the directed broadcast packet to the next hop.

Directed broadcast parameters must be enabled for a router that is directly attached to the specified network if it is to receive the directed broadcast packet and then forward it to all of the hosts on that network. If the network specified in the directed broadcast is subnetted, then all of the routers connecting the local subnets must have directed broadcasting enabled to ensure that all of hosts on the specified network receive the broadcast packet.

Directed broadcasts are in contrast to a limited or a local broadcast that is represented by 255.255.255.255. Limited or local broadcasts are not forwarded by routers. They are meant only for the local network. Note that the default broadcast address for NetWare IP configuration is 255.255.255.255. You can change this to a directed broadcast if required.

BootP Forwarding Configuration

BootP is a bootstrap protocol. When a TCP/IP workstation first boots, it gets its configuration information from a configuration file that typically resides on local storage media, for example, hard disk or floppy disk. For security or economic reasons some TCP/IP workstations are diskless. These workstations still have to get their configuration information from somewhere if they are to be functional. BootP facilitates this process. BootP's implementation begins in a workstation's PROM. A diskless TCP/IP workstation will issue a BootP request at boot time. This request might or might not include the station's IP address, depending on the implementation of BootP. A BootP server on the network will respond. This response will include a filename that enables the workstation to finish its boot process. For additional information on the BootP protocol refer to the original BootP RFC 951.

BootP configuration options are shown in figure 6.50.

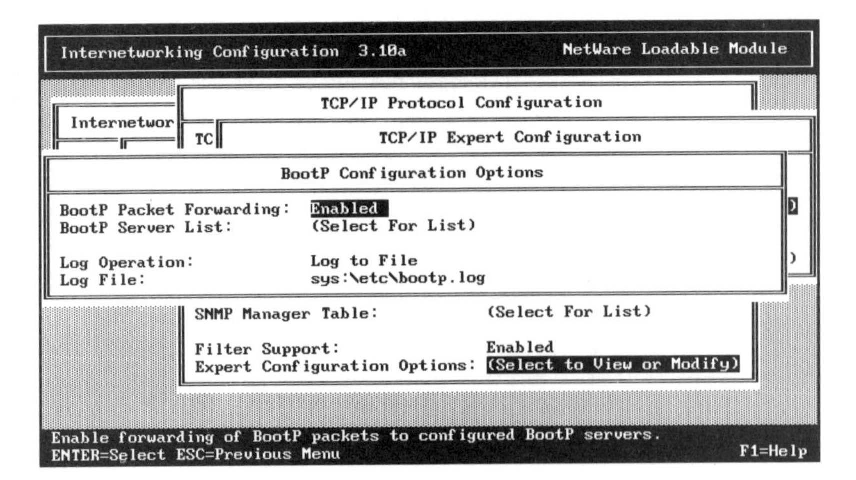

Figure 6.50

BootP configuration options.

BootP forwarding can be either Enabled or Disabled. Enabling BootP forwarding means that this router will forward BootP packets across the internetwork. The default for this option is Disabled. If you want to enable it, you must first enter the IP addresses of the BootP servers. This is done by highlighting the BootP Server list and pressing Ins (see fig. 6.51).

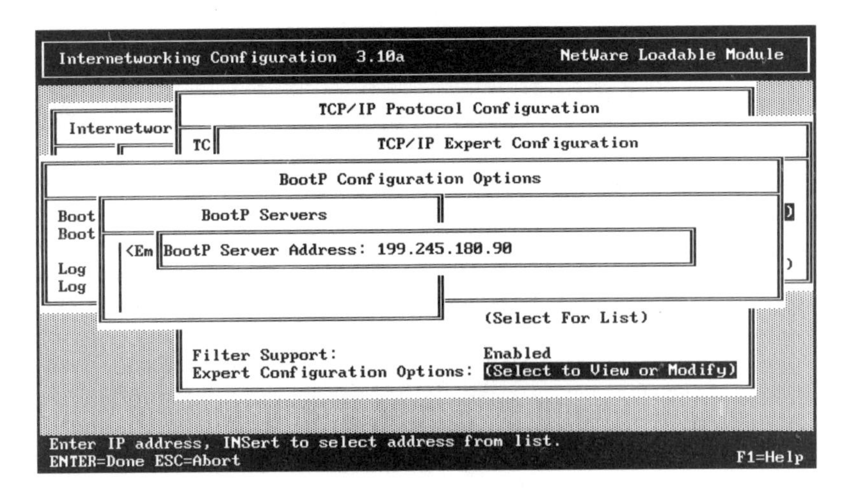

Figure 6.51

Specifying a BootP server IP address.

Up to four BootP servers can be configured. BootP Packet Forwarding cannot be enabled until at least one BootP server has been defined. An error message will result if an attempt is made to enable BootP forwarding without defining BootP servers. BootP configuration also enables you to specify a log file for BootP operations. The default log file for bootp.log is SYS:ETC directory.

EGP Configuration

If EGP is enabled, then the parameters shown in figure 6.52 need to be specified. These are explained next.

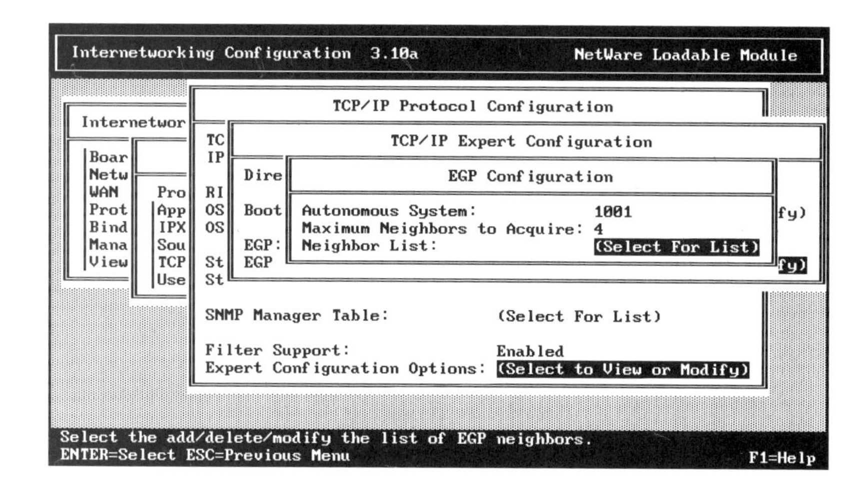

Figure 6.52

EGP configuration options.

- **Autonomous System.** EGP is a routing protocol that facilitates the exchange of information between large internetworks known as autonomous systems. The concept of an autonomous system or an autonomous management domain is the result of a tremendous growth of the original ARPAnet that led to the creation of the global Internet. It would be impossible for a global authority to manage the entire Internet down to individual routers and workstations of every connected network. Having an autonomous system means that the responsibility for network management can be decentralized. A large company with many routers could be assigned an autonomous system number. Autonomous system numbers for networks connected to the global Internet must be assigned by a global authority in a similar fashion that IP addresses are assigned.

  If autonomous systems are not connected to the global Internet, then administrators can choose their own AS numbers as long as they are in a range between 1 and 65535. A typical example for the need to run EGP between autonomous systems is when companies merge and they want to integrate their networks. Given, of course, some security parameters, each company would have to be assigned an autonomous system number if they did not already have one.

- **Maximum Neighbors to Acquire.** This parameter indicates how many other routers this server will be communicating with using EGP. When EGP is activated it performs what's known as neighbor acquisition. These neighbors come from the neighbor list that is defined by a network administrator. During the process of neighbor acquisition, routers agree that they will exchange reachability information with each other. Subsequent to becoming neighbors, routers continually test each other for reachability. Up to a maximum of eight neighbors are allowed.

- **Neighbor List.** Defining neighbors is done through a configuration screen shown in figure 6.53.

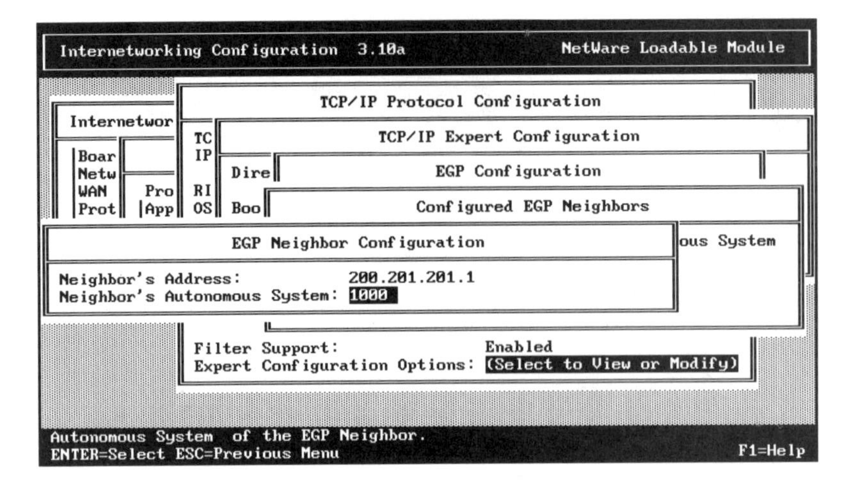

Figure 6.53
EGP neighbor configuration options.

Neighbor IP address and the autonomous system number need to be specified.

Configuration Files Affected by INETCFG.NLM

The configuration files created and maintained by INETCFG are stored in the SYS:ETC directory. NETINFO.CFG can be considered the primary configuration file. It contains the initial statements transferred from AUTOEXEC.NCF. It also contains configuration statements for additional boards defined through INETCFG, bindings to protocols, and LOAD commands for NLMs required to support the enabled protocols. The following is a sample NETINFO.CFG file:

```
#!VERSION=2.2
#!
#! -- WARNING -- WARNING -- WARNING -- WARNING -- WARNING -- WARNING ----
#! This file was created by the Internetworking Configuration Console.
#! It is intended to be modified ONLY by the configurator (INETCFG.NLM).
#! Tampering with this file may cause severe malfunctioning of the system.
#! The configurator will check for tampering and abort if it is detected.
#! ---------------------------------------------------------------------
#!
#!SERVERTYPE=NORMAL
#!SERVERNAME=BEST_SERVER
#!
#!BEGINGENLOAD
LOAD SNMP MonitorCommunity=MC_NAME ControlCommunity=CC_NAME TrapCommunity=TR_NAME
#!END
```

```
#!
#!BEGINTSMLOAD
#!END
#!
#!BEGINBOARD DRVR=TRXNET NAME=TRXNET_1 STATUS=ENABLED NUMPORTS=1 DRVRTYPE=LAN
VARIABLEPORTS=NO PORTPARAM=CHANNEL INT=2 PORT=2E0 MEM=D0000
#Transferred from AUTOEXEC.NCF
#!BEGINPORT NAME=TRXNET_1 NUMBER=1 STATUS=ENABLED FRAMES=YES NUMLINKS=1 MEDIA=RX-Net
WANFRAME=UNCONFIGURED
#Transferred from AUTOEXEC.NCF
#!REFCOUNT=2
LOAD TRXNET NAME=TRXNET_1_NRX FRAME=NOVELL_RX_NET INT=2 PORT=2E0 MEM=D0000
#!END
#!END
#!
#!BEGINBOARD DRVR=NE2000 NAME=NE2000_1 STATUS=ENABLED NUMPORTS=1 DRVRTYPE=LAN
VARIABLEPORTS=NO PORTPARAM=CHANNEL INT=5 PORT=300 RETRIES=5
#1st Ether segment
#!BEGINPORT NAME=NE2000_1 NUMBER=1 STATUS=ENABLED FRAMES=YES NUMLINKS=0
MEDIA=EtherTsm WANFRAME=UNCONFIGURED
#1st Ether segment
#!REFCOUNT=1
LOAD NE2000 NAME=NE2000_1_EII FRAME=Ethernet_II INT=5 PORT=300 RETRIES=5
#!END
#!END
#!
#!BEGINBOARD DRVR=NE2000 NAME=NE2000_2 STATUS=ENABLED NUMPORTS=1 DRVRTYPE=LAN
VARIABLEPORTS=NO PORTPARAM=CHANNEL INT=A PORT=320 RETRIES=5
#2nd Ether segment
#!BEGINPORT NAME=NE2000_2 NUMBER=1 STATUS=ENABLED FRAMES=YES NUMLINKS=0
MEDIA=EtherTsm WANFRAME=UNCONFIGURED
#2nd Ether segment
#!END
#!END
#!
#!BEGINPROTO PROTO=IPX STATUS=ENABLED
SET Reply To Get Nearest Server=ON
#
LOAD IPXRTR ROUTING=NLSP CFGDIR=SYS:ETC SEQ=2
#
LOAD IPXRTRNM SEQ=2
#
LOAD IPXFLT SEQ=2
#
LOAD SPXCONFG Q=1 A=540 V=108 W=54 R=10 S=1000 I=1200
```

```
#
SET IPX NetBIOS Replication Option=1
#
#!BEGINBIND STATUS=ENABLED
BIND IPX TRXNET_1_NRX NET=911FB366
#911FB366
#!END
#!END
#!
#!BEGINPROTO PROTO=TCPIP STATUS=ENABLED
LOAD Tcpip RIP=Yes Forward=Yes DIRBC=Yes
#
LOAD ipflt
#
LOAD IPConfig Screen=no
#
LOAD bootpfwd log=Yes file=sys:\etc\bootp.log server=199.245.180.90
#
#!BEGINBIND STATUS=ENABLED
BIND IP NE2000_1_EII ARP=Yes Mask=FF.FF.FF.0 Address=199.245.180.10
#199.245.180.10
#!END
#!END
#!
#!BEGINPROTO PROTO=APPLETLK STATUS=ENABLED
LOAD LLC8022
#
LOAD AppleTlk routing=Yes internal_net_mode=Yes net=33-33 zfile=Yes
#
LOAD atflt
#
LOAD adsp
#
LOAD aurp
#
#!END
```

INITSYS.NCF is an initialization file that executes the INITIALIZE SYSTEM command. Additional configuration files specifically related to TCP/IP include TCPIP.CFG, FILTERS.CFG, SNMP.CFG, and TRAPTARG.CFG. These files contain statements relating to OSPF, filter rules for routing protocols, and SNMP management. They store the values for IP addresses, autonomous system numbers, areas, and filtering rules configured through INETCFG described in the preceding sections. They are used to support the proper functioning of the protocols when they are enabled.

Changes made to configuration files through INETCFG are not effective until either the server is rebooted or the INITIALIZE SYSTEM command is executed from the server console.

Summary

INETCFG is a very versatile configuration utility for multiple network protocols on a NetWare server. INETCFG requires, however, that you plan your network configuration ahead of time and that you understand the parameters that are requested during the configuration. INETCFG will not protect you against wrong configuration decisions, but its menu-driven approach guards against syntax errors in the configuration files, and that's a big help in configuring network protocols.

Part II

TCP/IP Applications

NetWare/IP

The communication between a NetWare workstation and a NetWare server takes place using the IPX network layer (OSI layer 3) protocol. When NetWare was originally designed, Novell developed IPX based on the Internet Datagram Protocol (IDP) found in the Xerox Network System (XNS) network protocols used in Xerox networks. In the mid-1980s, TCP/IP, which originated as a protocol used on the old ARPAnet, became a de facto standard not only in universities and research organizations, but also in the commercial sector. Although TCP/IP has traditionally been used in Unix networks, it is not limited to running on Unix networks. Today, TCP/IP is available on all major computer/operating-system platforms ranging from microcomputers to mainframes. This chapter examines how a product called NetWare/IP can be used to provide access to NCP services using TCP/IP.

Understanding the Need for NetWare/IP

Novell began supporting TCP/IP at the NetWare server in 1988 using technology it obtained through the purchase of Excelan of San Jose. Today every NetWare 3.1x and 4.x server ships with a TCPIP.NLM that implements the TCP/IP protocol at the server. The TCPIP.NLM can be used to convert a NetWare server to an IP router and provide transport services for TCP/IP applications that can run at the server. An example of TCP/IP applications that run at the NetWare server is the NetWare Network File System (NFS) product. The NetWare NFS product must be purchased separately and implements NFS server, File Transfer Protocol (FTP) server, Unix-to-NetWare, and NetWare-to-Unix print gateways.

Until the development of NetWare/IP, there was no way to send NCP requests to a NetWare server using TCP/IP. The LAN Workplace products or third-party products from FTP Software, Chameleon, Beam & Whiteside, and so on can be used to talk to TCP/IP applications such as FTP, NFS, and print gateways at the server, but they cannot be used to obtain NCP services from a NetWare server.

NetWare/IP allows the native IPX protocol service to be replaced by the TCP/IP transport services (see fig. 7.1). Many organizations have a mix of TCP/IP and IPX protocols running on their networks. Typically, TCP/IP is used by engineering workstations and large machines, and IPX is used by NetWare workstations and servers. Network managers have to support and understand both types of protocols. With NetWare/IP, IPX can be replaced by TCP/IP and this allows an organization to support only one protocol: the de facto TCP/IP.

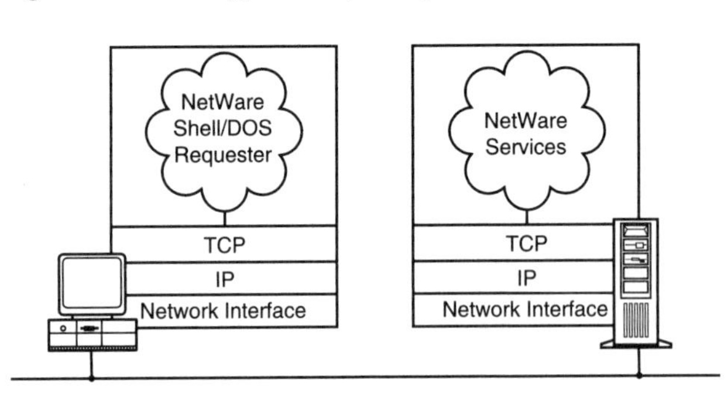

Figure 7.1
Use of TCP/IP in NetWare/IP.

NetWare/IP consists of a set of NLMs and client software that allows NetWare 3.1x and 4.x servers to use TCP/IP as their transport protocol for communicating with NetWare workstations. The NetWare workstations can be configured to use TCP/IP exclusively, or they can use TCP/IP in addition to the native IPX protocol.

NetWare/IP is currently not bundled with NetWare server software—it must be purchased separately. The NetWare/IP product comes with the DOS TCP/IP transport stack (TCPIP.EXE) from the LAN WorkPlace for DOS products.

Some of the benefits of NetWare/IP include the following:

- Network managers have the option of running IP-only networks. This is valuable for those organizations that standardized on TCP/IP as their protocol of choice. Routers on such networks can be configured to handle the IP packet only.
- Existing NetWare 3.1x and 4.x applications can continue to run and use TCP/IP as their transport protocol. These applications that use the standard NetWare APIs can run unmodified on a NetWare/IP node.
- Cost in managing network protocols is reduced because the network engineers who troubleshoot and configure network nodes have to understand and configure only one protocol—TCP/IP.
- NetWare/IPX and NetWare/IP networks can coexist. NetWare/IP has a feature called the NetWare/IP gateway that can be used to transparently connect native NetWare IPX networks with NetWare/IP networks. This gateway allows NetWare IPX clients to access NetWare/IP servers, and also allows NetWare/IP clients to access NetWare servers on the IPX network.
- The NetWare/IP gateway enables you to gradually convert NetWare clients to use NetWare/IP while allowing the network to function.
- NetWare/IP includes an application called XCONSOLE. This runs as an NLM at the server, and allows an X Windows terminal to act as a console from which NetWare/IP can be managed. Unix workstations or terminals that have X Windows can manage a NetWare/IP server. These Unix users have a choice of Windows manager such as MOTIF, OpenLook, or TWM.

Configurations Using NetWare/IP

Examples of network configurations that use NetWare/IP can clarify how NetWare/IP can be used. The following sections give some examples.

IP Backbone with IPX Islands

Consider an organization that standardized on using TCP/IP on its backbone network. A good reason for doing this, besides the fact that TCP/IP is now a de facto standard, is that the organization also has connectivity to the Internet, which is predominantly based on TCP/IP. It is also possible for such an organization to have a policy in which IPX can be used on local networks as long as the backbone only uses TCP/IP. Reasons for using TCP/IP exclusively on the backbone include the reduced costs of configuring backbone devices and of training personnel to administer the backbone. Another reason to use TCP/IP on the backbone is that TCP/IP has been proven to work efficiently on a WAN that has long delays in transmission and a variability in the delay. Local departments within the organization may, however, prefer the ease of configuration of IPX networks that do not require an explicit IPX network address assignment per workstation. Also, managers of NetWare LANs are traditionally unfamiliar with the configuration requirements of TCP/IP networks.

Because of this, it may be preferable for departmental networks to continue using IPX for accessing NetWare servers.

Figure 7.2 shows a campus network that has an IP backbone used to connect departmental networks. The departmental LANs run IPX to access NetWare servers. These departmental LANs can be joined to the IP backbone using the NetWare/IP gateway. This network configuration allows local departments to continue using IPX while IP is used on the backbone. The users in a department can continue using IPX locally and access servers in other departments using the IP backbone and the NetWare/IP servers configured as IPX-to-IP gateways.

Figure 7.2

IP backbone with IPX islands.

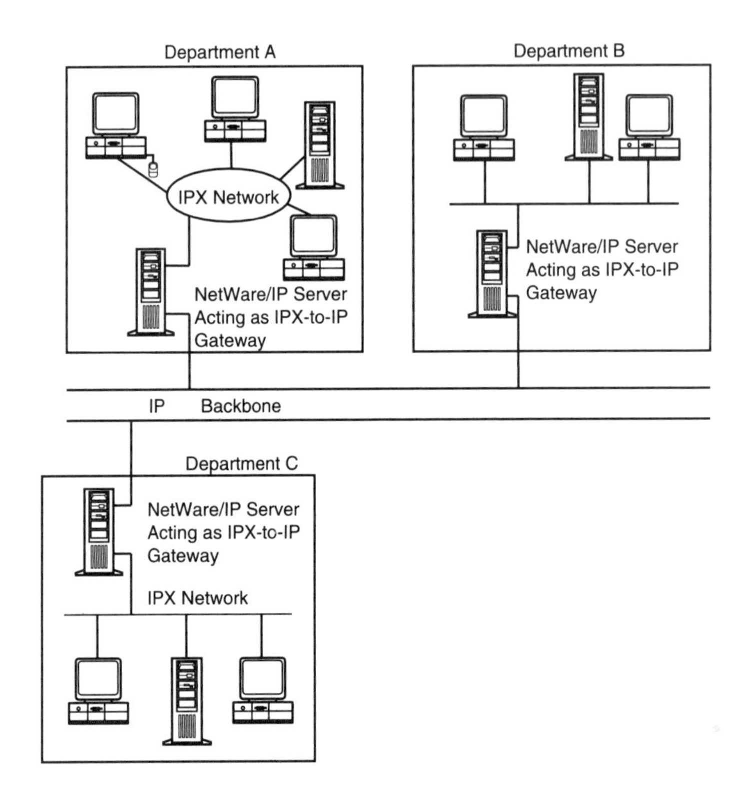

This configuration also gives the organization the option of gradually converting the local NetWare IPX environment to one based on using IP entirely. After all the servers in a department are converted to NetWare/IP servers, the workstations can be configured to use TCP/IP as their transport protocol. The NetWare/IP server configured as an IPX-to-IP gateway can then be configured as an IP router instead. Alternatively, you can replace the IPX-to-IP gateway function with a dedicated IP router.

An IP-Only Network

Figure 7.3 shows a network that uses IP only. This configuration can be used by a department that has many locations scattered over long distances. NetWare/IP allows each NetWare server and workstation to use the TCP/IP protocols, which work equally well on LAN and WAN links. The NetWare workstations at each location have access to all NetWare servers on the local network and other locations.

The networks in figure 7.3 also can support non-NetWare workstations and servers that also use TCP/IP protocols. This allows the entire enterprise to be based on a single TCP/IP protocol.

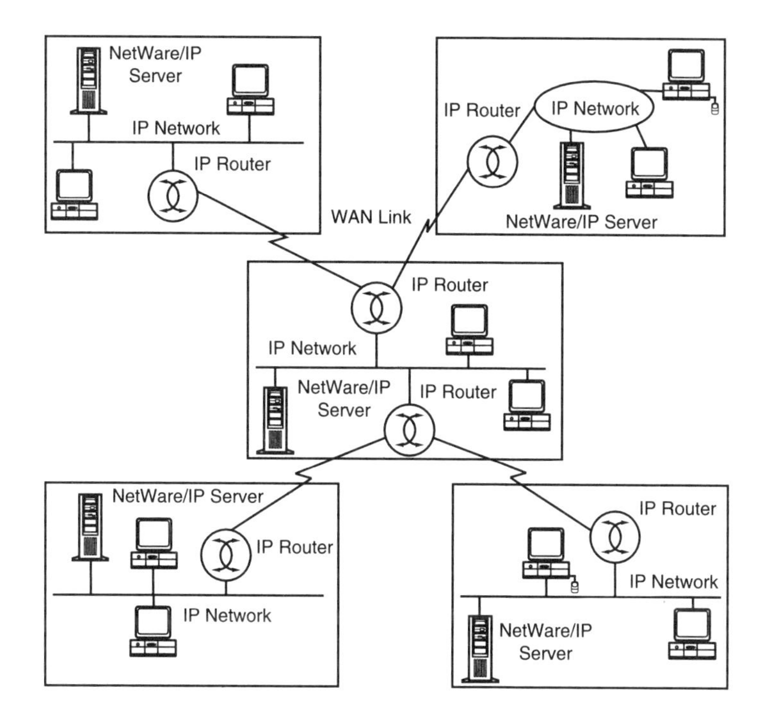

Figure 7.3
An IP-only NetWare

Examining NetWare/IP

NetWare/IP has the following components:

- **NetWare/IP server.** This is a series of NLMs that run on a NetWare 3.1x or 4.x server. These NLMs enable NetWare applications that previously used IPX to use TCP/IP as their transport protocol.

- **NetWare/IP client.** This allows a network workstation configured with an NIC to use TCP/IP protocols instead of (or in addition to) the IPX protocol. The NetWare client must be configured to use ODI drivers. The NetWare client support includes a TCP/IP stack implemented by TCPIP.EXE. Additional modules needed are NWIP.EXE, used for emulating the IPX Far Call interface, and a shell (NETX.EXE) or DOS Requester. If the VLMs are used, the NETX.VLM can be used to access bindery-based servers. To access NetWare 4.x servers, the DOS Requester VLMs are needed.
- **Domain Name System (DNS) server.** A NetWare server can be set up as a DNS server. The DNS server provides a distributed name look-up service that resolves symbolic names of hosts to their IP addresses. NetWare/IP clients use the DNS to look up the name of their nearest Domain SAP Servers (DSS).
- **Domain SAP/RIP Servers (DSS).** These are used as repositories of SAP/RIP information on the network. Service Advertising Protocol (SAP) is used in NetWare networks by NetWare services to advertise themselves to the rest of the network. Routing Information Protocol (RIP) is used to exchange IPX routing information. Using DSS, it is possible to partition networks into domains called NetWare/IP domains so that NetWare/IP clients and servers know of services in their NetWare/IP domain only.

Novell estimates, based on an internal study, that NetWare/IP provides comparable performance to NetWare IPX-based networks. On the average, the throughput of NetWare/IP is eight percent less than using IPX for the network transport. Most applications will not notice a performance loss.

Understanding NetWare/IP Domains

NetWare/IP domains should not be confused with DNS domains used in IP networks as a general purpose name look-up service for hostnames. Whereas DNS can be used by a mix of NetWare workstations, NetWare servers, and Unix-based machines, DSS is used only in NetWare networks. DSS and DNS servers can coexist on a network without any conflict.

Figure 7.4 shows an IP network for three separate departments of the hypothetical organization SCS. These department networks can be in different locations and are connected using IP routers. Department A has server NWS1 and workstation WS1; Department B has server NWS2 and workstation WS2; and Department C has server NWS3 and client WS3.

You can have one logical NetWare/IP domain encompassing the entire network or break the network into several logical domains.

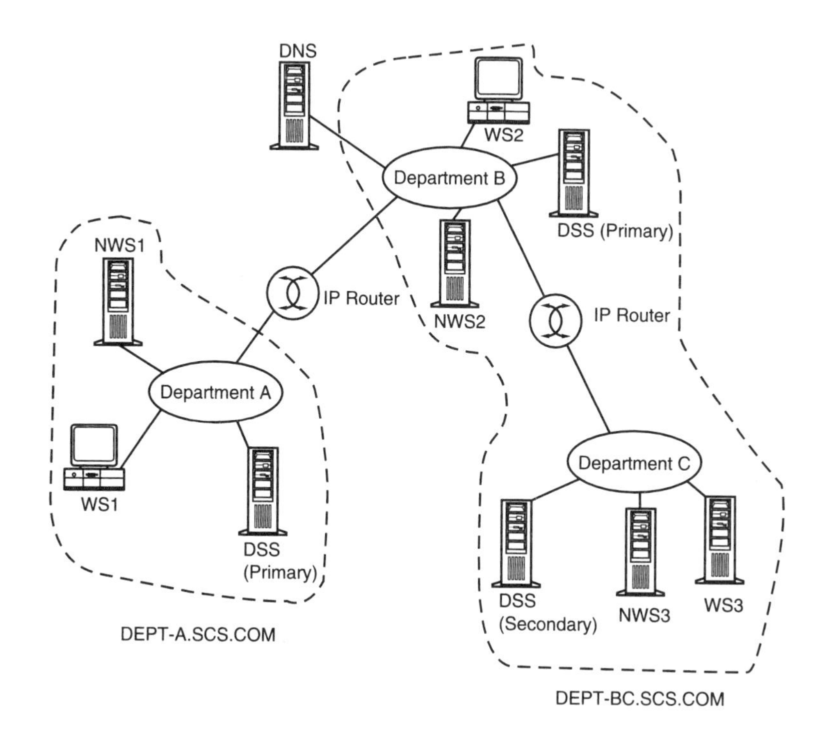

Figure 7.4

NetWare/IP domains.

The NetWare/IP domain must have at least one Domain SAP/RIP Server, called the primary DSS server. The DSS server acts as a repository for all SAP/RIP information. It broadcasts SAP/RIP information at periodic intervals to workstations and servers within the NetWare/IP domain. By performing this action, it emulates the requirements for SAP/RIP broadcasts for an IPX network. NetWare/IP nodes learn of services on a NetWare network from the DSS. NetWare/IP servers communicate with the DSS periodically to obtain and update SAP/RIP updates. When a NetWare/IP client uses commands such as SLIST (NetWare 3.x), NLIST SERVER (NetWare 4.x), or DISPLAY SERVERS (console command) that require SAP information, the NetWare/IP server responds with information obtained from a DSS server.

It is not necessary for a DSS server to also be a NetWare/IP server. In other words, the DSS server does not have to be running NWIP.NLM, the component that implements the NetWare/IP server. The NLM needed for implementing DSS is DSS.NLM.

The primary DSS server supports all NetWare/IP nodes (clients and servers) in its NetWare/IP domain. The NetWare/IP nodes use DNS to find the name of the nearest DSS for obtaining SAP/RIP information.

You might decide to divide the IP network into several logical NetWare/IP domains. Reasons for doing this include the following:

- ◆ To limit the amount of SAP/RIP information that must be maintained by DSS servers for a domain
- ◆ To reduce the processing overhead on a DSS server

You also can increase efficiency by spreading the processing load across multiple DSS servers deployed throughout the network.

Figure 7.4 shows a network divided into two NetWare/IP domains. One NetWare/IP domain encompasses the Department A network, and the other NetWare/IP domain encompasses the Department B and Department C networks. The NetWare/IP domains are shown with the following names:

- ◆ DEPT-A.SCS.COM (Department A network)
- ◆ DEPT-BC.SCS.COM (Department B and Department C networks)

The choice of names for the NetWare/IP domain such as DEPT-A or DEPT-BC is arbitrary. Use a convention that meets the needs of your organization. Novell documentation suggests Department B and Department C networks NWIP.SCS.COM and NWIP2.SCS.COM as names for the NetWare/IP domain.

The NetWare/IP domain DEPT-A.SCS.COM has a single primary DSS. The NetWare/IP domain DEPT-BC.SCS.COM has a primary DSS and a secondary DSS. The secondary DSS is located in the department C network. This makes it possible for the department C network to obtain SAP/RIP information by contacting a local DSS server rather than going across a router (and potentially slow and expensive WAN links) to obtain SAP/RIP information from the primary DSS server for domain DEPT-BC.SCS.COM.

If a NetWare/IP client in a NetWare/IP domain needs access to a server in another domain, you can use the NWIPMAP.EXE utility that comes with NetWare/IP to create a drive mapping to the server. In the example in figure 7.4, if WS1 needs to access the PUBLIC directory on server NWS2 in domain DEPT-BC.SCS.COM, it can do so by creating a drive mapping H: to the PUBLIC directory of S2 as follows:

```
NWIPMAP H: = S2/SYS:PUBLIC@DEPT-BC.NOVELL.COM
```

Figure 7.4 shows a DNS server outside the NetWare/IP domains. This emphasizes the point that NetWare/IP domains are used for NetWare-based networks, and DNS servers can be used by NetWare and non-NetWare nodes (Unix, VMS, MVS, and so on).

NetWare/IP Workstation Components

Figure 7.5 shows the NetWare workstation architecture that uses IPX only, and figure 7.6 shows the workstation architecture that uses TCP/IP to access NetWare services.

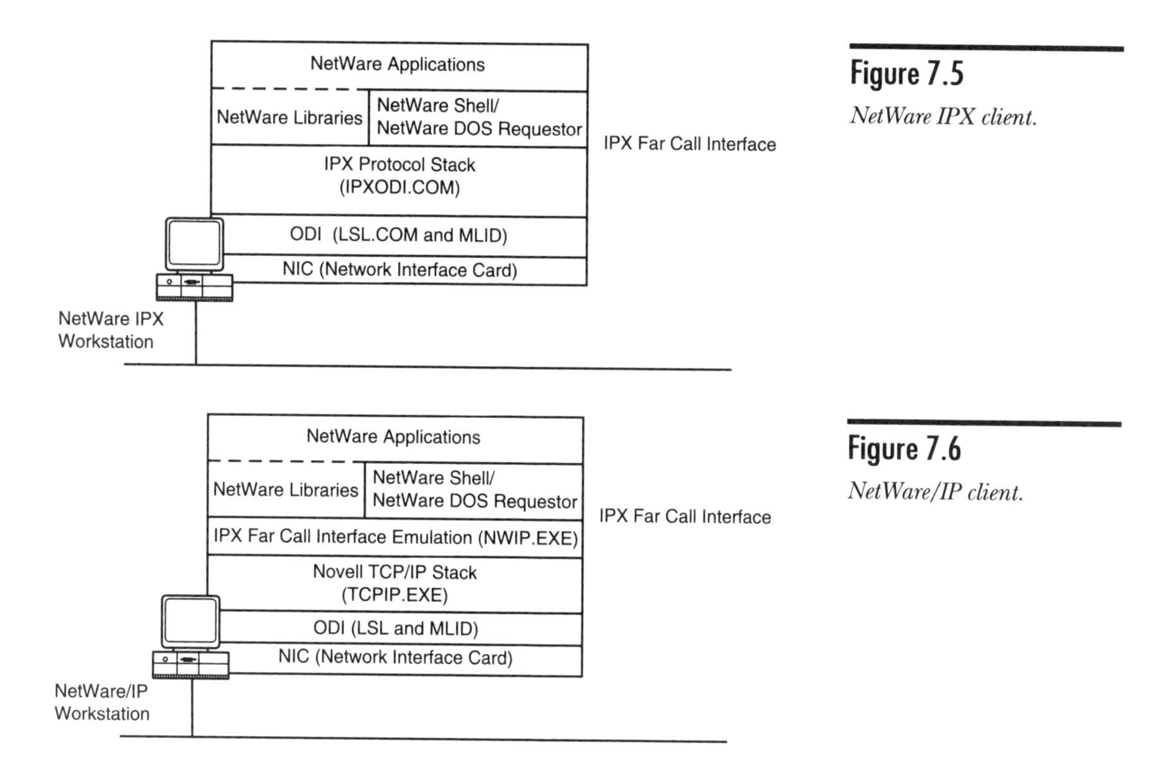

Figure 7.5
NetWare IPX client.

Figure 7.6
NetWare/IP client.

In figure 7.5, the bottom layer consists of the NIC hardware that represents layers 2 and 1 of the OSI model. The ODI interface is implemented by the Link Support Layer (LSL.COM), which communicates with the Multiple Link Interface Driver (MLID) for the NIC. The MLID communicates with the NIC hardware and with the Link Support Layer. The Link Support Layer provides a universal interface to the network adapter that allows a single protocol stack to establish communications with multiple NICs or multiple protocol stacks to communicate with a single NIC.

The IPXODI.COM implements the SPX/IPX protocols and provides the end-to-end transport protocols used by NetWare workstations. The IPXODI.COM exports an Application Binary Interface (ABI) called the IPX Far Call Interface that is backward compatible with earlier versions of IPX.

The NetWare libraries can be used by applications to access the transport protocols directly. The NetWare shell and the DOS Requester are special purpose applications that provide file and print redirection.

The IPX Far Call Interface mechanism is needed for future and existing applications to run over TCP/IP. It also ensures backward compatibility with earlier versions of IPX.

Comparing figure 7.6 with figure 7.5 shows that the IPXODI.COM is replaced with TCPIP.EXE. The TCPIP.EXE TSR implements the TCP/IP protocol stack. The TCP/IP protocol stack contains a transport layer (OSI layer 4) protocol called *User Datagram Protocol* (UDP). UDP is a simpler transport protocol than TCP and is more efficient for broadcasts and the request/reply nature of IP traffic.

Simple replacement of IPXODI.COM with TCPIP.EXE, however, is not sufficient to connect to a NetWare server, because the ABI used by TCPIP.EXE is different from that used by the shell/DOS Requester and other NetWare applications for using IPXODI.COM. The goal is to leave the existing applications unmodified and yet be able to use TCPIP.EXE, which uses a different ABI. Remember that IPXODI.COM exports the IPX Far Call Interface used by existing NetWare applications. A new module called NWIP.EXE interfaces with TCPIP.EXE and is used to export the IPX Far Call Interface. This allows existing NetWare applications to use the IPX Far Call Interface. NWIP.EXE translates this into the ABI used by TCPIP.EXE. This architecture allows future NetWare applications to work transparently with TCP/IP as long as they use the IPX Far Call Interface ABI. You can use the NETX.EXE or the NetWare DOS Requester with TCPIP.EXE.

The only limitation to the NetWare/IP architecture is applications that use IPX-based NetBIOS. NetBIOS applications use the IPX broadcast mechanism. If TCP/IP is used as the transport protocol, these broadcasts are confined to the local IP subnet because IP routers do not forward non-directed UDP/IP broadcasts to other IP networks.

The memory used by TCPIP.EXE and NWIP.EXE is 17.2 KB and 15.1 KB, respectively.

The TCPIP.EXE used in NetWare/IP is the same protocol stack used in the LAN WorkPlace for DOS product. Novell claims the following advantages/features in using this TCP/IP implementation:

- Support for 64 TCP and 32 UDP sockets
- IP support for up to four ODI interfaces
- Support for up to three default routers on each interface
- Duplicate IP Address prevention because of the Address Resolution Protocol (ARP) mechanism detecting this problem
- Support for network interfaces that use ODI Drivers for Ethernet, Token-Ring, FDDI, ARCnet, SLIP, PPP, and IBM Broadband
- IP configuration options through a choice of BOOTP, RARP, or ASCII text file
- Troubleshooting utilities and support for SNMP
- Support for NetBIOS over TCP/IP using the enhanced "B-node" implementation of RFCs 1001 and 1002
- Support for the BSD Socket interface and WinSock interface

The Domain Name System

NetWare/IP contains the file NAMED.NLM that implements the Domain Name System (DNS). DNS is a distributed name-to-IP address database used on many TCP/IP-based networks including the Internet. When a workstation issues a TCP/IP command such as the following:

```
ftp ftp.novell.com
```

the name of the host ftp.novell.com needs to be resolved to the IP address of the host. The IP address is then used by the TCP/IP protocols to interact with the host. Users in general find the symbolic hostname easier to remember than the IP address (32-bit number) of the host. The function of DNS is to translate the symbolic hostname to an IP address number that can be used by the protocol software. The term host refers to any machine that implements a TCP/IP stack. The resolution of the hostname to its equivalent IP address is performed by DNS protocols. These protocols and mechanisms are described in RFCs 1034, 1035, 1101, and 1183.

The IP address is a four-byte (32-bit) number assigned to every interface used by the IP protocol. If a NetWare server has two network interfaces to which IP is bound, a different IP address must be assigned to each of the boards. Most workstations have a single NIC, and if IP is used over this interface, a unique IP address must be assigned for the network interface.

The 32-bit IP address is usually written in a special format called the dotted decimal notation. In this notation, each of the four bytes that make up the IP address is expressed as a decimal number. The largest number contained in a byte is 255, and the smallest 0. Therefore, each of the bytes in the dotted decimal notation is a number between 0 and 255, inclusive.

The following is an example of an IP address in a dotted decimal notation:

```
144.19.74.201
```

The decimal number 144 corresponds to the most significant byte (left-most byte) of the 32-bit IP address, and the number 201 corresponds to the least significant byte (right-most byte) of the IP address. The dotted decimal number notation is much simpler to read than the 32-bit number translated as one decimal number. For example, the IP address also can be represented as the single decimal number: 2417183433.

DNS is implemented as a distributed database for looking up name-to-IP address correspondence. Another way of performing the name look up is to keep the name-to-IP address information in a static file. On Unix systems, this static file is the /etc/hosts file. On NetWare servers, this static file is kept in the SYS:ETC/HOSTS file.

A sample host file format is shown next:

```
# Local network host addresses
#ident "@(#)hosts    1.1 - 88/05/17"
#
127.0.0.1        local localhost
144.19.74.1      sparc1 sp1
144.19.74.2      sparc2 sp2
144.19.74.3      sparc3 sp3
144.19.74.4      sparc4 sp4
144.19.74.5      sparc5 sp5
144.19.74.6      sparc6 sp6
144.19.74.7      sparc7 sp7
144.19.75.1      sparc8 sp8
144.19.75.2      sparc9 sp9
144.19.75.3      sparc10 sp10
144.19.75.4      sparc11 sp11
144.19.75.5      sparc12 sp12
144.19.75.6      sparc13 sp13
144.19.75.7      sparc14 sp14
144.19.74.101    cdos
144.19.74.102    server1 s386 nw
144.19.74.103    spws sparcsrv sps ss
144.19.74.201    sparcc1 spc1
144.19.74.202    sparcc2 spc2
```

The IP address 127.0.0.1 is a special address called the *loopback address.* Packets sent to this address never reach the network cable. The loopback address can be used for diagnostic purposes to verify that the internal code path through the TCP/IP protocols is working. It also can be used by client applications to communicate with software programs running on the same machine.

Each <IP Address, Hostname> pair is expressed on a single line using the style shown in the host file. The multiple hostnames for the host are alias names. The protocol software, if configured to perform name resolution using this static host file, looks up the information for resolving a name. Consider the following command:

```
telnet sp14
```

The protocol software uses the following entry in the host file to resolve the name sp14:

```
144.19.75.7      sparc14 sp14
```

The name sp14 is an alias for the hostname sparc14. The corresponding IP address is 144.19.75.7. The protocol software resolves the name sp14 to 144.19.75.7. The preceding command then becomes the following:

```
telnet 144.19.75.7
```

A number of problems exist with the static host file approach. As the number of hosts on a network becomes large. It becomes increasingly difficult to keep this file up to date. Also, many organizations have more than one network administrator. It is difficult for these administrators to coordinate with each other every time host files need to be changed. Even keeping this information in a large central static file becomes quickly unmanageable as the number of entries in this file becomes large.

The DNS system was developed to overcome the problems of name resolution on a large IP network. It provides a distributed database of names and IP addresses. The names could be hostnames or names of mail exchanger hosts. It also has provisions for keeping text descriptions of hostnames and for providing name resolution for other protocol families besides TCP/IP (such as Chaos net, XNS, and so on). It is, however, used predominantly for resolving hostnames for the TCP/IP protocols.

Part of the scheme used in DNS refers to the use of hierarchical names, in which names are organized into a hierarchical tree. At the top of the tree is the root domain named by the period symbol (.). Because all names have this common root, the period is omitted when specifying the hierarchical name in most TCP/IP applications. Below the root domain are top-level domains (see fig. 7.7). These reflect how names are organized. Table 7.1 shows examples of top-level domains.

Table 7.1 Top-Level Domains

Top-Level Domain	Description
COM	Commercial organization
EDU	Education institution. Universities, schools, and so on
MIL	Military
GOV	Government (United States)
NET	Network provider
ORG	Organization
ARPA	ARPAnet; now historical; still used for inverse address mapping
US	Country U.S.A.
CA	Country Canada
UK	Country United Kingdom
DE	Country Germany
SE	Country Sweden
FR	Country France
IN	Country India
CN	Country China
JA	Country Japan

The two-letter designations are assigned to the country as per the CCITT standards. These are the same country designations used for specifying country objects in NetWare Directory Services. Below the top-level domains are middle-level domains. A number of middle level names can exist. Each name is separated from each other by use of the period (which can never occur as part of the name of a domain). The length of a complete domain name such as the following:

```
world.std.com
```

cannot exceed 255 characters. In the name world.std.com, the name of the host is as follows:

```
world
```

The following name is in the domain:

```
std.com
```

If another host is in the same domain whose name is "sparky," its Fully Qualified Name (FQN) is as follows:

```
sparky.std.com
```

Many of the middle-level names refer to names of organizations. An organization is free to define subdomains within the organization. If it does this, it should provide appropriate name services to resolve names in these subdomains. For example, consider the organization SCS that has the following domain name:

```
scs.com
```

If this organization has separate networks for its Corporate, Marketing, and Research arms, it can define three separate subdomains named CORP, MKTG, RESCH, and provide a DNS server or a number of DNS servers to resolve names on its networks. The domains in this case are as follows:

```
corp.scs.com
mktg.scs.com
resch.scs.com
```

Although a DNS server is not required for each domain, it is common to have one or more for each domain being served. Figure 7.7 shows several DNS servers for the root domain. These servers would know about names of the top-level domains such as COM, EDU, MIL, ORG, NET, and so on. Several DNS servers can be used for a domain to perform load balancing, avoid unnecessary network traffic, and for reliability in case the primary DNS server is not available. The COM domain would have one or more DNS servers that know the names of all commercial organizations in the COM domain. Within the COM domain, a subdomain such as IBM.COM has its own DNS servers for that domain. Hosts within a domain query the local DNS server for the domain to resolve names. For example, the host WORLD.STD.COM queries the DNS server for the domain STD.COM to find out the IP address of the host FTP.NOVELL.COM or the IP address of ATHENA.SCS.ORG. When this query is resolved, the results are usually cached locally for a configurable period of time.

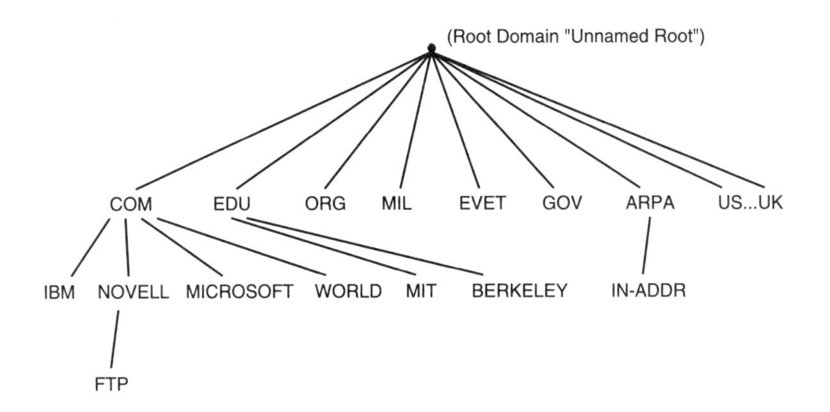

Figure 7.7

Hierarchical names in DNS.

The DNS servers for a domain need to resolve names of hosts in their domains. They do not need to know about hosts in subdomains if DNS servers are defined for subdomains. Secondary DNS servers in a domain must know the IP address of the primary server in the domain it can contact for resolving a name query. A DNS server must also know the IP address of the parent DNS server.

Relationship between DNS Domains and NetWare/IP Domains

A NetWare/IP domain is defined as a collection of NetWare/IP servers and clients that receive SAP/RIP information provided by one or more DSS servers in that domain. A NetWare network can be partitioned into multiple NetWare/IP domains. A NetWare/IP domain must exist in the context of a DNS domain. A NetWare/IP domain is created by creating a DNS subdomain with the following properties:

- The DNS subdomain must be a subdomain of an existing DNS domain.
- The DNS subdomain cannot have subdomains.

After creating the NetWare/IP domain, you must configure NetWare/IP nodes that belong to this domain with the NetWare/IP domain name.

The organization SCS has a registered domain SCS.ORG. This organization has two existing DNS subdomains for two separate networks for the Engineering and Marketing department as follows:

```
ENG.SCS.ORG
MKTG.SCS.ORG
```

SCS decides to have a NetWare/IP domain cover the entire Engineering network and two NetWare/IP domains for the Marketing network. To create these NetWare/IP domains, you must first create DNS subdomains. For the DNS domain ENG.SCS.ORG, you can create a NetWare/IP domain called the following:

```
NWIP.ENG.SCS.ORG
```

For the Marketing network, you must create two NetWare/IP domains. Therefore, you must first create two DNS subdomains of MKTG.SCS.ORG. You can do this by creating the following domains:

```
NWIP1.MKTG.SCS.ORG
NWIP2.MKTG.SCS.ORG
```

After creating these DNS subdomains, you must configure the NetWare/IP nodes and DSS servers that are in the NetWare/IP domain with the names of these subdomains.

Examining the DSS Server

To provide SAP/RIP information to a NetWare/IP network, you must have at least one DSS server in a NetWare/IP domain. The DSS server holds a database of SAP/RIP information for a NetWare/IP domain. The information in the DSS server can be replicated on multiple DSS servers to improve performance across WAN links and to increase reliability. This section helps you understand how the DSS server updates its information and how this information is disseminated to other NetWare/IP nodes. It also covers the issue of DSS database replication for improved reliability.

Updating DSS Servers

In a IPX-based NetWare server, NetWare services such as File, Print, and Database services advertise their existence using the SAP protocol. These services send SAP broadcast packets every 60 seconds. (The actual value is configurable, but 60 seconds is the default.) The broadcast packets are sent out over every network interface to which IPX is bound.

In NetWare/IP networks, NetWare services also advertise themselves using SAP. These SAP packets are sent directly to the DSS servers using UDP/IP packets.

When a NetWare server boots, it sends a SAP broadcast advertising its existence. If the server is configured as a NetWare/IP server, it also sends a SAP packet directly to the nearest DSS server using the UDP/IP protocol. The NetWare/IP server sends this information to the DSS server every five minutes (the value is configurable). If the DSS server does not receive the SAP refresh information, it times out the information.

Disseminating DSS Information

In an IPX-based network, NetWare servers listen for SAP packets and cache this information. They then create temporary bindery entries that list the services seen by the server. NetWare IPX clients and applications locate these services by looking up the bindery information stored on the server.

NetWare/IP servers also keep a list of available services in the NetWare bindery. They do this by periodically requesting a download of this information from the DSS server. The download occurs at a configurable time interval whose default value is five minutes.

Replicating the DSS Database

To increase the reliability and availability of the DSS information, you can have several secondary DSS servers in a NetWare/IP domain. If the primary DSS server is unavailable or too busy to respond to requests by NetWare/IP servers, the secondary server can be used to provide the desired information.

To provide consistency of the DSS information, the DSS database is replicated to all the DSS servers in the NetWare/IP domain. In a large network consisting of slow WAN links, performance can be improved by avoiding sending requests for DSS information across the WAN links. This can be achieved by installing a local DSS server on each network so that NetWare/IP nodes can query the local DSS server instead of querying a remote DSS server separated by the slow WAN link. The primary DSS server holds the master copy of the DSS server, and the secondary DSS servers hold a Read/Write replica.

SAP/RIP information can be received by DSS servers at different times. This can result in the DSS servers not having the same information. To keep the DSS servers synchronized, the secondary DSS servers contact the primary DSS server at periodic intervals to synchronize their information. If the DSS databases are out of synchronization, the synchronization process commences. If at any time, connectivity between primary and secondary DSS servers is lost, the secondary DSS server periodically attempts to establish a connection and initiate synchronization. If the secondary DSS server is activated after being down, it attempts to synchronize with the primary DSS when it comes up.

To ensure that synchronization is done correctly, each DSS server maintains a database version number for the information stored on it at any time. The database version number is changed whenever the database is changed by new information. The database version numbers help the DSS servers determine if the database is out of synchronization. During synchronization, the secondary DSS server uploads to the primary DSS any new records received since the last synchronization. It also downloads any records not in its database. Only changed, deleted, or new records are exchanged, and not the entire database.

Understanding NetWare/IP Installation

The amount of memory needed to run a NetWare/IP server depends on the components loaded at the NetWare server, and the number of NetWare/IP servers configured in its NetWare/IP domain. If *N* is the number of NetWare/IP servers, the server memory requirements can be calculated using the formulas in table 7.2. The amount of disk space needed on the NetWare server is about 2 MB on the SYS: volume.

Table 7.2 Memory Requirements on a NetWare/IP Server

Type of NetWare Service	Memory Requirements (Bytes)
NetWare/IP	*N**380 + 75000
DSS on NetWare 3.1x	*N**440 + 450000
DSS on NetWare 4.x	*N**440 + 710000

**N* = Number of NetWare/IP Servers in a NetWare/IP Domain

NetWare/IP at the workstation requires approximately 2 MB of free disk space for DOS and 3.2 MB of free disk space for Windows. The TCPIP.EXE requires 17.2 KB of RAM, and the NWIP.EXE requires 15.1 KB of RAM. Using memory managers, these components can be loaded in upper memory.

Installing NetWare/IP

You must log in as SUPERVISOR (NetWare 3.1x) or Admin (NetWare 4.x). If installing on a NetWare 4.x server, you must have the bindery context set using the following server console command:

```
SET BINDERY CONTEXT = context
```

The bindery context is normally set in the AUTOEXEC.NCF file. To view the current server bindery context, use the following command:

```
SET BINDERY CONTEXT
```

You can install the NetWare/IP from a DOS workstation or the NetWare server.

Installing NetWare/IP from a DOS Workstation

To install from a DOS workstation, you must have REMOTE and RSPX running at the server. This can be done using the following commands:

```
LOAD REMOTE password
LOAD RSPX
```

The steps for installing are as follows:

1. Log in with Supervisor access to the server.
2. Create a directory called NWIP1 on one of the NetWare volumes.
3. Use NCOPY to copy the disk labeled NWIP1 to the NWIP1 directory as follows:

   ```
   NCOPY A: SYS:NWIP1 /S /E
   ```

4. Run RCONSOLE.
5. Select the server to install NetWare/IP.
6. Enter REMOTE password to connect to the server console.
7. Proceed with instructions in the following section.

Installing NetWare/IP from a Server

The steps for installing are as follows:

1. At the server console, run the INSTALL program by issuing the following command:

   ```
   LOAD INSTALL
   ```

2. On a NetWare 3.1x server, make the following selections:
   - Select Product Options.
   - Press Ins.

   On a NetWare 4.x server, make the following selections:
   - Select Maintenance/Selective Install.
   - Select Product Options.
   - Press Ins.

3. When prompted to insert the disk, enter the disk or alternate location for the source files.

   On a NetWare 3.1x server, you can simply override the default source location (A:) by typing in the new path.

   On a NetWare 4.x server, you can press F3 to specify a different source (such as SYS:NWIP1).

4. You are informed about a README file. Press Esc to continue.
5. Select No when asked if you want to exit installation. Select Yes if you want to read the README file and start the installation again.
6. If TCP/IP has not been configured, you are asked to switch to the console screen and configure it. You should also make changes to the AUTOEXEC.NCF file to configure TCP/IP. Press Esc to continue.

   If you are performing installation locally at the server, press Alt+Esc to switch to the console.

   If you are performing installations remotely, use the numeric key pad <+> or <-> key on NetWare 3.1x servers, and Alt+F3 or Alt+F4 on NetWare 4.x servers.

To configure TCP/IP, perform the following commands:

```
LOAD LANDriver NAME=IPNET FRAME=ETHERNET_II (for Ethernet)
LOAD LANDriver NAME=IPNET FRAME=TOKEN-RING_SNAP (for Token Ring)
BIND IP TO IPNET ADDR=IPAddress
```

7. Enter the local hostname. The default is the name of the server. Accept the default.

   The INSTALL program begins copying the NetWare/IP files to hard disk and displays the filename being copied.

8. Enter the drive path for booting the server. This should be the C: drive on the NetWare server. Accept this value and press Enter.
9. Press Esc a few times to exit the INSTALL program. Confirm that you want to exit installation.
10. Make sure that your AUTOEXEC.NCF file contains the TCP/IP configuration.
11. Down the server.
12. Restart the server.

Proceed to the next section on configuring NetWare/IP software.

Configuring NetWare/IP

After you install NetWare/IP, it must be configured before it can be used. Configuring NetWare/IP involves a number of steps. One of the first steps is using the UNICON utility to perform the following:

- ◆ Configure NetWare/IP servers
- ◆ Configure DNS servers
- ◆ Configure DSS servers
- ◆ Monitor and fine-tune performance

Using UNICON

You can start UNICON by typing the following command at the server console:

```
LOAD UNICON
```

If asked to log in, specify the server name on which you want to perform NetWare/IP configuration. You must also specify the Supervisor account name and password.

Figure 7.8 shows the main UNICON screen. You can use the options on this screen to perform most NetWare/IP configuration tasks.

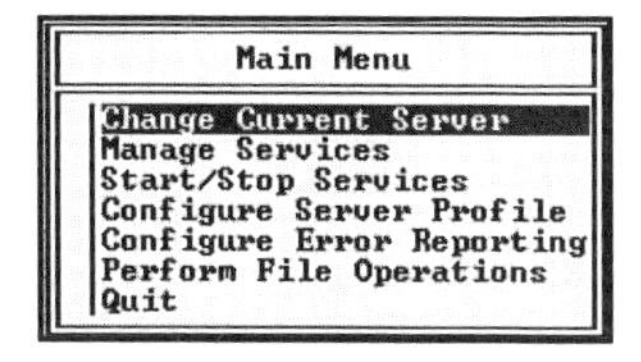

Figure 7.8

Main UNICON screen.

The Change Current Server option is used to log in to other NetWare servers for performing NetWare/IP configuration.

The Manage Services option is used to configure DNS server and Host information and NetWare/IP domains.

The Start/Stop Services option starts services not running, and stops services that are running.

The Configure Server Profile option is used to configure server parameters.

The Configure Error Reporting option is used to set the error reporting level for messages reported to the Product Kernel screen or the AUDIT.LOG file. It also can be used to specify the maximum size of the AUDIT.LOG file. Setting the error levels can be useful for troubleshooting NetWare/IP configuration.

The Performing File Operations option is used to copy files through FTP, edit files, set up the DNS name server database, and create text files from the database.

Configuring the DNS Server

The DNS server must be configured before a NetWare/IP server or DSS server can be activated. You can configure DNS servers in the following two ways:

- Configure DNS server to run on a NetWare server.
- Configure DNS server to run on another operating system. A sample choice is to use Berkeley Internet Domain Service (BIND) available on Unix or DOS (from FTP Software, Inc).

Configuring DNS on a NetWare Server and Creating NetWare/IP Domains

The DNS server must contain IP Address and Hostname mappings. You can enter these names directly into the DNS database. Each entry in the DNS database is called a *resource record.*

You must first create the DNS Master Database. You can do this by performing the following steps:

1. Load UNICON.
2. Select Perform File Operations (see fig. 7.9).

Figure 7.9

File Operations screen.

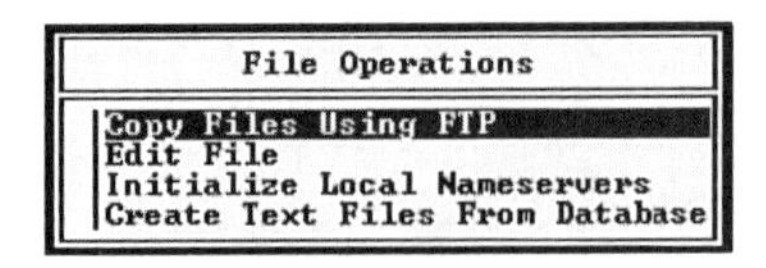

3. Select Initialize Local Nameservers (see fig. 7.10).

Figure 7.10

DNS Server Initialization Data screen.

4. Enter the Fully Qualified Name (FQN) for the DNS domain. The following is an example:

   ```
   SCS.COM
   ```

5. Wait a few seconds for the Please Wait message to disappear, and press Esc.
6. You are asked if you want to initialize the DNS database. Select Yes.
7. You see a status message similar to figure 7.11. Press Esc to continue.

   At this point, you created the database for the domain name and started the DNS server. The database initially contains just the hostname record for the NetWare/IP server.

Figure 7.11

DNS database creation status messages.

```
Generated zone SCS.COM. database.
Generated zone 19.144.in-addr.arpa. for address to hostname lookups.
Configured domain SCS.COM for DNS client access.
Successfully created DNS database.
Starting DNS Server.
Press <ESCAPE> to Continue
```

8. Press Esc a few times to get back to the main UNICON menu.

You can now enter hosts information for DSS severs in the domain that you just created by performing the following steps:

1. Select Manage Services.
2. Select Hosts. You should see a list of DSS server hosts in the DNS database (see fig. 7.12).

   You can display information about a specific DSS host by highlighting a host and pressing Enter (see fig. 7.13).

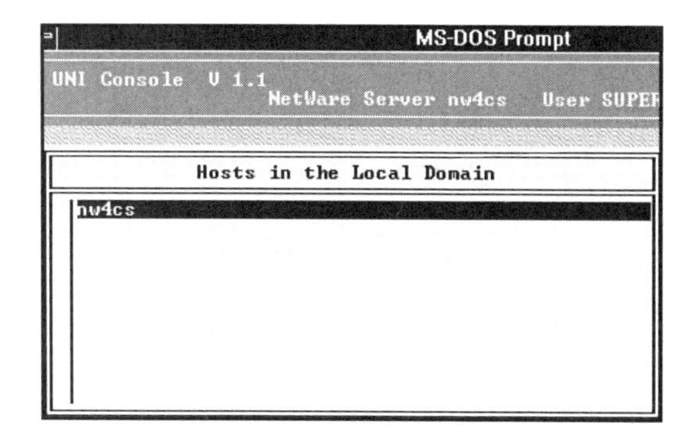

Figure 7.12

Hosts in local domain.

3. To add additional secondary DSS servers' hostnames, press Ins on the screen in figure 7.12. To modify entries for a host, use the screen shown in figure 7.13.

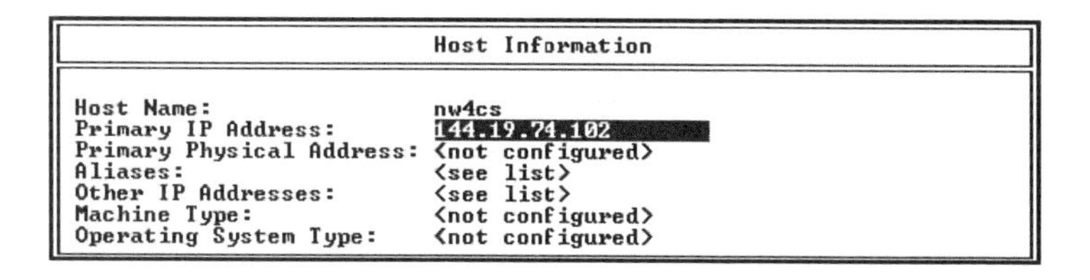

Figure 7.13

Host Information screen.

4. Go to the Manage Services menu option. (Press Esc if you have just performed step 2.)
5. Select DNS Server (see fig. 7.14).

Figure 7.14

DNS Server Administration screen.

6. Select Configure Master Database (see fig. 7.15).

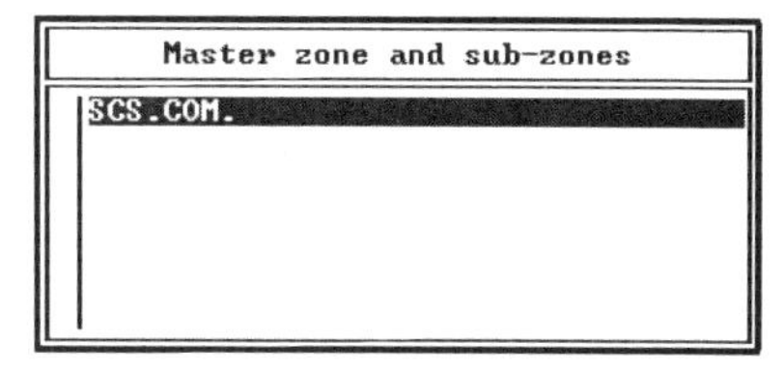

Figure 7.15

Master zone and sub-zone list.

7. The list shows the master domain you have just created. You need to add to it a DNS subdomain for the NetWare/IP domain. To do this press Ins and enter the name of the NetWare/IP domain. If the master domain zone name was SCS.COM., you can enter the NetWare/IP domain as follows:

   ```
   NWIP.SCS.COM.
   ```

8. Highlight the newly created NetWare/IP domain from the list of master zones and subzones and press Enter.

   You should see an empty list of name servers for this subdomain (see fig. 7.16).

Figure 7.16

Name servers in subdomain.

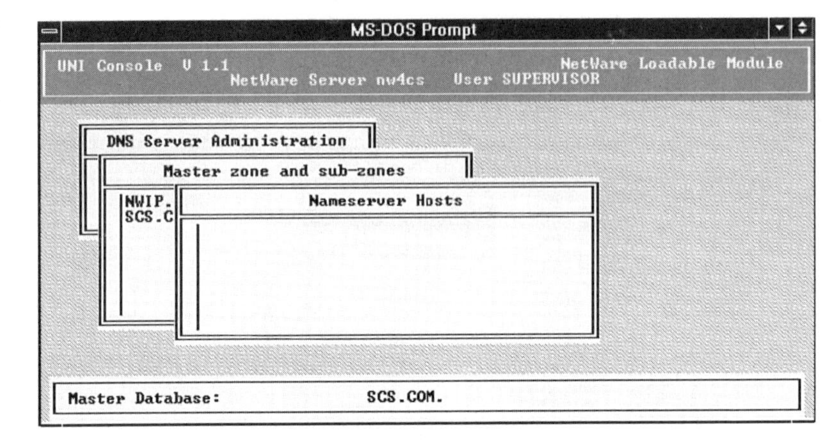

9. Press Ins.

   You are asked to enter the fully qualified name of the name server host (see fig. 7.17). Enter the name of the primary DSS server for the NetWare/IP domain. On a small network, this DSS server can be the same as the DNS server. For example, if the name of the DSS server is NW4CS, its fully qualified name is as follows:

   ```
   NW4CS.SCS.COM
   ```

   UNICON automatically appends a period for the root domain.

Figure 7.17

Adding a DSS server to the NetWare/IP domain.

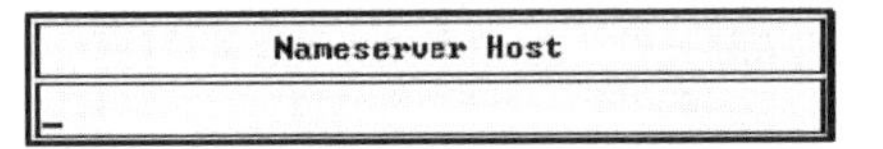

10. Press Enter after adding the name. You should see the name server added to the list of nameservers for the NetWare/IP domain (see fig. 7.18).

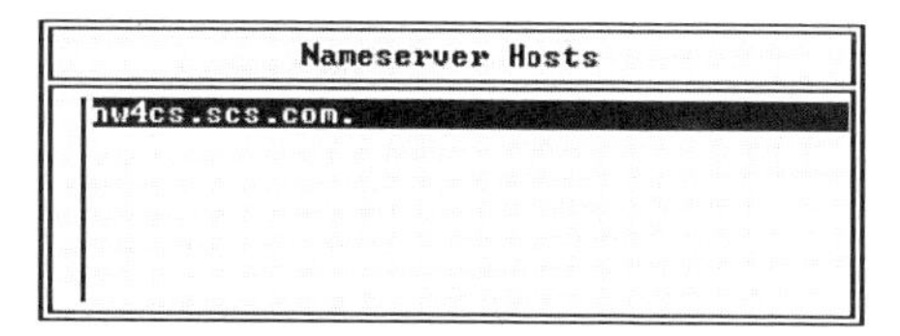

Figure 7.18

DSS server added to the NetWare/IP domain.

11. Repeat the steps 9 and 10 to add optional secondary DSS servers to the NetWare/IP domain.

12. Repeat steps 6 to 8 to create other NetWare/IP domains.

13. After creating a NetWare/IP subdomain (also DNS subdomain), you must inform the DNS server for the parent domain about the new DNS subdomain you just created. The parent DNS server can be on another node administered by someone else. You have to request the DNS administrator for the parent domain to add your subdomain to the parent's database. In the example in this guided tour, the parent DNS server is on the same server as the DSS server, and figure 7.19 shows that the master domain SCS.COM. knows about the subdomain (sub-zone) NWIP.SCS.COM.

```
Master zone and sub-zones
nwip.SCS.COM.
SCS.COM.
```

Figure 7.19

The master domain knows about the new NetWare/IP domain.

When a new domain record is added to the parent DNS server, the NetWare DNS server automatically links into the DNS hierarchy by using the information stored in SYS:ETC\DNS\ROOT.DB.

14. Any time you add records in the DNS database, you must restart the DNS service, so that it can initialize its cache with the new information.

To restart the DNS service, you must first stop it and then start it again. The following steps outline how you can accomplish this:

1. Go to the main menu of UNICON.
2. Select Start/Stop Services.
3. If the DNS service appears in the list of Running Services (see fig. 7.20), highlight it and press Del. Answer Yes to the query verifying if you want to stop the service.

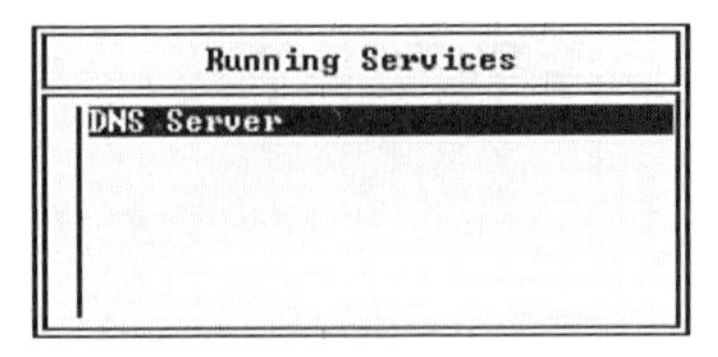

Figure 7.20

List of running services.

4. To start the DNS service again, press Ins on the list of running services. You should see a list of available services that you can run (see fig. 7.21). Highlight DNS Server and press Enter. This activates the DNS Service, and it appears in the list of Running Services.

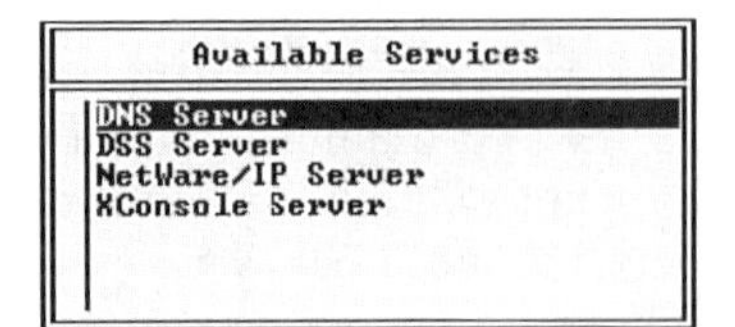

Figure 7.21

List of Available Services to run.

Creating a Replica of the DNS Database

For reliability, you may want to create one or more replicas of the DNS database on other servers. The following steps outline how you can do this:

1. Load UNICON.
2. Select Manage Services.
3. Select DNS Server.
4. Select Configure Replica Databases. You should see a list of replica databases that initially is empty.
5. Press Ins to create a replica of the DNS database on the server. A form for importing database information appears (see fig. 7.22).

   The Domain field specifies the name of the domain for which this replica has a copy.

   The Name Server field contains the IP address of the DNS master name server. Three Name Server fields are provided to enter IP addresses of additional DNS name servers.

   The Database Backup File field contains the name of the file that contains the backup copy of the database. The default filename is sys:etc/doc/zones.dbf. You can change this to specify a different filename.
6. After filling in the form, press Esc. If asked to save your changes, answer Yes.

```
Replica Database Information
Domain:                    <not assigned>
Name Server:               <not assigned>
Name Server:               <not assigned>
Name Server:               <not assigned>
Database Backup File:      sys:etc/dns/zone4.db
```

Figure 7.22

Replica Database Information form.

Configuring DNS Servers on Non-NetWare Platforms

If you are using a non-NetWare platform as a DNS server for a domain, you need to consult the documentation for DNS services for that operating system.

On Unix systems, DNS is implemented by BIND. On BSD-derived Unix, this is implemented by running the following program:

```
named
```

On SVR4 Unix, the following is implemented by the program:

```
in.named
```

DOS-based implementation of BIND is available from FTP Software, Inc. It runs as a TSR called NAMED.

BIND uses a file called /etc/named.boot that contains a list of other files for holding the zone records for the DNS database. FTP Software's BIND uses the filename NAMED.BOO.

The DNS zone files are text files and have a special format. You can refer to the DNS RFCs referenced earlier for information on the syntax of these text records, or consult your operating system's implementation.

If you are using non-NetWare DNS servers for the master domain, you must add a record in its database for the new subdomains that you created for NetWare/IP. This usually involves using a text editor and adding a record to the zone data file for the DNS server. If you created a primary DSS named nw4cs.scs.com (IP address 144.19.73.102) and a secondary DSS named ucs.scs.com (IP address 144.19.74.103) for the NetWare/IP domain nwip.scs.com, add the records shown in the following to the zone data file for non-NetWare DNS:

```
# Domain/Host     Class     RR Type     Data
nwip.scs.com.     IN        NS          nw4cs.scs.com.   # Primary DSS
nwip.scs.com.     IN        NS          ucs.scs.com.     # Secondary DSS
nw4cs.scs.com.    IN        A           144.19.74.102    # Host record
ucs.scs.com.      IN        A           144.19.74.103    # Host record
```

On most DNS implementations, you must restart the DNS service before the changes are registered.

Configuring the DSS Server

After the DNS server is configured, you can configure the DSS server. This involves configuring the primary and secondary DSS servers and starting the DSS service.

Configuring Primary and Secondary DSS Servers

The following steps outline the DSS configuration procedure:

1. Load UNICON.
2. Select Manage Services.
3. Select NetWare/IP.

   If your DNS server is set up on a different server from the DSS server, you see a form that enables you to make the DSS server a client of the DNS server (on another machine). This form has a DNS Domain field and three Nameserver fields.

   The DNS Domain field is used to specify the name of your DNS domain. The first Nameserver field specifies the IP address of the server to contact to resolve name queries. The other Nameserver fields represent the order in which other DNS servers are contacted to resolve names, if the answer is not found in the first name server.

4. Select Configure Primary DSS. The Primary DSS Configuration form appears (see fig. 7.23).

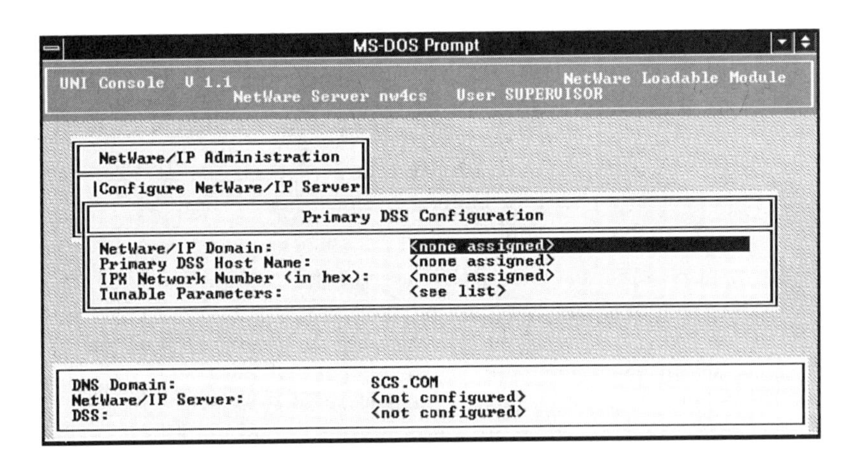

Figure 7.23
Primary DSS Configuration form.

The NetWare/IP Domain field contains the name of the NetWare/IP domain. All NetWare/ IP nodes (clients and servers) are members of this NetWare/IP domain. The NetWare/IP Domain, for example, can be the following:

```
nwip.scs.com.
```

The Primary DSS Host Name field contains the fully qualified name of the primary DSS host. For example, it can have a name such as the following:

```
nw4cs.SCS.COM.
```

The IPX Network Number (in hex) field contains the IPX network number assigned to the DSS service. This number must be different from the IPX internal network numbers assigned to NetWare 3.x and 4.x servers and from network numbers assigned to any IPX interface.

Selecting the Tunable Parameters field brings up a form for tuning DSS parameters (see fig. 7.24).

```
                    Tunable Parameters
UDP Port Number for NetWare/IP Service:        43981
SAP/RIP Database Synchronization Interval:     5          minutes
Maximum UDP Retransmissions:                   3
UDP Checksum?                                  No
```

Figure 7.24

Tunable DSS Parameters form.

The UDP Port Number for NetWare/IP Service field can be used to specify the UDP port number used by the NetWare/IP service. The default value is 43981. Two successive port numbers are assigned. The first port number 43981 (default) is used for packet transmission. The second port number 43982 (default) is used for SAP/RIP queries.

The SAP/RIP Database Synchronization Interval field can be used to specify how often a NetWare/IP server queries DSS for updated information. The value can range from 1 to 60 minutes with a default of 5 minutes.

The Maximum UDP Retransmissions field can be used to specify how often a packet should be resent if no acknowledgment is received for the packet. The value can range from 1 to 48 minutes with a default of three minutes.

The UDP Checksum? field determines whether the UDP packet uses the checksum field (set to Yes or No). The default value is No. LANs have a reliable transmission rate, and a value of No gives maximum performance. If you suspect that the physical network transport is unreliable, you may want to set the value to Yes. If set to Yes, UDP checksums are performed over the data packet. Checksum errors cause a packet to be rejected and retransmitted.

If any of the DSS tunable parameters are changed, you must stop and restart all DSS servers for the domain. You should also unload NWIP.EXE and reload it at each workstation.

5. After configuring the primary DSS, press Esc. If asked to verify that you want to set up this host as a primary DSS server, answer Yes.
6. The next step is to configure any optional secondary DSS servers.

To configure Secondary DSS servers make the following selections:

1. Select Managing Services.
2. Select NetWare/IP.
3. Select Configure Secondary DSS. A secondary DSS server form with the following fields appears:

Field NetWare/IP Domain contains the name of the NetWare/IP domain to which the secondary DSS belongs.

Field DSS Primary Host specifies the name or IP address of the primary DSS server.

After the DSS servers are configured, you must start them by performing the following steps:

1. Go to the main menu of UNICON.
2. Select Start/Stop Services.
3. If the DSS server appears in the list of Running Services, highlight it and press Del. Answer Yes to the query confirming that you want to stop the service.
4. To start the DSS service again, press Ins on the list of Running Services. A list of available services that you can run appears. Highlight DSS Server and press Enter. This activates the DSS Service, and it appears in the list of Running Services. Starting the DSS server also starts the DNS server (if the DNS server is not running).

Changing DNS Servers Associated with DSS Servers

UNICON provides a Server Profile Form that can be used to change DNS server names accessed by DSS servers.

To access the Server Profile form, perform the following steps:

1. Load UNICON.
2. Select Configure Server Profile from the main menu (see fig. 7.25).

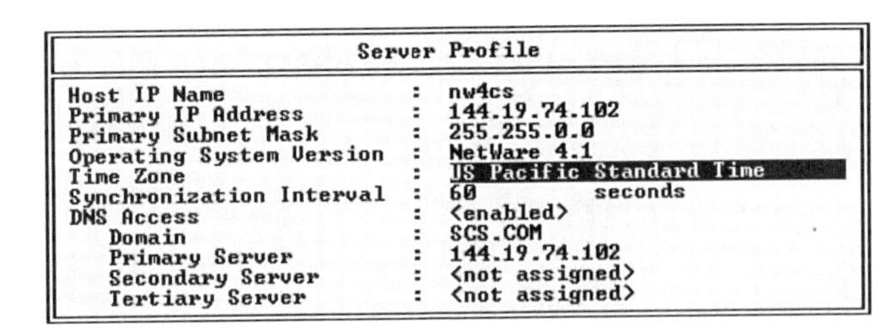

Server Profile

Host IP Name	:	nw4cs
Primary IP Address	:	144.19.74.102
Primary Subnet Mask	:	255.255.0.0
Operating System Version	:	NetWare 4.1
Time Zone	:	US Pacific Standard Time
Synchronization Interval	:	60 seconds
DNS Access	:	<enabled>
Domain	:	SCS.COM
Primary Server	:	144.19.74.102
Secondary Server	:	<not assigned>
Tertiary Server	:	<not assigned>

Figure 7.25

The Server Profile form.

The Host IP Name field contains the IP hostname of the NetWare/IP server created during NetWare/IP installation. This field cannot be selected. It is for informational purposes only.

The Primary IP Address field contains the IP address of the NetWare/IP server created during NetWare/IP installation. This field cannot be selected. It is for informational purposes only.

The Primary Subnet Mask field contains the subnet mask for the IP interface for the NetWare/IP server created during installation. This field cannot be selected. It is for informational purposes only.

The Operating System Version field contains the name of the operating system on the specified host. This field cannot be selected. It is for informational purposes only.

The Time Zone field is used to select one of the listed time zones. Selecting this field displays a list of available time zones (see fig. 7.26).

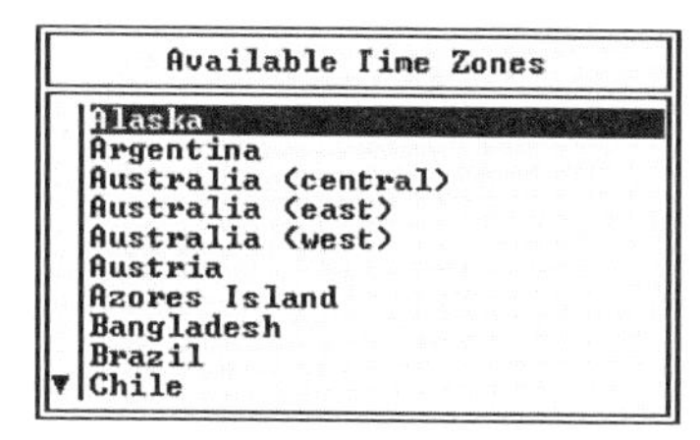

Figure 7.26

Time Zones for the NetWare/IP server.

You can add additional time zones by editing the text file SYS:ETC/TIMEZN. This editing can be performed by selecting the following options in UNICON:

1. Select Perform File Operations.
2. Select Edit File.

The contents of this file are as follows. The first column displays the hour offset and the second column the minute offset from GMT. Negative offsets are used for the Eastern Hemisphere, and positive offsets are used for the Western Hemisphere.

```
0     00    England
0     00    Portugal
-1    00    Austria
-1    00    France
-1    00    Germany
-1    00    Italy
-1    00    Spain
-2    00    Egypt
-2    00    Finland
-2    00    Greece
-2    00    Turkey
-2    00    Israel
-3    00    Kenya
-3    00    Saudi
-4    00    UAE
-5    00    Maldives
-4    30    Pakistan
-6    00    Bangladesh
-5    30    India
-6    00    Myanmar
-7    00    Thailand
-7    00    Indonesia
-8    00    Australia (west)
```

```
-9     30    Australia (central)
-8     00    China
-8     00    HongKong
-8     00    Singapore
-9     00    Japan
-9     00    Korea
-10    00    Australia (east)
-10    00    Guam
-11    00    New Caledonia
-12    00    Fiji
-12    00    New Zealand
11     00    Western Samoa
10     00    Hawaii
9      00     Alaska
8      00     US Pacific Standard Time
7      00     US Mountain Standard Time
6      00     US Central Standard Time
5      00     US Eastern Standard Time
9      00     US PST + daylight savings
8      00     US MST + daylight savings
7      00     US CST + daylight savings
6      00     US EST + daylight savings
4      00     Chile
4      00     Venezuela
3      00     Argentina
3      00     Brazil
2      00     Fernando de Noronha
1      00     Azores Island
-12    00    ¦ GMT -12 ¦
-11    00    ¦ GMT -11 ¦
-10    00    ¦ GMT -10 ¦
-9     00    ¦ GMT -9  ¦
-8     00    ¦ GMT -8  ¦
-7     00    ¦ GMT -7  ¦
-6     00    ¦ GMT -6  ¦
-5     00    ¦ GMT -5  ¦
-4     00    ¦ GMT -4  ¦
-3     00    ¦ GMT -3  ¦
-2     00    ¦ GMT -2  ¦
-1     00    ¦ GMT -1  ¦
0      00    ¦ GMT     ¦
1      00    ¦ GMT +1  ¦
2      00    ¦ GMT +2  ¦
3      00    ¦ GMT +3  ¦
4      00    ¦ GMT +4  ¦
5      00    ¦ GMT +5  ¦
```

```
6       00      ¦ GMT +6  ¦
7       00      ¦ GMT +7  ¦
8       00      ¦ GMT +8  ¦
9       00      ¦ GMT +9  ¦
10      00      ¦ GMT +10 ¦
11      00      ¦ GMT +11 ¦
12      00      ¦ GMT +12 ¦
```

The Synchronization Interval field is the number of seconds at which the NetWare/IP server checks the SYS:ETC\NFSUSERS, SYS:NFSGROUP, and SYS:NWPARAM files for changes. The first two files are used by the NetWare NFS product. The parameter ranges from 1 to 1,000 seconds and has a default value of 60 seconds.

The DNS Access field informs you if DNS is enabled or disabled.

The Domain field in the DNS Access group displays the DNS name configured during installation. You can enter a different value to change the domain name.

The Primary Server field in the DNS Access group can be set to the IP address of the first DNS server to contact for name resolution.

The Secondary Server field in the DNS Access group can be set to the IP address of the second DNS server to contact for name resolution if the other DNS servers fail to respond with the desired answer.

The Tertiary Server field in the DNS Access group can be set to the IP address of the third DNS server to contact for name resolution if the other DNS servers fail to respond with the desired answer.

Configuring the NetWare/IP Servers

After the DNS and DSS servers are configured, the next step is to configure the NetWare/IP servers.

The following is an outline of the steps needed to configure NetWare/IP:

1. Load UNICON.
2. Select Manage Services.
3. Select NetWare/IP.

   If your DNS server is set up on a different server from the DSS server, you see a form that enables you to make the DSS server a client of the DNS server (on another machine). This form has a DNS Domain field and three Nameserver fields.

   The DNS Domain field is used to specify the name of your DNS domain. The first Nameserver field specifies the IP address of the server to contact to resolve name queries. The other Nameserver fields represent the order in which other DNS servers are contacted to resolve names if the answer is not found in the first name server.
4. Select Configure NetWare/IP Server.

The NetWare/IP configuration form appears (see fig. 7.27). In the NetWare/IP domain field, you should enter the fully qualified NetWare/IP domain to which this NetWare/IP server belongs. In the example for this guided tour, this value is as follows:

```
NWIP.SCS.COM.
```

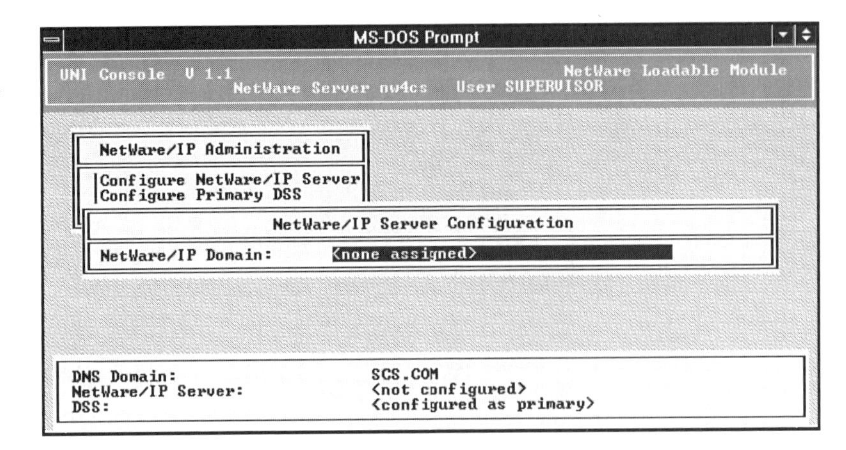

Figure 7.27
The NetWare/IP Server Configuration form.

If the NetWare server has two network boards to which the IP protocol is bound, you also see a Preferred IP Address field. You have the choice of associating any one of the IP addresses for the network interface with the NetWare/IP server. The decision to select the IP address must be based on the network interface through which you want NetWare/IP to communicate with the rest of the network.

5. Press Esc after you finish making changes and answer Yes to use this server as a NetWare/IP server. The status box at the bottom of the screen changes to indicate that the NetWare/IP server is configured.

You must start the NetWare/IP service. Before starting the NetWare/IP server, you must make sure that DNS and DSS are setup. To do so, follow these steps:

1. Go to the main menu of UNICON.
2. Select Start/Stop Services.
3. If the NetWare/IP server appears in the list of Running Services, highlight it and press Del. Answer Yes to the query verifying that you want to stop the service.
4. To start the NetWare/IP server again, press Ins on the list of Running Services. A list of available services that you can run appears. Highlight NetWare/IP Server and press Enter. This activates the NetWare/IP Server, and it appears in the list of Running Services.

Disabling the NetWare/IP Gateway

If the IPX protocol is bound to a network interface, the NetWare/IP server acts as an IPX-to-IP gateway. If you are on a purely IP-based network, you do not need the NetWare/IP gateway. You can disable this by unbinding IPX from the network interface. You can do this from the server console by typing the following command:

```
UNBIND IPX FROM network_board
```

Alternatively, you can comment out the BIND command in the AUTOEXEC.NCF files. You also can comment out the LOAD statement for the network drivers that use frame types used for IPX only.

Changes to AUTOEXEC.NCF

The NetWare/IP installation at the server adds a command called UNISTART.NCF at the end of the AUTOEXEC.NCF file. The UNISTART.NCF file contains the commands to start DNS, DSS, and NetWare/IP services. The following is an example of the contents of the UNISTART.NCF file:

```
load dispatch
load NAMED
load NISBIND
load NISSERV
load DSS
load NWIP.NLM
```

Installing and Configuring NetWare/IP Clients

The last phase in NetWare/IP installation is installing and configuring the NetWare/IP client. Before running the NetWare/IP client, you must do the following:

1. Set the CONFIG.SYS files to the following:

   FILES=40 (or higher)

   BUFFERS=20 (or higher)

2. Do not use the DOS APPEND command. To cancel any APPEND commands, you can use the following:

   ```
   APPEND ;
   ```

3. Disable the SHARE command, if it is in effect.

4. If you plan to run LAN WorkPlace or LAN WorkGroup, install these products before installing the NetWare/IP client. NetWare/IP is compatible with these products, but has files that include additional functionality.

Installing NetWare/IP Client

To install the NetWare/IP client software, perform the following steps:

1. Insert the disk labeled WSDOS_1 in drive A: and type the following command:

```
INSTALL
```

The INSTALL screen appears (see fig. 7.28).

Figure 7.28

NetWare/IP INSTALL screen.

```
STEP 1. Type target directory name for NetWare Client Files.
        C:\NWCLIENT

STEP 2. Client installation requires "LASTDRIVE=Z" in the
        CONFIG.SYS file and "CALL STARTNET.BAT" added to
        AUTOEXEC.BAT.  Install will make backup copies.
        Allow changes?  <Y/N>:  No

STEP 3. Do you wish to install support for Windows? <Y/N>:  No
        Windows Subdirectory:

STEP 4. Press <Enter> to install the driver for your network
        board.  You may then use arrow keys to find the
        board name.
        Press <Enter> to see list.

STEP 5. Press <Enter> to continue.

Esc-exit  Enter-select  ↑↓-move  Alt F10-exit
```

2. For step 1, type in the directory that contains NetWare/IP files. The default directory is C:\NWCLIENT.
3. For step 2, enter Y to have the INSTALL program modify the CONFIG.SYS and AUTOEXEC.BAT files. Enter N if you want to change these files manually.
4. For step 3, enter Y to install MS Windows support; otherwise, enter N. If you entered Y, enter the pathname where MS Windows is installed.
5. In step 4, select the driver for your interface board.

   If you already have a driver loaded, INSTALL recognizes it. You can install the latest version of this driver or continue with the next step.
6. In step 5, continue with the installation by pressing Enter. The second form showing the remainder of the steps appears (see fig. 7.29).

Figure 7.29

Rest of NetWare/IP INSTALL screen.

```
STEP 6. Provide the following information for configuring TCP/IP.

        TCP/IP Directory:             C:\NET
        Using Boot Protocol?          No
        Client IP Address:            <none assigned>
        Subnetwork Mask:              <none assigned>
        Default Router Address:       <none assigned>
        DNS Domain:                   <none assigned>
        Name Server Address:          <none assigned>
        Name Server Address:          <none assigned>
        Name Server Address:          <none assigned>

STEP 7. Configure this host to access NetWare/IP service.

        NetWare/IP Domain:            <none assigned>

STEP 8. Press <Enter> to install.
```

7. In step 6, enter the NetWare/IP client information in each field.
8. In step 7, enter the name of the NetWare/IP domain to which this NetWare/IP client belongs. Figure 7.30 shows some sample values.
9. In step 8, press Enter to continue with installation. Follow instructions to enter appropriate disks.

```
STEP 6. Provide the following information for configuring TCP/IP.

        TCP/IP Directory:              C:\NET
        Using Boot Protocol?           No
        Client IP Address:             144.19.74.44
        Subnetwork Mask:               255.255.0.0
        Default Router Address:        144.19.74.91
        DNS Domain:                    SCS.COM.
        Name Server Address:           144.19.74.102
        Name Server Address:           144.19.74.201
        Name Server Address:           <none assigned>

STEP 7. Configure this host to access NetWare/IP service.

        NetWare/IP Domain:             NWIP.SCS.COM.

STEP 8. Press <Enter> to install.
```

Figure 7.30

NetWare/IP Client Configuration values.

Checking Frame Types

The NetWare/IP client uses any of the following frame types for TCP/IP:

- Ethernet: ETHERNET_II or ETHERNET_SNAP
- Token Ring: TOKEN-RING_SNAP
- FDDI: FDDI_SNAP
- ARCnet: NOVELL_RX-NET
- PCN or PCN II: IBM_PCN2_SNAP

Checking the NET.CFG File

The NetWare/IP client installation modifies the NET.CFG file. The following is an example of the modified NET.CFG file:

```
#Link Driver CEODI
Link Driver CEODI
FRAME Ethernet_802.2
FRAME Ethernet_802.3
FRAME Ethernet_II
INT          5
PORT        300
MEM       d0000
SOCKET         1
IOWORDSIZE     16
```

```
SOCKETSERVICES     Y
CARDSERVICES     Y
Protocol IPX
bind 1
;    bind 2
NetWare DOS Requester
PB BUFFERS=4; Default is 3. 4 provides best throughput
FIRST NETWORK DRIVE = F
PREFERRED SERVER = NW4CS
NAME CONTEXT = "OU=CORP.O=ESL"
Link Support
Buffers     8 1500
MemPool     4096
Protocol TCPIP
PATH TCP_CFG         C:\NET\TCP
ip_address     144.19.74.44
ip_netmask     255.255.0.0
ip_router     144.19.74.91
NWIP
NWIP_DOMAIN_NAME     NWIP.SCS.COM.
NSQ_BROADCAST     ON
```

The new sections added are the Protocol TCPIP and the NWIP. These contain the IP address interface and the NetWare/IP domain information.

Checking the STARTNET.BAT File

The STARTNET.BAT file contains a line to load NWIP.EXE, the IPX Far Call Interface module.

The following is a sample STARTNET.BAT file:

```
C:\NET\bin\yesno "Load Networking Software? [y/n]"
@ECHO OFF
if errorlevel 1 goto nonet
C:
CD \NWCLIENT
SET NWLANGUAGE=ENGLISH
LSL
CEODI
C:\NET\BIN\TCPIP
NWIP
if errorlevel -1 goto err_loading_nwip
VLM
CD \
:err_loading_nwip
:nonet
```

Summary

This chapter covered the essential concepts needed to design, install, and configure NetWare/IP-based networks.

NetWare/IP solves a very important problem. It enables network designers to use the TCP/IP protocol for transport services on a NetWare network. This allows large networks currently based on TCP/IP to use this protocol for all their network services.

NetWare/IP also can be used as a gateway to link IPX networks with a backbone network based on TCP/IP only.

LAN WorkPlace and LAN WorkGroup

The increasing interest (and growing need) for communication with, and access to, TCP/IP-based hosts (on and off the Internet) has resulted in a demand for higher-level TCP/IP protocols such as File Transfer Protocol (FTP) and Terminal Emulation (Telnet) at the workstation level.

To utilize these high-level TCP/IP protocols on workstations, you need to implement TCP/IP workstation software (protocol stack). A number of products are available, and those products include support for DOS, Windows, OS/2, NT, Windows 95, and the Macintosh. In this chapter, Novell's workstation TCP/IP solutions: LAN WorkPlace 5 for MS Windows and DOS, and LAN WorkGroup 5 for MS Windows and DOS are discussed in detail. The following topics are covered:

- An overview of the Novell LAN WorkPlace 5 and LAN WorkGroup 5 products, along with some historical background. Differences between feature sets are highlighted.
- Installation procedures for LAN WorkPlace 5 and LAN WorkGroup 5.
- Configuration information and tips for the various LAN WorkPlace 5 and LAN WorkGroup 5 components, such as the Dialer and the BOOTP server.

- Usage tips and tricks on some of the more popular LAN WorkPlace and LAN WorkGroup applications, including Rapid Filer and Netscape Navigator.

History of Lan WorkPlace and LAN WorkGroup

LAN WorkPlace (LWP), originally developed by Excelan in 1985, became a Novell product in 1989 when Excelan was acquired by Novell. In the early days of PC-based TCP/IP implementation, LAN WorkPlace was just about the only product that could exist with NetWare on the same client. Through the years, Novell has enhanced the product and added more functionality. The version of LAN WorkPlace that goes on the NetWare file server is called LAN WorkGroup (LWG), although little else has changed in the product; there are additional modules in LAN WorkGroup that help administrators better and more easily manage their TCP/IP environments. These features are discussed later, in the section "Features of LAN WorkGroup 5."

LAN WorkPlace started as TCP/IP for PCs, which allowed PCs to emulate Unix terminals (DEC VT100s) so that they could communicate with TCP/IP hosts. A Macintosh version, LAN WorkPlace for Macintosh, was introduced later (as well as an OS/2 version). The main thrust of LAN WorkPlace, however, has always been on the PC.

The initial LAN WorkPlace code was implemented in conjunction with Excelan's own proprietary Ethernet card, which has an on-board coprocessor. Most of the LAN WorkPlace code was loaded and executed on this coprocessor. Although an expensive way (use of an intelligent network card) to provide TCP/IP support, this method provided a couple of important functions, as follows:

- To minimize the use of memory on the host PC (because memory management techniques and software weren't readily available until the early 1990s).
- It was the only way at the time (the late 1980s) to support multiple protocols (TCP/IP and IPX/SPX) on the same client.

When Novell acquired Excelan, most of the hardware lines were gradually sold off—including the intelligent Ethernet cards. Around the same time, however, Novell began development of the Open Data Link Interface (ODI) drivers, which made it possible for a client to support multiple protocols without the use of intelligent network cards.

Today, LAN WorkPlace and LAN WorkGroup work with any network adapter that has a certified ODI driver. This means LAN WorkPlace and LAN WorkGroup support Ethernet, Token Ring, and ARCnet, as well as FDDI.

Features of LAN WorkPlace 5

Novell shipped LAN WorkPlace for MS Windows and DOS version 5 in May, 1995. The following is a breakdown of its features:

- **Netscape Navigator.** An Internet browser and newsreader that enables users to retrieve information and communicate on the Internet. Users get point-and-click access to text, graphics, sound, and video files on the World Wide Web (WWW).
- **Windows-based Mailer.** Provides an interface for sending and receiving messages and files over TCP/IP networks, including the Internet; supports Simple Mail Transfer Protocol (SMTP) and the Post Office Protocol version 3 (POP3).
- **X-Server.** Enables users to run X Windows-based applications on remote hosts (over IP and IPX) from their desktop.
- **Windows-based Line Printer Daemon (LPD) and Line Printer Remote (LPR) print drivers.** Lets Windows and Unix systems share printers.
- **WinSock compliance.** Now all LAN WorkPlace Windows applications can be run on any WinSock-compliant TCP/IP stack. Similarly, any other WinSock-compliant application can be run on Novell's client TCP/IP stack, which is included along with the NetWare client for DOS and Windows (starting with v1.2 of the Client kit).
- **Graphical installation and configuration.** Enables users to easily install or reconfigure all LAN WorkPlace components, including the NetWare client and TCP/IP protocols, through a single interface.
- **Electronic documentation.** Online manuals, in DynaText format, provide help for quick answers.
- **Improved Windows TN3270 terminal emulator.** Gives Windows users easy access to mainframe resources.
- **Improved terminal emulation using Telnet.** Host Presenter now provides drag-and-drop keyboard remapping, enabling keystroke sequences to be simplified.
- **Integrated NFS client.** Gives users transparent access to files on any host supporting the Network File System (NFS). (NFS is covered in detail in Chapter 11, "Internetworking with NetWare NFS.")
- **Integrated Windows Dialer.** Provides remote users with on-demand dial-in over standard phone lines using Point-to-Point Protocol (PPP) or Serial Line Internet Protocol (SLIP).

Other than the above (which are all Windows-oriented), DOS versions of the higher-level TCP/IP protocol applications are also available. Examples of such protocols are TNVT220 for Telnet access and FTP and TFTP for file transfer.

Network administrators face two major issues on a constant basis. One is keeping application suites up to date. Because LAN WorkPlace is meant to be installed on individual workstations, keeping the software up to date can be a real chore—especially if the workstations are spread out over a number of geographic locations, or even on notebook and laptop computers. The second problem is the assignment and management of IP addresses in a TCP/IP environment. These two issues are addressed by the LAN WorkGroup product, as discussed in the following section.

Features of LAN WorkGroup 5

Novell began shipping version 5 of LAN WorkGroup for MS Windows and DOS in December, 1995. LAN WorkGroup 5 contains the same product feature set as LAN WorkPlace 5, but with the several additional NetWare server-based functionalities.

The server-based installation of LAN WorkGroup 5 means the application suite is installed once at the NetWare server. This lets network administrators manage the application suite from a central location, and makes it easier to keep applications up to date. LAN WorkGroup 5 eliminates the need for the administrator to update all network clients for installation and configuration.

The server-based installation also lets administrators have better control over which users will have access to the LAN WorkGroup applications (through NetWare file system security). This lets the administrator control software licensing issues.

LAN WorkGroup 5's central TCP/IP address assignment and administration capability means reduction in the time spent on (and cost of) system administration. By setting up the NetWare server as a BOOTP server, administrators can assign and administer IP addresses and other associated IP-related assignments (such as default routers) from a single location.

In summary, the two major differences between LAN WorkPlace 5 and LAN WorkGroup 5 are as follows:

- LAN WorkGroup 5 is a server-based installation, allowing all applications to be located on a NetWare server; LAN WorkPlace 5 is workstation-based.
- LAN WorkGroup 5 comes with a set of NetWare NLMs that allow central assignment and management of IP addresses via the BOOTP protocol.

Because of the NetWare server requirement of LAN WorkGroup 5, it can't be used in a non-NetWare environment. LAN WorkPlace 5 makes no assumption of the NetWare requirement, however, and can be used in a pure TCP/IP environment.

The following section details the procedures for installing LAN WorkPlace 5 and LAN WorkGroup 5.

Installing LAN WorkPlace 5 and LAN WorkGroup 5

The following sections walk you through installing and configuring the LAN WorkPlace 5 and LAN WorkGroup 5 products. Steps for Windows-based and DOS-based installation and configuration are provided.

Before installing the products, you should ensure you have the necessary computer hardware and software. It's also important you gather the information required to install and configure the products.

Hardware and Software Requirements

When installing LAN WorkPlace 5, make sure you have these minimum hardware and software requirements:

- The client workstation should be a 386-class or higher CPU.
- At least 4 MB RAM (to support MS Windows).
- Sufficient disk space to install the product. The exact amount of disk space required depends on the product components you select during installation. The installation program calculates and displays the amount of disk space required and shows you whether sufficient disk space is available (see fig. 8.1).

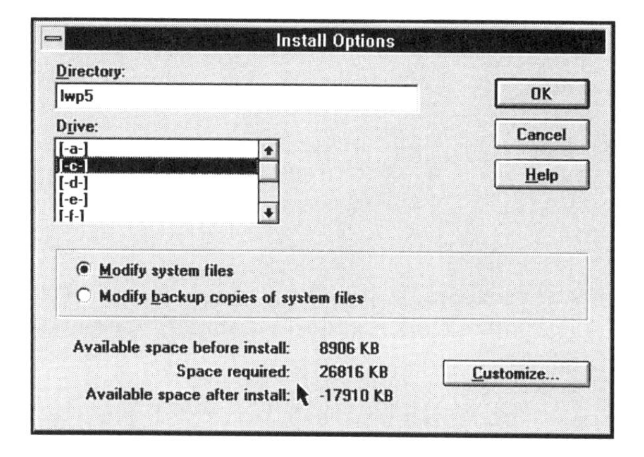

Figure 8.1

LAN WorkPlace 5's installation program determines the amount of disk space required and available.

- A full installation requires about 43.5 MB of disk space, which includes the DynaText online documentation. A partial (or custom) installation requires less space.
- At least 400 KB of uncompressed disk space for the installation program to use as temporary work space.
- VGA or higher display.
- CD-ROM drive or a 3.5-inch high density (1.44 MB) floppy drive for product installation. LAN WorkPlace 5 ships on 19 3.5-inch disks as well as on CD; LAN WorkGroup ships on 37 3.5-inch disks as well as CD. Installation is much faster via CD-ROM; a dual-speed or faster CD-ROM drive is recommended.
- An appropriate network card for the workstation, with a certified ODI driver. If you want to use the serial network connection features (such as PPP), you also need a modem. Most popular modem brands and models are compatible with LAN WorkPlace 5 and LAN WorkGroup 5. If you plan to access the Internet on a regular basis, modem speed of at least 14.4 Kbps is recommended.
- MS-DOS 3.3 or higher, DR DOS 6.0 or higher, or Novell DOS 7.0 or higher for the operating system.

- The workstation must be running MS Windows 3.1, or higher, in Enhanced mode—if you want to use the Windows applications from the LAN WorkPlace/LAN WorkGroup suite.

Note Although LAN WorkPlace 5 and LAN WorkGroup 5 aren't certified for Windows 95 or NT, Windows 95 does include its own TCP/IP stack and WinSock driver, letting you use Windows applications—such as Host Presenter—on Windows 95 machines. Novell will be releasing an update to LAN WorkPlace 5/LAN WorkGroup 5 in the near future for Windows 95 compatibility.

Installation for LAN WorkGroup 5 calls for similar hardware and software requirements, but with the disk space requirement from the NetWare server rather than from the client workstations. The NetWare server requirements for LAN WorkGroup 5 include the following:

- The NetWare server be running NetWare 3, version 3.12 or higher, or NetWare 4, version 4.1 or higher.

Note Although NetWare 3.11 is not officially supported by LAN WorkGroup 5, if your NetWare 3.11 server has all the latest NetWare updates, LAN WorkGroup 5 works fine.

- LAN WorkGroup 5 software needs about 70 MB of disk space on the NetWare server. If you choose not to install the online DynaText documentation, you only need to have 50 MB of disk space available.

The products come with a Configuration Workbook, which is a set of forms that helps you gather the information you need to install and configure LAN WorkPlace and LAN WorkGroup.

Tip The Configuration Workbook serves as a useful reference, should you later need to reconfigure or reinstall the product. You should complete the forms in the Workbook for later reference.

LAN WorkPlace 5 and LAN WorkGroup 5 can be installed from floppy disks or via CD-ROM. The following discussion on installation procedures assumes you're using a CD-ROM–based installation.

Installation of LAN WorkPlace 5

With LAN WorkPlace 5, applications are installed onto the workstation's hard disk. The source of the files can be local to the workstation or from a NetWare server. No changes to the installation procedures are required for network installation.

Note If you have previous versions of LAN WorkPlace installed, LAN WorkPlace 5's installation program protects your current configuration files, such as the HOSTS file, scripts, and profiles, while it updates the rest of the product directories with new LAN WorkPlace files.

You can install LAN WorkPlace 5 from Windows or DOS; both procedures are discussed in the following sections.

Windows-Based Installation Procedure

The Windows-based LAN WorkPlace installation program is invoked by executing the INSTALL.EXE or the SETUP.EXE program by selecting File, Run from Windows' Program Manager. The opening screen is Install Options (refer to fig. 8.1). From this screen, you can configure the following:

- The name of the directory into which the LAN WorkPlace files will be copied. The default directory name is LWP5.
- The disk drive on which the product will be installed. The default is drive C.
- If the install program is to modify system files (such as AUTOEXEC.BAT) for you. This is the default selection.
- Whether you want to do a Standard or Custom install. A Standard install copies all files (which amounts to about 43.5 MB of data). A Custom install lets you pick and choose the different product components to install. A Custom install is desirable if you have limited disk space or only need a subset of the applications. The default is Standard.

Note A Custom installation also lets you reinstall one or more components of the product, or install additional components at a later time.

To perform a Standard install, select the desired disk drive and directory name, then click on OK to proceed. To perform a Custom install, select the desired disk drive and directory name, then click on the Customize button. A screen similar to figure 8.2 appears.

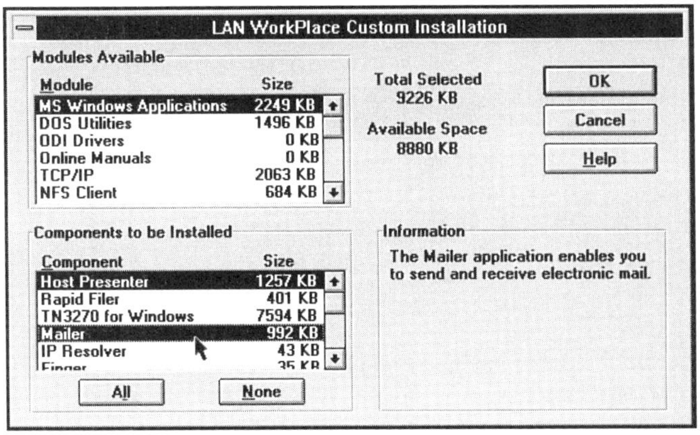

Figure 8.2

Selecting the product components to install.

From the Custom Installation screen, you can select which component of each module to install. To install only the Host Presenter and the Mailer components of the MS Windows Applications module, for example, follow these steps:

1. Click on MS Windows Applications to select the module.
2. Click on None (at the bottom of the screen) to deselect all components.
3. Click on the descriptions (in the lower window) to select the Host Presenter and the Mailer programs.

   Repeat the above steps for each module you want to customize.

4. Click on OK to return to the previous screen. Click on OK again (on the Install Options screen) to proceed with installation.

A status screen appears during the file copy process (see fig. 8.3). You can abort the install at any time by pressing F3 or by clicking on the Exit button on the lower right corner of the screen.

Figure 8.3

File copy status screen.

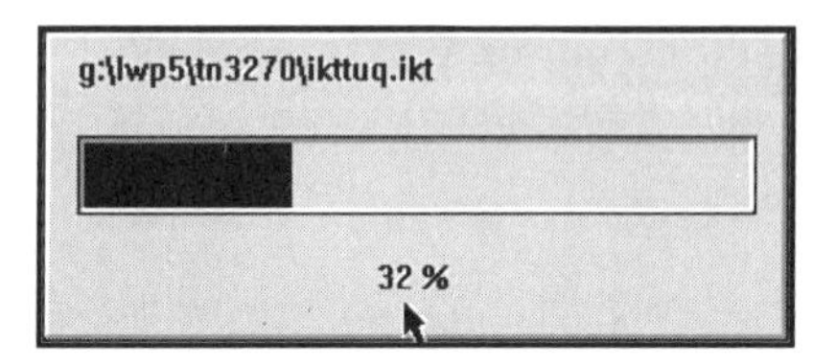

After the product files are copied, you're prompted to configure the product or exit Windows (see fig. 8.4). You must configure LAN WorkPlace before you can use most of its features. If you want to configure LAN WorkPlace or reconfigure LAN WorkPlace at a later time, you can use the Configuration program from the LAN WorkPlace DOS Utilities program group (see fig. 8.5) or from the LAN WorkPlace (where the Windows application icons are placed) program group.

Figure 8.4

You must configure LAN WorkPlace before you can use most of its features.

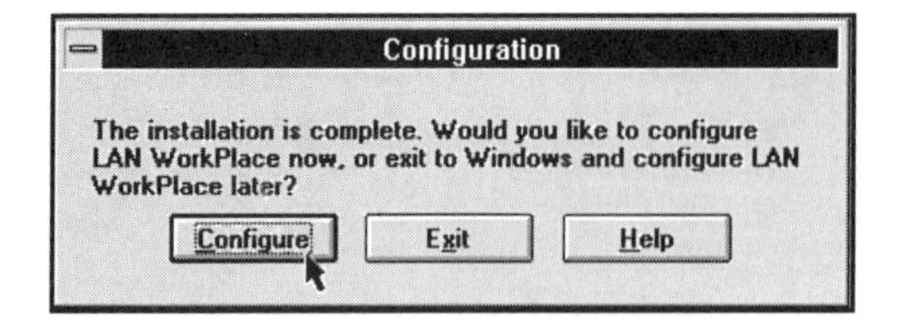

Stop

If you exit installation without running the configuration program, a message box asks you to exit Windows and reboot the workstation (see fig. 8.6). You *must* do so if you want to use any of the LAN WorkPlace applications without first running the configuration program.

The reboot is necessary for some more files to be copied (they couldn't be updated during the install process since they were in use).

If you're installing LAN WorkPlace files to a server, *do not* reboot the workstation right away. During the install, your workstation's AUTOEXEC.BAT is modified to execute a program called COPYACTV.EXE, which copies some files from the LAN WorkPlace 5 directory/disk drive (which is on your server) you selected during the install to your Windows directory and the final LAN WorkPlace 5 directory (which is also on your server). If you don't have the network drivers loaded before COPYACTV.EXE is executed, the update fails and results in an incomplete LAN WorkPlace installation. Examine and modify your AUTOEXEC.BAT as needed before rebooting.

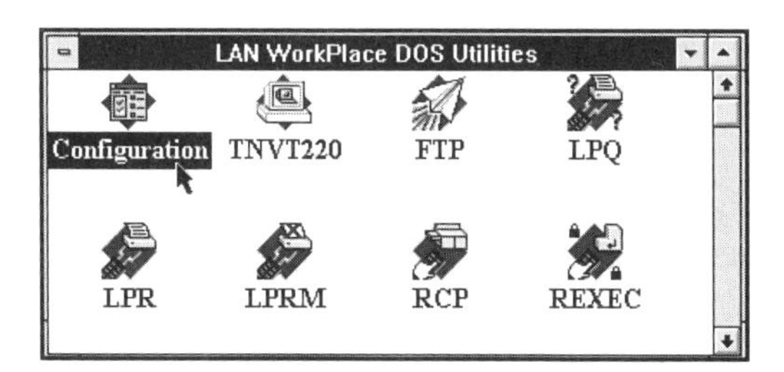

Figure 8.5

The LAN WorkPlace DOS Utilities program group.

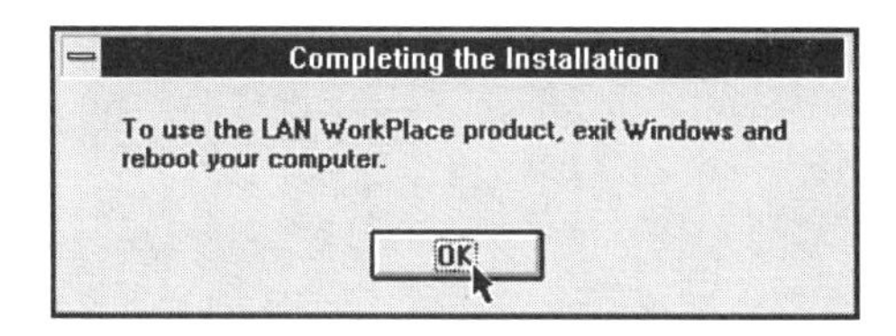

Figure 8.6

A reminder to reboot the workstation before using LAN WorkPlace 5 applications.

The configuration of LAN WorkPlace is discussed in the "Configuring LAN WorkPlace 5" section later in this chapter.

DOS-Based Installation Procedure

The DOS version of the LAN WorkPlace 5 installation program is invoked by running INSTALL.EXE or SETUPD.EXE at the DOS prompt. When the installation program starts, it displays the Install screen, as shown in figure 8.7.

Similar to the Windows version of the install program, you can select the following:

- Name of the directory into which the LAN WorkPlace files will be copied. The default directory name is LWP5.
- The disk drive where the product will be installed on. The default is drive C.

- If you want the install program to modify some system files (such as AUTOEXEC.BAT); this is the default selection.
- Select the modules (such as MS Windows Applications) to install.

The big difference between the DOS-based installation and the Windows-based installation is that the DOS version of the install program doesn't let you select which of the components within a module to install.

After the product files are copied, you're prompted to configure the product or exit to DOS. You must configure LAN WorkPlace before you can use most of its features. If you want to configure LAN WorkPlace or reconfigure LAN WorkPlace at a later time, you can use the Configuration program, LWPCFGD.EXE, located in the LWP's BIN directory.

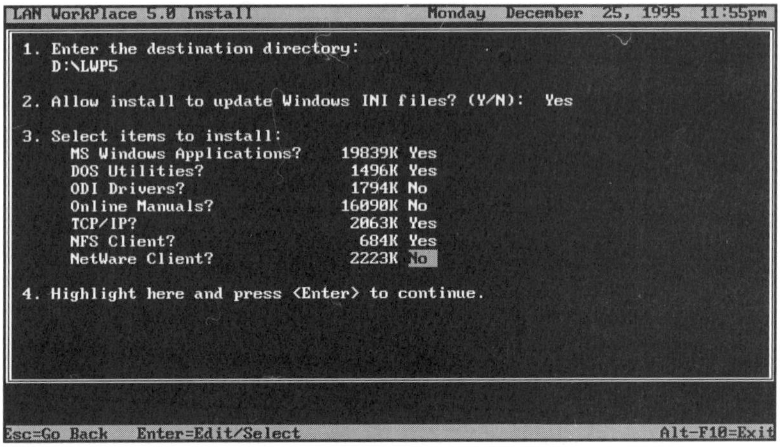

```
LAN WorkPlace 5.0 Install                      Monday  December  25, 1995  11:55pm

 1. Enter the destination directory:
    D:\LWP5

 2. Allow install to update Windows INI files? (Y/N):  Yes

 3. Select items to install:
       MS Windows Applications?     19839K Yes
       DOS Utilities?                1496K Yes
       ODI Drivers?                  1794K No
       Online Manuals?              16090K No
       TCP/IP?                       2063K Yes
       NFS Client?                    684K Yes
       NetWare Client?               2223K No

 4. Highlight here and press <Enter> to continue.

Esc=Go Back   Enter=Edit/Select                                        Alt-F10=Exit
```

Figure 8.7

The DOS version of the LAN WorkPlace 5 installation program.

Tip

If you need to revert back to your previous workstation and Windows configuration, a backup copy of AUTOEXEC.BAT, CONFIG.SYS, WIN.INI, SYSTEM.INI, PROGMAN.INI, and NET.CFG can be found in the LAN WorkPlace INSTALL directory. If you're reinstalling LAN WorkPlace, a backup copy of LWP.INI can also be found there.

Installation of LAN WorkGroup 5

Because LAN WorkGroup 5 is installed onto a NetWare server, the INSTALL.NLM is used to install the product. Here's the process:

1. Before you install LAN WorkGroup 5, ensure that TCP/IP is correctly configured on your server.
2. From the server console, type **LOAD INSTALL**.
3. Select Product Options from the INSTALL.NLM main screen.

4. Select Install a product not listed from Other Installation Options.
5. Press the F3 function key to specify the source of your LAN WorkGroup 5 files, if you're not installing from floppy disks using drive A. Specify the path where INSTALL can find the DISK1 directory of your LAN WorkGroup 5 files.

   You are prompted to select the volume onto which the LAN WorkGroup 5 files will be installed, and whether you want to install online documentation. Make sure you have at least 50 MB of free space for LAN WorkGroup 5 files, and about 70 MB if you plan to also install the online documentation.

Note If you're installing from a server-mounted LAN WorkGroup 5 CD-ROM, you'll also see a volume named LAN WorkGroup5 appear on the volume selection list. Don't select this volume; it's the CD-ROM volume.

6. The Installation Status Messages screen shows the file copy progress, as shown in figure 8.8. Unlike LAN WorkPlace 5, whose default top-level directory is LWP5, the LAN WorkGroup 5 files are installed into a NET directory, and subdirectories underneath it, starting from the root of the volume you've selected.
7. When the file-transfer process completes, the program displays a message indicating that the file transfer was successful. To continue, press Esc.
8. INSTALL then displays the RESOLV.CFG information form. If you don't have Domain Name System (DNS) information configured in the RESOLV.CFG file (located in SYS:ETC directory), the program prompts you to enter your domain name and name server address. If your network uses DNS, enter the appropriate responses and press Esc. If your network doesn't use DNS, leave this form blank and press Esc.
9. The next step is to create a group called LANWORKGROUP. To accomplish this, the INSTALL first prompts you to log in to NetWare Directory Services (NDS). Enter your NDS username and password. Then INSTALL prompts you to select the container in which to create the LANWORKGROUP group object. Select the appropriate container by typing an entry or by pressing Enter to use the browser. Press Esc to continue.
10. After the above is completed, INSTALL displays a message that tells you to reboot your server. Press Esc to continue.
11. Finally, you need to restart your server for the new changes to take effect.

The LAN WorkGroup 5 software is now installed and running. Before the software can be used, however, you must complete further configuration procedures outlined in the "Configuring LAN WorkPlace and LAN WorkGroup" section.

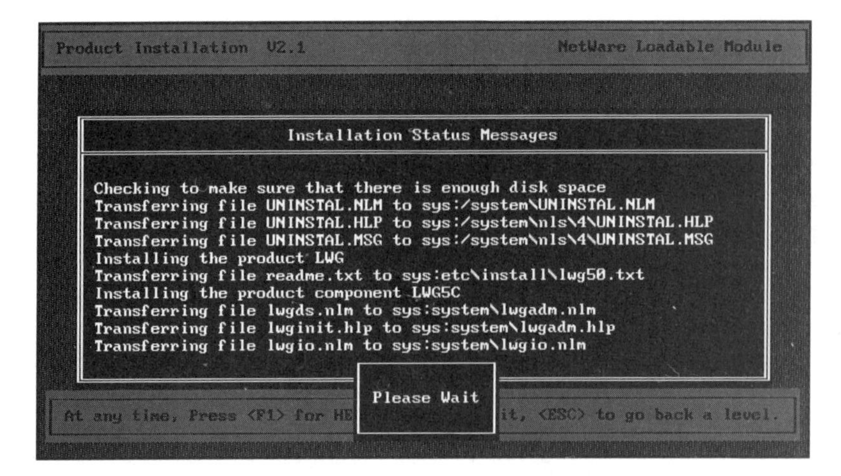
Product Installation V2.1
NetWare Loadable Module
Installation Status Messages
Checking to make sure that there is enough disk space
Transferring file UNINSTAL.NLM to sys:/system\UNINSTAL.NLM
Transferring file UNINSTAL.HLP to sys:/system\nls\4\UNINSTAL.HLP
Transferring file UNINSTAL.MSG to sys:/system\nls\4\UNINSTAL.MSG
Installing the product LWG
Transferring file readme.txt to sys:etc\install\lwg50.txt
Installing the product component LWG5C
Transferring file lwgds.nlm to sys:system\lwgadm.nlm
Transferring file lwginit.hlp to sys:system\lwgadm.hlp
Transferring file lwgio.nlm to sys:system\lwgio.nlm
Please Wait
At any time, Press <F1> for HE
it, <ESC> to go back a level.

Figure 8.8
The Installation Status Messages screen.

Note The one drawback of the LAN WorkGroup 5 installation process, as compared to LAN WorkPlace 5, is the lack of customization. You have to install all LAN WorkGroup application components.

Configuring LAN WorkPlace and LAN WorkGroup

The LAN WorkPlace configuration program takes information you provide about your network (such as IP address and subnet mask) and your workstation (such as ODI driver and frame type) and writes the data to the appropriate files (such as NET.CFG). Some information is required.

Note If you upgraded from a previous version of LAN WorkPlace, the existing configuration settings are automatically read by the configuration program.

To effectively use LAN WorkPlace and all the associated applications, the following information and applications need to be configured. Depending on your needs, some items must be configured; others are optional:

- Network card information (required)
- TCP/IP information (required)
- NetWare information (if you're IPX at the same time; optional)
- NetWare/IP information (if your servers are running NetWare/IP; optional)
- Hosts file information (optional)
- NFS Client information (optional)
- Link Support information (optional)

- Path information to tell LAN WorkPlace where to locate the various .INI and script files (required)
- Application information used by Talk, R-Utilities as well as X-Server font resolution (optional)
- Async dialer information (optional)
- Mailer information (optional)
- Netscape Navigator (optional)
- TN3270 session information (optional)
- BOOTP server information (optional)

These configuration topics, along with some tips, are discussed in the following sections.

Configuring LAN WorkPlace 5

The first nine configuration topics are handled by the LAN WorkPlace configuration program. You can use the Windows (LWPCFG.EXE) or DOS version (LWPCFGD.EXE). Because the interface between the two versions is similar, only the Windows version will be discussed here. Figure 8.9 shows the opening screen of the LWPCFG.EXE program.

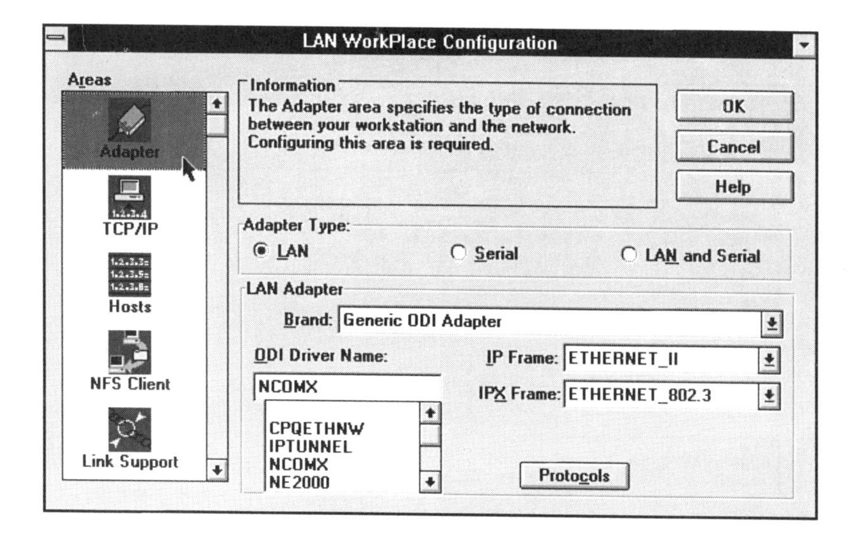

Figure 8.9

The Windows-based LAN WorkPlace 5 configuration program.

By selecting the icon along the left-hand side of the screen (titled Areas), you can configure the first nine configuration topics, ranging from Adapter to NetWare to Applications.

Note If you previously gathered the various network and TCP/IP information and recorded it in the Configuration Workbook shipped with your copy of LAN WorkPlace 5, configuring LAN WorkPlace 5 should take you less than 15 minutes.

Because each of the configuration options is self-explanatory and well documented with extensive online help, a detailed description of each is not covered here. Figures 8.10 and 8.11, for example, show the configuration of the TCP/IP information area.

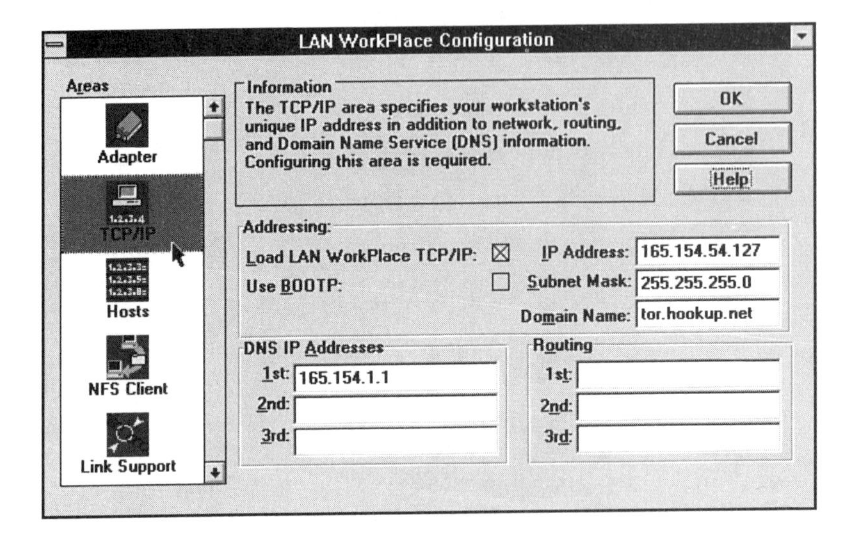

Figure 8.10

The TCP/IP configuration screen.

Configuration

File Edit Bookmark Help

Contents Search Back History Glossary << >>

Providing TCP/IP Information

Transfer the values from the TCP/IP section of your Configuration Workbook to the TCP/IP parameters (shown below). TCP/IP information includes IP address information for your workstation and may identify any name servers and routers with which your workstation communicates. LAN WorkPlace requires TCP/IP information to run.

To display the TCP/IP parameters, select the TCP/IP icon on the left side of the LAN WorkPlace Configuration window. For more information about a parameter, select the parameter from the example shown here.

Addressing:
Load LAN WorkPlace TCP/IP: IP Address:

Type the IP address written in your workbook here. If there is no IP address in your workbook, your network includes a BOOTP server. Make sure you check the Use BOOTP box.

DNS IP Addresses 1st: 2nd: 3rd:
Routing 1st: 2nd: 3rd:

Figure 8.11

Online help for the TCP/IP configuration screen.

The following is a sample NET.CFG file configured to support both for PPP using the Dialer and LAN TCP/IP connection:

```
Link Support
        Buffers        8    1500
        MemPool    4096
        Max Stacks 8
        Max Boards 8

Link Driver NCOMX
        INT        4
        PORT       3f8
        Frame      PPP

Link Driver CPQETHNW
        Frame Ethernet_II
        Frame Ethernet_SNAP
        Frame Ethernet_802.2
        Frame Ethernet_802.3
        Protocol IPX 0 Ethernet_802.3
        Protocol IP 0800 Ethernet_II
        Protocol ARP 0806 Ethernet_II
        Protocol RARP 8035 Ethernet_II

Protocol TCPIP
        PATH LANG_CFG    d:\lwp5\lang
        PATH SCRIPT      d:\lwp5\script
        PATH PROFILE     d:\lwp5\profile
        PATH LWP_CFG     d:\lwp5\hstacc
        PATH TCP_CFG     d:\lwp5\tcp

        TCP_SOCKETS      15
        UDP_SOCKETS      15

        ip_address       165.154.54.127  DialNet
        ip_netmask       255.255.255.0   DialNet
        ip_router        0.0.0.0         DialNet
        Bind NCOMX 1 PPP                 DialNet

        ip_address       123.0.0.13      LAN_CONNECTION
        ip_netmask       255.0.0.0       LAN_CONNECTION
        ip_router        123.0.0.1       LAN_CONNECTION
        Bind CPQETHNW 1 Ethernet_II      LAN_CONNECTION
```

If you set your IP_ADDRESS entry to 0.0.0.0 or omit it, the TCP/IP stack (TCPIP.EXE) tries to determine the IP address by first trying for a BOOTP server, then looking for a RARP (Reverse Address Resolution Protocol) server. If a RARP server doesn't respond, the workstation won't be assigned an IP address, and TCPIP.EXE fails to load.

Note The most recent version of TCPIP.EXE (including the version shipped with LAN WorkPlace 5 and LAN WorkGroup 5) does a duplicate-IP-address check when it loads. If TCPIP.EXE detects another device using the same IP address, it displays an error message and exits to DOS.

To use the Dialer for either PPP or SLIP connections, the NCOMX driver is used; previous versions of LAN WorkPlace and LAN WorkGroup used a driver called SLIP_PPP.

Note If you want to use a SLIP connection instead of PPP, the only change required in the NET.CFG is the BIND NCOMX statement in the Protocol TCPIP section—change PPP to SLIP. The frame type under the Link Driver NCOMX section should be left at PPP.

Generally, you only use one network at a time. There might be times, however, when you are connected to your local TCP/IP network and need to access a remote network via dial-up. The above sample NET.CFG helps you accomplish that. You need to pay attention to the order of the IP information in the Protocol TCPIP section; when you try to access an IP network that isn't local, the packets are routed through the first network specified in the Protocol TCPIP section. In the example above, if you try to access network 192.31.114.0, the packets are routed through the PPP connection (network 165.154.54.0) instead of the LAN connection.

The following drivers are needed to support the PPP or SLIP dial-up connection (note the recommended load order):

- **LSL.** The LSL driver is responsible for identifying the type of packet it receives and passing it to the appropriate protocol (TCP/IP in this case) stack for processing.
- **NESL.** The NESL driver is responsible for monitoring the connection status of the modem link. If you try to access the remote network and the link is down, NESL tries to reconnect.
- **NCOMX and NWREMOTE.** The NCOMX and NWREMOTE drivers make up the async COM port driver for serial communication.
- **TCPIP.** The TCPIP driver is the TCP/IP protocol stack.

Configuring the Dialer

The LAN WorkPlace Dialer enables you to connect to an Internet provider's dial-up port, or to another network, via either the PPP or SLIP connections. There are six configuration "pages" to the Dialer's configuration program (see figs. 8.12 and 8.13).

Figure 8.12

The LAN WorkPlace Dialer configuration program.

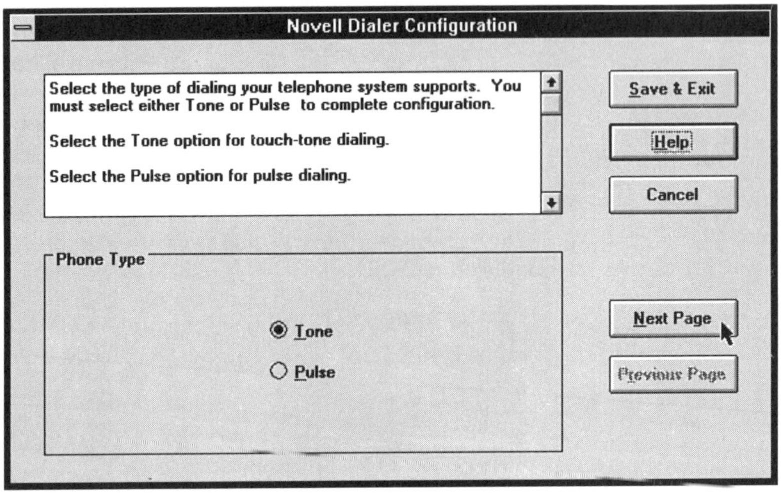

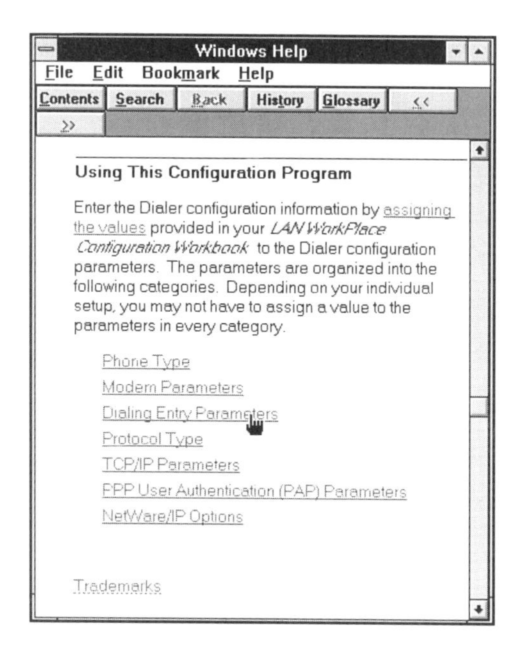

Figure 8.13

Online help for the LAN WorkPlace Dialer configuration program.

The first time you invoke the Dialer, the configuration program (DIALER_CFG.EXE) executes automatically. After that, you can change the parameters using the pull-down menu from the Dialer's screen (see fig. 8.14).

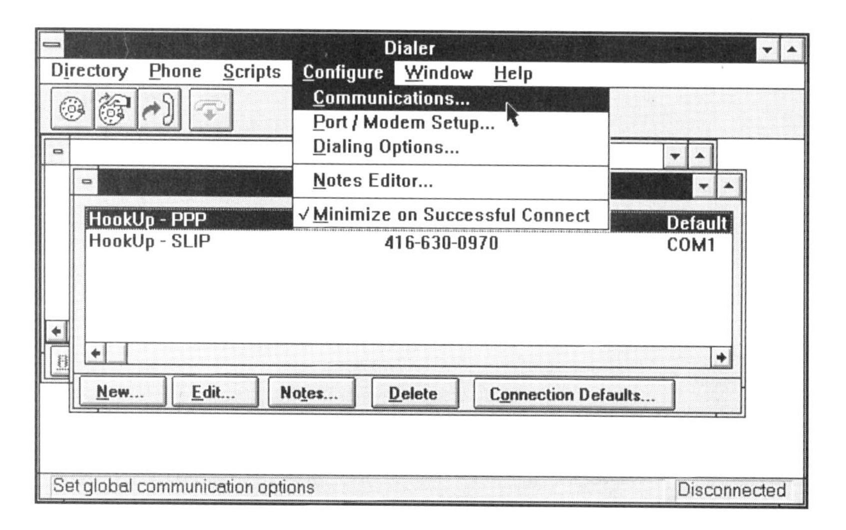

Figure 8.14

The LAN WorkPlace Dialer screen.

You can define a different Connection Directory entry for each remote network that you'll be dialing into. For example, you might have one entry for a PPP connection and another for a SLIP connection.

Other than the IP-specific settings, such as IP address, subnet mask, domain names, and so forth, you should be able to use the default settings of the Dialer to connect to your remote PPP and SLIP connections. Figures 8.15 through 8.18 show a sample Dialer configuration that can be used to connect to a local Internet Service Provider.

Figure 8.15

A sample Port Settings screen.

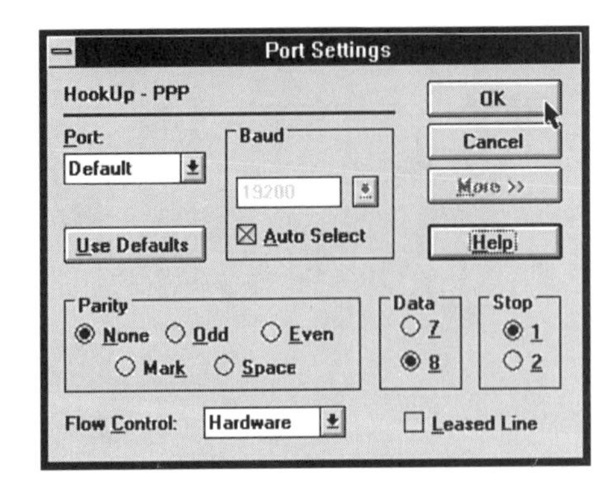

Figure 8.16

A sample PPP Network Settings screen.

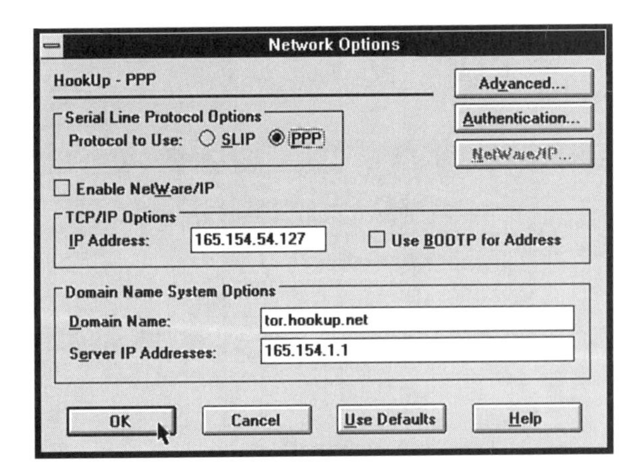

Note

If you're using BOOTP to obtain your IP address, make sure that on the Network Settings screen, you select the Use BOOTP for Address check box, and leave the IP Address box empty (see fig. 8.16). Also ensure that in your NET.CFG, the IP_ADDRESS field under the Protocol TCPIP section is set to 0.0.0.0 (for BOOTP) or omit the field entirely. Otherwise, you might encounter problems obtaining an IP address via BOOTP.

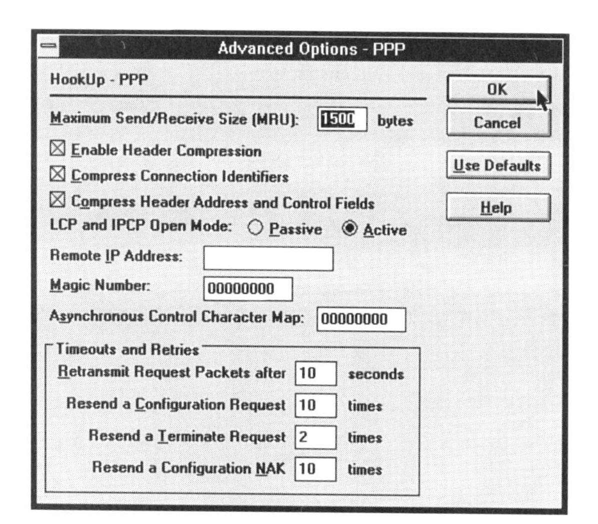

Figure 8.17

A sample Advanced PPP Settings screen.

Figure 8.18

A sample PPP Authentication Settings screen.

To activate a given connection, double-click the entry from the Connection Directory window. A Dialing window is displayed to show the status. When your network dial-in service answers the call, the Dialer switches to a Login window (see fig. 8.19) to let you complete the connection by interactively entering the login information.

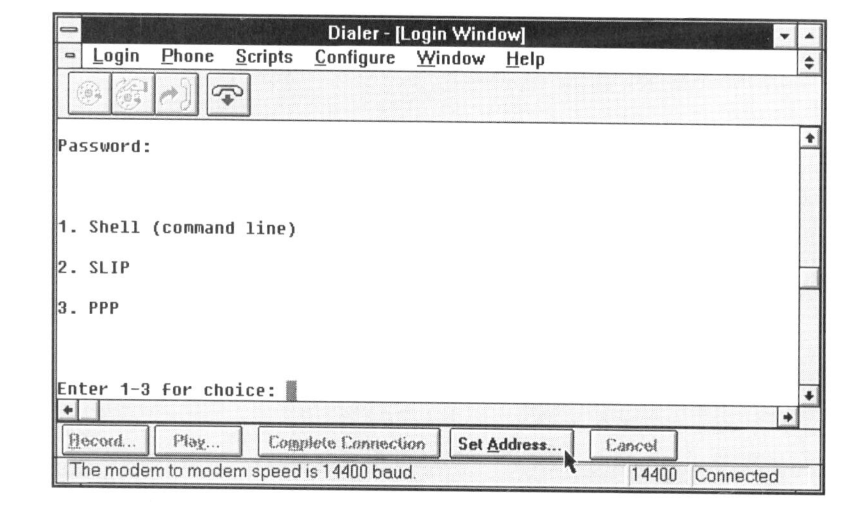

Figure 8.19

The Login window of the LAN WorkPlace Dialer.

You can automate your login process by playing back a script file. The easiest way to create this script is to turn on the record function (from the Login pull-down menu) while the Login window is active. You need to edit the recorded script file afterwards to remove unnecessary information, such as system messages and add-in commands such as WAITFOR (wait for message from remote) and WRITELINE (send output to remote).

Stop Because the script file also contains your login password, you should consider password-protecting the script.

The following is a sample login script file:

```
WAITFOR login:
WRITELINE your-username-goes-here
WAITFOR Password:
WRITELINE your-password-goes-here
WAITFOR Enter 1-3 for choice:
WRITELINE 3
HANDOFF
```

A useful configuration option in the Dialer is the idle timeout option. This lets the Dialer automatically disconnect the modem after a preset amount of time of inactivity on the modem. This is most useful in saving connection charges. The idle timeout setting is set by using the Communications command from the Configure pull-down menu on the Dialer's main screen (see fig. 8.20).

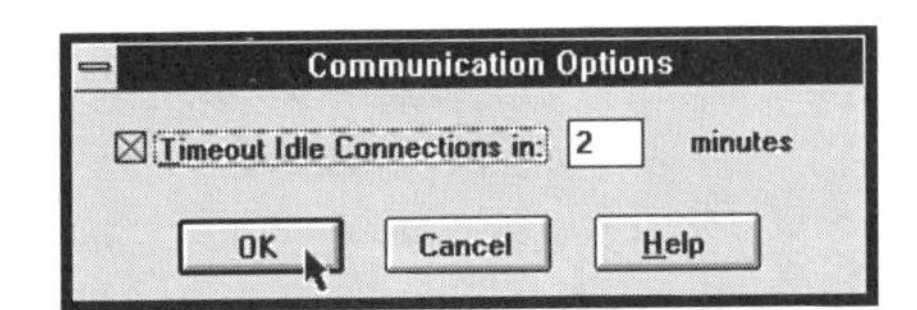

Figure 8.20
Setting the idle timeout value.

The Dialer includes an automatic connection capability (with the help of the NESL driver mentioned in the previous section). When you request a network resource from within a LAN WorkPlace application and a connection isn't already established, the application invokes the Dialer to open a connection for you. However, not all LAN WorkPlace 5 applications work with the automatic connection feature. The following applications support this feature:

- **Mailer**—when you send or check for incoming mail.
- **Rapid Filer**—when you ask to display the files of a remote file system.
- **Host Presenter**—when you try to log in to a remote host.
- **IP Resolver**—when you try to ping or resolve a hostname from the DNS server.

The following applications do *not* work with the automatic connection feature of the Dialer:

- Serving FTP (the FTP server software) doesn't bring up a connection automatically, since it's waiting for a connection and not initiating one.

- The Finger Daemon doesn't bring up a dial-up connection to make its information available to the network.
- When someone uses Talk to contact you, the dial-up connection won't be made since, again, you're not initiating the call. If you use Talk to contact others, however, you can connect automatically.

The automatic connection feature doesn't guarantee a connection 100 percent of the time. At times, the modem you are calling is busy, resulting in a failed connection. If the remote dial-in host is busy, the Dialer might timeout before a connection is made—again resulting in a failed connection. If your application cannot establish a connection on the first try, try again.

Configuring the Mailer

The Mailer is an e-mail application with special features for mobile users. You can read, compose, and prepare mail for delivery without being connected to your network. The first time you invoke the Mailer program, a screen similar to figure 8.21 is displayed for you to enter some configuration information.

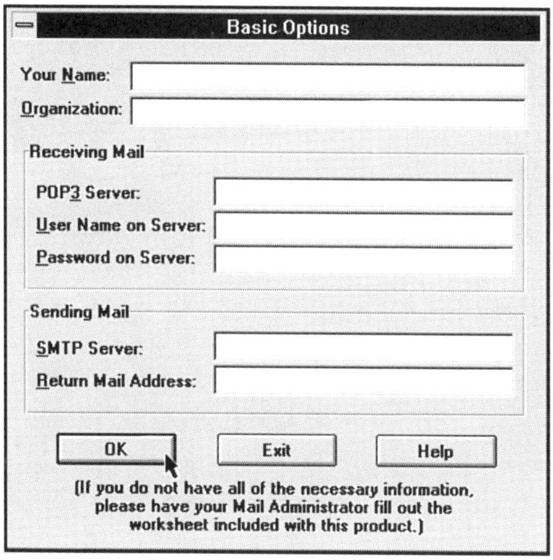

Figure 8.21

The Mailer configuration screen.

Depending on whether you are using POP3 or SMTP, up to seven pieces of configuration information are needed:

- **Your Name.** This is the name that will show up in the "From" area of a new message.
- **Organization.** This identifies your company.
- **POP3 Server.** This is the name of your POP3 mail server.
- **User Name on Server.** Enter your username on the POP3 mail server.
- **Password on Server.** Your POP3 mail server password.

- **SMTP Server.** The hostname of your SMTP mail server. For example, DreamLAN.COM.
- **Return Mail Address.** This identifies your return mail address, usually your username, an "@" sign, and your SMTP hostname. For example, Peter@DreamLAN.COM.

You can change any of these settings by selecting the Options pull-down menu, and then selecting the Basic option.

If you use the NetWare MHS transport for e-mail, you need to configure the MHS option. This is accessed by the seleting the MHS command from the Options pull-down menu (see fig. 8.22).

Figure 8.22

The MHS Options dialog box.

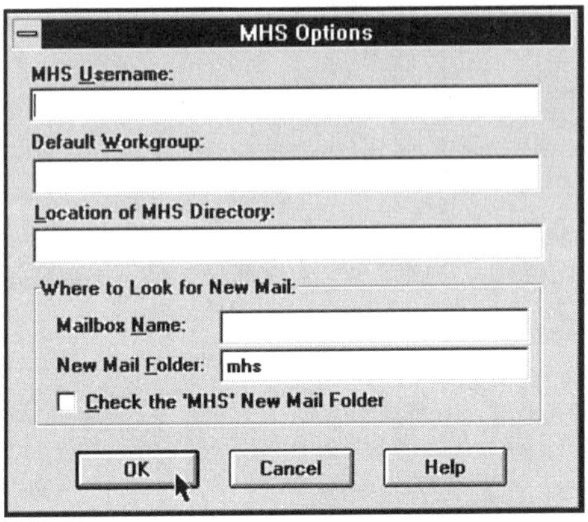

When you have incoming mail, it is first stored on your mail server. The Mailer later downloads your new messages to your workstation, using POP3. The default setting is such that the Mailer deletes each message from your mail server after copying it to your workstation. If you want to save your copies on the mail server, you need to change the Receive option, as follows:

1. Select the Receive option from the Options pull-down menu.
2. Deselect the Delete Messages on Server after Download check box (see fig. 8.23).

The Mailer operates in two modes: Deferred and Immediate. Deferred mode, the default, is designed for mobile users. In Deferred mode, you need to manually initiate sending and receiving mail messages (after you connect to your network). In Immediate mode, you can select how often the Mailer checks the mail server for new messages. (The default is every 10 minutes.) You can change it by using Receive Options, as discussed earlier in this chapter.

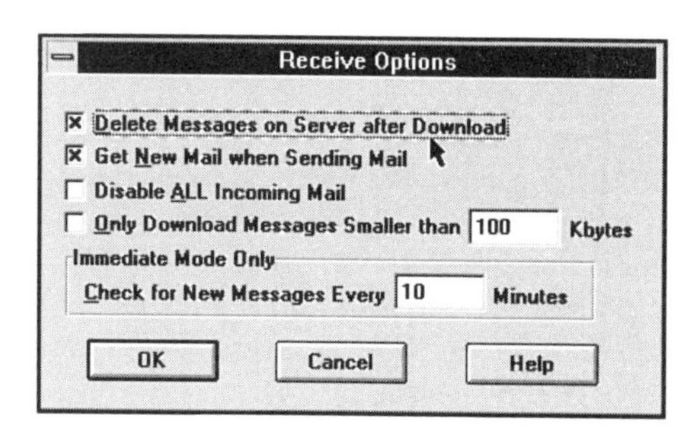

Figure 8.23

The Receive Options dialog box.

Note All outgoing (and incoming) messages are stored in the MAIL directory under the directory pointed to by the LWP_CFG path in your NET.CFG. For example, if your LWP_CFG points to D:\LWP5\HSTACC, the messages are stored in the D:\LWP5\HSTACC\MAIL directory.

You can easily switch the Mailer between Deferred and Immediate mode by selecting either the Deferred Mode option or the Immediate Mode option from the Options pull-down menu (see fig. 8.24).

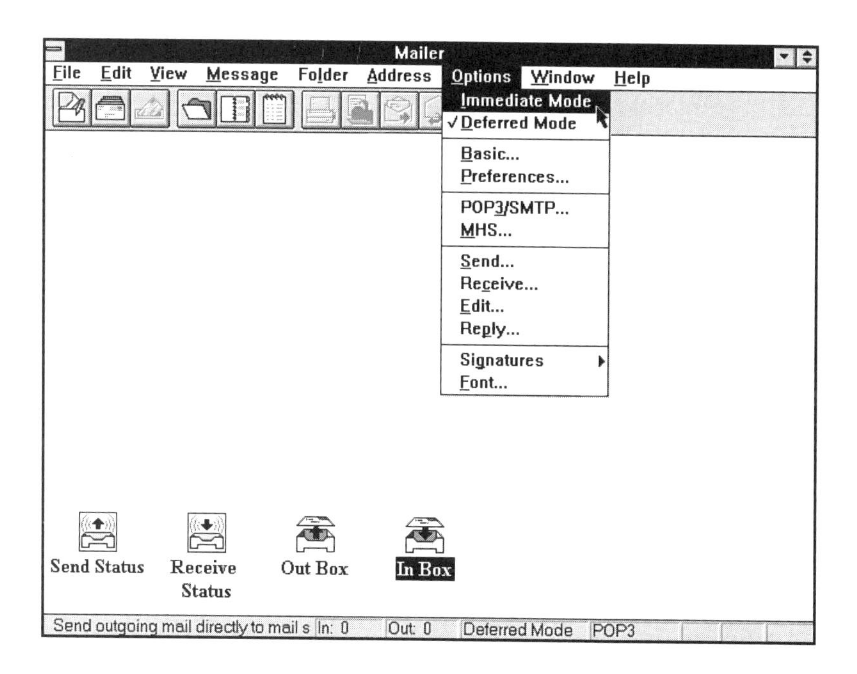

Figure 8.24

The Options pull-down menu.

Configuring Netscape Navigator

The Netscape Navigator, licensed by Novell from the Netscape Communications Corporation, comes with a number of default settings. You can use Netscape without much customization. If you want to Telnet to a remote host using Netscape, however, you need to inform Netscape of the name of your Telnet application. Because Netscape is a Windows application, the natural choice here is Host Presenter—it is a Windows application shipped as part of LAN WorkPlace/LAN WorkGroup. To configure Netscape, access the Options pull-down menu and select Preferences; a screen similar to figure 8.25 appears.

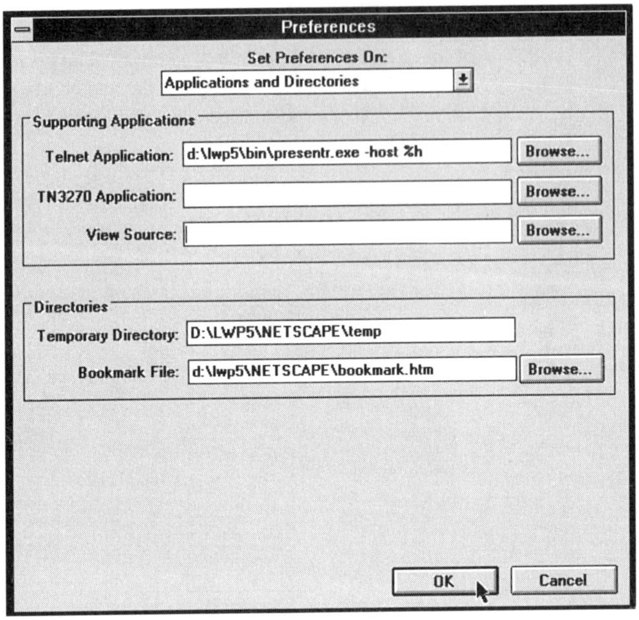

Figure 8.25

Netscape Navigator's Preferences screen.

If your screen isn't similar to that of figure 8.25, click on the down-arrow on the Set Preferences On field and select Applications and Directories.

You also need to tell Netscape where its temporary directory is and the location of its bookmark file.

From the Set Preferences On field, a total of eight (based on version 1.1NOV) different sets of preferences can be set. If you want to customize your color settings and character font displays, for example, you can use the Color and Fonts option to change them. In most parts, however, you can use the defaults.

Configuring TN3270 Sessions

Included with LAN WorkPlace 5 and LAN WorkGroup 5 is a TN3270 (3270 terminal emulation over TCP/IP using the Telnet protocol) emulator from Attachmate Corporation. In the 3270 mainframe world, you must define the session type (either a terminal or a printer session) before a connection to the mainframe can be made. The setup of TN3270 is accomplished using the TN3270 Configurator software (see fig. 8.26).

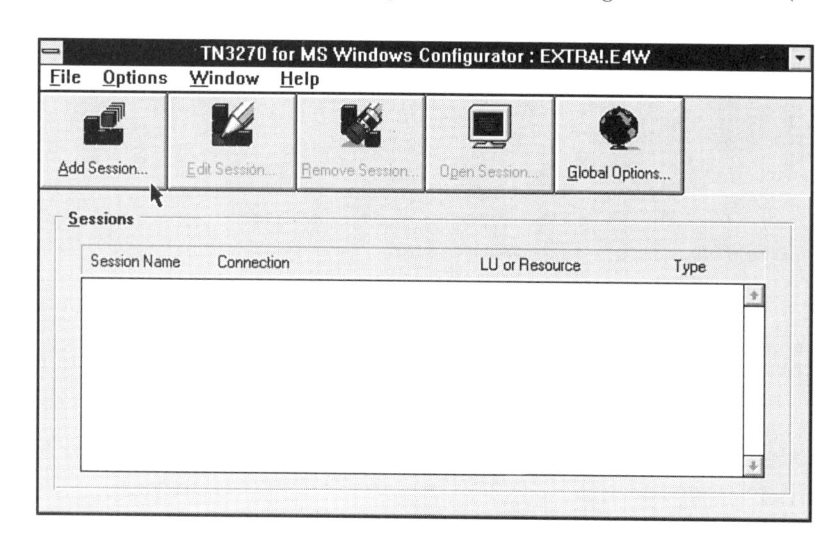

Figure 8.26
The TN3270 Configurator.

You can create a single new session by using the Add Session button from the Configurator menu or by using the Fast Configurations command from the Options pull-down menu to add a set of sessions at one time.

Here are a couple of configuration issues to be aware of. If you change a display or printer session configuration, and then start the same session using the one of the following procedures, your changes won't be reflected in the open session:

- Using Session Configurator, you edited a session, but did not save the changes.
- Using a display or printer session, you open the session that you just edited.

To avoid these problems, save the configuration before opening the session from the TN3270 for MS Windows program group. Or, simply open the edited session from the Session Configurator.

Note If you save a configuration but have an incorrect path in your WIN.INI file, the configuration appears to have been saved successfully, but actually is not saved.

Although not advisable because of performance issues, it is possible for you to run TN3270 under Windows Standard mode. To do this, you must manually install E4WTIMER.EXE (a standard mode device driver) by including it in your AUTOEXEC.BAT file and then rebooting. This driver allows your communications line to remain active when you shell out to DOS, or do task-switching with another DOS application.

The E4WTIMER.EXE driver remains in your workstation's memory even if you are not using TN3270. If you need to unload E4WTIMER.EXE to save memory, exit to DOS and type this command:

```
path\E4WTIMER /U
```

in which *path* is the path to the directory containing your TN3270 for MS Windows files.

You can obtain further configuration tips by using online Help.

Configuring LAN WorkGroup 5

You need to be aware of a number of planning issues when configuring LAN WorkGroup 5 services, including the following:

- Which users need to have access to LAN WorkGroup?
- Are these users on the same subnet?
- Are different workstation configurations being used throughout the network (Ethernet versus Token-Ring)?

During the LAN WorkGroup 5 installation, a NetWare group object called LANWORKGROUP is created. It's given file-system rights to the NET directory, where the LAN WorkGroup 5 applications and utilities are installed. For users who need access to LAN WorkGroup 5 applications, you need to make them members of LANWORKGROUP.

In almost all cases when LAN WorkGroup 5 is used, its BOOTP service is used to assign IP addresses to workstations. If you have multiple IP networks, you need to set up multiple subnet configurations for the BOOTP server to function correctly. The details are provided in the next section.

Last of all, certain configuration files, such as the Windows group files, need to be copied to user workstations. LAN WorkGroup 5 provides a WGSETUP utility to help you to perform that task. If you have different workstation configurations, you need to set up different "profiles." When you run the WGSETUP utility, you need to specify the correct workstation profile as the command-line parameter, so the proper NET.CFG section settings (such as the Link Driver) will be applied; if no command-line parameter is specified, the !Default profile is used. Furthermore, if your users have different application requirements (some need X-Server and some don't), you may need to plan more profiles.

Note Similar to LAN WorkPlace 5, a Configuration Workbook is also included to assist you in configuring LAN WorkGroup 5.

The workstation profiles are managed using the LWGCON.NLM utility. From the main menu of LWGCON, select Workstation Type. A default configuration (called !Default) is included with LAN WorkGroup 5. To modify an existing configuration, highlight the name and press Enter. To create a new one, press Insert. The following is a sample workstation profile setup:

```
-----------------------------------------------------------------------------
                          New Workstation
-----------------------------------------------------------------------------
Boot Drive:
Link Driver Setup:
   Name:
   Frame  Type For IP:
Optional Tuning Parameters:
   Buffer Size:                  1500
   Number of Buffers:            8
   Memory Pool Size:             4096
   Maximum Number of Boards      4
   Maximum Number of Stacks      4
Primary Terminal Emulation:
Xfonts:
Load LPR Print Client Driver:    No
NFS Client Configuration:        No
```

In the profile, you can do the following:

- Specify the drive letter that identifies the drive from which all workstations using this workstation type will boot. (Required)
- Select the proper ODI driver and its frame type(s). (Required)
- Change, if necessary for performance tuning reasons, the values for the buffer size, number of buffers, memory pool size, maximum number of boards, and maximum number of stacks.
- Select the primary emulation mode—async, NVT, and Telnet—for the Host Presenter application. (Required)
- Select the X-Server font resolution (75 or 100 dpi), if applicable.
- Install the LPR Print Client application.
- Install the NFS Client application.

After configuring the various workstation profiles, you also need to set up the global LAN WorkGroup options. From the LWGCON main menu, select the LAN WorkGroup Parameter option. On this form, specify the following:

- **Private Path.** This is the path and name of the directory where the workgroup users' personal configuration files are stored.
- **Shared Drive.** This is the drive letter to be mapped to the NetWare volume where the LAN WorkGroup applications and utilities are stored.
- **SYS Drive.** If the LAN WorkGroup software is installed on a volume other than SYS:, type the drive letter to be mapped to the SYS: volume on the LAN WorkGroup server.

Note If LAN WorkGroup is installed on the SYS: volume, the utility automatically displays the same drive letter as the one you entered in the Shared Drive field.

Finally, update your system login script so that users who are members of the LANWORKGROUP group receive the proper drive mappings when logging in to the server. For NetWare 3.1x servers, add the following to the system login script:

```
if member of "lanworkgroup" include sys:public\syslogin.lwg
```

For NetWare 4 servers, add the following to the container or profile login script:

```
if member of ".cn=lanworkgroup.ou=org_unit.o=org" include servername/
sys:public\dslogin.lwg
```

The login script file is not created until you configure the global LAN WorkGroup parameters using LWGCON, as discussed earlier in this section.

Configuring the NetWare Server as BOOTP Server

When a LAN WorkGroup client boots (assuming no IP address was configured in its NET.CFG), it broadcasts a BOOTP request for its IP address. When the BOOTP server receives the message, it checks its database to determine which configuration information to return. The BOOTP server then replies by sending a BOOTP reply message containing all TCP/IP configuration information required by the specific client that sent the request.

To configure the BOOTP service, perform these tasks:

1. If you have multiple subnets on your TCP/IP network, set up a subnetwork profile for each subnetwork using LAN WorkGroup services. Or, if your network doesn't use subnetting, set up a single subnetwork profile.
2. Set up a list of IP addresses that are to be assigned statically. This ensures a given workstation (based on the network card's hardware address) gets a specific IP address.
3. Set up a list of nodes that you don't want the BOOTP server to reply to.

These tasks are performed using the Subnet Profile option in the LWGCON.NLM utility. Figure 8.27 shows a sample subnet profile configuration.

The example shows that the Engineering subnet uses DNS, and the name servers are at IP addresses 123.45.6.77 and 123.45.6.88. The BOOTP server is to automatically assign all possible (legal) IP addresses to devices on this subnet on a first come, first served basis.

Note After the BOOTP server assigned an IP address to a device, the same device always gets the same IP address—until you reset the BOOTP database. This is a nice feature because it behaves as though you've manually assigned an IP address (at random) to each device. On the down side, when a device is moved from one subnet to another, you must clear that entry from the database. If you don't, the device won't be able to obtain an IP address from the BOOTP server, as it's now located on the wrong subnet. This causes some headaches for users of laptops and notebook computers.

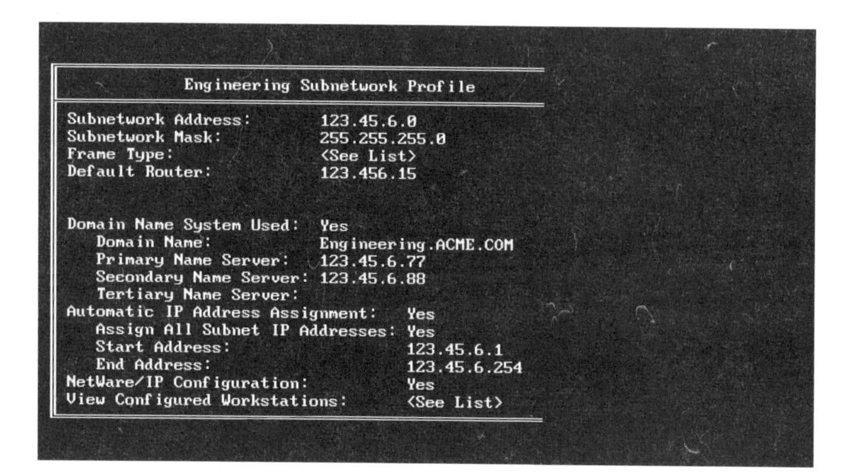

Figure 8.27

Sample subnet profile configuration.

If there are devices that you want to have a statistically assigned IP address (pre-determined address), you can use the IP Address Assignment option in LWGCON. You need to determine beforehand the hardware address of the device. If it's a workstation, you can log in to the server with it, then use USERLIST/A or NLIST USER/A to determine the hardware address. In the IP Address Assignment form, you enter a name (description), the desired IP address, the hardware address (physical address), and the name of the subnet profile it's to be associated with.

Tip The statistically assigned address is useful in pre-assigning devices, such as routers, hubs, and servers, and their IP addresses. This helps you have a numbering standard, and can help in troubleshooting.

A new feature introduced in LAN WorkGroup 5 is the capability to exclude certain devices from obtaining IP addresses from the BOOTP server. This is done using the Excluded Nodes option in LWGCON. Enter the hardware addresses of the devices you don't want to have an IP address assigned to by this BOOTP server. You can also use a wild card with the address' vendor code portion (the first six hex digits)—for example, 12:34:56:*.*.*. This prevents a particular vendor's hubs from obtaining IP addresses from this BOOTP server.

To activate the BOOTP server, at the NetWare server console, enter **LOAD BOOTPD**. You should include this LOAD command in the AUTOEXEC.NCF file.

Configuring NetWare Servers as BOOTP Forwarders

Although BOOTP is an effective method for sending TCP/IP configuration information to distributed client workstations from a central location, it has one major disadvantage. Because clients broadcast their BOOTP requests, the BOOTP server can only reply directly to workstations on the local subnetwork; the IP routers block all broadcast packets by default.

To extend the BOOTP service onto a different or remote subnetwork, you must set up a BOOTP forwarder. A BOOTP forwarder is a server or router that routes BOOTP requests (and replies between) the workstations on its local subnetwork and a BOOTP server on a remote subnetwork.

Note BOOTP requests can be forwarded across a maximum of five network hops (IP routers).

The BOOTP forwarder accepts BOOTP request broadcasts from workstations on its local subnetwork. In turn, the BOOTP forwarder generates a new BOOTP request on behalf of the client, which it sends directly to the remote BOOTP server. The BOOTP server determines the appropriate configuration information to return, based on the subnetwork on which the client resides. Then, the BOOTP server sends the BOOTP reply back to the BOOTP forwarder, and the forwarder sends the BOOTP reply on to the client.

Note A BOOTP forwarder can be an IP router, if it has that support. Most hardware-based routers, such as Cisco and Wellfleet, have that support. Depending on the vendor, this feature might be given a different name. For example, BOOTP Helper or Forwarder.

To set up a NetWare 3.1x server as a BOOTP Forwarder, you need to set it up as an IP router, and ensure BOOTPFWD.NLM and CSLSTUB.NLM are in its SYS:SYSTEM directory. You can find the necessary files (including updated TCPIP.NLM and SNMP.NLM) in the DISK1\SYSTEM\311 directory on your disk or CD-ROM. At the server console (or include the command in the AUTOEXEC.NCF file) enter the following:

```
LOAD BOOTPFWD -Fip_address
```

in which *ip_address* is the IP address of the BOOTP server.

Note When loading BOOTPFWD, you can also specify the -Q or -V parameter. The -Q option turns off the logging of error messages to SYS:ETC\BOOTP.LOG file. The -V (verbose) shows additional BOOTP transaction information to both the BOOTP screen and the log file.

Similarly, to set up a NetWare 4.1 server as a BOOTP Forwarder, load the BOOTPFWD.NLM with the appropriate parameter; the CSLSTUB.NLM is not required for NetWare 4.

Using LAN WorkPlace 5 and LAN WorkGroup 5

More than 50 applications and utilities are shipped with LAN WorkPlace 5 and LAN WorkGroup 5. It's not possible to cover every one here. The following are some of the most commonly used applications and utilities:

- Host Presenter and TNVT220
- Rapid Filer and FTP

- Mailer
- Netscape Navigator

Host Presenter and TNVT220

Novell provides two Telnet applications for users who need terminal-emulation access to remote TCP/IP hosts. The MS Windows version is called Host Presenter (PRESENTR.EXE); the DOS version is TNVT220.EXE. Host Presenter offers the following advantages over the DOS version:

- You can copy text between session windows.
- You can create profiles of TCP/IP hostnames and addresses and the terminal-emulation parameters for that host.
- You can cut-and-paste to facilitate repeating of commands on the host.

Both the MS Windows and DOS versions let you open multiple sessions with one or more hosts, print the data on the screen, and change text colors and display characteristics, such as tabs settings (see fig. 8.28).

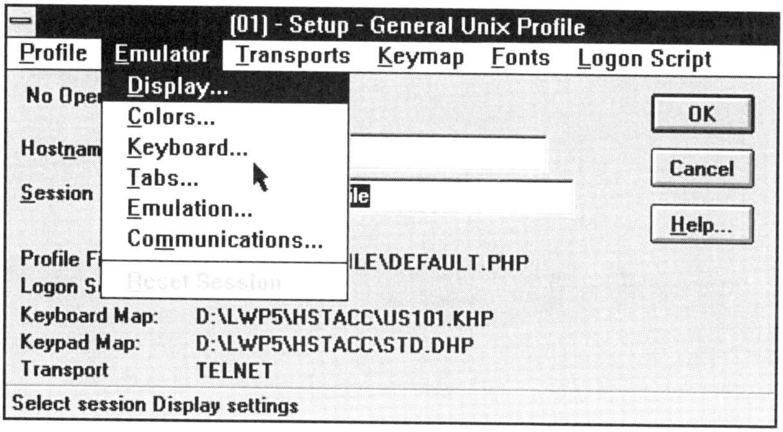

Figure 8.28

Configuring Host Presenter.

Figure 8.29 shows the configuration screen for TNVT220 (press Alt+S to activate). You can only bring up this screen under one condition: you must have established a Telnet connection.

Figure 8.30 shows the dialog box for opening a session with a host using Host Presenter. You can automate the connection process in two ways. First, you can create a profile for each of the hosts you'll be connecting to by specifying the IP address or hostname in the Hostname field (see fig. 8.31).

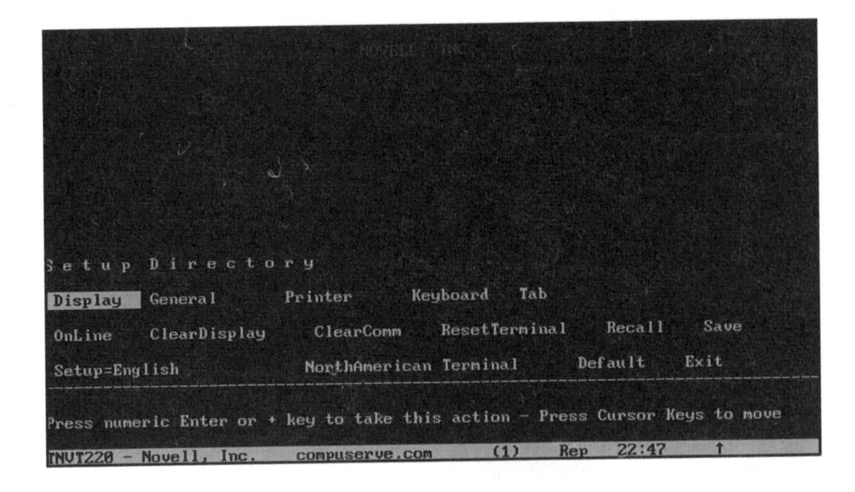

Figure 8.29
The TNVT220 configuration screen.

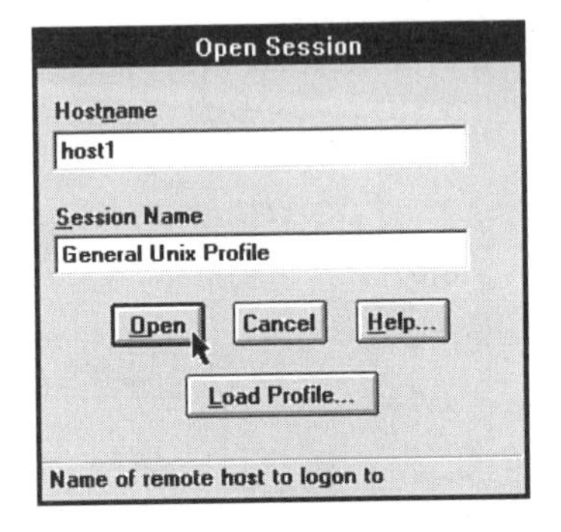

Figure 8.30
Host Presenter's Open Session dialog box.

Figure 8.31
Creating a Host Presenter profile.

You can also create a different Host Presenter icon for each host you'll be connecting to. The IP address, or the hostname of the remote host, can be specified on the Command Line property of the icon (see fig. 8.32). Therefore, the user will only have to double-click on the icon to activate the Telnet link to the host—without loading different profiles. You can also specify a profile using /PROFILE *profile name* as part of the command line.

You can initiate a Telnet connection using TNVT220 in two ways: TNVT220 *hostname*, or by using the OPEN command after you start TNVT220.

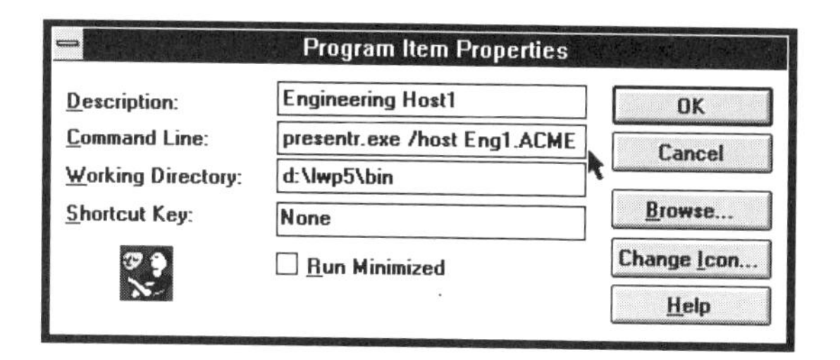

Figure 8.32

Use the /HOST option to automate a Host Presenter connection.

Rapid Filer and FTP

Other than remote terminal access to TCP/IP hosts, file transfer between hosts is probably the next most popular access method used on a TCP/IP network. FTP is the file transfer protocol of choice. LAN WorkPlace's and LAN WorkGroup's implementation is called Rapid Filer (RAPFILER.EXE) in MS Windows, and FTP.EXE under DOS. (Rapid Filer was known as File Express in earlier versions of LAN WorkPlace.)

Note Almost all TCP/IP packages have a command-line (DOS or otherwise) implementation of FTP called, appropriately enough, FTP. If you're not sure whether your system supports FTP, try entering FTP at the command prompt.

FTP is a secured file transfer protocol, meaning that you need to have a valid username and password on the remote host before you can perform any file-transfer functions. In many instances, however, an FTP server sets up a special username called "anonymous" and you can use any password with it. This is the equivalent of the GUEST userID on a NetWare server. In general, the anonymous user will have read-only access on the host and is restricted to a particular file system area for the purpose of downloading files. This is known as Anonymous FTP access.

Note The typical password for Anonymous FTP access is your e-mail address.

Rapid Filer is easy to use because you can drag-and-drop when copying files. Figure 8.33 shows the dialog box used by Rapid Filer to connect to a remote FTP server. You need to supply the IP address or the hostname of the FTP server, a valid username, and password.

Tip As you can with Host Presenter, you can also create profiles for Rapid Filer—one for each remote host you'll be accessing.

Figure 8.33

Connecting to a remote FTP server using Rapid Filer.

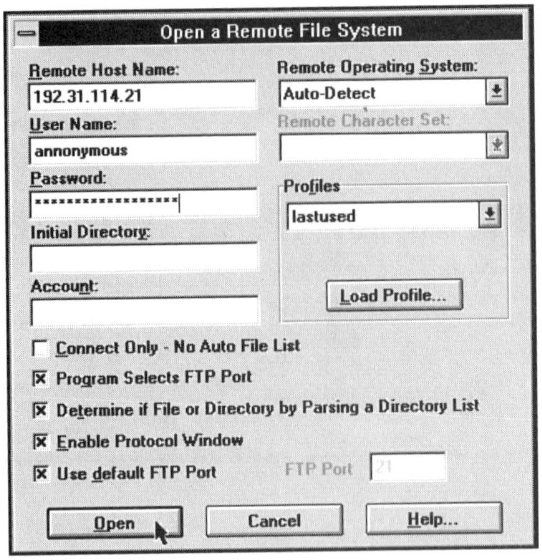

Rapid Filer displays your local file system on the top half of the screen and the remote file system on the lower half. To move files from one file system to another, select the desired files and "drag" them from one window to the other (see fig. 8.34). Rapid Filer has many features, including auto file type (ASCII or binary) detection and copy status screen, which aren't available in the DOS version. For example, Rapid Filer can auto-detect if a file is text or binary and set the transfer options automatically. In the DOS version, you need to manually specify the file type (see table 8.1) before files can be correctly transferred. The copy status screen is a pop-up window that shows you the number of bytes copied (see fig. 8.34).

Figure 8.34

Using drag-and-drop to copy a file to a remote host.

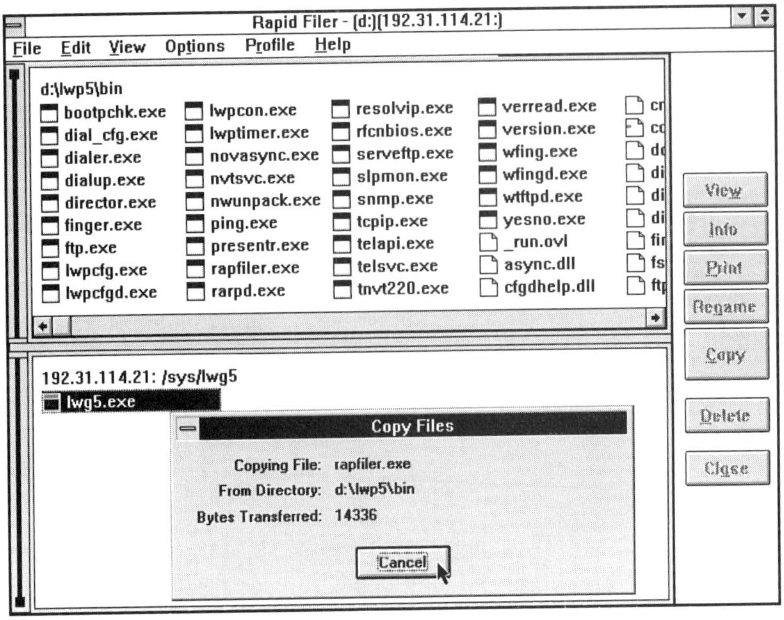

You can tune many of the parameters for Rapid Filer and other LAN WorkPlace/LAN WorkGroup Windows applications by editing the LWP.INI file. This file is copied to your MS Windows directory during installation.

There are more than 20 commands for FTP, most of which are straightforward. Normally, however, you use no more than 10 of them. Table 8.1 lists the most frequently used FTP commands.

TABLE 8.1 FREQUENTLY USED FTP COMMANDS

Command	Syntax	Description
ascii	ascii	Sets the type of file transfer to ASCII (text only)
binary	binary	Sets the type of file transfer to binary
bye	bye	Closes the FTP session and exits. Can use exit or quit.
cd	cd *directoryname*	Changes the remote working directory
get	get *filename*	Copies the file called *filename* from the remote host
hash	hash	Toggles the printing of a # character (hash mark) for each block of data transferred.
mget	mget *files*	Retrieves multiple files from host using wild cards. For example, mget *.dat will copy all files with the .dat file extension.
mput	mput *files*	Copies multiple files to the remote host using wild cards. For example, mput *.exe will copy all files with the .exe file extension from the local host to the remote host.
put	put *filename*	Copies the file named *filename* to the remote host

Typically, FTP displays the prompt `ftp>` to indicate that it is ready to accept commands. You can use Help or ? to get a list of supported commands from the application.

Figure 8.35 shows the commands (along with the replies from the FTP server) necessary to copy a file from the local host to a remote host using the DOS version of FTP. It's much more cumbersome than the drag-and-drop you can perform in MS Windows.

If you want to run FTP.EXE in an unattended mode, such as under a scheduler for periodic execution, you can create a script file with the appropriate commands and "pipe" it into FTP, as follows:

```
ftp -F -P -X < script.txt
```

The -F option tells FTP.EXE to try to determine the file type automatically if possible. Without it, FTP.EXE assumes all files to be ASCII (unless a "binary" command is issued). The -P option directs FTP.EXE to prompt for a password (if one isn't specified with the

USER command); the -X option tells FTP.EXE to exit if any command fails. The following is a sample script file that automates the file copy shown in figure 8.35:

```
open 192.31.114.21
user anonymous ********
dir
binary
hash
put d:\lwp5\bin\rapfiler.exe
exit
```

Figure 8.35

Using FTP.EXE to copy a binary file to a remote host.

```
C:\>ftp 192.31.114.21
FTP - Copyright (c) 1992-1995, Novell, Inc.

220 sjf-rsvp FTP server (NetWare v4.10) ready.
Remote User Name: annonymous
Remote Password:
ftp> dir
-rw-------  1        0        -2 29882163 Dec 04 11:09 lwg5.exe
ftp> binary
ftp> hash
Display # for each 1K bytes transfer.
ftp> put d:\lwp5\bin\rapfiler.exe
#############################################################################
####################################################
132512 bytes transmitted in 92 seconds (1440 bytes/s)
ftp> exit

C:\>
```

In the preceding example, the password (represented as "*") is purposely not shown. If you consider using a script file for automated FTP processing, give some thought to the security implications before you place the password into the script file.

You can automate some FTP procedures (if certain files are to be transferred on a constant basis) for your DOS users by using script files similar to the one listed above, by omitting the password field in the USER command, and by using the -P option to force the user to enter a password. Doing so provides automation while still maintaining security.

The following handy options are available in Rapid Filer (they are not available in FTP.EXE):

- **Copy Filenames to File.** There might be times that you need to get a record of the filenames on a remote host, but you don't have a printer handy. By first selecting the filenames of interest, you can then use the Copy Filenames to File command from the Edit pull-down menu to print the list of names to a file for later reference.
- **Search for File.** How often have you been given a filename to retrieve from an FTP server, but weren't provided the location of the directory in which the file is located? Using the Search for File option in Rapid Filer, you can easily locate the file (if it's in a directory you have rights to). This feature is similar to the Unix find command.

To search for one (or more) files using Rapid Filer, use this procedure:

1. Select the file system of interest by clicking the mouse cursor somewhere within the window that displays the file system.
2. Select File, Search.
3. Fill in the name of the file to search for in the Select Additional File box, and click the Add To Selection button. You can specify multiple files and use wild cards.
4. Fill in the starting directory for the search in the Start Search At box.
5. Click on the Search button to start the search process (see fig. 8.36).
6. After the file is found, all instances of it are listed in the Search Results dialog box (see fig. 8.37).
7. Highlight the desired file and click the Go To button. This makes the directory in which the file is found the current directory.

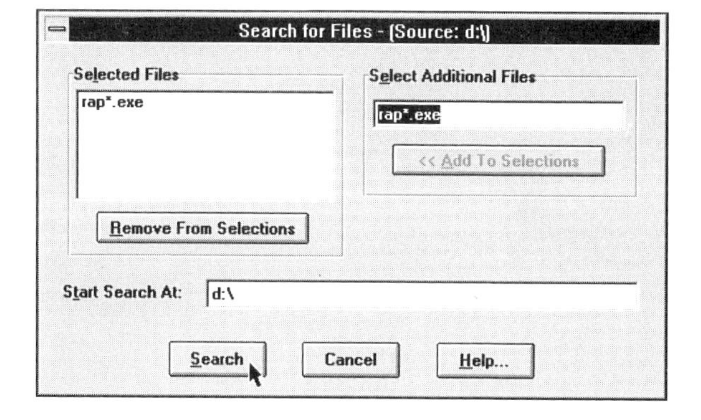

Figure 8.36

Searching for a file using Rapid Filer.

If your users are running MS Windows-capable machines, Rapid Filer is one sure way of forcing your users to learn about the cryptic Unix commands—and become productive in a short time.

Mailer

You can operate the Mailer in one of two modes: Deferred or Immediate. In Deferred mode, you read, compose, and prepare mail for delivery offline; you need to manually initiate the connection to your mail server to exchange mail messages. In Immediate mode, the Mailer connects to the mail server on a periodic basis to exchange mail (without your intervention). From a user's standpoint, using the Mailer in Deferred or Immediate mode is similar (except for the need to manually initiate the connection for mail exchange in the deferred mode). The discussion here will be mostly directed toward users of the Deferred mode—mobile users. Figure 8.38 shows how a typical mobile user processes mail.

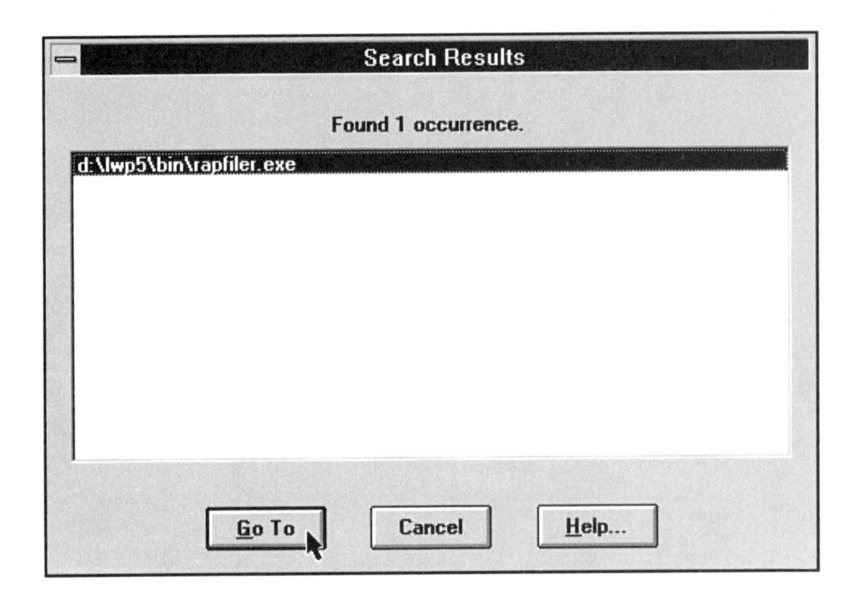

Figure 8.37

The Search Results dialog box.

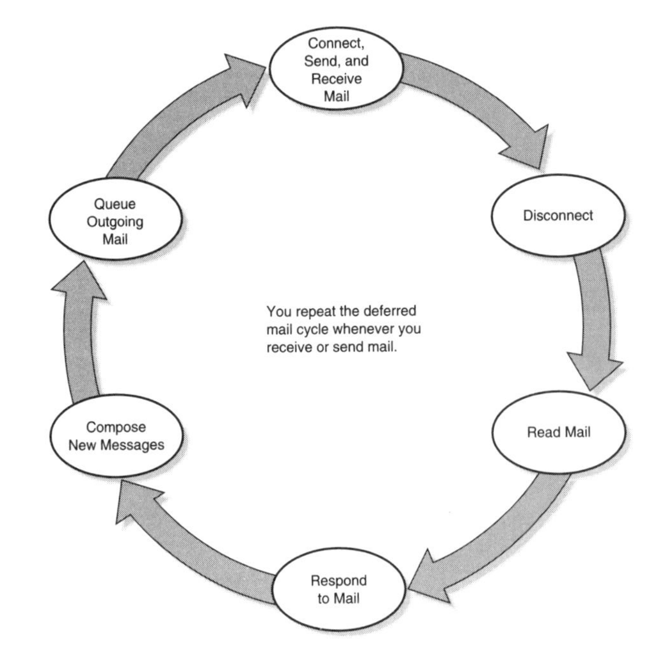

Figure 8.38

The deferred mail-processing cycle.

For a non-mobile user (for example, a user running Mailer in Immediate mode), the only deviation from the processing cycle is the connect and disconnect steps (see fig. 8.38); Mailer performes those steps automatically on preset time intervals.

When you start the Mailer, four status icons appear on the bottom of the Mailer window (see fig. 8.39).

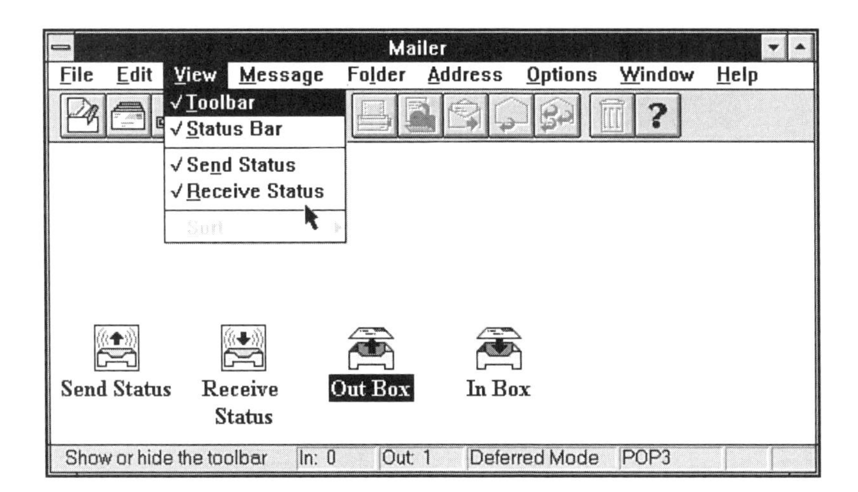

Figure 8.39

The Mailer main window showing the four status icons.

- **Send Status.** This displays the progress when you're sending outbound messages to your mail server (see fig. 8.40).
- **Receive Status.** This displays the progress when you're receiving new messages from your mail server (see fig. 8.41).
- **Out Box.** This displays any messages that are queued for sending (see fig. 8.42).
- **In Box.** This displays messages waiting to be read (see fig. 8.43). These message have already been downloaded to your workstation.

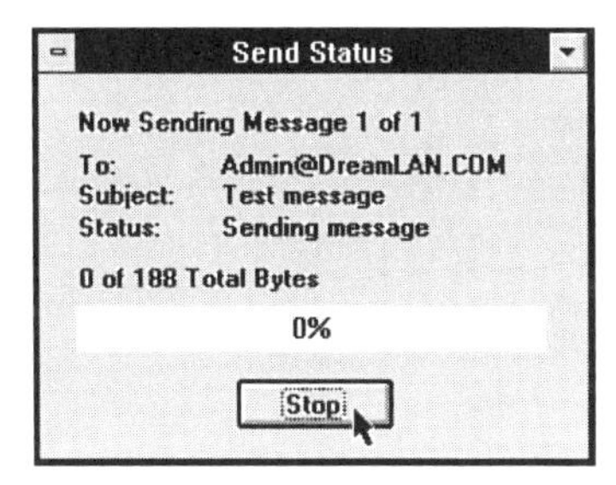

Figure 8.40

The Send Status screen.

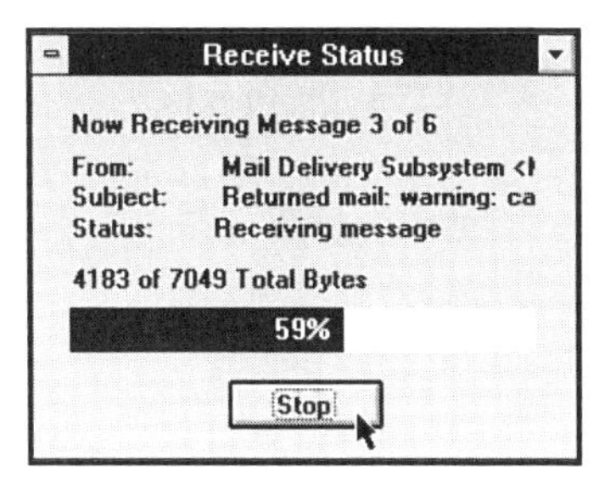

Figure 8.41

The Receive Status screen.

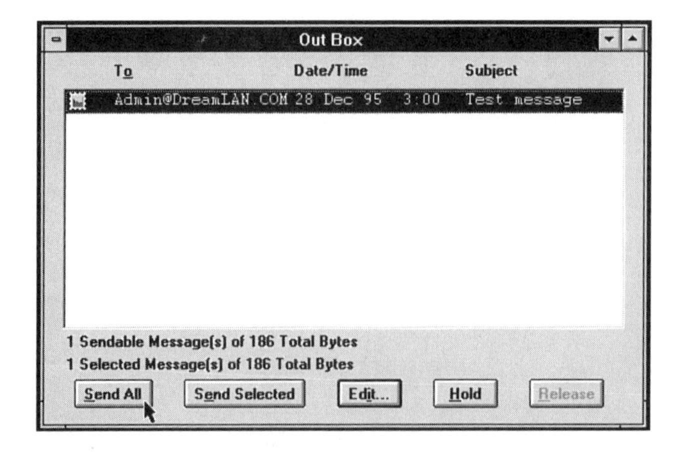

Figure 8.42

The Out Box screen.

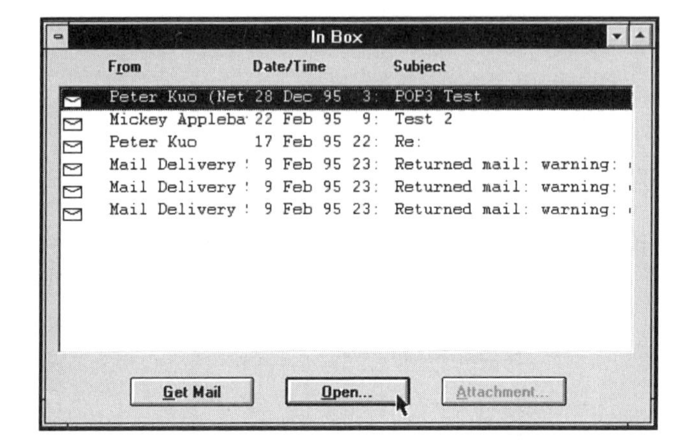

Figure 8.43

The In Box screen.

Tip

You can turn off the Send and Receive status icons by deselecting the Receive Status and Send Status options from the View menu (refer to fig. 8.40). (The default for both is ON.)

To read a message from your In Box, double-click on the message or highlight the message with a mouse click, then click on Open. The Next and Previous buttons enable you to move back-and-forth within the In Box without having to select the individual message (see fig. 8.44). If the message includes an attachment, the Attachment button is enabled (highlighted).

Each mail message has an icon or flag associated with it to indicate the status of the message.

- A *sealed envelope* means the message hasn't been opened.
- An *open envelope* indicates the message has been read.

- A *flag* means the message is urgent.
- A *paper clip* means the message has a file attachment.

You can use the Tools button to accomplish the same tasks. As you move the mouse cursor over each tool button, the bottom of the screen displays a one-line description of the button's function. When the mouse cursor is positioned over the left-most tool button, the description on the bottom of the screen indicates the button lets you compose a new message (see fig. 8.45).

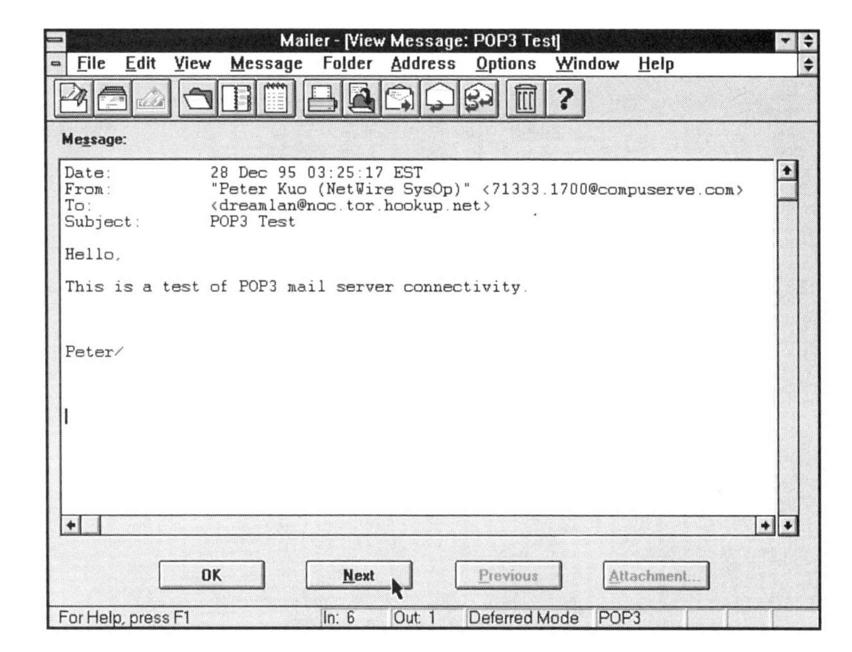

Figure 8.44

Reading incoming mail messages.

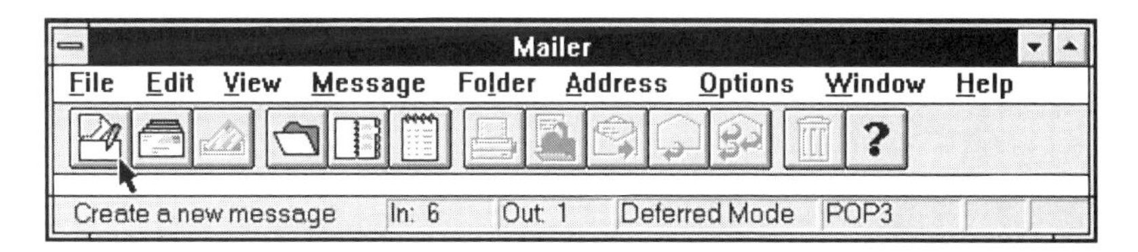

Figure 8.45

The Compose New Message tool button.

The rest of the user interface of the Mailer is very straightforward and doesn't require much discussion. You can also use the pull-down menu options to compose new messages, read new messages, and file messages from the In Box to folders for later retrieval.

Netscape Navigator

The version of Netscape Navigator that ships with LAN WorkPlace 5 is version 1.01, an out-dated version. Novell has released version 1.1NOV, which you can download free from

Novell's FTP sites (as well as CompuServe's NetWire forum. Do a search for the file LW50B1.EXE. LAN WorkGroup 5 ships with the updated Netscape version 1.1NOV.

Note You can always download the latest version of Netscape Navigator from Netscape Communications Corporation to work with LAN WorkPlace 5 and LAN WorkGroup 5. Your LAN WorkPlace 5 and LAN WorkGroup 5 license doesn't cover the versions from Netscape Communications, so you are responsible for the registration fee of these versions.

Netscape Navigator is easy to use, and its layout is intuitive. Figure 8.46 shows the opening screen of Netscape.

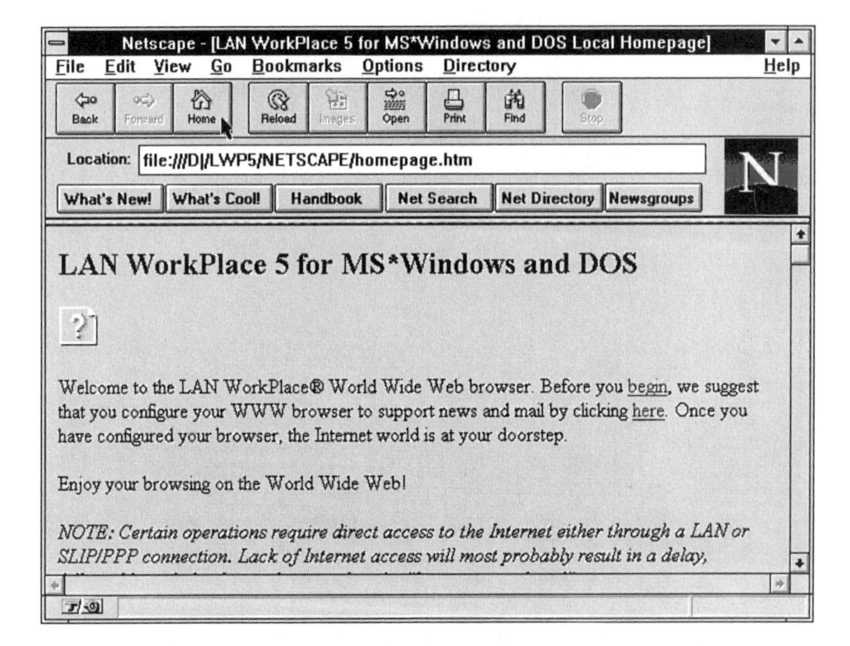

Figure 8.46

Netscape's opening screen.

A number of HTML pages are included with LAN WorkPlace 5 and LAN WorkGroup 5. They include information on general troubleshooting hints for LAN WorkPlace 5 and LAN WorkGroup 5, as well as a list of interesting Internet World Wide Web sites.

To attach to a specific Web site, you can use the Open button to specify the Uniform Resource Locator (URL; see fig. 8.47) in the form of

```
http://webserver_name.domain
```

For example, the URL for Novell's Web server is

```
http://www.novell.com
```

To access an FTP site from within Netscape, use the prefix of FTP instead of HTTP. For example, to access Novell's FTP server from within Netscape, use the following URL:

```
ftp://ftp.novell.com
```

To access a remote site via Telnet, use this syntax:

```
telnet://hostname.domain
```

Instead of using the Open button, you can edit the Location field at the top of the screen.

You can easily navigate an HTML page. In most cases, the hypertext links to other locations or pages are underlined and blue in color. When you move the mouse cursor over the hypertext link, the cursor changes into a hand, and the location name is shown at the bottom of the screen (fig. 8.48). After a link is accessed, the color changes from blue to another color, such as red or purple.

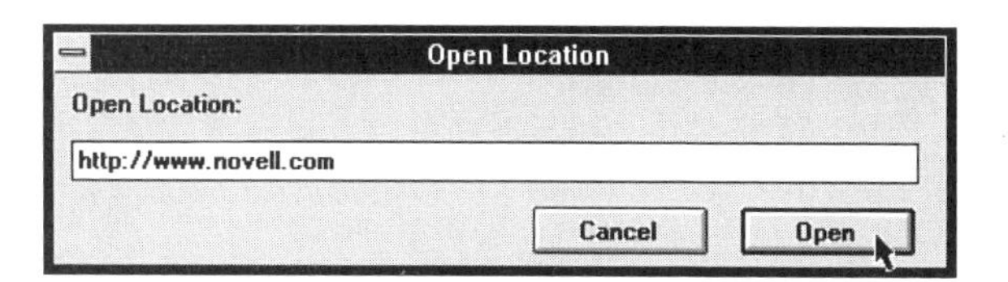

Figure 8.47

Accessing a Web site using the Open button.

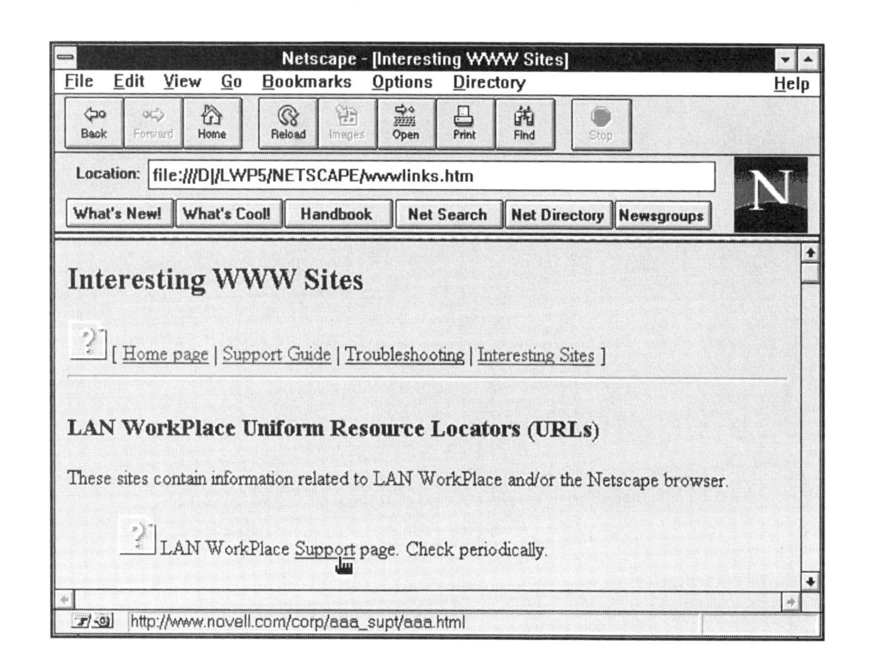

Figure 8.48

A sample hypertext link.

To go back to your previous link location, click on the Back button at the top-left of the screen. You can keep going back until you're back at your home page again. In the case of LAN WorkPlace 5 and LAN WorkGroup 5, the home page is an HTML file in your Netscape file directory.

If the network is slow, and you don't want to wait for the link to be established, you can click on the Stop sign button (top-right of the screen) to abort the connection.

If you come across a site of particular interest and you want to return to it later, you can "mark" it by using the Bookmarks menu. From the Bookmarks pull-down menu, select Add Bookmark (see fig. 8.49). To connect to it at a later time, select the name of the site from the bookmark list.

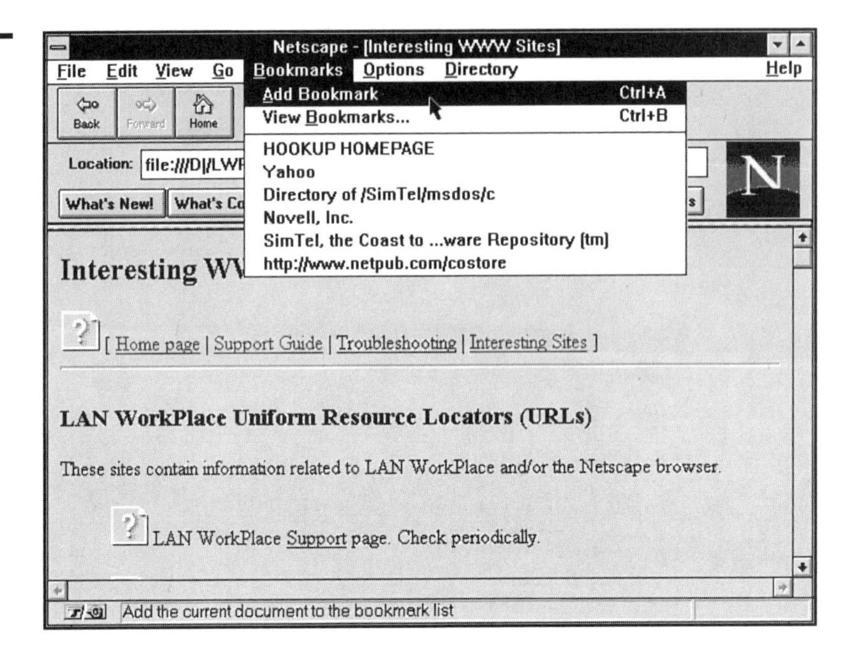

Figure 8.49

The Bookmarks option.

Summary

In this chapter, you received an overview on the product features of Novell's LAN WorkPlace 5 and LAN WorkGroup 5—along with a discussion of their differences. Also covered were these topics:

- Installation of LAN WorkPlace 5 and LAN WorkGroup 5.
- Configuration of LAN WorkPlace 5 and LAN WorkGroup 5.
- Configuration of the Dialer, Mailer, Netscape Navigator, TN3270 sessions.
- Setting up NetWare servers as BOOTP servers and as BOOTP Forwarders.
- Usage tips and tricks on Host Presenter, TNVT220, Rapid Filer, FTP, Mailer, and the Netscape Navigator.

Accessing Internet Services from a NetWare Environment

The Internet is the largest network in the world. Great interest in connecting to the Internet currently abounds, because the Internet offers a wide array of information services. Many organizations, such as Novell, Microsoft, DEC, and so on, have begun to offer their technical support services on information servers such as the World Wide Web (WWW) and Gopher servers.

This chapter discusses the different methods of gaining access to the Internet from a NetWare environment and from a mobile user environment.

What Is the Internet?

The Internet evolved from a network sponsored by the Department of Advanced Research and Project Agency (DARPA), called the ARPAnet. The former ARPAnet has gradually been replaced by the Internet.

The Internet is not a single network, but rather, is a conglomeration of several networks. The predominant protocols used are TCP/IP and the applications are TCP/IP-based. But not all networks on the Internet use TCP/IP, such as the BITNET and the CREN, which use IBM's SNA protocols. Before these networks can interact with other networks that use TCP/IP, protocol translations by gateways are necessary.

Internet Examples

Even though the Internet continues to undergo commercialization, it provides an incomparable test network for developing new protocols and application services. For example, a great deal of experimentation and research on OSI application services is conducted on the Internet.

Table 9.1 contains some of the networks that comprise the Internet. The list is by no means exhaustive, but rather, intends to give you an idea of the range of participation on the Internet by international communities.

TABLE 9.1 EXAMPLES OF NETWORKS ON THE INTERNET

Network	Description
NSFNET	National Science Foundation Network. Backbone network in the U.S.
CSNET	Computer Science Network. Affordable Internet services using X.25 for small schools and organizations.
Cypress Net	Provides low-cost and low-volume Internet access centered around Purdue University.
MILNET	U.S. Department of Defense (DoD) network. Originally part of ARPAnet.
BITNET	Because It's Time Network. Uses IBM Mainframes and low-cost 9600 bps links.
CREN	Consortium for Research and Education Network. Successor to CSNET and BITNET.
EARN	European Academic Research Network. Uses BITNET technology. Network for Europe, Middle East, Africa.
JANET	Joint Academic Network. Network for universities and Research Institutions in the U.K.
CDNet	Network services to Canadian research, education, and advanced development community.

Network	Description
NRCnet	Canadian National Research Council network. Modeled after NSFNET.
ACSnet	Australian Computer Science Network. Used by universities, research institutions, and industry.
Kogaku-bu	Established at University of Tokyo. Uses proprietary 100 Mbps fiber backbone network.

Internet Users

The earlier Internet community consisted of universities, such as Stanford University, UCLA, MIT, UCSB, University of Utah, University of Hawaii, University of California at Berkeley, and research organizations, such as SRI International, Rand Corporation, the Institute of Advanced Computation, and Bolt, Beranek, and Newman (BBN).

The Internet community now has expanded to include commercial organizations and individual users. The Internet community includes all major universities, research organizations, corporations, individual users, and Internet providers.

Internet Backbone

The National Science Foundation Network (NSFNET) was the original backbone of the Internet in the United States. Management of the NSFNET was contracted to Advanced Network Services (ANS). When commercialization of the Internet began, an ANSNET backbone was formed to carry the commercial traffic. ANS also managed the ANSNET backbone. Actually, both NFSNET and ANSNET traffic was carried over the same physical links, but two virtual backbones were run over it (see fig. 9.1).

Who Manages the Internet?

When people first use the Internet, they often ask who runs it. No one specific is really in charge. The closest thing to central management is the Internet Activities Board (IAB) and the Internet Society. The IAB is divided into groups that specialize in research and engineering activities related to the Internet. Figure 9.2 shows the interrelationship between the various bodies that have an impact on the Internet.

The IAB provides focus, direction, and coordination of TCP/IP-related protocols, and guides the evolution of the Internet. The IAB consists of the Internet Research Task Force (IRTF) and the Internet Engineering Task Force (IETF). The Federal Networking Council (FNC) is a U.S. government regulatory body that serves as an advisory body. As the Internet continues to get increasingly commercialized, the influence of the FNC will decrease even further.

The Internet Engineering Steering Group (IESG) manages the IETF. The IETF is, in turn, divided into areas, and those areas are divided into working groups. The IETF focuses on short-to-medium-term engineering problems.

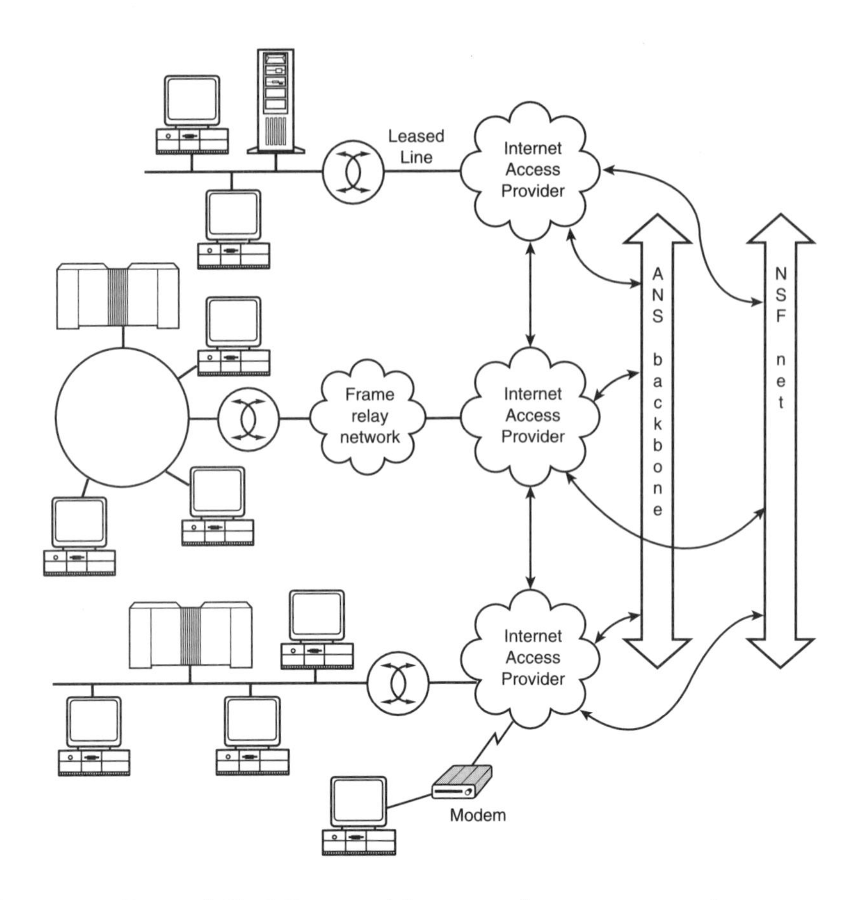

Figure 9.1

Internet access.

IRSG manages the Internet Research Task Force and focuses on long-term research problems.

The IETF has the following eight broad technical areas. The actual areas might change over time depending on the needs of the Internet.

- Applications
- Host protocols
- Internet protocols
- Routing
- Network management
- OSI interoperability
- Operations
- Security

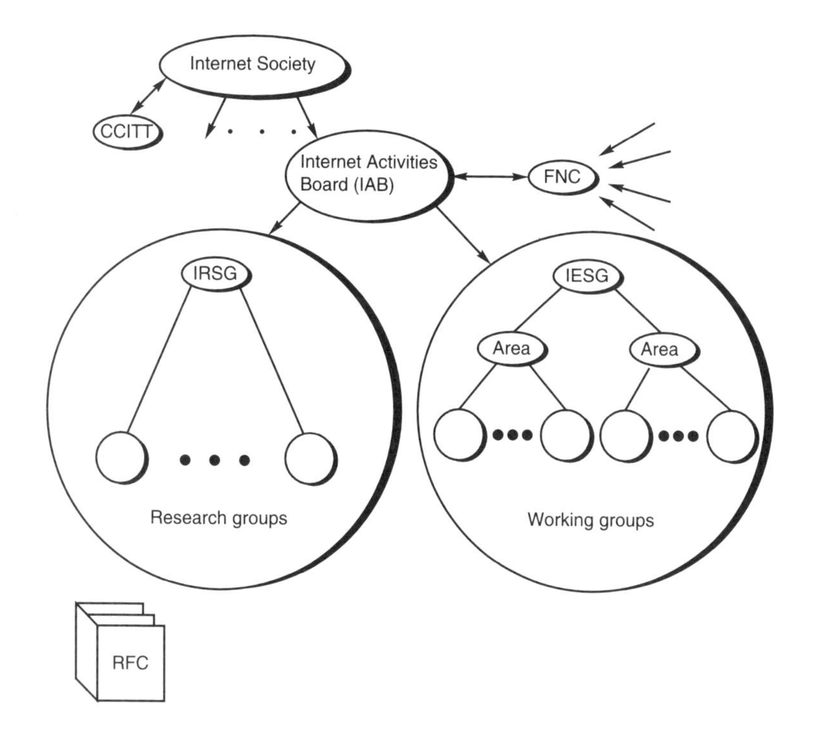

Figure 9.2

The structure of the IAB.

The IETF has many working groups, such as Authentication, Domain names, Dynamic host Config, Host requirements, Interconnectivity, Internet MIB, Joint management, Telnet, User documents, and so on.

A more recent development is the formation of the Internet Society. The Internet Society promotes the use of the Internet for collaboration on research topics on the Internet. It provides a forum for industry, educators, government, and users, and is involved in recommending procedures and technical standards for the global Internet and private internets.

Membership to the Internet Society is open to everyone at an annual membership fee. The regular membership is $70/year and $25/year for students (note: prices may have changed since the writing of this book). You can contact the Internet Society in the following ways:

- Postal Address:

  Internet Society
  Suite 100
  1895 Preston White Drive
  Reston, VA 22091-5434
  U.S.A.

- Internet E-mail: isoc@isoc.org
- Telephone: 703-648-9888
- Fax: 703-620-0913

Accessing the Internet

Internet access is provided through Internet Access Providers (IAP) and by government and military organizations. The government and the military were among the earliest Internet users. However, access to the Internet through the government and military organizations is denied for ordinary users. The majority of users who need Internet access must use one of the Internet Access Providers.

The Internet Access Providers consist of commercial organizations and universities that already have access to the Internet and provide commercial accounts. Tables 9.2 and 9.3 show a partial list of IAPs within the United States and outside the United States, respectively.

Table 9.2 Internet Access Providers in the United States

Internet Access Provider	Contact
AlterNet	UUNET Technologies, Inc. 800-488-6383 703-204-8000 alternet-info@uunet.uu.net
Internet Express	719-520-1700 ID "new", password "newuser" Local access area codes: 303, 719 klaus@usa.net
DELPHI	800-365-4636 Local access areas: Boston, Kansas City walthowe@delphi.com
Dial-in-cerf	Provided by CERFNET 800-876-2373 or 619-455-3900 Local access area codes: 213, 310, 415, 510, 619, 714, 818 help@cerf.net
NEARnet	617-873-8730 Local access codes: 508, 603, 617 nearnet-join@nic.near.net

Internet Access Provider	Contact
NETCOM	408-554-Unix nfo@netcom.com
NorthWestNet	206-562-3000 nic@nwnet.net
NYSERnet	315-453-2912 info@nysernet.org
PSInet	703-620-6651 all-info@psi.com
Well	The Whole Earth 'Lectronic Link 415-332-6106 ID "newuser" info@well.sf.ca.us
World	Software Tool & Die 617-739-9753 ID "new" 617-739-0202 office@world.std.com

TABLE 9.3 INTERNET ACCESS PROVIDERS OUTSIDE THE UNITED STATES

Internet Access Provider	Contact
ARnet	Alberta, Canada 403-450-5187 neilson@titan.arc.ab.ca
BCnet	British Columbia, Canada 604-822-3932 mike@bc.net
ONet	Ontario, Canada 416-525-9140 drake@mcmaster.ca
AARnet	Australia +61-6-249-3385 aarnet@aarnet.edu.au

continues

Table 9.3, Continued

Internet Access Provider	Contact
CNS	Chernikeeff Networking Services (CNS) UK +44-932-814-800 cns@chernikeeff.co.uk
Demon Internet Limited	UK +44-81-349-0063 internet@demon.net
Pipex	UK +44-223-250120 sales@pipex.net
EUnet	Austria, Belgium, Czech Republic, Germany, Finland, Spain, Portugal, Slovakia, Switzerland +31-20-592-5109 info@eu.net
Fnet	EUnet — France +33-1-45-21-02-04 contact@fnet.fr
Internet Initiative Japan	Japan +81-3-3580-3781 info@iij.ad.jp
SwipNet	Swedish IP NETwork info@swip.net
TIPnet	Sweden 90-400,08-688-20-00 info-eng@tip.net

When you connect to the Internet, the following types of connections are possible:

- ◆ Permanent direct
- ◆ On-demand direct
- ◆ Dial-up
- ◆ Mail only

Permanent Direct Internet Access

Permanent direct connection provides dedicated connections to the Internet (see fig. 9.3). The permanent direct connections are made via Channel Service Unit/Data Service Unit (CSU/DSU) to a router on the customer's LAN. The connection is made through the Internet Provider's network.

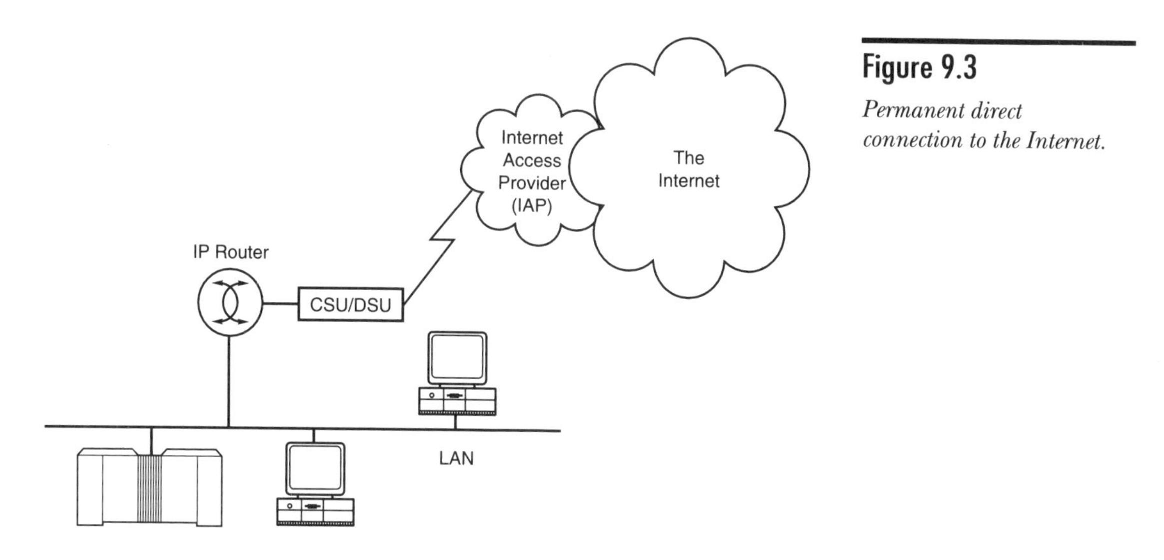

Figure 9.3

Permanent direct connection to the Internet.

The point-to-point connection between the CSU/DSU and the IAP is usually a high-speed connection, made over speeds of 56 Kbps or greater. A 56 Kbps leased line is the simplest of the connection types. The leased line usually can be ordered through the regional phone company. In some areas, alternative types of high-speed connections are available, such as ISDN, T1, Frame relay, and SMDS, and can range from speeds of 64 Kbps and higher.

You usually must meet a one-time installation cost for a leased line installation and a startup fee for a leased line connection. In the United States, startup cost can run between roughly $1,000 and $1,600. The recurring cost consists of a monthly service fee charged by the IAP ($800 to $1,500 per month) and the leased line cost. The router and CSU/DSU costs are an additional $1,000 to $5,000. You can purchase the router and CSU/DSU separately or through the IAP.

In the permanent direct connection method, the LAN administrator is responsible for assigning IP addresses using the IP network number obtained through the Internet Access Provider. The actual cost of permanent direct connection depends on location of access, but generally is the most expensive of the Internet connection methods. On the other hand, it gives you the maximum flexibility.

Permanent Direct Internet Access for NetWare LANs

If a number of users in an organization want to share an Internet connection, the permanent direct connection is the best option. The users can be connected by an internal network (such as a LAN) with an IP router and a CSU/DSU that they can use for Internet access.

In a NetWare environment, the workstations can run NetWare client software with an IPX and a TCP/IP protocol stack (see fig. 9.4). The workstations can use the IPX protocol for accessing the internal NetWare servers and TCP/IP for accessing the Internet and internal TCP/IP hosts.

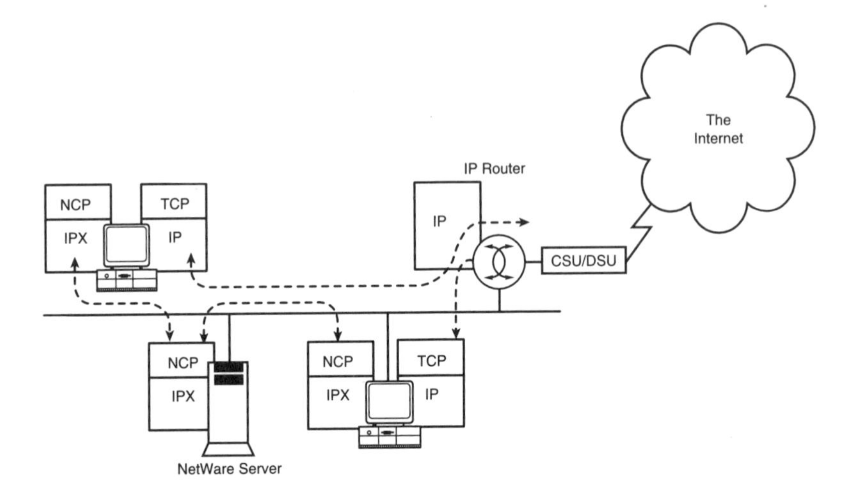

Figure 9.4

Dual protocol stack on NetWare clients for Internet access.

If the NetWare clients use the NetWare/IP product, they can replace the IPX protocol with the TCP/IP protocol stack, which they can then use to access NetWare servers, internal TCP/IP hosts, and the Internet (see fig. 9.5). Because TCP/IP enables NetWare server access, any host on the Internet can use TCP/IP to access the NetWare server, which is both an advantage and a disadvantage. The advantage is ease of access. Any legitimate user can access the corporate NetWare servers by connecting to the Internet. The disadvantage is that the NetWare servers are exposed to potential attacks by malicious users (see fig. 9.6).

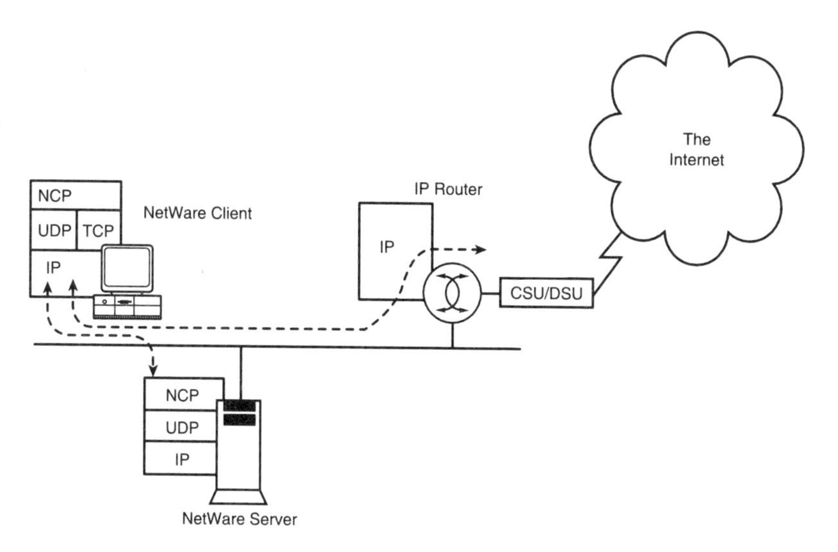

Figure 9.5

Single TCP/IP protocol stack on NetWare clients for Internet access.

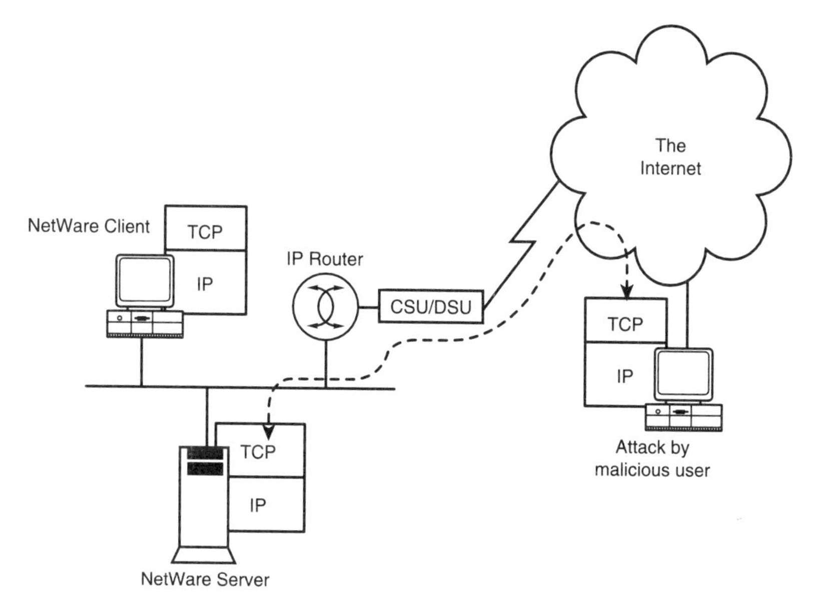

Figure 9.6

Exposure of NetWare servers through TCP/IP access.

Another way to connect NetWare users to the Internet using a single protocol stack but avoiding the exposure illustrated in figure 9.6 is to designate a single NetWare server to act as a TCP/IP application service gateway. The NetWare clients use a single IPX protocol stack (see fig. 9.7). The NetWare server that is designated as the gateway accepts the requests for Internet access and initiates the connections necessary for implementing the requests. Because the NetWare clients run the native IPX protocol stack, they do not have to be configured for TCP/IP. Assigning and maintaining unique IP addresses and dealing with IP subnetting issues can prove daunting for many network administrators. You can avoid these problems by using the IPX protocol stack. When you use IPX, no special IPX address assignments are required on the NetWare workstations. An example of a TCP/IP application gateway for NetWare is the NOV*IX product sold by Firefox Communications. The NO*VIX product runs as a series of NLMs on the NetWare servers and provides access to TCP/IP applications for IPX workstations.

Figure 9.7

Single IPX protocol stack on NetWare clients for Internet access.

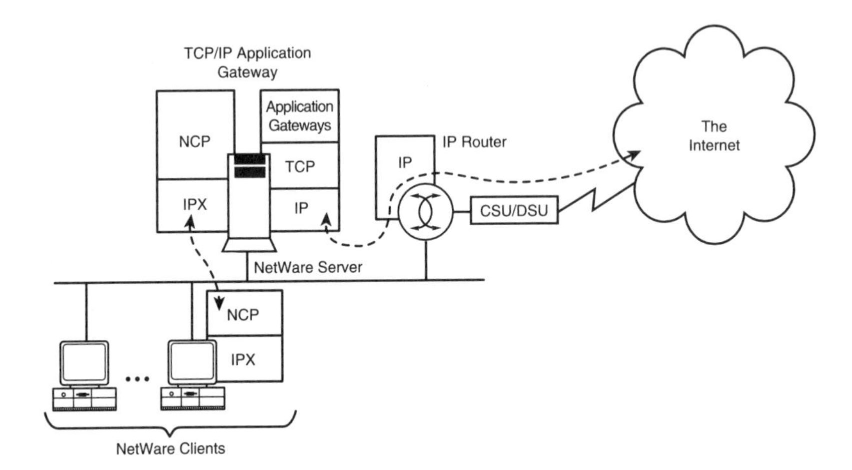

Only the NetWare servers that run the TCP/IP application gateway services are exposed to attack from the Internet. The other NetWare servers that do not have TCP/IP stack are protected from attacks, because the attack can only be transmitted on the Internet using TCP/IP.

On-Demand Direct Connection

On-demand direct connection allows a computer to be a full participant on the Internet on a temporary basis (see fig. 9.8). The computer can be connected (to a LAN) or stand alone. Typically, these computers are stand-alone computers designated for home or business use. If the computer is on a LAN, you can use the direct connection approach discussed earlier in the chapter.

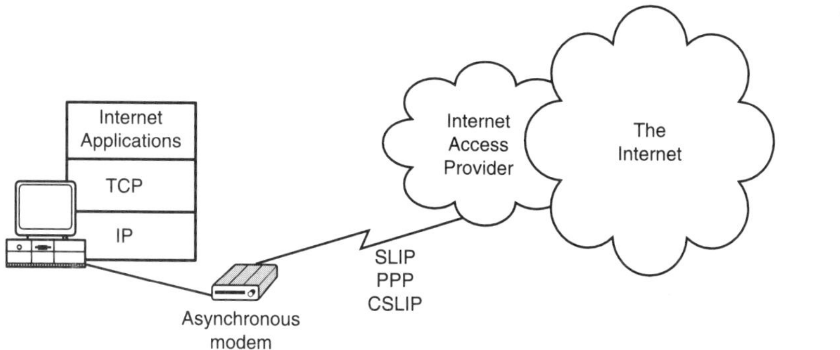

Figure 9.8

On-demand direct Internet connection.

The TCP/IP protocol stack runs on the computer, so you must assign an IP address to the line interface. This means that before you can install the TCP/IP software, you must have a basic understanding of installing and configuring TCP/IP software. You are responsible for configuring TCP/IP software and applications on your computer.

An IP address is assigned to the serial interface used to connect to the IAP using the modem. The IP address must be unique and is usually assigned by the IAP for the individual user. Some IAPs, such as PSInet, assign the IP address on a dynamic basis as connections are made to the IAP's network. For IBM PCs, the modem is an asynchronous modem attached to one of the serial interfaces on the computer. Alternatively, an internal modem can be used.

The line to the IAP is a dial-up line that uses an asynchronous modem. Typical speeds of such modems are up to 14.4 Kbps (V.32bis). Standards such as V.FAST promise speeds up to 28.8 Kbps. The data-link protocol used for sending the IP packets across the dial-up line is the Serial Line Interface Protocol (SLIP), Point-to-Point Protocol (PPP), or Compressed Serial Line Interface Protocol (CSLIP). You can obtain SLIP/PPP accounts from most Internet Access Providers at nominal cost.

Dial-Up Internet Access

Dial-up Internet connection involves using communications software to emulate a terminal connected to the Internet service provider's host (see fig. 9.9). Examples of the communications software used on the dial-up computer are PROCOMM, CrossTalk, and Qmodem. Important: The TCP/IP protocol and application services run on the IAP's host computer, not on the computer used for dial-up connections.

The dial-up computer runs only the communications software, so no IP addresses need to be set on the dial-up computer. The IAP provides TCP/IP software and Internet tools. The TCP/IP software typically runs on a Unix machine, and the users need to be familiar with basic Unix commands. Some Internet service providers use a simplified menu interface for users who are not familiar with Unix commands (see fig. 9.10).

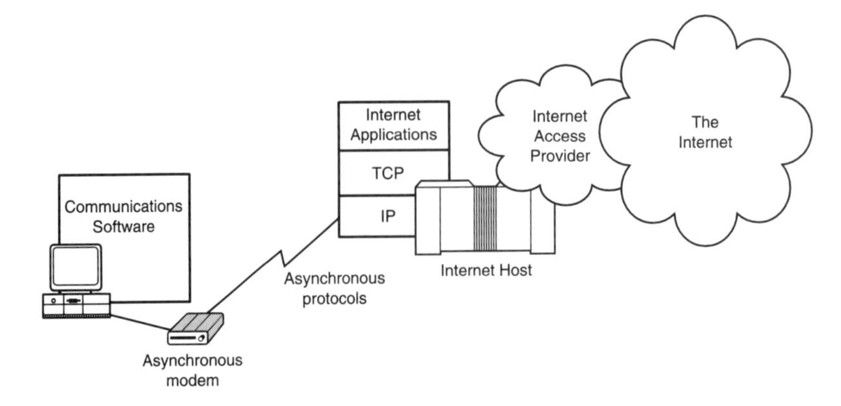

Figure 9.9

Dial-up Internet access.

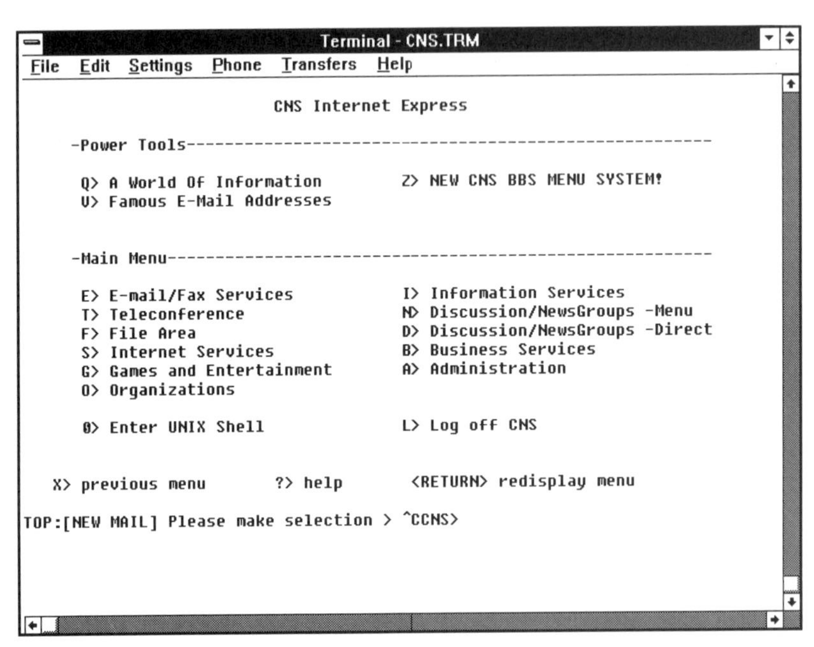

Figure 9.10

Simplified menu interface for dial-up accounts.

The dial-up accounts also are called *shell accounts.* The dial-up line to the Internet uses an asynchronous modem to transmit data using an asynchronous protocol.

A disadvantage of using dial-up connections is that a double download of files must be performed to copy the files to the user's workstation, because the TCP/IP software runs on the IAP's host and not on the user's workstation that runs the terminal emulation communications software. When FTP is used to copy a file from a remote host, it is copied to the IAP's TCP/IP host. The user then must download this file in a separate step, using file transfer protocols such as XMODEM, YMODEM, or Kermit. Figure 9.11 shows the double download necessary to copy files to a dial-up workstation. The following are examples of commands for copying a file from the IAP host to the user's dial-up workstation:

- Download a file using XMODEM: sx *filename*
- Download a file using YMODEM: sy *filename*
- Download a file using Kermit: sk *filename*

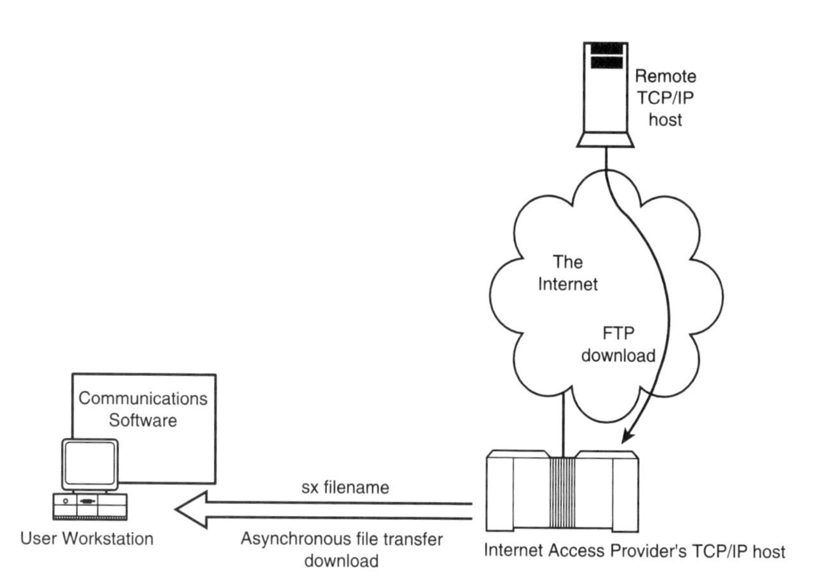

Figure 9.11

Double download for dial-up Internet connections.

Mail-Only Internet Access

Users on networks such as CompuServe, MCI Mail, and Sprint Mail can exchange e-mail with other Internet users by using an e-mail gateway connected to their networks. The mail-only Internet access is the cheapest of the Internet connections because there are no additional costs.

The e-mail gateway is an application-level gateway that converts e-mail messages from the proprietary format used by CompuServe, MCI Mail, and Sprint Mail users to the Simple Mail Transfer Protocol (SMTP) format used by Internet users.

Using NetWare Clients for Internet Access

Many TCP/IP client packages are designed to run in a NetWare environment using a dual protocol stack approach. This section describes two popular packages that can run on NetWare workstations: Chameleon NFS and LAN WorkPlace from Novell.

Using Chameleon NFS

Chameleon NFS is a TCP/IP software package from NetManage, and comes with a number of tools for Internet access. The software package runs in a DOS/Windows environment and can coexist with the NetWare drivers that NetWare client software uses. The TCP/IP protocol stack and the application programming interface to this protocol stack is implemented using Winsock (Windows TCP/IP sockets). A DLL called WINSOCK.DLL ships with the product.

The following is an outline of the steps for installing Chameleon NFS on a NetWare workstation:

1. Load the IPX drivers on the NetWare workstation. Chameleon NFS then recognizes that you are installing on a NetWare-based network.
2. Launch Windows. Insert the first Chameleon NFS disk in drive A: and run the SETUP.EXE program on this disk.
3. You are prompted to enter the name of the directory in which you should install Chameleon NFS. Accept the default location of C:\NETMANAG.
4. You are prompted to insert additional disks; do so in the order prompted.
5. Accept the prompts for updating the Windows SYSTEM.INI file.
6. Open the Chameleon NFS group. Figure 9.12 shows the different Internet services that you can access from the Chameleon NFS group.

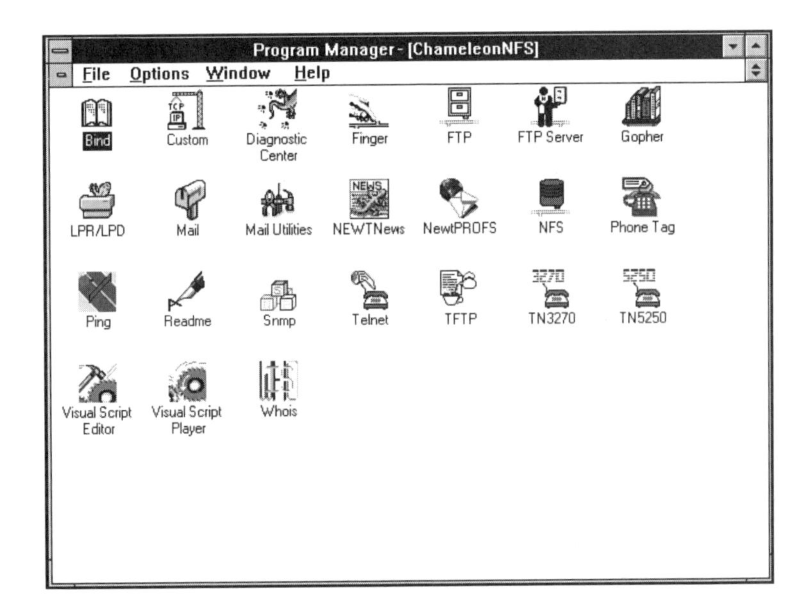

Figure 9.12
Chameleon NFS group.

7. Double-click on the Custom icon.
8. Highlight Ethernet0 and select Setup to verify (and if necessary, change) the following:
   - Ethernet Type: Ethernet/DIX.
   - IP address: Set a unique IP address for your workstation. Consult with your network administrator.

- Subnet mask: Assign a subnet mask for your network. Consult with your network administrator.
- Host name: Assign a symbolic name for your computer.
- Domain name: If you have a domain name, assign it.

9. Select Services from the Custom menu bar.

   Select Domain Servers.

   On the first domain entry, enter the name of the Domain Server or its IP address. If you have a Domain Name Server (DNS) on your network, you can specify its IP address. Otherwise, you can use the DNS server provided by your Internet Access Provider. You can specify up to three DNS servers. These DNS servers are consulted for name resolution in the order in which you specify them.

10. Select Services from the Custom menu bar.

    Select Default Gateway.

    Set the IP address of the IP router used to connect to the Internet Access Provider on your network.

11. Select File from the Custom menu bar, then select Save. Select File from the Custom menu bar, then select Exit.

The previous installation and configuration procedure has been described for a NetWare workstation. If you want to use Chameleon NFS for on-demand direct connection access to the Internet, you must configure the SLIP, PPP, or CSLIP interfaces.

Using LAN WorkPlace

LAN WorkPlace is a TCP/IP software package from Novell, and comes with a number of tools for Internet access. The software package runs in a DOS/Windows environment and can coexist with the NetWare drivers that the NetWare client software uses. The TCPIP.EXE TSR, which you must load before you can use the Internet tools, implements the TCP/IP protocol stack and the application programming interface to this protocol stack.

The following is an outline of the steps necessary for installing LAN WorkPlace on a NetWare workstation:

1. Start Windows. Insert the first LAN WorkPlace disk in drive A:, then run the INSTALL.EXE program.
2. Select the different LAN WorkPlace components that you want to install. Some of the components are required, such as ODI workstation services, TCP/IP transport services, and DOS applications. If you have MS Windows at your workstation, you should install the Windows applications.
3. After you make your selections, save your changes. Select the drive to which you will install the software.

4. Select the target directory in which you will install the software. Accept the default of C:\NET.
5. You are prompted to insert additional disks; do so in the order prompted.
6. Accept the prompts for updating the Windows SYSTEM.INI file. You also must specify whether the workstation boots from a file server.
7. Select the network driver to install and specify its hardware settings.
8. Specify whether BOOTP is used to specify the TCP/IP parameters. If not, you must specify the IP address of the workstation.
9. If subnets are being used, answer Yes to specify the subnet mask.
10. If a default router is used, answer Yes to specify that a router is to be used. You must then enter the IP address of the router. This IP address will be the address of the IP router used for connecting to the Internet Access Provider.
11. If a domain name server is used, answer Yes. You must then enter the IP address of the domain name server.
12. You must select the data-link layer format for IPX communications. For Ethernet your choices are Ethernet_802.3, Ethernet_802.2, Ethernet_SNAP, and Ethernet_II. For token ring, your choices are Token-Ring and Token-Ring_SNAP.
13. You must enter the username to be used with the Berkeley-r* utilities, such as the rcp, rexec, rsh, and so on.
14. After the files are copied, you receive a message that the installation is successful.

For more information about LAN WorkPlace (and LAN WorkGroup), see Chapter 8.

Using Internet Services

You can use a number of useful tools to access resources on the Internet. The following are some of the more common tools:

- Telnet
- FTP
- Archie
- WAIS
- Gopher
- Veronica
- WWW

- Lists
- Newsgroups

You can access any of the preceding services from a NetWare-based network. Most TCP/IP vendors provide some or all of the aforementioned tools to access these services. The following sections describe how to use each of these services.

Using Telnet Services

The Telnet service enables you to log in remotely to an Internet host; that is, you can use Telnet client software to log in to any TCP/IP host on the Internet. You must use a user account set up on the remote machine to log in. By default, the Telnet client software connects to TCP port 23 on the host machine that provides remote login access. However, you also can use the Telnet client software to access a service that resides on any TCP port on the remote machine (see fig. 9.13).

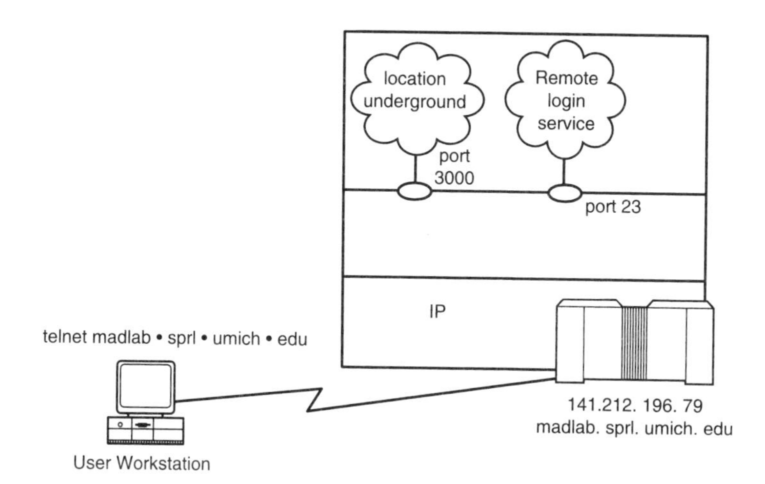

Figure 9.13
Using Telnet.

The general syntax of the Telnet command is as follows:

```
telnet hostname [port]
```

If you do not specify *port*, port number 23 is used. By specifying a different port number, you can access a service at that port number. Figure 9.14 shows that you can use the following command to contact the weather underground service at TCP port 3000 on the Internet host madlab.sprl.umich.edu:

```
telnet madlab.sprl.umich.edu 3000
```

Table 9.4 shows examples of services on Internet hosts that you can use Telnet to access.

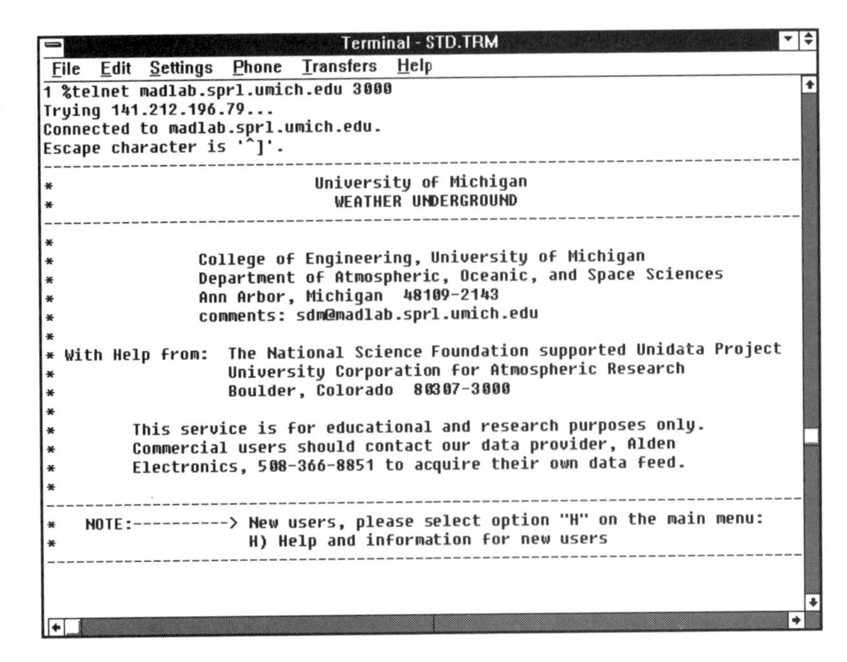

Terminal - STD.TRM
File Edit Settings Phone Transfers Help
1 %telnet madlab.sprl.umich.edu 3000
Trying 141.212.196.79...
Connected to madlab.sprl.umich.edu.
Escape character is '^]'.
University of Michigan
WEATHER UNDERGROUND
College of Engineering, University of Michigan
Department of Atmospheric, Oceanic, and Space Sciences
Ann Arbor, Michigan 48109-2143
comments: sdm@madlab.sprl.umich.edu
With Help from: The National Science Foundation supported Unidata Project
University Corporation for Atmospheric Research
Boulder, Colorado 80307-3000
This service is for educational and research purposes only.
Commercial users should contact our data provider, Alden
Electronics, 508-366-8851 to acquire their own data feed.
NOTE:----------> New users, please select option "H" on the main menu:
H) Help and information for new users

Figure 9.14

Accessing special services using the Telnet command.

Table 9.4 Sample TELNET Sites

Hostname	Port Number	Description
madlab.sprl.umich.edu (141.212.196.79)	3000	Provides weather service from the University of Michigan. Can be used for long-range forecasts, latest earthquake reports, severe weather, hurricane advances, international data, marine forecasts.
martini.eecs.umich.edu (141.212.99.9)	3000	Provides geographic information on cities.
nssdca.gsfc.nasa.gov (128.183.36.23)	23	Access to The National Space Science Data Center. NASA's educational division provides educational programs and materials for teachers and students from the elementary to university level.

Hostname	Port Number	Description
info.umd.edu (128.8.10.29)	23	University of Maryland information center.
nysernet.org (192.77.173.2)	23	User guide on resources on the Internet. Login: nysrview Password: nysrview
freenet-in-a.cwru.edu freenet-in-b.cwru.edu freenet-in-c.cwru.edu	23	Cleveland Freenet system

File Transfer Using FTP

The *File Transfer Protocol* (FTP) uses the TCP transport protocol to transfer files reliably between two computers. TCP is the transport protocol because it provides guaranteed delivery of services.

FTP enables the user to interactively access files and directories on remote hosts, and perform directory operations such as the following:

- Listing files in a remote or local directory
- Renaming and deleting files (if user has permission)
- Transferring files from remote host to local host (downloading)
- Transferring files from local host to remote host (uploading)

Figure 9.15 shows a transfer of a file from the local host to the remote host and outlines the FTP session to perform this transfer. The FTP session is initiated by the FTP client across a TCP/IP network. The computer used to log in is called the *FTP host*. The FTP host must have a software component (called the *FTP server*) that interacts with the file system of the host.

In general, before you can use FTP or any other TCP/IP application service, you must have a client version of the applications. Client TCP/IP applications are available on Unix hosts. You must purchase separate products for DOS clients, such as from Novell (LAN WorkPlace), FTP Software, Inc. (PC/TCP or OnLAN), Wollongong (Pathways), or from a variety of other vendors.

Figure 9.15

File transfer using FTP.

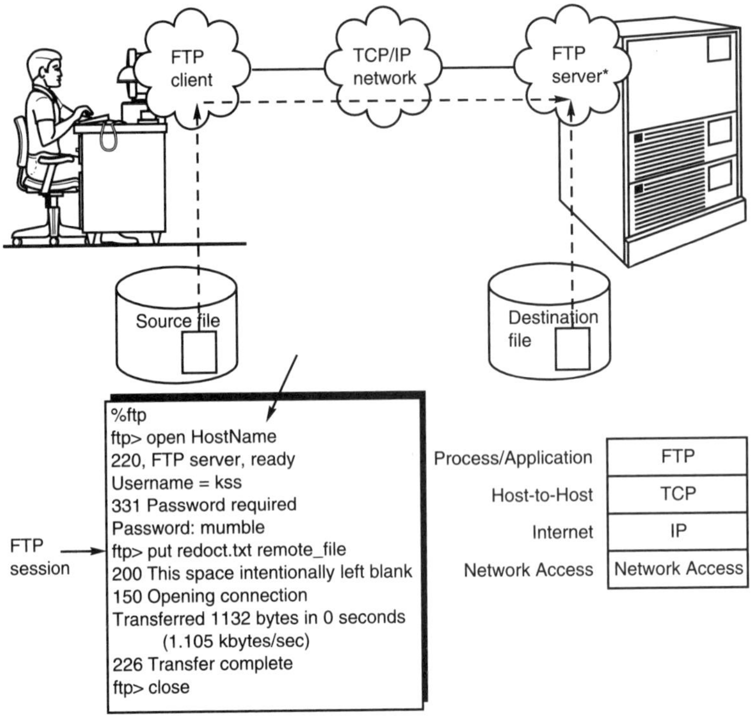

* FTP server is also called FTP daemon.

Performing FTP from the Command Line

Many FTP clients are command-line based, which means that you must use the FTP command to initiate an FTP session. To start an FTP session, you can use the following command:

```
ftp [hostname]
```

hostname represents the IP address of the host onto which you are logging. If you leave out hostname, you still can issue a number of FTP commands. If you type the HELP command or ?, you can obtain help on the FTP commands.

```
ftp> ?
```

The following listing outlines some of the FTP commands available when you are logged on to the INTERNIC.NET host (you can abbreviate commands):

!	delete	mode	rmdir
$	dir	mput	runique
account	diconnect	nmap	send
append	form	ntrans	sendport
ascii	get	open	status
bell	hash	prompt	struct
binary	help	proxy	sunique
blob	lcd	put	tenex
bye	ls	pwd	trace
case	macdef	quit	type
cd	mdelete	quote	user
cdup	mdir	recv	verbose
close	mget	remotehelp	?
cr	mkdir	rename	
debug	mls	reset	

If you want to perform an FTP session to the host INTERNIC.NET, you would use the command:

```
ftp INTERNIC.NET
```

If you know the IP address of the host, such as the FTP server for Novell, you can use the following command:

```
ftp 137.65.4.1
```

Please be aware that before you can connect to hosts outside your network environment, you need access to these hosts through a TCP/IP internetwork. An example of such an access is provided through the Internet.

You must specify a username and a password before you can log in to an FTP host. The FTP server uses the FTP host's underlying authentication mechanism to verify the privileges an FTP user should have. This means that if you have a user account, for instance Bob, on the computer acting as the FTP host, you can log in as user Bob, and use the same password that you would normally use to log on to that computer's native operating system. Many FTP hosts provide anonymous logins, which means that if you specify the username anonymous and a password of guest (some computers expect an e-mail address that contains the @ character), you can log in to the FTP host with a limited set of privileges determined by the system administrator of the FTP host.

The following is a short guided tour of an FTP session to the INTERNIC.NET host.

1. Type the ftp command and supply the name of the host.

   ```
   % ftp internic.net
   ```

   The % in the previous command is the default Unix prompt.

   The internic.net is the hostname, and uses the Domain Name Syntax discussed later in this chapter.

2. If the host is reachable, a message similar to the following appears. Details of the sign-on messages can differ. The following is an example of the sign-on message for the INTERNIC.NET host. This is the host on the Internet that is responsible for Internet Registration services.

   ```
   Connected to internic.net.
   220-*****Welcome to the InterNIC Registration Host *****
   *****Login with username "anonymous" and password "guest"
   *****You may change directories to the following:
   policy       - Registration Policies
   templates     - Registration Templates
   netinfo      - NIC Information Files
   domain       - Root Domain Zone Files
   220 And more!
   Name (internic.net:karanjit):
   ```

   As the message indicates, you can log in as the user anonymous with password guest.

3. Supply the username and password.

   ```
   Name (internic.net:karanjit): anonymous
   331 Guest login ok, send "guest" as password.
   Password:guest
   230 Guest login ok, access restrictions apply.
   ftp>
   ```

4. After you log in, you can use the ? or help command:

   ```
   ftp>?
   ```

   You can abbreviate commands. (Commands are listed previously in this section.)

5. The command to see your current directory on the FTP host is pwd.

   ```
   ftp> pwd
   257 "/" is current directory.
   ```

   The status of each FTP command is returned as a numeric code such as 257, and a text message accompanying it.

6. To see a listing of files in the current directory (as follows) use the ls or dir command.

```
ftp> ls
200 PORT command successful.
150 Opening ASCII mode data connection for file list.
bin
usr
dev
etc
pub
policy
templates
home
netinfo
domain
ls-ltR
netprog
archives
rfc
226 Transfer complete.
99 bytes received in 0.04 seconds (2.4 Kbytes/s)
```

The previous listing just lists the files and does not give information about the size of a file or whether it is a directory. To see this information, you should use the dir command as shown in the following:

```
ftp> dir
200 PORT command successful.
150 Opening ASCII mode data connection for /bin/ls.
total 22
drwxr-xr-x 2 root   1      512 Mar 22 21:40 archives
dr-xr-xr-x 2 root   1      512 Feb 25 1993 bin
drwxr-xr-x 2 root   1      512 Mar 9 1993 dev
drwxr-xr-x 2 root   1      512 Apr 1 1993 domain
dr-xr-xr-x 2 root   1      512 Feb 25 1993 etc
drwxr-xr-x 2 root   1      512 Mar 9 1993 home
-rw-r--r-- 1 root   1     9035 May 4 19:12 ls-ltR
drwxr-xr-x 2 root   1     1024 Apr 14 14:57 netinfo
drwxr-xr-x 2 root   1      512 Apr 1 1993 netprog
drwxr-xr-x 2 root   1     1024 May 4 19:11 policy
drwxr-xr-x 4 root   1      512 Apr 20 15:01 pub
lrwxrwxrwx 1 root   1        6 Aug 9 1993 rfc -> policy
drwxr-xr-x 2 root   1      512 May 3 19:54 templates
drwxr-xr-x 3 root   1      512 Feb 25 1993 usr
226 Transfer complete.
875 bytes received in 0.25 seconds (3.4 Kbytes/s)
```

The information is reported in the Unix style listing format, because you are logged on to a Unix system.

7. If you know that you are logged on to a Unix system that is acting as an FTP server, you can use the following useful trick:

   If you use the ls command, the Unix ls command is executed. You can supply any of the Unix options to the ls command, such as the -lR option that gives a recursive long form listing of files in subdirectories. The -lR option is not a part of the standard FTP commands, and works only for Unix FTP servers or FTP servers that emulate this behavior. The following shows the output of the ls -lR command. You can use this to get a quick overview of the files that are available on the FTP host.

```
ftp> ls -lR
200 PORT command successful.
150 Opening ASCII mode data connection for /bin/ls.
total 22
drwxr-xr-x 2 root      512 Mar 22 21:40 archives
dr-xr-xr-x 2 root      512 Feb 25 1993 bin
drwxr-xr-x 2 root      512 Mar 9 1993 dev
drwxr-xr-x 2 root      512 Apr 1 1993 domain
dr-xr-xr-x 2 root      512 Feb 25 1993 etc
drwxr-xr-x 2 root      512 Mar 9 1993 home
-rw-r--r-- 1 root        9035 May 4 19:12 ls-ltR
drwxr-xr-x 2 root      1024 Apr 14 14:57 netinfo
drwxr-xr-x 2 root      512 Apr 1 1993 netprog
drwxr-xr-x 2 root      1024 May 4 19:11 policy
drwxr-xr-x 4 root      512 Apr 20 15:01 pub
lrwxrwxrwx 1 root      6 Aug 9 1993 rfc -> policy
drwxr-xr-x 2 root      512 May 3 19:54 templates
drwxr-xr-x 3 root      512 Feb 25 1993 usr
      :
```

(listing continues)

```
      :
usr/lib:
total 576
-r-xr-xr-x 1 root     40960 Feb 25 1993 ld.so
-rwxr-xr-x 1 root     516096 Feb 25 1993 libc.so.1.8
-rwxr-xr-x 1 root     24576 Feb 25 1993 libdl.so.1.0
226 Transfer complete.
remote: -lR
9228 bytes received in 1.2 seconds (7.5 Kbytes/s)
```

8. To change your directory to a particular directory, such as rfc, use the cd command:

```
ftp> cd rfc
250 CWD command successful.
```

9. To see a listing of the files in the /rfc directory, use ls or dir, as follows:

```
ftp> ls
200 PORT command successful.
150 Opening ASCII mode data connection for file list.
asn.index
domain.index
index
master.index
network.index
rfc1009.txt
rfc1011.txt
rfc1031.txt
      :
```

(*listing continues*)

```
      :
226 Transfer complete.
496 bytes received in 0.045 seconds (11 Kbytes/s)
```

10. If you try to get a file that does not exist, such as the file rfc1365.txt, FTP indicates the following:

```
ftp> get rfc1365.txt
200 PORT command successful.
550 rfc1365.txt: No such file or _directory.
```

Remember that filenames under Unix are case-sensitive.

11. To copy a file from the FTP server to the local host, you use the following FTP command:

```
get remotefile [localfile]
```

remotefile represents the name of the file on the remote host and *localfile* the name of the file on the local machine. If you do not specify localfile, the local file is given the same name as the remote file.

For text files, FTP performs the proper carriage return to carriage-return/linefeed conversions between different operating systems, if the transfer mode is ascii. To use the transfer mode of ascii, use the FTP command ascii. To transfer binary files, use the FTP command image or binary to disable carriage-return/linefeed conversions.

The following demonstrates the FTP get command:

```
ftp> get rfc1400.txt
200 PORT command successful.
150 Opening ASCII mode data connection for rfc1400.txt (13009 bytes).
226 Transfer complete.
local: rfc1400.txt remote: rfc1400.txt
13404 bytes received in 0.78 seconds (17 Kbytes/s)
```

12. To close the current FTP connection, use the close command.

```
ftp> close
221 Goodbye.
ftp>
```

13. To exit out of FTP completely, use the bye command. The bye command also closes existing FTP connections before exiting FTP.

```
ftp> bye
%
```

Performing FTP Using a GUI Client

The preceding examples of FTP usage show you how to use FTP commands to transfer files. Some vendors offer a graphical interface for using FTP, such as NETMANAGE's Chameleon NFS and Novell's LAN WorkPlace/Workgroup products. Figure 9.16 shows NETMANAGE's graphical interface using MS Windows.

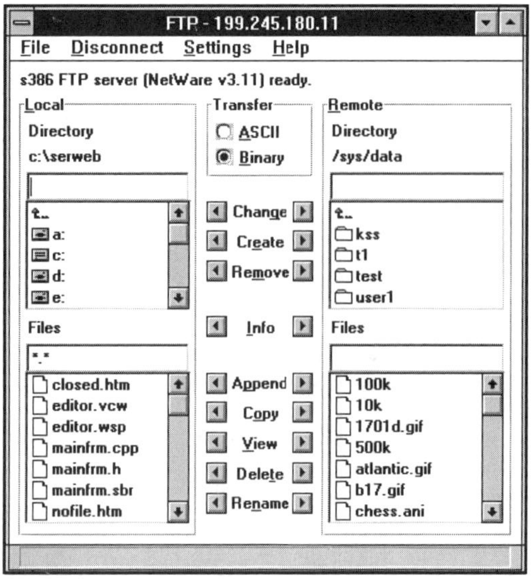

Figure 9.16

FTP graphical interface using Chameleon NFS product.

Using Archie

The Internet contains a vast body of information resources. One of the difficulties you experience is when you want to find the hosts on which a file is located, owing to the millions of computers on the Internet. Several tools, such as WWW, Gopher, and WAIS, have been developed to help find information on the Internet. An earlier tool is Archie.

Archie was developed at McGill University in Canada, and is a software tool that maintains an index of files on FTP sites in a searchable database. Archie consists of a server and a client component. An Archie server is responsible for periodically interrogating its own set of FTP hosts and building a database. The Archie client enables you to search for the text in filenames and directories.

You can access Archie by any of the following means:

- ◆ Telnet to an Archie server
- ◆ Archie client
- ◆ E-mail

Figure 9.17 shows how you can use Telnet to access an Archie server, and figure 9.18 shows the Archie server being accessed by an Archie client. Table 9.5 shows some of the commands that you can issue when logged on interactively to an Archie server using Telnet.

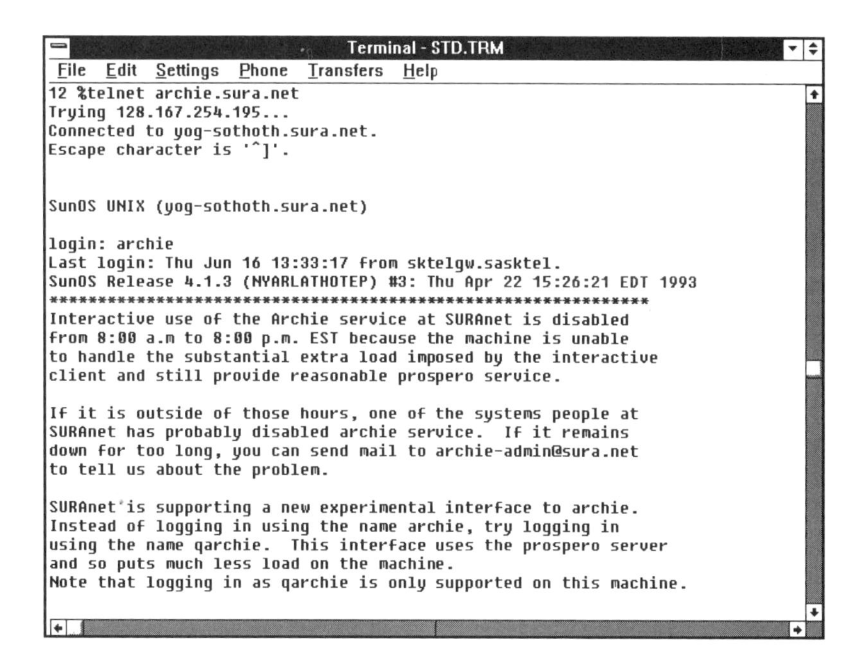

Figure 9.17

Using Telnet to access an Archie server.

Table 9.5 Sample Archie Commands

Archie Command	Description
prog searchstring	Searches for files and directories with specified search string
servers	Gets a list of all known Archie servers
site hostname	Lists all files available at the specified host via anonymous FTP
list	Displays a list of anonymous FTP servers that are indexed on the Archie server
help	Shows help on Archie commands

show variable	Shows value of Archie variable
	Example:
	`show search`
	`value of 'exact' means search string must match file exactly`
	`value of 'regex' means use of Unix style regular expressions`
	`value of 'sub' means substring search; case ignored`

set variable value	Used to set value of Archie parameter that controls Archie session
	Example:
	`set search regex (use regular expressions)`
	`set pager   (stop output when screen is full)`
	`set maxhits 100  (limits output to 100 matches)`
	`set mailto root@whitehouse.gov`

unset variable	Turns off a Boolean variable Example: `unset pager`
mail e-mail-address	Sends result of last search to an e-mail address; if e-mail address is not specified, value in mailto variable is used
whatis searchstring	Searches the Software Description Database (SDD) maintained by an Archie site; SDD contains a brief description of many of the files about which Archie knows

The option -s in the Archie client command (see fig. 9.18) means to ignore the case of the letters when searching for file and directory names. The -m6 option in the Archie client command means to look only for the first six matches.

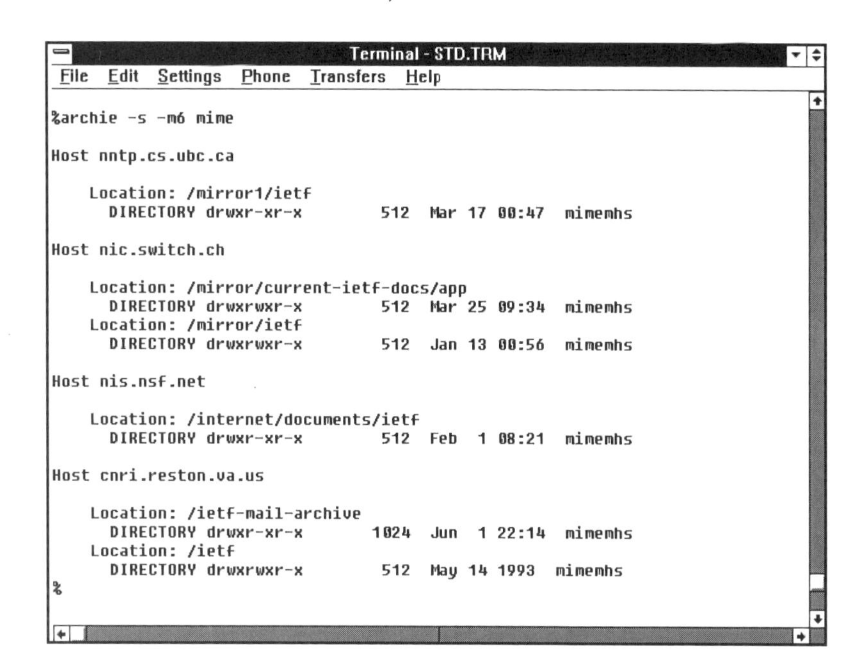

Figure 9.18

Using an Archie client to access an Archie server.

Internet users who only have e-mail can still access Archie servers by sending e-mail to an Archie server that contains Archie commands. The results are sent back by e-mail. In the e-mail request, the text placed in the subject and body of the e-mail message is treated as Archie commands. The following is a sample e-mail session:

```
mail archie@archie.rutgers.edu
Subject:
prog art              (searches for directory/files with text string "art")
compress               (compresses using Unix compress command. Uses
                        UUENCODE to convert to text. You must use
                        UUDECODE to recover output)
path kss@world.std.com      (specifies that result be sent to a different mail box)
quit                 (quits Archie)
```

To be considerate to the sites that provide Archie servers free of charge, you should avoid contacting Archie servers during the working hours for the time zone in which the Archie server resides. Table 9.6 shows commonly used Archie servers and the time zones in which these servers reside.

Table 9.6 Archie Servers

Archie Server	IP Address	Owner	Time Offset
archie.rutgers.edu	128.6.18.15	Rutgers University	GMT-6
archie.sura.net	128.167.254.179	SURAnet	GMT-6
archie.unl.edu	129.93.1.14	University of Nebraska, Lincoln	GMT-6
archie.ans.net	147.225.1.2	ANS	GMT-5
archie.au	139.130.4.6	Australian Archie server	GMT+9
archie.funet.fi	128.214.6.100	Finland	GMT+1
archie.doc.ic.ac.uk	146.169.11.3	UK	GMT
archie. thdarmstadt.de	130.83.128.111	Germany	GMT+2
archie.cs.huji.ac.il	132.65.6.15	Israel	GMT+5
archie.ncu.edu.tw	140.115.19.24	Taiwan	GMT+6
archie.sogang.ac.kr	163.239.1.11	Korea	GMT+7
archie.kuis.kyoto-u.ac.jp	130.54.20.1	Japan	GMT+8

Using WAIS

Wide Area Information Server (WAIS) is a text search system based on the American National Standard Z39.50:Information Retrieval Service Definition and Protocol Specification for Library Applications. WAIS servers maintain searchable indexes to documents. Every word in the text documents of a WAIS database is indexed, minus common words, called *stop words,* such as:

a, about, after, be, can, do

As a result of the WAIS search, matching documents, called hits, are scored, and the best match is given 1,000 points. The best match is the one with the highest score.

WAIS was developed by Thinking Machines Corporation, Apple Computer, and Dow Jones.

You can access WAIS in any of the following ways:

- Telnet to quake.think.com (192.31.181.1) and login as wais
- Use WAIS client software
- Use the Gopher menu selection Other Gopher and Information Servers

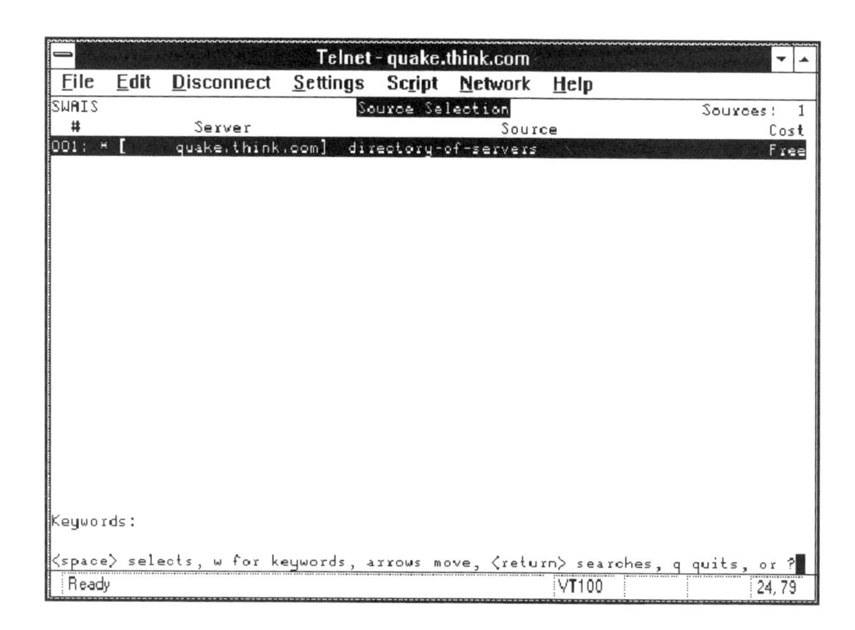

Figure 9.19

A sample WAIS session.

A sample WAIS session is shown in figure 9.19.

The limitations of WAIS are that it is less mature than other search tools, and the WAIS servers lack Boolean logic in searches, wild-card searches, and contextual search capabilities.

Using Gopher

The Internet Gopher tool enables you to navigate the Internet by selecting resources from menus. Gopher clients can perform Telnet and FTP sessions "behind-the-scenes" to retrieve resources.

The Gopher protocol and tool was developed at the University of Minnesota and the source code is available in the directory pub/gopher on the FTP server boom-box.micro.umn.edu. The RFC 1436 describes the Gopher protocol.

You can access Gopher through Telnet sessions to public Gophers. You can usually log in as the user gopher. Table 9.7 shows a partial list of Gopher sites and user logins necessary for accessing these gopher servers. Figure 9.20 shows a Telnet session to a public Gopher site, including the top-level menu for the Gopher site.

Table 9.7 Sample Public Gopher Servers

Public Gopher Site	IP Address	User Login Name	Location
gopher.uiuc.edu	128.174.33.150	gopher	North America
consultant.micro .umn.edu	134.84.132.4	gopher	North America
panda.uiowa.edu	128.255.40.201	panda	North America
gopher.sunset.se	192.36.125.2	gopher	Sweden
gopher.chalmers.se	129.16.221.40	gopher	Sweden
info.anu.edu.au	150.203.84.20	info	Australia
tolten.puc.cl	146.155.1.16	gopher	Chile
ecnet.ec	157.100.45.2	gopher	Ecuador

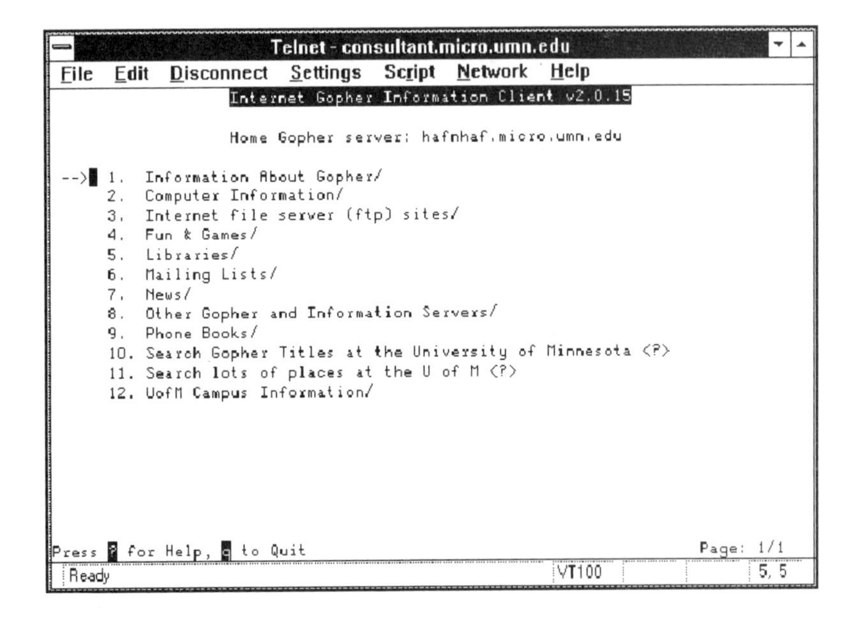

Figure 9.20

Telnet to a Gopher server.

Another way to access Gopher servers is to use Gopher clients. Figure 9.21 shows a Gopher client that has a graphical user interface. The menus appear in a graphical fashion. You can navigate through the menus and select the resources that you want to browse.

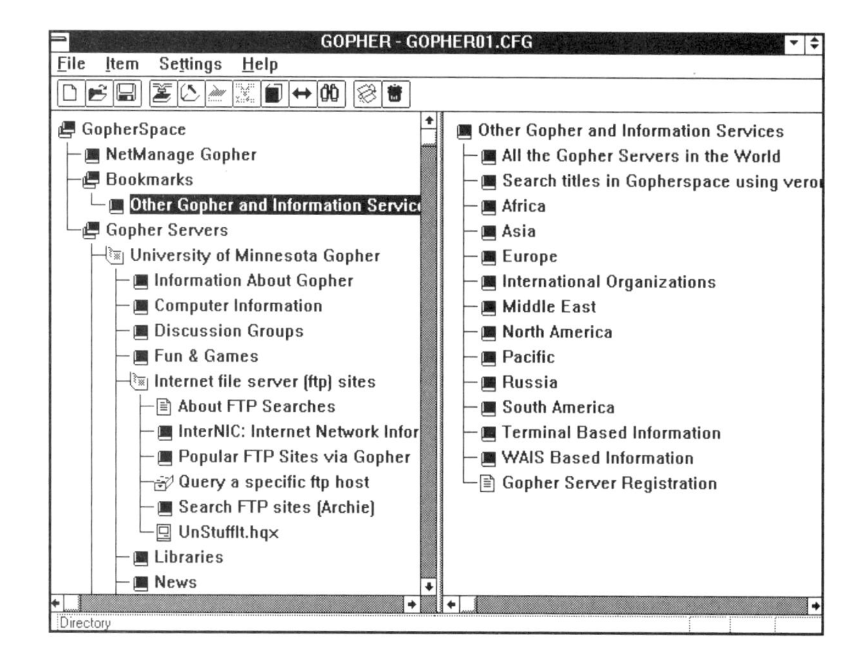

Figure 9.21

Using a Gopher client to access Gopher servers.

Using Veronica

A problem when you use the Gopher search tool is that you might not know how to find on Gopher servers all the menus that deal with a particular topic.

You can use a special tool, called Veronica (Very Easy Rodent-Oriented Network-wide Index to Computerized Archives), to search for menu items in the Gopher menus of different servers. Veronica was developed at the University of Nevada, and is used exclusively with the Gopher tool. Veronica searches menus on Gopher servers for keyword searches and builds a custom Gopher menu. You then can select from a Veronica-created Gopher menu and connect to the Gopher server that has the menu item.

You can use Veronica from the Gopher menu. The Veronica option on the Gopher menu is available as "Search titles in gopherspace using Veronica/." You might need to first select Other Gopher and Information Service first.

Veronica searches can build menus that contain Gopher directories only, or contain Gopher directories and information in Gopher directories. You also can use Boolean searches that consist of operators "and" or "or." For example, you can search for any of the following:

space *and* research

business *or* commerce

Figure 9.22 shows the Veronica option on a Gopher menu, and figure 9.23 shows the results of running a search for the word "ATM." The word "ATM" has many different meanings. All the menu items in the "gopher space" with the word "ATM" are listed.

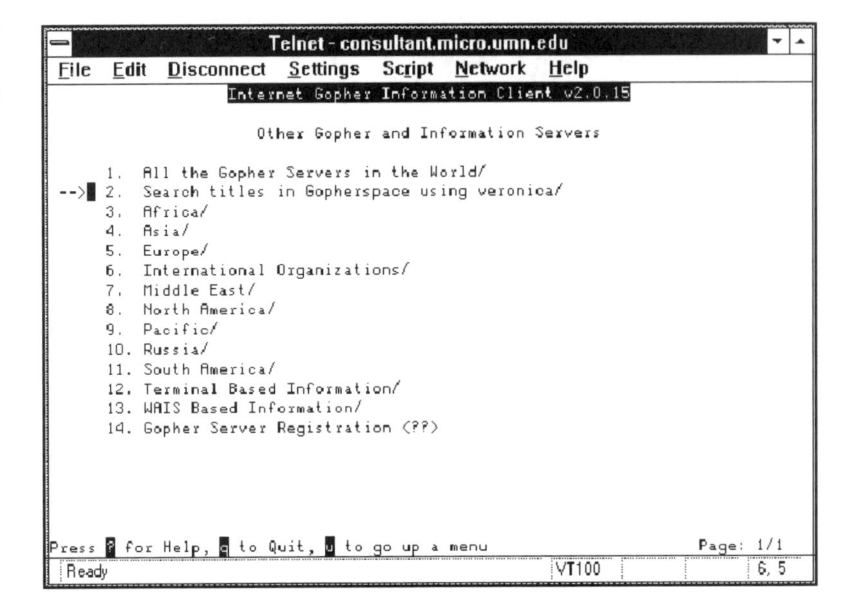

Figure 9.22

Veronica option on Gopher menu.

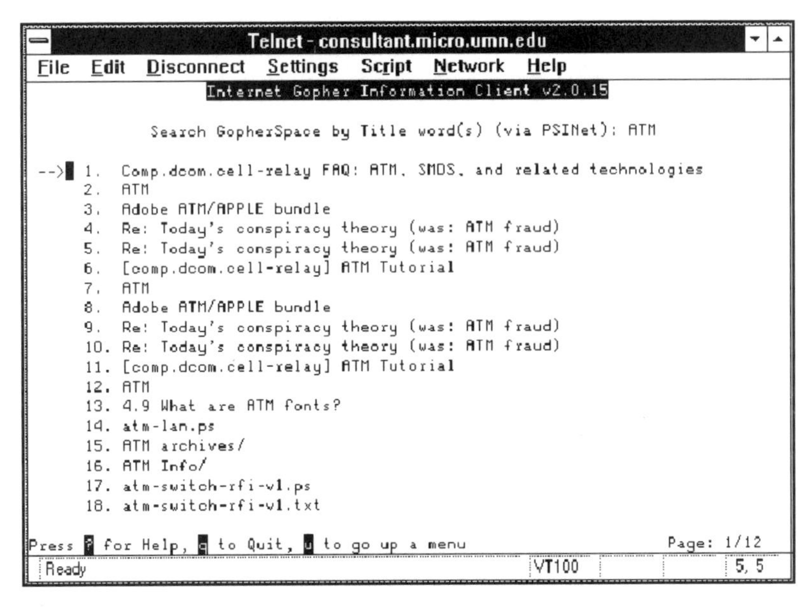

Figure 9.23

Results of Veronica search.

You can access Novell's Gopher server on the host Gopher.novell.com. Figure 9.24 shows some of the Gopher menu items on Novell's gopher server.

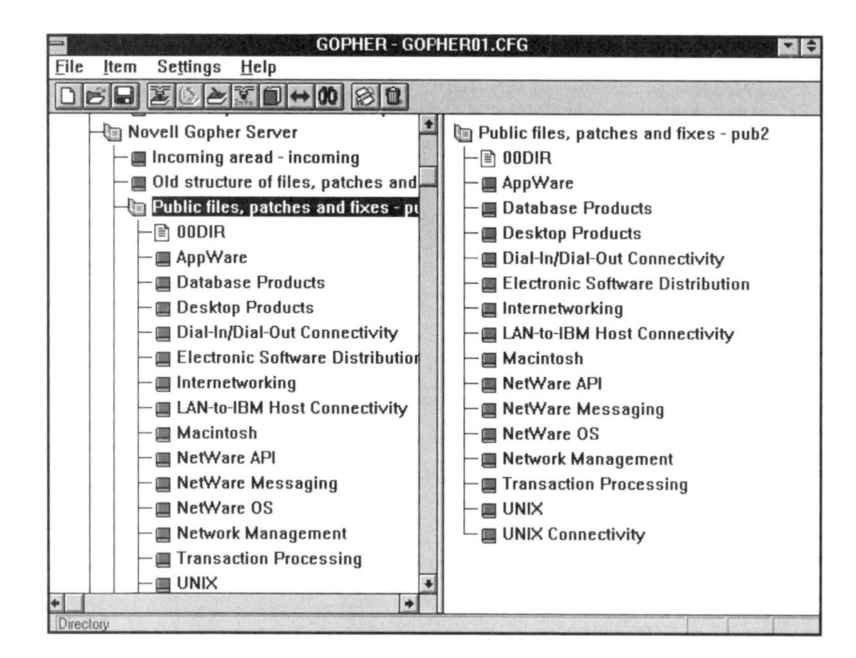

Figure 9.24

Novell's Gopher System.

Using WWW

The *World Wide Web* (WWW) lets you navigate the Internet by selecting marked phrases from text pages, called hypertext technology, instead of using menu-based search tools, such as Gopher.

Most of the development of the World Wide Web has taken place at CERN, the European Particle Physics Laboratory.

You can access WWW via a Telnet session to a WWW server. Examples of such Telnet sessions to actual WWW sites are shown next:

```
telnet  info.cern.ch

telnet  nxoc01.cern.ch

telnet  ukanaix.cc.ukans.edu
```

Figures 9.25 and 9.26 show Telnet sessions to the WWW server at CERN and the University of Kansas, respectively. The University of Kansas WWW server shows a Lynx client.

Figure 9.25

Telnet session to CERN WWW server.

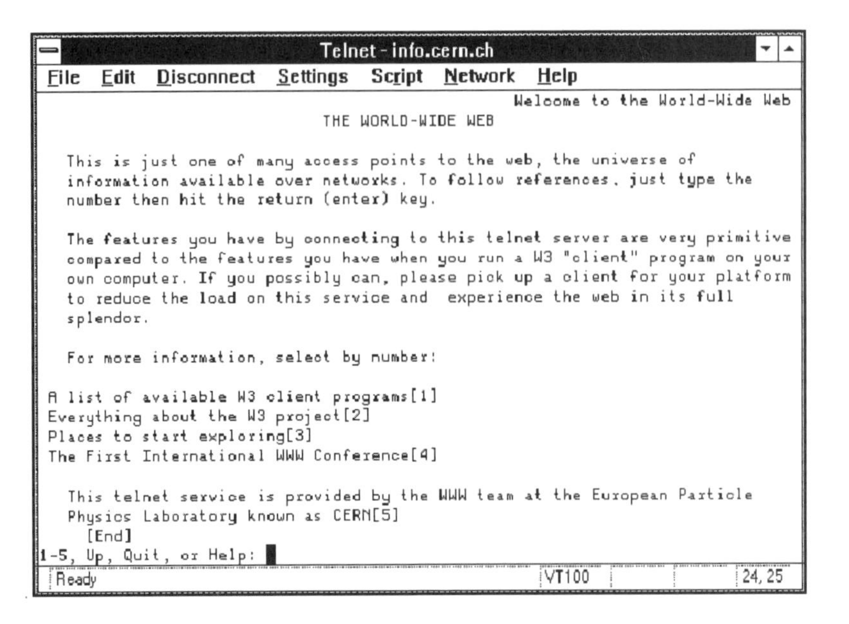

Figure 9.26

Telnet session to University of Kansas WWW server.

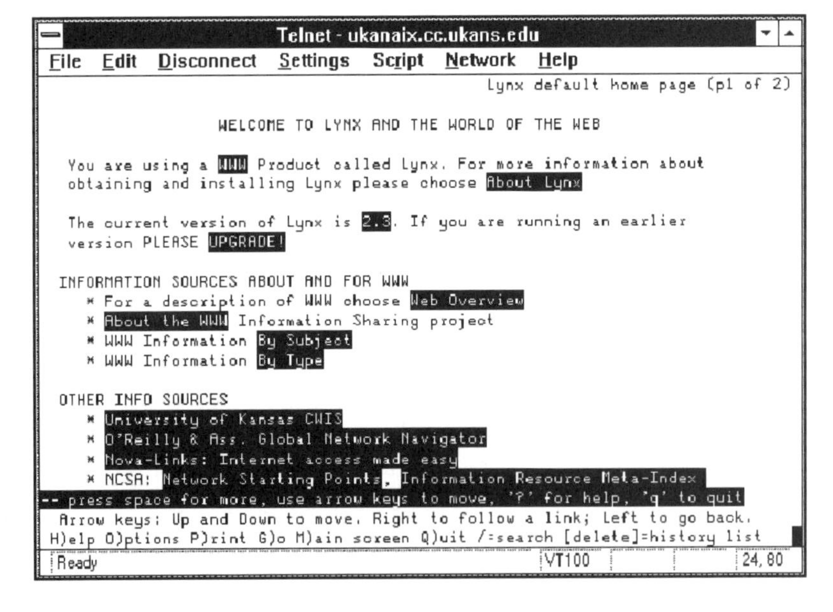

A more popular—but also more bandwidth intensive—method is to use a WWW client. Examples of such WWW clients are Mosaic, Cello, and Lynx.

Figures 9.27 and 9.28 show the use of the Mosaic client to access the Novell WWW server on the host www.novell.com.

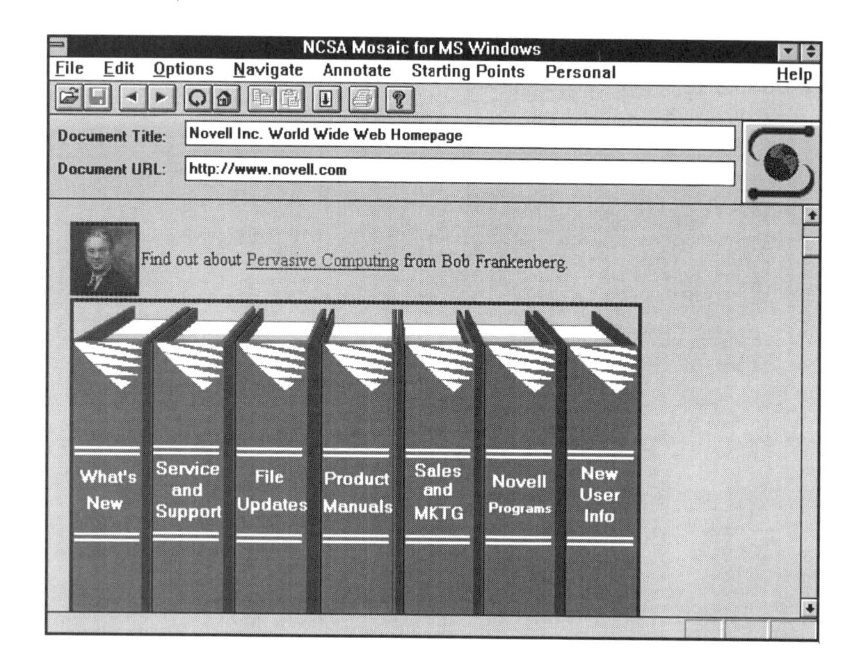

Figure 9.27

Home page for Novell's WWW server.

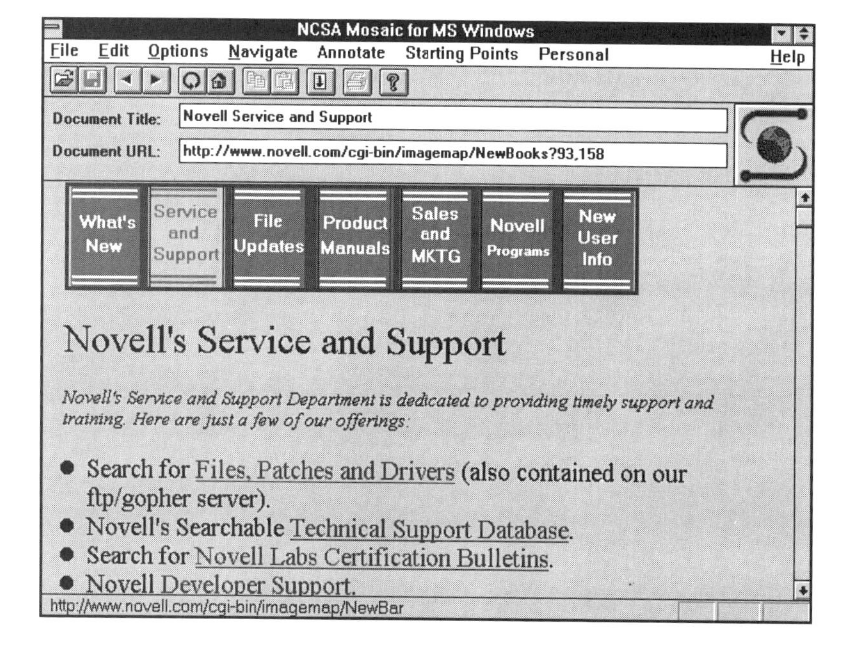

Figure 9.28

Service and Support page on Novell's WWW server.

The displays shown in figures 9.27 and 9.28 are called *pages*. These pages are described using a language called *HyperText Markup Language* (HTML). The protocol used between the WWW client and server is called *HyperText Transfer Protocol* (HTTP).

WWW documents are represented using HTML, which consists of ordinary text data that has embedded HTML tags. HTML tags are enclosed in <>. The following is an example of HTML use:

```
<TITLE>This is a title</TITLE>
<H1>This is a heading</H1>
```

In this example, the text between <TITLE> and </TITLE> will appear as the title of that page, and the text between <H1> and </H1> will appear as a level one heading. One can provide links to other resources by using anchor tags, which have the following syntax:

<A HREF= "URL name">hyperlink</A>

The URL name is the Uniform Resource Locator name that completely describes the location of the resource. The following is an example of an HTML page:

```
<TITLE>Title goes here</TITLE>
<H1>This is a level 1 heading </H1>
Welcome to the Serendipity Book Center (SPC)<P>
We provide books on a vast array of unusual and exciting topics.
Our worldwide centers are located in London, Paris, Stockholm, Los Angeles, Hong
Kong, New Delhi...
<P>
<B><I>For further information select </I></B> <A HREF="http://www.spc.com/
books.htm">more info</A>
<P>
```

The preceding HTML page, when viewed using a WWW client such as Mosaic, appears as shown in figure 9.29.

Using Lists and Newsgroups

You can exchange information and views on a topic of interest by subscribing to a LIST Server discussion group. You use e-mail to exchange information with other participants of the newsgroups. Using LIST Servers enables you to use the familiar e-mail interface, but you have less control over handling information compared to Newsgroups. On an active list discussion, your e-mail box can get cluttered quickly!

Another way to exchange information is to use newsgroups, also called Usenet news. If you participate in a newsgroup discussion group, you must use special newsreader programs. These newsreader programs give you greater message-handling flexibility.

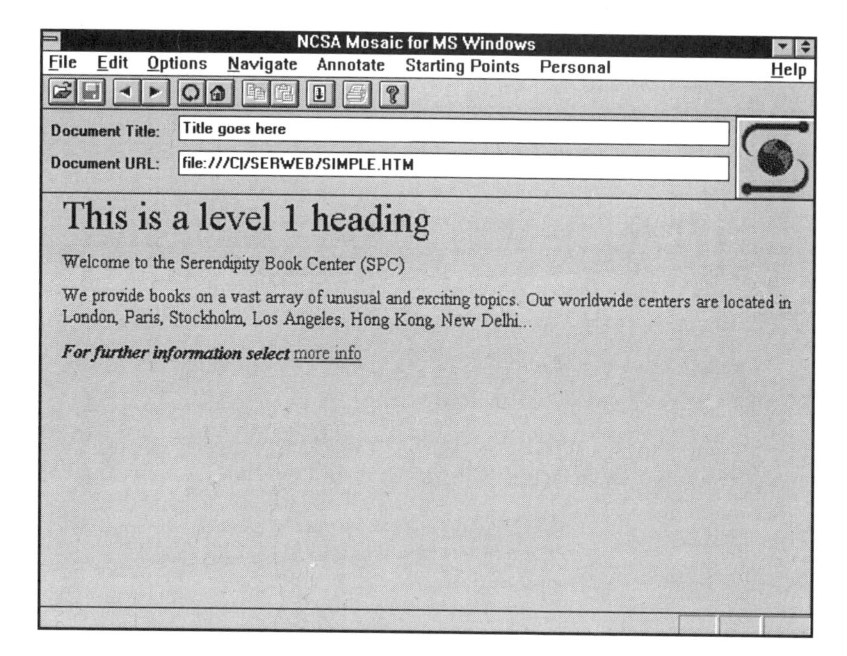

Figure 9.29

HTML example viewed using MOSAIC.

You can subscribe to a mailing list by sending mail to listserv@*listserverhost*, where *listserverhost* is the name of the host on which the LISTSERV software is running. The body of the message must contain the command:

```
subscribe listname  firstname lastname
```

You can abbreviate the keyword subscribe as "sub." Examples of list server subscription requests follow:

```
subscribe  new-list   Paul  Newman

sub             guns-l    John  Dillinger
```

If you get tired of receiving every individual response to a list server, and would rather receive one large mail block incorporating all the messages for the day, you can use the "digest" command. After you subscribe, you can send the following e-mail message, which enables you to receive a digest of all the messages for that day:

```
set listname digest
```

To unsubscribe from a list, send the following mail to LISTSERV, not to the list from which you are unsubscribing. The body of the message must contain the following command:

```
signoff listname
```

Avoid making the common mistake of sending requests to the list itself, which can send your unsubscription request to thousands of annoyed users. In other words, do not send the unsubscription request to *listname@listserverhost*; send it to LISTSERV@*listserverhost.*

Some sample mailing lists are shown in table 9.8.

Table 9.8 Sample Lists

List Name	Description
A+SCOMP	College of Arts and Sciences Computing Services
ADMUSERS	UVM Administrative Systems Group
ASIS-L	American Society for Information Science
BACKS-L	Research on lower back pain, disability, and rehabilitation
CHAOPSYC	Discussion list for Society of Chaos Theory in Psychology
CSAC-L	Computing strategies discussion list
SAFETY	On safety
SKIVT-L	Vermont Skiing and Snow Reports
ALBION-L	British and Irish history
AUDIO_L	Audio applications and equipment
CANINE_L	Discussion group for dog owners
PCBUILD	Discussion list on building PCs and upgrading hardware

If you participate in a newsgroup, you must have access to a news server (also called an NNTP server). The administrator of a Usenet computer that acts as a news server must decide which newsgroups to make available at a given site. To manage the overwhelming amount of data in newsgroups, news messages have an expiration date after which the news server deletes them.

A newsgroup's name describes its area of interest. Newsgroup names are arranged in topical hierarchies. Example top-level hierarchy names are alt, biz, comp, misc, news, rec, sci, soc, talk, and so on. Table 9.9 shows examples of some newsgroups. Examples of Novell-related newsgroups are:

```
comp.sys.novell

comp.unix.unixware
```

Table 9.9 Sample Newsgroups

Topic	Newsgroups
Agriculture	misc.rural
Astronomy	sci.[astro, astro.fits, astro.hubble]
Aviation	rec.aviation
Chemistry	sci.[chem, engr.chem]
Computer	comp.[ai,arch,cog-eng, compilers, Science compression, databases, editors, graphics, lang, multimedia, music, parallel, programming, protocols, realtime, research, robotics, security, simulation, specification, terminals, theory, windows]
Computing	comp.sys.[3b1, acorn, alliant, amiga.*, apollo, apple2, atari.*, att, cbm, cdc, concurrent, dec, encore, handhelds; hp48, hp, ibm.pc.*, ibm.ps2.*, intel, isis, laptops, m6809, m68k, m88k, mac.*, mentor, mips, misc, ncr, next.*, nirthstar, novell, nsc.32k, palmtops, pen, prime, proteon, pyramid, ridge, sequent, sgi, sun.*, super, tahoe, tandy, ti, transputer, unisys, xerox, zenith]
Cooking	rec.food.cooking
Engineering	sci.[engr, engr.chem, engr.biomed]
Health	sci.[med.aids, med.physics, med] k12.ed.health-pe
History	soc.history
Hobbies and Crafts	alt.[aquaria, magic, sewing] rec.[antiques, aquaria, collecting, crafts.brewing, crafts.misc, crafts.textiles, folk-dancing, gambling, gardens, guns, juggling, models.railroad, models.rc, models.rockets, photo, radio.amateur.misc, radio.amateur.packet, radio.amateur.policy, radio.cb, railroad, roller-coaster, wood-working]

Usenet news items are called news articles. Unlike messages in mailing lists, news articles do not arrive automatically at your mailbox. You must use a newsreader program to access the news articles.

When you start the newsreader program for the first time, all the newsgroups known to the news server are listed. You must use your newsreader program to subscribe to only the newsgroups that interest you. You can unsubscribe or subscribe to a newsgroup at any time. Usenet articles have sender, date, and subject fields. All the news articles that share a subject within a newsgroup comprise a subject thread. You can view articles by subject thread or by post date. Sample newsreader programs: rn, trn, tin, nn.

Setting Up a NetWare Server as an FTP Server

You can convert a NetWare 3.x or 4.x server to an FTP server that internal clients on the corporate network or external users on the Internet can access. The FTP Server components are bundled as part of the NetWare NFS product and the NetWare Flex/IP product. The following two NLMs can implement the FTP server:

- INETD.NLM
- FTPSERV.NLM

Figure 9.30 shows the operation of the NetWare FTP server.

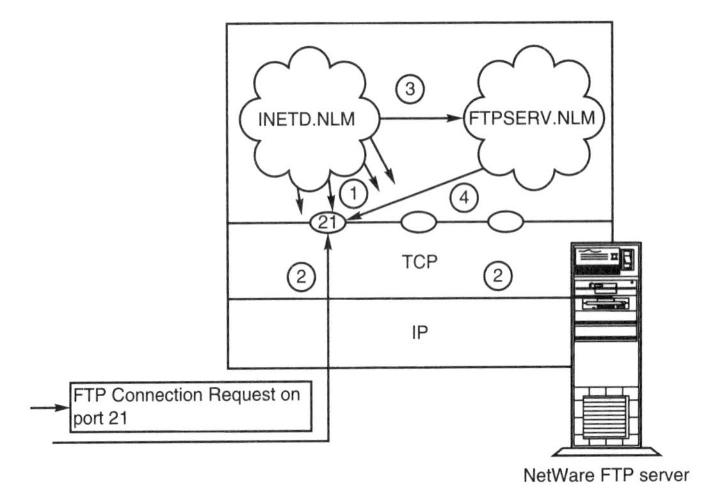
INETD.NLM
FTPSERV.NLM
3
1
4
21
TCP
2
2
IP
FTP Connection Request on port 21
NetWare FTP server
1 INETD.NLM listens for requests
2 FTP connection request arrives on well known port 21
3 INETD.NLM creates (loads) FTPSERV.NLM
4 FTPSERV.NLM listens on port 21 for further requests

Figure 9.30
FTPSERV.NLM and INETD.NLM.

The INETD.NLM is an implementation of the Internet Daemon used in Unix systems. The INETD.NLM listens on well-known ports, such as the FTP port 21, and waits for incoming connection requests. When INETD.NLM sees a TCP connection request on port 21, it knows that this is an FTP connection request, and it loads the FTPSERV.NLM.

FTPSERV.NLM remains in NetWare server memory as long as active FTP connections exist, but is automatically unloaded as soon as no more active FTP connections exist.

To enable the FTP server, you must load INETD.NLM, which you start by using the LOAD INETD command in the NFSSTART.NCF/UNISTART.NCF file. INETD.NLM requires that the preconfigured file SYS:ETC\INETD.CFG exist.

The following are the contents of the INTED.CFG file:

```
#svc    socktype protocol   program-name
ftp     stream   tcp        ftpserv
```

You should normally not have to change this file for FTP services.

To stop FTP services on the NetWare FTP server, unload INETD. If an active FTP connection exists, you must first unload FTPSERV.NLM. The following are the general commands for stopping FTP services on a NetWare FTP server:

UNLOAD FTPSERV

UNLOAD INETD

You use a special file called the SYS:ETC\FTPSERV.CFG configuration file to configure the FTP server. You can use this file to do the following actions:

- Define maximum number of FTP Sessions on the NetWare FTP Server
- Configure the default name space (DOS or NFS) accessed by FTP clients
- Define the default login directory for FTP users

The following is a sample of the SYS:ETC\FTPSERV.CFG file:

```
SESSION   20
NAME SPACE  NFS
USERDEF   /sys/data
GUESTDEF   /sys/data
```

Table 9.10 explains the FTPSERV.CFG Parameters.

TABLE 9.10 FTPSERV.CFG PARAMETERS

Parameter	Description
SESSION	Defines maximum number of concurrent sessions on the NetWare FTP server. Maximum sessions are limited to 75, and the default is 9.
NAME SPACE	Value can be DOS or NFS. Defines the default name space seen by the FTP user. The FTP user can change the default name space using the QUOTE SITE command. Volumes that do not support NFS name space can be accessed from the DOS name space only.
USERDEF	Defines the default directory regular users (nonguest) log in to when making a FTP connection. The default directory is /sys. Users who do not have rights to do a CHANGE DIRECTORY command (CD) to this directory are denied access. You cannot use / (root) as the default directory.
GUESTDEF	Defines the default directory anonymous users (guest) log in to when making an FTP connection. The default directory is /sys. Anonymous users can access only this directory (and its subdirectories).

NetWare Directory Name Convention

The FTP clients see NetWare pathnames and directory listings in Unix style format. The following examples of NetWare pathnames are seen and specified in the FTP client.

```
SYS:PUBLIC\DATA appears as /sys/public/data

VOL_A:APPS\DB\MEMOS appears as /vol_a/apps/db/_memos
```

The general syntax for converting NetWare style names is the following:

```
/volumename/pathname
```

volumename represents the NetWare volume name, and *pathname* represents the NetWare directory pathname. You must use these names in their lowercase form.

The NetWare FTP Server (FTPSERV.NLM) can handle pathnames of 255 characters or less. The FTP server also supports the Unix wild cards (*,?), which are useful in the FTP mget and mput commands that you can use to transfer multiple files with a single command.

The NetWare FTP Server (FTPSERV.NLM) supports the use of two periods (..) to refer to the parent directory. For example, the following FTP command makes the parent directory the current working directory on the NetWare FTP server.

```
cd ..
```

The NetWare FTP Server (FTPSERV.NLM) supports the tilde (~) character, which expands to the pathname of the NetWare user's home directory.

Viewing NFS Name Space

The NetWare FTP server supports the QUOTE SITE command, which enables the FTP client to view the FTP server's directories in the DOS name space or the NFS name space, regardless of the name space on the NetWare volume.

After initial configuration of the FTPSERV.NLM for NFS name space, file operations for volumes that do not have NFS name space take place in the DOS name space.

You can use the FTP QUOTE SITE command to specify the name space to use to view the files. The general syntax for this command follows:

```
QUOTE  SITE  { DOS ¦ NFS }
```

To view the name space as a DOS name space, use the following command:

```
QUOTE SITE DOS
```

To view the name space as an NFS name space, use the following command:

```
QUOTE SITE NFS
```

Figure 9.31 shows the alternate views of the FTP server's directories in the DOS or NFS name space. Figures 9.32 and 9.33 show the use of the QUOTE SITE DOS and QUOTE SITE NFS commands. Notice the message that appears when you use these commands. When you use the QUOTE SITE DOS command, the operations are only for volumes that support the DOS name space (all NetWare volumes support the DOS name space). When you use the QUOTE SITE NFS command, the operations are only for volumes that support the NFS name space. Also, note the differences in directory listing of the two name spaces. The NFS name space directory listing (fig. 9.33) shows the full long names of the files shown in figure 9.32.

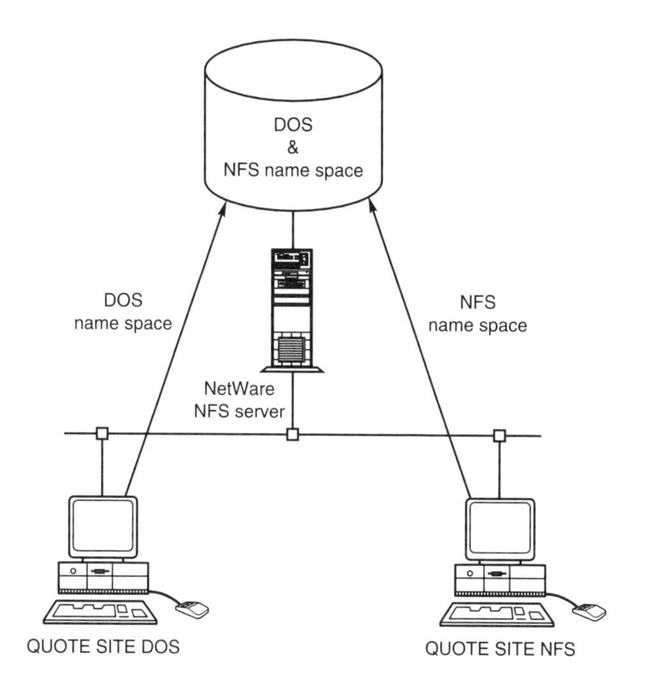

Figure 9.31

Using the QUOTE SITE command.

In many FTP clients, you can abbreviate the QUOTE SITE command to SITE.

In the DOS name space, text files transferred to DOS name space use a 2-byte <LF><CR> termination (<LF> signifying line feed, <CR> signifying carriage return). In the NFS name space text files transferred to NFS name space use a 1-byte <LF> termination.

Another difference between the DOS name space and NFS name space is the way symbolic links are handled in the two name spaces.

Figure 9.32

Using the QUOTE SITE DOS command.

```
Connected to nwcs.
220 s386 FTP server (NetWare v3.11) ready.
Name (nwcs:root): supervisor
331 Password required for supervisor.
Password:
230 User SUPERVISOR logged in.
ftp> cd user1
200 CWD command okay.
ftp> quote site dos
250-This connection is configured for dos namespace.
250 Operations are only for volumes that support dos namespace.
ftp> dir
200 PORT command okay.
150 Opening data connection for  (199.245.180.16,1062).
- [RWCEAFMS] nobody              0      May 15 06:58    accounti.fil
- [RWCEAFMS] nobody              0      May 15 06:58    account0.fil
- [RWCEAFMS] nobody              0      May 15 08:13    areapi2
- [RWCEAFMS] nobody              0      May 15 07:00    lengths1
- [RWCEAFMS] nobody              0      May 15 07:01    strange
- [RWCEAFMS] nobody              0      May 15 08:14    strange0
- [RWCEAFMS] nobody              0      May 15 07:01    strange1
- [RWCEAFMS] nobody              0      May 15 07:19    strange2
226 Transfer complete.
ftp> █
```

Figure 9.33

Using the QUOTE SITE NFS command.

```
ftp> quote site nfs
250-This connection is configured for nfs namespace.
250 Operations are only for volumes that support nfs namespace.
ftp> dir
200 PORT command okay.
150 Opening data connection for  (199.245.180.16,1066).
- [RWCEAFMS] nobody              0      May 15 06:58    accounting.files
- [RWCEAFMS] nobody              0      May 15 06:58    accountingdept.fi
- [RWCEAFMS] nobody              0      May 15 08:13    area=pi2
- [RWCEAFMS] nobody              0      May 15 07:00    length=s1+s2+s3
- [RWCEAFMS] nobody              0      May 15 07:01    =.=
- [RWCEAFMS] nobody              0      May 15 08:14    =
- [RWCEAFMS] nobody              0      May 15 07:01    =[]=
- [RWCEAFMS] nobody              0      May 15 07:19    =+
226 Transfer complete.
ftp>
ftp>
ftp>
ftp>
ftp>
ftp>
ftp>
ftp>
ftp> █
```

Symbolic Links in DOS and NFS Name Spaces

If a symbolic link is retrieved from the FTP server in the NFS name space, the file or directory that is the target of the symbolic link is returned, which is the expected behavior for Unix symbolic links. However, if a symbolic link is retrieved from the FTP server in the DOS name space, the file that is returned is the filename of the target of the symbolic link rather than the contents of the target file. This is because symbolic links appear in the DOS name space as text files that contain the name of the file or directory being pointed to.

Figure 9.34 shows a symbolic link /sys/data/test/memo.txt to the file /sys/data/utils/kss.txt. The contents of the file kss.txt are as follows:

```
"If you can keep your head about you when all are losing theirs..."
```

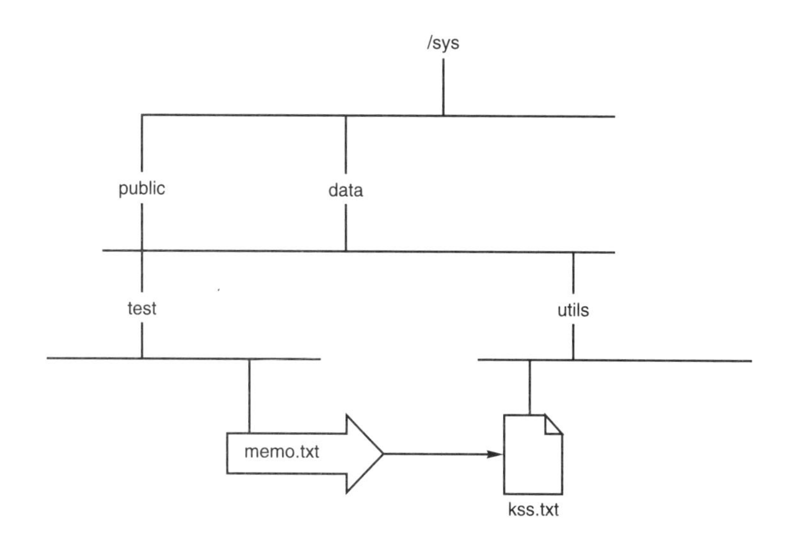

Figure 9.34

Symbolic links and NFS name space example.

Figure 9.35 shows an attempt to read the contents of the symbolic link file /sys/data/test/memo.txt that was transferred using the NFS name space. The contents that are displayed are the contents of the target file kss.txt.

```
331 Password required for supervisor.
Password:
230 User SUPERVISOR logged in.
ftp> cd /sys/data/test
200 CWD command okay.
ftp> ls
200 PORT command okay.
150 Opening data connection for  (199.245.180.16,1083).
l [RWCEAFMS] nobody              23       Dec 30 02:16    memo.txt -> /sys/
- [RWCEAFMS] nobody            1217       Dec 30 02:01    regfile
- [RWCEAFMS] nobody            1217       Dec 30 02:01    regfile.hardlink
226 Transfer complete.
ftp> quote site nfs
550 This connection is already configured for nfs namespace.
ftp> get memo.txt
200 PORT command okay.
150 Opening data connection for memo.txt (199.245.180.16,1084).
226 Transfer complete.
67 bytes received in 0.0028 seconds (24 Kbytes/s)
ftp> bye
221 Goodbye.
ucs# cat memo.txt
If you can keep your head when all about you are losing theirs...
ucs#
```

Figure 9.35

Symbolic links and NFS name space example.

Figure 9.36 shows an attempt to read the contents of the symbolic link file /sys/data/test/memo.txt that was transferred using the DOS name space. Contrast the results of figure 9.36 with figure 9.35. Notice that the contents that are displayed are not the contents of the target file kss.txt, but the name of the target symbolic link /sys/data/utils/kss.txt.

Figure 9.36

Reading symbolic link from the DOS name space.

```
331 Password required for supervisor.
Password:
230 User SUPERVISOR logged in.
ftp> cd /sys/data/test
200 CWD command okay.
ftp> ls
200 PORT command okay.
150 Opening data connection for  (199.245.180.16,1086).
l [RWCEAFMS] nobody              23       Dec 30 02:16     memo.txt -> /sys/
- [RWCEAFMS] nobody            1217       Dec 30 02:01     regfile
- [RWCEAFMS] nobody            1217       Dec 30 02:01     regfile.hardlink
226 Transfer complete.
ftp> quote site dos
250-This connection is configured for dos namespace.
250 Operations are only for volumes that support dos namespace.
ftp> get memo.txt
200 PORT command okay.
150 Opening data connection for memo.txt (199.245.180.16,1087).
226 Transfer complete.
23 bytes received in 0.0027 seconds (8.4 Kbytes/s)
ftp> bye
221 Goodbye.
ucs# cat memo.txt
/sys/data/utils/kss.txtucs#
```

The QUOTE STAT Command

Another extension of the NetWare FTPSERV.NLM is the QUOTE STAT command.

The QUOTE STAT command enables you to inquire about the status of the connection to NetWare FTP server and the best parameters for retrieving a file. The general syntax for QUOTE STAT is as follows:

QUOTE STAT [*pathname*]

Figure 9.37 shows that if you use the QUOTE STAT command without specifying pathname, information on the status of the connection appears. If you use the QUOTE STAT command on a file, it displays information about the best set of FTP parameters for retrieving the file in the following format (see fig. 9.38):

Type Format Stru Mode Pathname

Figure 9.37

The QUOTE STAT command.

```
ucs# ftp nwcs
Connected to nwcs.
220 s386 FTP server (NetWare v3.11) ready.
Name (nwcs:root): supervisor
331 Password required for supervisor.
Password:
230 User SUPERVISOR logged in.
ftp> quote stat
211-Status on s386
       Client node:          ucs
       Client name:          SUPERVISOR
       Directory:            /sys/data
       Type:                 Ascii Non-Print
       Structure:            File
       Mode:                 Stream
       Namespace:            NFS
211 End of Status.
ftp>
```

```
ucs# ftp nwcs
Connected to nwcs.
220 s386 FTP server (NetWare v3.11) ready.
Name (nwcs:root): supervisor
331 Password required for supervisor.
Password:
230 User SUPERVISOR logged in.
ftp> quote stat hangman.c
250 ANFS hangman.c
ftp> █
```

Figure 9.38

The QUOTE STAT filename command.

Table 9.11 explains the meanings of the preceding fields:

TABLE 9.11 DESCRIPTION OF OUTPUT FOR THE QUOTE STAT FILENAME COMMAND

Field	Meaning
Type	A for ASCII. I for Image (Binary). This is the data transfer type.
Format	Data transfer format. N for nonprint (used for ASCII and IMAGE), or a number specifying local byte size.
Stru	The transfer structure. F for file structure. R for record structure.
Mode	The transfer mode. S for Stream. R for record structure.

Accessing NetWare Servers that Lack FTP Support

The NetWare FTP server contains a feature that allows NetWare servers that lack FTP services to be accessed through the use of a NetWare FTP server. Figure 9.39 shows that the NetWare server NWCS has FTP services, whereas the NetWare server RAMU does not. The FTP client can access the NetWare FTP server, and through this connection access files on the NetWare server, RAMU, that does not have FTP services.

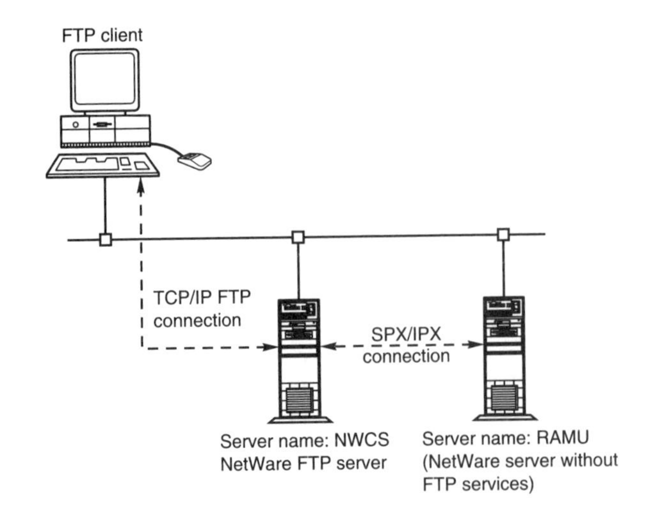

Figure 9.39
Accessing NetWare servers that lack FTP support.

To reference the pathnames for the NetWare server that lacks FTP services, you must use the following special syntax:

```
//netware_server_name/volume_name/file_pathname
```

For example, you would use the following name to reference the file RAMU/SYS:PUBLIC/DATA/MEMO.TXT:

```
//ramu/sys/public/data/memo.txt
```

Some restrictions and requirements, however, apply to accomplishing the connections shown in figure 9.39, as described in the following list:

- A NetWare account that has identical username and password to the NetWare FTP Server must exist on the NetWare server (that lacks FTP services). This applies to NetWare 3.x servers.
- Anonymous users cannot access files on NetWare server without FTP services.
- FTP clients can access only DOS name space on NetWare server without FTP services.
- To configure the NetWare server that lacks FTP services, you must use the following setting:

  ```
  SET REPLY TO GET NEAREST SERVER=ON
  ```

Anonymous Users in FTP

To support anonymous users on the NetWare FTP server, a NetWare user account called ANONYMOUS, which has rights to the directory specified by the GUESTDEF parameter in FTPSERV.CFG, is necessary.

If your NetWare FTP server is connected to the Internet, the NetWare FTP server can serve as a repository of files for anonymous users.

The FTP client who wants to use "guest" services on the NetWare FTP server can use the username anonymous to log in. The anonymous user can use only the directory specified by the GUESTDEF parameter. The ANONYMOUS user can supply any password, regardless of the actual password set for the NetWare user ANONYMOUS. In other words, the password supplied by the anonymous user is not checked against the password for NetWare user account ANONYMOUS.

A common convention is for the ANONYMOUS user to supply his or her identity, such as an e-mail address.

Denying Access to the NetWare FTP Server for Specific Users

You can place users' names in the SYS:ETC\FTPUSERS configuration file to deny access to them.

If the file FTPUSERS is missing or empty, any user who has an account on the NetWare FTP server can access the server.

The following example is a sample FTPUSERS file, where a command is used to display its contents:

```
F:\> TYPE \ETC\FTPSUSERS
HACKER
BILL
ANDY
RICHARD
MENAX
SAM
```

The users listed in the preceding example are denied access to the FTP service on the NetWare server.

The NetWare FTP Server Log File

The NetWare FTP server maintains a log file of all FTP server login attempts, which is a text file that is kept in the SYS:ETC\FTPSERV.LOG file.

The following is an example of sample FTPSERV.LOG file:

```
Sun Apr 5 14:50:51 1992No Such User.
Sun Apr 5 14:51:39 1992 KARANJIT login from ltrees1 without password.
Sun Apr 5 14:59:27 1992 USER1 login failed. Wrong password from ltree1.
Sun Apr 5 14:59:58 1992 KARANJIT login from ltree1 without password.
Fri Apr 17 20:22:21 1992 KARANJIT login from ltree1 without password.
Thu May 14 12:54:11 1992 USER1 login failed. Wrong password from ltree1.
Thu May 14 12:54:34 1992 USER1 login failed. Wrong password from ltree1.
```

```
Fri May 29 13:21:30 1992 USER1 login from ltree1.
Wed Jul 1 07:34:09 1992 KARANJIT login from 144.19.74.21.
Sun Jul 5 11:22:50 1992No Such User.
Sun Jul 5 11:23:03 1992 SUPERVISOR login from ltrees1.
Sun Jul 5 11:28:25 1992 SUPERVISOR login from ltrees1.
Mon Jul 6 08:55:15 1992No Such User.
Mon Jul 6 08:59:15 1992 SUPERVISOR login from ltrees1.
Wed Jul 8 12:38:39 1992No Such User.
Wed Jul 8 12:38:55 1992No Such User.
Wed Jul 8 12:39:07 1992 SUPERVISOR login from 144.19.74.202.
Wed Jul 8 13:00:20 1992No Such User.
Wed Jul 8 13:22:57 1992No Such User.
Wed Jul 8 13:23:41 1992 SUPERVISOR login from ltrees1.
Wed Jul 8 13:52:40 1992No Such User.
Wed Jul 8 13:52:53 1992 SUPERVISOR login from ltrees1.
Thu Jul 30 13:47:46 1992No Such User.
Thu Jul 30 13:48:29 1992 SUPERVISOR login from 144.19.74.21.
Thu Jul 30 13:49:54 1992 SUPERVISOR login from 144.19.74.21.
Thu Jul 30 17:19:02 1992 USER1 login from 144.19.74.21.
Thu Jul 30 17:34:34 1992 USER1 login from 144.19.74.21.
Thu Jul 30 17:39:51 1992 USER5 login from 144.19.74.21.
Thu Jul 30 17:41:13 1992 USER8 login from 144.19.74.21.
Thu Jul 30 17:59:49 1992 USER14 login from 144.19.74.21.
Fri Sep 25 20:48:28 1992 SUPERVISOR login from ltree1.
Sun Oct 11 12:36:03 1992No Such User.
Sun Oct 11 12:36:23 1992 SUPERVISOR login from 144.19.74.221.
Wed Dec 9 19:20:21 1992 SUPERVISOR login from ltree2.
Wed Apr 21 14:24:30 1993No Such User.
Wed Apr 21 15:19:33 1993 KARANJIT login from ltree1.
Wed Apr 21 15:33:10 1993 KARANJIT login from ltree1.
Wed Apr 21 15:39:26 1993No Such User.
Wed Apr 21 19:32:36 1993 KARANJIT login failed. Wrong password from ltree1.
Wed Apr 21 19:33:49 1993 KARANJIT login from ltree1.
Fri Apr 23 10:48:09 1993 SUPERVISOR login from ltree1.
Fri Apr 23 11:07:50 1993No Such User.
Sat May 15 13:13:42 1993No Such User.
Sat May 15 13:14:23 1993 KARANJIT login from ucs.
Sat May 15 16:57:49 1993 KARANJIT Name Space or Directory Error.
Sat May 15 16:58:35 1993 KARANJIT Name Space or Directory Error.
Sat May 15 17:00:13 1993 KARANJIT login from ltree1.
Sat May 15 17:15:49 1993 Guest login 'guest' from ltree1.
Sat May 15 17:29:19 1993 HACKER login from ltree1.
Sat May 15 17:30:53 1993 HACKER Denied Access.
Sat May 15 17:31:08 1993 KARANJIT login from ltree1.
```

```
Wed Dec 29 23:33:33 1993 KARANJIT login from ucs without password.
Wed Dec 29 23:34:07 1993 USER1 login failed. Wrong password from ucs.
Wed Dec 29 23:34:19 1993 USER1 login failed. Wrong password from ucs.
Wed Dec 29 23:34:40 1993 SUPERVISOR login from ucs.
Wed Dec 29 23:49:53 1993 SUPERVISOR login failed. Wrong password from ucs.
Wed Dec 29 23:50:10 1993 SUPERVISOR login from ucs.
Wed Dec 29 23:51:59 1993 SUPERVISOR login from ucs.
Wed Dec 29 23:57:52 1993 SUPERVISOR login from ucs.
Thu Dec 30 00:03:46 1993 SUPERVISOR login from ucs.
Thu Dec 30 00:30:25 1993 SUPERVISOR login from ucs.
Thu Dec 30 00:31:16 1993 SUPERVISOR login from ucs.
Thu Dec 30 00:42:24 1993 SUPERVISOR login from 199.245.180.9.
Thu Dec 30 00:59:06 1993 USER1 login failed. Wrong password from ucs.
Thu Dec 30 00:59:21 1993 USER2 login failed. Wrong password from ucs.
Thu Dec 30 01:07:24 1993 USER1 login from ucs.
Thu Dec 30 01:10:03 1993 KSS login from ucs.
Thu Dec 30 02:41:24 1993 SUPERVISOR login from ucs.
Thu Dec 30 02:42:41 1993 SUPERVISOR login from ucs.
```

Note the entry (in italics) for the user HACKER. An attempt to log in by user HACKER is shown in the following:

```
Sat May 15 17:29:19 1993 HACKER login from ltree1.
Sat May 15 17:30:53 1993 HACKER Denied Access.
```

The user HACKER was denied access because the name HACKER was listed in the SYS:ETC\FTPUSERS file.

Summary

In this chapter, you learned about the four different methods for accessing the Internet: direct connection, on-demand direct connection, dial-up, and e-mail. If you are on a NetWare-based network and want to share Internet access with other users connected to the network, the most flexible method to use for Internet access is the direct connection.

You were presented with a description and installation of two TCP/IP Internet software tools that you can use on a NetWare-based network for Internet access. You also learned about the different Internet tools that you can use to access information on the Internet, and how you can set up your NetWare server as an Internet FTP server.

Using NetWare for Internet Access

Since its inception in the early 1980s, Novell NetWare has captured the largest market share of the currently installed network operating systems. Estimates are that anywhere from 50 percent to 70 percent of the installed local area networks are running Novell NetWare. Novell's popularity in the local area network environment is due in part to the robust performance of its IPX/SPX protocol stack, which was designed and optimized for LAN operations.

With the tremendous growth and popularity of the Internet, it's only natural that NetWare LAN administrators will want to connect their networks to the Internet and provide NetWare users with access to Internet resources. The Internet, however, is based on the open TCP/IP protocol, which was designed and optimized for WAN traffic and is not compatible with IPX.

When network protocols are not compatible, they can still be made to work together. Making incompatible protocols work together is done either through a gateway that converts between the protocols or through protocol coexistence. Coexistence between network protocols is referred to as *dual protocol stacking* or *multiple protocol stacking*, depending on how many protocols are running or coexisting on the same device. Many commercial products are available that provide coexistence or convert between TCP/IP and IPX/SPX protocols. With TCP/IP being most popular in datagram-oriented WANs and IPX being the most popular LAN protocol, products that integrate TCP/IP and IPX are in demand.

Building Internet Servers Using NetWare

NetWare servers and workstations always run the IPX protocol stack. Optionally, you can configure a NetWare server to run the TCP/IP protocols for the purpose of protocol conversion between IPX and TCP/IP and for the purpose of supporting TCP/IP applications. When a server converts between the IPX and TCP/IP protocols it is acting as an IPX to TCP/IP protocol gateway. When a server is also running TCP/IP applications, these applications can be accessed from the workstations either through the gateway or directly over TCP/IP. The workstation must be running TCP/IP if it wants to communicate with the TCP/IP server application without going through the gateway. Given these configuration options, NetWare LAN administrators can configure their NetWare servers and workstations in at least three different ways to provide NetWare users with access to the Internet.

- Server as a TCP/IP to IPX gateway only
- Server as a TCP/IP to IPX gateway with TCP/IP applications
- Server and workstations running TCP/IP

Network administrators must determine which configuration is most applicable in their environments. Existing applications, user requirements, and organizational security requirements have to be taken into account when configuring a NetWare server for Internet access.

Server as a TCP/IP to IPX Gateway

This configuration is perhaps the simplest of the three ways in which a NetWare server can be used for Internet access. In this configuration, a NetWare server acts as a protocol gateway that converts between the IPX/SPX and TCP/IP protocols. Both TCP/IP and IPX protocols are running at the server. However, NetWare users are able to access the TCP/IP-based Internet with only the native IPX protocol running at their stations. Users do not have to have TCP/IP configured at their workstations in this "gateway only" approach.

Two gateway software components (server and client) are involved in this "gateway only" approach. The server component of the gateway is installed on the NetWare server in the form of an NLM. The client component of the gateway is installed on every NetWare station that needs to access the Internet.

The client component of the gateway runs at the workstations and intercepts all of the requests from the Windows-based, WinSock-compliant Internet applications (WWW, Mail, Gopher, and so forth), which are written specifically for TCP/IP. The client component of the gateway enables these request to be sent over the LAN in IPX packets instead of TCP/IP packets. These requests are requests for Internet services. At the NetWare server, the server component of the gateway translates the incoming, Internet-bound IPX packets received from the NetWare stations into TCP/IP packets. These TCP/IP packets are then sent from the NetWare server to their final destinations on the Internet.

TCP/IP packets coming from the Internet are converted into IPX packets at the NetWare server and sent via IPX to the NetWare stations. These IPX packets are first received by the client component of the gateway installed at the workstations and then passed on to an appropriate application at the workstation.

The TCPIP NLM must be loaded on the NetWare server to support the server component of the gateway. The NetWare server must also be correctly configured for TCP/IP. Figure 10.1 shows components of a NetWare network with the server acting as a generic Internet gateway. See the section "Overview of Internet Servers Using NetWare" for specific details on the configuration of a NetWare server as an Internet gateway using the Inetix Client and Gateway software from Micro Computer Systems.

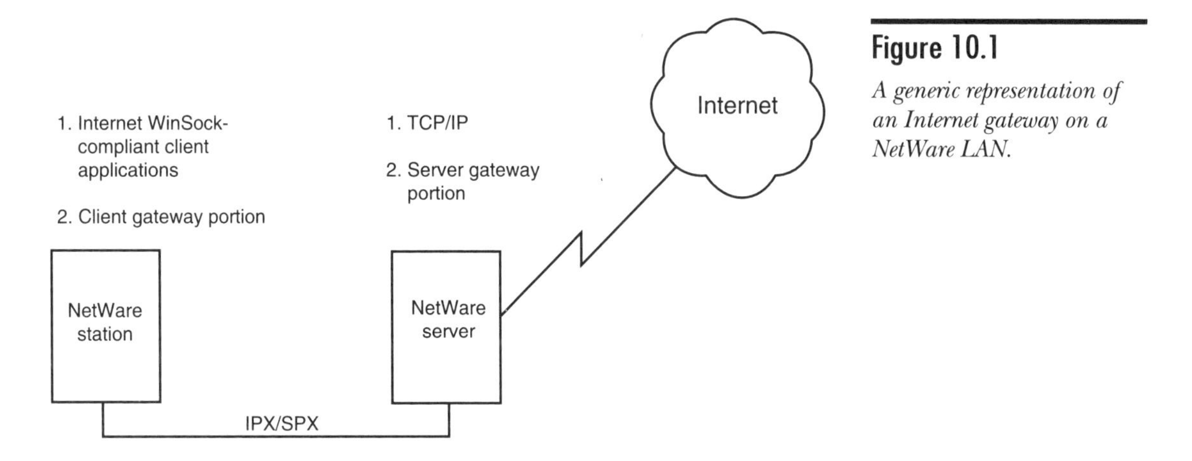

Figure 10.1

A generic representation of an Internet gateway on a NetWare LAN.

The "gateway only" approach enables LAN users to access the Internet without the NetWare LAN itself becoming part of the Internet. Only outbound connections from the LAN are allowed. No incoming connections from the Internet are permitted. Because much of the hacking and network penetrations take place over TCP/IP, there are security advantages to this approach. Of course good security measures can be implemented in the TCP/IP environment as well, but implementing security procedures demands time from already stressed network administrators.

Server as a TCP/IP to IPX Gateway with TCP/IP Applications

In this configuration, a NetWare file server runs the popular Internet TCP/IP client-server applications such as the WWW, Gopher, or Mail. These applications can then be accessed by the Internet users and by the local NetWare users as well.

Internet TCP/IP applications follow the client-server software model. In the client-server software model, the server component of an application must be loaded and running on the server and a client component of the application has to be loaded and running at a workstation.

To activate the server component of an Internet application, load one or more of the application NLMs at the server console. When loaded, these NLMs install the server portion of the WWW, Gopher, FTP, or Mail. Internet application NLMs can be loaded manually by the administrator each time the server is brought up, or the LOAD commands can be placed in the AUTOEXEC.NCF file. In addition to the Internet application NLMs, the NLM for the server portion of the TCP/IP to IPX gateway, and the TCPIP NLM (which comes with NetWare) must also be loaded on the server.

At the workstations, only the IPX protocol is active. Also, the client portions of the WinSock-compliant Internet applications, such as WWW, Gopher, or Mail, must be installed on all NetWare workstations that need access to the Internet. Additionally, the client portion of the TCP/IP to IPX gateway must also be installed. The function of the client portion of the gateway software is to take the output from the WinSock API and place it in IPX packets. If the client gateway software is not installed, NetWare stations would have to run IPX and TCP/IP concurrently to access the Internet or the TCP/IP applications installed on the NetWare server. This workstation configuration is similar to the approach described in the preceding section in which the server is acting as a TCP/IP to IPX gateway only and the clients are running IPX only.

Examples of commercial products that turn a NetWare server into an Internet server and gateway include the following:

- SiteBuilder (from American Internet)
- HTTPD-CLACI (from Great Lakes Area Commercial Internet)

Server and Workstations Running TCP/IP

In this approach, the Internet applications on the server are configured in the same way as described in the preceding section. The server portions of the WWW, Mail, or Gopher are activated by loading a series of NLMs. The difference in the server configuration between this approach and the approach described in the preceding section is that there is no need for an IPX to TCP/IP gateway at the server because both the server and the NetWare workstations are running IPX and TCP/IP.

At the workstations, both the IPX and the TCP/IP protocols need to be properly configured and bound to network interface card(s). For more details on binding IPX and TCP/IP to network cards, refer to Chapter 6, "Managing TCP/IP Protocols Using INETCFG."

As a network administrator, you must determine whether to use a single NIC or multiple NICs in the workstation for both IPX and TCP/IP traffic. A determining factor is the projected network traffic and the characteristics of the underlying network technology. If a certain number of users will be doing a lot research on the Internet (that is, surfing the WWW and downloading documents), for example, it is advisable from a network design point of view to have a separate cabling segment for the TCP/IP traffic for these users. Surfing the WWW involves transfer of images and text from WWW pages to a workstation. This creates a lot of network traffic, which could have a serious impact on the performance of other users. With two NICs in a workstation, the IPX protocol would be bound to one NIC and the TCP/IP protocol would be bound to the other.

Binding IPX and TCP/IP to different NICs means that you will have multiple cabling segments in your network but the traffic on each segment will be lighter than if both of the protocols were bound to the same network card. This results in better network response time for all users, which can translate into better productivity.

If you choose to have two network cards in your workstations, you will also want to have at least two network cards in the NetWare server—one card bound to IPX and the other card bound to TCP/IP. Because every NetWare server can also be configured as a TCP/IP router, and a router can act as a "firewall," your NetWare server can also be configured as a "firewall." A *firewall* is a security mechanism that separates networks. A network on one side of the firewall is considered exposed to outside intruders. A network on the other side of the firewall is considered to be secure. For more information on firewalls and Internet security, refer to *Implementing Internet Security* from New Riders.

The administration of TCP/IP addresses is considered to be more difficult than the administration of IPX addresses. In fact, there is no such thing as administration of IPX addresses at the workstations. Workstations obtain their IPX addresses by combining the network number with the workstation hardware address and a socket number of a software process. This means that IPX addressing at the workstation is dynamic and requires no involvement on the part of a network administrator.

If TCP/IP address administration is a consideration to not run both IPX and TCP/IP protocols at the workstation, consider a product that allows for dynamic workstation IP address management from the server. This means that when a workstation needs to establish a TCP/IP connection to the server, it gets an IP address from a pool of addresses centrally managed at the server. The available IP addresses are stored in a configuration file at the server rather than having a permanent address assigned to each workstation. Two protocols provide this central administration of IP addresses: BootP and DHCP. DHCP (Distributed Host Configuration Protocol) is considered to be an "auto configuration" protocol as opposed to a bootstrapping protocol such as BootP. BootP is a bootstrap protocol developed in the mid 1980s for use with diskless workstations. See Chapter 6 for more details on BootP.

Note The BootP program for NetWare servers comes with the LAN Workgroup product. On Technologies provides a DHCP implementation in a product called IP Track.

You must have a functional physical WAN connection to the Internet in all of the above described cases. The physical connection can be either a direct Internet connection (if you are fortunate enough to have your own official IP address), or it can be a connection through an ISP (Internet Service Provider). This connection can be an ISDN line, a fractional T1 line, a full T1 line, or any number of other wide area services depending on their cost and availability. In this chapter, the focus is on integrating NetWare into the Internet and not on the data communications and addressing aspects of Internet connectivity. Some options for physical connectivity to the Internet are covered in the section "Physical Connections to the Internet."

Note Internet Service Providers (ISPs) are companies that provide connection services to the Internet. ISPs are located worldwide and can assist you in securing a valid IP address and the necessary bandwidth to meet your organizational requirements.

Overview of Internet Servers Using NetWare

A number of commercial products allow a NetWare server to be configured as an Internet gateway or as an Internet server. Each of these products implements one of the three approaches to using NetWare for Internet access described in the preceding section. The following products are brought to your attention so that you can determine which approach to implementing a NetWare server for Internet access is most viable in your environment:

- Inetix Gateway from Micro Computer Systems
- SiteBuilder from American Internet Corporation
- GLACI-HTTPD from Great Lakes Area Commercial Internet
- WEBserv from Puzzle Systems
- NOV*IX from Firefox
- NetWare Web Server from Novell

Inetix Gateway

The Inetix Gateway from Micro Computer Systems turns your NetWare server into a TCP/IP to IPX gateway. The gateway product comes with a server and a client portion. Inetix also provides its own version of WINSOCK.DLL with the client portion of the gateway. The Inetix version of WINSOCK.DLL works in conjunction with the client portion of the gateway to intercept requests from TCP/IP applications on the workstations and uses the IPX/SPX NetWare protocols to carry these requests to the server. The client portion of the gateway establishes a "virtual circuit" SPX connection with the server portion of the gateway. The commands needed for the client and server portions of the gateway to communicate are contained in the first byte of the data portion of the SPX packet. At the server, these requests are converted into TCP/IP format by the server portion of the Inetix Gateway.

Before proceeding with the Inetix Gateway installation, the NetWare server must already be configured for TCP/IP. The server must also be configured to provide DNS (Domain Name Services). Inetix Gateway installation takes place from a client station that is running Microsoft Windows and is logged in to a NetWare server.

The default installation options are to install both the server and the client portions of the software. The server portion of the gateway is installed on the server and is represented by the Install Inetix Gateway Software option. The client portion of the Inetix software is installed on your local station and is represented by Install Inetix Gateway Configuration Software option.

The Inetix Gateway Software installation copies the INETIX.NLM into the SYS:SYSTEM directory and gives you the option to have AUTOEXEC.NCF modified to include the LOAD INETIX statement. The LOAD INETIX statement in AUTOEXEC.NCF will activate the Inetix Gateway every time the server is brought up.

The Inetix Gateway Configuration Software is loaded into a default C:\INETIX directory on the local workstation. This installation option also creates a Windows NETWORK program group. Clicking on the configuration icon in the NETWORK program group takes you to a screen with configuration options (see fig. 10.2). These options include the configuration of local clients and remote hosts, and the IP number of the NetWare server acting as the gateway. This screen also enables you to monitor the status of connections to the gateway. Figure 10.2 shows the current status of the gateway—up and running with 0 connections.

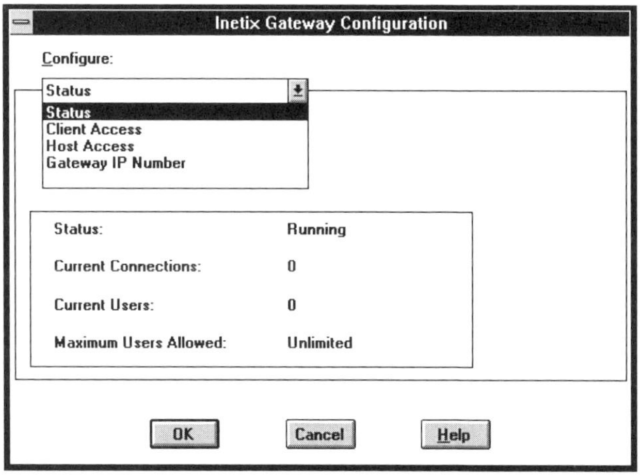

Figure 10.2

The Inetix Gateway status screen.

Clicking on Client Access causes the client configuration screen shown in figure 10.3 to appear.

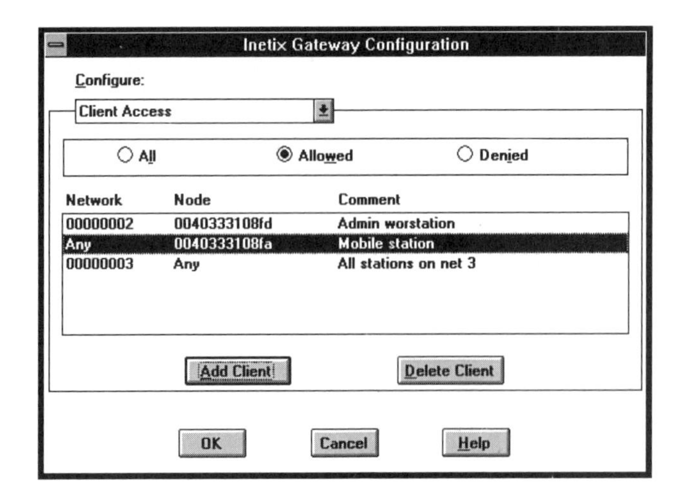

Figure 10.3

The Inetix Gateway client configuration screen.

The client configuration screen displays the following three options for controlling client access:

- **Mobile stations.** If you have a mobile station that attaches to a LAN anywhere on your internetwork, you can configure it to access the gateway from any network number. The word "Any" in the "Network" column in figure 10.3 indicates that the mobile station with a hardware address of 004333108fa can access the gateway from any LAN segment in the internetwork.
- **All stations on a cabling segment.** The word "Any" in the "Node" column in figure 10.3 means that all stations on net 3 can access the gateway. You can give access to any station on a specified network number as well as limit your clients to being on specific nets.
- **Specific station from a specific LAN.** When the network number and the node numbers are specified, it means that this particular node must be attached to this particular network number to access the gateway.

Hosts that are accessible through the gateway are configured through the Host Access option of the configuration screen (see fig. 10.4).

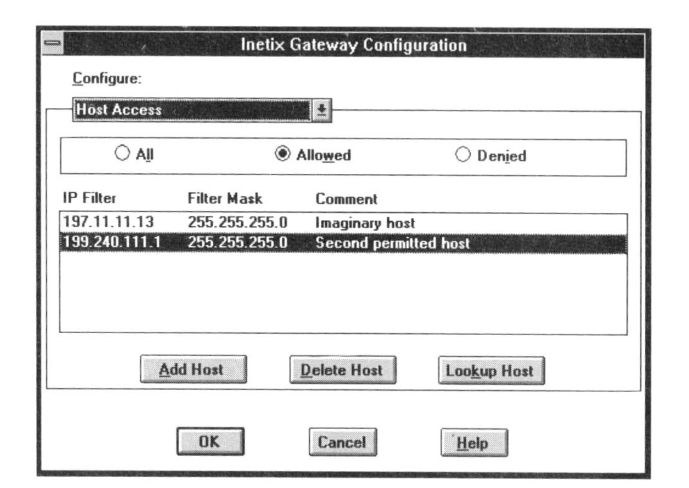

Figure 10.4

The Host Access option of the Inetix Gateway Configuration screen.

After the clients and hosts have been configured, you can use the Inetix Gateway client software to make connections to servers on the Internet. The gateway client software is invoked by clicking the MCS FTP icon in the NETWORK program group created during the Inetix Gateway installation. MCS FTP is an abbreviation for Micro Computer Systems File Transfer Protocol. FTP enables you to make a connection to a remote host via the gateway.

Click on the Connect option and a default connection screen appears, as shown in figure 10.5.

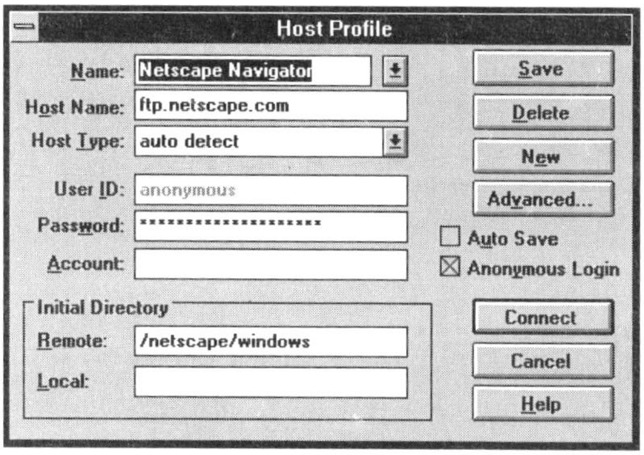

Figure 10.5

The MCS FTP screen with the default connection option.

The default connection screen shows that an attempt will be made to connect to the ftp.netscape.com host. The question is, Will this connection be successful given the host configuration shown in figure 10.4? The answer is that the host configuration shown in figure 10.4 would have to be modified to add the IP address of ftp.netscape.com to the "allowed" list, or the host configuration could be modified to allow connection to all hosts.

The MCS FTP program allows other Internet applications, such as Gopher and WWW browsers, to be used over the connection established via the Inetix Gateway. These Internet applications either can be installed in the default C:MCS_FTP directory, or you can change directories to have these application programs displayed and accessible from the MCS FTP screen.

The Inetix Gateway product is a viable solution for situations where you do not want to set up your own Internet server but still want to provide NetWare users on a local LAN with access to the Internet.

SiteBuilder

SiteBuilder, from the American Internet Corporation, implements an IPX to TCP/IP gateway and a WWW application. The SiteBuilder product is a client/server application with the server portion running on the NetWare server in the form of NLMs and the client portion installed on a local station under Windows.

You can install the server portion of SiteBuilder either from the file server console or from a workstation. For installation from the file server, SiteBuilder provides the SBINST NLM, which is loaded on the file server console from the first installation disk. After the SBINST NLM is loaded, it brings up an installation menu on the file server console. To install SiteBuilder from the file server console, you must have physical access to the file server.

Note Many network administrators regard installing programs from the file server as less desirable than installing programs from a workstation. The file server is the most critical component of your network; some network administrators consider it best to minimize physical access to and contact with the server. An inadvertent hand or foot motion can flip the file server power switch or unplug it from an electric outlet bringing your entire network down.

To install SiteBuilder from a NetWare workstation, the workstation must be logged into the file server under the SUPERVISOR (NetWare 3.x) or the ADMIN (NetWare 4.x) account. The workstation must also be running Microsoft Windows 3.x or higher. Installing SiteBuilder from the workstation is the standard installation procedure for Windows applications. The SETUP program from the installation disk is executed using the RUN option from the FILE menu. The installation program creates a directory structure on the file server for the SiteBuilder files. The files are then copied from the installation disks into these directories. The default installation directory is AIC on the SYS volume. This installation procedure installs the server portion of SiteBuilder.

The installation of the client portion of SiteBilder also takes place from the workstation but only after the server portion of SiteBuilder has been installed on the server. The SETUP program from the SYS:AIC\WINDOWS directory is executed from Windows to install SiteBuilder Control and IPAccess, which are the client portions of SiteBuilder.

After the server and workstation installation is complete, two NLMs, WEB and IPACCESS, must be loaded on the server. These two NLMs are installed by default in the SYS:AIC directory, which means that a full path to that directory must be specified at the time they are loaded, or the SYS:AIC directory must be added to the search path with the SEARCH ADD console command. These two NLMs turn the NetWare server into a WWW server accessible from the Internet and from the local NetWare stations. The WEB NLM displays a statistics screen on the file server console, as shown in figure 10.6.

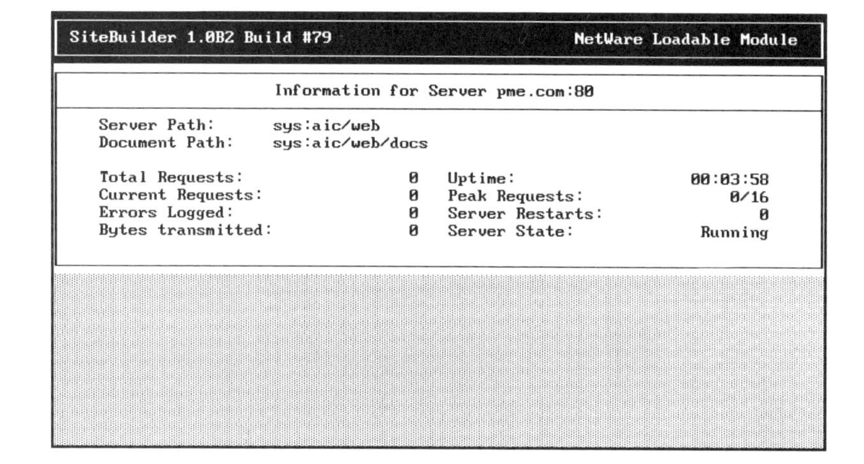

Figure 10.6

The file server console display after loading WEB and IPAccess NLMs.

When IPACCESS has been loaded on the server, the client portion of IPAcess works in conjunction with the IPACCESS NLM to enable the WinSock-compliant WWW browser running on workstations to use IPX packets to carry requests between the workstations and the NetWare server. The IPAccess part of SiteBuilder is a TCP/IP to IPX gateway employing the client/server architecture. This technique of carrying requests from TCP/IP applications in IPX packets is also referred to as *spoofing*. The client portion of IPAccess spoofs the TCP/IP application into thinking that it communicates over TCP/IP. There are future plans to enhance the WinSock API standard so that it has a direct built-in support for IPX.

After the WEB and the IPACCESS NLMs have been loaded, the SiteBuilder WWW server can be fully configured from a workstation through the SiteBuilder Server screen (see fig. 10.7).

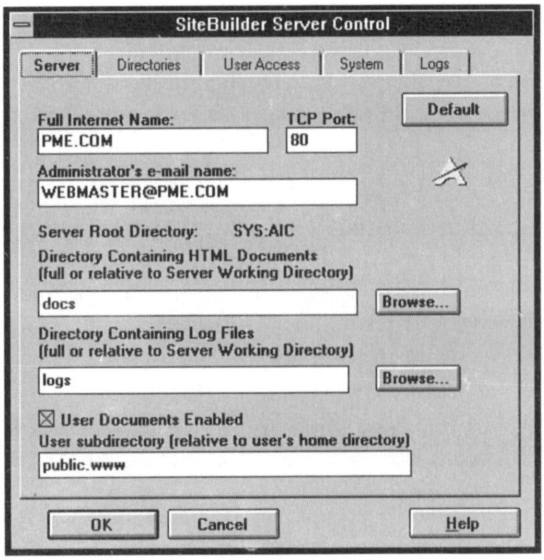

Figure 10.7

The SiteBuilder Server configuration screen.

In addition to the parameters shown in figure 10.7, the following configurations can be performed by clicking on the items at the top of the screen:

- **Directories.** Directories can be specified for the location of documents, images, and scripts.
- **User Access.** User access can be controlled by adding users to the authorized user list. Users can be selected either from the bindery or from the DNS depending on which version of NetWare is used and how it is configured. User access controls access for local users, not for Internet users (see fig. 10.8).

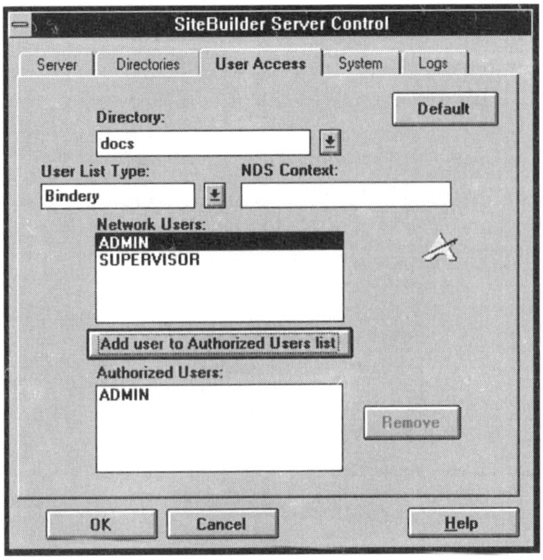

Figure 10.8

The SiteBuilder User Access configuration screen.

- **System.** System access can be controlled to limit access to the server directories for Internet users by specifying allowable Internet addresses (see fig. 10.9).

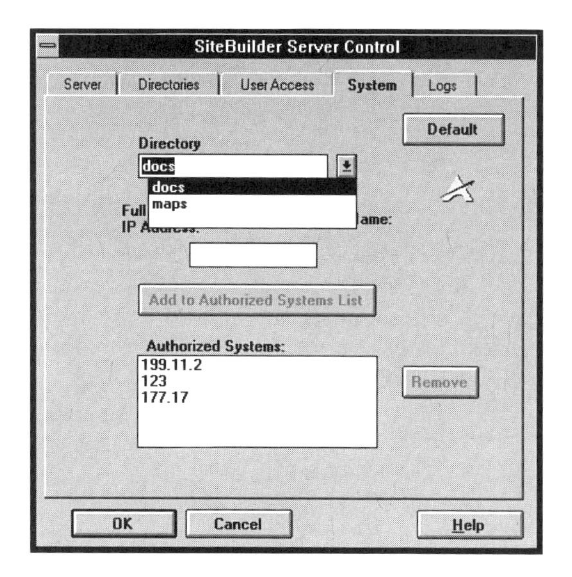

Figure 10.9

The SiteBuilder System configuration screen.

American Internet uses SiteBuilder to operate its WWW server on the Internet. At the time of this writing, the specs for the WWW site were a 486DX2-66 PC with 12 MB RAM, 400 MB hard disk, running NetWare 4.1.

GLACI-HTTPD

GLACI-HTTPD, from Great Lakes Area Commercial Internet, turns your NetWare server into a WWW server, but it requires that you configure TCP/IP at the workstation.

GLACI-HTTPD is installed by loading the HTSETUP NLM from the installation disk at the file server console. The installation procedure requires that you specify the location of the GLACI files to be installed. The HTTPD NLM turns the NetWare server into an Internet WWW server. HTTPD is copied by default from the installation disk into the SYS:SYSTEM directory.

Tip The SYS:SYSTEM directory is the default directory for NetWare NLMs. If a copy of HTTPD from another vendor already resides in the SYS:SYSTEM directory on your server, it will be overwritten during this installation. Be careful to save your old version of HTTPD if you are just experimenting with the software.

When HTTPD is loaded from the file server console, a status display message appears on the server, as follows:

```
CLACI-HTTPD 2.01
Copyright Dec 1995
```

```
Root document directory set sys:/etc/htdocs
Home page is set to welcom.htm
CGI executable directory is SYS:/ETC/CGI-BIN
Logging to file sys:/etc/httpd.log
HTTPD binding to TCP port 80
```

Note HTTPD is the HyperText Transport Protocol Daemon NLM. HTTP is the protocol that is used to access the WWW.

The configuration parameters for GLACI HTTPD are stored in a HTTPD.CFG configuration file, which resides in the SYS:ETC directory. These parameters define the location of files and security parameters. GLACI HTTPD supports flexible security by allowing and denying access to and from specific hosts or networks. Consider, for example, the following statements from the security section of the HTPPD.CFG configuration file:

```
ipdeny 199.245.180.2
ipallow 199.245.180.*
ipdeny *.*.*.*
```

"ipallow" and "ipdeny" are keywords used to build an IP access filter to restrict access to the WWW server. The keywords are followed by an IP address to allow or deny access. Any octet of the address can be replaced with the * (asterisk) wildcard character to permit or deny access to entire networks or subnets. When an attempt is made to connect to the server, the server starts at the top of the list and compares the connecting address with each line in the access list until a match is found or the end of the list is reached. If no match is found, the connecting system is allowed access. In the above example, all hosts on the 199.245.180.* network, except the host with an IP address of 199.245.180.2, are allowed access. All other networks are denied access.

Note The order of the ipdeny and ipallow statements in the HTTPD.CFG configuration file is important. Specific ipdeny statements without any wildcards should be first, followed by an ipdeny statement to all networks, as illustrated in the preceding example. This order results in the minimum number of statements. If, in the preceding example, the first ipdeny statement was skipped, it would require that an ipallow statement be included for every host on the network 199.245.180, except for the host 199.245.180.2. This would make the configuration file considerably longer and more difficult to manage.

GLACI-HTTPD does not come bundled with any client software. You can use GLACI-HTTPD with any package that allows WWW access from a NetWare workstation (Chameleon NFS from NetManage, for example). Chameleon NFS comes with its own WWW browser and a complete suite of TCP/IP utilities that are installed on a workstation. Be sure to install the ODI driver that comes with Chameleon at the workstation.

WEBserv

WEBserv from Puzzle Systems does not rely on the spoofing techniques that enable WinSock-compliant applications to use IPX for traffic between the workstation and the server running both TCP/IP and IPX. WEBserv uses dual stacking, which is not difficult to implement for PC clients running Windows for Workgroups, Windows 95, Windows NT, or Unix, or for MacIntosh clients. Dual stacking means that IPX and TCP/IP are implemented at the client workstations.

Configuring WEBserv on a NetWare server allows workstation IP addresses to be centrally managed from the server. When a workstation makes a request to access the Internet or a TCP/IP resource on the server, the workstation's IP address is picked up from the list of addresses on the server and a TCP/IP connection is made.

Figure 10.10 shows the initial WEBserv installation screen. The WEBserv installation takes place from a workstation by invoking the SETUP program using the Run option in the Windows File menu.

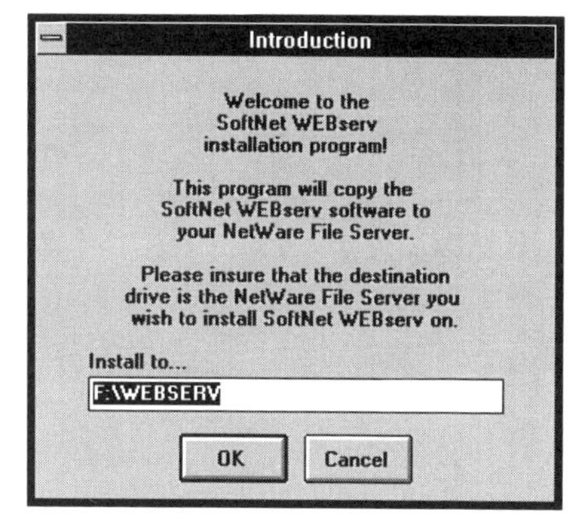

Figure 10.10

The initial WEBserv installation screen.

The default installation directory for WEBserv is the WEBSERV directory on the SYS volume. The next installation screen, shown in figure 10.11, requests that you supply the following:

- An IP address and domain name for your NetWare server
- An Internet IP address, which would very likely be an IP address supplied to you by an ISP
- An authorization key

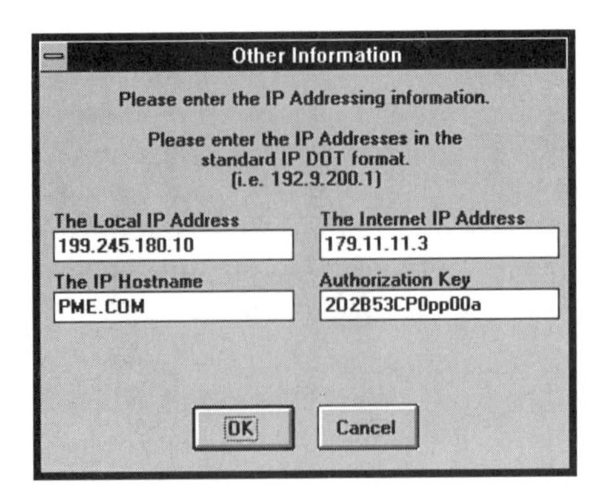

Figure 10.11
WEBserv's second installation screen.

The WEBserv installation program now copies all of the files to your server and presents you with an option to create a Windows program group called WEBserv (see fig 10.12).

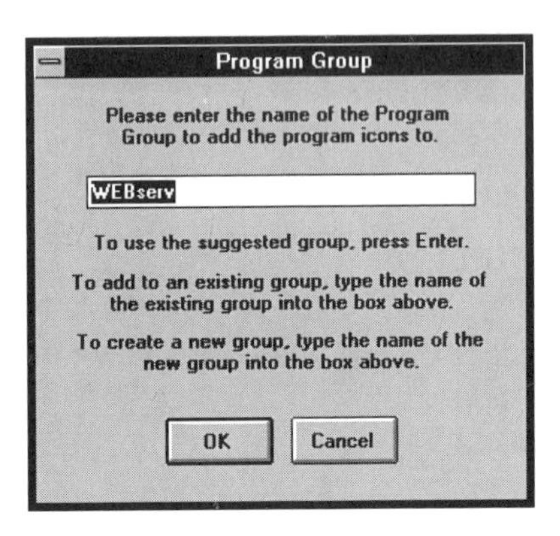

Figure 10.12
WEBserv's third installation screen.

After clicking on the OK button, the WEBserv program group under Windows is created (see fig. 10.13).

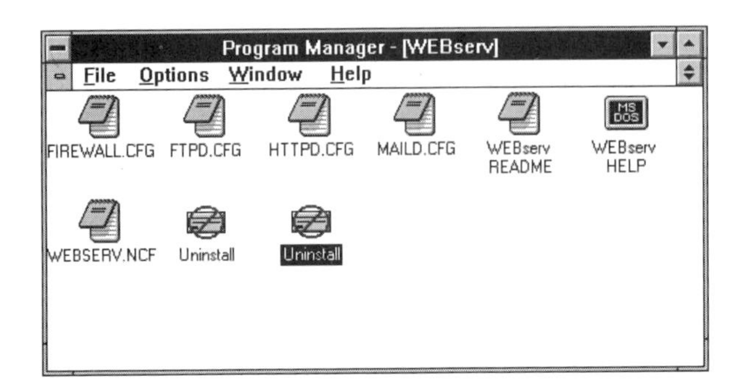

Figure 10.13
The WEBserv program group.

Note that most of the icons shown in figure 10.13 have to do with the configuration of WEBserv TCP/IP services. WEBserv installation also creates a WEBSERV.NCF file in the SYSTEM directory. This file needs to be appended to the AUTOEXEC.NCF file if you want the WEBserv NLMs to be loaded each time your NetWare server is brought up. The NLMs loaded from WEBSERV.NCF include NLMs for Mail, FTP, and WWW server support. Thus, in addition to allowing access to the Internet, WEBserv can also turn a NetWare server into a WWW server, an FTP server, a DNS server, a BootP/DHCP server, and an e-mail server (SMTP and POP3), as well as a firewall for incoming user access. You can configure all of these services from the workstation.

WEBserv supports commercial and freeware Internet WWW browsers (such as Mosaic and Netscape) and e-mail packages (such as Eudora or Pegasus mail). Optionally, WEBserv can be bundled with an Emissary TCP/IP client from Wollongong.

NOV*IX

NOV*IX for NetWare from Firefox is a collection of products that facilitate access from Novell networks to TCP/IP hosts either on a local internetwork or on the global Internet. The suite of products consists of the NOV*IX server software and NOV*IX client software. The client options include NOV*IX Elite, NOV*IX for Internet, NOV*IX for Workgroups, and NOV*IX for Client/Server. Only the NOV*IX server software and the NOV*IX Elite and NOV*IX for Internet clients are discussed here.

NOV*IX Server Software

The NOV*IX server software is installed on a NetWare file server from a workstation. The workstation must be logged in as a SUPERVISOR (NetWare 3.x) or as ADMIN (NetWare 4.x). The workstation must also be running Microsoft Windows and be equipped with a CD-ROM and a 3.5-inch floppy drive. To begin installation, execute the SETUP program from the NOV*IX CD. An initial installation screen appears, as shown in figure 10.14.

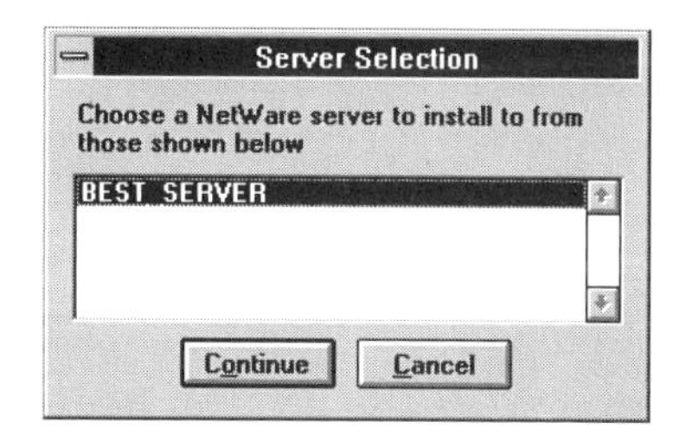

Figure 10.14

*The initial NOV*IX installation screen.*

You are given a choice to select the NetWare server on your internetwork on which to install the NOV*IX software. A subsequent screen (not shown here) gives you a choice to select a NetWare volume. Figure 10.15 shows the NOV*IX TCP/IP services that can be installed.

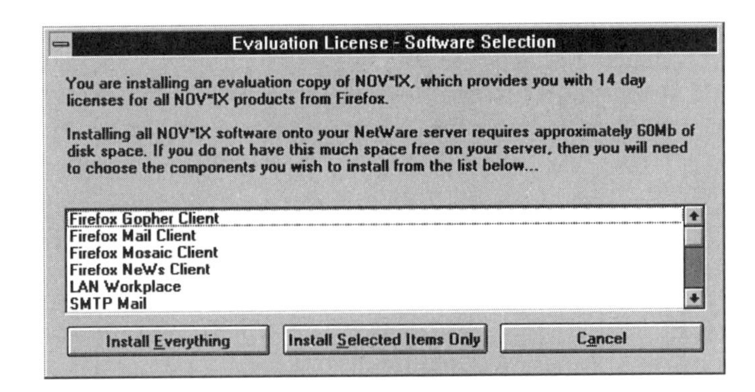

Figure 10.15
*The list of available NOV*IX services.*

The TCP/IP services shown in figure 10.15 are only a partial list of all of the services available through the NOV*IX software. The rest of the available services can be viewed by scrolling through the display window (during installation, of course). Several descriptions of the available services have the word "client" in them, as shown in figure 10.15. Installing client services software components on the server means that the files for these client components are uploaded to the server from the installation CD and are stored on the server hard disk. The actual client installation on a workstation takes place by running the DOWNLOAD.EXE file from Windows, which resides in the FIREFOX directory on the server.

Figure 10.16 shows the installation screen with the NOV*IX product options. Client components, such as Gopher and Mosaic, are bundled in more than one product. NOV*IX Elite and NOV*IX for Internet, for example, both include Gopher and Mosaic. Note the option to install the online manuals. Online documentation comes in very handy during the subsequent NOV*IX configuration on your network.

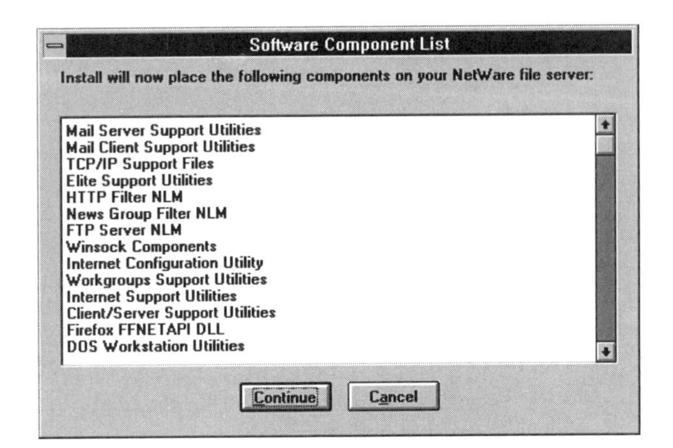

Figure 10.16
*The NOV*IX client options selection.*

The installation program then proceeds to display specific software components that will be installed to support your previous choices (see fig. 10.17). You need to have at least 100 MB of free space on the server to proceed with a complete installation of all of the client options and online documentation.

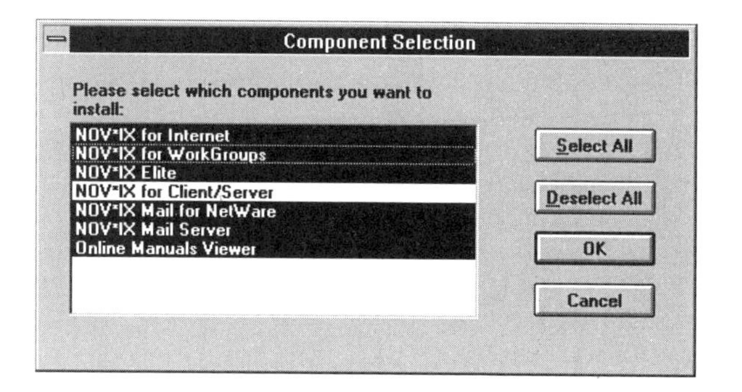

Figure 10.17

*The NOV*IX software component list.*

After the installation to the server has been completed, you have to load the NWPSRV and NOVIX NLMs and execute the BIND command at the server to activate the NOV*IX Gateway. The NWPSRV NLM is a NetWare Print Services Library NLM that must be loaded before the NOVIX NLM will load. When the NOVIX NLM is loaded, it will list the names of the available network cards that can be bound to it. You must then issue a BIND command binding NOVIX to one of the available cards. The NOV*IX gateway at the server is now operational.

NOV*IX Client Software

After all of the chosen software components are installed on the server, you can configure the workstation by running the DOWNLOAD.EXE program residing in the FIREFOX directory on the server. This program download to the your workstation the client portion of the product options shown in figure 10.16.

*NOV*IX Elite*

The NOV*IX Elite product option is for NetWare users who want access to TCP/IP hosts to transfer files (FTP sessions), to do terminal emulation for interactive terminal traffic (Telnet), and to print. A NetWare LAN that needs to be connected to a TCP/IP LAN is an example of an environment where NOV*IX Elite can be used.

*NOV*IX for Internet*

NOV*IX for Internet is a collection of Internet client software including the WWW browser Mosaic, Mail, Gopher, News, and FTP. These client components give NetWare users access the Internet via the NOVIX gateway at the server. NOV*IX for Internet can also be used locally if the local NetWare server is configured as a WEB, Mail, Gopher, or FTP server.

NOV*IX Management

The program used to configure the NOV*IX TCP/IP options and services is FFTCPW.EXE. It resides in the SYSTEM\NOVIX directory on a NetWare server. The NOV*IX TCP/IP configuration information also resides on the file server rather than in individual configuration files at the workstations. Having the TCP/IP configuration files reside on the file server means that the TCP/IP configuration is centrally managed. The NOV*IX IP address management, for example, offers considerable flexibility. IP addresses can be allocated to individual users who are identified by NetWare user names. IP addresses can be allocated to workstations that are identified by the workstation hardware addresses. IP addresses can also be part of a pool of addresses available to anyone on the network. An IP address can also be assigned to a NetWare group.

NOV*IX security can be implemented for both inbound and outbound connections. For both inbound and outbound connections, specific TCP/IP hosts identified by IP addresses, specific TCP/IP port numbers and NetWare groups on your local internetwork can be combined to allow or disallow a connection.

Novell Web Server

Novell has come up with its own Internet solution: the NetWare Web Server. The NetWare Web Server is an integrated product that includes a single license of the Netscape Navigator WWW browser, WordPerfect Internet Publisher, and two CGI script interpreters, PERL and BASIC. CGI (Common Gateway Interface) scripts are programs that are used to collect information from forms embedded in HTML (HyperText Markup Language) documents. Forms are used to solicit information from users visiting WWW sites and can be used for taking orders online, feedback from customers, surveys, and so forth. NetWare Web Server relies on the NetWare Directory Services security features to provide secure access to the NetWare Web Server site.

Physical Connections to the Internet

All of the products discussed in the preceding section require a proper physical connection to the Internet to provide your NetWare users with a functional Internet access. The kind of physical connection to the Internet and the kind of service you choose will in all likelihood depend on where you live and how much money you are willing to spend for it. The options include the following:

- A dedicated digital line
- Dial-up lines
- Direct router connections

A Dedicated Digital Line

A dedicated digital line can take the form of the following:

- **T1 line.** T1 offers 1.544 Mbps bandwidth.
- **Fractional T1 line.** A fractional T1 line is composed of one or more 64 Kbps digital channels that are bundled together, up to a maximum of 24 channels. When 24 digital 64 Kbps channels are bundled together, the fractional T1 becomes a full T1.
- **ISDN line.** The basic rate ISDN service offers 128 Kbps bandwidth.

A T1 line, a fractional T1 line, or an ISDN line can be connected directly to a corresponding adapter card installed in the NetWare server. The line can also be connected to a dedicated router that is connected to the LAN with a LAN interface and has a T1, fractional T1, or ISDN interface as well. Having a dedicated IP router increases the cost of your installation. If you forgo a dedicated router, however, you will need to install the software-based NetWare Multi Protocol Router (MPR). The dedicated line will most likely terminate at the site of your ISP.

Dial-Up Lines

Dial-up lines can take the form of the following:

- Dial-up analog lines
- Dial-up digital lines
- Dial-up ISDN lines
- Dial-up X.25 line

Dial-up services are less expensive than having a dedicated line; you pay for the service only when you use it. In certain parts of the world, it is not possible to get a dedicated line, in which case dial-up lines are the only option. Dial-up lines are slower than dedicated lines and make sense for occasional use. With dial-up lines, you will still most likely be dialing to an ISP.

Direct Router Connections

A connection to a router that is already part of the Internet is feasible for those companies that are already connected to the Internet. If your company has an IP router that is already connected to the Internet, and if it is possible to connect your NetWare LAN to an available port on that router, you will not have to deal with an ISP.

Summary

Many commercial products allow a NetWare server to be configured either as a gateway to the Internet or as an Internet server. As a NetWare LAN administrator, you will have to determine whether or not your NetWare server will be used as a gateway only or whether it will also be configured as an Internet server. There are costs and security considerations involved in making that decision. The products discussed in this chapter facilitate both approaches. Whatever the approach, all of the products discussed in this chapter enable users to access the Internet. Physical connectivity to the Internet is required by each of the commercial products discussed. The kind of the physical connectivity and service you choose will depend on the availability of the service from your telephone company and on the cost of the service. Internet Service Providers can help you with making your Internet connection.

Internetworking with NetWare NFS

This chapter discusses NetWare NFS's features and how to the install and configure NetWare NFS. You will learn to monitor and control NetWare NFS servers from DOS NetWare clients and Unix clients. You also will learn to manage the NetWare NFS server's system security.

You will learn several aspects of NetWare NFS, such as adding and removing name space, and mapping rights for Unix NFS clients to the equivalent NetWare rights.

An Overview of NetWare NFS

NetWare NFS consists of NetWare Loadable Modules (NLMs) that run on a NetWare 3.x or NetWare 4.x server. Because the NFS protocols are dependent on protocols such as UDP and IP, the NetWare server must be properly configured for TCP/IP transport services. For details on configuring the TCP/IP transport for the NetWare server, see Part One of this book.

NetWare NFS Components

Figure 11.1 shows the components of the NetWare NFS server. The NetWare NFS server consists of a number of modules dealing with network file services, including lock management, status monitoring, Unix-to-NetWare print services, NetWare-to-Unix print services, File Transfer Protocol services, and Xconsole services.

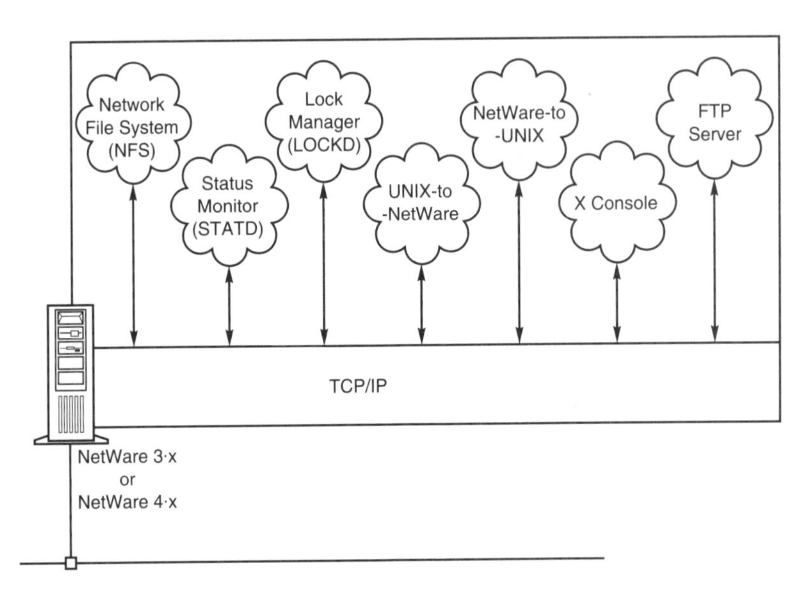

Figure 11.1
NetWare NFS services.

At first sight it may seem strange to see Unix-to-NetWare and NetWare-to-Unix print services, FTP services, and Xconsole services as part of a product that includes the name "NFS." After all, NFS deals with remote file access. The core service provided by NetWare NFS is the Network File System protocol, originally developed by Sun Microsystems. The other services are bundled with the NetWare NFS product to make the product more useful and attractive.

NetWare NFS provides Unix and NetWare integration. Most users who mix Unix and NetWare networks will also be interested in printing from a Unix workstation to a NetWare printer, or printing from a NetWare workstation to a Unix printer. These services are provided by the Unix-to-NetWare and NetWare-to-Unix print services. The NetWare NFS server can also act as an FTP server, enabling NetWare files to be accessed by any FTP client.

Most NetWare system administrators are familiar with the RCONSOLE utility for managing the NetWare server console from a remote NetWare workstation. The Xconsole service enables the NetWare server console to be managed from a Unix workstation running the X Window System graphical interface.

Table 11.1 summarizes the different NetWare NFS components. The OSI reference model helps you better understand how the different NFS components fit together.

Table 11.1 NetWare NFS Components

NetWare NFS Component	Description
NFS	Provides NFS clients with transparent access to files on the NetWare server. The files on the NetWare server also can be shared by non-Unix clients such as DOS, OS/2, FTAM, Macintosh, and Windows NT.
Lock Manager	Implements file locking for the NFS file system on the server. This is compatible with Lock Manager (lockd) on Unix systems. Unix systems perform advisory (logical) locking. These advisory locks will be enforced on all non-Unix clients such as DOS, OS/2, FTAM, Macintosh, and Windows NT.
Status Monitor	Restores the status of file locks if the NetWare server is brought down and rebooted. This service is compatible with Status Monitor (statd) on Unix systems.
Unix-to-NetWare	Enables Unix client systems Print Service to print jobs on the NetWare server. The NetWare NFS server implements the Line Printer Daemon (lpd) service. This enables Unix clients to submit jobs to this line printer daemon. Once the Unix job arrives in a NetWare queue, it can be sent to any NetWare printer to which the queue is assigned.
NetWare-to-Unix	Enables NetWare clients to print gateway print jobs on a Unix printer. The NetWare clients that can access a printer on a Unix host include DOS, OS/2, and Macintosh clients.
File Transfer Protocol	Converts NetWare server to an FTP server. FTP clients can transfer files between themselves and the NetWare FTP server. FTP clients include DOS, Unix, OS/2, Macintosh, VMS, and so on. The FTP client service for non-Unix machines must be purchased as a separate add-on product. If a client already has NFS client

continues

Table 11.1, Continued

NetWare NFS Component	Description
	services, NFS provides a more transparent way to access the NetWare server files. On clients without NFS clients that have FTP client services, the FTP server on the NetWare NFS server can be used to exchange files with the NetWare server.
Xconsole	Enables Unix workstations to remotely manage a NetWare server using the X Window System graphical user interface.

NFS Protocols

NFS consists of a number of protocols that act together to implement a transparent file system. NFS was developed by Sun Microsystems in early 1980s and has been licensed to over 200 vendors. The NFS protocol is documented in RFC 1094.

The NFS protocol has become the de facto protocol for providing transparent remote file services on Unix systems.

NFS was designed for local area networks. Although it can be used over a wide area network, there are several characteristics of NFS that are not suited for the lower transmission bandwidth and unpredictable and longer delays associated with WANs. Another protocol called the *Andrew File System* (AFS) has been designed by researchers at Carnegie Mellon University. AFS is available as a product from Transarc Corporation but does not have the widespread acceptance that NFS enjoys.

Figure 11.2 shows the different NFS protocols in relationship with the OSI and DoD models (see Chapter 2 for discussion of the DoD model), and table 11.2 contains a description of these protocols.

OSI Model	NFS Protocols	DoD Model
Application	Network File System (NFS)	Process/Application
Presentation	External Data Representation (XDR)	
Session	Remote Procedure Call (RPC)	
Transport	User Datagram Protocol	Host-to-Host
Network	Internet Protocol (IP)	Internet
Data-Link	Token-Ring, ARCnet, Ethernet	Network Access
Physical		

Figure 11.2

The NFS protocols.

Table 11.2 The NFS Protocols

NFS Protocol Stack Component	Description
Token-Ring, Ethernet, ARCnet	Includes the DoD network access layer and the data link and physical layers of the OSI model. The NetWare server uses ODI (open data link interface) drivers to access the network adapters.
Internet Protocol (IP)	Provides datagram service between the NFS client and the NFS server. Its primary function is to route, fragment, and reassemble datagrams.
User Datagram Protocol (UDP)	Provides an unreliable (unguaranteed), connectionless delivery service used by NFS. Application messages can be sent without the overhead of an explicit acknowledgment and the overhead of maintaining a virtual circuit connection. The NetWare TCP/IP transport bundled with the NetWare 3.*x* server provides UDP and IP services.
Remote Procedure Call (RPC)	An Application Programming Interface (API) that transparently enables clients to execute programs residing on remote machines. Developers can purchase NetWare RPC separately.
External Data Representation	Defines a format by which various data types (integers, floating-point numbers, characters) can be represented in a uniform manner across the network regardless of the operating system and machine platform.
Network File System (NFS)	Enables users to mount directories across the network and treat those directories as if they were local.

At the data link and physical layers of the OSI model (the Network Access layer of the DoD model), NFS supports the wide variety of available technologies, including Token-Ring, ARCnet, and Ethernet LANs. Because NFS uses UDP and IP, it can run on any data link layer technology that supports IP.

At the network layer of the OSI model (the Internet layer in the DoD model), NFS uses the Internet Protocol (IP). Recall that IP uses datagrams and fragments datagrams to accommodate the maximum packet size limitations of the underlying network. The IP datagrams, if fragmented, are reassembled by the receiving end.

At the transport layer of the OSI model (the Host-to-Host layer in the DoD model), NFS uses the User Datagram Protocol (UDP). UDP is typically used when the underlying network is inherently reliable, and as such does not provide any packet sequencing. Recall that packet sequencing reorders packets at the destination in the order in which the packets were transmitted by the sender. UDP does provide, however, an optional checksum.

The optional checksum is highly recommended when running NFS on a network that is not very reliable, such as a network running SLIP (Serial Line Interface Protocol) on unshielded twisted-pair wiring.

At the session layer of the OSI model (part of the Process/Application layer), NFS uses the Remote Procedure Call (RPC) protocol. There exist a number of quite different RPC protocols, but they are all called RPC. NFS's RPC is often called Sun-RPC to distinguish it from other RPC protocols. RPC enables NFS services at the server to be accessed using the "procedure-call" paradigm familiar to programmers. RPC provides high-level access to NFS services without getting involved with details of communication protocols. Programmers who use RPC do not have to be communication experts to use the networking services that can be accessed using RPC.

At the presentation layer of the OSI model (part of the Process/Application layer), NFS uses the External Data Representation (XDR) protocol. The XDR provides a uniform way of representing data. For example, number data is represented using two's complement notation; if a system uses a different number representation, conversion is done by XDR.

At the application layer of the OSI model (part of the Process/Application layer), NFS uses the Network File System (NFS) protocol. The NFS protocol provides services such as writing to a file, creating a file, reading a file, and so on at the NFS server.

The application layer also consists of a number of support protocols, such as the mount and portmapper protocols. The mount protocol implements the NFS mounting procedure, and the portmapper protocol provides clients who need access to a service with the port number for the service. The portmapper uses the well-known UDP port number 111. An NFS client who wants to access a particular service sends a request to the UDP port number 111. Server programs that want to provide a service register with the portmapper. On receiving a request for a registered service, the portmapper responds with the port number of the service to which the requests should be sent.

NFS Remote Procedure Calls

NFS implements 18 remote procedure calls. The software code for these procedures resides at the NFS server. The NFS procedures are used by NFS clients to access the network file services implemented by the NFS server. An NFS client accesses these procedures through the RPC mechanism.

The RPC protocol contains a program number and a procedure number. The program number identifies the service being accessed. For example, the NFS service has the program number 100003. Within the program there are 18 procedures, numbered from 0 to 17. For instance, procedure 6 deals with reading a file. An NFS client that needs to read a file will send an RPC request containing the program number 100003 and the procedure number 6 (see fig. 11.3). Other parameters for the read operation will also have to be supplied in the NFS client's RPC request packet.

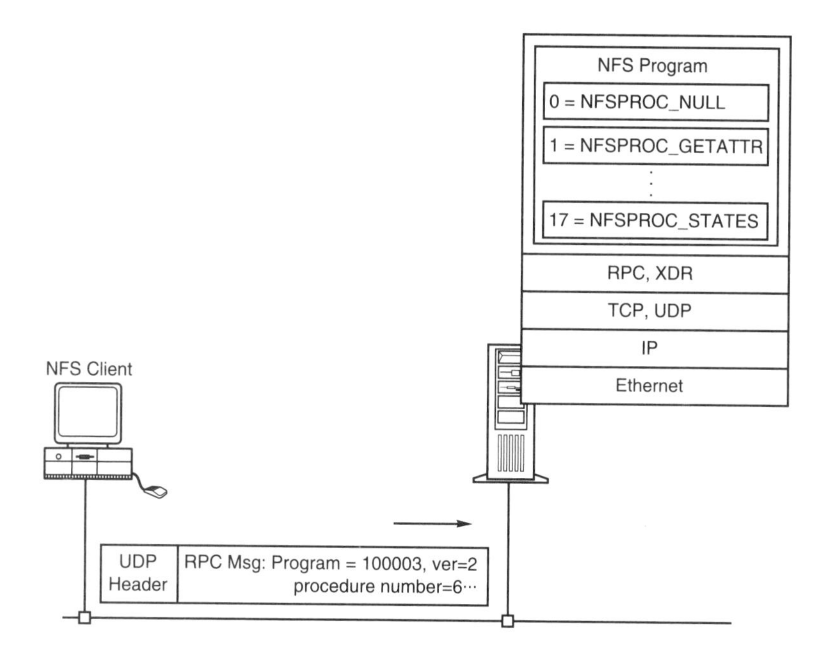

Figure 11.3
An RPC call.

The RPC request also specifies the version number of the program that should provide the service. All programs that advertise their services have a version number. The version number gracefully enables old and new versions of a program service to coexist. This supports existing NFS clients using the older service, while newer NFS clients can access the newer (and hopefully better) version of the program.

Table 11.3 lists and briefly describes the different procedure numbers for the NFS program.

Table 11.3 NFS Remote Procedure Call (RPC) Numbers

Procedure Number	NFS Procedure	Description
0	NFS_PROC	Diagnostic check.
1	NFS_GETATTR	Gets the attributes of a file/directory, such as owner and group owner permissions.
2	NFSPROC_SETATTR	Sets the attribute of a file/directory, such as owner and group owner permissions.
3	NFSPROC_ROOT	Now obsolete. Handled by the mount protocol.
4	NFSPROC_LOOKUP	Obtains a file handle to a file in a specific directory.
5	NFSPROC_READLINK	Reads contents of a symbolic link.

continues

Table 11.3, Continued

Procedure Number	NFS Procedure	Description
6	NFSPROC_READ	Reads from a file.
7	NFSPROC_WRITECACHE	Used in NFS version 3 to write to cache.
8	NFSPPROC_WRITE	Writes to a file.
9	NFSPROC_CREATE	Creates a file.
10	NFSPROC_REMOVE	Removes a directory entry from a directory.
11	NFSPROC_RENAME	Renames a file.
12	NFSPROC_LINK	Creates a hard link to a file.
13	NFSPROC_SYMLINK	Creates a symbolic link to a file.
14	NFSPROC_MKDIR	Creates a directory.
15	NFSPROC_RMDIR	Removes a directory.
16	NFSPROC_READDIR	Reads a directory.
17	NFSPROC_STATFS	Gets the file system attributes.

If an RPC request is sent to procedure 0, the procedure simply returns the request to the sender. In other words, procedure 0 acts as a simple "echo" service. Many NFS clients use this "echo" feature as the basis for providing a diagnostic utility called *nfsping*. When the hostname or IP address is supplied as a parameter to the nfsping utility, it sends an echo request to procedure 0 for the NFS program and awaits a reply. The following is the syntax for using nfsping:

```
nfsping hostname
```

If the NFS service is active at the host, a reply will be received; otherwise, you can conclude that the service is not available or the host is unreachable.

File Sharing between Unix and NetWare

Applications such as WordPerfect, Framemaker, dBASE IV, AutoCAD, and Lotus 1-2-3 have been ported to both DOS and Unix environments. These applications maintain the same data file structure on DOS and Unix platforms. The NetWare NFS server can be used to share these application data files and make them available to both DOS clients and Unix NFS clients.

Text File Differences between DOS and Unix

Besides the previously mentioned application data files, text files containing ASCII data can be shared between Unix NFS clients and DOS clients.

Both Unix and DOS use the ASCII code character set for text files. They differ in how an end-of-line is represented on the two systems. DOS uses a two-byte line-feed/carriage return combination consisting of the ASCII codes 10 and 13 to terminate a line and begin a new line. Unix, on the other hand, uses a one-byte line-feed (ASCII code 10) to terminate a line and begin a new line (see fig. 11.4).

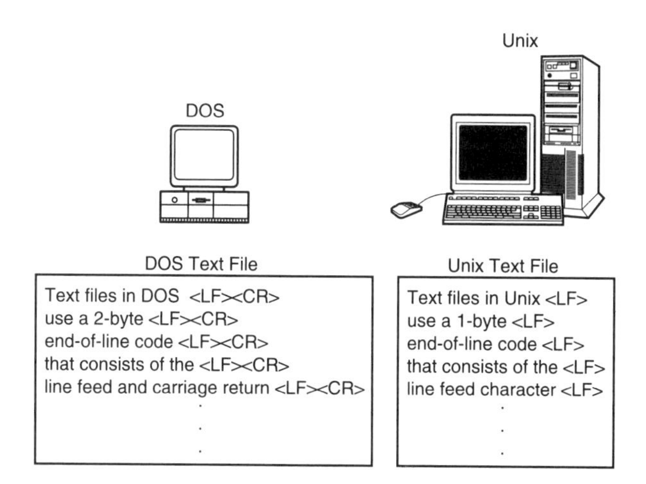

Figure 11.4
End-of-line conventions in DOS and Unix.

Note For internationalization, you can use an extended character set called International Alphabet 5 that supports characters in the European languages for creating text files.

If a file is copied from a Unix to a DOS system, it is missing the carriage return at the end of each line. If the contents of such a file are displayed on a DOS system, it appears as shown in figure 11.5. This figure shows the Unix password file, /etc/passwd, copied to a DOS system. Notice that because the carriage return is missing, each new line is displayed immediately before the last line ended (causing improper wrap-around), and does not start from column 1 of the display.

```
C:\PUBS\ICPNFS>TYPE PASSWD
root:*:0:0:System Administrator:/root:/bin/tcsh
                                        daemon:*:1:1:System Daemon:/root

sys:*:2:2:Operating System:/tmp:/bin/csh
                                bin:*:3:7:BSDI Software:/usr/bsdi:/bin/
sh
  operator:*:5:5:System Operator:/usr/opr:/bin/csh
                                          uucp:*:6:6:UNIX-to-UNIX Copy:
var/spool/uucppublic:/usr/libexec/uucico
                                games:*:7:13:Games Pseudo-user:/usr/gam
s:
  nobody:*:32767:32766:Unprivileged user:/nonexistent:/dev/null
                                                      karanjit:*:0:0:K
ranjit Siyan:/root:/bin/tcsh
                         user1:*:100:50::/home/user1:/bin/csh

C:\PUBS\ICPNFS>
```

Figure 11.5
A Unix text file displayed on a DOS system.

If a file is copied from a DOS to a Unix system, it has an extra carriage return at the end of each line. If the contents of such a file are displayed on a Unix system, you do not see anything unusual in the display, because the extra carriage return simply starts the new line from the first column. This is something that Unix does in any case when it sees a line feed at the end of the line. However, if such a file is edited using a text editor such as vi, you see the extra ^M characters at the end of each line (see fig. 11.6).

```
This is a DOS text^M
file that was copied ^M
over to a UNIX system to^M
see how the file is displayed^M
in a text editor such as vi.^M
^M
Notice that there are extra carriage ^M
return characters that appear^M
as the control-M symbol.^M
^M
^M
~
~
~
~
~
~
~
~
```

Figure 11.6

A DOS text file in a Unix text editor.

Because DOS and Unix use different end-of-line conventions, the end-of-line in text files from the other system needs to be converted to the native end-of-line format.

Tip

When transferring text files using FTP, you should set the transfer mode to ASCII. To set this transfer mode, enter ascii at the FTP prompt. When you set the transfer mode to ASCII, FTP performs the end-of-line conversions for you.

DOS uses a two-byte line feed and carriage return combination for the end-of-line character. Unix uses a one-byte line feed for the end-of-line character.

Using the DOS2UNIX and UNIX2DOS Utilities

The NetWare NFS product includes the source code for two utilities written in the C language that you can use to convert text files between the two systems. These files are called DOS2UNIX.C and UNIX2DOS.C. The compiled versions of these files for DOS are DOS2UNIX.EXE and UNIX2DOS.EXE. These two files are installed in the SYS:PUBLIC directory during the NetWare NFS server installation.

To convert a DOS text file to a Unix text file, enter the following command:

```
DOS2UNIX dostextfile > unixtextfile
```

To convert a Unix text file to a DOS text file, use the following command:

```
UNIX2DOS unixtextfile > dostextfile
```

The output redirection symbol (>) is needed because these utilities display the output on the standard output device (the console).

NetWare NFS provides the source code versions of these utilities so that you can compile them under Unix to have the Unix version of these utilities. The DOS2UNIX.C and UNIX2DOS.C files are installed in the SYS:ETC directory. You can transfer these files to Unix using any of the following methods:

- **FTP.** Use FTP on DOS and enable the FTP Server on Unix.
- **NFS.** Use a DOS NFS client (for example, PC/TCP's Interdrive from FTP Software, Inc.) with the Unix system acting as the NFS server.
- **Disk.** Copy the files to the Unix system on a floppy disk. Many Unix systems provide methods to read DOS-formatted floppy disks. Consult the vendor's system documentation for the Unix system.

After you copy the files DOS2UNIX.C and UNIX2DOS.C to the Unix system, you must compile them. To compile these files, use the following command:

```
cc -o dos2unix dos2unix.c
cc -o unix2dos unix2dos.c
```

The cc command invokes the C compiler. The -o option produces the executable output in the specified file. If the executable output file is not specified, the C compiler produces the executable output in a.out. You must move this file (use the mv command) to a filename that you are using for the utility.

Figure 11.7 shows the output of compiling the DOS2UNIX.C and UNIX2DOS.C files on a Unix system. The ls command shows the details of the executable images that are produced.

```
ucs# cc -o dos2unix dos2unix.c
ucs# cc -o unix2dos unix2dos.c
ucs# ls -l dos2unix unix2dos
-rwxrwxr-x  1 root  students  32013 Aug  2 14:47 dos2unix
-rwxrwxr-x  1 root  students  31997 Aug  2 14:47 unix2dos
ucs# █
```

Figure 11.7

Compiling DOS2UNIX.C and UNIX2DOS.C on a Unix system.

Figure 11.8 shows the DOS2UNIX program converting the file dosfile.txt. When the command is run by itself (see fig. 11.8), it displays a brief message showing how to use the program.

```
ucs# ./dos2unix

  Usage: dos2unix source_file [ > dest_file]
ucs# ./dos2unix dosfile.txt > unixfile.txt
ucs# █
```

Figure 11.8

Using DOS2UNIX on a Unix system.

Notice that the command used in figure 11.8 to run DOS2UNIX is "./DOS2UNIX". The "./" is used so that Unix will look for the filename in the current directory. In Unix, the current directory is not automatically included in the path name. Once you compile a program, you can move it to a directory containing executable programs that is on the path environment variable for the users. If the directory containing the program is on the path, you do not have to precede the executable path name with a "./".

For example, if /usr/local/bin is in the shell path, you can use mv DOS2UNIX /usr/local/bin to move the DOS2UNIX program.

If you always want the current directory to be used in the path and also be the first directory searched, you can set the path name as follows for the C shell:

```
set path = ( . $path)
```

If you are using the Bourne or Korn shell, you can use

```
PATH=.:$PATH
```

If you have set the previous command in a Bourne or Korn shell script, you must add the export PATH command, so that the value of the PATH environment variable will be "visible" outside the script.

Similarly, to convert a Unix text file that contains a listing of all files on the Unix system (produced by the ls -lR / command) for direct use on a DOS system, you can use the UNIX2DOS program (see fig. 11.9).

Figure 11.9

Using UNIX2DOS on a Unix system.

```
ucs# ls -lR / > allfiles
ucs# ./unix2dos

  Usage: unix2dos source_file [ > dest_file]
ucs# ./unix2dos allfiles > allfiles.dos
ucs# █
```

Using awk to Convert between DOS and Unix Text Files on Unix

If you do not have access to a C compiler or the source code of the UNIX2DOS.C and DOS2UNIX.C programs, you can use a utility called *awk,* available on most Unix systems.

The awk tool is named after its developers, Aho, Weinberger, and Kernighan. The awk tool uses an interpretive text-processing language based on C language constructs and the use of regular expressions. A new version of awk called *nawk* is available on many systems (starting with System V, Release 3). The Free Software Foundation GNU project's version of awk is called *gawk.*

The following awk command will convert the *unixfile* to a *dosfile*:

```
awk '{FS = "$"; print $1 "^M"}' unixfile > dosfile
```

To enter the ^M (control+M), press Ctrl+V and then Ctrl+M.

The awk program reads each line of the unixfile. For each line of this file it applies the commands within the brackets. Generally, you can specify that the commands within the brackets apply when a certain condition is true:

```
condition      { ... }
```

If the *condition* is not specified (as is true in the previous example of using awk), the statements in the braces are executed unconditionally.

Each line is treated as a record that consists of fields separated by the field separator character. The default field separator character is a space. The FS = "$" sets the field separator after the record has been read to the end-of-line. The print $1 refers to the entire record consisting of a single field, and the ^M adds the carriage return to the end of the line. The print statement displays the output on the standard output file, and redirection must be used if you want the output to go to a file other than the "standard output."

The awk tool is available for Unix systems. If you are interested in a DOS version of this utility, you can contact MKS Systems, Inc.

You can create a shell script that uses the previous awk command to convert Unix text files to DOS text files. To do this you must enter the following line in a text file, called, say, "*todostext*":

```
awk ''{FS = ""$""; print $1 ""^M""}'' $1 > $2
```

The *unixfile* and *dosfile* filenames have been replaced by the shell arguments $1 and $2 that will be supplied to the shell script.

The Unix shell arguments $1, $2, . . . passed to the script file are similar to the %1, %2, . . . arguments that are used in DOS batch files.

You must now flag the script file as executable using the chmod command (see Chapter 7).

```
chmod 755 todostext
```

To run the script file, use the following command:

```
todostext  unixfile > dosfile
```

Figure 11.10 shows the creation and use of this script file. The todostext script file performs the same function as the UNIX2DOS command. The vi editor could be more easily used to create this script file. Figure 11.10 shows the use of the cat command to create this file, much the same as the COPY CON command is used in DOS. To enter the ^M (carriage return), press Ctrl+V followed by Ctrl+M. At the end of typing the awk line, you must press Ctrl+D to end the standard input (similar to the use of the F6 key in DOS).

Figure 11.10

Creating and using an awk script file to perform Unix-to-DOS text-file conversion.

```
# cat > todostext
awk '{FS="$"; print $1 "^M"}' $1 > $2
# chmod 755 todostext
# ./todostext allfiles allfiles.dos
# █
```

To create a shell script to convert a DOS text file to a Unix text file, place the following in a shell script file:

```
awk '{p=index($0,"^M"); print substr($0,1,p-1)}' $1 > $2
```

Flag the file as executable and, using a script file named tounixtext, use the following:

```
tounixtext dosfile > unixfile
```

Figure 11.11 shows the creation and use of this script file. The tounixtext script file performs the same function as the DOS2UNIX command. Enter the ^M by pressing Ctrl+V followed by Ctrl+M. At the end of typing the awk line, you must press Ctrl+D to end the standard input.

Figure 11.11

Creating and using an awk script file to perform DOS-to-Unix text-file conversion.

```
# cat > tounixtext
awk '{p=index($0,"^M"); print substr($0,1,p-1)}' $1 > $2
# chmod 755 tounixtext
# ./tounixtext dosfile.txt unixfile.txt
# █
```

Using a Text Editor to Convert a DOS Text File to a Unix Text File

If you do not have access to a C compiler or the awk program, you can use a text editor to convert between DOS and Unix text files on Unix.

To convert a DOS text file to a Unix text file, create a text file called "unixsubst" and place in it the following lines of text:

```
%s/.$//
wq
```

The first line contains a global command to delete the last character at the end of each line. The second line saves the file and quits the editor.

Now use the editor ex on the file to be converted (*dosfile*) and pass to the editor the "unixsubst" commands as input.

```
ex dosfile < unixsubst
```

The substitutions will take place in *dosfile* itself, and this file will be modified.

NetWare NFS Installation and Configuration

This section discusses the installation and configuration requirements and procedure for NetWare NFS. While you can install and configure NetWare NFS as part of the same installation procedure, it is easier to install the software first and configure it as a later step (once you know that your installation has been successful). Configuring NFS may also involve configuring NetWare-to-Unix and Unix-to-NetWare print services. It is therefore best to perform this configuration step at a later time.

NetWare NFS Installation Requirements

NetWare NFS installation requirements depend on the version of NetWare NFS you are installing.

Hardware Requirements for NetWare NFS

If you are installing NetWare NFS 1.2, the Novell documentation states that you need 5 MB of RAM at the server and 1 MB of free disk space on the SYS volume. Other documentation on the product says that you need 3 MB of free disk space on the server.

If you are installing NetWare NFS 1.2c, the Novell documentation says that you need 2 MB of RAM in addition to the base requirements of the server, and 1 MB of free disk space on the SYS volume.

For best server disk performance, you should use a volume block size of 8 KB for NetWare 3.x, and a volume block size of 64 KB for NetWare 4.x.

In addition, you need a network interface card that supports TCP/IP. The Novell documentation lists that TCP/IP support is available for Ethernet, Token-Ring, and ARCnet. Although not listed in the Novell documentation, TCP/IP support is also available for FDDI.

Software Requirements for NetWare NFS

You need the NetWare NFS product disk and a NetWare server that is configured for TCP/IP.

In NetWare NFS 1.2, the installation procedure tries to configure your server for TCP/IP if it is not already configured for TCP/IP. It does most of the TCP/IP installation correctly, but it does not specify a frame type of ETHERNET_II when loading the Ethernet driver for the second time. This causes TCP/IP not to load when an attempt is made to activate the NetWare NFS server. In NetWare NFS 1.2c, the NetWare NFS installation does not try to configure your server for TCP/IP. If the NetWare server is not configured for TCP/IP, the NetWare NFS installation will stop and ask you to configure the NetWare server for TCP/IP before proceeding.

Additionally, you need the frame types listed in table 11.4 for the different network boards.

Table 11.4 Required Frame Types for NetWare NFS

Network Board	Frame Type
Ethernet	ETHERNET_II or ETHERNET_802.2
Token-Ring	TOKEN-RING_SNAP
ARCnet	RX-NET

Some of the Novell documentation lists ETHERNET_802.2 as a frame type encapsulation for TCP/IP. An attempt to bind IP to ETHERNET_802.2, in the existing Novell's TCP/IP implementation, however, fails with the warning that ETHERNET_802.2 is not one of the supported media types for IP. You can, however, bind IP to a driver using the ETHERNET_SNAP frame type.

It is possible to run TCP/IP on ETHERNET_802.2, but this is not currently supported by Novell's TCP/IP.

Installation Requirements for NetWare 4.x

NetWare 4.x server must be set up with bindery emulation for the NetWare NFS installation to work correctly. Briefly stated, a bindery context is defined in NetWare 4.x as the container whose objects are emulated as bindery objects. In addition, a bindery user SUPERVISOR is defined, who has the same password as the initial password specified for the Admin user of the NDS (NetWare Directory Services) tree.

The bindery context is set by the SET BINDERY CONTEXT console command. You can place this command in the AUTOEXEC.NCF file so that it takes effect every time the server starts. For example, if the bindery context is to be set to OU=PUBLICWORKS.O=E&L, use the following server console command:

```
SET BINDERY CONTEXT = OU=PUBLICWORKS.O=E&L
```

You can view the current context (if set), using the following server console command:

```
SET BINDERY CONTEXT
```

NetWare NFS requires the user GUEST. While this user is created automatically in NetWare 3.x, it does not exist in NetWare 4.x unless you have upgraded your NetWare 4.x server from a NetWare 3.x server. In the latter case, the user GUEST will be created as an NDS user object.

If NetWare 4.x does not have the GUEST user object, you must create one in the container that is used for the bindery context.

Installing NetWare NFS When the NetWare NFS Gateway Product Is Already Installed

NetWare NFS Gateway is a product that provides TCP/IP services to IPX clients. If this product is already installed, it may have been configured to bypass the use of the local files in the SYS:ETC directory. The files in SYS:ETC are needed for NetWare NFS. To enable the use of the files in the SYS:ETC directory, you must enter the following lines at the end of the SYS:ETC/NFSPARAM file:

```
[NETDB]
WRITELOCALFILES 1
```

Installing NetWare NFS

Figure 11.12 provides an overview of the NetWare NFS installation procedure. You can use this as a quick review of the detailed procedure that follows.

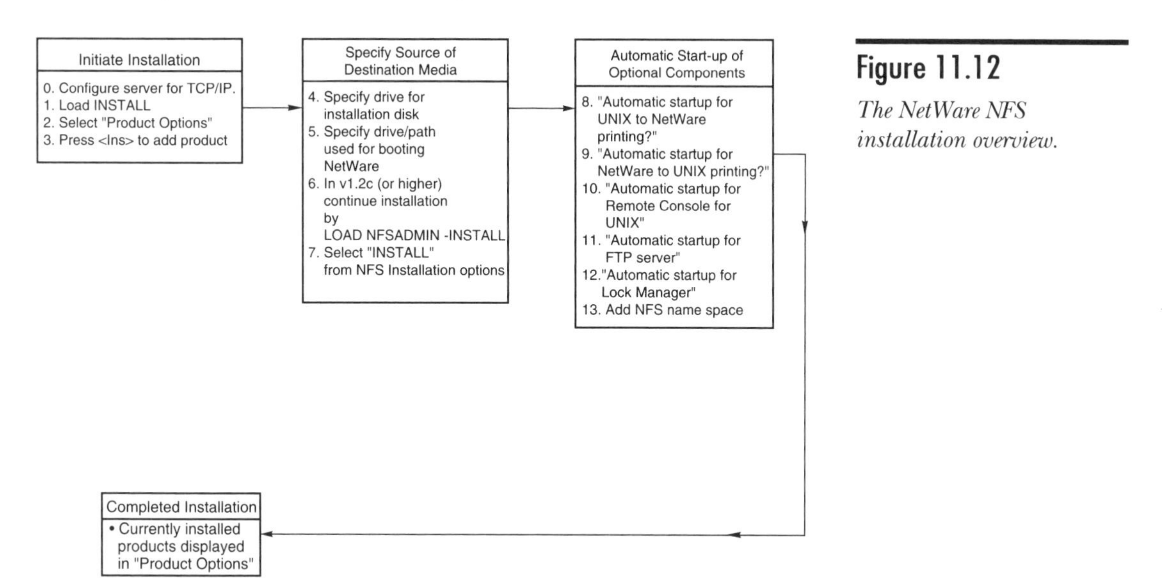

Figure 11.12

The NetWare NFS installation overview.

1. Start your NetWare server.
2. From the server console, run INSTALL NLM by entering **LOAD INSTALL**.
3. On a NetWare 3.x server, select "Product Options" to display a list of currently installed products.

   On a NetWare 4.x server, select "Maintenance/Selective Install" first, and then select "Product Options" to see a list of currently installed products.

If you have not installed a product previously using "Product Options," you will see an empty list.

4. Press the Insert key to add a new product.

5. At the prompt, enter the name of the drive from where you will be installing. This could be the A: drive, or another directory on which you have installed NetWare NFS distribution files.

   On a NetWare 3.x server, to specify an alternate source, simply type the new location and press Enter.

   On a NetWare 4.x server, to specify an alternate source, press F3, and type the new location and press Enter.

   You will see a "Please Wait" message, and the namespace NLMs will be transferred to the SYS:SYSTEM directory.

6. Depending on the version of NetWare NFS you are installing, you may see a message informing you about a README.TXT file. You will have to stop the installation to read the README.TXT file, and continue later. You can skip reading the README.TXT file, however.

7. In NetWare NFS 1.2c (and higher), if the server is not configured for TCP/IP, the installation will not proceed unless you switch to the system console and configure TCP/IP.

   Alternatively, you can exit the installation, configure TCP/IP, and restart the installation.

8. When prompted to "Enter drive and/or path name for booting NetWare," enter the path name of the directory containing the SERVER.EXE program (C:\SERVER.311, C:\SERVER.312, or C:\SERVER.40, and so on).

   In NetWare 1.2c (and higher), if the hostname has not been defined for the server, you will be prompted for it.

   The files are copied, and the NFS namespace modules NFS.NAM and V_NFS.NLM used by VREPAIR are placed in the boot directory containing SERVER.EXE.

9. If you are installing with NetWare NFS 1.2c (or higher), the installation program will complete and ask you if you want to exit at this point. Select "Yes."

   You must add the NFS space as shown in step 21, and the Installation is now complete, but the NetWare NFS server is not ready to use unless properly configured. NetWare NFS configuration for version 1.2c (or higher) can be started using the command LOAD NFSADMIN -INSTALL.

10. If installing with NetWare NFS 1.2, you should see the NFS Installation Options menu. Select the "Install" option.

    The NFS support NLMs, database files, and utilities are placed in the SYS:SYSTEM, SYS:ETC, and SYS:PUBLIC directories, respectively.

The Installation program also adds the following statements to the beginning of the AUTOEXEC.NCF file:

```
LOAD PATCHMAN
LOAD NFSFIX
```

The following command is added to the end of the AUTOEXEC.NCF file:

```
NFSSTART.NCF
```

The PATCHMAN.NLM in NetWare NFS 1.2 is for NetWare 3.11. If you are installing NetWare NFS 1.2 on a NetWare 3.12 (or higher) server, you will have to obtain a PATCHMAN.NLM for NetWare 3.12 (or higher) from Novell in order to run NetWare NFS.

11. If the NFS configuration finds that certain files, such as HOSTS and EXPORTS, already exist, you can choose to overwrite these files.

    If the SYS:ETC\HOSTS file already exists, do not overwrite it. It probably has the IP addresses set up correctly. You can edit this information after installation.

    If the SYS:ETC\EXPORTS file already exists, you may want to overwrite it if you will be setting up different export pathnames.

12. If TCP/IP has already been loaded, skip this step. Otherwise, enter the following information:

    ```
    Internet Address:
    Hostname:
    Subnet Mask:
    Maximum Packet Size:
    Minimum Receive Buffers:
    LAN driver:
    ```

    Press Esc and answer Yes to update the configuration files.

13. At the prompt, you will be asked the question, "Automatic Startup for Unix to NetWare Printing?"

    Answer No, unless you are already knowledgeable about this and understand the procedure.

14. At the prompt, you will be asked the question, "Automatic Startup for NetWare to Unix Printing?"

    Answer No, unless you are already knowledgeable about this and understand the procedure.

15. At the prompt,you will be asked the question, "Automatic Startup for the Remote Console for Unix?"

    Answer Yes, because this allows a Unix station to manage your server console. If you don't want a Unix station to use the X Window System to manage the NetWare console, select No.

16. At the prompt, you will be asked the question, "Automatic Startup for FTP server?"

    Answer Yes, if you want the NetWare server to act as an FTP server; otherwise, answer No.

17. At the prompt, you will be asked the question, "Automatic Startup for Lock Manager?"

    Answer Yes. This adds the commands to load the LOCKD.NLM and the STATD.NLM to implement file/record locking for the NetWare NFS server.

18. Press Esc to exit the NFS Installation Options menu. Then press Esc again to exit NFS Installation.

    You should see the list of configuration modules for the NFS product.

19. Press Esc to exit the list of currently installed products.

20. Use Alt+Esc to switch to the system console.

    There should be messages on the console informing you of the modules loaded during NetWare NFS Installation. You should see messages indicating that NFS.NAM, NFSFIX.NLM, and PATCHMAN.NLM have been loaded.

21. Add the NFS name space from the system console.

    ```
    LOAD NFS                (if not already loaded)
    ADD NAME SPACE NFS TO SYS
    ```

22. Shut down your server and restart it to verify that NetWare NFS installation works correctly. To shut down your server, use the DOWN command from the server console. Restart it by executing the SERVER program from the DOS partition.

    On a NetWare 4.x server, you can use RESTART SERVER after the DOWN command from the server console prompt.

23. When the NetWare server boots, supply the password for the REMOTE console.

24. If you see any error messages, make sure that the network driver is being loaded with the correct frame type. Remember that for Ethernet, you must use ETHERNET_II frame encapsulation for binding IP to the network interface.

NetWare NFS Configuration

After you have installed NetWare NFS, you must configure it. This section shows you where and what the NetWare NFS configuration fields are.

NetWare NFS Installation Directory Structure

Figure 11.13 shows the directories where NetWare NFS files are installed.

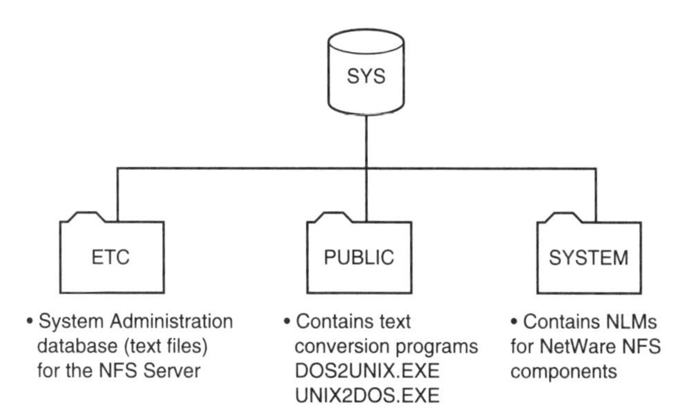

Figure 11.13
The NetWare NFS directories.

The SYS:SYSTEM directory contains the NLMs for NetWare NFS. Table 11.5 shows the NLMs and support files used by the different NetWare NFS services.

Table 11.5 NFS Services and Support files

NFS Service	Support Files
NFS Server	NFSSERV.NLM NFSADMIN.NLM NFSADMIN.HLP RPCSTUB.NLM
FTP Server	INETD.NLM INETD.CFG FTPSERV.NLM
Unix-to-NetWare Print Service	PLPD.NLM PLPDCFG.NLM PLPDMSG.HLP FLTRLIB.NLM FILTER.NLM
NetWare-to-Unix Print Service	LPR_GWY.NLM LPR_PSRV.NLM
NFS Name Space Support	NFS.NAM V_NFS.NLM (for NetWare NFS 1.2 you need PATCHMAN.NLM and NFSFIX.NLM)
Lock Manager	LOCKD.NLM STATD.NLM
Xconsole	XCONSOLE.NLM

continues

Table 11.5, Continued

NFS Service	Support Files
NetWare Command File (NetWare NFS 1.2)	NFSSTART.NCF NFSSTOP.NCF
NetWare Command File (NetWare NFS 1.2c)	UNISTART.NCF UNISTOP.NCF

The SYS:ETC directory contains the database configuration files for NetWare NFS. Some of the files, such as SYS:ETC\HOSTS, are shared and used by both the NetWare TCP/IP transport and NetWare NFS.

The SYS:PUBLIC directory contains the NetWare utilities (UNIX2DOS.EXE, DOS2UNIX.EXE) needed to convert between Unix and DOS text files.

The following sections supply you with a conceptual understanding of what the different file components provide for each service.

NFS Name Support Modules

Figure 11.14 shows the NFS name space support NLMs. The NFS name space adds a Unix directory entry for each file or directory in the volume to which name space has been added. All the DOS and Unix directory entries for a file point to the data area for that file (see fig. 11.14).

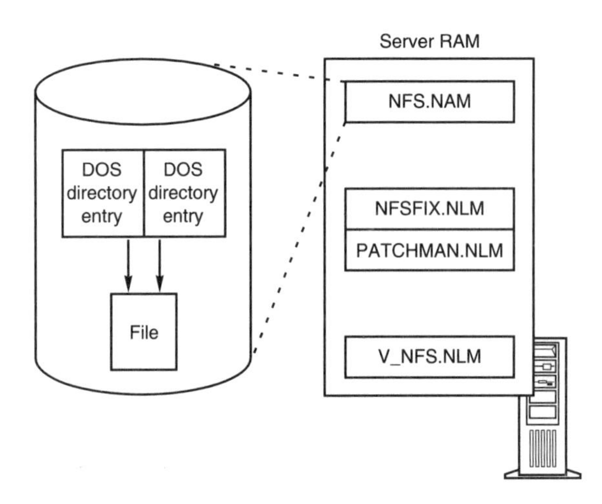

Figure 11.14
NFS name space support modules.

The knowledge of the Unix directory entries (called *NFS name space*) is implemented by NFS.NAM. The NFS.NAM provides a view of the NetWare File System as an NFS file system.

The NFSFIX.NLM is used in NetWare 1.2 to fix a bug in NFS. This patch is applied dynamically to NetWare NFS when it is running in server RAM. The PATCHMAN.NLM is a general-purpose NLM used in NetWare to apply patches implemented in modules such as

NFSFIX.NLM. The NFSFIX.NLN enables DOS users (who have the appropriate permissions) to delete hard links created by Unix NFS clients.

V_NFS.NLM provides NFS name support for VREPAIR. This enables VREPAIR to perform volume repairs on the NFS name space.

The NFS Server and Configuration Modules

Figure 11.15 shows the NFS server and configuration modules. The NFSSERV.NLM implements the NFS server. The NFS server requires the RPC protocol, which is implemented by RPCSTUB.NLM. This is a shared module that can be used by other applications that use RPC.

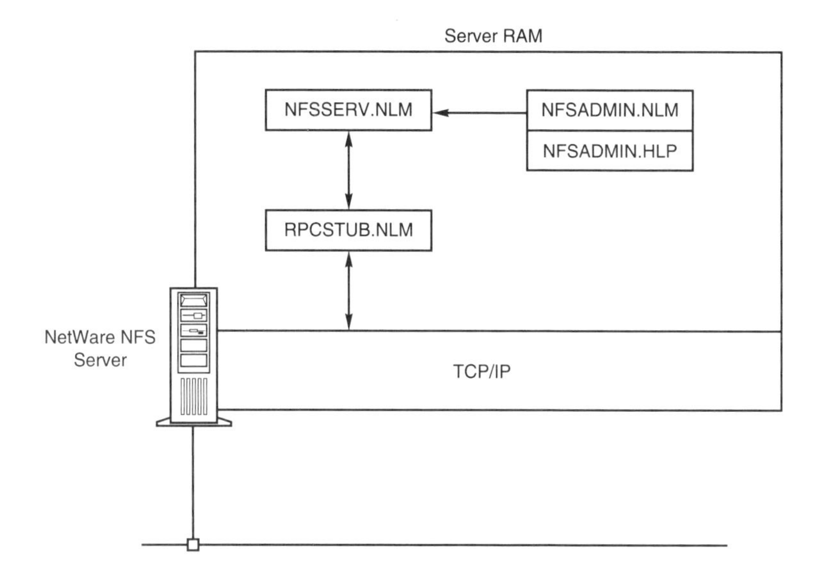

Figure 11.15
NFS server and configuration modules.

The NFSADMIN.NLM is a configuration module for configuring the NetWare NFS server component (NFSSERV.NLM), and the NFSADMIN.HLP file is a help file that is used by the NFS administration program.

Unix-to-NetWare Print Service Modules

Figure 11.16 shows the modules needed to implement Unix-to-NetWare print services. The PLPD.NLM implements the line printer daemon. The line printer daemon is a print server process that Unix line printer clients can use to send print jobs.

The PLPDCFG.NLM is a configuration module for configuring the PLPD.NLM, and the PLPDMSG.HLP file is a help file used by the PLPDCFG.NLM configuration program.

The FILTER.NLM implements the NFS print filters. Print filters include filters to translate a print job to PostScript format or to provide end-of-line translations for text file print jobs.

The FLTRLIB.NLM implements the print filter library. This is a set of support library routines used by the FILTER.NLM.

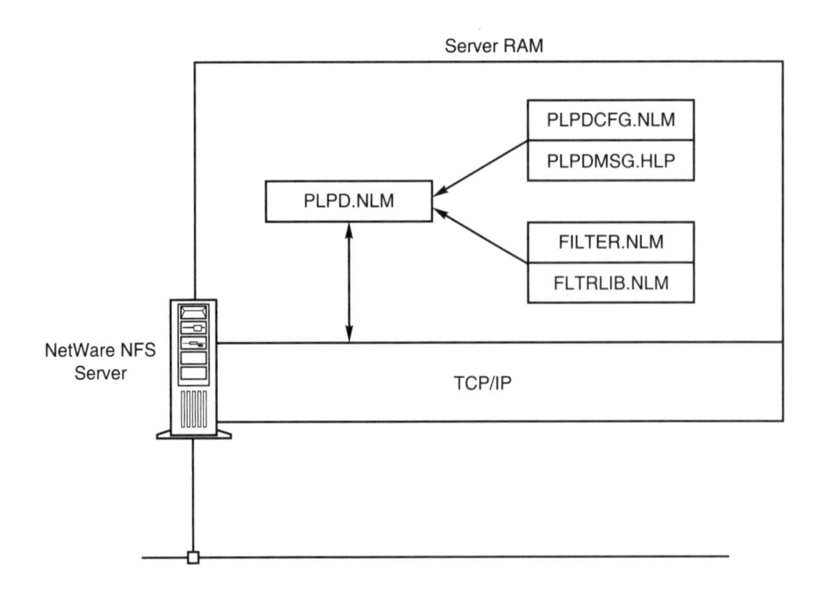

Figure 11.16

Unix-to-NetWare printer modules.

NetWare-to-Unix Print Service Modules

Figure 11.17 shows the modules needed to implement NetWare-to-Unix print services. The LPR_GWY.NLM is used to provide the conversion between NetWare print jobs and Unix print jobs. This gateway takes print jobs from a NetWare queue, translates them to a Unix print job format, and sends them to a Unix printer. The gateway acts as a Unix lpr client for the purpose of sending the NetWare print job.

The LPR_PSRV.NLM provides print server functions that are needed to send the print job to Unix.

Figure 11.17

NetWare-to-Unix print modules.

```
% ls -l | grep kss
drwx---r-x  2 65533  students      512 Dec 21  1993 kss
% █
```

Lock Manager

Figure 11.18 shows the modules needed to implement the lock management functions. LOCKD.NLM is used to provide file and record locking for NetWare NFS. STATD.NLM (status monitor daemon) is used to re-establish locks in the event of a server crash.

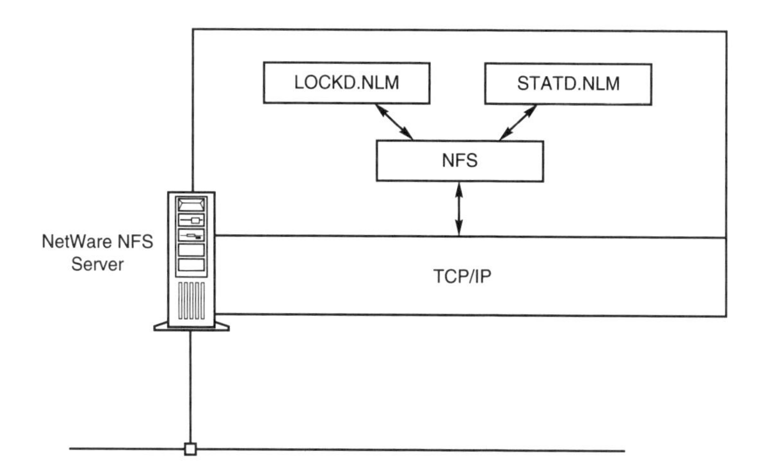

Figure 11.18

The Lock Manager and Status Monitor.

The FTP Server Components

Figure 11.19 shows the modules needed to implement FTP server components. The INETD.NLM implements the Internet Daemon. The Internet Daemon process monitors well-known ports waiting for a connection request. In the case of FTP, if an open TCP connection request is received for FTP services, it loads and starts the FTPSERV.NLM.

The file INETD.CFG is a configuration file used by the INETD.NLM.

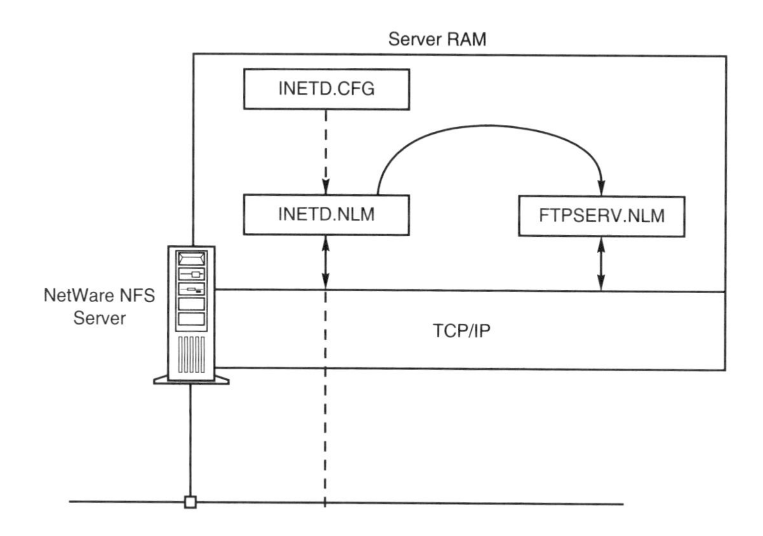

Figure 11.19

FTP server components.

NetWare Command Files for NFS

When NetWare NFS is installed or configured, it automatically creates two NetWare command files. One of the files is used to start NFS and the other is used to stop NFS services.

In NetWare NFS 1.2, the start-up NetWare command file is NFSSTART.NCF, and the NetWare command file to stop services is NFSSTOP.NCF.

Starting with NetWare NFS 1.2c, the names of these files have changed. The start-up NetWare command file for NetWare 1.2c (and higher) is UNISTART.NCF, and the NetWare command file to stop services is UNISTOP.NCF.

The following are the contents of a sample NFSSTART.NCF/UNISTART.NCF file. The actual details depend on the NFS service you have installed. For example, if you have not configured Unix-to-NetWare print services, the PLPD.NLM will not be loaded.

```
load nfsserv
#Set up Unix-to-NetWare Print Service
load plpd
#Set up NetWare-to-Unix Print Service
load lpr_psrv
load lpr_gwy
#Set up remote console for Unix
load xconsole
#Set up inetd to start FTP server
load inetd
#Set up Lock Manager and status monitor
load statd
load lockd
```

The NFSSTART.NCF/UNISTART.NCF is placed at the end of the AUTOEXEC.NCF file, at the end of the NetWare NFS installation. For NetWare NFS 1.2, the following additional commands are placed at the beginning of the AUTOEXEC.NCF file:

```
load patchman
load nfsfix
```

The following are the contents of a sample NFSSTOP.NCF/UNISTOP.NCF file. The actual details depend on the NFS service you have installed. For example, if you have not configured Unix-to-NetWare print services, the PLPD.NLM will not be unloaded.

```
unload ftpserv
unload inetd
unload plpd
unload lpr_gwy
unload lpr_psrv
unload plpdcfg
unload nfsadmin
unload lockd
unload statd
unload xconsole
unload nfsserv
```

NFS Support Files

The SYS:ETC and SYS:PUBLIC contain a number of support files for NetWare NFS. These files and their functions are explained in tables 11.6 and 11.7.

Table 11.6 SYS:ETC Files for NetWare NFS

Filename	Description
EXPORTS	A database of directories to be exported.
HOSTS	A database consisting of hostnames and their IP addresses.
NFSERROR	A configuration file for NFS error messages.
NFSPARAM	Defines the values of NFS tunable parameters.
NFSUSERS	Contains mappings between Unix uids and NetWare user accounts.
NFSGROUP	Contains mappings between Unix gids and NetWare groups.
INETD.CFG	The configuration file for the INETD.NLM.
FTPSERV.CFG	The configuration file for FTPSERV.NLM.
DOS2UNIX.C	The source code for converting a DOS text file to a Unix text file.
UNIX2DOS.C	The source code for converting a Unix text file to a DOS text file.

Table 11.7 SYS:PUBLIC Files for NetWare NFS

Filename	Description
DOS2UNIX.EXE	A DOS program for converting a DOS text file to a Unix text file.
UNIX2DOS.EXE	A DOS program for converting a Unix text file to a DOS text file.

Removing NetWare NFS

If the installation of NetWare NFS was unsuccessful and you would like to start again, or you must install a product that conflicts with NetWare NFS, you may want to remove NetWare NFS from your server.

You can remove NetWare NFS by performing the following steps:

1. Load INSTALL.NLM.
2. Select Product Options from the Installation Options menu.
3. Highlight the product to be removed and press Del.

Configuring the NFS Server

Configuring the NFS server consists of a number of tasks. These tasks are listed below:

- Mapping Unix uids to NetWare user accounts (SYS:ETC\NFSUSERS).
- Mapping Unix gids to NetWare groups (SYS:ETC\NFSGROUP).
- Modifying the Host table (SYS:ETC\HOSTS).
- Exporting NetWare directories (SYS:ETC\EXPORTS).
- Setting the file attributes (SYS:ETC\EXPORTS).

Many of the previously listed tasks can be performed by directly editing database text files contained in SYS:ETC (listed in table 11.6). However, this requires you to be knowledgeable about the special syntax of these files. A preferred way of making these changes is to use NFSADMIN.

The NFSADMIN program can be started using the console command LOAD NFSADMIN.

Figure 11.20 shows the main options of the NFSADMIN NLM.

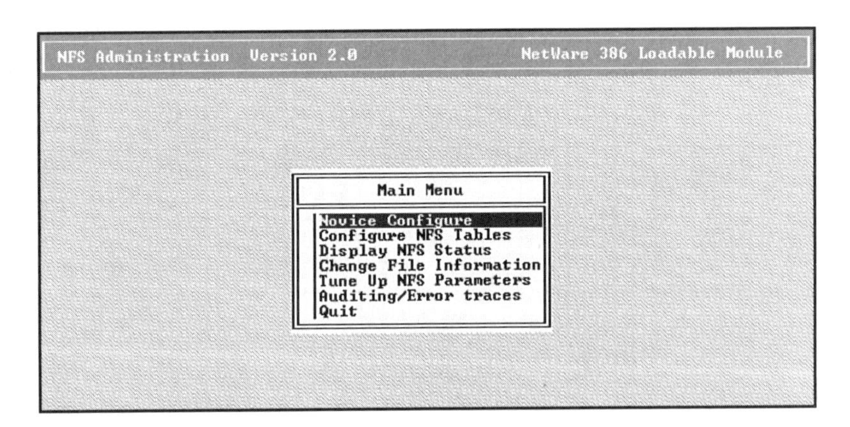

Figure 11.20
The NFSADMIN Main Menu.

If you select the Novice Configure option from the NFSADMIN Main Menu, it systematically leads you through the following procedures. You have the option at each step to say "Yes" or "No" to perform the indicated procedure (see fig. 11.21).

1. Map Unix uids to NetWare user accounts.
2. Map Unix gids to NetWare groups.
3. Map TCP/IP hostnames to IP addresses.
4. Define NetWare directories that can be exported.
5. Set file attributes for exported directories.
6. Configure NetWare-to-Unix print gateway.

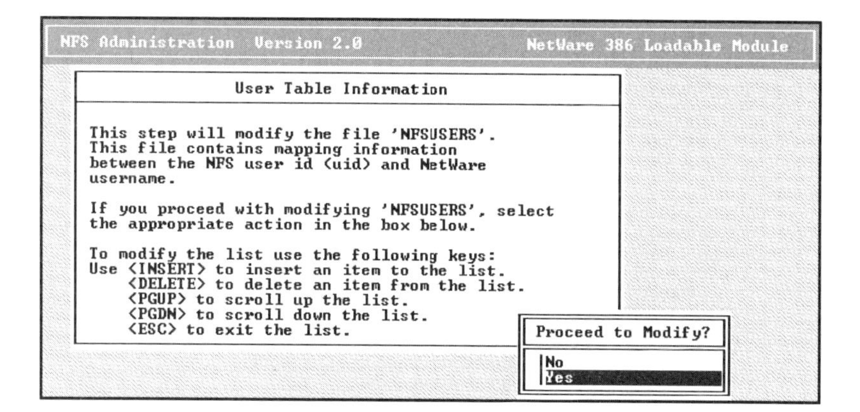

Figure 11.21

Selecting the Novice Configure option.

Alternatively, you may prefer to perform the previously listed tasks by using options from the NFSADMIN Main Menu. For example, many of the previously listed tasks can be performed by selecting Configure NFS Tables or Change File Information from the Main Menu.

Mapping Unix Users to NetWare Users

Because NetWare NFS runs on a NetWare server, the NFS client must be assigned a corresponding NetWare user account. Doing so assures that the NFS client will have its permissions controlled through a NetWare user account. By changing the file system Trustee rights on the NetWare user account the NetWare NFS administrator can control the rights an NFS client is allowed.

An "escape" mechanism exists so that NFS users who are not explicitly mapped to a NetWare user account are assigned a mapping to the user account NOBODY. The NetWare NOBODY user account must be created, and by default user NOBODY has limited rights.

The mapping between NFS clients and NetWare accounts is maintained in the SYS:ETC\NFSUSERS file. The following is a sample NFSUSERS file:

```
# "NFS uid", "NetWare Username"
-2          nobody
0           supervisor
100         ANUMENOS
101         ZNUMENOS
102         RGWAUXLN
```

The NFS client user is represented by the Unix uid. In the NFSUSERS sample file, the uid 0 maps to the NetWare Supervisor account. Recall that a uid of 0 is assigned to the Unix root user (superuser). These users automatically have supervisor privileges on the NetWare server.

If the Unix system administrator is different from the NetWare supervisor, you may want to map the uid 0 to a non-supervisor account. You should also restrict the Write (W) right to the SYS:ETC\NFSUSERS file in order to prevent unauthorized users from modifying this file.

In the previous example, the Unix uid 100 maps to the NetWare user account ZNUMENOS, the Unix uid 101 maps to the NetWare user account ANUMENOS, and the Unix uid 102 maps to the NetWare user account RGWAUXLN.

The user NOBODY is created automatically when you first enter the "User Information" option from NFSADMIN. Figure 11.22 graphically shows this mapping.

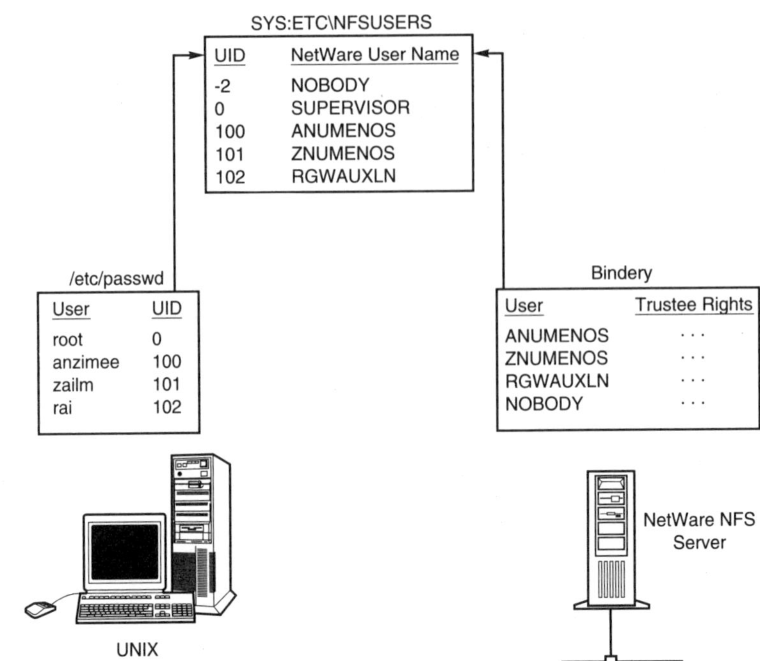

Figure 11.22

Mapping between Unix uids and NetWare user accounts.

You can map Unix users to NetWare user accounts by selecting Configure NFS Tables, User Information from NFSADMIN.

Figure 11.23 shows the screen for mapping NFS users to NetWare user accounts. You can press the Insert key to add a new mapping, the Delete key to delete a user mapping, or the Enter key to edit a mapping.

The NFSUSERS file can be modified using NFSADMIN or a text editor. If you use NFSADMIN to create a user mapping for a NetWare user that does not exist, NFSADMIN automatically creates the NetWare user in the bindery. If you use NFSADMIN to delete a user mapping, the corresponding NetWare user is not deleted.

If you use a text editor to create or delete a user mapping, the corresponding NetWare user is neither created nor deleted.

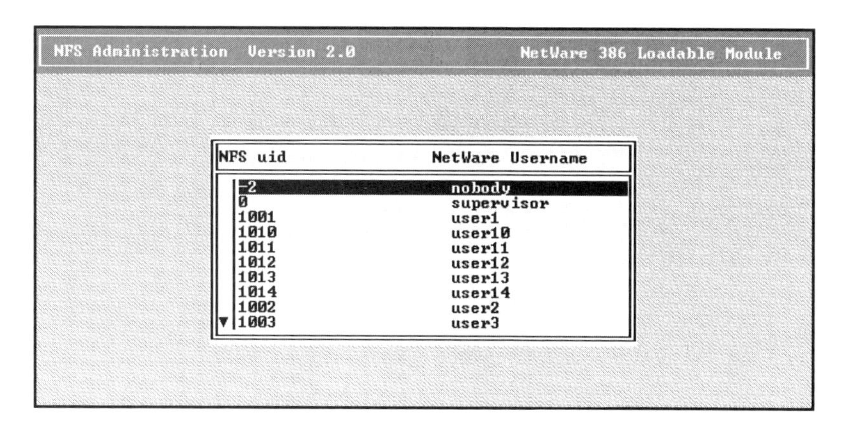

Figure 11.23

The NFSADMIN screen for mapping between Unix uids and NetWare user accounts.

Mapping Unix Groups to NetWare Groups

The NFS group permissions need an equivalent concept on the NetWare NFS file system. A file or directory in Unix has a user owner and a group owner, and both can have a different set of rights.

NetWare NFS provides a mapping between Unix gids and NetWare groups. The NetWare NFS user looks up gids in a table to determine group ownership permissions for files and directories. This mapping table is kept in the SYS:ETC\NFSGROUP file.

NFS groups not explicitly specified in the SYS:ETC\NFSGROUP file are assigned a mapping to the group NOGROUP. The NOGROUP NetWare group must be created, and by default the NOGROUP has limited rights.

A sample NFSGROUP file follows:

```
# "NFS gid", "NetWare Group Name"
50      ENGINEERS
51      MARKETING
52      CORPORATE
800     nfsgroup
-2      nogroup
```

The NFS group account is represented by the Unix gid. You should also restrict the Write (W) right to the SYS:ETC\NFSGROUP file in order to prevent unauthorized users from modifying this file.

In the previous example, the Unix gid 50 maps to the NetWare group ENGINEERS, the Unix gid 51 maps to the NetWare group MARKETING, and the Unix gid 52 maps to the NetWare group CORPORATE. The group NOGROUP is automatically created when you first enter the "Group Information" option from NFSADMIN. Figure 11.24 shows this mapping.

Figure 11.24

Mapping between Unix gids and NetWare groups.

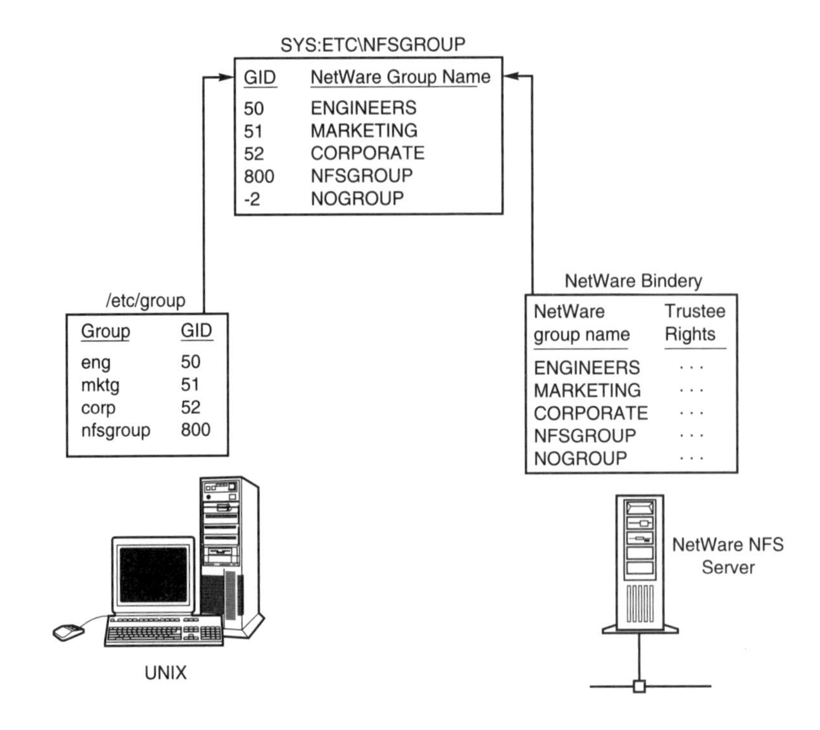

You can map Unix group owners to NetWare groups by selecting Configure NFS Tables, Group Information from NFSADMIN.

Figure 11.25 shows the screen for mapping NFS gids and NetWare groups. You can press the Insert key to add a new mapping, the Delete key to delete a user mapping, or the Enter key to edit a mapping.

Figure 11.25

The NFSADMIN screen for mapping between Unix gids and NetWare groups.

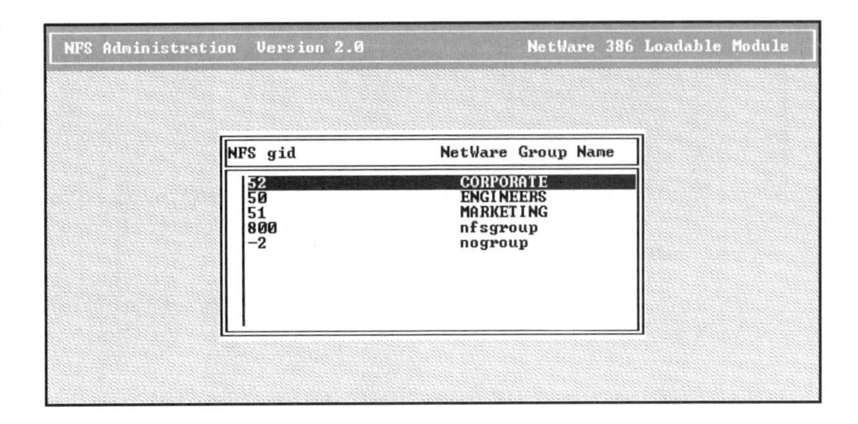

The NFSGROUP file can be modified using NFSADMIN or a text editor. If you use NFSADMIN to create a group mapping for a NetWare group that does not exist, NFSADMIN automatically creates the NetWare group in thc bindery. If you use NFSADMIN to delete a group mapping, the corresponding NetWare group is not deleted.

If you use a text editor to create nor delete a group mapping, the corresponding NetWare group is neither created nor deleted.

Mapping Hostnames to IP Addresses

The Hosts file is used to translate a symbolic name for a machine to its IP address. This file is kept in SYS:ETC\HOSTS file. This file is typically used to keep the hostnames of NFS clients who have access to the NetWare NFS server.

A sample SYS:ETC\HOSTS file follows:

```
# "IP Address", "Hostname"
127.0.0.1 localhost loopback lb
133.123.74.91 bantu
199.245.180.11 s386 nwcs
199.245.180.16 ucs bsd
```

You can add hostnames by selecting Configure NFS Tables, Workstation IP Address from NFSADMIN.

Figure 11.26 shows the screen for mapping hostnames and IP addresses. You can press the Insert key to add a new mapping, the Delete key to delete a user mapping, or the Enter key to edit a mapping.

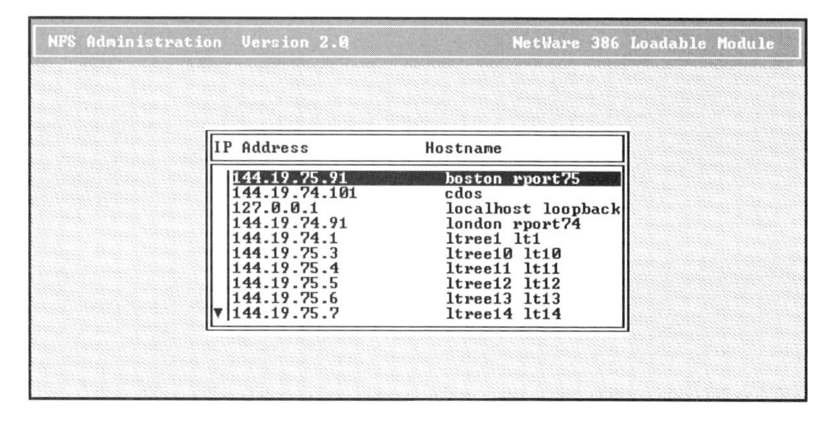

Figure 11.26

The NFSADMIN screen for mapping hostnames to IP address.

Defining the Export Table

The export table contains a list of directories on the NetWare server that can be mounted by NFS clients. The process of "mounting" by a Unix NFS client consists of accessing the NetWare directory as if it were local to the NFS client.

The exported directories are listed using Unix syntax. For example, /sys/data is used to export the NetWare directory SYS:DATA. Similarly, to export VOL_A:APPS, you would use the syntax /vol_a/apps, and to export SYS:PUBLIC/APPS, you would use /sys/public/apps.

The exported directories are stored in the text database file SYS:\ETC\EXPORTS.

A sample SYS:ETC\EXPORTS file follows:

```
# "Field 1: ", "Field 2: "
/sys/data  -root=ltrees1 ltrees2, -trustee_rights=create, -_dos_attributes=modify
/sys/etc   -trustee_rights=create, -dos_attributes=modify
```

The syntax is similar to the BSD Unix /etc/exports file, but the attributes are specific to NetWare NFS.

You can change or add export options by manually editing the SYS:ETC\EXPORTS file. This is not recommended unless you are knowledgeable about special syntax for export options.

A better way to modify the SYS:ETC\EXPORTS file is to use NFSADMIN. To do this, follow these steps:

1. Select Configure NFS Tables from the NFSADMIN Main Menu.
2. Select Export Information from the Configuration menu.
3. Highlight the exported path and press Enter.

Figure 11.27 shows the screen for setting export options.

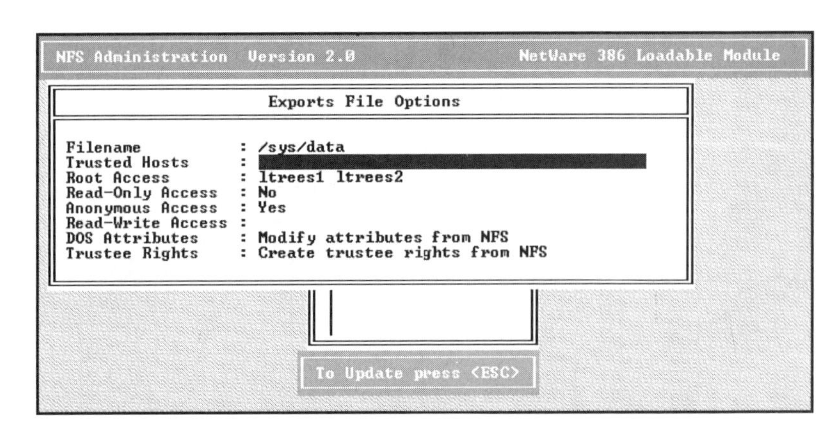

Figure 11.27
The NFSADMIN screen for editing export options.

The different export options are described in table 11.8.

Table 11.8 Export Options

Export Option	Description
Filename	The directory for which export options need to be set. You must use Unix style path names, for example, /sys/data or /sys/public/docs. You cannot export subdirectories of paths that already have been exported.
Trusted Host	This lists the hostnames that have access to the exported directory. Leave this field blank to enable NFS clients to have access. Otherwise, list the hostnames that have access. Separate hostnames with commas or blanks.
Root Access	Lists each hostname whose root user is allowed supervisor privileges to the exported directory. If this field is left blank, root access is denied. If root access is granted to a directory, the Unix root user has full access to that directory structure. The Unix client hostname for the root user must have access to the exported path.
Read-Only Access	If set to No (the default), NFS clients can write to this directory. To disable writing to this directory, set Read-Only access to Yes. The Read-Write Access parameter can override this for specified hostnames.
Anonymous Access	If this field is set to Yes (the default), Unix users whose uid is not found in the NFSUSERS database are mapped to user NOBODY. If this field is set to No, such users are denied access.
Read-Write Access	Used to specify hosts that are allowed write access to the exported directory if Read-Only Access is set to Yes.
DOS Attributes	Can be set to "Do not modify attributes from NFS" (the default) or "Modify attributes from NFS." If set to "Do not modify attributes from NFS," NFS clients cannot change NetWare file attributes. If set to "Modify attributes from NFS," NFS clients can change file attributes.
Trustee Rights	Can be set to "Create trustee rights from NFS" (the default) or "Do not create trustee rights from NFS." If set to "Create trustee rights from NFS," explicit trustee assignments are made for the NetWare owner, group, and everyone when a file or directory is created based on the current setting of the umask. Also, if NFS client issues a chmod, chown, or chgrp command, explicit trustee assignments are made to the NetWare file/ directory. If set to "Do not create trustee rights from NFS," the chmod, chown, and chgrp commands have no affect on NetWare trustee rights. If trustee rights cannot be created from Unix, access to files are determined by the effective rights that flow down through the NetWare directory structure.

Understanding Permissions Mappings between the NFS and NetWare Environments

Unix and NetWare implement directory and file permissions differently. These differences require that there should be a mapping between the NFS permission concepts and NetWare file system rights concepts.

Figures 11.28 and 11.29 show how a Unix owner and Unix group owner of a NetWare file are determined. The mapping is calculated each time an access to a NetWare file is made, to account for any changes that may have been made since the last access to that file.

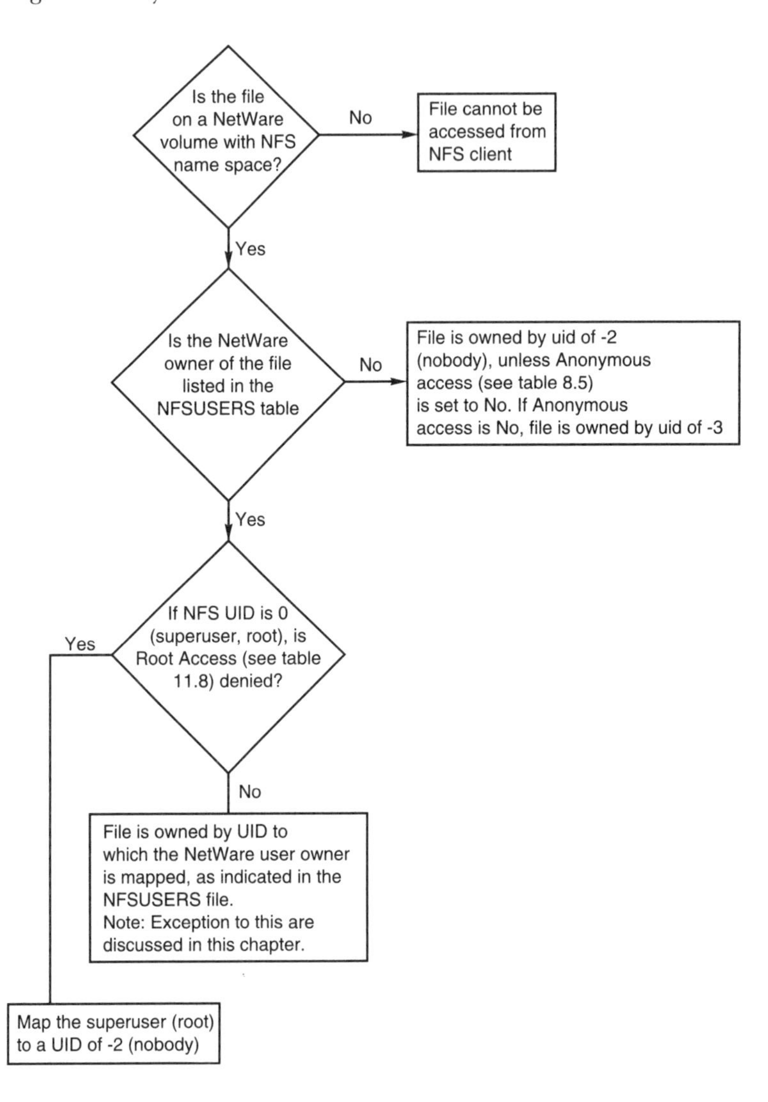

Figure 11.28

Determining the NFS user owner (uid) for a NetWare file.

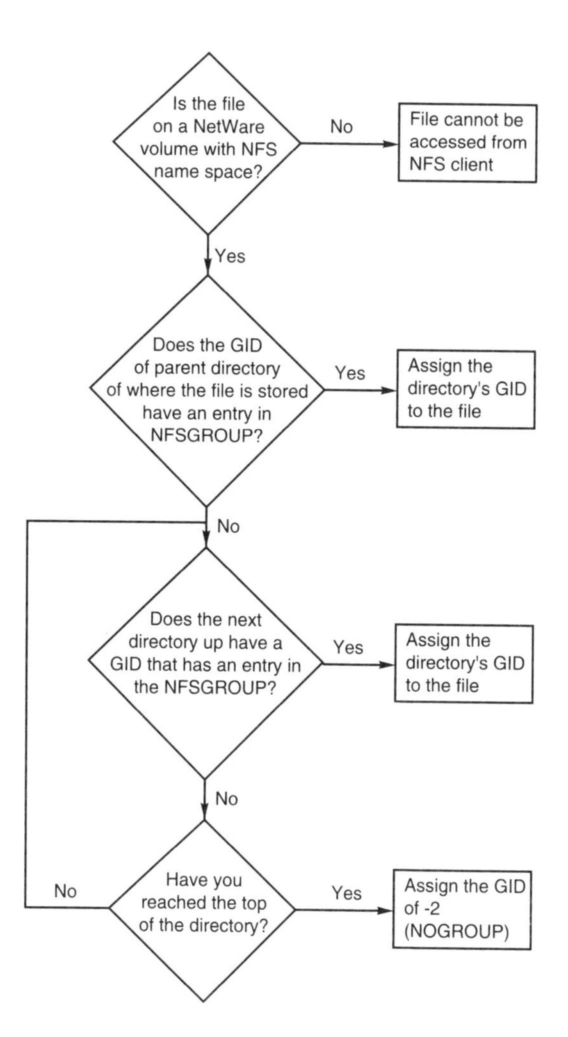

Figure 11.29

Determining the NFS group owner (gid) for a NetWare file.

In Unix (and NFS, because NFS uses Unix permissions), a group is associated with a file or directory. Such a group is called the *group owner* of that file or directory. NetWare enables many groups to be granted access to a file or directory. Because of this basic difference between groups in Unix and NetWare, figure 11.29 shows that the NFS group is determined by examining the gid (group ID) of the file's ancestor directories.

The "others" group in Unix (NFS) is mapped to the NetWare group EVERYONE. Figure 11.30 summarizes the user owner, group owner, and others mapping to corresponding users and groups in NetWare.

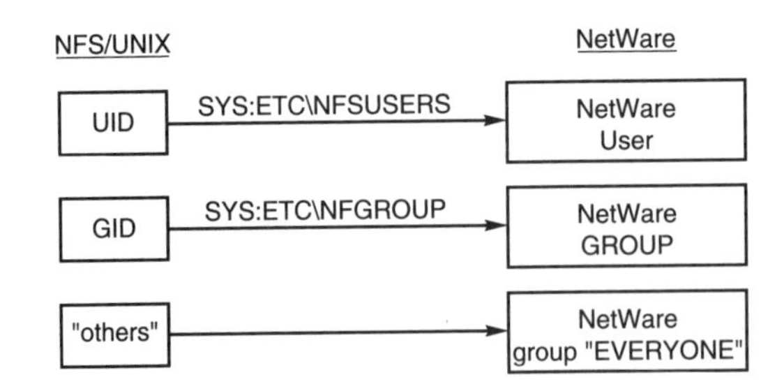

Figure 11.30
Mapping NFS's uid, gid, and others to the equivalent NetWare concepts.

UID/GID Mapping Exceptions

Figure 11.28 shows some exceptional situations when the uid for the NFS file for a user maps to a uid of –2 or –3. Because a uid of –3 is not normally listed in the NFSUSERS table, such a user will have no mapping to a NetWare user, and therefore no rights.

The exceptions are in the following list:

- If the root (superuser) user accesses a NetWare NFS file system and the "Root Access" is set to No for the NetWare NFS server, the root user is mapped to a uid of –2. Because a uid of –2 is nominally mapped to the NetWare user NOBODY, the root user's rights will be controlled by the rights assigned to user NOBODY.
- If "Anonymous Access" is set to No for the NetWare NFS server, there is no mapping of the user in NFSUSERS, and the NFS uid is mapped to –3.
- If the NFS user maps to NOBODY and there is no user NOBODY defined, the NFS uid is mapped to –3.
- If the NetWare user owner of the file does not have the NetWare Access Control (A) right, the uid is mapped to –3.
- If the exported directory has the option "Modify DOS attributes from NFS," the owner of the parent directory will be mapped to a uid of –3 if any file in that directory has the NetWare Delete Inhibit (DI), Rename Inhibit (RI), or Transactional (T) attribute, or if any subdirectory has the NetWare Delete Inhibit (DI) attribute.
- If the exported directory has the option "Do not modify DOS attributes from NFS," and any file in that directory has the NetWare Read-Only (Ro) attribute, the owner of both the file and the parent directory will be mapped to a uid of –3.
- If the exported directory has the option "Modify DOS attributes from NFS," and any file in that directory has the NetWare Transactional (T) attribute, the owner of the parent directory will be mapped to a uid of –3.

General Rules for NFS Permissions to NetWare Permissions Mappings

The following general guidelines will help you understand NFS permissions to NetWare permissions mappings.

- The NFS owner of a file must be assigned the NetWare Access Control (A) right, because the root user and owner of a file on some Unix systems can issue the Unix chmod command to change permissions. In NetWare a user can only change rights (permissions) if a minimum of the Access Control (A) right is given. Therefore, an NFS owner of a file must have the Access Control (A) right.
- If you remove the Access Control (A) NetWare right for a file or directory, the uid on the NFS side will be changed to –3.
- Consider USER1 who has the Access Control (A) right in SYS:DATA/KSS. You can use the RIGHTS /T command in NetWare 4.x to examine its trustee rights. These rights are shown as in figure 11.31. (On a NetWare 3.x server you will use the TLIST command.)

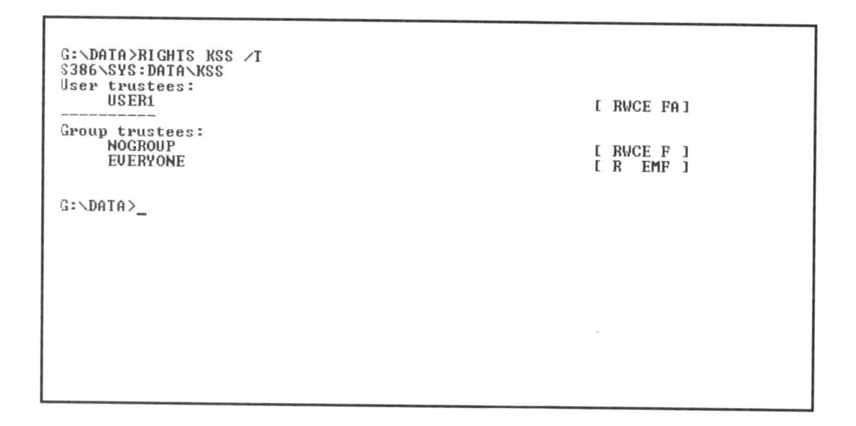

```
G:\DATA>RIGHTS KSS /T
S386\SYS:DATA\KSS
User trustees:
     USER1                                           [ RWCE FA]
----------
Group trustees:
     NOGROUP                                         [ RWCE F ]
     EVERYONE                                        [ R   EMF ]

G:\DATA>_
```

Figure 11.31

The trustees for a NetWare NFS exported directory.

- Figure 11.32 shows that the Access Control (A) right is revoked from the directory SYS:DATA/KSS. The command that is shown is for a NetWare 4.x server. On a NetWare 3.x server, you would use the command REVOKE A FOR SYS:DATA\KSS FROM KSS.

```
G:\DATA>RIGHTS KSS -A /NAME=USER1

S386\SYS:DATA
Directories                                                  Rights
------------------------------------------------------------ ---------------
KSS                                                          [ RWCE F ]

Rights for one directory were changed for USER1


G:\DATA>
```

Figure 11.32

The trustees for a NetWare NFS exported directory.

- Figure 11.33 shows that the owner uid has changed to –3, as mentioned in the rule. Figure 11.34 shows the directory listing for the same directory from the Unix NFS client. In figure 11.34 the uid for the file is shown as having a value of 65533. This represents a value of –3 using a 16-bit unsigned number. Similarly, a uid or gid value of –2 appears as the 16-bit unsigned number 65534.

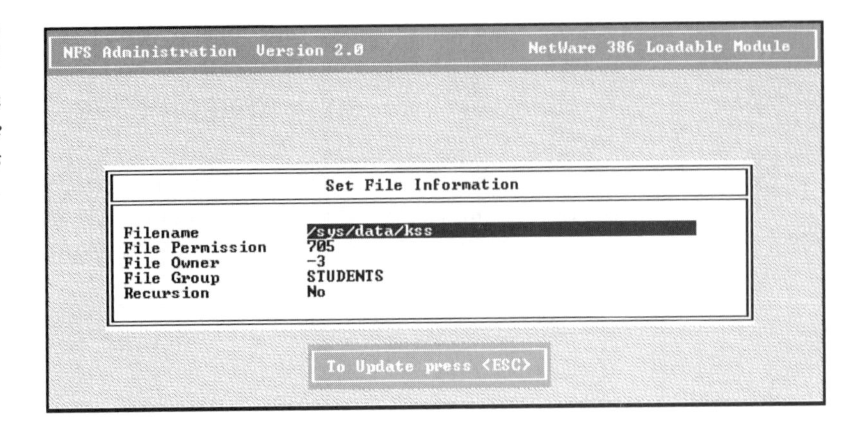

Figure 11.33

Changing the owner for a directory whose NetWare Access Control right is revoked.

Figure 11.34

The directory attributes for a Unix NFS client whose NetWare Access Control right is revoked.

```
% ls -l | grep kss
drwx---r-x  2 65533  students      512 Dec 21  1993 kss
%
```

◆ If Erase and File Scan rights are to be set for a directory as a result of modifying the rights from an NFS client, these rights need to be set for all files in that directory, but not in subdirectories.

The first time you create files and directories, the following rules apply:

◆ The IRM (Inherited Rights Mask for NetWare 3.x) or IRF (Inherited Rights Filter for NetWare 4.x) for newly created files and directories is set to [SRWCEMFA] if the uid/gid of the file/directory is the same as that for the parent directory; otherwise, the IRM/IRF is set to [EMF].

◆ The Erase NetWare right is granted for a newly created file or directory if the user has the "w" NFS permission in the parent directory.

◆ The File Scan NetWare right is granted for a newly created file if the user has the "rx" NFS permission in the parent directory.

◆ The Modify NetWare right is granted for a newly created file if the user has the "wx" NFS permission in the parent directory.

Tables 11.9 and 11.10 show how rights translate from NFS to NetWare, and from NetWare to NFS. When an exact mapping is not possible between the systems, a conversion is made in favor of greater restrictions. Because the NFS file system is implemented on a NetWare server, the final access control information is based on the NetWare permissions.

TABLE 11.9 TRANSLATING NFS PERMISSIONS TO NETWARE TRUSTEE RIGHTS

File/Directory	NFS Permission	NetWare Trustee Right
File	r (read)	R (read)
File	w (write)	W (write)
File	x (execute)	Not Applicable
Directory	r (read)	R F (Read, File Scan)
Directory	w (write)	W C E (Write, Create, Erase)
Directory	x (execute)	R F (Read, File Scan)

TABLE 11.10 TRANSLATING NETWARE EFFECTIVE RIGHTS TO NFS PERMISSIONS

File/Directory	NetWare Right	NFS Permission
File	R (Read)	r (read)
File	W (Write)	w (write)
File	C (Create)	Not meaningful for a file
File	E (Erase)	Parent's "w" (write)
File	M (Modify)	Not applicable
File	F (File scan)	Parent's "rx"
File	A (Access control)	No direct match
File	S (Supervisor)	Not applicable
Directory	R (Read)	Not applicable
Directory	W (Write)	Not applicable
Directory	C (Create)	"w" granted if NetWare directory also has Erase (E)
Directory	E (Erase)	"w" granted if NetWare directory also has Create (C)
Directory	M (Modify)	Not applicable
Directory	F (File scan)	"rx" (read, execute)
Directory	A (Access control)	No direct match
Directory	S (Supervisor)	Not applicable

Setting File Attributes

You can set the NFS permissions for exported directories using NFSADMIN. To set the NFS permissions, use the following steps:

1. Select Change File Information from NFSADMIN's Main Menu.
2. Select Get File Information to view the current settings for an exported path.
3. Select Set File Information to change settings.

   If you selected Get File Information prior to this step, the current permission settings for the directory are displayed.

Figure 11.35 shows a sample Set File Information screen. The fields are described in table 11.11.

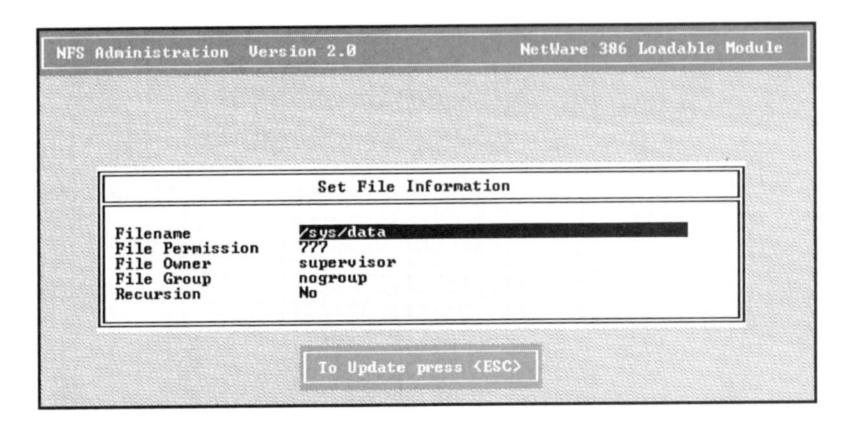

Figure 11.35
The Set File Information screen.

Table 11.11 The Set File Information Fields

File Information Field	Description
Filename	The complete path name of directory or file. Wild cards (*, ?) are allowed.
File Permission	Use the octal permission notation for the directory/file. For example, 755 means "rwx" by owner, "rx" by group and others.
File Owner	The uid or NetWare user account for the directory or file.
File Group	The gid or NetWare group for the directory or file.
Recursion	If set to Yes, any changes affect all files and directories. If set to No, the changes apply only to the current directory.

Configuring a NetWare Server: A Guided Tour

In this guided tour, you learn how to complete the configuration of a newly created NetWare NFS on your student machine.

Case Study

This guided tour will be done in the context of a case study.

You have been assigned the task of integrating a NetWare-based network with an existing Unix-based network using NetWare NFS.

The users on the Unix host that need to access the NetWare server are shown in the following table. The table also shows the equivalent NetWare user accounts to which the Unix users need to be mapped.

Username	Login Name	UID	NetWare User
Bill Joy	bill	101	USER1
Drew Heywood	drew	102	USER2
Steve Weiss	steve	103	USER3
Karen Opal	karen	104	USER4
Tim Huddleston	tim	105	USER5

The Unix host has a gid of 50 defined on it, and members of this gid must be assigned permissions to the NetWare group EVERYONE.

In addition to the IP Address and Hostname mappings that may already exist in the SYS:ETC\HOSTS file on the NetWare server, the server needs to know the following hostnames and their IP addresses.

IP address	Hostname
199.245.170.50	intellicom_snmp
199.245.170.16	ucs
199.245.170.15	rama
199.245.170.17	sita

The NetWare server should export the paths SYS:PUBLIC and SYS:.

The exported path SYS: should be configured in the following manner:

Trusted hosts:	ucs
Root Access:	ucs, rama
Read-Only Access:	Yes
Anonymous Access:	No
Read-Write Access:	ucs
DOS Attribute:	Modify attributes from NFS
Trustee Rights:	Create trustee rights from NFS

The exported path SYS:ETC should be configured as shown below:

Trusted hosts:	(Leave blank to allow all hosts)
Root Access:	(Leave blank to disallow root access)
Read-Only Access:	No
Anonymous Access:	Yes
Read-Write Access:	ucs
DOS Attribute:	Do not modify attributes from NFS
Trustee Rights:	Do not create trustee rights from NFS
File Permission:	755
File Owner:	supervisor
File Group:	everyone
Recursion:	Yes

The following is a guided tour for achieving the objectives of this case study.

1. Start your NetWare NFS server.
2. From the server console run NFSADMIN NLM by entering **LOAD NFSADMIN**.

   At any time during this configuration/exploration, you can use the help key (F1) to find out additional information on the options.
3. Select "Configure NFS Tables." You should see a list of the Configuration options.
4. Select "User Information" from the Configuration menu. You should see a table of NFS uid and NetWare Username mappings. This table is used to provide a mapping between Unix user accounts (uids) and NetWare accounts. When a Unix user logs in, the user is assigned the rights of the corresponding NetWare user.
5. Note any initial user mappings and, using the information in this chapter, review their purpose.
6. Use the information provided in the case study to enter the uid and NetWare user mappings. To enter a mapping, press the Insert key and enter the uid and NetWare user information. Press Esc when you are done, and answer Yes to save your changes.
7. Select "Group Information" from the Configuration menu. You should see a table of NFS gid and NetWare Group Name mappings. This table is used to provide a mapping between Unix groups (gids) and NetWare groups. When a Unix user logs in, the group permissions for the user are based on the corresponding NetWare group.
8. Use the information provided in the case study to enter the gid and NetWare group mapping. To enter a mapping, use the Insert key and enter the NFS gid and NetWare group. Press Esc when you are done, and answer Yes to save your changes.

9. Select "Workstation IP Address" from the Configuration menu. You should see a table of IP Addresses and Hostnames. The information entered here is saved in the SYS:ETC\HOSTS file.
10. Use the information supplied in the case study to provide a mapping between IP addresses and hostnames. To enter a mapping, use the Insert key and enter the IP address and hostname. Press Esc when you are done, and answer Yes to save your changes.
11. Select Export Information from the Configuration menu. You should see a list of exported paths. Initially this list should be empty. This list is used to specify the paths that can be mounted by NFS clients.
12. Use the information provided in the case study to specify the exported paths.

    Remember that pathnames must be entered using the Unix style convention. Thus SYS: becomes /sys.

    To enter an Exported Path, use the Insert key and enter the Unix-style name of the NetWare directory to be exported.

    Press Esc when you are done, and answer Yes to save your changes.
13. Select Export Information again to see a list of exported paths entered in the previous step.

    Highlight each exported path and press Enter to further configure the exported path.

    Use the information provided in the case study to configure each of the exported paths.

    When done, press Esc a sufficient number of times to return to the main menu.
14. You have set the export path options but not the Unix permissions an NFS client will have for the exported paths. You must perform this step next.
15. From the main menu, select Change File Information. You should see the File Information MENU.
16. Select "Get File Information" from the File Information menu.

    Specify the exported path /sys/etc.

    Note the permission settings for /sys/etc.

    Press the Esc key to return to the File Information menu.
17. Select "Set File Information." You should see the file information for the /sys/etc directory.

    Enter the permission information for /sys/etc as indicated in the information provided in the case study.

    Press Esc enough times to return to the main menu.

In this section, you set the NFS_THREADS and TIME_ZONE information.

1. Select "Tune Up NFS Parameters" from the Main Menu.

   Change NFS_THREADS and TIME_ZONE as indicated in above.

   Save the settings and exit the NFSADMIN utility.

2. Shut down the server and start it again for the settings to take effect.

3. Examine the contents of the SYS:ETC\EXPORTS file to observe how the exported paths are represented. You can do this from the server console by entering **LOAD EDIT SYS:ETC\EXPORTS**

   Examine the contents of other files that were modified by the configuration tasks that you performed from NFSADMIN. These files are indicated in the following list:

   SYS:ETC\NFSUSERS

   SYS:ETC\NFSGROUP

   SYS:ETC\HOSTS

Monitoring the NetWare NFS Server

Monitoring the NetWare NFS server includes any of the following tasks:

- Observing clients that have mounted the NetWare NFS server file system.
- Observing the services (RPC) that have been registered at the NetWare NFS server.
- Observing NFS statistics.

You can perform many of these tasks using NFSADMIN. You can also use the Unix NFS client to perform monitoring operations.

Using the NetWare NFS Server from Unix NFS Clients

Once you have used the procedures outlined earlier in this chapter to export the NetWare NFS server's directories to the network, any NFS client can access these file systems by performing an operation called *mounting the file system.* If the NFS client is a Unix computer, you mount the NetWare NFS file system using the mount command. The general syntax of the Unix mount command is

```
mount [options] exportpath mountpoint
```

The mount command is found in the /etc directory on older BSD Unix systems. On most newer Unix systems it is located in the /sbin directory. Figure 11.36 shows the relationship between the *exportpath* and the *mountpoint.*

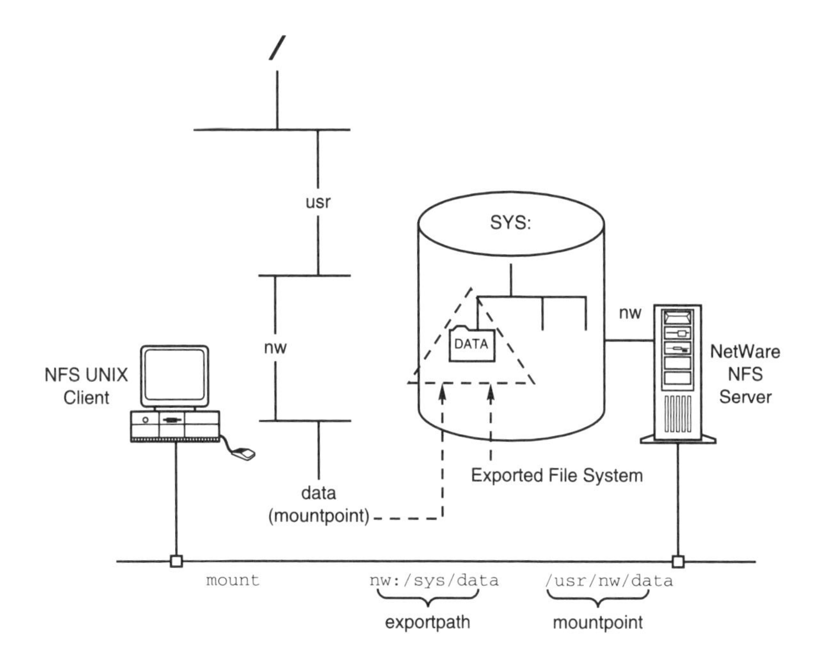

Figure 11.36

Unix NFS client mount.

The *exportpath* is the path name of the exported directory, and the *mountpoint* is the location in the NFS client's local file system, where the remote file system is "attached" or "grafted."

To accomplish the mount in figure 11.36 for SunOS, use the following mount command:

```
mount nw:/sys/data  /usr/nw/data
```

The "nw" refers to the hostname of the NFS server. The exportpath is nw:/sys/data and the local mount point is /usr/nw/data.

On 4.4 BSD Unix and Linux, use the following command:

```
mount -t nfs nw:/sys/data  /usr/nw/data
```

On Unix System V Release 4, use the following command:

```
mount -F nfs nw:/sys/data  /usr/nw/data
```

Another option that can be used with the mount command is the following:

```
-o  [ro] [,soft] [,hard] [,retry=n]
```

The ro option is for mounting the NFS file system as read-only. The soft option returns an error if the server does not respond. The hard option (default) retries the operation indefinitely until the server responds. The retry=*n* option retries the mount operation up to *n* times.

The following is an example using the mount command on SunOS:

```
mount -o ro,soft,retry=6 nw:/sys/data /mnt
```

If the NFS server does not respond, the mount operation will be tried up to six times, and return an error message on the screen each time it fails. The export path nw:/sys/data is mounted at the local directory /mnt.

To dismount a file system, use the umount command. The general syntax of the umount command is the following:

```
umount mountpoint
```

For example, to dismount the file system that was mounted at the mountpoint /mnt, use the following command:

```
umount /mnt
```

You can use the mount command by itself to see all the file systems that have been mounted by the Unix NFS client. Figure 11.37 shows the results of executing the mount command by itself. Notice that there are two NFS mounts to nw:/sys/data and nw:/sys/etc. The hostname nw is the name of the NFS server. The local mountpoints are /usr/nw/data and /usr/nw/etc.

Figure 11.37

Using the mount command to view mounted file systems.

```
% mount
/dev/sd0a on / (local, NFS exported read-only)
/dev/sd0h on /usr (local, NFS exported)
nw:/sys/data on /usr/nw/data
nw:/sys/etc on /usr/nw/etc
% █
```

Examining NFS Mounts Using the /etc/fstab and /etc/mtab Files

If you want automatically to mount a file system during Unix system boot, you can list the file system in the /etc/fstab file for BSD-derived Unix. Figure 11.38 displays the contents of /etc/fstab. The last two lines in this file list the NFS file systems that are to be mounted on system boot.

If you want to see file systems that are currently mounted, you can, as explained previously, use the mount command by itself without any arguments. Alternatively, you can display the contents of the /etc/mtab file on a SunOS system. File systems that are currently mounted on the Unix system are kept in the /etc/mtab file.

On a SunOS system, you can output the currently mounted file systems in the /etc/fstab format using the following command:

```
mount -p > /etc/fstab
```

The -p option displays the format in the fstab format, and this output can be redirected to /etc/fstab.

```
% cat /etc/fstab
#
# File system mount information belongs in this file.  Each
# line is of the form:
#
#  device        mount_point     type    flags   dump_interval   fsck_pass
#
# The following are sample entries for wd0 and sd0 root/usr partitions:
#
# /dev/wd0a      /       ufs     rw      0 1
# /dev/wd0h      /usr    ufs     rw      0 2
#
/dev/sd0a        /       ufs     rw      0 1
/dev/sd0h        /usr    ufs     rw      0 2
#
# The following will set up a memory based filesystem for /tmp
# /dev/wd0b      /tmp    mfs     rw,-s=4000      0 0
# /dev/sd0b      /tmp    mfs     rw,-s=4000      0 0
#
# NOTE: No comment lines are allowed in the real fstab at this time!
#
nw:/sys/data     /usr/nw/data    nfs     rw      0  0
nw:/sys/etc      /usr/nw/etc     nfs     rw      0  0
%
```

Figure 11.38

The /etc/fstab file.

Viewing NetWare Clients from NFSADMIN

To view clients that are mounted from NFSADMIN, from the NetWare console, enter the following:

```
LOAD NFSADMIN
```

Next, choose Display NFS Status, Clients Mounted. Figure 11.39 shows the NFS clients that have been mounted. This figure shows that the NFS client ucs has mounted two file systems on the NetWare NFS server.

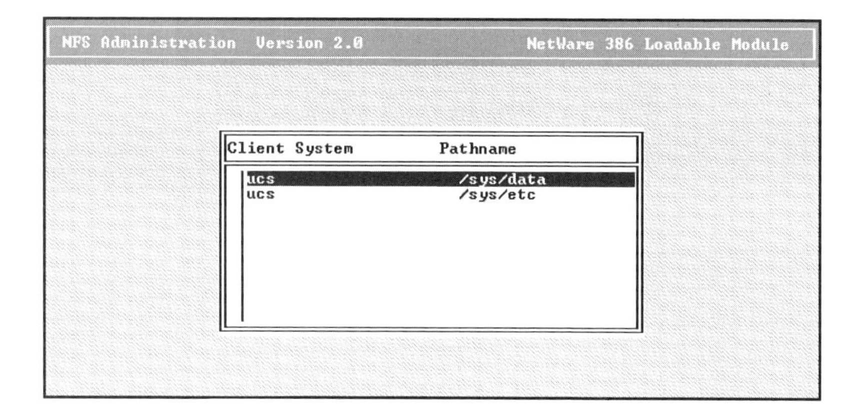

Figure 11.39

Viewing NFS clients that have been mounted.

You also can view the contents of the SYS:ETC\RMTAB file from a NetWare client to see the NFS clients that have mounted a file system on the NetWare NFS server. Figure 11.40 displays the contents of a sample SYS:ETC\RMTAB file. The lines in this file list that the client ucs has mounted the NFS files /sys/data and /sys/etc.

Figure 11.40

The SYS:ETC\RMTAB file.

```
G:\ETC>TYPE RMTAB
# "Client System", "Pathname"
ucs:/sys/data
ucs:/sys/etc

G:\ETC>
```

Viewing NetWare NFS Clients from an NFS Unix Client

You also can view the clients that have mounted a file system on an NFS server, by using the showmount command with the -a option. The following is the general syntax of this command:

```
showmount -a nfserver
```

The following command shows all NFS clients that have mounted a file system on the NFS server "nw":

```
showmount -a nw
```

Figure 11.41 shows the output of the previous command. This figure shows that the /sys/data and /sys/etc commands are mounted by the client "ucs."

Figure 11.41

The showmount command with the -a option.

```
% showmount -a nw
All mount points on nw:
ucs:/sys/data
ucs:/sys/etc
%
```

Viewing Exported File Systems from an NFS Unix Client

You also can view all file systems that are exported on the NetWare server by using the showmount command with the -e option. The following is the general syntax of this command:

```
showmount -e nfserver
```

The following command shows all exported file systems on the NFS server "nw":

```
showmount -e nw
```

Figure 11.42 shows the output of the previous command. This figure shows that the /sys/data and /sys/etc commands are available for exporting by "Everyone."

```
% showmount -e nw
Exports list on nw:
/sys/data                              Everyone
/sys/etc                               Everyone
% █
```

Figure 11.42

The showmount command with the -e option.

Monitoring the Services Registered at the NFS Server

You can monitor the RPC services registered at a NetWare NFS server from a Unix NFS client or by using NFSADMIN.NLM at the NetWare NFS server.

Using an NFS Unix Client to Monitor Services Registered at an NFS Server

The Unix NFS client software comes with a program called rpcinfo that can be used to find information on RPC services running on the network. The following is the general syntax of the rpcinfo command to find RPC services registered at a specific host:

```
rpcinfo -p [hostname]
```

The -p option causes rpcinfo to probe the portmapper (on UDP port 111) on *hostname* and print a list of all registered RPC programs. If *hostname* is not specified, it defaults to the value returned by the command hostname (local host). Figures 11.43 and 11.44 show the results of examining the RPC services on the local host and on the host "nw." The information on the RPC services contains the program number, the program's version number, the transport protocol and port number at which the service is registered, and the symbolic name (if any) of the registered service.

```
ucs# rpcinfo -p
   program vers proto   port
    100000    2   tcp    111  portmapper
    100000    2   udp    111  portmapper
    100003    2   udp   2049  nfs
    100003    2   tcp   2049  nfs
ucs# █
```

Figure 11.43

Using rpcinfo -p to monitor local RPC services.

The -b option can be used with rpcinfo to make an RPC broadcast to procedure 0 of the specified program and version using UDP. It reports all hosts that respond. For example, to find all "nfs" RPC program numbers with a version number of 2 that are on the network, use the following command:

```
rpcinfo -b nfs 2
```

Similarly, to find program number 100005 (mountd), version 2, use the following command:

```
rpcinfo -b 100005 2
```

And to find the program status, version number 1, use the following command:

```
rpcinfo -b status 1
```

Figure 11.45 shows the outputs of the previous commands. Use the interrupt key (^C) to stop the display; otherwise, these commands broadcast requests for the services indefinitely. The first command shows that two hosts at IP address 199.245.180.11 and 199.245.180.16 have the "nfs" RPC service. The other two commands show that the "mountd" and "status" RPC services were found on host 199.245.180.11 server only. The host at 199.245.180.11 is a NetWare NFS server.

Figure 11.44

Using rpcinfo -p to monitor RPC services on host "nw."

```
ucs# rpcinfo -p nw
   program vers proto   port
    100000    2   udp    111  portmapper
    100000    2   tcp    111  portmapper
    100005    1   udp   1026  mountd
    100005    2   udp   1027  mountd
    100003    2   udp   2049  nfs
    300055    1   udp   1028
    100024    1   udp   1030  status
    100024    1   tcp   1026  status
    100021    1   udp   1031  nlockmgr
    100021    2   udp   1032  nlockmgr
    100021    3   udp   1033  nlockmgr
    100021    1   tcp   1027  nlockmgr
    100021    2   tcp   1028  nlockmgr
    100021    3   tcp   1029  nlockmgr
ucs# █
```

Figure 11.45

The rpcinfo -b command.

```
ucs# rpcinfo -b nfs 2
199.245.180.16 ucs
199.245.180.11 nwcs
199.245.180.16 ucs
199.245.180.11 nwcs
^C
ucs# rpcinfo -b 100005 2
199.245.180.11 nwcs
199.245.180.11 nwcs
^C
ucs# rpcinfo -b status 1
199.245.180.11 nwcs
199.245.180.11 nwcs
^C
ucs# █
```

On BSD Unix systems the following commands can be used as an RPC "PING" test to see whether a service is alive:

```
rpcinfo [ -n portnum ] -u host prognum [ versnum ]

rpcinfo [ -n portnum ] -t host prognum [ versnum ]
```

These commands send a message to procedure number 0 of the indicated program (and version), and check whether a reply was received. Recall that procedure 0 of all RPC programs returns a reply when a call is made to it. The -u option indicates that the UDP port number specified by the -n option is used. The -t option indicates that the TCP port number specified by the -n option is used. If the -n option is not used, the message is sent to the portmapper port number, which has the well-known value of 111.

Using NFSADMIN to Monitor Services Registered at a NetWare NFS Server

To use NFSADMIN to monitor RPC services registered at the NFS server, from the NetWare server console, enter the following command:

```
LOAD NFSADMIN
```

Next, choose Display NFS Status, Services Registered. Figure 11.46 shows the NFSADMIN display, showing the RPC services.

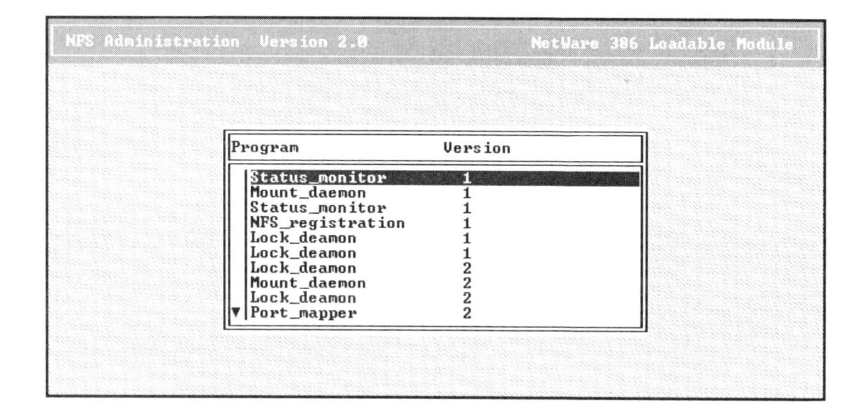

Figure 11.46

Viewing registered RPC services from NFSADMIN.

Viewing NFS Statistics

You can view NFS statistics for the NetWare NFS server from a Unix NFS client or by using the NFSADMIN.NLM at the NetWare NFS server.

Using NFS Unix Client to View NFS Server Statistics

The Unix NFS client software comes with a program called nfsstat that is used to display statistics on the NetWare NFS server.

Figure 11.47 shows the output of the nfsstat command. The nfsstat command with no arguments displays details of the nfs statistics at the client.

Figure 11.47

NFS statistics for Unix

```
ucs# nfsstat | more
Client Info:
Rpc Counts:
  Getattr    Setattr      Lookup  Readlink        Read       Write
        0          0           0         0           0           0
   Rename       Link     Symlink     Mkdir       Rmdir     Readdir
        0          0           0         0           0           0
Rpc Info:
 TimedOut    Invalid X Replies   Retries    Requests
        0          0         0         0           0
Cache Info:
Attr Hits     Misses Lkup Hits    Misses BioR Hits      Misses B
        0          0         0         0         0           0
BioRLHits     Misses BioD Hits    Misses DirE Hits      Misses
        0          0         0         0         0           0

Server Info:
  Getattr    Setattr      Lookup  Readlink        Read       Write
        0          0           0         0           0           0
```

To see a summary of the client and server statistics, every five seconds, you can use the following:

```
nfsstat -w 5
```

Figure 11.48 shows the output of the previous nfsstat command.

Figure 11.48

Viewing NFS statistics for a Unix NFS client and server.

```
ucs# nfsstat -w 5
         Getattr   Lookup Readlink    Read   Write   Rename    Link  Read
Client:        1        1        0       0       0        0       0
Server:        0        0        0       0       0        0       0
Client:        0        0        0       0       0        0       0
Server:        0        0        0       0       0        0       0
Client:        1        0        0       0       0        0       0
Server:        0        0        0       0       0        0       0
Client:        0        0        0       0       0        0       0
Server:        0        0        0       0       0        0       0
Client:        0        0        0       0       0        0       0
Server:        0        0        0       0       0        0       0
Client:        2        5        0       0       1        0       0
Server:        0        0        0       0       0        0       0
Client:        0        0        0       0       0        0       0
Server:        0        0        0       0       0        0       0
Client:        0        0        0       0       0        0       0
Server:        0        0        0       0       0        0       0
^C
                        0
```

Using NFSADMIN to Monitor NetWare NFS Server Statistics

To use NFSADMIN to monitor the NetWare NFS server statistics, from the NetWare server console, enter the following command:

```
LOAD NFSADMIN
```

Next, choose NFS Statistics, Display Statistics. Figure 11.49 shows the NFSADMIN display, showing NetWare NFS statistics.

NFS Administration Version 2.0 NetWare 386 Loadable Module

Event Name	# of calls	Total Ticks Used	Seconds/Call	Total
NFSPROF_NULL	0	0	0.0000000000	0.0
NFSPROF_GETATTR	4	6	0.0750000000	0.3
NFSPROF_SETATTR	0	0	0.0000000000	0.0
NFSPROF_ROOT	0	0	0.0000000000	0.0
NFSPROF_LOOKUP	6	4	0.0333333333	0.2
NFSPROF_READLINK	0	0	0.0000000000	0.0
NFSPROF_READ	0	0	0.0000000000	0.0
NFSPROF_WRITECACHE	0	0	0.0000000000	0.0
NFSPROF_WRITE	1	0	0.0000000000	0.0
NFSPROF_CREATE	1	1	0.1000000000	0.1
NFSPROF_REMOVE	0	0	0.0000000000	0.0
NFSPROF_RENAME	0	0	0.0000000000	0.0
NFSPROF_LINK	0	0	0.0000000000	0.0
NFSPROF_SYMLINK	0	0	0.0000000000	0.0
NFSPROF_MKDIR	0	0	0.0000000000	0.0
NFSPROF_RMDIR	0	0	0.0000000000	0.0
NFSPROF_READDIR	4	0	0.0000000000	0.0
NFSPROF_STATFS	1	0	0.0000000000	0.0

Figure 11.49
Viewing NFSADMIN's NFS Statistics.

In figure 11.49, # of calls is the number of times a remote procedure was called; Total Ticks Used is the total time in ticks (1/18.28 second) spent executing the RPC procedure; Seconds/Call is the average number of seconds spent executing a procedure; and Total is the total time in seconds spent executing the procedure.

Viewing the NetWare NFS Server Audit Log File

The NFS Audit Log is kept in SYS:ETC\AUDIT.LOG but is locked when NFS server is running. To view the NetWare NFS Audit log file, from the NetWare console, enter the following:

```
LOAD NFSADMIN
```

Next, choose Auditing/Error traces, Display Audit Log. Figure 11.50 shows the results of performing these actions.

To view or edit the Audit default settings, from the NetWare console, enter the following:

```
LOAD NFSADMIN
```

Next, choose Auditing/Error traces, View/Edit Defaults. Figure 11.51 shows the result. The audit log defaults show the maximum size of the audit log file. It also shows the actions (display to screen, log to file) to be performed when the different classes of errors (error, warning, information, debugging) are encountered.

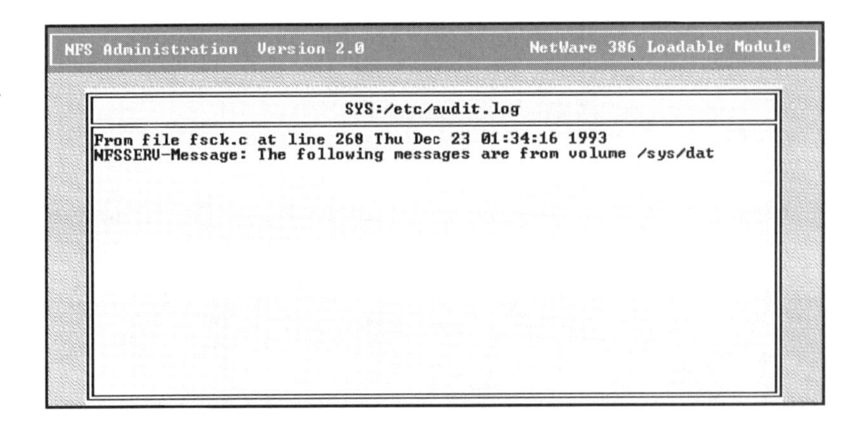

Figure 11.50

Viewing the audit log using NFSADMIN.

```
NFS Administration  Version 2.0                NetWare 386 Loadable Module

                 View/Edit Error Display Default
         Error Class   Output To File   Output To Screen
         ERROR         Yes              Yes
         WARNING       No               Yes
         INFORMATION   No               No
         DEBUGGING     Yes              No

         FILE LIMIT    10240
```

Figure 11.51

Viewing the audit log defaults using NFSADMIN.

To clear NetWare NFS Audit log, from the NetWare console, enter the following:

```
LOAD NFSADMIN
```

Next, choose Auditing/Error traces, Clear Audit Log.

Tuning NetWare NFS

You can fine-tune a number of NetWare NFS parameters to optimize the NetWare NFS server performance. To tune NetWare NFS from the server console, enter the following:

```
LOAD NFSADMIN
```

Next, choose Tune Up NFS Parameters. Figure 11.52 shows the result. You can edit the parameters using NFSADMIN (see fig. 11.52) or edit the NFS parameters stored in the text file SYS:ETC\NFSPARAM.

A summary of NFS's tunable parameters is shown in table 11.12.

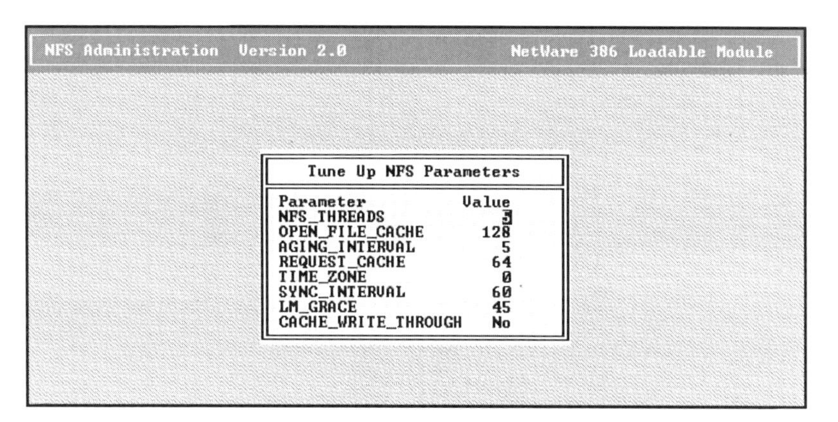

Figure 11.52

Tuning up NFS parameters using NFSADMIN.

TABLE 11.12 NFS PARAMETERS

NFS Parameter	Description
NFS_THREADS	The number of NFS requests that can be processed simultaneously (called *interleaved* by Novell). The default value is 3. The range is 1 to 5 for NetWare NFS 1.2, and 1 to 20 for NetWare NFS 1.2c (and higher).
OPEN_FILE_CACHE	The number of NFS files that the NFS server can have open simultaneously. The range is from 32 to 1,024, with a default value of 128. Increasing this value means that files accessed by NFS clients are more likely to be found in the server cache.
AGING_INTERVAL	The time in seconds that the NFS server keeps information on a file cached in memory. While file information is cached in memory, the file is unavailable to non-NFS clients such as DOS and Macintosh. Therefore, larger values improve NFS performance but degrade DOS and Macintosh user performance for shared files. The range is from 1 to 2,000, with a default of 5.
REQUEST_CACHE	The number of requests that the server remembers at any time. This enables the server to ignore duplicate requests that have been processed. If cache is too small, the server may not be able to determine that a request is a duplicate, and this can cause error warnings to appear on the NFS Message screen. The range is from 64 to 256, with a default value of 64.
TIME_ZONE	The number of hours from GMT. Range is from -12 to +12, with a default value of 0 (GMT).
SYNC_INTERVAL	The time interval in seconds that the NFS server checks the files NFSUSERS, NFSGROUP, HOSTS, NFSPARAM, and EXPORTS for changes. If changes are detected, the file is reread by the

continues

Table 11.12, Continued

NFS Parameter	Description
	server. This parameter applies to changes made using a text editor; changes to these files made from NFSADMIN take effect immediately. The range is from 1 to 1,000, with a default of 60.
LM_GRACE	The time interval in seconds that the Lock Manager waits for NFS clients to reclaim locks if server fails.
CACHE_WRITE_THRU	When set to Yes, information written to the file cache is immediately written to disk and then an acknowledgment is returned to the NFS client. If set to No, information written to the cache is written in the background by a *lazy cache write* process, but acknowledgment is returned to NFS clients without further delay. The default is No. For diskless clients and critical database server applications running without UPS support at the NFS server, set this parameter to Yes.

Some of the parameters in table 11.12 are explained in greater detail in the sections that follow.

The NFS_THREADS Parameter

The NFS_THREADS parameter determines the number of NFS client requests that can be handled simultaneously (see fig. 11.53). Increasing the number of NFS threads can result in quicker response for NFS clients at the cost of affecting normal NetWare services and overall server performance. Starting with NetWare NFS 1.2c, the maximum for this value has been increased to 20.

The OPEN_FILE_CACHE Parameter

Figure 11.54 shows that information about NFS files that are open at any given time are cached in server memory. The size of this table determines the number of files that can be opened simultaneously. Increasing the value of OPEN_FILE_CACHE increases the size of this table, increasing the probability that the information about a file being accessed is found on this table. You should monitor the files that need to be opened simultaneously by user applications before adjusting this value. Making the value of OPEN_FILE_CACHE larger than is necessary can waste server memory.

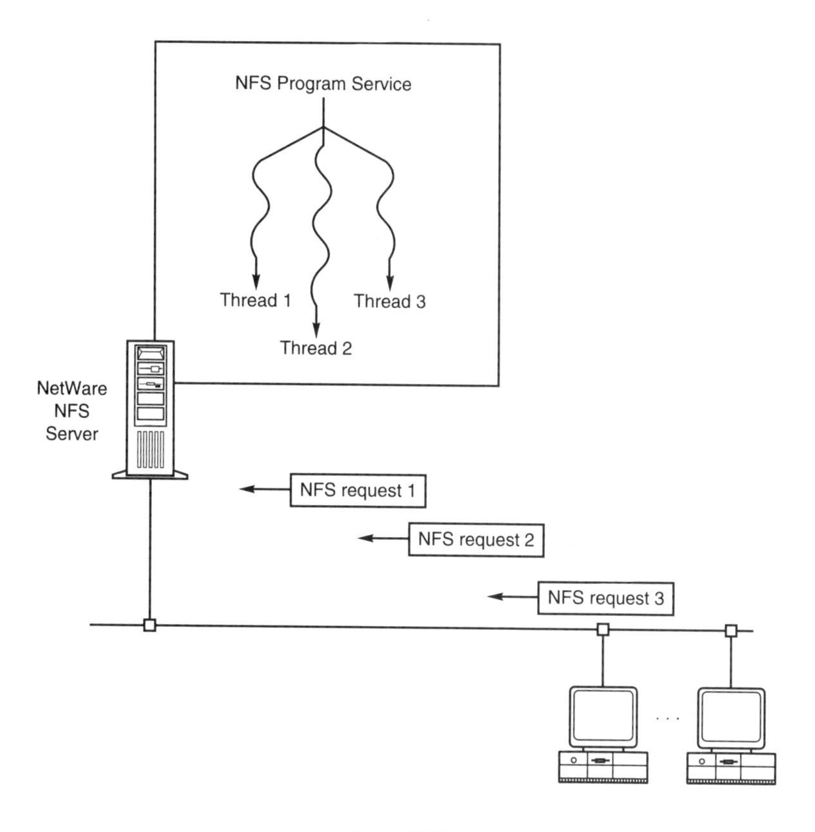

Figure 11.53

Using the NFS_THREADS parameter.

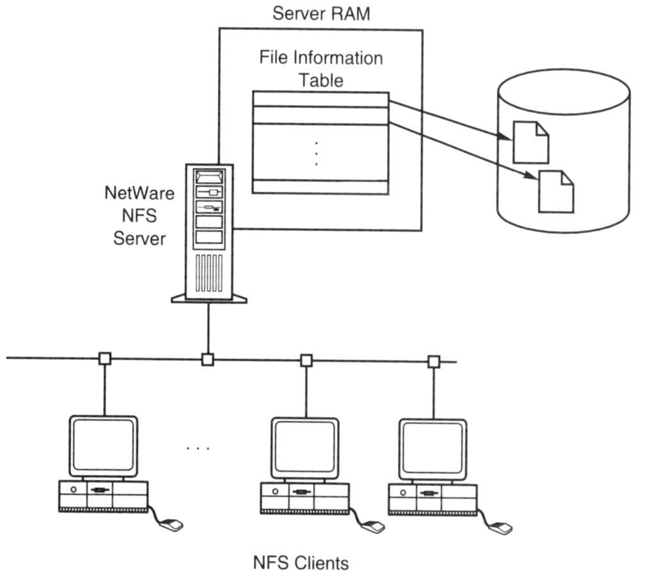

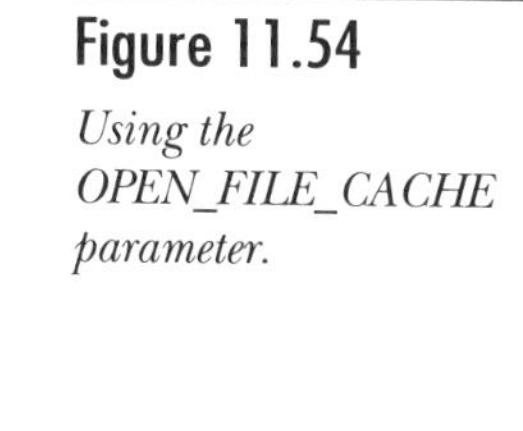

Figure 11.54

Using the OPEN_FILE_CACHE parameter.

The AGING_INTERVAL Parameter

Figure 11.55 shows that a time-out value is kept with each entry in the file information table. This time-out value is the AGING_INTERVAL, and it is the length of time information on the file is kept in memory. During the time that the file information is kept in memory, the file is not accessible by non-NFS clients (that is, other NetWare workstations). Increasing the value of AGING_INTERVAL will produce better performance for NFS clients, at the cost of making the files unavailable for long intervals of time for non-NFS clients.

If you set the AGING_INTERVAL to 0, the NetWare NFS server will close the file immediately after a read/write, thus making the file available to non-NFS clients for read/write operations.

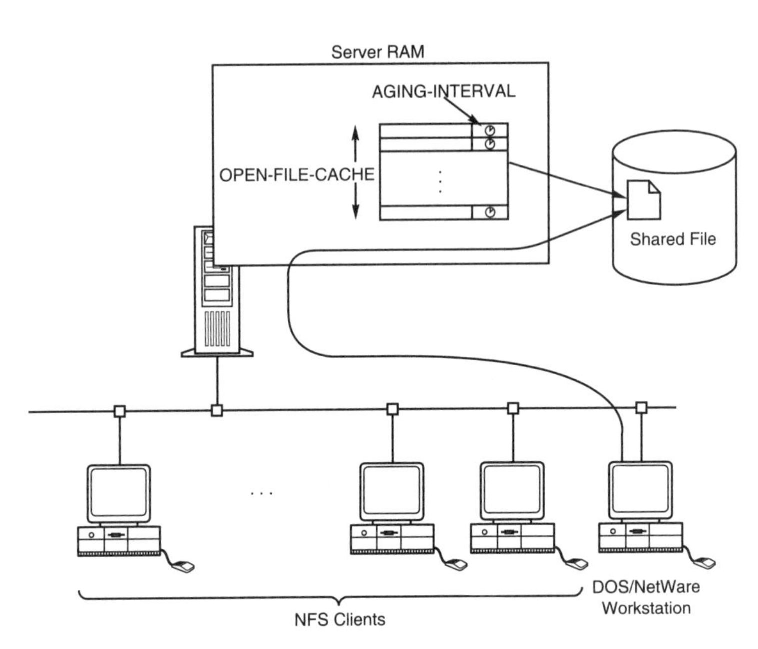

Figure 11.55

Using the AGING_INTERVAL parameter.

The REQUEST_CACHE Parameter

Figure 11.56 shows that the NFS request and its reply is cached in the server. This allows the server to respond to duplicate requests directly from its request cache. If the request cache is too small, and the server is busy handling many requests, the entries in the request cache can be overwritten quickly. If the NFS client does not receive a reply from a server within the expected time period, the NFS client will send a duplicate NFS request. The server would normally re-send the reply from its request cache. However, if the original reply has been overwritten by newer NFS request/replies, the server will report an error.

The request cache needs to be large enough to handle duplicate cache requests for a given network configuration. The default value of 64 is sufficient for most networks. You can increase this value when the server starts reporting errors concerning insufficient request cache size. However, making the REQUEST_CACHE larger than necessary will waste server memory.

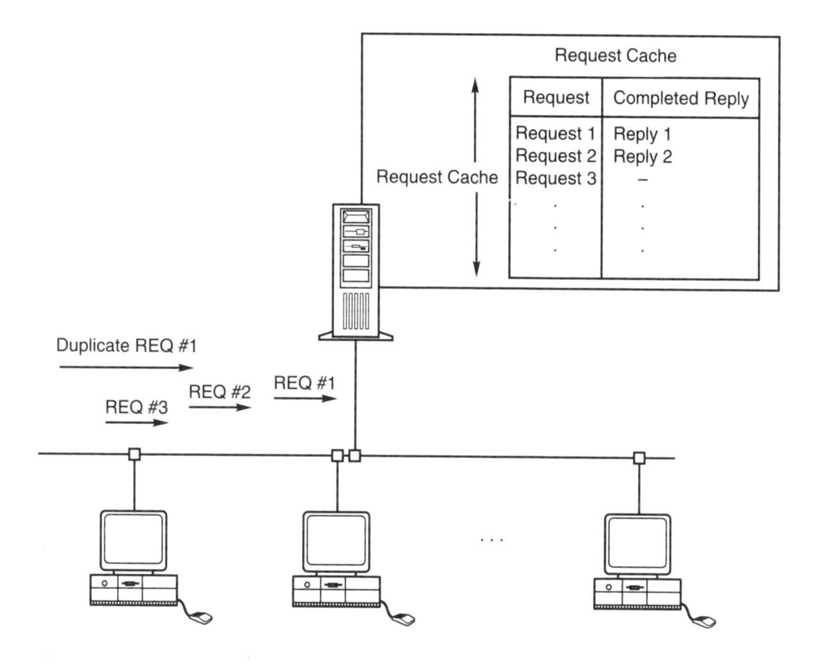

Figure 11.56

Using the REQUEST_CACHE parameter.

The TIME_ZONE Parameter

Figure 11.57 shows that the time zone is the number of hours from GMT (Greenwich Mean Time). Locations west of GMT have a positive time offset (EST = 5 hours, PST=8 hours), and locations east of GMT have a negative offset.

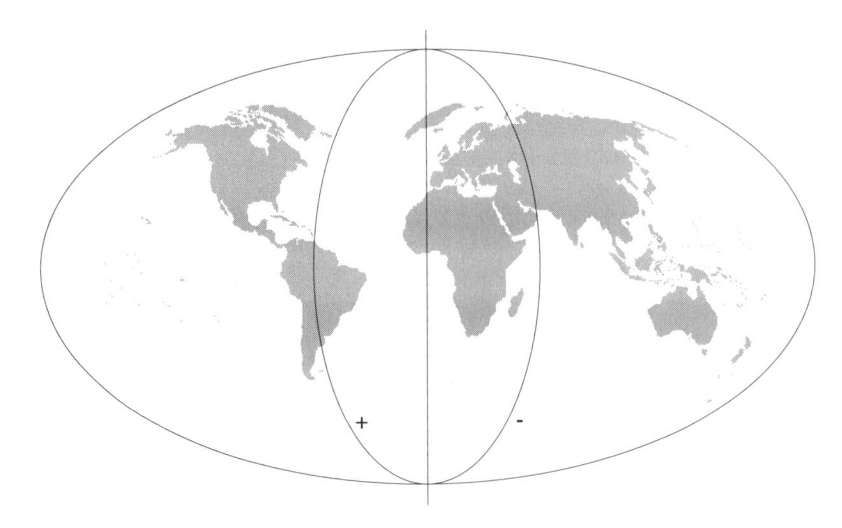

Figure 11.57

Using the TIME_ZONE parameter.

The SYNC_INTERVAL Parameter

The NetWare NFS server periodically checks the files NFSUSERS, NFSGROUP, NFSPARAM, EXPORTS, and HOSTS to see if changes have been made. If a change is detected, the file is read and the server is initialized with the changes. Figure 11.58 shows that the SYNC_INTERVAL controls the length of time in seconds that the server checks the database files.

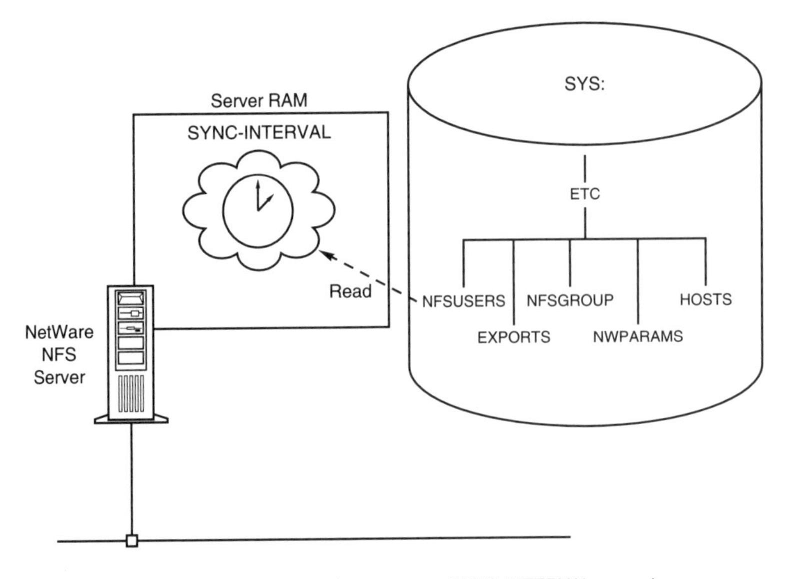

Figure 11.58

Using the SYNC_INTERVAL parameter.

The CACHE_WRITE_THRU Parameter

To improve the performance of write requests, the server can cache these requests and write them to disk at a later time by a background process called the *lazy cache write process* (see fig. 11.59). Setting CACHE_WRITE_THRU to Yes implies that the caching is disabled, and write requests will be immediately written to disks. For database applications that need the assurance of a "true write," you may want to disable write cache. If the write cache is enabled (CACHE_WRITE_THRU = No), you will see a substantial improvement in performance of write operations, at the risk that data in memory and on disk may not be synchronized in the event of server failure.

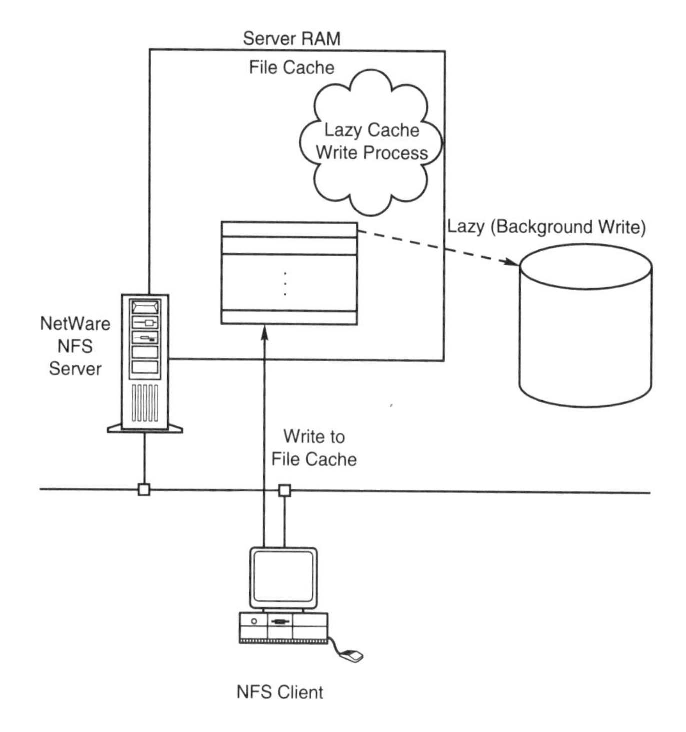

Figure 11.59

Using the CACHE_WRITE_THRU parameter.

NetWare NFS Locking and the LM_GRACE Parameter

To understand the remaining parameter, LM_GRACE, you must understand the stateless behavior of NFS and NFS file and record locking issues.

NFS as a Stateless Protocol

NFS is often called a stateless protocol. *Stateless* refers to the fact that the NFS server does not keep state information about prior requests. NFS requests and replies are constructed so that the NFS server does not have to remember the previous NFS requests to perform a current NFS request. The NFS request contains complete information for the execution of the request at the NFS server. If the NFS server were to crash (see fig. 11.60), the NFS client repeats the request until the server is up again. The server, on coming up, responds to the NFS request without any memory of the previous crash or a previous request.

Figure 11.60

The NFS server's stateless properties.

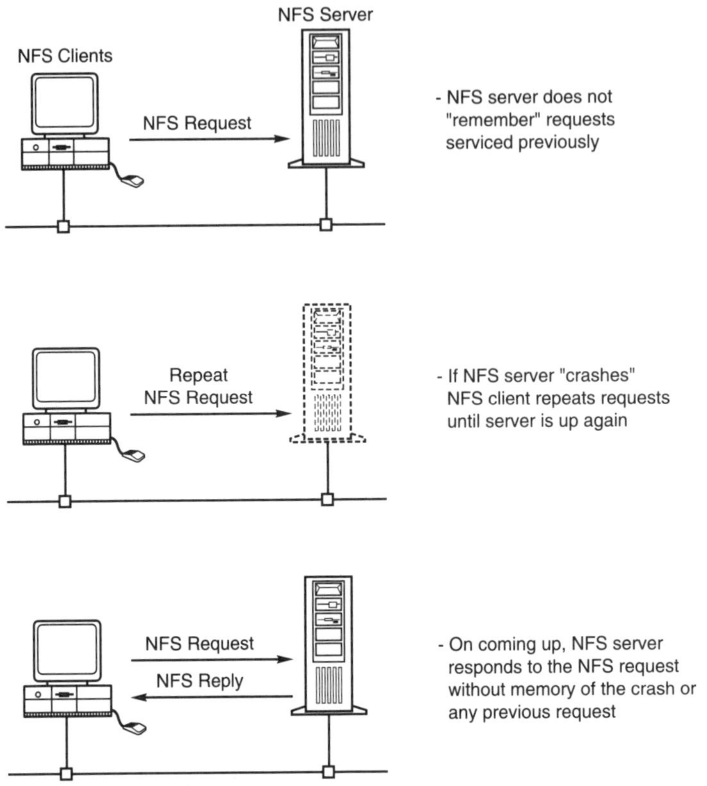

NFS Server
NFS Clients
NFS Request
- NFS server does not "remember" requests serviced previously

Repeat NFS Request
- If NFS server "crashes" NFS client repeats requests until server is up again

NFS Request
NFS Reply
- On coming up, NFS server responds to the NFS request without memory of the crash or any previous request

Although the stateless property of NFS is useful for crash recovery, it cannot be used to implement file and record locking because file and record locking are inherently stateful operations. When a file or record lock is made, subsequent operations are often dependent on this fact. Because the server has to remember the prior operations, file and record locking are not stateless. Hence these operations are called *stateful* to distinguish them from *stateless* operations.

Implementing Locks in NetWare NFS

File and record locking are commonly used in database applications. To support database applications on an NFS file system, a different RPC service, called LOCKD, is used to implement locking services. On a NetWare NFS server, the Lock Manager daemon service (see fig. 11.61) can be started using the following command:

```
LOAD LOCKD
```

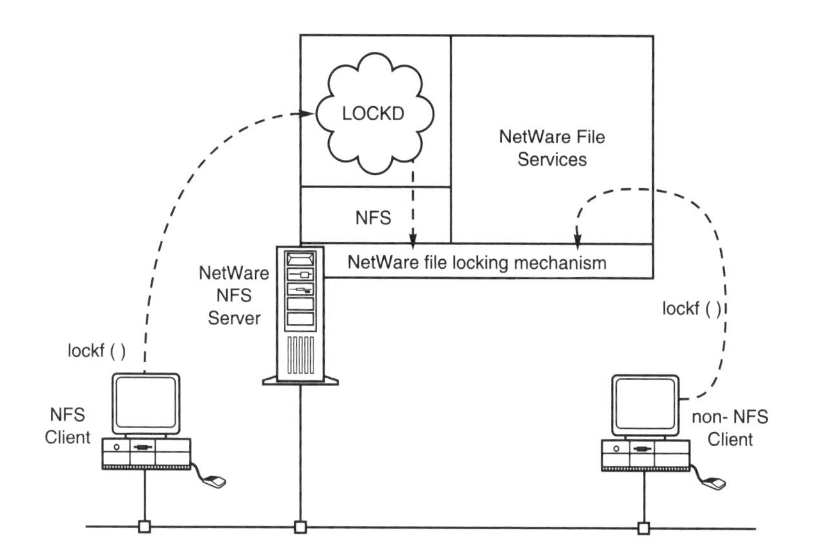

Figure 11.61

The NFS Lock Manager (LOCKD).

The Unix lock shown in figure 11.61 is an *advisory* locking mechanism. The advisor, or *logical lock,* will work only if other applications cooperate by using special system services to check for the lock. However, lower-level input/output functions can bypass the locking mechanism.

Unix Advisory Locks versus NetWare Physical Locks

NetWare uses *physical locks* for locking resources. This means that the NetWare operating system issues the locks, and this locking does not depend on cooperative behavior between applications.

In NetWare NFS, the Unix advisory locks are implemented by NetWare NFS as NetWare physical locks. The implications of this include the following:

- Non-NFS clients cannot write to a file that is locked by an NFS client.
- NFS clients cannot write to files locked by Non-NFS clients.

Both NFS client and non-NFS client locks are implemented by NetWare's physical locks. If a file is locked using physical locks, no other clients, NFS or non-NFS, can access a file that has been physically locked.

Restoring Locks after an NFS Server Crash

Figure 11.62 shows how the NFS server restores locks in the event of an NFS server crash. By definition (as a stateless protocol), the NFS server does not maintain a record of operations performed. However, the NFS server remembers the clients that have mounted the server's directories.

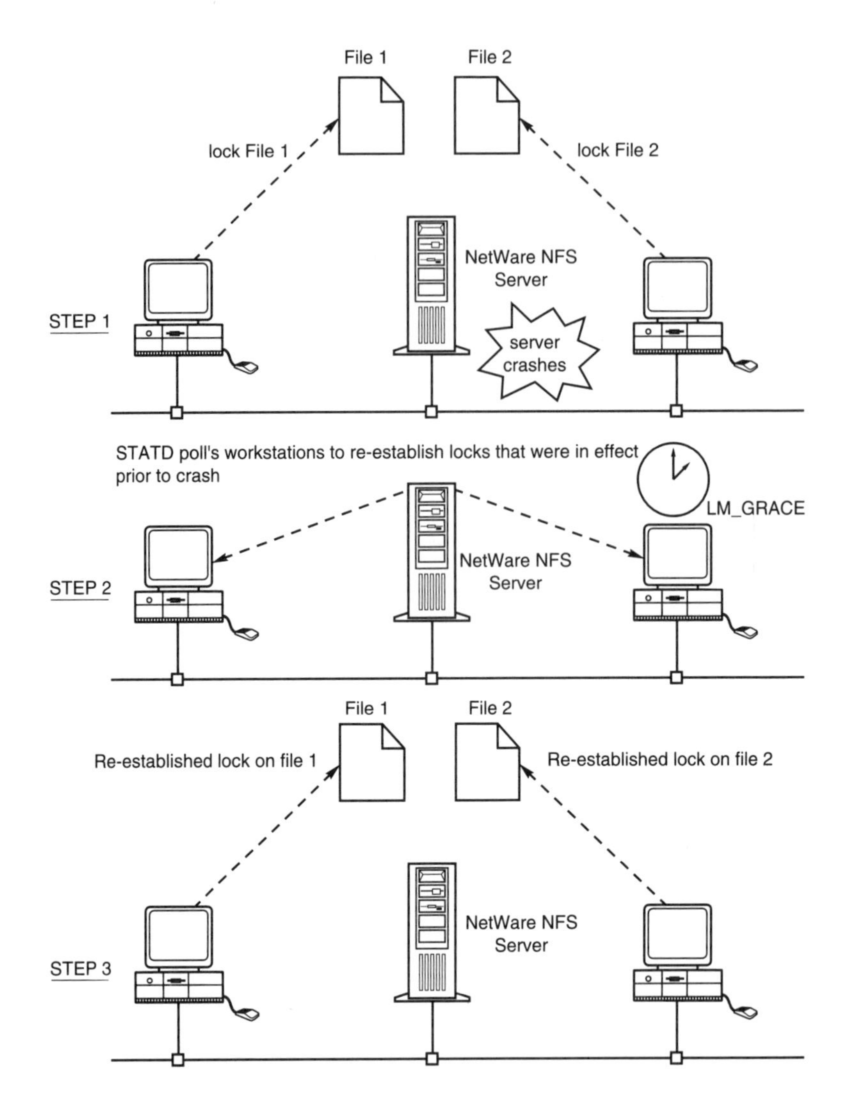

Figure 11.62

The role of STATD in restoring NFS locks.

After recovering from a system crash, the NFS server refuses all requests for file locks for a period of time set by the LM_GRACE tunable parameter. During this interval, the status monitor daemon (STATD) polls all mounted NFS clients and determines which locks were in effect at the time of the crash and reestablishes these locks (see fig. 11.62).

After the expiration of LM_GRACE period (the default is 45 seconds; the range is from 10 to 60 seconds) the Lock Manager accepts lock requests from other NFS clients.

You start the Status Monitor from the server console by entering the following command.

```
LOAD STATD
```

The LM_GRACE parameter, which controls the duration of time that the NFS server ignores any lock requests on recovering from a crash, can be set using the NFSADMIN NLM or by directly editing the SYS:ETC\NFSPARAM using a text editor.

NetWare NFS Name Space

Each NetWare server client is able to view the NetWare file system using its local file system conventions. In figure 11.63, the Unix, OS/2, DOS, and Macintosh workstations maintain their own view of the NetWare file system. The different client operating systems are able to have their own view of a common file system because of the alternate name spaces that NetWare can have on any of its volumes.

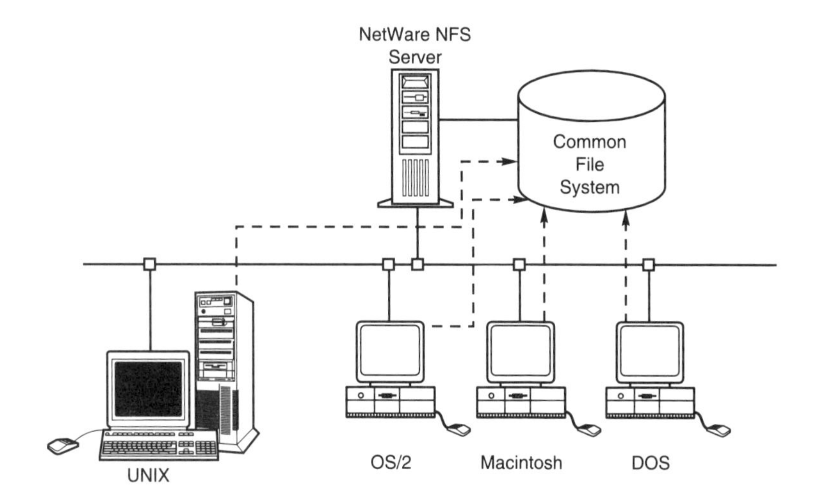

Figure 11.63
NetWare's name space support.

By default, NetWare provides the DOS name space for each of its volumes. Besides the DOS name space, NetWare can provide alternate name spaces for the client operating systems by extending the volume's directory tables to implement the file system attributes for each client file system. The file system for non-DOS clients is called *name space support.* NetWare provides name space support for NFS (Unix), OS/2, Macintosh, FTAM (OSI's Application layer File Transfer and Access Management), and Windows NT.

Adding NetWare NFS Name Space

The Unix name space support is implemented by the NFS.NAM NetWare Loadable Module. To add the NFS name space to a volume, enter the following commands from the server console:

```
LOAD NFS
ADD NAME SPACE NFS TO volumename
```

You need to add the NFS name space to a volume only once. When you install NetWare NFS, the LOAD NFS.NAM command is inserted in STARTUP.NCF, and the NFS.NAM is copied to the server's boot directory.

Figure 11.64 shows the effect of adding the NFS name space to a NetWare volume. Before adding the NFS name space, the DET (Directory Entry Table) contains entries for DOS name space only. After adding the NFS name space to a volume, each DOS file or directory entry is also visible from a NFS Unix client. Because Unix has different file and directory attributes, additional DETs are added for the Unix name space, even though they point to the same data file.

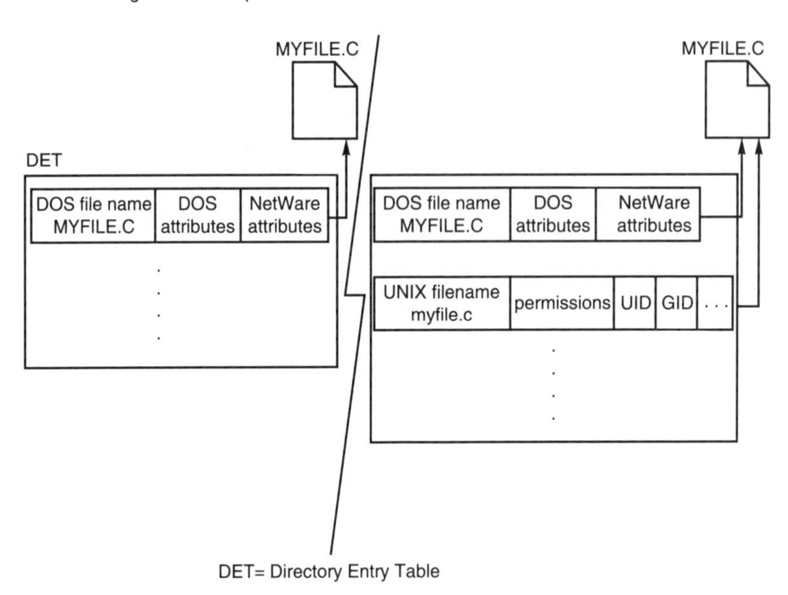

Figure 11.64
Adding NFS name space.

Name Space and the VREPAIR Utility

If there is a minor problem with a NetWare volume, the VREPAIR.NLM can fix most of these problems. However, to run VREPAIR on a volume to which the NFS name space has been added, you need the V_NFS.NLM that works in conjunction with VREPAIR to correct problems with the NFS name space.

Before you can run VREPAIR on a volume, you must dismount the volume. VREPAIR will not work on a mounted volume. To use VREPAIR on a NetWare NFS file system, enter the following commands:

```
DISMOUNT VOLUME volume
LOAD  bootdrive:V_NFS
```

Then run VREPAIR until no errors are found.

Loading VREPAIR autoloads V_NFS if V_NFS is not loaded, and loading V_NFS autoloads VREPAIR if VREPAIR is not loaded.

An alternative sequence which also works is to load VREPAIR or V_NFS prior to dismounting the volume. This enables you to load these NLMs from the SYS:SYSTEM directory, if they exist in this directory only. You can then switch to the system console screen (using Alt+Escape or Ctrl+Escape) and dismount the volume. You can then switch back to the VREPAIR screen and run VREPAIR.

Removing NFS Name Space Using VREPAIR

You may, on occasion, need to remove an added name space such as the NFS name space. You may want to do this if you have decided to uninstall the NetWare NFS server. In this case the NFS name space may not be needed, and you can reduce the amount of server memory needed by the DET tables by removing the NFS name space.

To remove the NFS name space using VREPAIR, at the console enter the following:

```
DISMOUNT  VOLUME  volume
LOAD  bootdrive:V_NFS
```

Then perform the following steps:

1. Select Set Vrepair Options.
2. Select Remove Name Space Support from the Volume.
3. Enter the name space to remove from the list of name spaces supported at the server.
4. Go to the previous menu and select Repair a Volume.
5. Exit Vrepair when done.

NFS-to-DOS Name Space Translation

On adding NFS name space to a NetWare volume, the Directory Entry Table (DET) contains an additional NFS entry linked to a DOS name-space entry. Changes made to file contents and permissions in one name space affect the other name space. As pointed out earlier, the permissions for Unix are computed dynamically when a file or directory is accessed. This ensures that the latest changes made to NetWare rights and attributes by non-NFS clients are reflected in the NFS name space.

Rules for Converting NFS and DOS Filenames

Because NFS filenames can be longer than DOS filenames and support special characters, filename conversion may be necessary. Figure 11.65 summarizes the filename translation rules. Table 11.13 gives some examples of the application of these rules. Notice that if the filename contains non-DOS characters only, the Unix name for the file is STRANGE. If a second file is created in that directory that also contains non-DOS characters only, this file is named STRANGE0; and the next strange file will be named STRANGE1, and so on. Also, note that if the Unix file contains multiple dots (.), the last sequence of characters after the dot are used for the DOS name extension.

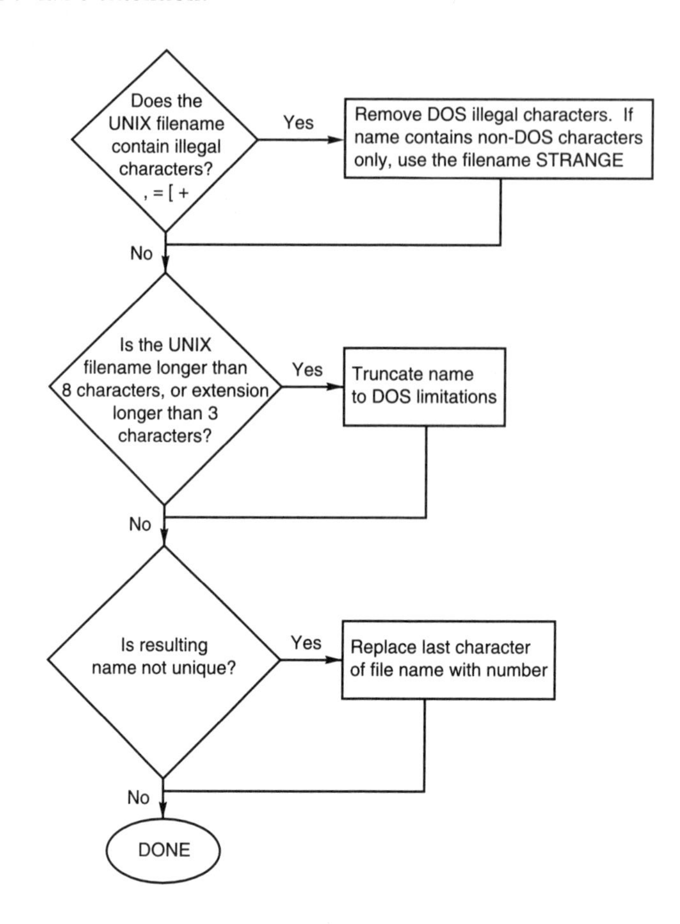

Figure 11.65

The rules for converting between NFS and DOS name spaces.

Table 11.13 Some Examples of Unix-to-DOS Name Translation for Files in the Same Directory

Unix Name	DOS Name
AveryLongFileName.text	AVERYLON.TEX
Averylongfilename.text	AVERYLO0.TEX
averylongfilename.text	AVERYLO1.TEX
Month=October	MONTHOCT
File.With.Extensions	FILE.EXT
File.With.Another.Extension	FILE0.EXT
Length=S1+S2+S3	LENGTHS1

Unix Name	DOS Name
=.=	STRANGE
=+	STRANGE0
Area=PI**2	AREAPI2
+=	STRANGE1
=[]=	STRANGE2

Viewing Long Filenames on a NetWare DOS Client

The FILER utility can be used to examine long names. Follow these steps to use the NetWare 3.x FILER utility.

1. Select Select Current Directory, and set it to the directory containing the file.
2. Select "Directory Contents."
3. Select the file.
4. Select View/Set File Information.
5. Select the Long Name field.
6. If multiple name spaces have been installed, select the NFS name space.

For NetWare 4.x FILER, the steps for viewing long names are the following:

1. Select "Current Directory," and set it to the directory containing the file.
2. Select "Manage Files and Directories."
3. Select the file.
4. Select View/Set File Information.
5. Select "Long Name."
6. If multiple name spaces have been installed, select the NFS name space.

Figure 11.66 shows the above operations performed to view the long name for the DOS name space file LENGTHS1. Notice that the NFS long name space for this file is length=s1+s2+s3.

You can also use NDIR with the /LONG option to view long names. Figure 11.67 shows the long name space for LENTHS1 using the NetWare 3.x NDIR utility. This figure shows the long name for the NFS and FTAM name space (which was installed in addition to the NFS name space). The NetWare 4.x NDIR command to see long filenames is the following:

```
NDIR SYS:DATA\USER1\LENGTHS1 /LONG
```

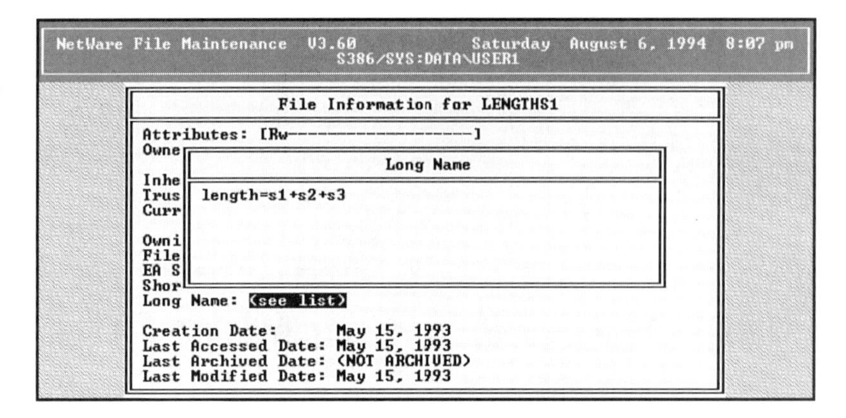

Figure 11.66

Viewing a long name using FILER.

Figure 11.67

Viewing long names using NetWare 3.x's NDIR /LONG.

```
G:\PUBLIC>NDIR /LONG SYS:DATA\USER1\LENGTHS1
S386/SYS:DATA\USER1

Files:                                       Size     Last Updated
----------------------------------------- ------------ ---------------
LENGTHS1                                           0  5-15-93   7:00a
   NFS:  length=s1+s2+s3
  FTAM:  length=s1+s2+s3

            0 bytes in     1 files
            0 bytes in     0 blocks

G:\PUBLIC>
```

Summary

This chapter discussed NetWare NFS features and how to install and configure NetWare NFS. You learned about the differences between DOS and Unix text files and how to convert between them. You learned to monitor and control NetWare NFS servers from DOS NetWare clients and Unix NFS clients. You were presented with several examples of the Unix commands and NFSADMIN administration procedures needed to manage NetWare NFS.

You also learned about the fundamental differences between Unix and NetWare permissions and how permission mappings between the two systems are performed.

Index

Symbols

A

B

C

E

F

G

H

I

J-K-L

M

O

P

Q-R

S

T

V-W

X-Y-Z

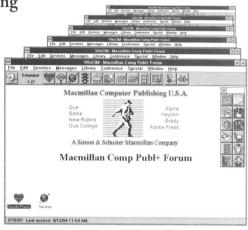

REGISTRATION CARD

Internetworking with NetWare TCP/IP

Name ______________________ Title ______________________

Company ______________________ Type of business ______________________

Address ______________________

City/State/ZIP ______________________

Have you used these types of books before? ☐ yes ☐ no

If yes, which ones? ______________________

____

How many computer books do you purchase each year? ☐ 1–5 ☐ 6 or more

How did you learn about this book? ______________________

Where did you purchase this book? ______________________

Which applications do you currently use? ______________________

____

Which computer magazines do you subscribe to? ______________________

____

What trade shows do you attend? ______________________

____

Comments: ______________________

____

____

Would you like to be placed on our preferred mailing list? ☐ yes ☐ no

☐ **I would like to see my name in print!** You may use my name and quote me in future New Riders products and promotions. My daytime phone number is: ______________________

New Riders Publishing 201 West 103rd Street ◆ Indianapolis, Indiana 46290 USA

Fax to **317-581-4670** Orders/Customer Service **1-800-653-6156**

Fold Here

PLACE
STAMP
HERE

NEW RIDERS PUBLISHING
201 W 103RD ST
INDIANAPOLIS IN 46290-9058